HENRY CLAY

HENRY CLAY

THE ESSENTIAL AMERICAN

David S. Heidler and
Jeanne T. Heidler

RANDOM HOUSE

NEW YORK

Published in the United States by Random House, an imprint
of The Random House Publishing Group, a division of
Random House, Inc., New York.

RANDOM HOUSE and colophon are registered trademarks
of Random House, Inc.

LIBRARY OF CONGRESS CATALOGING-IN-PUBLICATION DATA

Heidler, David Stephen
Henry Clay: the essential American / David S. Heidler and Jeanne T. Heidler.
p.   cm.
Includes bibliographical references and index.
ISBN 978-1-4000-6726-8
eBook ISBN 978-1-5883-6995-6
1. Henry Clay, 1777–1852.   2. Legislators—United States—Biography.   3. United States.
Congress—Biography.   4. United States—Politics and government—1815–1861.   I. Heidler,
Jeanne T.   II. Title.
E340.C6H45 2010   328.092—dc22   2009027872
[B]

Printed in the United States of America on acid-free paper

www.atrandom.com

2 4 6 8 9 7 5 3 1

First Edition

Book design by Victoria Wong

For
Sarah Daniel Twiggs,
mother to us, friend to all,
in calm laughter and gentle grace,
like Lucretia

Contents

Prologue

BEFORE THE CLOCKS struck noon, Washington's church bells began to toll, a signal to the capital that it was over. The telegraph sent the news across the country, and bells began to ring in cities and towns from the Atlantic coast to the deep interior. One of those first telegrams was sent to Lexington, Kentucky: "My father is no more. He has passed without pain into eternity."[1] Soon that message was speeding to the house nearby called Ashland, where an old woman at last had the hard news she had been expecting for months. Her husband of more than fifty years was dead. Lucretia Clay was a widow. The bells in Lexington were already ringing.

Henry Clay was dead. Shop owners across the country paused to stare briefly into the distance before pulling shades and locking doors. Men reflexively pulled watches from their vest pockets and noted the time. The immediacy of the news was sobering. Clay had died at seventeen minutes after eleven that very morning of June 29, 1852. Only a few years before, reports of his death would have seeped out of Washington only as fast as the post office and knowledgeable travelers could carry them. People on rivers would have heard about it first, possibly in days, but days would have stretched into weeks before most people learned that the greatest political figure in the nation was dead. Time would have cushioned the blow, weakening its power until it became a piece of history, something that had happened a long way off, a long time ago.

The telegraph made the news of Clay's death instant and therefore indelible. Only hours passed before cities from Maine to Missouri began draping themselves in crepe and men from Savannah to St. Louis began pulling on black armbands. Washington, already slowed by summer's heat, came to a halt. President Millard Fillmore shut down the government, and Congress immediately adjourned. Members scattered to boardinghouses, hotels, and taverns, some to draft eulogies they would deliver the next day in the legislative chambers that

Henry Clay had deftly managed for almost a half century. Even after sunset, the bells continued to ring. Cannon at the Navy Yard were firing.[2]

On June 30, the House of Representatives and the Senate heard recollections of Henry Clay. His passing was not unexpected—he had lain ill in his rooms at the National Hotel for months, and his visitors had been on what amounted to a deathwatch for weeks—but the expectation did not make its actual occurrence any less piercing. The sense that Clay's death was ending a momentous chapter in the country's history was also sobering. A little more than two years before, Clay's celebrated contemporary John C. Calhoun had died, and another, Daniel Webster, was gradually succumbing to maladies that were soon to carry him off as well. These three had become the fabled Great Triumvirate of American government. More than mere symbols of the Republic, they became personifications of it. The South Carolinian Calhoun was the South with its growing frustrations and emerging belligerency over the slavery issue. New England's Webster had become the conflicting ambiguities of the North with its moral repugnance over slavery and its allegiance to a country constitutionally bound to slavery's preservation. And the Kentuckian Clay was that national ambiguity defined. He was a westerner from the South. Yet he was not southern, because he deplored slavery. His owning slaves, however, meant that he was not northern. When an admirer said that "you find nothing that is not essentially AMERICAN in his life," it was meant as a compliment in a divisively sectional time, but in retrospect it was also a warning to the country. Like Henry Clay, it could not long continue to own slaves while denouncing slavery.[3]

When Congress met on June 30, however, it was more in the mood to celebrate Clay's life than to find portents in his death. Some members quoted poetry; some of it was good. Several remarked on his humble birth and his admirable efforts to rise above it, a theme that had already become an American political staple by the mid-nineteenth century, an obligatory credential for establishing one's relationship with "the people." And though in some cases, such as Clay's, it was an exaggeration for election campaigns, he had indeed risen, and no less spectacularly because he started from relative comfort rather than poverty. His success resulted from ceaseless labor and fastidious attention to detail. Kentuckian Joseph Underwood reminded the Senate that Clay had been neat in everything from his handkerchiefs to his handwriting. Underwood was not just talking about wardrobes and penmanship.[4]

All realized, some grudgingly, that Clay had become a great statesman. They also had to admit—again, some grudgingly—that he had been usually a jovial adversary with his opponents and always an endearing companion to his friends. New York Whig William Seward, destined to become Abraham Lin-

coln's secretary of state, did not particularly like or admire Clay, but he nevertheless dubbed him "the Prince of the Senate" and recalled that his "conversation, his gesture, his very look, was persuasive, seductive, irresistible." A House
Democrat paid tribute to the peerless orator for "the silvery tones of his bewitching voice," and a Kentucky Whig said "he reminded us of those days when there
were giants in the land," concluding with Shakespeare's Antony describing Caesar with "say to all the world, *This was a man!*"[5]

The reference to Caesar was ironic. The closest thing to an American Caesar
in Clay's time had been his most implacable foe, Andrew Jackson. "For near a
quarter of a century," Virginia's Charles Faulkner observed, "this great Republic has been convulsed to its centre by the great divisions which have sprung
from their respective opinions, policy, and personal destinies."[6] But that didn't
say the half of it. Andrew Jackson's shadow had cast a pall over Clay's political
life for more than a quarter century in some way or other, starting with Clay's
criticism of Jackson's foray into Florida in 1818, their rivalry in the 1824 presidential contest, and clashes during Jackson's presidency that included the titanic
struggle over the national bank, a political brawl so devastating that it was called
a war. Clay had lost that war. In fact, he had lost almost every time he challenged
Andrew Jackson, and worse, he was defined for many Americans by the accusation Jackson and his friends leveled at Clay in 1825. He had, they said, entered
into a "corrupt bargain" with John Quincy Adams to give Adams the presidency
in exchange for Clay's appointment as secretary of state, a presumed springboard to the presidency. This example of what Americans now call the politics
of personal destruction was called by Clay's generation simple candor by his
foes, base slander by his friends. The argument over who was right would out-
live both Jackson, who died in 1845, and Clay, but as his colleagues took the
measure of his life on that hot June day, the question momentarily became irrelevant. When John Breckinridge, a young Democrat from Clay's Kentucky, proclaimed that Clay had been "in the public service for fifty years, and never
attempted to deceive his countrymen," it was a slightly oblique jab at Jackson
and the charge he had perpetuated. Walker Brooke reminded the Senate and
James Brooks the House of Clay's famous response when advised to modify his
principles for political advantage: "Sir, I had rather be right than be President."
Clay's repeated failures as a presidential aspirant are evidence that he apparently meant it.

Yet Clay's principles had never made him inflexible or doctrinaire, an ineffective posture for a party leader. Twenty years earlier, he had shaped the faction
opposed to Andrew Jackson into a political party. Its members became known
as Whigs because just as the Whigs of England had objected to the unchecked

power of the throne, the American Whigs resisted "King Andrew's" excessive assumption of authority. Abraham Venable noted that Clay was a highly successful party leader, his "plastic touch" almost always shaping Whig plans and purposes. Another speaker praised his ability to "relax the rigor of his policy" if it endangered the government and the nation.[7] Those traits had earned his reputation as a political peacemaker. He was the "Great Compromiser" and the "Great Pacificator," labels applied as tributes to a man who had always pursued political goals within the limits of the possible. Congress had the evidence for that in the most recent clash over slavery that had almost destroyed the Union. Clay, gravely ill and fading daily, had helped to save the country from that crisis in his last public act. These men now contemplating his death were ready to see that gesture as one of singular selflessness, a labor that had hastened a frail old man's demise, making him a martyr to the cause of Union, "a holy sacrifice to his beloved country."[8]

We know now what they could not imagine. Clay's sacrifice was ultimately in vain, and the ungainly compromise he had helped cobble together was already unraveling as he died. The country had no more compromises in it, and only nine years later, the Union that Clay knew and loved would disappear. The congressional eulogies on June 30 contained subtle hints of the divisions that would finally split that Union and turn its political arguments into a civil war. Of the thirteen eulogies in the House of Representatives, all but three were delivered by Whigs, and they were mostly from the East. Not a single New Englander rose to praise Henry Clay, and aside from two representatives from Kentucky, only congressmen from Tennessee and Indiana, both Whigs, spoke for the West. No representative from the Deep South spoke for Clay. The only southerners who did so were from Virginia, North Carolina, and Maryland. Many in the House apparently followed the rule that when unable to say anything good, one should say nothing at all.

The time was fast coming—perhaps it had already arrived—when even a Great Pacificator could not soothe such troubled political waters. One Democrat even tinged his remarks with mild spite. Virginia senator Robert M. T. Hunter was still smarting from the bruising fight over the Compromise of 1850 and could not keep from reciting a series of backhanded compliments that damned with faint praise: Clay was not well educated but had managed to achieve success anyway; clearly past his prime, he had soldiered on; never bright or prescient, he at least had never exaggerated matters for political effect. Hunter closed by inviting the Senate to gaze upon the ghost of the Democrat Calhoun, the man Hunter clearly regarded as a genuine intellect and great statesman.[9] Some muttered about Clay's popularity in death spanning the political breach and took small comfort in the reality that it was bad form to speak ill of the dead. Four days after the congressional eulogies, Democrat newspaper editor Francis Preston Blair privately groused that Democrats had made the best speeches but had apparently forgotten that Clay was a Whig.[10]

Nobody could forget, however, that Clay was a friendly, persistently cheerful man whose mark on the country was as indelible as his influence on its politics was profound. "The good and great can never die," said Walker Brooke, and Maryland's Richard J. Bowie observed that Clay's "name is a household word, his thoughts are familiar sentences." But Alabama senator Jeremiah Clemens, who happened to be a Democrat, spoke the simplest and most poignant sentiment, because it was the most personal. He had disagreed with Henry Clay about almost everything, but that was of no relevance now. "To me," Clemens said simply, "he was something more than kind."[11]

THE NEXT MORNING Clay came to the Capitol for the last time. Overnight, Washington had dressed its buildings in black. As dignitaries spent the morning gathering at the National Hotel, the church bells resumed their tolling, and the cannon at the Navy Yard began firing as they had the previous night, one report every sixty seconds, hence their label as minute guns. All flags were at half-staff. It was 11:00 A.M., and the day was steaming hot, making black attire even more oppressive.

It took an hour to organize everyone, but at noon the procession finally moved out for the Capitol, only a few blocks to the east. It headed up Pennsylvania Avenue behind two military companies and a regimental band setting a slow pace with dirges and muffled drums. The Senate Committee on Arrangements, wearing white scarves, and the Senate pallbearers with black scarves, led the funeral car, an elaborate creation covered in black cloth, its corners decorated by gilded torches wrapped in crepe, silver stars fastened to its sides, and a canopy of intertwined black and white silk arching over the coffin. Six white horses, each attended by a groom dressed in white, pulled the car up the avenue. A silent multitude lined the route. The slow pace took the procession almost an hour to cover the short distance to the Capitol's portico that opened to the Rotunda.

President Fillmore, cabinet officers, and the diplomatic corps entered the Senate chamber at 12:20 P.M., and shortly afterward they were followed by the congressional chaplains, the pallbearers and the casket, Clay's son Thomas, friends, senators, representatives, Supreme Court justices, judges, senior military officers, mayors from Washington and other major cities, civic groups, and militiamen. The absolute silence of such a large gathering, especially among the citizens packing the gallery above, was eerie. As the casket was brought in, the imposing figure of Senate chaplain Charles M. Butler, clad in high canonical robes, stepped forward and broke the hush: "I am the resurrection and the life, saith the Lord."[12]

The coffin was placed in the center of the chamber. It was a distracting novelty, made of metal shaped to resemble the human form and with weighty silver mountings and handles. A large, thick silver plate bore the inscription HENRY CLAY, and another just above it could be removed to reveal the corpse's face under a glass pane, a practice to make sure that the encased body really was lifeless in order to avoid the nineteenth century's greatest nightmare, being buried alive. The president and Speaker of the House sat nearest the coffin at the center. Senators, diplomats, family, and friends formed a semicircle just beyond. Congressmen and visiting dignitaries filled the outermost circles.[13]

The Reverend Dr. Butler was Clay's friend. He performed the service as much from affection for the deceased as from his official duty as the Senate's chaplain. He began by noting how different people would remember different Henry Clays. There was the Clay of youth and ambition, the Clay of great accomplishment and renown, the Clay of the sickroom, feeble but cheerful, and the Clay who rose to defend the beleaguered Union. But there was also the Henry Clay who had embodied all that was great and good about America. Butler invoked Jeremiah, chapter 48, verse 17, to describe this universal recollection of Henry Clay as "the strong staff" adorned with "the beautiful rod" of patriotism. He spoke of a nation in mourning, its cities silent but for pealing bells, an entire country swathed in crepe, its commerce stilled and its citizens reflecting on the sobering loss and the finality of burying Henry Clay. *"Burying* HENRY CLAY!" Butler roared. "Bury the records of your country's history—bury the hearts of living millions—bury the mountains, the rivers, the lakes, and the spreading lands from sea to sea, with which his name is inseparably associated, and even then you would not bury HENRY CLAY—for he lives in other lands, and speaks in other tongues, and to other times than ours."[14]

As Butler spoke, Francis Preston Blair in the gallery scanned the assembly. His eyes found Daniel Webster among the cabinet, the last of the Great Triumvirate, now in his final days serving as Millard Fillmore's secretary of state. Blair saw in Webster's face haunting, inconsolable sadness.[15] Daniel Webster himself had less than four months to live.

The service ended. Attendants quietly removed the silver plate covering Clay's face. President Fillmore paused only briefly to look on Clay for the last time. Tuberculosis had made him more skeleton than man and had drained the vitality out of his expressive face, but visitors in his last days had still seen something of the old spark, even at the very end. Now that was gone too, and what remained was only an effigy. Those who knew him well did not linger now to gaze upon it. At first, the plate was removed at stops on the lengthy journey home whenever Clay lay in state for public viewing, but the practice was soon discontinued. The remains had not been embalmed, and it was summer. In any case, those who knew him preferred to keep their memories unimpaired. When he arrived in Lexington, his family would leave the plate in place.[16]

The coffin was soon moved to the Rotunda and set atop a bier. Despite its enormous size, the Rotunda was quickly crammed with a confused, shoving crowd. Outside, the throng overflowed the portico and public grounds. Grief, curiosity, and the limited time almost turned the scene into mayhem as the jostling and rising murmur of the mob alarmed the U.S. marshal and his deputies. The confusion was understandable. Henry Clay was the first American to lie in state at the Capitol. No other official of the government, not even a president, had ever been accorded that honor. Procedures for managing the resulting crowd did not exist, and the marshal and his assistants took a while to restore order and establish the proper decorum. At last the crowd formed an orderly file that entered the Rotunda and parted into two queues on either side of the funeral bier, never pausing, steadily passing to catch a glimpse of the shadowed face in the odd coffin. Americans would not do this again for thirteen years. Then it would be for Abraham Lincoln.

AT 3:30 THAT afternoon it was time for Clay to start home. The Committee on Arrangements and the honorary pallbearers, led by four military companies and followed by a large crowd, accompanied the casket to the railroad station where a locomotive was standing by. At the station, thousands of men and women stood silently as the coffin was placed in a special car. The entire train was trimmed in crepe. The six senators selected to take Clay home prepared to board, a strange bunch split evenly between Whigs and Democrats. They included the venerable Lewis Cass, at seventy the eldest, and Tennessee's James C. Jones, a youngster at forty-three. Sam Houston, the flamboyant Tennessee transplant to Texas, confidant of Andrew Jackson, was part of the group, as was New Jersey's Robert F. Stockton, whose grandfather had signed the Declaration of Independence. The train's whistle wheezed to a full roar, and its wheels began their slow turns, easing out of Washington like a black snake, bound first for Baltimore.

It was a mark of Clay's importance that this last journey home began by heading away from it. The family agreed to allow the body to travel a much extended, roundabout route from Washington to Lexington, though Clay's son

Thomas dreaded the prospect of it all. "Oh! how sickening is the splendid pageantry I have to go through from this to Lexington," Thomas wrote to his wife.[17] In addition, the funeral procession was unprecedented. The funeral party would cover more than a thousand miles by train and steamboat, first to Baltimore and Wilmington and Philadelphia and then swinging north to New Jersey and New York, arcing over to Buffalo before heading south through Ohio to Kentucky. The journey consumed nine days—a direct passage could have taken Clay home in a fraction of that time—and attracted huge crowds in large cities and drew out the entire populations of towns. Aside from the journey's obvious symbolism, it held subtle significance too. When Clay first traveled from Lexington to Washington, the trip took weeks of hard trekking on horseback and rickety stagecoaches. That was in 1806, when Thomas Jefferson was president. The enormous continental heartland called Louisiana had only just been added to a country that was still mainly a wilderness crossed by trails, many only paths hemmed by trees and undergrowth. When Clay headed home four and a half decades later, he passed through a land unrecognizably altered and marked by unparalleled expansion and improvement. Americans had turned trails into roads, some paved with wooden planks or broken stones to make them passable in all weathers, allowing coaches to cover twenty, sometimes thirty miles a day. Travelers who decades before had slept under the stars now could stay in moderately comfortable lodgings.

Americans now call such wonders "infrastructure," but Clay's generation called them internal improvements. He had been their constant champion through both private initiative and public subsidies. Internal improvements, he preached, could speed American commerce, bolster American security, refine life on rough farmsteads, transform remote villages into thriving townships. With such encouragement, engineers had scoured harbors and dredged rivers. Where there were no rivers, they dug them in the form of canals that could float keelboats heavy with freight and passengers into the interior. Along the way, steam revolutionized water traffic to allow packets to strain against American rivers and moor in spacious harbors, courtesy of the Army Corps of Engineers. Steam radically changed ground travel as well. When Clay first came to Washington, he would have heard only the wind in the trees, the songs of birds, the rush of untamed waters. On his last journey home, in 1852, the pounding cylinders of his locomotive joined a chorus of machined progress that had become an American expectation, a march that rarely paused for anything. It paused only briefly for Clay's passing. Americans felt in their bones the inevitability of material improvement as they saw the future dance to the music of roaring steam whistles atop grand riverboats and heard the pinging of spikes driven for new

iron rails and more locomotives. That summer evening in 1852, one of those locomotives pulled Henry Clay into the American twilight, a full moon waxing.

THE TRAIN ARRIVED at Baltimore's outer depot on Poppleton and Pratt
streets at 6:00 P.M. Attendants placed the coffin on an ornate hearse that slowly
made its way up Pratt Street between a vast crowd toward the towering domed
rotunda of the Exchange, a building owned by a joint stock company of Baltimore merchants. There the coffin was placed on a large draped catafalque. Its
faceplate was removed, and the men of the local militia, in this case the Independent Greys, managed the slow-moving lines that passed in tribute well into
the night.[18]

At 10:15 the next morning, a large procession escorted the coffin to the
Philadelphia Depot. By 11:00 the train was on its way to Wilmington, where it
stopped before proceeding at 7:00 P.M. to Philadelphia. A large crowd was gathered at that city's Baltimore Depot when the train arrived at 9:00, and a torchlight procession conveyed the remains to Independence Hall. That night into the
next morning, Philadelphians filed passed the funeral bier, military guards at its
corners. No one seemed to have noticed the coincidence of the date, especially
the year. Clay came to this room exactly seventy-six years, almost to the day,
after the Declaration of Independence had been signed there in the year 1776.

On Saturday, July 3, the body was escorted to Kensington and placed on the
steamboat *Trenton* bound for New York City. New York closed down and turned
out on Broadway to see the makeshift parade that bore Clay to City Hall. He lay
in state there for the rest of the day and all of the next, July 4, a Sunday.[19]

Despite a veneer of organization, almost everything about this funeral journey was impromptu and planned on the fly. It was a testament to the resourcefulness of the senators accompanying the remains. In New York City, for
example, there was no set time for departure, and the city planned to have Clay
lie in state "until the Congressional delegation determine to proceed onward."[20]
After the Fourth, after tens of thousands of New Yorkers had paid their respects,
the congressional delegation decided it was time to move on. Another grand
procession conveyed the remains and the funeral delegation to the *Santa Claus,*
a Troy passenger steamer, which promptly headed up the Hudson River to Albany. The *Santa Claus* made only a few brief stops, but all the towns along the
way paid respects anyway. As the steamer neared Poughkeepsie at 5:00 P.M., it
slowed to allow citizens in small boats to hand up flowers for the coffin. Albany
was alerted and ready for their arrival. By the time the *Santa Claus* docked, a
general din of steamboat whistles, church bells, and firing guns had broken out.
Preparing to disembark, the funeral party was startled to see the gigantic crowd

that stretched into the dark distance of Albany's streets. After all, it was 11:00 at night.[21]

At 8:30 the next morning, the body and its growing entourage were escorted to the Erie Railroad Station, where another special funeral train began a slow journey to Buffalo, briefly pausing for large crowds at towns along the way. Like Albany, Buffalo remained up for the train despite its late arrival, greeting it with a torchlight procession that conveyed the coffin to the *Buckeye State,* an enormous steamboat of the first class, almost three hundred feet long and boasting powerful engines that made her one of the fastest of the Great Lakes packets. She was soon under way, lighted from bow to stern, heading down the Erie shore toward Cleveland.

SOME FIVE HUNDRED miles to the west, as the *Buckeye State* sped toward Cleveland, citizens and officials in Springfield, Illinois, were doing what countless towns across America were doing—gathering to mourn the death of Henry Clay. In Springfield, plans for such ceremonies had been made the evening of Clay's death at a public meeting presided over by the young lawyer Abraham Lincoln. The next day a special committee set the following Tuesday as the day for the commemoration and the Illinois statehouse as the place. Stephen T. Logan, Lincoln's former law partner and a leader in Illinois politics, was to deliver the eulogy. Before July 6, however, Lincoln was tapped to take Logan's place. It has never been clear why this was done, but Lincoln must have been ambivalent about it. He was tired, having just returned from a long trip riding the Illinois judicial circuit, and he was busy preparing the defense of a Mexican War veteran, an amputee, who stood accused of stealing from the U.S. mails.[22] It was also extremely short notice, and Lincoln's previous experience at writing a eulogy—he had delivered one when President Zachary Taylor died two years earlier—had been a frustrating disappointment.

He was likely troubled by the task for other reasons as well, for he admired Clay more than he did any other man on the American political scene, describing him later as "my beau ideal of a statesman."[23] He had never met Clay, but he had devoured his speeches and had even heard him speak on one memorable occasion at Lexington in 1847. Lincoln had been visiting his in-laws, the important Robert Todd family, who knew Clay quite well. Clay was a frequent dinner guest in the Todd home, and Lincoln's wife, Mary, as a girl had once taken her new pony to Ashland to show it off to Clay.[24]

Tackling this important and unexpected task, Lincoln hurriedly consulted Clay's own writings and published speeches for inspiration, even searching for a model eulogy to imitate, but he could find nothing helpful. When the observances opened on July 6 at the Springfield Episcopal Church before moving to the hall of the state House of Representatives for his speech, Lincoln felt ill prepared and showed it. He spoke for just under an hour and was as disappointed as his listeners with a lackluster, pedestrian effort. He was especially frustrated because Clay meant so much to him, and Lincoln obviously meant it when he noted how Clay's failed quests for the presidency had not diminished him in the slightest, how those who had won the office "all rose *after,* and set long before him."[25] Most of all, though, Lincoln strained to describe Clay as a champion not only of the Union but of human freedom, from his support for Latin American and Greek independence to his advocacy of gradual emancipation of American slaves and their colonization in Africa. Lincoln found both courses wise and sensible. He did not say so on July 6, 1852, but he was convinced, like Clay, that only gradual emancipation would end slavery without destroying the Union, and only colonization would remove freed slaves from the enduring bigotry of white Americans.

Although Lincoln's speech was strangely disappointing and its effect unmemorable, there was a seed of great meaning and portent in it. Haste and the emotion of the moment seemed to have overwhelmed his talent for soaring rhetoric, his flair for muscular prose, a talent that appeared in some of Clay's best speeches, a gift that had helped make Clay Lincoln's political idol. That July day in the Springfield statehouse, the task proved too much for Lincoln, and he confessed as much about understanding Henry Clay's appeal: "The spell—the long-enduring spell—with which the souls of men were bound to him, is a miracle," he said. He then asked, "Who can compass it?"[26]

Lincoln was asking how such a miracle could be understood, and on that day he clearly did not know the answer. But the echo of Clay's words would sound in Lincoln's mind through the years and eventually find voice in Lincoln's own words, when it really mattered. Lincoln would in the end manage to compass the miracle that puzzled him that day. It would be later, when it really mattered.

THE *BUCKEYE STATE* reached Cleveland, where a train waited to transport the funeral party south, at last heading toward Clay's home, passing through Columbus and arriving at Cincinnati at 11:00 A.M. on July 8. The large gathering at the station there included citizens, military companies, local lodges of Masons and Oddfellows, and firemen. Immediately a long procession formed to convey the body and its growing number of companions to the wharves on the Ohio. It took two hours to reach the river and the steamer that would take Clay to Louisville. The boat, a special charter, had delayed its scheduled departure by an hour.

The earliest French explorers called the Ohio "the beautiful river," and most travelers ever since have agreed. The waters were clear and almost always smooth, resembling polished glass except when southerly breezes rippled them for a few hours, usually at midday. Before there were steamboats, those winds had allowed travelers to make sail and beat upriver against the current. At night, the river caught starlight like a mirror and reflected the rising moon in a long shaft that chased the hulls of watercraft and mesmerized their occupants.[27] Clay had traveled the Ohio many times. This last trip would carry him on it for the rest of Thursday and into dawn on Friday. Along the way, emerging national greatness was evident in bustling towns that had sprung up on the river's banks and trim farms cultivating its fertile valley. They were lively places usually, but that Thursday they were subdued as the steamboat passed, steadily ringing its bell to signal its approach. Occasionally church bells and cannon answered from communities wrapped in black.

The steamer was the *Ben Franklin,* a U.S. mailboat that regularly made the Louisville run. Two years earlier, Ralph Waldo Emerson had taken the *Ben Franklin* out of Cincinnati on the way to visit Mammoth Cave, and indeed the trip was often festive with tourists bound for excursions. But on this run all was quiet except for the ringing bell, the thrashing waters under the boat's paddle wheels, the reciprocating pistons of its engine sending a rhythmic thrum through its decks and cabins. The Senate delegation and others who had started this journey eight days earlier must have been exhausted, and everyone was certainly crowded and uncomfortable as the entourage had grown, increased along the way by delegations joining the trip to Lexington.

Yet the *Ben Franklin* had been only a few hours under way when something remarkable happened. The ringing bell suddenly stopped, and curious passengers crowded to the boat's starboard rail. Indiana was off to the right, and just ahead on a community wharf stood more than two dozen ghosts, white shadows in the lowering sun. The regular beat of the bell having stopped, the silence was unsettling as the steamer glided closer. Gradually the passengers could see that the figures were not ghosts but girls. There were thirty-one of them, each to represent a state of the Union, and all but one dressed in white. The one in black was Kentucky. Behind them, off the wharf, the population of their town was gathered and hushed.

No one said a word, and the *Ben Franklin* continued downriver. Its bell began ringing steadily again, and the passengers moved away from the rail. The crew, familiar with the towns along the route, could have told them the name of the place with the girls. It was Rising Sun, Indiana.[28]

———

THE *BEN FRANKLIN* completed the 133-mile run to Louisville at six on Friday morning. Four hours later the funeral party departed on a train that stopped at Frankfort and finally at dusk arrived in Clay's hometown of Lexington. A large crowd carrying torches silently escorted the coffin through the black-cloaked town. Lexington's population was about nine thousand ordinarily, but in the first week of that July it became the most populous place in the state. It was impossible to make an accurate count, but at least thirty thousand—and some say as many as a hundred thousand—were gathered to pay respects to Clay.

A procession conducted the coffin to the Ashland estate, where it arrived at eight o'clock that evening and was placed in the large dining room. The Senate committee along with the family filled the house. Clay's son Thomas had made the grueling journey with his father's remains, and he was now joined by his brothers James and John and his mother, Lucretia. She was seventy-one and feeble, an intensely private woman who had never publicly shown much emotion or displayed much affection, masking what her family and friends knew to be a turbulent and loving heart. The years had made her resemble a frail bird, her eyes hard as diamonds. She had many devoted friends in Lexington, but now she had lost her best one, the only person in the world who had ever thoroughly understood her. She, the boys, and their families stood next to the coffin that night. Just five years earlier, Lucretia had been sitting down to dinner with her family in this same room when she had received devastating news about one of her sons. Now, surrounded by fine china and crystal gleaming in the candlelight, she gazed at her husband's coffin. The family did not remove the faceplate; they did not need to. Clay was not really in that metal container, but he was there in that room. And for the rest of the night so was Lucretia.[29]

The Clay Guard that had come down from Cincinnati stood vigil through that night as thousands continued to stream into Lexington for the funeral the next day, Saturday, July 10. At 10:00 A.M. the Reverend Edward F. Berkeley, rector of Clay's church in Lexington and the man who had baptized him only five years earlier, read a sermon and eulogy in a small outdoor service at Ashland. The coffin was then taken to Lexington in a grandly designed car drawn by eight horses, each as white as snow and wearing silver-fringed crepe. Lucretia watched the procession leave in the rising heat of the July morning before going back into the house and closing the door. She did not feel well, she had said simply. She would not go to the cemetery.

In Lexington a spectacular pageant grew to immense proportions, the procession extending farther and farther as muffled drums beat the cadence toward the Lexington Cemetery. The now familiar sounds of bells and cannon echoed out from the city across the countryside. Lucretia would have heard them. The crowd overflowed the cemetery's grounds, many out of earshot of Berkeley's reading of the Episcopal service and unable to see the ritual by the local Masons. During the ceremony, they placed on his coffin a Masonic apron, a gift to Clay from the Marquis de Lafayette, removing it just before the coffin was placed in its vault.

And so it ended, nine days and more than a thousand miles from where it had begun with the death of Clay and the beginning of his extraordinary journey home. The man whom *The New York Times* had judged "too great to be president" had been given a farewell to make a monarch envious. The London *Times* spoke of Clay's "antique greatness" and said that Clay's death deprived many Americans of something noble and fine, something connected to the beginning of the country, spanning from the Revolution through the tumult and strain of first creating and then building an American dream.[30]

Henry Clay's part in that adventure had been always central and often crucial. But there was more to it than that. Lincoln had described the enduring affection for Clay as a miracle, as mysterious as it was tangible. Lincoln and many of his fellow Americans could not fully grasp it, he said, but they certainly felt it, and Lincoln would draw on it to help him save the country when the time came. Some of those girls in Rising Sun would later send off fathers, husbands, and sweethearts to fight and die for their country, and for the same reason that they had wrapped themselves in peculiar clothes and waited on a hot wharf that July afternoon for a steamboat.

In 1852 all of the country mourned Clay's passing, marking a rare instance of agreement among people who had gotten into the habit of disagreeing about almost everything. He was a titanic symbol of Union to the very end, promoting compromise to prevent his country's demise and the slaughter he was certain would follow. He saved his country until its muscles and sinews could weather a terrible civil war, until "fair seed time" and his example could produce a man like Lincoln, who when Clay died was yet straining to understand what it all meant, to understand the miracle that stemmed from Clay's life, a life that had begun seven and a half decades earlier amid Virginia's swampy rills. Clay's life began in the midst of a war that was, as Lincoln's would be, for national survival.

Losing Henry Clay was a uniquely personal event for the nation because his life had been the mirror of his country and its aspirations. In that, it was an extraordinary life. "I will forgive your weakness," wrote a student at Yale, who could have been speaking for the entire country, "if you bow your head and weep for the departure of his noble spirit."[31]

HENRY CLAY

CHAPTER ONE

The Slashes

I N THE YEAR 1777 the United States was less than a year old and at war. It was also deeply divided over the wisdom of that war and doubtful in the main about its conclusion. And yet for much of the country the war was a distant event. Britain chose to focus on what it regarded as the hotbeds of pro-war sentiment, which were in the Northeast. The strategic decision to isolate New England kept the war centered on New York and made it remote for the rest of the thirteen erstwhile colonies, at least for a time. Now styling themselves as sovereign states united for the purpose of fighting this war and not much else, the new United States confronted the complicated and divisive nature of their enemy. The rebellion that had become the Revolution also became a civil war. Little wonder that many did not hold out much hope for success.

This was the world that greeted Henry Clay on April 12, 1777, two years almost to the day after the shedding of first blood at Lexington and Concord in Massachusetts that marked the beginning of the shooting war with Britain. In that respect, he and his country were intertwined in both origin and destiny.

Henry Clay was a member of the sixth generation of a family that had been in colonial Virginia for more than a hundred and fifty years. John Clay was the first of that line, emigrating from England around 1612. Descendants maintained that John was the son of a Welsh aristocrat, but there is no definitive proof of the claim. If John's pedigree was unremarkable, though, his industry once he arrived in the New World was admirable. Hard work and two good marriages brought him property and prominence. His marriage to Elizabeth—his second, her third—produced Charles in 1645. Ten years later, when John died, he left a considerable estate. Charles married Hannah Wilson and commenced something of a Clay tradition for producing large families. He and Hannah had seven children, three of them girls, though the female children had a distressing way of dying young, a peculiarity that tragically repeated itself in subsequent generations. Charles's boys, however, were not only hale, two of them were well-nigh immortal. Charles Jr., born in 1676, lived to see ninety, and his older brother, Henry, born in 1672, nearly matched that endurance, dying in 1760 at age eighty-eight. Such longevity was rare anywhere in the world, let alone in hardscrabble colonial Virginia.

The elder Charles was a prosperous planter whose lands lay on the Virginia frontier, vulnerable to hostile Indians and persistently ignored by the colonial government in Jamestown. For those beyond the sight line of the eastern elite, prosperity did not necessarily mean security, and success did not breed prudence when it came to their relations with the Crown's neglectful representatives. Sir William Berkeley's administration proved indifferent to mounting protests, and Charles Clay joined Nathaniel Bacon's rebellion in 1676 that chased Governor Berkeley to the Eastern Shore of Virginia and briefly set up a rival government for the colony. Bacon's Rebellion did not last long, but its occurrence made an impression on the royal administration. Charles Clay emerged from the event unpunished.

Clay lands were originally in Henrico County, a large district that spanned both sides of the James River. In 1749, the Virginia Assembly had established Chesterfield County out of Henrico, making it the new district within which sat "The Raels," the Clay plantation that belonged to Charles's son, the long-lived Henry. While in his late thirties, Henry married teenaged Mary Mitchell sometime before 1709 and began a family that would also number seven children. The youngest, John, survived Henry by only two years, dying young at forty-one in 1762. Around 1740, though, he married affluent Sarah Watkins and had two sons with her before her untimely death at age twenty-five; the elder of them, also named John, was Henry Clay's father.

John Clay was born in 1742 and at age twenty inherited his father's plantation, "Euphraim," in Henrico County with about twelve slaves. Three years later, he married fifteen-year-old Elizabeth Hudson, the daughter of a substantial Hanover County family. The Hudsons owned roughly five hundred acres of cultivated fields and pasturage three miles from Hanover Court House and sixteen miles north of Richmond. Elizabeth and her older sister, Mary, were to inherit this property in equal portions, a legacy sure to enhance John's already impressive holdings.

John and Elizabeth lived at Euphraim and in characteristic Clay fashion began working on a large family. Sadly, they had limited success, for their children died with a frequency remarkable even for a time when it was frightfully easy for children to die. They lost their first girl, Molly, so quickly that she does not even appear in many genealogical charts or biographical accounts. Their second child, Betty, lived only a little more than ten years, and the third, a boy named Henry after his paternal great-grandfather, only about eight years. Even the subsequent children were for the most part frail or just unlucky: George, born in 1771 and named after Elizabeth's father, did not reach twenty, and Sarah, born some three years later, died at twenty-one.

George Hudson's estate technically belonged to Mary and Elizabeth after his death in 1773, but his will also stipulated that their mother could remain on the farm in Hanover County for the rest of her life. She herself was elderly and feeble, and her need for care and companionship probably prompted the Clays to move from Euphraim to the Hudson farm in early 1777. Elizabeth was heavy with her seventh child, who turned out to be her fourth son. Thus it happened that Henry Clay was born at the Hudson home in Hanover County on April 12. They named him in remembrance of both his ancestor and his dead brother.

JOHN MADE ARRANGEMENTS to establish sole ownership of the Hudson farm by buying out the interest Mary and her husband, John Watkins, had in the property. It was there, his birthplace, that Henry would spend his first years. He responded to a question many years later about its exact location by casually observing that his memory was sketchy about the matter because "I was very young at my birth." But he could approximately place it as having been "between Black Tom's Slash, and Hanover Court-house."[1] The farm sat in that part of Hanover County called "the Slashes" because of the swampy terrain covered with thick undergrowth. The house was probably much like the one at Euphraim in Henrico County, though possibly more accommodating for a growing family. The Hudson home was a clapboard structure of one and a half stories, three prominent dormer windows resembling doghouses jutting from the sloping roof and offering a pleasant view through old growth trees of nearby Machump's Creek. Two large masonry chimneys of either stone or brick rose prominently on each end of the house, a mark of affluence when poor farmers had only one chimney, often made of logs.

The old Hudson place, which John and Elizabeth named Clay's Spring, was modest in comparison with the grand mansions of the Virginia Tidewater. Clay's forebears had at one time owned thousands of acres, but successive generations had divided the lands among numerous heirs. Earlier, until Virginia abolished entail in 1776, eldest sons inherited the lion's share of estates, relegating their siblings to the ranks of lesser planters. Except for his father, most of Henry Clay's paternal ancestors had not been eldest sons.

Clay's Spring was a handsome establishment, though. In addition to the main house, an extra room had been added around one of the chimneys, and the yard was fenced. Various outbuildings helped in the workaday business of growing corn, tobacco, and wheat as well as livestock, all with the labor of about twenty slaves. The income from the farm and Euphraim, left in the hands of an overseer, supported a growing family. In addition to John Clay (born around 1775) and young Henry, Elizabeth bore another son, in 1779, whom they named Porter.

Little remains to draw a clear picture of Henry Clay's father, John Clay. No physical description survives, nor is there any detailed recollection of memorable events in his life. He might have been an imposing man with an air of authority, characteristics suggested by references to him in legal records of Hanover and Chesterfield counties as "Sir John Clay." Neither he nor any of his American ancestors had been knighted, and even the supposition that the title was an honorific out of respect for the family's aristocratic British ancestry makes little sense. Years later Henry explained away the title as merely "a sobriquet" his father had somehow acquired. It was a credible explanation suggesting that like the honorary Kentucky colonel, John Clay was respected enough by both neighbors and the courts to merit the mark of natural nobility. It was, in any case, destined to be something of a family trait.[2]

It was not an easy life, but it must have seemed a good one, with God not only in His heaven but also very much in the household and life of the Clays. Generally, religion was not as important for Virginians as for, say, New Englanders. The rural setting with scattered, sparse populations meant that churches tended to be isolated in both material and spiritual ways. People wed in their parlors, christened their children in their homes, and buried family in graves dug on their farms rather than among orderly headstones in church cemeteries. Noah Webster, visiting from New England, observed these practices with sniffing disdain when he noted that Virginians placed "their churches as far as possible from town and their play houses in the center."[3]

John Clay expended considerable effort trying to correct that. Around the time of his marriage he received "the call." Eventually he became the Baptists' chief apostle in Hanover County, working to change attitudes that were not necessarily irreligious but did find the Church of England emotionally unsatisfying and spiritually moribund. After the Great Awakening swept its revivalist fervor across the country, Virginians found the mandatory nature of Anglican worship—dissenters could be fined and even imprisoned—infuriating, and a simmering discontent over the lack of religious freedom helped stoke dissatisfaction with other aspects of British rule. Presbyterians became the dominant denomination in literate areas as converts in the Tidewater and Piedmont were matched by Scots-Irish migrations from Pennsylvania into the Shenandoah Valley. In the region between—Henrico, Chesterfield, and Hanover counties—the less literate gravitated to the Baptists, whose services were long on emotion and short on complicated liturgical teachings.[4]

Because of this, the number of Baptists markedly increased in the 1760s and 1770s, particularly among lower-class whites and slaves. Preachers could be unschooled and were always uncompensated, at least by any hierarchical authority. They came to their pulpits after an extraordinary religious experience referred to as "the call." After John Clay received the call, he organized churches in Henrico and Hanover counties, including a large congregation at Winn's Church in 1776. Most of his flock comprised a sect known as New Light Baptists, not exactly economic levelers but noted for simple attire and the practice of calling each other "sister" and "brother" regardless of social rank or economic status. They were clearly more democratic than class-conscious Anglicans, and congregations even allowed slaves to participate in worship services. That eccentric practice alone caused Anglican planter elites anxiety over the influence of Baptists, a troubling, troublesome lot who made even Presbyterians look respectable.[5]

Baptists took such contempt as a badge of honor. They and the Presbyterians grew increasingly angry about the power of establishment Anglicans, in particular evidenced by onerous taxes and reflexive persecution. At least once John Clay himself felt the weight of Anglican anger when he was jailed for his dissent. Such experiences, though, fueled rather than suppressed enthusiasm for religious liberty. As protests over British taxes became more strident, calls for spiritual freedom matched them. The drive for independence gained momentum, and the calls for disestablishing the Church of England became more vocal.[6]

Even though the fighting was far away, Virginia was in the middle of the American Revolution from the start, and no part of Virginia more than Hanover County. The county's burgess in the Virginia Assembly, after all, was for years the famous firebrand Patrick Henry, who had been calling the king a tyrant for more than a decade when the shooting started. For his part, John Clay openly supported independence, tying it to Anglican disestablishment and helping to circulate a Baptist petition in 1776 pledging support to the new nation if it would stand for religious as well as political liberty. John and Elizabeth were notably fiery patriots in a region known for its radicalism.[7]

Then, in 1780, John became sick. It only took him a few months to deduce that his illness was fatal, though no one has ever been able to tell what exactly was wrong with him, only that it brought about an exceedingly untimely end to his life. He was only thirty-eight years old and had been hearty enough to make Elizabeth pregnant just before falling ill. Yet his decline was rapid and remorseless. We can only guess the pall it cast over the household. Aside from the emotional distress, there were sobering practical considerations: six children, the oldest only nine and the youngest an infant, would be dependent on a thirty-year-old expectant mother. Adding to these heartbreaking burdens, Elizabeth's elderly mother was seriously ill as well. And there was more. Reports told of British raids in the area. As Clay's Spring became the scene of two wrenching deathwatches, the Revolutionary War came to Virginia.

On November 4, 1780, John Clay summoned several neighbors to witness his last will and testament, a simple document that named Elizabeth custodian of both plantations until the children grew up or she remarried. He wanted the estate kept intact until the children came of age in any case, which was eighteen for the girls and twenty for the boys. The oldest, George, was to inherit Euphraim, and Clay's Spring was to be sold and the proceeds divided among all the male children. Each child, including the girls, was to have an equal share in the livestock. John left two slaves, specified by name, to each child. Henry was to inherit James and Little Sam.[8]

It was as thorough a document as the modest patrimony of John Clay warranted. The settlement of the estate's land on the oldest son sustained the habit of primogeniture. Clay anticipated Elizabeth's remarriage as likely for a young widow and consequently made modest provisions for her maintenance, lending for her use the Henrico County property slated for George, obviously in the certainty that he would take care of his mother should she remain a widow.

His affairs in order, John Clay lingered through his last winter. He had started it "very sick & week [*sic*]" and never regained any lost ground.[9] He and his mother-in-law sank together—she would survive him by only a few months—and when spring came, shortly after Elizabeth bore him another child, he died. The child, a girl, died too.

AS CLAY'S SPRING mourned these losses, the war came not just to the Slashes but to Elizabeth's doorstep. The British had been in Virginia for months, starting when former American general Benedict Arnold completed his transformation into turncoat by accepting a British general's commission and setting out on a hunt for forces under the Marquis de Lafayette. Then Lord Cornwallis abandoned his indecisive southern campaign to head north out of the Carolinas. By the spring of 1781, the war's focus had shifted to Virginia as these varied British contingents converged in the state. In the fall, the war would end there as well, when Cornwallis surrendered to George Washington and the Comte de Rochambeau at Yorktown.

That spring, however, Washington was encamped outside New York City,

Rochambeau was at Newport, Rhode Island, and Lafayette was on the run from Cornwallis's superior numbers. Virginia was extremely vulnerable, especially its isolated western settlements. The campaign mounted by Cornwallis had as its primary objective a storage depot at Point of Forks on the upper James River, and he dispatched a large force to that place. A smaller one under Lieutenant Colonel Banastre Tarleton was to harry the countryside by destroying its farms, a legitimate military objective because those farms could feed Patriot forces. Tarleton's other goal was to disrupt Virginia's government, which had repaired to the supposed safety of Charlottesville when the British entered the state.

Tarleton began by burning several buildings in Hanover Court House before fanning his men out across the county.[10] They came to Clay's Spring in late May, possibly the day after the family had buried John Clay. As Tarleton's dragoons approached, Elizabeth hurried her overseer—a white man running the farm during John's illness—out the back door, sending him scampering into the woods to avoid capture. It was a wise move. Tarleton's men meant business.

That business was one of proficient if random destruction and simple theft. The British soldiers shouldered their way into the house, ransacked it for valuables, and packed away any food they could not eat on the spot. They smashed furniture and slashed open feather beds. It snowed feathers in the yard as they emptied the mattresses out the windows. Others chased chickens to kill and throw across their saddles. They rounded up some of the slaves to take away. Spying the new grave, they inspected it for hidden treasure by running their swords into the freshly turned earth.

Elizabeth Clay watched all this with Porter and Henry clinging to her skirts. The children were terrified. It is difficult to know how much of what happened next was embellished by family legend and postwar patriotic fervor. Possibly Clay's campaign biographers later exaggerated events; it's hard to resist a good story. Clay himself was quite young (only four), but the event remained understandably vivid for him for the rest of his life: the sight of those strangely costumed men on snorting horses with flashing swords that cut up the family's beds and stabbed at his father's grave, the smashing of furniture, the chaos of shouting men, squawking chickens, and the frightened slaves standing amid the prancing, crisscrossing horses, all under the soft snowfall of the mattress feathers; and his mother, her arm tight around his shoulder, pressing him to her side, Porter crying, her voice rising in anger, and the man they later learned was "Bloody Ban" himself—a name given him for having massacred Abraham Buford's surrendering Patriots just a year earlier in the Carolina Waxhaws, an act that had made the phrase "Tarleton's Quarter" a description for warfare without mercy. Possibly Elizabeth angrily denounced Tarleton, as family lore was to recall. But it is doubtful that he paused, as was later said, to pull from his pocket a small pouch from which he emptied a clutch of coins onto a table, explaining as he stalked out to mount his horse that it was to make up for the mess.

The raid was brief because the British had more important quarry. Tarleton and his men were soon heading for Charlottesville, where they put the Virginia Assembly to flight and nearly captured Thomas Jefferson at his home, Monticello. They had indeed left Clay's Spring a mess. Grandchildren later told how Elizabeth scorned Tarleton's gesture as much as she had him. She swept up the coins, they would say, and angrily hurled them into the fire.[11] This scene of this quaint family legend almost certainly did not happen. Yet, given what Elizabeth Clay faced that spring and how she managed it all, there is no reason to doubt her capacity for defiance. The destruction of her house was quite real, a grim accompaniment to the destruction of her life with the loss of her husband and baby on top of the burden of tending to her dying mother while taking care of six children. There is not a single recollection, however, of Elizabeth Clay's ever uttering a word of complaint, let alone showing any self-pity, as she put her family's life back together. Instead, she immediately commenced rebuilding the farm and her children's future. She must have wept as she faced the insurmountable odds, braced for her mother's death, and buried her husband and baby, but Henry did not see it. This remarkable woman probably did not throw Tarleton's money into the fire, because he probably did not leave any, but in the months that followed she performed quiet deeds of even greater courage.

At least the war did not come back. In only a few months, in fact, word filtered back from the east of the British surrender at Yorktown. Yet the good luck of peace or even her personal fortitude would not better Elizabeth's situation. For one thing, when John died he had not finished paying John and Mary Watkins for their share of Clay's Spring. This did not pose a problem—the Watkinses were moving to Kentucky and did not want the property—but it did become a complication when Elizabeth remarried less than a year after John's death.

The brevity of her widowhood was not unusual in a world framed by essential material want. She could not long have provided for her family otherwise. And Elizabeth herself presented an attractive prospect to suitors, a still youthful woman in possession of some measure of an estate that included salable property. As it happened, her suitor did not have to go far to find her, and she did not have to wait long to be found. He was Henry Watkins, the younger brother of her sister's husband, John. In fact, he was even more family than that: John Clay's mother and Henry Watkins's father were sister and brother, making him John Clay's first cousin. The family connections were not coincidences, nor should they be ridiculed as resulting from the ignorant practices of the inbred. Rather, they were a demonstration of the clannish nature of colonial Virginia, where the most elite families often included married cousins because of the scarcity of marriageable upper-class prospects. For the Clays and Watkinses, it was evidence of the interwoven nature of communities in rural settings.

For reasons not clear, Elizabeth delayed probating John's will. When she remarried, however, the will stipulated the termination of her role as custodian of the plantations, the sale of Clay's Spring, and the distribution of the assets to the children. In February 1782, everyone agreed to let the court sort the matter out. The judge ordered the property sold to retire the debt on it, with the remainder going to the heirs. Everyone apparently anticipated this sensible solution, and Elizabeth's new husband quickly resolved the matter of debt and distribution by purchasing Clay's Spring from the estate, a belated wedding present for his bride.[12]

Henry Watkins was a captain in the Virginia militia, a pleasant young man, Hal to his friends. He was also a man of good prospects as well as current substance, as his purchase of Clay's Spring indicated. He brought to the marriage seventeen slaves (the family now owned a total of twenty-five) as well as livestock and two carriages. An affront to modern sensibilities, the presence of slaves was in that time simply another aspect of daily life. The aspiration to live as English country gentlemen was only just that for colonists in the decades before Henry Clay's birth, but the wealth of the great tobacco barons and their reliance on slave labor to build grand fortunes created a southern oligarchy that lived in material grandeur and moral ambiguity. The middling farms with the modest clapboard houses—the place in the social pyramid of the Clays and the Watkinses—also relied on slavery for more than a source of labor. Social status came with owning slaves, determining everything from the circles one moved in to the girls one could court and marry.[13]

Years later, when it became politically prudent to claim impoverished origins framed by hardship, Henry Clay would say that he grew up an orphan in straitened circumstances. Campaign biographies took the cue and succeeded in creating the myth that he came of age with callused hands and in chronic want, his good character the result of his efforts to claw his way out of it. Central to that story was the depiction of him as riding a horse laden with sacks of dried corn to a gristmill on the Pamunkey River and dutifully bringing back the meal to his mother. Hanover County neighbors were said to have taken to calling Henry "the Millboy of the Slashes," and it became a staple of credulous biographers to hang his youth on the hook of that nickname. But it was all an invention of later years, and the poverty it implies was simply never the case. Henry would have done chores, as expected of any boy on a farm, but hard toil on a plantation with twenty-five slaves, as well as long trips to a local gristmill, were not likely. Archaeological evidence indicates that there was a mill on the Clay-Watkins property in any case. Henry Clay was not an orphan, was not impoverished, and was not the Millboy of the Slashes.[14]

Rather, he lived in relative comfort with enough leisure time to learn the fiddle, spend languid afternoons fishing in nearby streams, and become an excellent horseman. He lived in an area with few towns, and what appeared to be villages were actually parts of plantations, their buildings in small clusters bordering cultivated fields. These self-sufficient establishments made towns unnecessary. Place names referred to trail crossings or churches or small county seats denoted as such by having Court House attached to their names, as in Hanover Court House. Roads were often only trails that crossed the region to speed travel and commerce between plantations that lay along rivers, the easiest avenues for trade, the real roads of empire. The county seat had a small store that doubled as a tavern. In Hanover Court House it was Tilghman's Ordinary, owned by Patrick Henry's father-in-law. There was also a courthouse with a little jail attached. The monthly court session or periodic militia muster transformed these somnolent places into centers of festivity and retail. At Tilghman's, men gathered to play cards, discuss politics and horseflesh, and drink. During elections, the courthouse green became the setting for political speeches, some of them memorably delivered by the county's renowned orators, Patrick Henry foremost among them. Novice speechmakers honed their skills by watching such masters and trying out material and techniques before the squinting faces of discerning crowds. Young Henry grew up observing these performances and how they played before audiences, marking what persuaded listeners and, more important, what did not. He was a quick study.[15]

Often the most learned man in the community was the local preacher, and a youngster's first semblance of formal education would be under his guidance. John Marshall took lessons from the Reverend Archibald Campbell in the generation before Clay's, and Nathaniel Hawthorne a generation afterward first learned from a country preacher as well.[16] Clay probably received a few years of schooling at the Vestry House of St. Paul's Church near his home, but details are lacking. As he grew older, he was allowed to go in to Hanover Court House, where a transplanted Englishman named Peter Deacon ran a field school in a one-room log cabin. Clay spent three years at Deacon's school, where the basic elements of the fabled Three Rs (readin', ritin', and 'rithmetic) formed the essentials of a bare-bones curriculum designed to teach children under nearly impossible conditions. The product was a serviceable amount of learning, but nothing more. It was the only formal schooling of Clay's youth, and he always lamented the deficiencies that resulted and admonished children, both his own and those of friends, to mind their books.

In Deacon's school, students widely ranging in age and background were assembled at the same time in that one room, making for a disciplinary challenge even more daunting than the pedagogical one. Deacon had a past clouded by strong drink, and he often took the edge off the day with liberal doses of peach brandy. Mild inebriation made him an easy mark for mischievous boys, but it could also make him irascible. Deacon once struck Henry with "a magisterial blow" that left a mark for "a long time."[17]

Much of Clay's learning took place outside the classroom. In addition to studying the budding and established politicians of Hanover County, he soaked up the culture of the planter class that included a near obsession with horse racing and gambling of all kinds. He saw how men drank—Deacon was a cautionary example—how they joked, and how they argued. Boys sneaked out to drink and smoke; they tried to compromise girls, some willing but most disappointingly chaste. Mischief was usually harmless, if exasperating. And most boys were expected to go out on their own early, to become self-sufficient and ready to shoulder responsibility at an earlier age than in our time. The Revolution taught a generation that lesson with a vengeance, as youngsters had taken up arms to grow up fast with war a harsh tutor. The concept lauded by Thomas Paine in *Common Sense* of America separating from the parentage of Britain had practical application in the changing relations of parents and children in this new, boundless country.[18]

IN ONE SENSE, then, it was not unusual that Henry Clay would leave his family at an early age and strike out on his own. But in another sense, the circumstances that brought this about were peculiar.

It had to do with his mother and stepfather's move to Kentucky. In the mid-1780s, John and Mary Watkins moved to Kentucky's Woodford County. Soon they were sending back stories about the region's potential and their success in it, none of it an exaggeration. John was acquiring significant amounts of land and was well on his way to becoming a leader in the growing region. In 1792, he helped establish the town of Versailles (named after the French palace, a tribute actually to Lafayette, but with the Americanized pronunciation of "Versayles"). He would participate in the convention that drafted Kentucky's state constitution and would serve in the first state legislature. In a few short years, he became eminent in the new state's affairs while growing rich to boot, an example that beckoned Hal to follow.

The need to support his family was the deciding factor. He and Elizabeth had added a daughter and a son of their own to a growing brood strained by the diminishing chances available in Virginia. The best lands were taken, tobacco had depleted the soil of the rest, and even the fertile Shenandoah Valley was filling up with settlers coming south from Pennsylvania. Kentucky was a place of seemingly infinite opportunity and limited risks. The decision to go was simple.

Not so simple were the matters of disposing of their Virginia property and deciding who would make the journey. As for the property, it became a case study of how estates, children, and remarriage could complicate the simplest arrangements. The eldest Clay child, George, died in 1787 (possibly 1788) before coming of age. He therefore never took possession of Euphraim, the Henrico County plantation. Apparently forgetting the provision that only loaned Euphraim to Elizabeth until she remarried, Hal and Elizabeth sold the property along with Clay's Spring as they prepared to leave Virginia. Yet John Clay's will clearly instructed that if George were out of the picture, the proceeds from Euphraim were to go to the other Clay children. In short, John and Elizabeth kept the money from the sale of property that did not belong to them. That they meant no injury to the children was proven years later when the mistake was corrected by a friendly lawsuit to have the property restored to John, Henry, and Porter Clay. The suit was the work of Henry, by then a successful lawyer, a career that confirmed the decision John and Elizabeth made about his future as they left for Kentucky at the end of 1791.[19]

Hal Watkins was a good man who never sought to take John Clay's place for his children but instead worked hard to provide them with all their material needs while setting an example and acting as a friend. By all accounts, the Clay children responded affectionately to this amiable, even-tempered man who made their mother happy. Given that picture of a contented home, it has never been adequately explained why Hal and Elizabeth decided to leave Henry behind when they moved to Kentucky. The tradition of young men starting life early might answer except that John Clay, two years older than Henry, went to Kentucky with the other Clay siblings, Porter and Sarah. Henry could not have wanted to stay behind. He no doubt felt very much as Horace Greeley would years later when his family left Vermont after placing him in an apprenticeship. Emotionally devastated by the separation, Greeley would recall the long walk to his new place of work as the most wrenching moment in his life.[20]

Henry Clay was never so frank in his recollection of this pivotal event in his life. Possibly he better understood the reason for it. Just before leaving Kentucky, Hal Watkins took Henry to Richmond and placed him in the employ of Richard Denny, who ran a successful emporium. Hal told his stepson that this job would be temporary. Hal had taken the measure of Henry's magnetic personality, his quick mind and easy smile, and his ability to work hard without turning tasks into drudgery. Something about the gangly fourteen-year-old next to him in the carriage on the way to Richmond had convinced Hal that Henry should not go to Kentucky.

To that end, Hal pulled some strings and called in some favors. Colonel Thomas Tinsley, delegate to the state legislature from Hanover County and acquainted with Watkins through their militia service, had a brother named Peter who was the clerk of Virginia's High Court of Chancery in Richmond. Using these connections, Hal Watkins secured for Henry an assistant clerkship when one came available. Until then, he would work at Denny's store. Hal left Henry there, returned to Hanover County, and soon afterward set out westward with his family.

Although she went to Kentucky, Elizabeth Clay Watkins never really left Henry, even though they would not see each other again for six years. She loved him and seemed always confident that he would do well, that his natural talent would surmount all obstacles, that his happy manner would best all adversity. His career does not seem to have dazzled her, possibly because she had expected him to be successful. For his part, he loved her in a quiet but no less profound way. The day before he died, he would see her in his room at the National Hotel, even though she had been dead more than twenty-two years. "My mother, mother, mother," he would murmur, perhaps trying to find with his small hand the skirts he had gripped so many years before when "Bloody Ban" had come calling and she had been so brave; or possibly it was a greeting at the end to close the circle from the farewell, here at the beginning, on the day that he and Hal set out for Richmond, leaving his mother and his brothers and sisters at the little clapboard house in the Slashes.[21]

CLAY WORKED IN Denny's store for about a year, stocking shelves and running errands. When business was brisk, usually when the legislature was in session and the town filled with people, he helped behind the counter. Making deliveries gave him a chance to explore the city, which was at first big and imposing for a country boy. Richmond was divided into two sections. The lower town ran along the James River, the commercial center of the city, where wharves jutted into the river and played host to ships up from Norfolk, their holds full of luxurious items from all over the world as well as ordinary goods. Everything about the lower town seemed fresh, new, and substantial, because it was. A devastating fire had leveled almost the entire district in January 1787, the flames leaping from building to wooden building, consuming them as though they were matchboxes. In four short years, the lower town had risen from the ashes like a brick phoenix, masonry the now preferred, fire-resistant construction standard. Richard Denny's store sat on what was called "Brick Row" on Main Street and sold everything from bonnets to books as well as playing cards and liquor.[22]

Henry's errands and deliveries also took him to Richmond's other section, which sat on a range of hills and was called the upper town. There fashionable ladies and gentlemen of the merchant and governing class lived in fine homes, and there Virginia's state government operated out of impressive buildings in varying stages of completion. Atop Shockoe Hill, the largest with the most commanding vista, the capitol was taking final shape after a design Thomas Jefferson had worked out while serving as minister to France. Jefferson based his plans on a Roman temple to which he had added Greek influences to create the "Temple of Liberty" that awed travelers. Citizens were proud of its immensity and elegance, and young Henry, who had never seen a man-made structure nearly so large, was surely impressed.[23]

In 1792, an assistant's place opened in the Chancery, and as promised, Clay was summoned to fill it. The job was important, at least for him. It was certainly a step up from the shop where he pushed a broom and ran errands. It was a step up in situation as well, taking him to the upper town. The post was modest, to be sure—assistant clerks were at the bottom of a long pecking order—and being the newest of the assistant clerks would place him lowest among the lowly boys who toiled at tedious chores that were as mindless as they were endless.

Henry's clothes were a measure of the importance he placed on the impression he hoped to make. His suit, according to some reports, had been made by his mother, her farewell present to help him make a good start in his new life as she embarked on hers. These were his best clothes, then, and though they were not as fine or as elegant as he would have wished, he made sure they were cleaned and pressed.

Thus armed with the optimism that comes with looking one's best, but also with the ambivalence and self-consciousness of a teenaged boy about to launch himself into a new and challenging job, young Clay entered the offices of the Chancery. The boys in the assistant clerk's office were not much older than he, if at all, but they were quite different, a fact evident at first glance. They were jaunty, exuding a worldliness that had them surveying him with a mixture of indifference and contempt. The gulf separating them was instantly apparent in his clothes. Henry's suit was a cotton and silk blend, salt-and-pepper "Figginy" (slang for Virginia homespun). It would never have seemed shabby in the Slashes, but the boys in the Chancery looked as if they expected it to shed hayseeds. Worst of all, Henry had tried to spruce up the coat by liberally infusing it with starch, and the unexpected result was that the coattails jutted out at absurd angles. On his gangly frame, the coat made him look like a tall bird with its tail feathers splayed. Henry's disheveled blond hair, so fair it looked white, topped off the effect. The boys were soon laughing at him.

He laughed too. When they teased him about his clothes, he agreed that they were absurd. When they mocked his use of quaint country phrases or his mispronunciation of a word, he joined the merriment. Gradually the smart jests at his expense didn't seem so amusing. In fact, the boys were soon disarmed by their new companion, particularly when they discovered he could take ribbing with the best of them. They were equally delighted to discover that he could dish it out just as well, summoning the hilariously appropriate ad lib effortlessly. It was clear that they had a first-class wit in their ranks, one a good deal quicker than many of them.[24]

Henry was lucky that two of these boys were from Hanover County. They eased him into the routines of the office, and everyone was soon showing him heretofore undiscovered pleasures of the city. An early biographer claimed that Henry's resolve to improve himself through constant study left him little time for frivolity, but that is simply a fabrication.[25] About the most harmless of Richmond's amusements was the theater, where some good and many bad productions could be enjoyed fairly cheaply. Other diversions were riskier and more expensive, and could be corrosive. The most popular pastimes were drinking and gambling, the latter evidently irresistible for Virginians of all classes but particularly among gentlemen. Mid-eighteenth-century colonial governor Francis Fauquier was said—likely an exaggeration—to have single-handedly popularized Virginians' addiction to games of chance, especially dice. The somber burdens of the American Revolution had curbed the enthusiasm for gambling, but ensuing years had revived it with a vengeance.[26] In Clay's time, cards had replaced dice as the preferred way to part fools from their money, and he developed in these years a lifelong passion for card games. Gambling had become so rampant by the time Clay arrived in Richmond that the legislature, shocked by the spectacle of substantial citizens ruining themselves at gaming tables, enacted a law in 1792 prohibiting the loss of more than twenty dollars a day. It was no use, though. Even legislators who had passed the law and magistrates charged with enforcing it continued merrily to wager their way to ruin, earning the city the distinction of having more gambling "than any place the same size in the world."[27]

Clay did not have a great deal of money, and prudence seems to have kept his gambling ventures from getting out of hand. Others were not so fortunate. A man could lose a week's earnings on the turn of a card. Worse, when such stakes were mixed with strong drink, wagers could lead to fisticuffs, even murder. These were sobering lessons indeed.[28]

The biographer who depicted Clay as always bent over a desk deep in study was exaggerating, but the young man did not completely neglect his improvement. Richmond made him aware of the many things he did not know, a valuable lesson in itself. In Clay's case, it spurred him to an intellectual program of his own devising. He would never match Jefferson's single-minded discipline in this regard: even given the time, Clay did not have the temperament for twelve-plus hours of daily reading or the systematic disposition to arrange his studies in clearly delineated categories. He did read, of course, but he preferred less solitary forms of refinement. He joined a rhetorical society formed by young men eager to practice public speaking and sharpen their debating skills. These were exhilarating times, as the administration of George Washington coped with the French Revolution and the European war it had spawned. Arguments about how best to repair the economy and fund a stable currency stimulated debates about the new constitutional government. The club accordingly discussed history, philosophy, and economics but usually filtered the topics through the exciting aspect of current affairs.

As a member of this club, Clay found himself in the company of talented men. Edwin Burrell, Littleton Waller Tazewell, Walter Jones, John C. Herbert, Bennett Taylor, Philip Norbone Nicholas, and Edmund Root were members, and it is notable that in such a gifted group he gained the reputation for being the most effective if not the most learned speaker. Dubbed by its members the "Democratic Club," they fancied themselves daring radicals as they applauded the success of the French Jacobins' supposedly democratic reforms. They endorsed, as though it mattered, the Democratic-Republicans, led by fellow Virginians Thomas Jefferson and James Madison and condemned, as though it mattered, the Federalists within Washington's administration for their ties to the British.[29]

Yet it was neither his reading nor his debating skills that helped Clay move from his lowly post as an assistant clerk up to the main Chancery office in only a year. It was his handwriting. Clay later credited Peter Tinsley with putting him through the penmanship drills that produced his clear, neat script, ever afterward the delight of correspondents as well as historians. The claim was possibly another invention to paint his youth as less privileged. A 1793 letter indicates that Clay's penmanship was actually quite good before he went to the Chancery. Written just weeks after he was purportedly under Tinsley's instruction, the letter shows young Henry's handwriting to be, if anything, more flamboyant, and his signature, adorned with scrolls and flourishes, more ornate than the clear, simple style he later adopted. Either he was a very quick study or, more likely, the "ritin'" rudiments of Peter Deacon's school had corrected his student's hen-scratched scrawls. It is also likely that Henry's mother influenced him in this regard, for her handwriting was also quite neat.[30] In any case, attractive, read-able handwriting came to the attention of the judge of the High Court of Chancery himself, none other than the great George Wythe, signer of the Decla-ration of Independence, possessor of a peerless legal mind, and a man suffering from a distracting tremble as well as gout in his right hand. He needed an amanuensis—the equivalent of a stenographer—and Clay's handwriting caught his eye. Wythe asked Tinsley if he could spare the boy, and Tinsley said of course. He likely would have said so even if Clay had become indispensable, for Tinsley suspected that this was an opportunity of incalculable value to young Henry. He was right.

CHARLES DICKENS COULD just as well have drawn these characters and the circumstances that brought them together. George Wythe was a great man whose legal accomplishments were legendary and whose mentorship had shaped the characters of many who would figure prominently in both Virginia and the nation's affairs. He acquired an extraordinary classical education, learn-ing at first with the help of his mother, but applying himself with diligence to mastering Greek and Latin. Thomas Jefferson, whom many regarded as the best classical scholar in Virginia, judged Wythe his superior. For years this smallish, courtly man had lived in Williamsburg, where he practiced and taught law. As with Clay in 1793, Wythe had noticed thirty years earlier the penmanship of a tall red-haired youth with a splash of freckles on his face. Good handwriting had made Tom Jefferson useful then in the same way that Clay later would be. Jef-ferson became Wythe's most famous student and was instrumental in having his teacher named professor of law at the College of William and Mary in 1779, the first such professorship in a country then lacking a systematic legal curriculum for aspiring attorneys. "Preach, my dear Sir, a crusade against ignorance," Jef-ferson had urged him.[31]

Wythe did just that before becoming a judge on the state's High Court of Chancery in 1789 and soon afterward, as the only judge on that court, the state's chancellor. "Such philanthropy for mankind," it was said of him, "such simplic-ity of manners, and such inflexible rectitude and integrity of principle, as would have dignified a Roman senator, even in the most virtuous times of the Repub-lic."[32]

From the start, Clay charmed the old man, and Wythe captivated Clay. As had happened to other young men over the years, Clay's initial awe steadily gave way to admiration and affection. Wythe had counseled the greatest men of his age, including two future presidents (Jefferson and James Monroe), a future U.S. attorney general (John Breckinridge), a future judge of the Virginia Supreme Court (Spencer Roane), and two governors of Virginia (Wilson Carter Nicholas and Littleton Waller Tazewell). Yet all of these relationships had become easy and enduring friendships, for Wythe was not only brilliant but kind, unpretentious, and, even at nearly seventy, when Clay met him, youthful.[33]

Clay spent four years in Wythe's employ and essentially became his private secretary. Clay's primary duty was to take Wythe's dictation of Chancery decisions and reports. After Wythe reviewed the copy, Clay made corrections and revisions and incorporated the literary references, usually in Greek, that Wythe often included in his decisions. This mild form of "pedantry," as one writer has described it, was a small vanity on Wythe's part but big trouble for Clay. He had absolutely no knowledge of Greek, and he had to copy with meticulous care the characters as though drawing hieroglyphics. The task added hours to his chores, but he never complained, and his work was always on time and neatly accomplished.[34]

Wythe noticed both the attitude and the industry. He opened his library to the boy and loaned him books as a way of suggesting what to read. He apparently avoided quizzing Clay about the subjects in order to prevent the acquaintance with books from becoming a chore rather than a pleasure. Instead, he encouraged free-ranging discussions that included everything from religion to politics, covering subjects from comportment to conscience, all framed by the meditations of great authors in great books. Thus while laboring at a copy desk Henry Clay received not just room, board, and a modest wage, but also a worldview broader than any vista he could have otherwise imagined, his guide not so much the chancellor of Virginia but a kind old man whose watery eyes saw promise in the gangly bumpkin with a ready smile and practiced pen. Clay always remembered that George Wythe had "the courtliest bow I have ever seen," one that the boy took to imitating for the same reason that he emulated the speaking techniques of effective orators. After four years with Wythe, Clay's deficiencies in formal schooling as well as in his manners were almost eliminated. When he left Wythe, Clay knew how to converse in intellectual company and how to act in the best circles of society.[35]

What exactly did Henry Clay learn from this remarkable teacher? Though he enjoyed listening to the old man read Greek, Henry never showed any facility for languages and never learned Greek or Latin, always to his regret. And despite Wythe's passion for learning as an end in itself, Clay never developed an intellectual curiosity beyond the goal of learning a thing for its practical benefits. Wythe's library was surely important in the formation of the adult Henry Clay, but the example of Wythe himself proved more central to Clay's education.

Wythe's role in the founding of the new nation and in securing Virginia's ratification of the Constitution were admirable endeavors, but his desire to have the very idea of America serve a broader purpose was nothing short of exhilarating. Liberty in America could become an opportunity for all humanity! That was a notion so compelling that it could merit a life's work. To preserve and to improve the Founders' gift to the world, thereby to promote the progress of people everywhere by preserving the liberty of men at home, made the struggling young republic a dazzling experiment.[36]

But it was a troubling one as well. In those four simple words—"the liberty of men"—an idea explained in Jefferson's majestic Declaration as an inalienable right direct from the hand of God—rested the most troubling contradiction in the American experiment, in which the grand quest for human freedom was soiled by human slavery. Wythe clearly noted the incongruity, as did many others of his time, but he was unique in the way he resolved it, at least as it touched his own life. He reconciled for himself the clash of freedom and slavery sooner rather than later, in fact immediately: he did not liberate his slaves in his will, as several Founders would do, but freed them outright with a stroke of a pen. More than that, he prepared them for freedom by having them taught trades to match their talents and inclinations. A few stayed with him, but only as employees earning fair wages, such as his elderly cook, Lydia Broadnax. A young mulatto named Michael Brown was another. Wythe taught Michael to read and write.

Henry Clay already technically owned slaves through his father's bequest, although one apparently went to Kentucky with the Watkinses, while the fate of the other is unknown. Yet what he saw in the Wythe household must have puzzled him. It was a bold challenge to the established order of things in the only world he had ever known, one that included slavery as a natural consequence of skin color and birth. Free blacks lived in Virginia, but laws restricted their freedom, prohibiting them, for instance, from bearing arms or voting. Clay mostly knew blacks only as slaves, an exotic people not just because of their color but because of their language, often a Creole pastiche of African tongues and Old World English that could make them difficult to understand. More than that made them difficult to understand, though. Clay's youth in Hanover County had etched strong impressions into him about blacks as people, whether slave or free, and those impressions would prove deep-seated and enduring. He would never surmount the prevailing opinions of his time that deemed blacks to be intellectually inferior and morally compromised. Yet Wythe's example proved as persuasive as it was puzzling. Like the old man, Clay came to view slavery as a blight, its proponents monstrous to the degree of their enthusiasm for it, its victims the prisoners of a foul travesty, everyone trapped by the cruel hoax it revealed in a land celebrating liberty.

Moreover, Clay knew that George Wythe had apprenticed his slaves to prepare them for freedom. He watched Michael Brown learn his letters. Clay would remember that.[37]

WHILE MANY OF the lessons Clay learned under the guidance of George Wythe concerned how to make a life, one of the most important had to do with how to make a living. Age had not dulled Wythe's legal expertise, and Clay watched the old man's mind work with growing admiration.

One case that came before the High Court of Chancery was especially instructive because it showed how the law was a constant bulwark even when challenged by popular sentiment. Several Virginians brought suit seeking relief from debts owed to English creditors, claiming that the British government's partial violation of the 1783 Treaty of Paris canceled those obligations. It was a clever dodge, disguising transparent self-interest by playing on anti-British prejudice, but Wythe was not convinced. He ruled against the debtors, insisting that the Crown's failures to honor other parts of the treaty had nothing to do with Americans' commitments to private English creditors. The debtors promptly appealed to the federal circuit court, and the case was heard by Chief Justice John Jay in his capacity as a circuit judge. The appellants brought in formidable legal talent. Patrick Henry and John Marshall argued their side before a packed courthouse. Henry Clay watched wide-eyed as these celebrated champions presented their arguments with compelling oratory. Patrick Henry was at the height of his spellbinding powers. When speaking to juries he had no equal in Virginia, and his very appearance, his dour expression, hawk nose, and broad, thin mouth emphasized by surprisingly large eyes, fascinated beyond the power of his inimitable voice, and that alone was powerful enough. He relied on his magnetic personality and way with words rather than study and application, for Patrick Henry was indolent to the point of laziness. Juries did not care. His ability to draw, as Edmund Randolph noted, not so much from the law as "from the recesses of the human heart" was irresistibly persuasive, at least for juries. John Jay, however, was not swayed by the approach. Wythe's decision was soundly based in the law, and Jay sustained it.[38]

Clay was mightily impressed, though, by all points of the law and its practitioners. Here was a profession that provided opportunities for grand public gestures yet was also anchored in the rituals of procedure and traditions of precedent. The law offered an avenue to prominence and achievement, and Clay resolved to travel it. He would certainly have wanted George Wythe to be his teacher in this new project, but the formality of the undertaking made it far more taxing than pointing out some books and chatting about them in idle moments. Wythe's duties as chancellor consumed too much time, and taking on a new student was out of the question.

Although efforts to systemize legal training into a standard mode of instruction were already emerging in certain parts of the country, they were random and rare. That Wythe himself was the first professor of law in the United States evidenced the newness of formal legal training, and most lawyers came to the craft by "reading" law under a practicing attorney. The system had many failings. Uneven instruction was an obvious one, and the possibility that lawyers would exploit students by turning them into glorified copyists was another.[39]

Ideally, the aspiring student performed clerical duties in return for access to law books and individual guidance, the idea being that such work exposed the mind to the forms and formulas of the law and fixed those elements by rote and repetition. After achieving an adequate level of proficiency, the apprentice was ready for examination before the bar by a panel of three judges from either the General Court or the High Court of Chancery, sometimes both. The questioning took place in open court and was usually more casual than rigorous, with queries probing a candidate's character as much as his knowledge. Successfully negotiating this bar examination was only a step to another stage of apprenticeship, the equivalent of moving to the status of journeyman in the legal guild. Newly licensed lawyers practiced in the lowest tier of courts. Only leading attorneys argued cases in the appellate courts, a slight concession to the irregular quality of lawyers the system produced.[40]

In late 1796, Wythe asked Robert Brooke to teach Clay the law and thus saw to it that Clay had an earnest, conscientious teacher with excellent credentials. Robert Brooke had just completed a term as governor in 1796 and had become the state attorney general. When Clay moved out of the back room of the Chancery, he was again physically moving up in the world. It was the custom for a law student to join the household of his teacher, and for the next few months, Clay would live in the home of the state's highest legal officer.[41]

Brooke found Henry a quick student. Building on the preliminary readings and stenographic work Clay had done for Wythe, he moved the boy rapidly along. In less than a year, Clay was ready for his examination. On November 6, 1797, Paul Carrington, William Fleming, and Spencer Roane, all judges of the Virginia Court of Appeals, found Henry Clay competent to practice law in the commonwealth of Virginia and granted him his "legal certificate."[42]

At twenty years of age, he was now Henry Clay, Esquire. Richmond was less than twenty miles from the Slashes, but it could not have been farther from the limits of that place had it been a mountain on the moon. The transformation from bumpkin in the swamps of Hanover County to attorney at the Virginia bar was only one facet of the change in Henry Clay during the pivotal six years he spent in Richmond. Physically he had not so much blossomed as grown like a weed, his stature accentuated by his spare build. Yet what had once been a gangly and ill-clothed boy had become, under careful observation and the tutelage of good men, an agile and tastefully dressed young man. Young Clay had come to Richmond with a winning way and an easy smile, but his mentors and companions taught him the etiquette of the drawing room as well as the rough pleasantries of the gaming table. He learned what to drink and, more important, how to be drink's master rather than its servant. He moved in circles that included the best minds of the passing, current, and coming generations, and integrated their sense of celebrity and purpose into his own persona. His white-blond hair, always a tad tousled, was never ponytailed in a cue but always worn short, in what was called "the French style," as befitted a true republican. He modeled his gestures and speaking style on the great orators he had seen on Richmond's stages and in its courtrooms, using his long-fingered hands and baritone voice to persuasive effect, in the manner of Patrick Henry. He pondered the moral dilemma of human bondage and came to regard it, as did his mentor George Wythe, as a repugnant evil, an opinion no less sincere because it was freighted with the prejudices of his time. And his gift for friendship had pulled elders and contemporaries alike into his embrace. Francis Taliaferro Brooke (Frank to his friends), his teacher's younger brother, and Tom Ritchie (the Brookes' brother-in-law), who would become an influential newspaper editor, were among them, as were the boys in the clerk's office at the Chancery, the men of his debating society, many destined for a measure of greatness themselves, and countless others who were part of an ever-widening circle of acquaintance and friendship.

And yet for all that, Clay knew even as he stood before his examiners that November day that his time in Richmond—in Virginia, in fact—was at an end. The city boasted an embarrassing abundance of lawyers, and a new one's ascent would certainly be slow. Even grand achievement brought rewards modest in the scale of things. John Marshall lived moderately well only because he had logged long days and built an enormous practice, the work of years, too long for a young man in a hurry. Virginia friendships could take one only so far as well, for they would always be trumped by family connections, often more essential for success than merit.

So Clay was packing even as he framed his new law license. His destination was never in doubt, for the appeal of his own family connections determined it from the start. To the west was Kentucky, where his mother and Hal had set up Watkins Tavern in Versailles and had made it one of the largest and most praised hostelries in the state. His brother John was a prosperous merchant in Lexington, the fastest-growing city in Kentucky. Just over those mountains, the ones dimly visible as a blue cloud just above the horizon, was the new place of Clay's family. It would be the place of his future.

In 1797 he started out, laden with his belongings, the accumulated experience of the previous six years, and the always ready smile that started at the side of his wide mouth before broadening into a fetching grin. A host of his mannerisms were adopted from admired men and close acquaintances, including the studied self-confidence with which he set out for Kentucky. At this early stage of his life, those mannerisms were really more affectations than self-realized qualities. Except for the smile. That was his own.[43]

CHAPTER TWO

"My Hopes Were More than Realized"

WITHIN DAYS OF receiving his law license in Richmond, Clay packed his meager belongings, mounted his only horse, and set out for Kentucky. He traveled the Wilderness Road, the path taken by pioneers for more than two decades toward a place once called "the Dark and Bloody Ground" because Indians had so persistently fought over it. The road began west of Richmond, skirted south of the Shenandoah Valley through the Cumberland Gap along the Tennessee line, and then headed north into the heart of Kentucky. There it followed the route called Boone's Trace because Daniel Boone had carved it from the wilderness in the 1770s. The road split at Hazel Patch, Kentucky, its northwest fork stretching toward Louisville, its north fork toward Lexington. It was still a hard journey when Clay made it in 1797. Winter added to its hazards.[1]

At least the road was never empty, for the lure of Kentucky hypnotically drew immigrants regardless of the season. Like Clay, some trekked to join family members, earlier migrants already attracted to fertile soil and a buzzing economy. They came by the thousands, enduring all manner of hardships, certain that their fortunes lay in this western Eden. One young traveler who had passed along the route a year earlier described his journey and the people along it as a peculiar mixture of hope and despair. A few inns along the way offered good food and comfortable beds, but for long stretches travelers suffered from appalling want and exposure. Often the only available lodging was wretched. At one stop, seventeen people, women and children included, crowded into "a small Hutt . . . 12 feet square." The throngs of migrants touched his heart, for they too were often wretched. "Noticeing the many Distres.d familes," this traveler haltingly asked, "Can any thing be more distressing to a man of feeling than to see woman and Children in the Month of December. Travelling a Wilderness through Ice and Snow passing large rivers and Creeks with out Shoe or Stocking, and barely as maney raggs as covers their Nakedness, with out money or provisions[?]"

And yet they were seldom despairing. "Ask these Pilgrims what they expect when they git to Kentuckey," he remarked, "[and] the Answer is Land. Have you any. No, but I expect I can git it. . . . Here is hundreds Travelling hundreds of Miles, they Know not for what . . . except its to Kentucky."[2]

In 1797, everything about Kentucky was new, exciting, and until recently a little dangerous, for white settlement had only lately taken root. When whites first wandered into the Dark and Bloody Ground, Indians had been hunting the region's bountiful lands for as long as humans could remember. That was in the years before the American Revolution. These first whites were hunters too, a unique type labeled "long hunters" for their extended rambles west of the Blue Ridge that tested their resourcefulness and stamina and made them irritating interlopers to the Indians. The most famous long hunter was North Carolina's Daniel Boone, who trekked with companions into Kentucky, lived off the land for months while collecting pelts, and returned east to sell the hides and tell stories about the lush, lovely land beyond the mountains. Soon men with money were eyeing distant Kentucky as an investment opportunity. Richard Henderson of North Carolina joined with other backers—merchant Thomas Hart was a typical investor—to purchase Kentucky from the Indians and sell it to settlers. The project took shape under the auspices of the Transylvania Company and so stubbornly ignored Virginia's claims to Kentucky that Virginia's courts would eventually intervene, but not before settlers had begun moving into the area to build block houses, clear fields, and clash in sharp skirmishes with Indians as unimpressed with the Transylvania Company's claims as Virginia was.[3]

The American Revolution slowed settlement, particularly when the British allied with Indians intent on eliminating white encroachment. The Revolution's end did not stop Indian conflicts, but it did prompt a new wave of white settlers. In 1792, the Virginia county of Kentucky established itself as a state of the Union, and three years later General "Mad" Anthony Wayne forced Indians north of the Ohio River to sign the Treaty of Greenville, which terminated Indian claims south of the Ohio and put Kentucky at peace. With statehood and relative tranquillity as encouragements, Kentucky's wave of settlement became an overwhelming flood, and Henry Clay floated in on it.[4]

AFTER ENTERING KENTUCKY, Clay turned north along the Wilderness Road toward the Bluegrass region of the state, an area in north central Kentucky where his mother and stepfather lived in the small town of Versailles. The country was breathtaking, as fertile as it was beautiful and home to the state's fastest-growing population. In the Bluegrass, people boasted with good reason about the hottest land speculations and the highest land prices. There was no brag if everything was fact: the place was at once lovely and affluent, affordable only for those with enough money to buy the best. It consequently became the center of a ready-made body of elite landowners and professionals, people who had fled Virginia's practice of primogeniture and low tobacco prices but had brought many of Old Virginia's social customs with them.[5]

Clay arrived at his parents' tavern in Versailles for a joyous reunion. He had not seen anyone in his immediate family for six years, almost a third of his life, and much had changed. Some of it was sad. His older sister Sarah had died shortly after marrying their cousin John W. Watkins.[6] Henry, however, found younger brother Porter eighteen years old and healthy, and he would soon see his older brother, John, a merchant in Lexington about thirteen miles away. His two oldest half siblings, Martha and John Hancock Watkins, were frozen in his memory as small children, but they of course had grown up, and he met two new half brothers, Francis Hudson and Nathaniel Watkins, who had been born in Kentucky.[7]

Versailles was a pleasant town of shaded streets where Watkins Tavern served as Woodford County's social center. Future U.S. senator and Kentucky governor Thomas Metcalfe had built the impressive two-story stone building. Its second floor balcony and the frame wing off the back were its distinctive features. A popular hotel for travelers and a social and political gathering place for locals, the tavern made Hal Watkins prosperous and consequential. He was justice of the peace and owned a farm three miles outside of town, lots in Versailles, five horses, and eleven slaves. He now returned "Little Sam," bequeathed to Henry in John Clay's will, to his stepson.[8]

Founded in 1792, Versailles was certainly agreeable and even bustling in its own way, but the very success of Watkins Tavern proved that for most people the community was a place on the way to somewhere else. So it would be for Henry Clay. After visiting his family, he set out for Lexington, the seat of Fayette County, a dynamic town that described itself as "the Athens of the West" despite being less than twenty-five years old. If that claim was a bit overblown, the town did have reason to describe itself as the Rome of Kentucky, for every road in the north central part of the state passed through Lexington to connect it with villages throughout the Bluegrass. Founded during the American Revolution and named for its first battle, Lexington was also the largest town west of the Alleghenies, with one thousand citizens and counting. In fact, it would double in size during Clay's first five years there.

Lexington was also thoughtfully arranged, representing a great deal more urban planning than many eastern cities at the time. Wide, straight, tree-lined streets met at right angles. Crowds of people moved easily along these spacious avenues where dozens of shops carried the finest merchandise from the East and Europe. Taverns and inns served excellent food, fine wines, and the kind of liquor whose quality had already made the state famous. Vestiges of rusticity were rapidly disappearing as brick buildings and handsome homes replaced the few remaining log structures. Wealthy merchants and successful attorneys lived in fine two- and three-story brick houses that fronted lovely gardens or on country estates just outside of town. Those houses were always placed near the city because Lexington's business required regular attendance and its pleasures always beckoned.[9]

Virginia transplants were committed to making Lexington a vibrant cultural and educational center, giving substance to the Athenian boast. They established the Lexington Immigration Society to attract farmers and skilled artisans to the area and extolled the virtues of the region by placing advertisements in eastern newspapers. In 1795 John Breckinridge, John Bradford, Thomas Hart, and James Brown were among those former Virginians who set up a lending library on the second floor of Andrew McCalla's apothecary shop, conscientious citizens kicking in $500 of seed money to boost the project. By the time Clay arrived, they had committed to the even more ambitious venture of turning Transylvania Seminary into the first university west of the mountains, a feat sure to burnish Lexington's intellectual luster. Seminary students and local groups staged amateur theatricals and concerts that attracted people from miles around.[10]

John Bradford, one of the leaders who established the library, founded Kentucky's first newspaper, the *Kentucky Gazette,* in 1787 when town trustees voted him a lot on which to set up a printing press. Bradford typified the Virginian who became a brash Kentucky booster, and the pages of his twice-weekly paper often described the state with blissful rapture. More traditional fare filled out the rest of Bradford's paper, which regularly featured essays produced by local writers and borrowed from the works of celebrated authors, a standard journalistic practice of the day. There were advertisements, of course, and local and national news stories, particularly about politics.[11]

Lexington men engaged in and debated political affairs with remarkable fervor, and Henry Clay soon plunged into the discussions with enthusiasm. Shortly after arriving in town, he joined the Lexington Rhetorical Society, a club previously called the Kentucky Society for Promoting Useful Knowledge, more informally simply the Junto. Primarily composed of young men, many of them freshly minted attorneys, the Junto met at local taverns like Satterwhite's Eagle or the Sign of the Indian King or the Free and Easy to debate whatever struck the group's fancy. Wide-ranging discussions touched on politics, religion, law, slavery, and literature. The society sometimes held mock trials to polish court-room skills.[12]

As a new member, Clay just listened. One day the debate was about to end with a vote for the best argument when he muttered to himself that aspects of the topic remained unexplored. A member sitting nearby heard him and impulsively shouted to the assembly, "Mr. Clay will speak!" He hesitated as all eyes turned to him. He stood up, a towering six feet one, and began with the incongruous opening "Gentlemen of the jury," an obvious mistake. (In private, Clay had been rehearsing opening and closing arguments before an imaginary jury.) He paused; he even stammered; but he quickly gathered himself to repeat the phrase, "Gentlemen of the jury," as if it were an intentional rhetorical flourish. He then launched into an exhaustive speech whose lucid conclusion brought the club to its feet, cheers mingling with prolonged applause. A member of the Junto would always claim that this first effort was the best speech of Clay's life, but that judgment was likely caused by an impression common among listeners hearing Henry Clay for the first time. His voice sounded melodious baritone notes that were unexpectedly captivating in themselves, regardless of the words they formed. In fact, the words sometimes got in the way, which is why, we are told, that even those of Clay's speeches that do not read well were stunning when he spoke them. In person, listeners hung on his friendly, colloquial cadence that gave the peculiar impression that he was speaking directly to each of them, giving each person individual attention, no matter how large the audience or setting, making each one feel that for Henry Clay the most important thing in the world at that moment was to talk person to person, not as to a member of an audience, but individually. It was something no amount of observation could teach or practice achieve. It was the stuff of nearly irresistible persuasion, almost like magic, sometimes like lightning, often bringing men reflexively to their feet and women to tears. It happened for the first time that evening in Lexington.[13]

THE YOUTHFUL CHEERS of the Junto were pleasing, but they paid no bills. To earn a living, Clay had to impress the more mature members of Lexington's community. His Virginia law license gave him bona fides before most Kentucky courts and made the application for a Kentucky law license a formality, but Clay did not immediately enter the Kentucky bar. Instead, he offered his services to Lexington's established attorneys in order to acquaint himself with the state's legal system by preparing their paperwork. He chose his new mentors carefully, gravitating to former Virginians, especially protégés of George Wythe. Thus did George Nicholas, James Brown, and John Breckinridge become his guides and his friends. George Nicholas was even a Hanover County man, a resonant link for a fellow raised in the Slashes. George was also the brother of prominent Virginian Wilson Cary Nicholas, an intimate of Thomas Jefferson. James Brown attended the College of William and Mary before moving to Lexington in 1789, where he achieved eminence in the new state government and married Anne Hart, always "Nancy" to her friends, a circle that included just about everybody who ever laid eyes on her. She belonged to one of the town's wealthiest families, its patriarch the formidable Thomas Hart, yet people would have found sparkling Nancy irresistible had she been a pauper. Her husband was eleven years older than Henry Clay, but the young man's eagerness to learn the ropes struck James as exceptional. His initial respect for his protégé blossomed into a deep and enduring friendship.[14]

After two months of diligent preparation, Clay presented his Virginia license to the Lexington Court of Quarter Sessions and received a Kentucky license on March 20, 1798. Clay had already begun taking on clients and later remembered his great relief upon receiving his first fee. He had worried about getting along, but he recalled that soon "my hopes were more than realized."[15] With plenty of cases to go around, he was pleasantly surprised by how easily a determined lawyer could earn a handsome living, for circumstances made Kentuckians a litigious lot. Conflicting land claims sprouted like weeds because Virginia had never bothered to have its western expanse properly surveyed before selling portions of it. Overlapping claims abounded and usually wound up in court. Even otherwise unencumbered grants or purchases suffered from antique surveys in which trees, creeks, and boulders marked confused boundaries. Creditors and debtors were another abundant source of legal work, and out-of-state creditors were unusually good clients. Kentucky was a remote and difficult destination for such lenders, and they hired local attorneys to collect debts on commission—5 percent of the recovery was the standard fee—or to take delinquent borrowers to court, which could mean even larger fees.[16]

Land cases were profitable in other ways because they too based fees on a percentage, sometimes in recovered acreage. Clay's work on one land case, for example, earned him a fee of 1,050 acres on the Licking River, a tract that he could keep for investment or sell for cash. Effective and methodical attorneys could swell their bank accounts and become squires in the bargain by specializing in debt collection and land disputes. Clay was especially methodical and effective.[17]

His unique talents, in fact, were most obvious in debt cases, in which diplomacy was frequently more important than legal expertise. One of his first cases required that he travel to a small town south of Lexington to collect a debt from a farmer. When he arrived, he learned that his man was at a political rally, a touchy situation that placed his quarry among friends not likely to be sympathetic to a stranger wanting money. Clay went to the meeting anyway and was not there long before someone asked what he thought of the candidates. They were all local men about whom Clay knew absolutely nothing. He did know, however, that one could never go wrong praising Daniel Boone to a Kentuckian. He commenced a stem-winder celebrating the name and exploits of Boone that soon had everyone shouting full-throated hurrahs and slapping him on the back. The farmer smiled as he handed Clay the cash.[18]

These occasionally dramatic instances were rare, for most debt cases were routine affairs that involved clerkship rather than confrontation. Clay also engaged in the profitable work of commercial law as he represented eastern businessmen in their relations with Lexington merchants. One wholesaler, Baltimore merchant William Taylor, paid Clay more than $7,000 in fees over a ten-year period, a sum amounting to more than $100,000 in today's money. It was dull work, but Clay attended to its complexities with such thoroughness that other attorneys often recommended him as indispensable in such transactions. His practice grew.[19]

Criminal law was not lucrative enough to support an attorney in a community happily short of serious criminals. Hog stealers, horse thieves, and drunken brawlers were the norm, and murders were so infrequent that the cases could not match the large fees produced by the drudgery of land conflicts, debt collection, and business deals. Yet Clay's magnetism was uniquely suited to the courtroom, and when a good criminal case came along, he couldn't resist it. Sensational cases drew large crowds to court, and newspapers painted colorful performances with broad strokes. Clay's fluency, his commanding baritone, and his uncanny ability to make each juror feel personally connected to him made him a spellbinder. When there was a jury, he seldom lost.

One murder case earned Clay early acclaim in Lexington legal circles. Doshey Phelps killed her husband's sister in front of witnesses who saw the entire horrible episode unfold. The two had been arguing over money. As the quarrel grew more heated, Doshey fetched a musket and wordlessly shot her sister-in-law in the chest. "Sister, you have killed me," were the victim's last words.[20]

Most would have hoped only to save Mrs. Phelps from the gallows, but Clay tried to keep her from serving life in the state penitentiary as well. He employed one of the first known instances of an insanity defense, arguing that his client had been in the throes of "temporary delirium." In a memorable closing argument, he told the jury that Doshey had been driven to uncontrollable, blinding rage and was unable to stop herself. Moreover, Doshey's husband had forgiven the poor woman for killing his sister, Clay said. Could the jury do less? The jury, as it happened, finally decided to do a bit more, but its guilty verdict was for the lesser crime of manslaughter, and Doshey's sentence was only five years in the Frankfort penitentiary.[21]

In Harrison County he defended a father and son, German immigrants, for murder. After persuading the jury to convict for manslaughter, Clay audaciously moved for an "arrest of judgment," meaning that his clients should be set free. That was too much for the prosecutor, and it took another full day of arguments for Clay to convince the jury that his clients should not go to prison.[22]

Audacious tactics became his trademark. In the Abner Willis murder trial, Clay sufficiently punctured the prosecution's case that the jury could not reach a verdict. As was customary, a hung jury sent Willis to a second trial, but at its start Clay argued that his client had already been tried for the offense and this second proceeding violated the U.S. Constitution's ban on double jeopardy. The judge promptly ruled that it did no such thing. The trial began its preliminaries, but Clay paid no attention. Instead he calmly gathered his papers and stalked out of the courtroom. Everyone—jurors, spectators, prosecutor, judge, even Abner Willis—sat in shocked silence. After pondering this novel development, the judge sent a messenger for Clay and then ruled that, on second thought, double jeopardy was indeed a factor. He released Willis from custody.[23]

It wasn't the only time that Clay used a seemingly greater understanding of legal procedure and technicalities to cow a judge. He once argued that his client's arrest was invalidated by an improperly drawn warrant. The judge studied the document, the clock ticked, and Clay and his client sat in silence. Finally, Clay turned to his client and shouted in exasperation, "Go home!" The man sat frozen. He stared at Clay in wide-eyed disbelief. Clay shouted even louder, "Go home!" The defendant scampered out of the room. The judge did nothing to stop him.[24]

THESE MEMORABLE COURTROOM appearances paid little, but they paid off. Ordinary folk gradually perceived Clay as the defender of the little man rather than a corporate lawyer earning hefty fees for debt collections and land cases. His following among Kentucky's less affluent citizens was the beginning of a political base that would endure for a half century.

Clay had developed a heightened political awareness in Richmond as he moved quietly among Virginia's political elite, listening and watching, and he took an interest in Kentucky politics from the start. Before he arrived, Kentucky was debating whether to revise its 1792 constitution. Two favorable votes in as many years were required even to assemble a convention, but the 1797 referendum seemed to quash the matter at its outset. Despite a palpable desire among many to democratize state government, a majority of Kentuckians did not want to revise the constitution. Proponents of increased democracy remained unsatisfied, though, and they became more vocal in the face of this setback. More than that, by the time Henry Clay rode into Lexington, the movement had taken up the potentially explosive issue of slavery in Kentucky.[25]

This early emancipation movement was fueled as much by populism as altruism. Many Kentuckians wanted to abolish slavery in order to end the large slaveholders' monopoly on economic and political power. In short, small farmers stood to prosper if the institution of slavery went away. Clay came to this argument with views shaped by his mentor George Wythe—views that were tempered by practicality, particularly about the advantages of gradual over immediate emancipation. He approached the issue both as a humanitarian eager to resolve the conflict of slavery and freedom and as an advocate for Kentucky's poorer farmers. He also believed that sensible men would not be threatened by the prospect of gradual emancipation, even in Kentucky's most aristocratic, conservative county. He was wrong.

The state's economic and political elite (really one and the same) were not opposed to the *idea* of democracy. Most were good Jeffersonian Republicans, just like Clay, and founded groups like the Democratic Club to show solidarity with the French Revolution. They were exuberant members of the Republican choir that criticized Federalist centralizing schemes, extolled individual liberty, and imagined that the highest Federalist of all, Alexander Hamilton, privately whiled away the hours admiring himself wearing a crown. But having controlled Kentucky's government from the time of its formation, they bristled at the suggestion that their noblesse oblige was heavy on privilege and short on obligation. By allying himself with aggressive democratic activists, Clay was sure to upset these people and possibly even alienate new friends such as Breckinridge and Nicholas. And Clay's public stance for democratic reforms did trouble them, but that was only half of it. It was bad enough that he wanted to eliminate Kentucky's Electoral College that selected state senators and the governor (an elitist contrivance in the 1792 constitution), and replace it with direct election. When he started talking about doing away with slavery, he seemed to have lost his mind.[26]

Clay and *Kentucky Gazette* editor John Bradford understandably believed, however, that the relatively small number of slaves in Kentucky made emancipation socially and economically feasible, offering a unique but vanishing opportunity to strike down the institution. After all, slave owners themselves admitted that the presence of slavery mocked high-flown talk of human liberty. Yet most Kentuckians joined elite planters to condemn even the most gradual emancipation as too radical. Clay had not reckoned on a fearsome obstacle to emancipation, which was the universal desire for lofty social rank. Slaves were badges of white affluence, and those who owned the most slaves wielded the most influence. People who had never owned a slave coveted that.[27] Anyone who threatened to block that avenue to riches and power had simply lost his mind.

Clay persisted, though. Using the pen name "Scaevola"—a republican legalist of ancient Rome venerated for his bravery and patriotism—Clay published in Bradford's sympathetic *Kentucky Gazette* the first of his essays supporting the gradual abolition of slavery in Kentucky. Clay talked about the injury that slavery would eventually inflict on Kentucky's democratic institutions, but most notably he denounced its cruelty. "Can any humane man be happy and contented," he asked, "when he sees near thirty thousand of his fellow beings around him, deprived of all the rights which make life desirable, transferred like cattle from the possession of one to another . . . when he hears the piercing cries of husbands separated from wives and children from parents. . . . [?]" No, he answered, not "the people of Kentucky, enthusiasts as they are in the cause of liberty."[28] But he tempered his condemnation with practicality, for Clay disagreed with radicals calling for immediate abolition. Gradualism was not only more realistic (it would be less economically disruptive for slaveholders) but more desirable because slaves could be educated and trained in skills essential for making a living. Slaves had to be prepared for the very state of being free.[29]

The practicality of gradual emancipation left old heads unimpressed, and they criticized Clay as an impractical dreamer, one of a pack of "beardless boys," according to George Nicholas, a charge that must have stung a lad just past his twenty-first birthday. John Breckinridge, a member of Kentucky's lower house and a future United States senator and attorney general, answered Clay and other radicals by linking their calls for abolition to redistributionist land schemes. But Clay was not unsettled by the establishment's disapproval. Instead, the "beardless boy" spit on his palms. In February 1799, Scaevola (everyone knew it was Clay by then) fired back at Breckinridge's criticism. Nobody wanted to redistribute anyone's land, Clay insisted, and gradual emancipation was the best way to do away with an evil that would soon be too entrenched to eliminate.[30]

In the first round of this bout, Clay and his reform cohort won on points when the legislature grudgingly ignored the prior year's negative referendum and called for the election of delegates to a constitutional convention. It was scheduled for that summer, and Clay joined reformers in zestfully campaigning for the election of delegates sympathetic to their cause. Many in the ruling class had to admit that the boy had pluck, and one paid him the highest compliment a Kentuckian could receive by calling him "the best three-year old [*sic*] he had ever seen on turf."[31] But Fayette County's elite planters were determined to dominate the upcoming convention, and they handed Clay and his friends their beardless heads in the election. Voters soundly thrashed gradual emancipationists John Bradford and James Hughes to send James McDowell, Buckner Thruston, John Breckinridge, and John Bell to the convention in Frankfort. All opposed the abolition of slavery, gradual or otherwise. Fayette County's decision was mirrored in other counties that sent comparably disposed delegations, and the result was foreordained: slavery was untouched by the new constitution.

Delegates did, however, establish direct elections for state senators and the governor. They had at least heard the voice of the people, such as it was, on that procedural point of enhanced democracy for ordinary folk. To the "piercing cries of husbands separated from wives and children from parents," they were deaf. They remained chronically so in years to come. The impairment would cost their beloved Bluegrass State dearly one day, when families would divide and brothers would stride off in different directions to settle the matter with daggers rather than debates. Henry Clay's sons and grandchildren would be among them.[32]

ALTHOUGH THEY SQUABBLED over the future of their state, Kentucky's Democratic-Republicans found common cause in opposing the direction of the nation's foreign and domestic affairs. In fact, such issues firmly united them, and even Clay's drift toward the radicals on constitutional reform and gradual emancipation did not completely estrange him from the political elite. He regularly rubbed legal elbows with Breckinridge and Nicholas, and he eagerly joined other Lexington Jeffersonians who were furious with the Federalist Congress and the John Adams administration.

The European war that grew out of the French Revolution in the early 1790s always threatened to involve the United States. The two principal antagonists, Great Britain and France, were uniquely positioned to cause America trouble: Britain understandably provoked reflexive American anger, and France early invoked American military obligations under the Franco-American alliance of 1778. But George Washington steered the country to neutrality, a move that irritated Francophiles like Thomas Jefferson and his faction, who believed that Washington's prudence ill served the cause of liberty, not just in France but for all the world. More, they believed that Alexander Hamilton—whom they accused with some justification of being an Anglophile—was pushing America into the British camp in defiance of a legitimate treaty, not to mention in disobedience to America's commitment to freedom.

This dispute grew more rancorous at home and gradually caused political factions to harden into political parties, but it also grew more hazardous abroad. By 1798, French petulance over America's lack of help turned to belligerence. The ensuing French naval war against American merchant shipping was undeclared (it would eventually be called the Quasi War), but it was destructive to American commerce and thereby altered the course and purpose of domestic policy. The Democratic-Republican fear that Federalists would harass pro-French Jeffersonians was realized with a vengeance in late summer of 1798 when Congress passed the Alien and Sedition Acts. John Adams signed into law this incredible legislation, which included provisions to prosecute and imprison critics of the government. Adams gave his approval reluctantly, but reluctance made the terms no less odious. Americans, including veterans of the Revolution whose wounds still ached on cold nights, were being told by their government to shut up, or else.

When news of the Alien and Sedition Acts arrived in Lexington, it spread like wildfire and led to a spontaneous gathering at Maxwell's Spring south of town. A smattering of Federalists came out in support of the measures, but angry Democratic-Republicans were an overwhelming majority. Lexington's most outspoken Jeffersonian, George Nicholas, stood on a wagon bed serving as a makeshift platform and sneered at the unconstitutionality of making it a criminal offense to publish anything deemed "false, scandalous, and malicious" about the government. Nicholas proudly reminded his listeners that he had been a member of the Virginia ratification convention in 1788 and consequently knew full well what the Constitution really meant. The assembly cheered, but Nicholas was lucky to be preaching to the choir, because neither his manner nor his meaning was necessarily persuasive. People hardly needed reminding about his role in ratifying the U.S. Constitution, and his recollection about protecting unfettered political speech was chronologically off: the First Amendment did not exist in 1788.[33]

It didn't matter. The crowd cheered as its outrage intensified. Out of the din, someone shouted for young Henry Clay to speak. Men lifted him up onto the wagon, where he began an impromptu address that lasted an hour and put the already emotional crowd through the wringer, making it applaud and reflect by turns, making it laugh at the absurd attempt to quash a fundamental liberty, making it tremble at the implications of losing that fundamental liberty. It was a medley in baritone, condemning Federalists' efforts to make unnecessary war

on France and predicting that they would use, if they could, the military for domestic repression. By the time he was done, Clay had won the crowd's deafening approval, and it was in no mood to listen to rival suitors. A couple of
Federalists tried to crawl into the wagon, but men rushed them with hard looks
and clenched fists. Clay and Nicholas leaped up to restore calm and finally persuaded everyone that pummeling a Federalist violated the very principle they
had all turned out to support. That seemed fair enough on reflection, but nobody
wanted to spoil this rendezvous with an unexpectedly dashing champion by listening to Federalist rot, so the gathering adjourned in celebration. Clay and
Nicholas were borne aloft on shoulders that carried them to a waiting carriage.
Cheers accompanied their impromptu parade through Lexington. It was Clay's
first public address. By any measure, it had been a success.[34]

Lexington's Democratic-Republicans were not alone in their alarm at Federalist actions. Rallies throughout the state protested the Sedition Act and the
move toward war with France. Men wore the French tricolor cockade on their
hats as they marched and cheered orations condemning the Federalists. Clay
continued to speak out on the subject. And the legislature passed what became
known as the Kentucky Resolutions, a formal protest secretly drafted by
Thomas Jefferson. The first set of resolutions that passed in the fall of 1798
(even stronger ones followed in December 1799) were less intense than protests
adopted in Virginia, but they all essentially asserted the rights of a state to judge
the constitutionality of federal laws. Kentucky even declared that a state had the
right to interpose its authority to prevent federal enforcement of unconstitutional legislation.[35]

Clay supported Kentucky's stance, but he played a minor role in these
events. He was not shy about speaking his mind, whether in support of Jeffersonian Republican protests against Federalist excess or of gradual emancipation
in Kentucky, but he was young, newly arrived, and without significant family
connections to the ruling elite. He threw himself into his work, hoping that success and resulting affluence would give him entrée to influential circles.

Yet he didn't work all the time. During the winter of 1798–99, Clay began
visiting the home of Thomas Hart, one of Lexington's wealthiest citizens. Hart
had also been one of Richard Henderson's original partners in the Transylvania
Company. He did not move to Kentucky until 1794, but his family had been an
important factor in Kentucky's development from the start. Hart's brother
Nathaniel blazed trails for settlers to come to Kentucky before he died fighting
Indians at Boonesborough in 1782. The Harts hailed from Virginia—Hanover
County, in fact, which gave him and young Clay something to talk about.[36] After
marrying Susannah Gray, Thomas moved first to North Carolina and then to

Hagerstown, Maryland. Along the way his family grew to seven children and his merchant business grew a tidy fortune. Nancy Hart Brown, wife of Clay's mentor James, was one of his older girls, and the youngest daughter was Lucretia, born in Hagerstown in 1781. Hart affectionately dubbed her his "Little Marylander."[37]

After settling in Lexington, Hart established himself as a leading wholesaler and retailer and soon made so much additional money that he diversified into manufacturing by opening a ropewalk and nail factory. The Harts' imposing brick house at the corner of Mill and Second streets was opulent, furnished with the finest fixtures and carpets money could buy, brought either across the Atlantic from Europe or simply across the Blue Ridge from the most skilled craftsmen in the eastern United States. The home also radiated cultural refinement, with an extraordinary library and paintings by the nation's best artists. The Harts owned the first piano in town. Lucretia loved to play.[38]

Henry Clay became a regular visitor, but he had in mind something other than reminiscing about his and Hart's boyhood home. It was obvious from the start that Clay had taken an interest in the Little Marylander.

The ritual dances of this irresistible impulse are universal for any generation, many unchanged from when apples hung in Eden. But courtship for the middle and upper classes at the turn of the nineteenth century had taken on freer forms than those of previous decades. Parents, particularly fathers, still had the ultimate say regarding whom their daughters could see in the first place and marry in the end, but the girls of Clay's generation enjoyed more liberty than had their mothers about suitable beaux and serious intentions. Parents set general rules and daughters exercised judgment within them, making the hovering chaperone an increasingly quaint figure and priggish vigilance a disappearing custom. Courting couples could speak privately at properly supervised tea parties and dances, and they could even walk alone in the garden on brief promenades that were closely but not too obviously timed by monitors. A young man who proved himself trustworthy and relatively serious about a girl could eventually expect to see her alone for short interludes in her parents' parlor, where pocket doors were kept just slightly ajar and conversation was supposed to be fairly constant. One day, after everybody knew what her answer would be, he would have a talk with her father.

As winter moved toward spring in Lexington that year, Henry Clay and Lucretia Hart moved through the required steps of this timeless dance, the frequency of his calls making apparent his purpose, and the awkward early silences that always mark boy-meets-girl episodes gradually giving way to the easy but exhilarating familiarity of young people who have plainly arrived at an understanding. In the parlor of the big brick house on Mill and Second, they sat alone and talked. He arranged to meet with Mr. Hart.[39]

Nobody ever described Lucretia Hart as a beauty. She was an angular girl in face and body. The sharp edges of her high cheeks and brow were unfashionable for her day, and her thin figure was too slight, even bony, to people of a time that put a premium on plumpness. Likely she would be more agreeable to modern times, when motion pictures value chiseled, photogenic faces, and the measure of good looks is that described by the Duchess of Windsor, who famously remarked that a woman can never be too rich or too thin—two qualities that Lucretia Hart had in abundance. Contemporaries speculated that it was her family's money and status that attracted Henry Clay, landing a climber and a wallflower in a passionless marriage that pathetically rescued her from spinsterhood only because it would abruptly elevate him to a privileged circle. After all, her own father described her as "a fine sprightly, active girl . . . well accomplished in her education."[40] The less artful formulation is that a girl has a good personality, shorthand understood by boys everywhere, and at any time, to mean homely.

In cold point of fact, Henry Clay probably would not have wooed this slight, quiet girl had she not lived in a lavish house or hailed from a wealthy family. Clay's rising star in Lexington was not an accident, and all of his actions bear the mark of calculation: his humble entry into legal circles, his associations with important men, his displays of oratorical prowess, his diligent toil in dull but lucrative casework, his flamboyant courtroom performances, even his challenging the elite on democratic reform and gradual emancipation, all indicate a young man scaling a ladder one social, economic, and political rung at a time. From that perspective, a wife from the wealthiest circle, the daughter of a community leader, would simply be another step up. It is more than likely that such a consideration is precisely what brought Henry Clay calling at the house on Mill and Second.

Yet it is unfair from that hard reality to freeze the girl who sat quietly in that parlor into the shape of a plain, humorless biddy. She was a spare girl, to be sure, and even repeated pregnancies and age would not make her stout, but Clay does not seem to have minded and in fact might have preferred it. Years later he warned the young daughter of a friend not to allow her affections to be too easily "engaged" because youth tempted the "susceptible" heart. Above all he admonished her to look beyond appearances.[41] There was something about Lucretia Hart that people who took the trouble to know her—or more accurately, whom she took the trouble to know—found endearing, even captivating. Those who saw Henry Clay at all stages of his life reported that he too was physically unattractive, until he spoke or smiled, until something animated his features in a way that no portrait could really capture. For her part, Lucretia's mass of auburn hair, her soft eyes, small hands, and girlish feet, were fetching in their own way. She was clever, educated like most girls of her social class, and especially fond of playing the piano for family and guests. As the years rolled by, she would be something of an enigma to the outside world, but never to her family and friends, for Lucretia was kind, caring, and occasionally droll. But she was also an intensely private woman married to an intensely public man. That contradiction in temperament made her and Henry Clay different but not distant. He had undoubtedly first come calling that winter looking for money and status. In the end, he found Lucretia.

On April 11, 1799, one day before Clay turned twenty-two and shortly after Lucretia's eighteenth birthday, the two married in the parlor of the Hart home. They moved into a small brick house next door and just a stone's throw from Nancy and James Brown.[42] It was a normal arrangement that placed the Clays in the midst of a traditional system of family, a culture in which kinship through blood or marriage meant automatic acceptance in a community. Yet marriage was also in transition during these early years of the new republic. In middle- and upper-class unions, the "companionate ideal" held that couples should be friends as well as lovers, each respectful of the other's distinctive but equally important part in creating a stable family. A husband was the head of the family and its breadwinner, but a wife's role as manager of the home and molder of the children's character made her contributions to a stable society prestigious and indispensable. Child-rearing methods were also changing. Enlightenment philosophy informed educated people in their belief that everyone was inherently good and ultimately perfectible. Rather than treating exuberant children like rambunctious colts in need of breaking, mothers sought to guide them toward their potential. Thus were produced responsible members of a community, dependable citizens of the country. The companionate ideal, with its emphasis on properly raising children and its goal of a stable society, made the nuclear family the growing norm in the early American Republic.[43]

Henry and Lucretia Clay's growing brood epitomized the ideal nuclear family, but they also functioned within the traditions of kinship, for they both came from large, affectionate families whose ties of devotion were unaffected by time or distance. They began one of their own right away.

Clay had been busy with his legal practice before marriage, but his new father-in-law was soon steering cases his way and recommending him to other prominent Kentuckians. Thomas Hart's large land holdings and extensive business affairs gave Clay plenty of work that further enhanced his reputation among his peers. When prominent attorney John Breckinridge entered the United States Senate in 1801, he turned over a large part of his practice to Clay, a boost in his client list that was unabated over the next ten years. Clay invested in land and business ventures himself and became a man of standing and property. He soon adopted the simple signature of "H. Clay" rather than the more elaborate one of his younger days. Status could afford simplicity.[44]

His taxable income in these years is a clear indication of his growing wealth and importance. When he married Lucretia in 1799, Clay owned a house, three slaves, and two horses. The 1802 tax rolls still list him with two horses, but he had increased the number of slaves he owned to five; he also owned two wheeled vehicles (perhaps a carriage and a wagon) as well as two lots in town. In 1803, his land holdings jumped to four town lots and 6,525 acres of land in several counties throughout the state. Also in that year, he owned six slaves and five horses. Two years later, he began building a brick home on one of his town lots because his family—now numbering three children—had outgrown the small house next to the Harts. By then Clay owned eight slaves, more than 6,500 acres of land, and eight horses. Reflecting a growing passion for horse racing, he would more than quadruple the number of horses in his stables over the next three years.[45]

Family ties extended Clay's connections to other states. He had cousins in Virginia who became future business associates and political allies, and the Louisiana Purchase in 1803 lured many Kentucky friends and relatives south to new opportunities. His older brother, John Clay, moved to New Orleans in the hope that the fresh start would help him recover from his stalled business projects in Lexington, and Porter eventually, though only temporarily, followed him. By then, John had married Julie Duralde, the daughter of prominent Creole businessman Martin Milony Duralde, establishing another important family connection for Henry Clay in the Louisiana Territory.[46]

Any practical benefits from these departures by friends and family were in the future. At the time, they were emotionally taxing for the young couple who remained in Lexington and watched their circle diminish. The most wrenching farewell for Henry and Lucretia was when James Brown was appointed secretary of the Louisiana Territory, meaning that he and vivacious Nancy would also be moving to New Orleans. Lucretia was close to her brothers, John, Thomas, and Nathaniel, and another sister, a widow, Susannah Price, affectionately called Suky. (Another older sister, Eliza, had married Dr. Richard Pindell in Maryland and died in 1798.) But Lucretia was especially close to Nancy.

Everybody hated to see the Browns leave. There would be visits, of course, but distance and bad roads made trips novelties rather than routines. And good health was always a delicate uncertainty in a time when even a minor illness could suddenly become something serious and lethal. Leave-taking in such a setting meant more than the prospect of missing loved ones; it could mean truly losing them. Henry Clay inherited much of James's legal practice and was appointed to his vacated position as professor of law at Transylvania University, but he would rather have had his friend stay in Lexington.[47]

Clay's appointment to Transylvania's law professorship in 1805 continued a line of George Wythe protégés in that post that included George Nicholas and James Brown. By then the former Transylvania Seminary had been a university for six years and was a constant philanthropic project for boosters aware of its civic benefits. Clay was the school's attorney and promoted its need for a strong faculty, which he now joined. In addition to conducting his classes, he became acquainted with all students—the school's enrollment was small enough to make that possible—but he worked particularly closely with the little cadre of young men studying law, taking many of them into his small brick office on Mill Street after graduation to train them in the profession. Among those students who studied with Clay were future U.S. senator and Kentucky chief justice George Robertson, future U.S. congressman and Kentucky governor Robert P. Letcher, and Robert Smith Todd, whose daughter would marry Abraham Lincoln. Clay's increasing legal and political responsibilities caused him to resign his professorship in 1807, but his strong attachment to the university kept him affiliated as a member of its board of trustees, and he often mentored its graduates in his practice.[48]

Meanwhile, the Clays were doing their part to boost Lexington's population. Fourteen months after their vows, Lucretia gave birth to a little girl they named Henrietta, but she died just short of her first birthday, one of seven children they would lose over the course of their lives, heart-wrenching events that left painful emotional scars. A little over a year after Henrietta's death, on July 3, 1802, Lucretia gave birth to the first of their five sons, Theodore Wythe Clay, named in part for Clay's beloved mentor George Wythe. The following year, Thomas Hart Clay was named for his grandfather, and eighteen months afterward, his sister Susan Hart Clay was named for her Aunt Suky. The two-year delay before their next child was apparently the result of Clay's absence for several months in Washington as a United States senator, but soon enough there was another daughter, Anne Brown Clay, named for her aunt Nancy who had moved to Louisiana. Finally the parents had namesakes in Lucretia Hart Clay, born in February 1809, and Henry Clay, Jr., born in April 1811. Eliza Hart Clay arrived in July 1813 and was named after Lucretia's dead sister.

Eliza was to be the last for a while, but only because Henry was away in Europe on important diplomatic missions. After he returned in late summer of 1815, Laura Clay arrived like clockwork in October 1816, but they lost her in only a few months. One year later, James Brown Clay was born, and then in February 1821 John Morrison Clay marked the end of Lucretia's childbearing. After all, she was forty years old by then. Nevertheless, the Clays were remarkable for their time, when many upper- and middle-class couples had begun to practice some form of birth control, such as abstinence, to limit the size of families, in part for convenience. In what has been described as their marriage of "convenience," Henry and Lucretia Clay obviously, and repeatedly, had something else in mind.[49]

THE LEGAL PRACTICE and income grew along with the family. In addition to work for his father-in-law, Clay occasionally took a criminal case, his performances always drawing crowds to the courthouse. Clay also rode a legal circuit with other attorneys to county seats throughout the state to attend monthly court days, and he was often in the state capital at Frankfort representing clients before the state court of appeals and the United States District Court. When Fayette County was between regular prosecutors, he temporarily stepped into that post. His most famous case involved a slave on trial for murdering his overseer. Numerous witnesses established the defendant's guilt beyond question; Clay easily won a conviction, and the slave was hanged. Yet Clay always regretted the episode. The overseer had been infamously brutal, and it was hard to see how justice was served by killing his killer.[50]

Clay's travels throughout the state and to Frankfort gave him the chance to indulge a raucous streak, and he soon gained a reputation for heavy drinking and reckless gambling. In Richmond, young Clay had been quite the man about town, a convivial chum and boon companion, and he continued his revelries in Lexington. Out on the Kentucky circuit, he was always ready for a drink or a dance, and he could produce his fiddle in the blink of an eye or apply his rich baritone to popular songs. His gambling was legendary, and his antics with his fellow attorneys were celebrated in gossip, much of it true, if occasionally a bit embellished. On the circuit, the temptations for fun were many, and the drive to combat boredom was constant. Lawyers spent their days in stuffy courtrooms, and at night they ate flavorless food in fetid country inns and slept in crowded rooms, two and three to a bed. When the inn was pleasant and the food tasty, these lawyers could make an evening memorable, and Henry Clay was often at the center of the story. Once in Frankfort, a wild night of drink and cards stretched past dawn. Clay was due in court that morning. One of his law students was horrified to find him just leaving the card table, disheveled and bleary-eyed. He calmed his student: nothing to fret about, he said; an hour's rest and a splash of water on his face would make him good as new. Clay appeared that morning in court and won his case.

But the most notable exploit occurred in the Frankfort tavern Sign of the Golden Eagle after a convivial supper and considerable whiskey. Everyone was preparing to rise from the sixty-foot banquet table when Clay leaped from his chair, vaulted onto the table, and began a whirling dance down its length. His fellow diners ducked and dodged as crockery and glasses and flatware went flying, dissolving into hilarity as Clay executed a graceful *"pas seul* from head to foot of the dining table." The following morning the owner presented Clay with a bill for the breakage. He promptly paid the $120. It had been worth every penny.[51]

Such exploits soon had associates calling Clay "Prince Hal," a reference to the wild ways of young Henry V when he had frolicked with Falstaff. His daily recreation consisted of card games such as brag in which players bet on each of three cards, a quick pastime that rewarded bluff as much as chance. He also liked poker and whist and was quite accomplished at all three.[52] Lucretia once responded with a sly smile to a meddlesome matron who asked how she could abide Clay's gambling. She did not mind it at all, she said, because "he 'most always wins."[53]

When not riding the circuit, Clay spent from four to six evenings a month at local taverns treating himself to drink, games, and song. While the stakes in some of his gambling exploits could grow astonishingly high, wagers between friends were not really as alarming as the figures suggest. One night at a local tavern, for instance, he won $40,000 in IOUs from newspaper editor John Bradford. The two happened on each other the next day, and Bradford awkwardly told Clay that everything he owned would not pay half the debt. Clay instructed Bradford to give him a "note for $500" and the rest would be forgotten. A few days later, when Bradford bested Clay for $60,000 in IOUs, he took back his $500 note and called it even.[54]

Prudence born of maturity would gradually diminish Clay's affinity for this sort of thing, but even in the early days he never let gambling or drink become his master, and he drew a stark distinction between the high jinks of trading thousands by way of IOUs with an old friend and the activities of professional sharps who were as likely to mark cards as count them. When a local judge in 1804 fined a professional gambler $25, Clay agreed. He even wrote to the newspapers to defend such penalties as necessary for "preserving the morals of society and suppressing [the] pernicious practice" of gambling.[55] There were those, however, who did not like Clay and understandably regarded the contradiction between his pious pronouncement and profligate behavior as hypocritical.

KENTUCKY'S FUTURE SEEMED boundless in these years, but that very potential signaled looming changes. The Bluegrass region's economic power had always made it politically dominant, but commercial progress and population increases in other parts of the state challenged that supremacy in the early 1800s. Henry Clay's oratorical talent made him a natural choice to counter that challenge, and his Lexington friends put him forward in August 1803 as a candidate for the state legislature. Clay later claimed that he was away resting in the mountains when these friends initiated his first bid for public office and that they had therefore done so without his knowledge, but that is unlikely. He did seem, however, to approach the matter quite casually. Balloting took place in Lexington over three days in August, and Clay was nowhere to be found for the first two. He, Lucretia, and the Harts usually spent the hottest part of the summer at Olympian Springs, a resort that Thomas Hart had built forty-seven miles east of Lexington, and nervous friends wondered why he had inexplicably gone there at this crucial moment. Clay's supporters had counted on his appeal to ordinary as well as elite voters, but all the charm in the world was meaningless if absent.[56] They anxiously watched his opponents work the crowds, buying drinks and making promises. Finally, at the end of the second day of balloting, Clay appeared and mingled with voters clustered around the courthouse. He made an impromptu speech that had townspeople and rural farmers alike laughing at its folksy good humor.[57] It was yet another example of how "the depth and sweetness of his voice . . . has no compeers; and in the gracefulness of his enunciation and manner, few equals."[58]

He spent the next day making such speeches, but crowds were not always pliant. At one appearance a frontiersman clad in buckskins shouted, "Young man, you want to go to the legislature, I see." Clay said indeed he did.

"Are you a good shot?" asked the man.

"The best in the country!" Clay answered.

"Then you shall go to the legislature," said the man, "but first you must give us a specimen of your skill. We must see you shoot."

All eyes settled on Clay and squinted suspiciously when he insisted that he could shoot well only with his own rifle. The frontiersman strode forward with a Kentucky rifle and handed it to Clay. "If you can shoot any gun," he bellowed, "you can shoot Old Bess.'"

Clay paused but finally shouted, "Well, put up your mark!"

Men hurried to place a target about eighty yards in the distance, more curious now to see this boy from the city shoot than they were to hear him speak. Clay raised Old Bess to his shoulder and fired. The target was pierced almost at dead center. The crowd erupted in cheers, but one skeptic insisted that it was just a lucky shot. Clay should have to do it again. He certainly would, Clay told the man, if he could match the feat himself. The doubter skulked away. It was great theater, and it is likely that the accuracy of Clay's aim was a piece of singular luck. Later Clay could not resist embellishing the story by chuckling over how that was the first and last time he had ever fired a rifle. It was a peculiar claim for a boy who had grown up hunting in the Slashes.[59]

Speeches backed by such pluck won Clay election to the Kentucky House in his first bid for public office, and in November 1803, he took the seat he would hold for the next six years. In his first session, the legislature gathered on the second floor of the stone capitol in Frankfort abuzz with rumors of looming war with Spain.[60]

The purchase of Louisiana from Napoleonic France had set off celebrations only months before, but soon disturbing reports began circulating that the deal was hardly certain. Spain was insistent that it had ceded Louisiana to Napoleon only on the condition that France not sell it to the United States. Cash-strapped Napoleon, however, sold the province to Thomas Jefferson's administration so quickly that Spain was still in possession of it. Now Spain threatened to block its transfer to the United States. The entire West rose up in arms. Clay arrived in Frankfort that November as Kentucky militiamen were assembling with fight in their eyes, and he was quickly caught up in the war fever. He certainly knew that political laurels would likely result from participating in a campaign against the Spaniards, and he immediately signed on as an aide to the militia's commanding general, Samuel Hopkins. The militia's preparations had hardly begun, however, before word reached Kentucky that Spain would turn over Louisiana after all. The excitement died down as quickly as it started, disappointing more than a few boys who were spoiling for a fight, especially against Spaniards. Nobody liked Spaniards.[61]

The distraction of a possible war removed, the legislature began its work in earnest. Most of the session's business was routine. Divorce petitions took up a fair amount of time, because a marriage could be dissolved in Kentucky only after an act of the legislature allowed the suit to be brought in the courts.[62] Voting aid to veterans of the Revolution and Indian wars was a high priority, while placing bounties on wolf pelts answered farmers' complaints about losing livestock to predators. But there was also residual rancor over old disputes with Federalists. The Democratic-Republican majority eagerly embraced any scheme to reduce Federalist clout, and Clay took a leading role in the project even though he was a new member. In fact, Clay's first important legislative initiative was a proposal to gerrymander Kentucky Federalists out of presidential politics. Four of Kentucky's six electoral districts would be eliminated to swallow up Federalist enclaves and prevent even a single Federalist elector from being chosen in the 1804 presidential election.[63]

Thomas Jefferson had handily won Kentucky in 1800 and was predicted to win the state again in 1804, but Federalist gains in the state concerned his supporters. Joseph Hamilton Daveiss was a rising star in this Federalist revival and became an irritating opponent for Republicans. Friends called Daveiss "Jo." Clay was not among them. In fact, earlier in the year Clay had again appeared in the public prints as "Scaevola" to dispute Daveiss's claim that he was running for Congress on Jeffersonian principles. Clay's redistricting bill sought to make sure that such upstart Federalists could never wield influence in the state.[64]

More than party maneuvering roiled Kentucky politics. Frustration with Bluegrass dominance of state affairs made the region south of the Kentucky River especially restive. It was called the Southside and had able spokesmen, especially a young firebrand named Felix Grundy, whose thunderous voice and natural fluency made him a formidable opponent in debate. Clay did not encounter this fearsome adversary during his first legislative session because Grundy had recently changed districts and was not eligible to sit in the 1803 legislature. That would change the following November. In 1804, Grundy not only returned to Frankfort but also carried his part of the state's collective chip on his shoulder.

Grundy was not just popular. His image as an ordinary man who looked out for ordinary Kentuckians earned him extraordinary regard among grateful constituents. In legislative sessions before Clay's election, Grundy had helped to ram through measures touted as reforms, though sometimes they were nothing more than sops pandering to class resentment. For example, he played on the universal disdain of lawyers and their supposed double-talk to accuse Kentucky's judges of being in league with elite attorneys. This demagogic indictment of the state's legal system resulted in a "reform" that required the state circuit courts to seat two lay judges who, without a smidgen of legal training, had veto power over decisions rendered by the real judge. Common sense instead of lawyerly tricks would now decide cases, crowed Grundy's supporters.[65]

Felix Grundy had an even bigger target in his sights when he reentered the state legislature in November 1804. Three years earlier, the legislature had chartered the Kentucky Insurance Company to underwrite cargo vessels on the Ohio River. Its charter, however, also allowed the firm to issue notes that could circulate as currency, a privilege that essentially made the company Kentucky's first state bank. The scarcity of banknotes and government specie (the term for coins, i.e., minted precious metals), often made it next to impossible to do business in Kentucky. The Kentucky Insurance Company's stable currency seemed a sensible way to eliminate primitive bartering and encourage investment. Others saw something more sinister. They perceived the company's banking function as an attempt to concentrate all economic power in the Bluegrass region and keep down the state's poorer sections.[66]

Riding such resentment, Grundy and his supporters planned to revoke the Kentucky Insurance Company's banking privileges by arguing that many legislators had voted for the charter unaware that it contained such objectionable provisions. They never would have voted for something so contrary to republican institutions, Grundy said, and he commenced the well-rehearsed complaint that a bank concentrated power in the hands of an elite few who then imposed their will on the defenseless people.[67] Clay rushed to the company's defense. Part of his motive was regional loyalty (the company was based in Lexington), part was family allegiance (his father-in-law was on the board of directors), and part was self-interest (Clay owned stock in the company), but those factors were hardly the stuff of compelling arguments. Instead, Clay praised the company's role in stimulating Kentucky's economy and argued that canceling any part of its charter before it expired in 1818 would violate the constitutional prohibition on impairing contracts, an argument that anticipated a U.S. Supreme Court decision by fifteen years.[68]

Clay won this first round when Grundy's proposal was defeated by one vote. James Brown congratulated his brother-in-law from New Orleans, saying that he was "happy that the Bank has had the means of resisting the attacks of that unprincipled demagogue Grundy."[69] But the one-vote margin was a troubling indication that the Bluegrass bank was hardly safe. Grundy was sure to spend the coming year organizing for the second round in the next legislative session. In the meantime, he had another plan to reduce Bluegrass power.[70]

Under the U.S. Constitution at that time, state legislatures chose U.S. senators, and in that matter, as in virtually all others, Kentucky's senators were men of the Bluegrass. Senators John Brown and John Breckinridge were currently in office, and Brown was set for reelection. His mere existence irked Southsiders who rankled over Brown's aristocratic ways (he purchased an elegant coach and four during a visit to his New York in-laws), his elegant home called Liberty Hall, and his presumption of privileged leadership. Following Grundy's lead, they were determined to replace Brown with one of their own, nominating John Adair of Mercer County. Efforts to hold on to Brown's Senate seat were complicated by doubts among his own supporters about his political viability. Those dissatisfied with Brown nominated Buckner Thruston, dividing Bluegrass votes and giving Grundy and his supporters a good chance to elect Adair. Clay was loosely related to Brown by marriage (John was James Brown's brother), but he realized the danger, shifted his support to Thruston, and applied "artful management" to persuade enough legislators to give Thruston the seat. In the rough-and-tumble world of intrastate politics, Clay balanced the protection of family against the protection of regional interests. Regional interests won out on this occasion.[71]

Yet saving the Senate seat was a Pyrrhic victory, at least as far as the fortunes of the Kentucky Insurance Company were concerned. Thruston and Breckinridge not only represented the Bluegrass, they were both from Lexington, a fact that stoked Southside resentment and gave Grundy reason to renew his attack on Bluegrass dominance in the next legislative session. At the urging of Clay and its other supporters, the Kentucky Insurance Company tried to enhance support for its banking function by offering generous loans. Even though Kentuckians were struggling to pay new federal taxes on lands and eagerly took advantage of these liberal lending policies, resentment against the Bluegrass and anything associated with it was unabated. When Grundy returned to the legislature in the fall of 1805, he came with a crowd.[72]

It was clearly to be Clay versus Grundy, however, and when the House considered the disposition of the Kentucky Insurance Company's charter, the capital hummed over the prospect of the bout. On the day the two were to address the House, the state Senate adjourned to allow its members to watch the fireworks, and as it turned out, the debate became quite a show. Grundy and Clay circled and jabbed at each other for two days, repeating earlier arguments in a display that would have become tedious had it not been so fascinating. Behind all the drama, however, lay the inescapable fact that Grundy now had the votes to strip the company of its banking function, and no amount of debate, even from the dazzling Mr. Clay, could change that. When all was said and done, Grundy's measure passed the House, sailed through the Senate, and was dropped on the governor's desk for his signature, a result that everyone, counting the bill's legislative majorities, marked as certain. Much to everyone's surprise, however, Governor Christopher Greenup vetoed the bill, citing Clay's argument about the sanctity of contracts as the deciding factor. Grundy and his supporters railed at this executive effrontery and promptly overrode the governor's veto in the House. The Senate, however, considered an override with more deliberation, and the pause gave Henry Clay his chance. He had one more trick up his sleeve.

As the Senate deliberated, Clay introduced a measure in the House demanding immediate payment from speculators who had bought state lands along the Green River on credit. The debt to the state was an old one, but the speculators had managed to avoid paying it because of back-scratching bargains in the legislature. The arrangement had a smell to it, and the speculators had earned the label "Green River Band" because of their shady practices that smacked of influence peddling and cronyism. The Green River Band was accordingly an easy target, but it was also an inviting one because many of its members were often in Grundy's camp, rattling for his reforms and applauding his attacks on the privileged elite. Clay turned the tables to accuse them of acting more privileged than any Lexington tycoon, what with their sweetheart legislative deals and unpaid debts to the people of Kentucky. Clay's initiative so alarmed the Green River speculators that they pressured the Senate to let the governor's veto stand. The banking function of the Kentucky Insurance Company survived, and Clay quietly dropped his demand for immediate payment of the Green River debt.[73] Without losing a thing, Clay had won. His deft political maneuver had old political hands tugging at their chins and reassessing the tall young man with the impressive voice. Clearly there was more to him than words. "Henry is like a lion's whelp; who shall rouse him up?" asked one, mingling Old and New Testament verses. "The sound of his voice is terrible; yea, it is like the voice of many waters."[74]

Clay saved the Kentucky Insurance Company with last-minute heroics, but many legislators had already concluded that banks were actually quite useful. They soon created the Bank of Kentucky, an institution explicitly sanctioned by the state to act as a bank. Nevertheless, Clay's defense of banks worried some. He sometimes sounded like a Federalist, and the charge would be repeated in the years to come. Meanwhile, "that unprincipled upstart Grundy,"[75] as James Brown now called him, received an appointment to the Kentucky Court of Appeals and within months became the state's chief justice. But he soon decided to move to Nashville, Tennessee. Felix Grundy wryly explained that "Kentucky was too small for both him and Henry Clay."[76]

CLAY WOULD ALWAYS be associated with the Bluegrass and its interests, but his promotion of certain other measures gradually gained him a following throughout Kentucky. To help litigants appealing to U.S. circuit courts, he pushed a resolution through the House and Senate calling for the creation of a United States circuit west of the Blue Ridge. Clay urged that Kentucky finance internal improvements to boost commerce in all parts of the state, foreshadowing his life's work on the national scene.[77] He demonstrated an ability to bring together seemingly irreconcilable factions through compromise, and he became wedded to the idea that the key to political success was to promote the possible and avoid the unattainable ideal. Often that was accomplished through sleight of hand, sometimes with the simplest solutions. When he chaired a select committee on raising revenue, for example, a bill was proposed to tax billiard tables at $200 each. It was likely that such a measure would not generate much revenue but would instead make owning a billiard table beyond the means of taverns. Clay had the amount reduced to $50 but with an amendment naming the bill "an act more effectually to suppress the practice of gaming." Critics groused that he was more interested in saving billiards than promoting morality, but the tables survived, and the treasury profited.[78]

There were a few missteps. He offended Frankfort's citizens by repeatedly trying to have the state capital moved to Lexington. Frankfort was too small, he said; it lacked the radiating road system for which Lexington served as a hub. All of this was true, but it was impolitic to say so. Clay was never able to muster the two-thirds vote necessary to move the capital, but it was not for want of trying.

It was only one way in which he tried to boost Lexington's fortunes, only one facet of the project of civic improvement that he would pursue for the rest of his life. Clay was unabashedly proud of Lexington. He watched with satisfaction as the town grew in sophistication, population, and prosperity. By the early 1800s, it had become the center of education, commerce, and culture for the entire state. Lexington had three boarding schools for young ladies, several day schools for boys, and Transylvania University. Numerous taverns catered to every imaginable taste, offering freshly brewed beer, aged wines, whiskeys, and cordials. Gentlemen of the town had even established a coffeehouse, a euphemism for a tavern, that served the upper class, where a yearly rate of $6 could buy subscriptions to forty-two newspapers and periodicals from all over the United States. Henry Terrass ran this upscale tavern and also operated a public garden behind his house. Called Vauxhall, the garden was canopied by "a most luxuriant grape arbour." On Wednesday evenings, he hired musicians for dances.[79]

By 1805, Lexington had about five hundred houses, and the smell of freshly cut lumber, the sound of saws and pounding hammers, and the bustle of new houses and businesses springing up gave evidence of a prosperous place on the move while remaining a delight for the eyes. "The country around Lexington, for many miles in every direction," said a keen-eyed observer, "is equal in beauty and fertility to anything the imagination can paint."[80] Another traveler described the streets as "wide and airy." Moreover, the town was "as handsome" as Philadelphia but with a prettier countryside surrounding it. People in Lexington had "a glow of health, and an animation to their faces." Something about the air, something about the water, something about the place made its girls pretty and its boys strong.[81]

Henry Clay would never be able to bring himself to call any other place home. James and Nancy Brown beckoned him to move his family to New Orleans with alluring descriptions of waiting fortunes and balmy winters, but the Clays would not leave Lexington. Clay's economic and political future looked bright, and the town's destiny seemed a metaphor for his own. He was among the top attorneys in the state and could charge fees that even Virginia lawyers would have considered steep. In 1804, he began purchasing land outside of town to build a country home even as construction continued on a larger house in Lexington for his growing family. The twin projects strained the family's finances, but that was the price of living as a gentleman in the Bluegrass.[82]

The acreage outside of town and the house on it would be his "Ashland," a name he took from the large forest of ash trees that shaded the property. He situated the house on a gentle rise of land from which he could see the cupola of Lexington's courthouse and the steeple of Christ Church, home of the town's Episcopal congregation that Clay had helped to establish but would not join himself until forty years later. In 1805, on that gently sloped hill, a graceful house arose in the Federal style that Clay would remodel and add to in coming years, most notably by attaching two flanking wings to its center. He would also put up numerous outbuildings, for Ashland was to be a working farm. It was to be even more: Clay intended for it eventually to be a refuge, serene with shaded lawns, pleasing with native and imported plants. Its barns and pastures would be home to fine livestock, its stables full of fast horses, its fields lush with rows of hemp, wheat, and corn, and its pastures covered in the thick-bladed, hearty bluegrass that made cows fat and soil rich.[83]

Eventually all of that would happen just as he imagined it. For now, he watched the house and the first of his ideas grow from the ground. Because of Ashland, he would later count himself more fortunate than Moses. "He died in sight of and without reaching the Promised Land," Clay would say. "I occupy as good a farm as any he would have found had he reached it."[84]

CHAPTER THREE

"Puppyism"

I N THE SPRING of 1805, Aaron Burr came to Kentucky. His generous advocacy for western interests in the 1790s had always made him popular beyond the Blue Ridge, but his messy public and private life did not play well in the East, and by 1805 his political career had come crashing to earth with a resounding thump. When he resigned the vice presidency a few days before his term expired on March 4, 1805, he was under indictment for murder in not just one but two states.

Burr was an enigmatic man whose complexities have bedeviled modern attempts to understand him as much as they bewildered the people of his time. Charming and suave, he could enchant women and sway men with equal ease, often clouding their better judgment. His many friends defended him as a misunderstood patriot wronged by his many enemies. Those enemies just as vehemently described him as a sinister opportunist whose oily charm was only a mask for dark motives. People still argue over who was right about Aaron Burr. Possibly they all were, as Henry Clay would have occasion to discover.

Burr's problems began with the presidential election of 1800. The Electoral College gave both Thomas Jefferson and Burr, ostensibly the vice-presidential candidate, the same number of votes and threw the election into the House of Representatives. Because Burr refused to step aside, it took multiple ballots and some maneuvering to elect Jefferson, whose bitterness about Burr's behavior irreparably estranged them.[1] President Jefferson effectively excluded Burr from any meaningful role in his administration, and the Democratic-Republicans dropped him from the ticket in 1804, a rebuke made all the more obvious by Burr's replacement, George Clinton, another New Yorker. Burr tried to recover his career by running for governor of New York, but political rival Alexander Hamilton helped to defeat him. The two engaged in a mounting quarrel that ended on July 11, 1804, at Weehawken, New Jersey, as they faced off with cocked pistols. The most famous duel in American history killed Hamilton. In terms of his career, it killed Burr too.

New Jersey and New York indicted him for murder. Burr fled, eventually returning to Washington where he presided over the Senate, an odd figure of defiant innocence and putative guilt, shielded from arrest and punishment by the fact that murder was not a federal crime and extradition was unlikely, partly fortified by the fact that Hamilton had been pointing a pistol too, and by the fact that many, after all, hated Hamilton. But it was not enough to clean the stain of putative guilt, so Burr said good-bye to the Senate and headed west to Pittsburgh. He floated down the Ohio River on a large, well-appointed flatboat, stopping along the way to warm greetings and friendly faces. The farther west one went, the more Hamilton was hated by those who also remembered Burr as their region's champion. The farther west Burr went, the friendlier were the faces.

One of Burr's first stops was Blennerhassett Island, home of wealthy Irish immigrants Harman and Margaret Blennerhassett. Their beautiful Palladian mansion in its charming pastoral setting was a world apart, and Burr basked in its serenity. He was a delightful and fascinating guest, and everyone got on famously. The Blennerhassetts often visited Kentucky, where their many connections included prominent families such as the Harts and the Browns, so adding Burr to their collection of acquaintances seemed both natural and advantageous. When he left after a few days, they were sorry to see him go and eager for his return. They had no way of knowing that his visit would change their lives, that his plans would destroy their home and ruin their island.[2]

Burr headed for Cincinnati and then to Kentucky, meeting along the way with people interested in digging a canal around the rapids of the Ohio River. In fact, the wealthy and famous greeted him wherever he turned up. At Frankfort he stayed at former U.S. senator John Brown's Liberty Hall, and in Lexington he attended a concert at the popular hotel Traveller's Hall. Also in Lexington he met a young attorney named Henry Clay. As he did everyone else, the handsome and dashing Burr captivated Clay.[3]

From Lexington, Burr traveled overland to Mercer County to meet with Kentucky U.S. senator John Adair. In Nashville, Burr met Tennessee militia general Andrew Jackson and commissioned him to build boats, a hint that Burr's trip had purposes other than social. Another was his meeting with the United States Army's senior officer, James Wilkinson, at Fort Massac on the Ohio. The two knew each other from their service together during the Revolutionary War, and Wilkinson gave Burr letters of introduction to important people in New Orleans, where Burr's three-week stay, beginning on June 26, saw him feted at parties and honored by local dignitaries. The Mexican Association, a group that advocated the annexation of Mexico to the United States, was particularly enthusiastic. The association's president was also the mayor of New Orleans, Dr. John W. Watkins, who happened to be Henry Clay's first cousin and former brother-in-law.[4]

By the time Burr left New Orleans on July 14 to travel back through Tennessee and Kentucky, his journey was attracting attention. Kentucky's Federalist minority was a small group, but it was vigilant, especially Humphrey Marshall, one of Lexington's first settlers in the 1780s, and Joseph Hamilton Daveiss, who had become Kentucky's United States attorney. Both men had crossed swords with Clay, whose redistricting bill in the state legislature had gerrymandered Jo Daveiss out of his seat. These Federalists were well connected: Humphrey Marshall was U.S. Supreme Court chief justice John Marshall's cousin, and both he and Daveiss had married sisters of John Marshall. Because they were good Federalists, they reflexively opposed Kentucky Republicans, but they differed in their response to the implacable Republican majority. Marshall was such a snob that he made the highest Federalist look positively egalitarian, and he nursed a blinding hatred of political opponents. Some have explained Marshall and Daveiss's obsession with Burr as stemming from their desire to avenge Alexander Hamilton, whom Jo Daveiss so admired, it was said, that he took "Hamilton" as his middle name in tribute. Daveiss did admire Hamilton, but his middle name came from family, not fawning adulation of the arch-Federalist, and Marshall's primary reason for impugning Burr was not to exact revenge for Hamilton's death but to discredit Kentucky Republicans.[5] On the other hand, Daveiss was as much a patriot—something he ultimately proved with his life—as a partisan. Long irritated by Republican attacks on Federalists' patriotism, he smelled something rotten about Burr, squinted at his travels, and grew dimly aware, he thought, of his plans. In due course, Daveiss believed he had stumbled on a monstrous conspiracy to detach part of the western United States and violate federal law by invading Spanish territory in the Southwest. For his part, Marshall believed that implicating Republicans in these plans would show everyone a thing or two about who the real patriots in Kentucky were.

By early 1806, Burr was back east raising money for some sort of adventure, and Daveiss believed he could prove it was nefarious. He alerted the national government about his suspicions in a January 1806 letter to Jefferson. At the very least, Daveiss said, Burr and prominent westerners intended to take Spanish Mexico by force. Beyond that, they probably planned to separate the western part of the United States to make it part of Burr's new empire. The fact that Daveiss said he had the names of conspirators gave weight to his charges, but the list was simply incredible, a Who's Who of western politicians visited by Burr in his travels. Daviess claimed he could implicate federal district judge Harry Innes, U.S. congressman John Fowler, senior United States Army general James Wilkinson, Kentucky appellate court judge Benjamin Sebastian, U.S. senator John Adair, Indiana territorial governor William Henry Harrison, Jefferson's attorney general John Breckinridge, and even Henry Clay. In a later letter he admitted that he no longer believed Breckinridge and Clay were conspirators, but even so the list remained sobering. If true, this was a monstrous conspiracy indeed.[6]

Humphrey Marshall very much intended to make people believe it was true. That summer of 1806 he brought editor John Wood from Richmond to establish a Federalist newspaper in Frankfort. Joseph Street, a young clerk Wood had met in Richmond, became his partner in the *Western World,* a paper that Marshall filled with allegations about Aaron Burr and his Kentucky friends, all Republicans. The paper revived old rumors from the 1790s that accused Kentucky Republicans of involvement in the so-called Spanish Conspiracy, one of many shadowy schemes, it was whispered, to separate the West and join it to Spain's southwestern empire. The Louisiana Purchase, not patriotism, had made such plots irrelevant, said the *Western World,* which darkly reminded its readers that Republicans had not always been the true-blue Americans they now only pretended to be.[7]

By the time Burr returned to the West in the fall of 1806, the *Western World* had given rise to alarming stories about large numbers of men assembling on Blennerhassett Island, the construction of boats there and elsewhere, and the purchase of arms.[8] The *Western World* fanned the flames, and U.S. Attorney Daveiss felt the increasing heat. Reports about food being stockpiled on Louisville's wharves and boats nearing completion in its dockyards caused him to make an anxious trip to Louisville to see for himself, and what he saw did anything but calm him. News that hundreds of men had gathered on Blennerhassett Island in fact convinced him that Burr's plans were about to launch. He urged U.S. district judge Harry Innes on November 5, 1806, to arrest Burr for plotting an invasion of Spanish territory. Innes, who had been on Jo Daveiss's original list of conspirators, was not so sure.[9]

Meanwhile, Aaron Burr heard that Jo Daveiss wanted him thrown in jail. He raced from Lexington to Frankfort to hire a lawyer, and the man he sought out agreed to represent him. It was Henry Clay.

AFTER THINKING ABOUT Daveiss's request for several days, Innes ruled against issuing a warrant without a proper investigation: nobody should be arrested simply because Jo Daveiss thought he might be guilty. As the judge was reading this decision, Aaron Burr strode into the courtroom followed by Henry Clay and other prominent Republicans, all clearly tired of the *Western World*'s rumor mongering and the widespread innuendo it had encouraged. Taking the offensive, they demanded a grand jury investigation, confident that it would settle the matter once and for all. Innes wanted it settled too. He ordered a grand jury impaneled on November 12, 1806.[10]

People thronged into Frankfort from all over the Bluegrass to see a first-rate show. On November 12, Burr appeared in court accompanied by Clay and local counsel John Allen. The crowd scrambled for the few remaining seats, Judge Innes began his instructions to the grand jury, and Jo Daveiss stood up to ask for a postponement. The crowd groaned as Daveiss explained that one of his key witnesses had not arrived. Davis Floyd was a member of the Indiana territorial legislature, Daveiss weakly explained, and that body was still in session. A wave of laughter swept over the assembly as it realized the man Daveiss believed to be the quartermaster for Burr's army was at that moment helping to govern Indiana. Innes dismissed the jury and then granted Burr's request to address the court. Just a few days before, Burr said, Henry Clay had offered Burr's help in summoning witnesses, but Daveiss told Clay that the court would see to it. Burr demanded that the avoidable fiasco perpetrated by the U.S. attorney be recorded as the reason for the grand jury's dismissal.[11]

Burr's audacity was effective theater, but it only spurred Daveiss to greater efforts. Assured that Floyd would come to Kentucky, and armed with a list of other potential witnesses, Daveiss asked Innes to convene another grand jury on December 2.[12] From Louisville, Burr asked Clay to represent him at the new hearing, but this time Clay said no.

The young attorney hesitated, because his situation had dramatically changed. Just a week after the abortive grand jury incident, the Kentucky legislature selected Clay to replace Senator John Adair in Washington. Adair was a replacement himself, having been appointed to fill John Breckinridge's seat when Jefferson tapped Breckinridge for attorney general. Adair unexpectedly resigned in a huff when the legislature elected John Pope for the term beginning March 1807, a gesture Adair took as a personal rebuke, and Kentucky thus needed a short-term stand-in. Young Clay, thought the legislature, was just the man.[13]

Now that he was to be a United States senator, if only briefly, Clay worried about the propriety of representing a man suspected of violating federal law and possibly even plotting treason. Burr promised a handsome fee and assured Clay that Congress never conducted important business until the first of the year, but

Clay remained cautious. Only after friends convinced him it would be dishonorable to abandon Burr did he consider relenting. A letter from Burr vowing that he had "no design, nor have I taken any measure, to promote a dissolution of the Union or a separation of any one or more States from the residue" finally resolved the matter for him. Clay went to Frankfort.

It was a mistake.[14]

When the second grand jury convened on December 2, 1806, Burr confidently entered the crowded courtroom with Clay and Allen. After Innes instructed the grand jury and it had retired, Clay stood to address the court. The entire proceeding, he said, was simply a case of political grandstanding by Daveiss. Clay cast doubts on the reason the first grand jury had been fruitless, intimating that Daveiss had not wanted Burr present to defend himself; Daveiss had asked for a postponement so that he could wait until Burr left Kentucky. Only then, Clay said, had Daveiss asked for this grand jury, before which he planned to slander an absent Burr. But Burr had not left Kentucky and was very much a presence in the courtroom, a fact painfully evident when Daveiss slowly rose to ask for another postponement. The crowd groaned as it had before while the U.S. attorney explained that Davis Floyd was present as requested, but two other important witnesses, including former U.S. senator John Adair, had not arrived.[15]

Henry Clay leaped to his feet, loudly protesting this thoughtless treatment of his client. He angrily called the first grand jury proceeding a "farce and pantomime" and asked if Burr was again "to have his time and attention diverted from his own affairs, to be tortured and obliged to account to this court for every action, even those of the most trifling nature, in order to gratify the whim and caprice of the Federal Attorney?"

Jo Daveiss lost his temper. Clay, he barked, was interfering with the court's duty to conduct its investigation, and he informed the grumbling crowd that no statute required the authorities to inform Clay or his client about a grand jury proceeding.

Now Clay lost his temper. He shouted that his client could not help but be concerned about the U.S. attorney's overreaching to destroy the reputation of an honorable and patriotic American. Did the U.S. attorney mean to say, Clay asked, that Burr had no right to be present? He reminded the crowd as much as the court that this whimsical calling and dismissing of grand juries was unprecedented. If the court now sanctioned such capricious procedures, innocent men would lose the protection of the law, everyone would be subject to prosecutorial persecution, and soon Daveiss would be indicting people completely on his own, never bothering to call a grand jury.

Innes gaveled down this free-ranging exchange. Daveiss could have another postponement, he said, but only until the next morning. He looked levelly at the U.S. attorney and expressed regret over dismissing the November 12 grand jury. At least then, Innes mused, Daveiss was missing only one witness; now he was missing two.[16] That night Judge Innes spent a delightful evening dining at Liberty Hall with host John Brown and his guest of honor, Aaron Burr.

The next morning the U.S. attorney was all business. He began the day by handing the grand jury foreman an indictment against John Adair, the very man whom Daveiss had cited the day before as an essential witness and the reason for delay. Daveiss also made clear his intention to question all witnesses before the grand jury, a practice Clay had already protested as unprecedented.[17] The jurors had enough aptitude, Clay said, to ask their own questions without being steered by Daveiss's "ingenious and dangerous novelties."

"The only novelty which I see in this court," Daveiss snapped, "is Mr. Clay."

There was a pause as Clay slowly drew a large breath. "I presume, sir," he said solemnly, "that if on this occasion I be thought to indulge too freely in expressing the honest sentiments of my mind with regard to the extraordinary request of the Attorney, a desire of preserving the rights of my fellow citizens will be the only cause imputed to me. For their rights and for the liberty of my country I shall never cease to contend." The baritone rose as though to shake the windowpanes: "The woods of Kentucky, I hope, will never be made the abode of inquisitors, or our simple establishments exchanged for the horrid cells of deception and tyranny." He concluded with the definitive insult: even a British court would not allow what Daveiss was proposing.[18]

Nor would New York, said Burr, his observation rendered from his years as the state's attorney general, but coming after Clay's rousing performance, something of an afterthought. Innes ruled that Daveiss could not question witnesses but only answer jurors' inquiries on points of law.[19] Daveiss tried another tactic the following day. He proposed to provide jurors with slips of paper containing appropriate questions to ask the witnesses. Clay and Allen were in the process of protesting this new ploy when Burr, who had been shuffling through the slips, quietly said he had no objection to the questions or their manner of presentation.

Burr was right about the questions, at least. The grand jury returned to the courtroom at about 1:00 P.M. to report that the evidence was insufficient to indict John Adair. Daveiss promptly handed the foreman an indictment of Burr, and the jurors retired to begin questioning witnesses, but it was not until the following morning, when the jurors said they wanted to interview the *Western World*'s editors, John Wood and Joseph Street, that the inquiry seemed near concluding.

Neither Wood nor Street had been on Daveiss's witness list—strange omissions, because for months they had been printing extravagant claims about damning evidence that would convict Burr and his Kentucky Republican friends. Now, before a grand jury and under oath, Street and Wood sheepishly admitted that they had no such evidence at all. Wood, recently estranged from his young partner, even declared that as far as he knew, Burr was completely innocent.[20] At 2:00 P.M. the grand jury issued the legally stipulated declaration that the U.S. attorney's indictment was "not a true bill," but added the forceful statement, "The grand jury are happy to inform the court, that no violent disturbance of the public tranquility, or breach of the laws, has come to their knowledge. We have no hesitation in declaring, that having carefully examined and scrutinized all the testimony which has come before us, as well on the charges against Aaron Burr [and] John Adair, that there has been no testimony before us, which does in the smallest degree criminate the conduct of either." The courtroom erupted into shouts and applause as the jubilant crowd escorted Burr, Clay, and Allen from the building. Humphrey Marshall, who had written most of the *Western World*'s now admitted fabrications, sneered that the grand jury's statement sounded as if it had been written by the scoundrel Burr or, worse, his Republican attorneys, very likely that rascal Clay.[21]

CLAY HURRIED HOME to Lexington, not even pausing to attend the ball celebrating Burr's vindication. He had to pack and make arrangements to turn his legal practice over to fellow attorney William T. Barry before setting out for Washington. The second grand jury had delayed him two weeks, and he would already arrive several weeks after the final session of the Ninth Congress had convened. Before Clay departed, Burr came to Lexington to thank him for his efforts. Clay was more certain than ever that Burr was innocent. He refused to take a fee.[22]

Clay had won election to his first, short stint in the national legislature handily, 68 to 10 over George Bibb, a testament to his popularity in the Kentucky statehouse. Even Felix Grundy had voted for him.[23] Now he was eager to reach the nation's capital, where he looked forward to "dining on oysters at the city on Xmas day."[24] His route took him across the Ohio River to Chillicothe, Ohio, and from there to Wheeling, Virginia (now West Virginia), by boat. A long ride in a stagecoach completed the journey. He traveled alone except for a manservant because Lucretia was too far along in her pregnancy, her fifth in eight years of marriage, to risk the trip, which was a wretched ordeal by any standard. Clay took note of the country's miserable roads as uncomfortable stagecoaches bounced him along, and he concluded that something should be done about the nation's primitive transportation system. With that first journey to Washington, he felt the glimmer of an idea, a project for a life's work.

He also suffered a slight pang of alarm, one that became an even more nagging worry the closer he came to Washington. At every stop, starting with Chillicothe, he heard disturbing rumors about Aaron Burr and troubling stories about his plans. In Ohio, Clay continued to defend Burr and cited the Kentucky grand jury's decision. He assured people that Burr was merely planning to colonize lands he had bought in Louisiana. Shortly after he left Chillicothe, however, Clay heard that President Jefferson had issued a proclamation that certain citizens were planning an unlawful attack on Spanish territory. Moving out of the insular world of the Bluegrass, Clay could assess Burr's reputation east of the Blue Ridge, where he was detested by eastern Republicans as vehemently as he was hated by western Federalists. Clay considered the possibility that Burr was capable of anything, a notion that was perhaps more than the deluded idea of an obsessed, partisan prosecutor. Jefferson's proclamation gave Clay pause. As he embarked on this next stage of his rising career, he realized the sickening possibility that he had begun it with a serious mistake.[25]

Reports about Burr's unraveling plans dogged Clay's journey, and he entered Washington nervously a few days after Christmas in 1806. Possibly because he was preoccupied, Clay never recorded his first impression of the capital, but we know from other travelers during this time that it was anything but imposing. Its enormous size alone—"magnificent distances" was one charitable description—made its scattered, partially finished public buildings look raw and isolated. Washington was not much of a town at the end of 1806, let alone a national capital. Clay entered it through the small village of Georgetown. He crossed Rock Creek and rode past the President's House up the grandiosely named Pennsylvania Avenue, which was often a sluice of mud, toward Capitol Hill. The Capitol itself was still under construction, its perimeter littered with building materials and scrap. The weather was cold, and the swampy Potomac bottoms bordering the town to its south that fouled the air and sickened people in summer made the chill penetrating and bitter in winter. The town would fill out gradually, and Clay would be there to see it. The weather in both summer and winter, however, remained unpleasant at its extremes.[26]

Clay arrived so late in the session that he had difficulty finding a room in the boardinghouses scattered across Capitol Hill. After two weeks of living like a vagabond, he moved into Frost and Quinn's boardinghouse with his cousin Matthew Clay, a congressman from Virginia.[27] By then, Clay had presented his credentials to the Senate, and on December 29, 1806, he took his seat. Some senators noted his youth, but no one apparently minded that Clay was only twenty-nine years old, too young by more than three months to be a United States senator. Senator William Plumer of New Hampshire described Clay on his first day in the Senate as "a young man—a lawyer—his stature is tall & slender." Plumer instantly liked Clay. He "had much conversation with him, & it afforded me much pleasure. He is intelligent, sensible & appears frank & candid. His address is good & manners easy. So much for the first impression—I hope a further & more intimate acquaintance, will not weaken, but add force, to these favorable impressions." Plumer was a keen observer and had ample opportunity as a fellow boarder at Frost and Quinn's to take the measure of the affable young Kentuckian with a flair for camaraderie, regardless of political party. By the end of the session, Plumer, a Federalist, was describing the Republican Clay as "my friend."[28]

The Senate chamber was on the ground floor of the Capitol, "an elegant apartment, with handsome furniture" that was "adorned with full length portraits of the late unfortunate king and queen of France [Louis XVI and Marie Antoinette]."[29] Senators sat at wooden desks on chairs cushioned by red leather with a beautiful new carpet underfoot. Despite these stylish touches, the building was poorly constructed, and falling plaster frequently flecked their desks and the new carpet.[30]

For all his ease as he began attending Senate sessions, Clay was vaguely unsettled by the persistent rumors about Aaron Burr. On his first day, Clay told William Plumer that he had been reluctant to represent Burr before the second grand jury hearing. He showed Plumer the letter from Burr asserting his innocence. Clay assured Plumer that Daveiss had been overzealous, that the grand jurors were of the highest character, that everyone in Kentucky except for partisans knew Burr was guiltless. Clay, in short, whistled with a somewhat strained certainty as the dark gathered around Burr, possibly to dim the reputation of his former counsel as well.[31]

It soon got worse. When Clay called on Thomas Jefferson, the president showed Clay a sheet with cryptic markings, a key to a code for sending secret messages, and told him that its author was Aaron Burr. For Jefferson, this "cipher letter" sealed Burr's infamous role as the author of a treasonous scheme; but many now doubt that Burr had anything to do with the letter. Jefferson, however, embraced it as proof positive of Burr's guilt. Clay's little twinge became a swirling panic. He wrote home, whistling ever more forcefully, that surely no one could blame him or his friends for Burr's treachery.[32]

The question of Burr's treachery—its nature, its breadth, even its very existence—has never been settled, but Henry Clay now believed that Burr was guilty of something and had duped him into swearing otherwise. He never forgave him. He would not see Burr again until 1815, when Clay was touring some courtrooms in New York City and happened upon him, an encounter Burr apparently planned. Clay did not recognize the aged Burr at first. Burr walked toward him, his hand extended. Clay refused to take it. They made awkward small talk punctuated by pauses until Burr impulsively said that he would like a private meeting. Clay told Burr where he was staying, but Burr did not visit, and they never saw each other again. The refusal to shake hands, the uncomfortable conversation with its silent gaps, the proffer of an address but no specific appointment, all told Burr what he already knew. Clay would never forgive him.[33]

BURR WAS A cloud over the start of Henry Clay's national political career, the association making the president suspicious and Clay's Senate colleagues wary. The consummate gambler, however, bluffed his way through. On his third day in the Senate, he made his first speech, a demand that the West be given its due with the creation of a federal circuit court for Ohio, Kentucky, and Tennessee. Federal district courts in the region were badly overburdened, and appeals to the U.S. circuit courts required expensive and time-consuming travel over abysmal roads to the East. Clay headed the committee that considered his proposal and returned a bill creating a new U.S. circuit that would in turn require a new Supreme Court justice. The bill passed, one triumph made better by another when Thomas Todd, Clay's political friend and Harry Innes's brother-in-law, became the new associate justice. "The ardent, eloquent and chivalrous Henry Clay" had brazened his way through the first crisis of his legislative career.[34]

But the consequences of his relationship with Burr persisted. Convinced by the cipher letter that a crisis loomed, Jefferson issued a proclamation calling for Burr's arrest and asked Congress to suspend habeas corpus.[35] Clay's role as Burr's Kentucky counsel had already made him a curiosity for newspapers throughout the country, and they began implying that Clay had used "improper measures to vindicate" the man the president was now accusing of treason. Clay found himself in a quandary about how to respond to Jefferson's actions. He privately told William Plumer that he did not see the necessity of suspending the writ, but that "the delicate situation in which, he as (late councilor for Burr) would not only prevent him from opposing it, but oblige him to vote for it."[36] It would be one of the very rare occasions that Clay did not vote his conscience.

He continued to brazen his way through. Just as he had in Kentucky, Clay became a passionate advocate for government-sponsored internal improvements. He wanted a canal on the Kentucky side around the falls of the Ohio River and managed to surmount adamant Republican opposition to such local projects by creating a committee, chaired by him, to study the issue. Clay also supported a toll bridge across the Potomac River and a canal connecting Delaware and Chesapeake bays.[37] Yet in many matters he remained loyal to Republican principles of limited government. His proposed constitutional amendment to limit federal judicial power over land disputes within the states died in Congress, but it illustrated his thinking that the states should retain fundamental rights in the federal system. Even his growing nationalism over the years would never weaken his commitment to that standard.[38]

His outspoken manner earned the admiration of some. When Clay made an impassioned speech against continuing slave importations, Senator John Quincy Adams of Massachusetts wrote that Clay was "quite a young man—an orator—and a republican of the first fire."[39] His new friend William Plumer commented that Clay "as a speaker is animated—his language bold & flowery" and that he often spoke "with great ability & much eloquence."[40] George Hoadley, a visitor to Washington from Connecticut, wrote home that there was "a great dearth of [oratorical] talent" in Congress, but that "Mr. Clay a young man from Kentucky" had made a considerable splash during his first term in the Senate. According to Hoadley, Clay used "correct language" and spoke "with very great capacity."[41]

Others, however, found his manner arrogant and grating for one so young and untried. Indeed, Clay was often more impressed by his performances than even his admirers were. He boasted to his father-in-law about his warm reception in Washington and how he had been praised for scoring points in several Senate debates.[42] Yet fellow Kentuckian Buckner Thruston complained that although Clay was "a damned good speaker . . . he never says anything touching the questions."[43] Plumer admitted that Clay "does not reason with the force & precision of [James] Bayard [of Delaware]." And Senator Uriah Tracy once scoffed at the young man "in the plenitude of puppyism" as he tried to intimidate Clay into shutting up, if only for just a while. Tracy might as well have tried to dam the ocean. The young Kentuckian gained the floor and mockingly recited a poem:

> Thus have I seen a magpie in the street,
> A chattering bird, we often meet;
> A bird for curiosity well known,
> With head awry
> And cunning eye
> Peep knowingly into a marrow-bone.[44]

Clay's theatrics rather than clear, concise logic drew the most comment and occasional disdain, and such behavior would have been fatal in a body that placed a high premium on collegiality and ordered itself on hardening rules of seniority. Yet Clay earned grudging respect for his ability to work for hours on the most detailed matters, in committee and in full session, staying at tasks well into the night and coming away refreshed rather than weary. Over the years, his endurance became legendary, but in this first session he proved his willingness to take on any task and tackle any chore. He chaired two Senate committees, served on two others, and got his way as much by wearing down his opponents physically as by swaying them with dazzling speeches.[45]

His stamina carried over to his socializing. He brashly told Plumer that he had come to Washington for "pleasure" and to make money. Kentucky clients placed him on a $3,000 retainer to argue their cases before the Supreme Court, and he spent most evenings at Washington's gaming tables. Plumer found Clay's compulsive amusements disconcerting, and he could be an insufferable braggart. He told Plumer that in one night at cards he won $1,500, and on another evening he lost $600. Despite his homely appearance, Clay was "a great favorite with the ladies" and attended "all parties of pleasure—out almost every night—gambles much here—reads but little."[46] Senator Tracy had a point about puppyism.

Plumer complained that Washington's leading men were too miserly to entertain and that dinner invitations were rarer than hen's teeth, but Clay could always find a party, likely because he often became the life of it. These gatherings threw him together with many who became enduring admirers, including more than a few ladies. Margaret Bayard Smith, whose husband was the founding editor of the *National Intelligencer,* the administration's unofficial newspaper, was well on her way to dominating the capital's social scene. Quick in conversation and clever with a pen, she became one of Clay's dearest friends. Clay also met the wife of Secretary of State James Madison, Dolley Payne Todd Madison, one of those cheerful people always ready to embrace instant friends. Dolley had family in Hanover County, Virginia, and though she and Clay were not related, they decided to become unofficial cousins. For the rest of their days, she would always greet him across crowded rooms as Cousin Henry and throw back her head with a throaty laugh when he shouted back a hello to Cousin Dolley.[47]

WHEN CONGRESS ADJOURNED, Clay remained in Washington to attend the Supreme Court's early spring session before heading home. Lawyers from all over the country crowded the boardinghouses, including Frost and Quinn's, and Clay was mildly surprised to find among them Humphrey Marshall, whom he would oppose in one of the cases before the Court. They conducted themselves with cool cordiality, but when Marshall proved formidable and Clay asked for a rehearing, the Federalist angrily accused Clay of acting from personal rather than legal motives.[48]

It was a sour way to end his first, and to his mind otherwise successful, venture in national politics. A temporary senator in the truest sense, a brief replacement for a replacement, Clay had occupied his seat for only a few weeks, but the men who had watched him breeze into town, charge through its legislative halls and social salons, and then vanish again into the West knew they had seen someone remarkable and that they would see him again.

Clay was glad to get home. His return in April was more than usually merry because a baby was waiting for him, a little girl whose birth he had just missed. She was his second daughter. They named her Anne Brown Clay after her aunt Nancy Brown in New Orleans, a good choice because like Aunt Nancy, Anne would become a vivacious, clever girl. Clay cherished all of his children, but something about Anne always made him especially happy. A man who had countless friends, he would come to regard this daughter as among his very best.

The difficulties over Aaron Burr nevertheless troubled Clay's homecoming. Neither Humphrey Marshall nor Jo Daveiss believed that Clay was guilty of any criminal act, but his defense of Burr was embarrassing now that Burr had been arrested like a thief in the night and was slated for a treason trial in Richmond. Kentuckians who had earlier sung Burr's praises now denounced him as a scoundrel and a traitor. Clay continued to reassure them that no one had been imperiled by Burr's recklessness, but it was a hard sell, especially when he discovered that Burr had defaulted on most of his debts and many of his backers were financially ruined. Luckless Harman Blennerhassett was one poignant example. Clay found him penniless in a Lexington jail, his home lost, his island swarming with Virginia militia, his fortune consumed by the bottomless maw of Burr's shadowy scheme.[49] No other attorney would touch this political pariah, but Clay took his case.

While Clay was negotiating for Blennerhassett's freedom, larger trouble loomed for the Irishman. He too had been indicted for treason and would be taken to Richmond to stand trial. Ironically, newly minted Supreme Court associate justice Thomas Todd heard the case in his capacity as the new U.S. circuit judge, his place on that bench a result of Henry Clay's recent legislative achievement. Clay wanted to fight Blennerhassett's extradition—he was genuinely concerned that Blennerhassett would be physically harmed on the way to Richmond—but the poor man wanted the chance to exonerate himself. Clay appeared before Todd on July 16 to say that his client would make the trip but also to declare that the warrant for Blennerhassett's arrest was of dubious legality and his safety uncertain. Todd had little leeway about the warrant, but he did arrange for an armed guard to escort Blennerhassett to Richmond. There Harman Blennerhassett's luck would change to the extent that a jury's failure to convict Burr made all of his alleged accomplices unlikely targets for prosecution. Finally given his freedom, Blennerhassett never managed to rise from poverty, and the years dealt him one blow after another. More than thirty years later, Clay learned that his widow, Margaret, was living in a New York tenement where she was struggling to support her severely afflicted son. He tried to persuade Congress to give her some money, a small compensation for the destruction of her home on the Ohio River so many years before. Congress tabled the matter, however, and she died before it could be reconsidered, another casualty, even after all those years, of Burr's obscure plans and her husband's bad judgment.[50]

NOW UNDER THE sole editorial guidance of Joseph Street, Humphrey Marshall's *Western World* attacked Clay during the summer of 1807, but he easily won election to the state legislature. As Clay entered the House that fall, so did Marshall, its solitary Federalist, setting the stage for a series of clashes between the two that became the stuff of legend.[51]

The Kentucky House made Clay its speaker at about the same time that Aaron Burr again emerged as a source of controversy. His acquittal in Richmond had only spurred the Jefferson administration to greater efforts to try him on other charges, possibly in Kentucky, where many of his misdeeds had supposedly occurred. Jefferson's new attorney general, Caesar A. Rodney—another Clay friend from his time in Washington—asked Clay to prosecute Burr in some western venue, but Clay declined. He did not have the time, he said, and there were also ethical issues. Clay had no doubts about Burr's guilt, but attorney-client privilege barred further involvement with his case.[52]

Humphrey Marshall clearly intended to make trouble, and he began by taking aim at Judge Harry Innes. The *Western World* charged that Innes had favored Burr in the grand jury proceedings because he was mixed up in Burr's conspiracy. For good measure, Street renewed rumors about the infamous "Spanish Conspiracy" of the 1790s, placing Innes in the thick of it. Armed with these unfounded accusations, Marshall insisted that the Kentucky legislature demand that Congress begin impeachment proceedings to remove Innes from the federal bench. Speaker Clay could not engage in debate under a strict interpretation of the rules of order, so he simply established a new precedent, one he would later employ when he became Speaker of the House in Washington. He temporarily stepped down from the Speaker's chair, took the floor, and mounted a spirited attack on Marshall's resolutions.[53]

He disparaged them as groundless in the first place and prejudicial in the second. When charges against Innes had first appeared in the *Western World,* the judge had requested an investigation to clear up the matter, and now Clay helped frame a compromise in which the Kentucky House merely called for a congressional investigation.[54] Innes's friends, however, were riled up. Thomas Bodley, the judge's son-in-law, accused Marshall of land fraud, perjury, and altering court records. The House appointed a committee to investigate, selecting eleven committee members itself and leaving it to Speaker Clay to choose the remaining five.

The land fraud charge was pointless because such an accusation could be leveled against virtually every legislator, but the committee's inquiry into his behavior otherwise turned out badly for Marshall. With an 11 to 4 vote, the committee recommended his expulsion from the House for "moral turpitude." Although the entire House failed to follow through, citing insufficient proof, Marshall was humiliated at home and disappointed by Washington, where Congress that spring voted to leave Innes alone. Emboldened, Innes sued Joseph Street for libel, another potential setback for Marshall, who had written many of Street's articles.[55]

Yet Marshall and Street were unrelenting. In the spring and summer of 1808, when John Allen ran for governor, they smeared him as a Burr accomplice and predicted that if elected, he would be Henry Clay's puppet. Clay took up the gauntlet to defend Allen and lament how candidates for public office had become the target of vicious personal attacks. Clay explained that many who did not believe Burr to be guilty in the fall of 1806 now believed that he was, and that Allen should not be blamed for being among that sizable majority.[56]

Allen lost the election, but at least he lost to a fellow Republican, Charles Scott, giving Clay some measure of satisfaction. Furthermore, Federalist attacks did not hurt Clay among his constituents. His popularity had never been higher, and he easily won reelection to the Kentucky House in the summer of 1808. Humphrey Marshall, neither expelled nor repentant, won reelection too. During the previous session, before everything had turned personal, it had been devilishly difficult to make the legislature productive. Now, in an increasingly contentious setting, it was doubly so.[57]

That reality was highlighted when Clay returned to the Kentucky House in the fall of 1808 to face a serious challenge for the Speakership. When he lost 36 to 31 to William Logan, Clay's friends tried to soften the defeat by saying that members had wanted him unrestrained by House rules to speak out against people like Humphrey Marshall. But the Speakership had not prevented Clay from challenging Marshall in the previous session. Federalists saw Clay's defeat as a rebuke and chortled over his disappointment. Now he was back on the floor and separated from Marshall by only one seat, where a big, jolly German immigrant named Christopher Riffe sat between them.[58]

WHEN THE SESSION opened, the legislature received a message from the governor that President Jefferson had requested all state militias readied for possible war with either Great Britain or France. It was a grave response to the worsening international situation. After selling Louisiana to the United States in 1803, Napoleon had rekindled war with Britain, a conflict that did not end for another eleven years and eventually embroiled Americans in a nasty war of their own. In the meantime, increasing troubles abroad plunged them into spiteful arguments at home.

During the first two years of this new round of European warfare, America's merchant shippers basked in their country's neutrality while growing rich from a bountiful commercial carrying trade. That abruptly changed in 1805 when a British fleet under Lord Nelson demolished a combined French and Spanish force off Spain's shores at Trafalgar. The resulting British domination of the world's oceans made them an inevitable enemy to American mariners. In that same year, at Austerlitz, Napoleon smashed Austrian and Russian armies to make himself master of all Europe. Thus Britain's fleet controlled the oceans but was powerless to assail Bonaparte, and Napoleon with his victorious army could only sullenly gaze at the sea.

The result was a peculiar war of indirection: beginning in 1806, Britain issued a series of decrees called the Orders in Council, which authorized the seizure of ships bound for French-controlled ports unless those ships first stopped at a British port to pay fees, submit to inspection, and obtain permission to proceed. Napoleon responded with his own decrees that sanctioned seizing any merchant ship that had entered a British port when it arrived at one he controlled. The state of affairs was from the start an exasperating affront to American pride.

The British managed to achieve an even more infuriating insult. They crewed their ships through impressment, simply another word for compulsory conscription, a venerable policy that the Royal Navy applied with great energy during the war with the French. Officers and their burly, club-wielding hearties—press gangs, they were called—combed pubs for drunkards and other likely wastrels on British soil, but the Royal Navy also sought out able-bodied seamen on American merchant ships at sea, confident that American crews were riddled with British deserters. In many cases that was true, but it is likely that more than several thousand American citizens fell victim to British impressment during the Napoleonic Wars. Such abductions were simply intolerable to the young nation.

An uneasy situation became much worse because of a serious incident off the Virginia coast. In June 1807, HMS *Leopard* stopped USS *Chesapeake* and insisted on boarding her to search for British deserters. When the American captain refused to submit to this indignity, the *Leopard* fired three broadsides into the *Chesapeake,* killing three of her crew. Royal Marines then boarded the *Chesapeake* and took off four men, only one of whom, it turned out, was a deserter. The country exploded as news of this incident spread, and Jefferson could successfully have sought a declaration of war, but he instead employed what he believed would be effective commercial measures, specifically, a thorough embargo on all foreign trade.

Clay fervently supported Jefferson's policies. Humphrey Marshall, however, did not. For several weeks, he successfully prevented a vote on Clay's pro-administration resolutions with procedural tricks and various motions of his own. Despite efforts to appease Marshall by amending Clay's motions, the final vote was 64 to 1, the stubborn Federalist alone dissenting.[59]

Clay and Marshall's disputes by now had become quite personal, and their colleagues watched with grim fascination and vague apprehension as the two neared their boiling points. The subject that finally brought the two to blows seemed trivial at first. As soon as he could afford it, Henry Clay had become one of the best-dressed men in the state. He bought only the finest imported English broadcloth and linen and employed only the best tailors. The results were trim, tasteful suits and crisp linen shirts, obviously expensive though fashionably subdued. During this session, however, Clay began wearing a homespun denim suit, a conspicuous gesture to promote American goods for American consumption. He made his intention even more apparent on January 3, 1809, with his "Homespun Resolution" calling for legislators to wear only American clothes from thread to garment. The following day, Marshall made a gesture of his own. Entering the House chamber clad in the best imported British broadcloth, he called Clay a demagogue for making an issue of foreign manufactures. Clay questioned Marshall's patriotism. Marshall called Clay a liar.[60]

That did it. The two were about ten feet apart. Clay turned as though stunned and then lunged toward Marshall, his arms extended and hands clenched. Members rushed between them, several holding Clay as he thrashed wildly. Trying to free himself, he accidentally punched an innocent bystander. The big German Christopher Riffe stepped between Clay and Marshall, his booming voice shouting, "Come poys, no fightin here, I vips you both."

Clay, panting, regained his composure and was released. He immediately apologized to the House but disdainfully stared at Marshall as he declared that he had been provoked to violence because Marshall was not an honorable man. Marshall shouted, "It is the apology of a poltroon!" He was wrong on both counts: it was not an apology, and Clay was not a coward. That evening as Clay returned to his lodgings, he foolishly resolved to prove that.[61]

"After the occurrences in the House of Representatives on this day," he wrote to Marshall, "the receipt of this note will excite with you no surprise. I hope on my part I shall not be disappointed in the execution of the pledge you gave on that occasion, and in your disclaimer of the character attributed to you. To enable you to fulfill these reasonable and just expectations my friend Maj. [John B.] Campbell is authorized by me to adjust the ceremonies proper to be observed."[62]

These "ceremonies proper to be observed" meant a fight with weapons, potentially to the death—in short, a duel. The practice was banned by most states, including Kentucky, but duels were not uncommon, particularly for men of the upper class with their sensitive pride and sharpened honor. Duels were sometimes seen as the only respectable way to resolve a truly serious dispute, particularly one involving questions of character. The words Clay and Marshall had swapped made this an essential question of character for both. Clay had said that Marshall was a tacit traitor, a dishonorable scoundrel. Marshall had called Clay a liar, a sneaking coward. Clay on the night of January 4, 1809, believed he had no choice but to challenge Marshall to a duel. Marshall believed he had no choice but to accept.[63]

Their seconds—representatives who made the arrangements, Major John B. Campbell for Clay and Colonel James F. Moore for Marshall—set the appointment for January 19 and drew up the rules. Clay and Marshall would stand ten paces apart and hold their fire until hearing the command "Attention! Fire!" A misfire would be counted as a discharge. If one fired before the other, he had to remain in position until the other man fired. The seconds themselves would strictly enforce these rules by shooting down the man who violated them.[64]

Occasionally everything about these affairs was for show, easily stopped by the fabled "mutual friends" who engineered a reconciliation, at least for public consumption. This was not one of those affairs. For two weeks Clay and Marshall grimly and deliberately prepared to kill each other. Although the choice of weapons was customarily the province of the challenged party, Clay wanted to acquire a pair of pistols. Pistols, as it happened, were fine with Marshall. He was spending his days diligently practicing with one at the home of a friend.[65]

As the day neared, Clay and Marshall went to Louisville. The two with their respective companions separately crossed the Ohio near Shippingport to avoid the bad form of spilling blood in their home state. Indiana would do for a killing. Early on January 19, everyone met in a clearing near Silver Creek. A physician was present.[66]

Back in Lexington, Lucretia's sister Susannah Price was deeply troubled by the news. She could only imagine the strain on Lucretia, now far along in yet another pregnancy. Worried about how the shock of bad news would affect her sister and the baby, Suky Price hurried out to Ashland. If Henry Clay got himself killed up in Indiana, Lucretia would be a twenty-seven-year-old widow with four children under the age of eight and another on the way. Yet Suky found both Lucretia and Ashland strangely calm. The sisters visited as Lucretia tended to routine household chores. Neither woman mentioned the duel. Suky wondered with growing unease whether Lucretia possibly did not know what was happening that day somewhere north of the Ohio River. She could not bring herself to tell her. The hours passed. Late in the afternoon, a rider turned from the main road into Ashland's drive and approached the house. It was a messenger from town. He handed Lucretia a note.

THAT MORNING, HER husband and Humphrey Marshall had gone through with their duel. At the measured distance they stood sideways to make themselves smaller targets and at the command fired almost simultaneously. Marshall missed, but Clay slightly grazed Marshall along his abdomen near the navel. Both men wanted a second shot. This time Clay's gun misfired, and again Marshall missed. Both wanted a third shot, and in this round, Marshall finally hit his target by wounding Clay in the thigh, causing Clay's shot to go wide. Clay stumbled while shouting that he wanted another round. The physician, however, insisted on examining the wound. Although Clay was lucky that the bullet had not struck bone, he was clearly in no shape to continue. His friends ended the fight.[67]

They took Clay back across the river to Louisville, where Dr. Frederick Ridgely patched him up at the home of a friend. After all the excitement, Clay could not rest, and that same day he wrote to a friend to describe the duel and to say that he was already on the mend. It is very likely that he also wrote to Lucretia—it would have been most out of character for him not to—but no letter to her from him survives.

It almost seemed an afterthought, then, that a member of the legislature remembered Lucretia at Ashland and sent the messenger whom she and Suky watched approaching the house that afternoon. Lucretia read the note and passed it to her sister. "Thank God," Lucretia quietly breathed, "he is only slightly wounded." Suky quickly scanned the note. She looked at her sister in amazement. Lucretia had known all along. Suky exclaimed in gushing, laughing relief about Lucretia knowing all along, after all. She stared at her sister—calm, brave young woman.[68]

The seconds, Campbell and Moore, each wrote narratives of the affair that were published in the newspapers. Clay and Marshall, they proudly reported, had behaved honorably. The Kentucky legislature censured them for conduct unbecoming to members, but that was only an expected shrug of official shoulders, and the two resumed their seats without further ado. In fact, friends gave Clay backslapping congratulations along with chuckled regret that he had not finished Marshall off.[69]

Beyond her stoic words of relief to Suky, there is no evidence as to how Lucretia felt about all of this, but she must have been churning with anxiety before and greatly relieved afterward. And it would have been normal for her to be very angry at the risk her husband had selfishly taken, honor and reputation aside. In a few weeks, she had their third daughter. They named her Lucretia Hart Clay, after her calm, brave mother.

WHILE CLAY RECOVERED, the legislative session ended. He returned home to oversee the last stages of construction on the main part of the Ashland mansion, but he would soon expand it even more. In late 1813, he began two wings that flanked and were connected to the main house at right angles, a plan supplied by famed architect Benjamin Latrobe. Clay's growing fame eventually made Ashland a destination for admirers who were as pilgrims drawn to a shrine. Aside from its rising renown as a Bluegrass showplace, Ashland was to be a working farm where grains, hemp, and blooded livestock could flourish. With several other Kentuckians, Clay purchased a thoroughbred named Buzzard, making this expensive stallion the first horse in the United States to be owned by a syndicate. Buzzard earned his owners considerable sums in stud fees and established Ashland as the home of racing champions. By 1811, Clay owned sixty-five horses.[70]

From the very beginning and throughout Henry and Lucretia's lives, Ashland rang with the laughter and shouts of children. Everyone who knew her smiled on Lucretia, quiet and unassuming in society but warm and loving with children, whether her own or those of friends or eventually her grandchildren. That made what happened to Theodore, their oldest son, all the more tragic. The date is unfixed, but the event itself was vividly etched in his parents' memories. Theodore fell and suffered a severe head injury. Convinced that Theodore would otherwise die, Lucretia's brother-in-law Dr. Richard Pindell took drastic action. He relieved the pressure on the child's brain with a procedure called trepanning, the drilling of a hole in the patient's skull to drain fluid from the cranium. The procedure was as dangerous as it was grotesque, but Theodore survived it and seemed to get better. Henry and Lucretia were greatly relieved. And that too made what later happened to Theodore all the more tragic.[71]

Relatives were important to the Clays. Henry regularly visited his mother and stepfather at Versailles and handled their legal affairs. Clay's half sister, Martha "Patsy" Watkins, lived in Lexington, most likely with the Clays for a time, before she married William Blackburn. Lucretia's family too remained close even across great distances. James and Nancy Brown in New Orleans were always in touch, although Nancy joined a family chorus complaining about Lucretia's unreliability as a correspondent. In one instance, Nancy "was delighted at finding that Lucretia had overcome her repugnance to writing" and celebrated the rare event with an immediate reply.[72] Yet Lucretia's dislike of writing was only seldom shaken off, and then as the years passed not at all. Clay finally explained to a friend that Lucretia "is so out of the habit of writing that she now hardly ever writes to me."[73]

In June 1808, Lucretia's father died at his home on Mill Street. Clay and Thomas Hart's oldest son, Thomas Jr., were named executors of the enormous estate, and its extensive land holdings would take years to sort out. Hart left the house to his wife and settled upon her a generous allowance. The remainder of the estate was distributed to his surviving children and sons-in-law, and Lucretia's portion significantly increased the Clays' assets.[74]

Thomas Hart, Jr., died unexpectedly in 1809, and Clay had to shoulder the responsibilities of settling his brother-in-law's estate as well.[75] Such obligations with business dealings and political activities would have overwhelmed most men, but Clay's industry and stamina saw him through. He even expanded his holdings, investing in local manufacturing concerns and in 1808 purchasing Traveller's Hall, the place built in 1802 for "Genteel Guests Only," the hotel where Aaron Burr had attended a concert on his first visit to Kentucky. Clay renamed it the Kentucky Hotel and leased it for $900 a year to Cuthbert Banks, who had run Olympian Springs for Thomas Hart and who had sold to Clay the first 125 acres outside of town that became Ashland. At the age of thirty-one and with a bullet scar on his thigh, Henry Clay was one of the wealthiest and most influential men in the region. He had worked hard for it all. Lucretia could have said the same.[76]

CLAY RETURNED TO the Kentucky House of Representatives in December 1809 for the last time as a member. In only a few weeks the legislature had to replace Buckner Thruston in the U.S. Senate because he had resigned to accept a judicial appointment. Henry Clay and the current speaker, William Logan, stood for the post, with Clay winning 63 to 31. He was again to be a replacement, but with more longevity this time, as fourteen months remained on Thruston's term. Clay immediately resigned from the state legislature, with compliments to Logan on his honorable conduct during their brief contest, and headed home to pack his bags. He started for Washington in the dead of winter. The lateness of the season kept Lucretia from making the trip.[77]

Clay took his seat on February 5, 1810, as the capital was concluding its first year of James Madison's presidency. "Cousin Dolley" was now First Lady, and she had established a tradition of Wednesday evening parties at the President's House, lively affairs with food, drink, and spirited conversation. The rigors of brutal cold and wretched accommodations on Clay's journey, however, had made him sick. The nightly revels of his previous stay in Washington were unappealing on this trip.[78]

Instead, he threw himself into his work in the Senate. Considerable opposition to Jefferson's Embargo had developed in the closing days of his presidency, particularly in New England and Mid-Atlantic states dependent on shipping. Clay had considered the domestic consequences of the Embargo as the price of patriotism, the only way short of war to maintain American honor. Popular upheaval, however, compelled the Embargo's repeal. The Non-Intercourse Act was passed early in Madison's administration to replace the Embargo. It reopened U.S. trade to the world except for Great Britain and France.

When Clay entered the Senate, Congress was discussing the impending expiration of the Non-Intercourse Act. Because the law had proved distressingly easy to skirt, many in Congress wanted to replace rather than renew it. Yet a considerable number of Republicans had lost their enthusiasm for economic retaliation. Everyone hated the Embargo, and both Great Britain and France had laughed at Non-Intercourse. In addition, government revenues plummeted with the decline in trade, unbalancing the Treasury's books and nudging budget-conscious Republicans toward mild panic. As the Federalist minority cried for a return to free trade, Republican factionalism made it difficult for Congress to unite behind a policy. In fact, the Eleventh Congress began to dither and derange itself with such abandon that one observer called it a bunch of "blathering bitches." Virginian John Randolph, one of its more acerbic members, simply stated that "a more despicable set was never gathered together."[79]

The House sent a bill to the Senate that would close U.S. ports to British and French merchant vessels and warships, although the measure was obviously aimed at Britain: the Royal Navy's blockade kept French ships from reaching American ports. But the real purpose of the bill was to open trade for American ships with any nation. A sliver of the restrictive policy, and barely a sliver at that, remained in the proposal with the pledge to reopen U.S. ports to Britain and France when they stopped violating American neutrality. As an instrument of coercion, it wasn't much of a bill to begin with, but the Senate completely emasculated it by removing all retaliatory commercial sections. This newest version of the bill sniffed that British and French warships could not come into U.S. ports, but admitted both nations' merchant vessels.[80]

Clay watched this unfold with mounting disgust. His first speech in the Eleventh Congress foreshadowed those of the next two years. At first his fiery voice would be a lone one as it urged a more belligerent policy, but in due course he would lead a chorus.[81] He did not like the House bill, but he thought it far better than what the Senate had produced. The nation had tried peaceful resistance to European arrogance, Clay shouted; "when this is abandoned, without effect, I am for resistance by the *sword*." He preferred "the troubled ocean of war, demanded by the honor and independence of the country, with all its calamities, and desolations, to the tranquil, putrescent pool of ignominious peace." He scoffed at those who whined that the nation's economy could not sustain a war against Britain, a strutting commercial tyrant that compounded conceit with man stealing. Americans had the armed power in its militia to conquer British territory unaided: "the militia of Kentucky are alone competent to place Montreal and Upper Canada at your feet." Those who defended the British by saying their navy protected Americans from French aggression were merely submitting "to British slavery upon the water, that we may escape French subjugation upon land." He appealed to America's Revolutionary spirit and envisioned its renewal for the current generation in the forge of war.[82]

Clay's lone voice could not defeat the bill in the Senate, but the House refused to accept it. A new round of blathering finally produced a real monstrosity, Macon's Bill No. 2, a hodgepodge of measures that reopened unrestricted trade with everyone in the world, including Britain and France. If either the British or the French dropped their restrictions, Congress crowed, the United States would renew nonintercourse with the other. In short, Congress abandoned a policy that had consistently failed to shape events, but in the same breath pledged to implement it again, this time as much as a reward for good behavior as punishment for bad. Even North Carolina representative Nathaniel Macon, who reported the bill out of committee, hence its name, opposed it. It passed both houses, though, and Madison signed it into law.

Macon's Bill No. 2 dismayed Clay, but he continued to work for federally sponsored internal improvements, greater military preparations, and domestic industries. In Kentucky, the Embargo and Non-Importation Act had encouraged infant manufacturing concerns, and their investors wanted Congress to protect them from foreign competition. Clay and others tried to persuade Congress to take a small step in that direction.[83] On March 22, 1810, his fellow Kentucky senator John Pope proposed an amendment to a naval appropriations bill that would have required the secretary of the navy to favor the purchase of domestic naval supplies. Pope's goal was to boost Kentucky's hemp farmers, whose cordage could be used to rig the American navy, but the idea raised New Englanders' suspicions. When James Lloyd, Jr., of Massachusetts tried to remove Pope's amendment, Clay jumped to his feet and made a lengthy plea to support domestic manufacturing and promote American self-sufficiency. Casting his gaze beyond Kentucky hemp growers, Clay soared into a sweeping nationalism that decried conflicts between the country's producers and merchants that often put different sections at odds. Lloyd's New England depended on foreign commerce for its wealth, and Clay observed that "Dame commerce will oppose domestic manufactures. She is a flirting, flippant, noisy jade, and if we are governed by her fantasies, we shall never put off the muslins of India and the cloths of Europe." The producing sections of the nation, he predicted, would nevertheless manufacture all the goods the American people needed sooner rather than later.[84]

Clay's rejoinder to Lloyd struck a chord throughout the country. Many newspapers reprinted it as an indisputable case for national self-sufficiency, and it became a cornerstone for what Clay later dubbed the American System, a program for national unity and prosperity through internal improvements and domestic manufactures.[85]

Near the end of the congressional session, Clay concluded that he did not much like the Senate. Its constraining rules and staid style meant that few ever said what they actually meant, and many sugared their words into palatable but empty confections. Although certain that a full term in the Senate was his for the asking, Clay was unhappy. He discussed his feelings with friends and decided instead to seek election to the House of Representatives in the Twelfth Congress. A vacancy had recently occurred in his district, and he could have it right away, but he did not want to make Kentucky choose yet another replacement for the Senate with only one session remaining. Instead, William T. Barry stood in a special election for the House seat in the remainder of the Eleventh Congress. Clay meanwhile remained in the Senate, but he also stood for election in his district for the congressional term commencing with the Twelfth Congress. Clay easily won this contest and for a brief interval held the unique position of being a sitting senator as well as an elected congressman.[86]

IN JUNE 1810, off the Florida Keys, a British warship, HMS *Moselle,* mistook USS *Vixen* for a French warship and opened fire. The British captain apologized for the mistake, but Clay was furious that the American commander had not defended the flag. When a man is hit upon the nose, Clay muttered, he does not first ask "the person giving it what he means" before "avenging the insult."[87] Meanwhile, Americans were doing some insulting of their own. A group of settlers in Spanish West Florida staged a revolt to seize control of Baton Rouge and all the land from the Perdido to the Mississippi rivers. They asked the United States to annex the region. With Congress out of session until the fall, Madison consequently had to make some important decisions. He annexed the area seized by rebels in West Florida, claiming that the territory had been a part of the Louisiana Purchase, and planned to ask Congress to endorse his judgment. Most important, however, was the president's reaction to Napoleon's startling announcement in late summer that he would respect U.S. neutrality. Bonaparte was lying to make Madison invoke the terms of Macon's Bill No. 2, but the president lunged at the gesture nonetheless. Accordingly, the United States announced its intention to resume nonintercourse against the British if they did not rescind the Orders in Council in three months.

Clay was late in returning to Washington from Kentucky that fall. He brought Lucretia with him, and because she was about five months pregnant, they set a slower pace than was his habit. Lucretia took no pleasure in lively social scenes, but she soon met her husband's new friend, the vibrant hostess Margaret Bayard Smith, who found Lucretia to be "a woman of strong natural sense, very kind and friendly." The quiet woman from Kentucky was the polar opposite of her spirited husband. She had "no taste for fashionable company or amusements, and is a thousand times better pleased, sitting in the room with all her children around her . . . than in the most brilliant drawing room."[88] It was true that Lucretia was thoroughly devoted to her children, and apparently some had remained at Ashland, a cause for both Clays to worry. In any case, Washington society did not impress her much. Unadorned and unaffected, Lucretia clearly did not care whether Washington society was impressed with her. She radiated an unshakable sense of self. Margaret liked her.[89]

THE SENATE COMMITTEE on Foreign Affairs studied the portion of President Madison's message dealing with West Florida and framed a bill to make it part of the Territory of Orleans. The effort started a lively debate over territorial expansion, and Clay waded into it. A lengthy discourse by Delaware Federalist Outerbridge Horsey opposed adding West Florida to the United States, and Clay responded on December 28, 1810. He traced the region's history back to the seventeenth century to prove that everything west of the Perdido River was always part of Louisiana and was thus included in the 1803 purchase.[90]

Territorial expansion at the expense of Spain might seem unjust, especially because Spain was fighting Napoleon, but Clay pointed out that it was a predatory world: better the United States claim the land than someone else. He responded to fears that American behavior could provoke war with Britain by asking, "Is the time never to arrive when we may manage our affairs without the fear of insulting His Britannic Majesty? Is the rod of British power to be forever suspended over our heads?" In point of fact, Clay, like other westerners, saw this modest extension of American dominion as only a beginning. He declared a "hope to see, ere long, the *new* United States (if you will allow me the expression) embracing not only the old thirteen States, but the entire country East of the Mississippi, including East Florida and some of the territories to the north of us also."[91] It was an impetuous statement. Worse, it would prove an impolitic one.

On December 31, Massachusetts Federalist Timothy Pickering challenged Clay's assertion that the part of West Florida in question was in the Louisiana Purchase. Pickering waved a letter that Jefferson had submitted to the Senate in 1805, a communication from Maurice de Talleyrand, at the time Napoleon's foreign minister, clearly stating that Napoleon never intended that any portion of West Florida would be included in the Louisiana Purchase. The Talleyrand letter was indeed definitive proof that Clay was wrong, but Jefferson had given it to the Senate with the understanding that it would remain secret. To change the subject, Clay pounced on that facet of Pickering's evidence. He moved that the Senate censure Pickering for violating a pledge of secrecy. By then the hour was late, and New Year's loomed. The Senate voted to take the matter up again on January 2, 1811.[92]

Clay began that day by reading an amended resolution for censure, setting off an acrimonious debate that accomplished precisely his goal of diverting attention from the substance of the Talleyrand letter to the dubious process by which it had come to light. After lengthy discussions that at one point focused on whether to include the words "palpable violation" versus "unintentional violation" and even stalled on the possibility of removing the syllable "un" from "unintentional," Clay got his relatively mild censure through the Senate. Federalist newspapers knew their men had been gulled and called for the "censuring of Clay for his censorious resolution."[93]

In the wake of all this, the Senate postponed extending the Orleans Territory. The following day, however, President Madison requested secret authorization to seize every acre of Spanish Florida if military necessity required it. Clay chaired the Senate committee that recommended granting the administration's request, and a bill doing so passed both houses on January 15, 1811.[94] Like his pro-expansion speech, his role in this questionable initiative would come back to haunt him.

Clay tended to be testy and impulsive at this stage of his political career, prone to speak first and reflect later, but he was also ill during these weeks. A nagging cold along with a painful inflammation of his gums may have blunted his better political instincts.[95] The eventful final session of the Eleventh Congress had already put him on record several times in ways he would later rue, but his effort to prevent the recharter of the Bank of the United States would eventually cause him the most regret.

Congress had chartered the Bank of the United States in 1791 for a term of twenty years. The Bank was the brainchild of Treasury secretary Alexander Hamilton, who wanted a financial institution to stabilize the currency and fund the country's enormous national debt. The Bank was controversial from the start. Jefferson and Madison and their followers, later labeled Democratic-Republicans, opposed it because they believed it was unconstitutional. The Bank worked, however, a practical fact that diminished Jefferson and Madison's distaste for it during their presidencies. Their secretary of the Treasury, Albert Gallatin, had come to see it as indispensable to a sound economy and urged its recharter as it neared expiration in 1811. Congressman James Madison had been the most vociferous critic of the Bank at its creation. President James Madison was now silent about it.

Opposition to the Bank nonetheless persisted across the country. Old Republicans continued to fear that interpreting the Constitution so loosely would set a pattern to make it eventually meaningless. Others had less abstract reasons for opposing the national bank. Many states—Kentucky was one of them—eased credit and solved chronic currency shortages by chartering their own banks. These state banks both competed with and were forced to submit to the Bank of the United States, whose control of credit almost always struck freewheeling state bankers as shortsighted and overly restrictive. State governments also taxed state banks and chafed at the national bank's policies that impinged on their state institutions, sometimes to diminish their revenue. The irritation translated into reflexive opposition to the Bank of the United States, and in no place more vigorously than Kentucky, which flatly instructed its congressional delegation to oppose its recharter.[96]

Clay held stock and served on the board of Kentucky banks opposing recharter, but he was guided by more than plain self-interest. In time, he was less consistent in opposing federal initiatives, especially when they benefited the West, but in 1811 Clay still believed in states' rights and strict constitutional construction. In February, when the Senate began debating recharter, he sincerely thought that the Bank was unconstitutional.

In the Senate, William Harris Crawford of Georgia, a close friend of Albert Gallatin, took the lead in urging recharter. A native Virginian like Clay, Crawford was burly, ruggedly handsome, and popular, with a reputation for making careful arguments in an affable way. He was an effective advocate for the Bank, and a formidable adversary for those opposing it. On February 11, 1811, Crawford made a strong case for the Bank's constitutionality. Three days later the Bank's opponents began their case with Virginia's William Branch Giles's uncertain challenge of Crawford's argument. Possibly because Giles was Gallatin's political enemy, he framed his case against recharter in an especially cautious manner. In fact, many who listened to the first part of his speech were not sure whether Giles opposed or supported recharter. Not until his conclusion did he timorously declare that the Bank charter should expire.[97]

It was precisely the sort of performance that Clay found so exasperating about the Senate. On February 15, he was acerbic and unkind as he sarcastically lampooned Giles for his irresolute approach. Giles had "discussed both sides of the question, with great ability and eloquence, and certainly demonstrated to the satisfaction of all who heard him, both that it is constitutional and unconstitutional, highly proper and improper to prolong the charter of the bank." He compared Giles's speech to a fabled performance by Patrick Henry. Busy with numerous cases, Henry entered a courtroom one day forgetful of which side he was representing. He set forth a brilliant case, but it was against his client, who finally caught Henry's attention and whispered that he had "ruined" him. Henry paused before muttering not to worry. He immediately launched into a dazzling oration refuting everything he had previously said, and won the case.[98]

Clay's flashy impudence was unfortunate. If only because he could, he chose to make Giles squirm and the Senate uncomfortable, but his reputation as an enfant terrible would be hard to live down, particularly when enemies later recalled it as foreshadowing a dismissive arrogance of those less quick and less clever in floor debates. He was that day very much the puppy Senator Tracy had disparaged, in all its plenitude.

Yet he was also that day the shrewd lawyer who could marshal a broad array of persuasive reasons why the Bank of the United States was dangerous to American liberty. State banks were smaller, less centralized, and easier to control, he said. He co-opted his opponents' arguments in the Kentucky Insurance Company debates to describe the hazards of a national money power. He assailed Crawford's claims about "implied powers" giving Congress the authority to charter a bank. The formulation was too elastic and too prone to abuses that would make the states servile rather than sovereign. The speech was well argued, but the mean-spirited barbs at the beginning were its most memorable parts, and therein lay a high irony. Eventually, Henry Clay would behave in exactly the way he had described Patrick Henry. Eventually, every attack he made that day against the Bank he would later try to refute with glittering praise of it. Those who had looked down when Clay made Giles twist on his wit would remember. They would not let Clay forget.[99]

The Senate evenly divided on the question at 17 for and 17 against, leaving it to the elderly, ineffectual Vice President George Clinton to break the tie. Everybody had anticipated this awkward possibility, and Clinton fortunately had a speech ready explaining why he would side with the nays to kill the Bank of the United States. Clinton's words sounded strangely familiar, though, and some suspected that Clay had ghostwritten the speech the night before the vote. Clay's innocent smile and insistence that he had only taken Clinton's dictation to help an old man were unconvincing. The Senate was not altogether sorry to see Clay go.[100]

CONGRESS ADJOURNED ON March 3, 1811, and the Clays rushed back to Kentucky, as Lucretia now appeared ready to have her baby. Henry and Lucretia spent anxious days on the road but finally arrived at Ashland at the end of the month. In a downstairs room that would become the dining room after a subsequent remodeling, Lucretia had a healthy boy on April 10 "with less inconvenience . . . than she ever before experienced."[101] They named him Henry Clay, Jr., a pledge of great promise and a bright future; a pledge in that name also of great expectations, a heavy burden. Henry Clay the elder was certain the boy would be up to it.

CHAPTER FOUR

The Hawk and the Gambler

THAT SUMMER AT Ashland, Henry Clay judged war to be inevitable. French violations of American neutrality continued, but he believed the fight would be with Great Britain. While tending to a mountain of business and legal work, Clay queried his neighbors about the overwrought international situation and what it meant for American security, especially on the frontier.[1] Westerners resented British attacks on American shipping and the impressment of American seamen, and they were convinced that the British were encouraging Indians in the Michigan, Illinois, and Indiana territories to make war on American settlers. The charismatic Shawnee warrior Tecumseh and his brother Tenskwatawa (whites called him "the Prophet") were uniting northwestern tribes to block white expansion, and westerners imagined that British schemes abetted that effort. Actually, the Indians did not need Britain to rile them up over American encroachment on their lands, but such subtleties were easily buried under reflexive anger at Redcoats and raw terror caused by angry warriors. The West had a simple solution: conquering Canada was the best way to get rid of the British.

Clay intended to have Congress address these concerns when he returned to Washington in the fall to take his seat in the House of Representatives. The growing crisis prompted Congress to convene in early November, and Clay hurried to put his business affairs in order as he planned the trip for his family. Lucretia had not liked leaving the children (now six with the addition of Henry Jr.) at Ashland the previous winter, and she insisted that she would go to Washington only if they came too. He so wanted her with him that he agreed, although taking the whole family over the narrow, rutted roads to the capital promised to be a memorable ordeal.

Clay also carefully packed a sample of Kentucky wine made from Madeira grapes as a gift for President Madison. In 1807, a similar offering to Thomas Jefferson had mortified Clay when the president served it with considerable ceremony to a large gathering only to discover that the wine had gone quite bad.

Clay made certain that this batch slated for Cousin Dolley's table would do credit to Kentucky's vineyards, tangible evidence of western sophistication and industry.[2]

Clay returned to a very different Congress from the one he had left in March. Irate constituents embarrassed by the doings of the "blathering bitches" had turned out many representatives. The result was that almost half of the membership was new and inexperienced. The Twelfth Congress was also remarkably youthful. A considerable majority were under forty, and, like Clay, most were under thirty-five. One Federalist described them as "young politicians, half hatched, the shell still on their heads, and their pin feathers not yet shed."[3] They became quite well organized, though, unlike their opponents, even earning a label, a sure indication of a coherent faction. Caustic John Randolph called these new members War Hawks. He did not mean it as a compliment.

The Clays lodged at a boardinghouse with congressmen who all held similar views, especially the prickly one that Britain had insulted American honor long enough. They were a fire-breathing lot, soon known as the War Mess, an extraordinary group of young men who lived, ate, and worked together in such compatibility that they could finish each other's sentences. With the exception of South Carolinian Langdon Cheves and fellow Kentuckian George M. Bibb (who had taken Clay's place in the Senate), Clay was the oldest, but both Cheves and Bibb were senior by only a year, and Clay immediately became the leader of the group that included Felix Grundy, now a congressman from Tennessee, and two other South Carolinians, John C. Calhoun and William Lowndes, both only twenty-nine years old. Calhoun was late arriving because Floride (pronounced "Florida") Calhoun was giving birth to their first child, but the War Mess wasted no time in making plans for the upcoming session. On Sunday, November 3, the day before Congress convened, a caucus of Republican members, most of them freshmen, got their first look at the War Hawks in action when they drummed up support for Clay to be elected Speaker. The following day, Clay's friends tossed him into a contest that included several aspirants, the veteran Georgia congressman William W. Bibb prominent among them. Clay won going away, taking the Speakership with a 75 to 38 vote. The War Hawks had mobilized swiftly.[4]

Some members were already calling this tall Kentuckian "the Western Star" in tribute to his truly meteoric rise to the Speakership. Clay's election to the post was unprecedented. At thirty-four, Clay was the youngest Speaker of the House, his closest rival for that honor being Jonathan Dayton, whose service in the mid-1790s had begun when he was thirty-five. Sworn in by William Findley of Pennsylvania, Clay made brief remarks, settled into the ornate Speaker's chair, and got down to the business of filling House committees and appointing their chairmen. In this regard, Clay as Speaker wielded considerable power to steer the House's direction. He was careful to appear balanced in distributing appointments across the political spectrum, but he made sure that there were War Hawk majorities and friendly chairmen on key committees. John Randolph was so senior, for instance, that he had to have a place on the Foreign Relations Committee, but Clay also appointed New York War Hawk Peter B. Porter chairman and chocked the committee with other War Hawks to suppress Randolph's obstructionism if not smother his voice. Clay also appointed compliant chairmen to head other committees central to addressing the British crisis and provided them with War Hawk majorities as well. He placed messmate Langdon Cheves at the head of Naval Affairs, loyal Republican Ezekiel Bacon at Ways and Means, and South Carolina War Hawk David R. Williams at Military Affairs.[5]

Clay's hand in shaping these committees was not exceptional in itself, but the level of control he exerted was remarkable and innovative. Before Clay, Speakers were primarily parliamentarians issuing rulings on points of order and determining who held the floor during debates. They did not vote except to break ties and did not engage in debate. As for the latter custom, Clay resolved to depart from it early and often as the House confronted crucial foreign and domestic policy issues, a practice he had resorted to as the Kentucky Speaker of the House. When necessary, Clay temporarily left the Speaker's chair and the House became the "Committee of the Whole" while he participated in debate. His most significant innovation, though, rested in changes to House procedures that allowed him to control its operations through the deft use of his appointive power. As a result, committees conducted congressional business based on his priorities. He reshaped House routines by establishing new standing committees in addition to select committees and increasingly referred questions to both. The practice increased efficiency while enhancing his control over the legislative agenda.[6]

Clay was unfailingly fair as a presiding officer. He was nevertheless iron-fisted when dealing with the most vocal critics of an aggressive foreign policy. Federalists tried to impede the War Hawks at every turn, but their numbers (37 of 142 congressmen) hampered these efforts. In the face of that towering majority, Federalists like Josiah Quincy of Massachusetts contemplated giving Clay and his friends as much rope as they needed to embark on an unsuccessful war, discredit themselves in the process, and make way for a Federalist resurgence. But regardless of party, senior congressmen were stunned by this group of unknowns led by the upstart Clay. These veterans griped about the rapid, undeserved rise of the War Hawks. Quincy was typical in his contempt: Clay, he said, was "bold, aspiring, presumptuous, with a rough overbearing eloquence, neither exact or comprehensive, which he cultivated and formed in the contests with half-civilized wranglers in the county courts of Kentucky, and quickened into confidence and readiness by successful declamations at barbecues and election-eering struggles."[7]

John Randolph, nominally a Republican, was fearlessly nasty and tireless in opposing the War Hawks. Randolph was usually uncontrollable under the best of circumstances, and previous Speakers had simply resigned themselves to his legislative antics and personal crotchets. Randolph had started his political ca-reer as an ardent Republican and fervent supporter of fellow Virginian Thomas Jefferson, his distant cousin, yet he gradually came to judge President Jeffer-son's nationalism as heresy. By Jefferson's second term, Randolph had drifted into an informal alliance with Old Republicans, called such because they em-braced small government and strict constitutional construction, but also called Tertium Quids (meaning "third somethings") or just Quids, because they were neither Republican nor Federalist. These untethered Quids, with Randolph at their fore, feared that war with Great Britain would imperil the country, increase federal power, and cost a pile of money. They were right about all three, of course, and Randolph's relentless warnings were effective enough to take some-thing of the shine off the War Hawk agenda.

Aside from being a tireless Cassandra, Randolph was a peculiar character. Occasionally he could act as if he were stark raving mad. Either a childhood ill-ness or an affliction later labeled Klinefelter's syndrome had made him a beard-less, high-voiced, sexually impotent adult (this last confirmed by a postmortem in 1833).[8] But most of all, his odd condition made him irritable and vicious, quick to anger, and usually spoiling for a fight. In fact, conflict was mother's milk to Randolph as he galloped up to Washington from his Virginia plantation, Roa-noke, swigging brandy and erupting over perceived insults to his politics or his person, his hair-trigger temper as likely to be touched off by one as the other. He took an instant dislike to Henry Clay and quickly tested the new Speaker's will.

Randolph regularly brought his hounds into the House chamber, turning them loose to lope among the desks and lounge in the aisles. When Congress-man Willis Alston of North Carolina once complained that the large dogs were in the way, Randolph strode over to a startled Alston and rapped him with a cane, and that was the end of that. Clay's predecessor, Joseph Varnum of Mass-achusetts, watched this violent show of temper, weighed Randolph's reputation for wrath, and decided that discretion was the better part of parliamentary pro-tocol. Randolph's dogs remained a House fixture at the pleasure of their owner. Clay had been Speaker only a few weeks when Randolph bounced into the

House chamber, a huge dog at his heels. Clay immediately summoned the door-keeper and quietly told him to remove the animal from the House of Representatives. Everyone fell silent as the doorkeeper did Clay's bidding. Randolph was silent as well. He never brought a dog into the House again, but he never forgot the last day he had, and never forgave the man in the Speaker's chair who had not blinked.[9]

OVER TIME, CLAY'S transformation of the Speakership would become legendary, showing future Speakers how to exploit appointive and parliamentary authority in previously untried ways. Not until after the Civil War, though, would the country see another leader utilize the post's potential to the same extent as did Henry Clay. He augmented the Speaker's clout gradually, achieving it through many trials and occasional errors rather than through the systematic application of a preconceived plan.[10] When he was done, he had transformed the latent potential of the job into a lively dynamism of power and purpose. His friend William Plumer, observing that the post was "an office you did not want, but an office that wanted you," had predicted that Clay would "preside with dignity over" the House. Nobody could have known that he would also direct its affairs with such certainty that it would be the start of his reputation as a legislative dictator.[11]

Clay would have called it leadership. In the Kentucky statehouse, he had refused to be a mere enforcer of rules, a glorified ringmaster bringing order to fractious debates and controlling factious debaters. The legislature held pride of place in a government featuring a ceremonial executive, and Clay brought that philosophy of legislative supremacy to Congress from the start. The formula was syllogistic: the Speaker is the head of the majority party, the legislative majority should shape government policy, ergo the Speaker should coordinate and direct the government's course.[12]

Passive presidents are targets of contempt in the modern American political setting, and too often that relatively recent attitude is projected back to criticize the seemingly submissive executives of the early Republic. Yet the Framers, with good reason, had established the legislature in the *first* article of the Constitution, and George Washington himself had described Congress as the *first* wheel of government. The Revolutionary generation's contempt for kings stemmed from that generation's fear of unchecked power. A chief executive submitting to the will of the people in the form of a dominant legislature was not just the normal but the desirable form of government in an enlightened age. The locus of power in the presidency tended to subvert that ideal, of course, but the principle existed in any case, and the political establishment embraced it.

Thus Clay's views on legislative supremacy were in step with those of President Madison, who led House Republicans in the 1790s but never became Speaker because he could not envision melding the roles of floor leader and presiding officer. Becoming the president had not altered his opinion that Congress should take the initiative on most political matters. Madison's annual messages to Congress (what today are called State of the Union addresses) presented his observations about issues, but he believed the legislature should craft the policies to address them. The year 1811 brought into Congress a Speaker who intended to lead rather than simply moderate, steering the course of a government whose president was only too happy to let him.[13] The coincidental convergence of the aggressive legislator and the acquiescent executive makes it easy to overvalue Clay's part in reshaping the Speakership as an institution, for the situation was in many ways simply a result of complementary personalities and temperaments. Other Speakers would not have Clay's ability to lead, to speak, and to maneuver; other presidents would not be so willing to yield to anyone else on policy matters.[14]

While Clay insisted that the British revoke the Orders in Council or face war, tension on the western frontier erupted into actual fighting. In the fall of 1811, Indiana territorial governor William Henry Harrison advanced on a large Indian settlement at Prophetstown near Tippecanoe Creek. For almost three years followers of Tecumseh and Tenskwatawa had been gathering to swell Prophetstown's population. Nervous settlers finally demanded military protection from the perceived Indian threat that everyone suspected was a dark British project. Harrison's expedition was ostensibly to negotiate an understanding with these Indians and lessen strains on the frontier, but both sides were armed and edgy. Tecumseh was not at Prophetstown that fall, but his brother and his warriors attacked Harrison's forces, precipitating a disastrous battle for the Indians. As a military engagement, the fight was indecisive, but as a symbolic event with momentous consequences it had few peers. Tecumseh surveyed the setback at Tippecanoe Creek and resolved to cement an alliance with the British. Most westerners mistakenly assumed that such an alliance had existed for years. It did now.

Americans celebrated the battle as a victory, but the news was alloyed for Clay and his neighbors. Many Kentuckians had marched with Harrison, and some would never return. Jo Daveiss died leading a charge against an Indian position. Clay and Daveiss had not only settled their differences from the Burr affair but had become friends, serving together as members of Lexington's Masonic Grand Lodge of Kentucky (Daveiss was the eighth Grand Master). Clay turned over much of his legal practice to Daveiss when departing for the

Eleventh Congress and tried to secure government contracts for him. In the end, Daveiss died a hero in what amounted to the first engagement of the coming war. Clay often invoked his name as a martyr to American security and American honor, another reason to bring low the British.[15]

But it was another event that sent the capital into mourning that winter and had members of Congress tugging on black armbands. The day after Christmas, the Richmond Theatre in the Virginia state capital was consumed by a fire that started late in the evening performance. The raising of a chandelier onstage was the cause, its candles touching off the flammable scenery. The blaze quickly spread, and the audience responded in panic to the classic terror of fire in a crowded theater. As everyone clawed toward a single exit, women and children were trampled in the chaos. About seventy of the more than five hundred patrons perished, most burned beyond recognition. Governor George William Smith and former congressman and senator Abraham Bedford Venable were among the dead, as was Mary Clay, the young daughter of Henry's cousin and fellow congressman Matthew Clay, who collapsed as if dealt a hard physical blow when he received the news. Henry hurried to Matthew's rooms and sat with him through the night as his cousin shook with grief. For once, the Speaker was at a loss for words.[16]

CLAY BEGAN THE push to challenge Britain by letting others make the case. Over John Randolph's protests, the Foreign Relations Committee called for a more muscular military. Randolph screeched that a sizeable army was necessary only to implement plans to wrest Canada from Great Britain, and privately he mused that the War Hawks' real goal was to overtake the presidency. Meanwhile, when Madison asked Congress to authorize 10,000 additional regular army troops for a three-year term, the Senate more than doubled the number, a move by Madison's enemies to embarrass him. Republican members such as William Branch Giles disliked the president and detested Secretary of the Treasury Albert Gallatin. They knew that the government could never raise 25,000 men and could not pay for them if it did, and that any bill trying to authorize it would demonstrate the administration's incompetence.[17]

Clay realized that a large military increase could break the budget, but he also liked the boldness of the Senate's 25,000-man figure. The House received the Senate bill on Monday, December 30, 1811, and the following day went into the Committee of the Whole so that Clay could come down to the floor and discuss it. He began with a small concession to those fearful of its costs by proposing a scheme to stagger the appointment of officers to new regiments. As for complaints that 25,000 new recruits was excessive, Clay admitted the number was unwarranted for a country at peace but was, if anything, too small for a country likely to be at war. Yes, he said, the American militia had always been dedicated in their defense of the nation, but trained regulars were indispensable in a fight against the seasoned veterans of a militaristic enemy. To the question "What are we to gain by war?" he responded with his own question: "What are we not to lose by peace?" and promptly answered it: "Commerce, character, a nation's best treasure, honor!" He dismissed the claim that Britain was doing the world's work by fighting Napoleon: "We are called upon to submit to debasement, dishonor, and disgrace—to bow the neck to royal insolence, as a course of preparation for manly resistance to" a French invasion! "It was not by submission," he thundered, "that our fathers achieved our independence."[18]

The British goal, said Clay, was not only to deprive Napoleon of supply. Great Britain also aimed to dominate all the world's commerce by compelling the United States to submit to Britain's maritime regulations.[19] Allow the English navy to control trade between foreign ports, he warned, and soon it would control trade between New York and New Orleans. "When the burglar is at our door, shall we bravely sally forth and repel his felonious entrance, or meanly skulk within the cells of the castle? . . . Shall it be said that . . . we pusillanimously cling to our seats here rather than boldly vindicate the most inestimable rights of the country?"[20] Stoked up against the image of British burglars, the House agreed that an additional 25,000 constables seemed about right. After the Senate made a few minor changes, President Madison signed the military expansion bill into law on January 11, 1812.

Madison was not done, though. He had requested 50,000 short-term volunteers in addition to the regulars, prompting a debate in the House on the constitutionality of sending the militia into Canada, which was after all foreign territory. Clay again came down from the Speaker's chair to say that the president had the power to use the militia as a preemptive defensive force. Clay supported, he proclaimed, "an exertion of the national energies in every form, in prosecution of the war in which we are about to engage." John Randolph boiled. Preemptive defensive force? America about to wage war? Such belligerence, he raged in a letter to a friend in Virginia, proved "the depravity of my species!"[21]

As the War Hawks continued their preparations for war, even Republicans began to wonder about the speed and scope of the effort. Langdon Cheves's Naval Affairs Committee drafted a bill for the construction of twelve 74-gun ships and twenty frigates. The proposal marked such a startling departure from traditional Republican objections to large, costly navies that the legislative world of the House of Representatives almost halted on its axis. Naval expansion and the taxes it required during Federalist John Adams's presidency had united Republicans who had then and thereafter always resisted such initiatives as a pillar of Jeffersonian small government philosophy. Federalists slyly smiled as old and some young Republicans alike looked askance at a world now turned upside down. A committee headed by a Republican and dominated by Republicans envisioned a naval building program far more ambitious than anything the Federalists had ever proposed. Aside from reflexively balking at the enormous cost, many Republican members, particularly westerners, insisted that the naval project was quite unnecessary. They could fight the British in contiguous Canada, they said, and the country hardly needed a navy to do that. That was the course of debate when "the Western Star" again came down from the chair on January 22, 1812, to express his views on the proposed bill.

He agreed that the war should be taken to the British in Canada, but any hesitation, he said, as to whether it concerned American military might on land or sea sent a message of weakness to London. Clay reminded the House that the martyred Jo Daveiss had written that a larger navy was essential to protect American commerce, a crucial element of western development. Without a navy, Clay said, the United States could not secure the Gulf of Mexico and protect New Orleans. Losing New Orleans would block the mighty Mississippi River, the route to the world's oceans, and collapse the West's economy. Clay's arguments persuaded some, but not enough to win passage for massive naval expansion. Congress eventually passed a smaller appropriation for naval construction, while the original bill went down to defeat 62 to 59. Having been given enough rope by the Federalists, the War Hawks seemed to be reaching the end of it.[22]

In fact, the prospect of an expensive war made even some of Clay's allies nervous. When Secretary of the Treasury Gallatin proposed new taxes and loans to address shrinking government revenues, opponents doubted the War Hawks would agree to them. Randolph sneered privately that their incessant jabbering reminded him of "the talk of children," but Clay came out so resolutely for Gallatin's plan that most Republicans followed his lead and passed the measure.[23]

Clay's legislative successes during these months have caused historians to debate the weight of his role in bringing about the American declaration of war in 1812. Some see his accomplishments against long odds and traditional Republican scruples as proving that he was the prime mover. Others insist that he only directed the legislative side of a coordinated effort between the War Hawks in Congress and the executive branch, where President Madison and Secretary of State James Monroe were just as effective behind the scenes as Clay was on the public stage.[24] At the time, opponents of war were convinced that Henry Clay was pushing Madison into war rather than cooperating with him, and they imagined plots and cabals surrounding the effort. Clay, they deduced, used the Republican congressional caucus presidential nomination as leverage, delaying its choice of Madison for a second term and even threatening to support another candidate if Madison did not toe the War Hawk line. Rumors in February 1812 told of "a grand Caucus" that had already secretly met to nominate DeWitt Clinton of New York for president and Clay for vice president.[25] Yet the source who declared that Clay was holding the nomination hostage was Federalist Josiah Quincy, hardly a Clay confidant. Clinton would have been an especially odd choice for a Clay cabal in any case. He unsuccessfully challenged Madison in 1812, but on a ticket supported by the Federalists and the antiwar Republicans, a coalition completely incompatible with the War Hawk program.

President Madison began to dispel uncertainty about his attitude when he released a set of documents to Congress that were soon notoriously known as the John Henry letters. In 1809, Canada's governor-general James Craig had employed Henry, an Irish rogue with dubious claims of being an accomplished spy, to meander around New England evaluating Federalist anger over Madison's policies. Henry planted himself in Boston for several months, whence he dispatched increasingly fanciful messages to Governor Craig, such as the prediction that Massachusetts would ally itself with Britain in the event of war. Craig died before Henry could collect for his services, and nobody else in the British government would pay him any attention, let alone pay him any money. The Madison administration was not so cautious. By early 1812, Henry was desperate for cash and offered to sell his information to the American government. Secretary of State Monroe persuaded Madison to pay Henry the government's entire secret service fund of $50,000 for his letters. After several weeks, Madison released the documents to Congress, and they caused a sensation. The damaging allegations of New England disloyalty and the British desire to exploit it inflamed the country. A few temperate voices pointed out that the letters really did not say anything, certainly did not pin names to any misdeeds, and were likely the work of an audacious fraud, but the War Hawks drowned out such prudence with the "proof" of British perfidy and Federalist treason.[26]

A few days later, on the morning of March 15, Clay met with Monroe. Apparently they discussed how to persuade the nation to make war, for later that day Clay sent Monroe an aide-mémoire summarizing what to do if Britain maintained the Orders in Council and continued impressment. He noted that while awaiting the USS *Hornet,* due soon from Europe with intelligence about British intentions, the president should ask Congress to impose a thirty-day embargo to allow American ships to return home unmolested, after which Congress would declare war on Britain. It was an extraordinary plan, for it proposed that both Congress and the president move into uncharted territory. After the American Revolution, the United States had traded blows with France, Barbary pirates, and Indian tribes, but the country had never fought a declared war. Clay pointed out to Monroe that the Constitution clearly placed the authority for going to war with Congress, but that it was "within the scope of the President's constitutional duty to recommend such measures as he shall judge necessary and expedient."[27]

The uncharted, complicated nature of these actions was further demonstrated by the fact that even as the United States rattled its saber at Britain, merchant ships under American flags ferried supplies to British troops fighting Napoleon on the Spanish peninsula. Reports that French corsairs were attacking these American merchant ships prompted Madison to ask Congress for a sixty-day embargo on U.S. trade (twice the length Clay had requested) to provide more time for news of British plans to arrive. Again the House went into the Committee of the Whole, and Clay joined the debate to support the measure "as a direct precursor to war." After the thorough efforts to ready the nation for a fight, Clay was astonished that some would cover the country "with shame and indelible disgrace by retreating." In fact, Clay said that if French attacks persisted, Americans should face down proud Napoleon too. At that, John Randolph had heard more than enough. He leaped to his feet. These calls to belligerence were too perilous, he bellowed, to let pass without deliberation. A proper pause and reflection would show everyone that the United States was far from prepared to fight a war with anyone, let alone powerful Britain, and certainly not both the British and French empires. Clay responded. Randolph retorted. Followers of each spoke on their respective champion's behalf, giving the impression in their vehemence that the issue was closely joined, but when the votes were counted, it was not really close at all. Clay's side won, 70 to 41. The Senate extended the embargo to ninety days, the House concurring to avoid additional delay, and Madison signed the bill on April 4. By his own plain declaration, Clay meant for this action to be a preliminary to war. Congress agreed that it was likely to be perceived that way and called for a hundred thousand volunteers for a six-month enlistment.[28]

Then everyone waited for the *Hornet,* none more anxiously than British minister Augustus John Foster, whose usual affability was being greatly strained by events. Foster hosted pleasant gatherings at which he listened attentively to American complaints, but he could not for the life of him make out what all the fuss was about. Clay especially bewildered Foster. He respected Clay's talent and understood the reason for his influence, but he was flummoxed by Clay's treating the European crisis as if it were "the Game of Brag." Clay told Foster

that for Americans, war was necessary in the same way that a duel was necessary "to a young officer to prevent his being bullied and elbowed in society."
Likewise, said Clay, the end of the war, like the conclusion of a harmless duel,
"would probably leave them both better friends than they had ever been before."
Foster listened in amazement and could only nod, frowning, when Clay told him
that France would either compensate America for its maritime losses or face
American guns as well. Young Mr. Foster did not understand young Mr. Clay at
all.[29]

IN APRIL A series of editorials calling for war appeared in the *National Intelligencer,* their language so combative that many were convinced that Clay had
written them to manipulate Madison. The Federalist press condemned him for
trying to drag the country into an unnecessary war, but the editorials were actually the work of Secretary of State Monroe. Madison had already made up his
mind on the matter as well. He was convinced that any news from Great Britain
held out only a dim hope for peace.[30]

The Republican congressional caucus had nominated Madison almost unan-
imously for a second term, but the death of the elderly vice president George
Clinton a few weeks earlier complicated the selection of a running mate. Clinton had not presided over the Senate in weeks because of his illness, making
necessary the appointment of a president pro tempore, Clay's friend William
Crawford. When the caucus nominated seventy-year-old John Langdon of New
Hampshire, another elderly Republican, he declined, forcing the party to turn to
Elbridge Gerry of Massachusetts, who was very much a friend of the War Hawk
agenda. By then, the *Hornet* had arrived from Europe. The news was not good.

Britain had no intention of changing its policies, and no meaningful arrangement had been made with the French. Clay dismissed the problem with France
as a mere diplomatic delay, a minor setback, but he railed at Britain's continuing determination to assail American merchant ships and abduct sailors. He was
confident that sooner or later Congress would have to declare war.[31]

He worked hard to make it sooner. At some point between May 25 and May
29, Speaker Clay and a group of congressmen met with President Madison. The
date is uncertain because the meeting was extremely private, but shadowy reports of it later described Clay as browbeating the president into sending Congress a war message. Such impertinence was highly unlikely, however, even if it
had been necessary, which it was not. Madison was already in agreement with
the War Hawks, as evidenced by his administration's covert but no less effective
editorializing by its principal foreign officer, James Monroe. Actually, Clay
most likely only assured Madison that he had the votes for a war if Madison

wanted one. Private meeting aside, word soon leaked out that Madison would send a war message to Congress. John Randolph intended to challenge it. Clay and the War Hawks were ready for him.[32]

Clay was adept at using floor managers to shut down long-winded opponents who stalled proceedings with rambling speeches. A prearranged signal or a pre-conceived plan prompted designated members to call for a point of order or to ask the Speaker to apply a pertinent rule, giving Clay parliamentary cover to gavel down obstructionists. John Randolph had transformed obstruction into an art form, and on May 29, 1812, he planned a virtuoso performance, convinced that Madison's message could arrive at any moment. When Randolph gained the floor, Clay had temporarily turned over the chair to William Bibb of Georgia, which proved to be a mistake, for Randolph was able to get well along with his plan to snarl matters up before Clay could do anything about it. No motion was under consideration, but Randolph announced that he had heard "rumors to which he could not shut his ears," and that these rumors "impelled him to make a last effort to rescue the country from the calamites, which he feared, were impending over it."

Then he was off to the races: Napoleon was as much to blame for attacks on American shipping as were the British, Randolph was intoning, when one of Clay's floor managers, John C. Calhoun, saw what was happening and objected that Randolph was speaking against a motion that did not exist. Instead of snapping down his gavel, Bibb ruled that Randolph had indicated that he intended to make a motion of his own, if in a vague sort of way, and therefore he could continue. Across the chamber, Clay stopped his conversation and stiffened. He whirled and strode purposefully to the Speaker's platform, where he more or less shooed Bibb out of the chair, settled into it himself, and immediately recognized Calhoun, who repeated his objection. Clay told Randolph either to make a motion or to sit down. Randolph indignantly appealed Clay's ruling to the House, but it sustained the Speaker. Left with no other alternative, Randolph sullenly moved "that it is not expedient at this time to resort to war against Great Britain." Clay then declared that House rules required Randolph's motion to be put in writing. This was really too much, Randolph sputtered; he again appealed to the House, and again lost. Exasperated, he barked in protest over being compelled to make his motion in writing. Clay idly mused that no, actually Randolph was not compelled to do anything. He did not have to make the motion at all.

Randolph was already furiously scratching his motion on a piece of paper. He handed it up to Clay, who read it to the House. Thinking all protocols now satisfied, Randolph ostentatiously announced he would at last begin the debate on the motion, but Clay recognized Hugh Nelson—a delicious irony for the Speaker, because Nelson was a member of Randolph's own Virginia delegation. Nelson helpfully reminded Clay of a House rule requiring a vote on whether to consider a motion before it was debated. Clay seemed reflective, innocently admitting that he had completely forgotten about that particular rule, but nodding that Nelson was almost certainly correct. Randolph was stunned. On the verge of being thwarted with procedures, blocked by colleagues, shut up by the Speaker, he wailed that his right of free speech was being violated. "The meanest beggar," he shouted, "has a right to come here and state his grievances," which was neither exactly true nor clearly pertinent. Nevertheless he lectured the House, claiming that his lengthy service made him thoroughly knowledgeable about its rules. Clay broke in to remark curtly that Randolph's seniority was irrelevant to the propriety of a Speaker's ruling. Other members piped up to say that Clay was in the right, and Randolph decided not to lodge a third, equally futile appeal. Clay, victorious, could not let it lie—a bad habit. He delivered a brief but sanctimonious lecture of his own that patiently explained that orderly debate required a strict adherence to parliamentary rules. Coming at the end of the remarkable procedural contest, the House vote of 72 to 37 not to consider Randolph's motion was anticlimactic.

It was Friday afternoon, and the House adjourned for the weekend. For two days Washington buzzed with talk of the dramatic showdown on Capitol Hill. On Monday, June 1, however, everyone had something even more spectacular to talk about. A message from President James Madison arrived in Congress. It asked for a declaration of war.[33]

CLAY IMMEDIATELY REFERRED the president's communication to the Committee on Foreign Relations, and two days later Chairman John C. Calhoun reported a bill declaring war on Great Britain. Clay wanted the ensuing debate to be open to the public, but Madison did not, and Clay reluctantly agreed to have the House clear the galleries and close its doors. Federalists protested, Randolph stormed, and Clay wavered, sensing that secrecy at this juncture would mark a bad start for a perilous undertaking. He was also likely disappointed over not having the chance to be center stage at an impressive spectacle. But Madison had his reasons, and though it has never been clear what they were, they were persuasive enough to make Clay rule that debate would occur in closed session. The following day, on June 4, 1812, the House passed a declaration of war by a vote of 79 to 49. The Senate deliberated longer but finally passed a slightly different declaration 19 to 13 on June 17. The House planned to take up the Senate bill the following day.[34]

That evening the Madisons held a levee attended by all of the important people of Washington, including Augustus John Foster. The British minister found Madison polite and hospitable but "ghastly pale." Clay and Calhoun, on the other hand, mingled among the guests with supreme confidence. The next day the House voted 85 to 44 to accept the Senate's minor changes, and later that day Madison signed the bill. *"We shall have War,"* Clay exulted in letters clearly meant for publication, *"and, as I think it ought to be at present, War with England alone."* He firmly believed everyone was as enthusiastic as he was. "Every patriot bosom," he sang, "must throb with anxious solicitude for the result. Every patriot arm will assist in making that result conducive to the glory of our beloved country."[35] Yet from the very start of the war, patriots' bosoms were precious few, throbbing or otherwise. Federalists opposed the war almost to a man, and some in New England tried to impede the war effort.

John Randolph published a pamphlet describing the events of May 29, when Clay had cut him off, as a plot to stop debate and stifle free speech. Clay answered in the *National Intelligencer* that he had only enforced House rules, that members had repeatedly sustained him, and that to allow endless speeches without regard for procedure prevented the House from conducting its business. Randolph had taken the maneuvers to silence him quite personally, but Clay's response intensified his wrath, especially because he thought Clay was a boor beneath his notice. Clay's rulings, he said, had been inconsistent and his conduct a flagrant abuse of power, "prostrating, from motives of caprice, temporary convenience, or party spirit," the basic principles of free government.[36] Beneath all the bombast was a kernel of truth, for Clay had indeed used parliamentary procedure to silence opponents, a practice that would eventually give him a reputation as a dictator. But Randolph's anger was not just bluster. Clay had made a dangerous enemy.

For the moment, however, Clay had his hands full controlling his friends. Even his allies were worried about paying for the war they had just authorized. Anxiety over raising taxes caused some to suggest eccentric alternatives, such as lifting trade restrictions against Great Britain to fatten the Treasury with import taxes on British goods. Only days had passed since Congress had declared war on the British, but half the members of Congress saw nothing incongruous about reestablishing trade with them: the vote was 60 for and 60 against. Clay announced that the tie gave him the satisfaction of casting the deciding vote "to manifest his decided opposition to the measure."[37]

The long session was coming to a close just in time. In early June, Lucretia had gone home with the children, accompanied by her brother-in-law Dr. Richard Pindell, and Clay already missed her. During all the tumult leading to war, Lucretia had been Lucretia—hushed, unassuming, and kindhearted. Margaret Bayard Smith counted this "good woman [and] most devoted mother" her friend, pondering how she preferred to sew and play with her children rather than trade empty jests with fashionable company. When Margaret Smith fell ill, Lucretia took in the Smith children to let Margaret rest. Once Lucretia brought all the Clay children to the Smiths' house, where they spent an afternoon making flower wreaths, Lucretia cheerfully enjoying the fun as much as any of the youngsters. Margaret liked to hear Lucretia play the piano and smiled at how the children danced around her. Lucretia liked Margaret too, for she had little to do with those she did not like, and in Mrs. Smith's company Mrs. Clay did not even mind carriage rides to pay social calls. Yet she was always eager to return to Ashland.[38]

The congressional session did not end until July 2. Clay lived as a bachelor as he tied up loose ends in the capital. He rode horseback each morning out to Georgetown to sip mineral water at Dr. John Ott's soda fountain—young people giggled that it could make one "high"—and worked with renowned architect Benjamin Latrobe on plans for new buildings at Transylvania University. The final social function he attended before heading for Kentucky was a dinner the War Mess generously held for Augustus John Foster, who was also leaving Washington for Halifax and from there for London. Foster could have been excused for being more bewildered than ever. He had received his passport after the declaration of war and was grateful for the party, but he noted that Clay "was very warlike." Mr. Foster did not understand Mr. Clay at all.[39]

Yet matters were to become even more bewildering. As Congress was voting for war, an ocean away the British government was suspending the Orders in Council. The British saw the repeal of the Orders as a major concession, but the gesture did not change anything for Americans. There was still impressment to resist, and preparations for war continued.[40]

ON HIS WAY to Lexington, Clay was glad to hear that American armies were already on the march with an invasion of Canada led by General William Hull, a veteran of the Revolutionary War and Michigan's territorial governor. Lexington celebrated Hull's exploits, Congress's actions, and Henry Clay in particular at a public dinner on July 27. Toasts to Clay, the war, and Congress continued well into the evening. No one entertained the slightest doubt about the country's certain triumph.[41]

Clay wrote frequently to Secretary of State Monroe, with whom he had developed a close working relationship, and to Secretary of War William Eustis. Clay wanted western volunteers deployed, if for no other reason than to bolster the region's morale with the sense that it was being useful. He became a champion of Indiana territorial governor William Henry Harrison and took every opportunity to tout Harrison's military skills and universal popularity. Clay had always preferred that Harrison be placed in command of western troops, and that feeling only strengthened when word arrived in Kentucky that William Hull had called off his invasion and was retreating to Detroit. Clay was pleased that Kentucky troops sent to reinforce Hull's forces were at last going to get into the fight. Clay addressed volunteers as they were about to head north, reminding them that "they had the double character of Americans and Kentuckians" to uphold.[42]

The news coming from Hull's army was troubling, though. Aside from the obviously aborted invasion as a military setback, Clay worried that the administration's political enemies could point to it as proof that the country had not been prepared for war. As the news from Detroit grew darker, Clay warned the government that a disaster could be in the offing. He would take no pleasure in being right.[43]

Clay had little regard and less respect for William Eustis. Madison had appointed him to the War Department after first taking office in 1809 because Eustis was that rare animal, a loyal Republican from New England. He was adequate in his position in peacetime, but he lacked the organizational skills to manage his department during a war. By the fall of 1812, Clay's voice was among a chorus seeking his removal. Clay's frustration over clear evidence of incompetence in Washington was combined with impatience over slow communication between the West and the federal capital. He stood it as long as he could—which was not very long—before taking at least some matters into his own hands.[44] At Clay's urging, Governor Charles Scott summoned Kentucky's most important political figures to a meeting on August 25, 1812. They planned to discuss the military situation in the Northwest, but in the end they did considerably more. The group, which included Clay and Governor-elect Isaac Shelby, advised Scott to appoint William Henry Harrison a brevet major general of Kentucky militia with instructions to reinforce Detroit. After this astonishing action by this extraordinary meeting, Clay wrote to Monroe admitting that Kentucky had no authority to take such a step but insisting that the emergency at Detroit made it necessary to bypass the War Department. Nobody seemed to mind that Harrison was not from Kentucky.[45]

Despite its audacity, Kentucky's initiative was already too late. Over the strenuous protests of his officers, William Hull surrendered Detroit and its garrison to British general Isaac Brock on August 16, 1812. By the time Kentucky heard about this, the state also had bad news about the evacuation of Fort Dearborn (modern-day Chicago) and the massacre of many of the refugees by Indians. Harrison sped the pace of his preparations and recruiting. He chose Lucretia's younger brother, Nathaniel Hart, to serve as his brigade inspector, and he asked Lucretia's husband to accompany the expedition to the Northwest as his adviser. Clay obviously declined—though we do not have his response to Harrison, he did not go with the army—but he stayed in touch with Harrison to offer advice and encouragement.[46]

Clay thought that Hull's surrender was utter treachery and urged that he be tried and executed. Despite the fact that he had never swapped an angry word with an Indian, Clay was full of advice about the best way to fight them. While Lucretia packed for their return to Washington, Clay frantically attended to business details. In early October, they set out with their three youngest children. The three older children were in school.[47]

Clay found the government virtually paralyzed by military calamities. Unexpected American naval victories in single-ship fights with Royal Navy frigates bolstered spirits somewhat, and the recent capture of HMS *Macedonia* by the *United States* under Stephen Decatur was reason for celebration. At a grand ball, the *Macedonia*'s colors were placed at Dolley Madison's feet, but the depressing performance of American armies remained a cloud over otherwise merry events.[48] Intent on ignoring that cloud, Clay redoubled his efforts to support the administration, encourage American commanders, and fend off the unrelenting criticism from Federalists and John Randolph. The second session of the Twelfth Congress was a short one, but Clay left the chair to speak on the floor with even greater frequency, always optimistic, always confident. To friends in private, however, he was gloomy. Military operations had been wretchedly planned, and President Madison's "mild & amiable virtues" were "wholly unfit for the storms of War."[49]

That was in private. Clay's public posture was intent on stiffening American resolve, even if he had to assume an occasionally illogical position to do so, such as the one he took in early December. Nonimportation against the British in 1811 had included provisions for the policy's termination if Britain repealed the Orders in Council. American merchants in Europe, unaware of the declaration of war, consequently responded to the British repeal in June 1812 by gleefully purchasing British goods and shipping them to the United States. Yet the war meant that nonimportation was not lifted, and customs officials accordingly seized these cargoes when they arrived in U.S. ports. The distress of American shippers was palpable, and sympathy with them was easy because they had not imagined themselves doing anything in the least wrong. Clay's ally Langdon Cheves argued that these merchants should be compensated for their losses.

On December 7, the House was constituted into the Committee of the

Whole, and Clay spoke at length against compensation. He conceded that these Americans abroad had not known about the declaration of war, but that ignorance did not absolve them from obeying the law until they were officially informed that it was no longer in force. He would bend only to the extent of partial compensation for a very few, recommending that in all other cases the law be enforced.[50] It was a muddled performance further marred by a nonsensical solution. All the shippers had obviously acted from the same ignorance, so it was both pointless and unfair to accommodate only a few and punish the rest. Congress enacted a very lenient measure that fully compensated most of the merchants. Most representatives did not go so far as John Randolph—he privately called Clay's speech a "rant of which the delivery was as bad as the matter," and then parsed it for grammatical errors—but they plainly dismissed Clay's reasoning as deeply flawed.[51]

It was a small crack in the Speaker's armor, but a chink even so. As the House considered a bill to swell the army by twenty regiments, Randolph and Federalist Josiah Quincy did not confine their acerbic remarks to private letters. Only great exertions by Clay's floor managers kept those comments brief and to the point. Keeping them civil was impossible. Beginning on January 5, Quincy used his speech opposing army expansion to attack the war and to describe James Madison, James Monroe, Albert Gallatin, and even Thomas Jefferson as French lapdogs. The administration's supporters, said Quincy, were "sycophants, fawning reptiles, who crowded at the feet of the president, and left their filthy slime upon the carpet of the palace."[52]

That language set off a two-day outpouring of Republican outrage, concluding with the House resolving itself into the Committee of the Whole and Speaker Clay taking the floor. He began disingenuously with the claim that he was quite unwell and unprepared to speak. He then commenced one of the most commanding and effective discourses of his career, one that spanned the next two days. The tour de force dispelled any doubt about Clay's armor and arsenal; in this recital he proved himself quite well armed and very dangerous indeed. As he disdainfully mocked instances of Federalist disloyalty, furiously narrated examples of British perfidy, and laced his remarks with sweeping expressions of patriotism, the Western Star made his friends gleam and his enemies squirm. "If we are united," Clay roared, "we are too powerful for the mightiest nation in Europe, or all Europe combined. If we are separated and torn asunder we shall become an easy prey to the weakest of them. In the latter dreadful contingency, our country will not be worth preserving." It was the kind of rhetoric schoolboys would commit to memory and budding politicians would try to imitate. Twenty-five years later, Abraham Lincoln would deliver a speech to the Springfield

Lyceum that spoke of combined European armies being unable to take a drink from the Ohio or place a track on the Blue Ridge, words that echoed his hero Henry Clay.[53]

Clay turned on Quincy with menacing fury. How dare he attack the venerable patriot Thomas Jefferson! When Quincy "shall have mingled his dust with that of his abused ancestors, when he shall be consigned to oblivion," Clay boomed, everyone will yet remember the greatness that is and always will be Jefferson. Clay turned on the Federalists. He sneered at their delicate and recently recovered devotion to liberty, certainly absent in 1798 when they had shamelessly trampled on their country's most basic civil rights. On he went, the hours passing, until he dramatically asked for everyone's indulgence. He was too exhausted to continue, he croaked, collapsing theatrically into a chair, insisting that he had more to say, promising to continue on the morrow.[54]

Throughout the evening the news tore through the capital about what Clay had done on the floor of the House that day and that there was more to come. Throngs of people streamed up muddy Pennsylvania Avenue and crowded into the Capitol. As Congress opened the day's session, House galleries sagged and groaned under the weight of a multitude. Clay stood and waited for the silence, breaking it with a cadenced repetition of his earlier attack on Quincy, his baritone rising to the ceiling as he accused the Federalist of outraging "all decency." Spectators and representatives alike sat forward. This was going to be good.

Clay did not disappoint. He outlined the causes of the war and dismissed the false optimism of thinking that Britain's repeal of the Orders in Council changed anything. The Orders were only part of the reason for war, he explained, as he narrated the grievances that had finally compelled the fight to preserve American honor. The country required, said Clay, the means necessary to fight a successful war and secure a principled peace. He ended, his voice pounding to a crescendo: "In such a cause, with the aid of Providence, we must come out crowned with success; but if we fail, let us fail like men, lash ourselves to our gallant tars, and expire together in one common struggle, fighting for *'seamen's rights and free trade.'* "[55]

He basked in the whistles, shouts, and applause, Western Star rising. The bill passed.

The Republican press lauded Clay and denounced Quincy as "dead to every honorable and every patriotic feeling of the human heart."[56] Quincy's friends warned him that Clay was trying to goad him into a barbaric southern duel. He simply responded to Clay's attacks by politely calling the Speaker a liar.[57]

Unfortunately, terrible news about the war soon began to trickle into Washington. In the Northwest, winter weather had stopped Harrison's offensive as isolated American forts were besieged. On January 22, an American force that included many Kentuckians ranged too far from the main army and was captured at Frenchtown (near modern-day Monroe, Michigan) on the River Raisin after suffering heavy casualties. Clay's cocounsel in the Burr trial, John Allen, was among those killed. The British marched away most prisoners but left the wounded under Indian guards supervised by a few British soldiers.

Captain Nathaniel Hart, Lucretia's younger brother, was only slightly injured in his knee, but was unable to march with the other captives. When the Indians commenced what would be known as the infamous River Raisin Massacre, Nathaniel bought his life with a bribe. One of the Indians agreed to take him by horseback to safety, but on the way, he was shot and scalped. His youthful widow had two little boys. The younger was named Henry Clay Hart.[58]

THE SHORT SECOND session of the Twelfth Congress came to a close, and Clay prepared to return with his family to Ashland. The unrelenting bad news had put him on edge, and at a dinner in his honor hosted by French minister Louis Sérurier, he was gloomy and rude. Clay spoke privately to Sérurier in sharp terms. If the United States did not have evidence of French friendship soon, he snapped, Americans would have to look for friends elsewhere.[59]

Madison had already announced his plans to call a special session of the new Thirteenth Congress to meet at the end of May 1813, so Clay's time in Kentucky would be brief. In addition, getting to Kentucky seemed to take a lifetime because Lucretia was five months pregnant with their eighth child. After reaching Lexington, though, Clay was not altogether sorry he would soon be going back to Washington. Many Kentuckians were disillusioned with the war. The battle and massacre on the River Raisin, where so many beloved neighbors had been killed or captured, left communities deflated and somber. Clay was beginning to doubt Harrison's abilities. That he had been Harrison's unstinting champion was disquieting.[60]

In early May, the Clays headed back to Washington and found everyone's mood a bit brighter because of diplomatic rather than military developments. When Napoleon invaded Russia in 1812, Czar Alexander I was more than chagrined that Britain would be distracted by an American war. He offered to mediate the Anglo-American conflict as soon as it started, a proposal that finally reached the American government in the spring of 1813. Madison leaped at this potentially happy way to end this most unhappy war. He immediately sent Treasury secretary Albert Gallatin and Delaware Federalist James A. Bayard to Russia, where they and U.S. minister John Quincy Adams would, Madison hoped, sit down with British counterparts under the benevolent gaze of the Czar of all the Russias. As it happened, none of this would be so easy—the Senate rejected Gallatin's nomination because his appointment ostensibly left the Treasury untended, and the British simply rejected the Russian mediation offer as mischievous meddling—but at least the prospects for a negotiated peace appeared to be improving.

The Thirteenth Congress, however, was in a foul mood from the start. Some of the president's strongest opponents, including Randolph and Quincy, were not there, either by their choice or because of their constituents' displeasure. Randolph claimed that he was happy to be "no longer under the abject dominion of Mr. H. Clay & Co."[61] In the place of those implacable foes came others, though, such as New Hampshire Federalist congressman Daniel Webster, a young man with an imposing dark, broad brow and a voice as deep and commanding as Clay's. Madison would hear more vocal criticisms from Republicans too, especially in the Senate. Clay had a job of work maintaining support for the administration in this Congress.

The House convened on May 24 and again selected Clay as Speaker, but the vote was 89 for Clay to 54 for Connecticut Federalist Timothy Pitkin, with five votes scattered among other candidates, an indication of slipping support for the war and the man seen as its principal advocate.[62]

Clay selected the reliable War Hawk John C. Calhoun to head the Foreign Relations Committee, which would handle most of the president's message to the special session, but the Speaker was anxious and quick-tempered. One portion of Madison's message covered Britain's military reliance on Indians, with details about alleged atrocities in the northwestern theater of war. Clay made what Webster called "a furious speech" insisting that a select committee look into these matters. Clay also ejected from the floor of the House a stenographer who worked for the *Federalist Republican,* an anti-administration newspaper published in Georgetown by arch-Federalist and Maryland congressman Alexander Hanson. Hanson's vigorous opposition to the war at its beginning had sparked riots in Baltimore in the summer of 1812, and the mob that had destroyed his press very nearly killed him and his associates. Now Clay's banishment of Hanson's reporter to the gallery (four others from friendly newspapers remained on the floor) ignited considerable controversy. Calhoun defended the action, but the Federalist press knew who was responsible. They berated Clay for "petty tyranny" and upbraided him for favoring only reporters who approached him "in the submissive style of supplication."[63]

Clay had a larger problem than hostile newspapers. Opponents and friends alike were certain to be unhappy about what Madison really wanted from the special session, which was for Congress to address the looming financial crisis.

The government simply had to have more money to finance the war.[64] Albert Gallatin had asked for new taxes before leaving for Russia, and Madison's message to the special session imparted urgency to the subject. Republicans instinctively opposed direct taxes, and Clay carefully approached the problem of persuading them to accept the need for new revenues. He called caucuses to address groups and cajoled individuals in the House cloakroom and the capital's taverns. He quashed Federalist proposals to tax only special interest groups, an obvious ploy to divide Republicans, and he honed his skills for conducting informal negotiations and brokering confidential deals.[65]

Many things in Washington were done then as they are done now, but the town was more intimate and relationships could be quite informal, especially because the population was small, even when Congress was in session. People greeted each other on the street by name, visited in homes or rooming houses, attended the theater together, and did much of their politicking at social events. An urgent matter could merit an unannounced call at a cabinet member's home where a cool drink on a porch in the day or cigars and brandy in the evening helped to hash things out. Clay became a master at this friendly type of negotiation in both private and social settings, and the elegant levees and dinners hosted by the Madisons presented the perfect opportunity to persuade the reluctant and reassure the faithful.[66]

During the early part of the summer of 1813, however, James Madison contracted an intestinal ailment so serious that Dolley darkened the executive mansion and cleared her crowded social calendar. For several weeks the president could not leave his bed, and the entire capital hung on every word of news, fearful that he might die. Congress consulted with Vice President Elbridge Gerry as the British began raids in Chesapeake Bay that brought them up the Potomac River within fifty miles of the capital. Lucretia had just given birth to Eliza Hart Clay, and Henry made plans to send everyone to safety at Margaret Bayard Smith's place in the country. Nancy Hart Brown was also in Washington with her husband, James, a new senator from Louisiana, and she planned to go to the Smiths' as well if the British marched on Washington. Everyone relaxed when the British tide ebbed back into the Chesapeake. The capital was safe, for the time being.[67]

And slowly it looked as though Madison was too. His recovery was gradual, though, keeping him indoors, preventing his return to social events, and spawning rumors that his convalescence was less than hopeful. As Congress approached the end of the special session, Clay's enemies worried that Madison's death might put the Speaker in the presidency, because fate had ironically realigned the line of succession. Elbridge Gerry was almost seventy, seven years older than Madison, and occasionally ill himself. The line of succession specified that the death of the president and vice president would bring to office the Senate's presiding officer, the president pro tempore, an arrangement that sustained as much as possible the stability of vice-presidential succession. If the post of president pro tempore were vacant, however, the Speaker of the House became president. To ensure that no such vacancy existed, vice presidents routinely relinquished the chair to a president pro tempore during the final days of a session in order to have that post filled should a catastrophe occur during the congressional recess. Yet that summer, Gerry did not like what he saw at all. He weighed the prospects of Madison's recovery, gauged his own frailty, and presumed that the Senate would elect obstreperous William Branch Giles, an avowed enemy of the administration, president pro tempore. Gerry broke tradition and did not step down, thereby making the selection of a president pro tempore unnecessary. Alexander Hanson's *Federal Republican* raged that if Madison died, Clay would likely murder Gerry to become president, but Gerry was willing to risk it. A lung hemorrhage, not a homicidal Speaker, killed Gerry a year later, and by then Madison had fully recovered. Yet had both Madison and Gerry died while Congress was in recess, Henry Clay would have become president of the United States. It was perhaps the best chance he ever had.[68]

THAT OCTOBER, THE Madison administration learned that the British had rejected the Russian mediation offer but had substituted a proposal for direct negotiations either in the Swedish city of Gothenburg or in London. The proposal coincided with improvements in the American military situation. In September, Commander Oliver Hazard Perry defeated a British naval squadron on Lake Erie, securing those important waters for the United States. Losing control of Erie meant that the British had to flee the Northwest, and William Henry Harrison was close on their heels to defeat them on the Thames River. Tecumseh reportedly was killed in this engagement, supposedly by Clay's friend Richard Mentor Johnson of Kentucky, shattering the Anglo-Indian alliance and paving the way for American control of the frontier. Yet a failed expedition against Montreal alloyed these triumphs, and Madison gloomily contended with ongoing criticism. He eagerly searched for an honorable end to the war.

On January 6, 1814, Madison accepted the British offer for direct negotiations at Gothenburg, but slow communications over great distances subjected the process of bringing together British and American commissioners to frustrating delays. Bayard and Gallatin, in Saint Petersburg since summer (Gallatin had ignored his rejection by the Senate), already knew about the British offer and left frigid Russia that January for London. There they awaited instructions, thinking their presence might speed negotiations. John Quincy Adams remained at his post in Saint Petersburg, so the American commissioners themselves were spread across Europe.

Madison was committed to retaining this team. After appointing Senator George Washington Campbell to take over at Treasury, he again placed Gallatin's name before the Senate, this time successfully. Madison also considered including U.S. Minister to France William H. Crawford on the peace commission, but Napoleon had suffered a devastating defeat at Leipzig in October 1813 and nobody knew what the future held for France. Madison thought it best to keep Crawford in Paris. Instead, the president turned to Henry Clay, his most reliable champion in Congress and the man whose imprimatur on any peace would ensure its acceptance as honorable. Clay was reluctant to leave the country indefinitely, but duty won out. Finally, veteran diplomat Jonathan Russell, the newly appointed minister to Sweden, would also be on the American peace commission because Sweden would host the negotiations.

French minister Sérurier was thrilled that Clay would be part of the commission, allaying concerns that the administration might concede too much to the British. Federalists, suspecting that Clay would indeed be just that inflexible in negotiations, would have blocked his confirmation if they had possessed the votes, but they comforted themselves that the Kentuckian would have to defer to Adams, the former Federalist and loyal protector of New England's interests.[69]

Clay stepped down from the Speakership and resigned from Congress on January 19. As South Carolina War Hawk Langdon Cheves took his place, the House voted 144 to 9 to commend Clay for his service as Speaker, the 9 "composed of those whose approbation . . . Henry Clay never courted, if he desired it."[70] He arranged for Lucretia and the children to return to Ashland, received his instructions from Secretary of State Monroe, and headed for New York to join Russell and set out for Sweden. Clay was confident that everything would be settled in months.[71]

The *John Adams* sailed from New York on February 25 to commence a horrendous journey over persistently mountainous seas lashed by freezing rain. Clay, Russell, and the delegation's secretary, Christopher Hughes, Jr., bore up fairly well in the cramped and malodorous quarters. All were game pranksters, as it turned out, and youthful "Kit" Hughes (he was twenty-eight) was as fond of puns as he was openly excited about the adventure before them. Unfortunately the ship's captain fell ill and became deranged, adding to the nightmares of the seven-week passage that finally deposited the American commissioners and staff at Gothenburg on the west coast of Sweden. For all their trouble, they discovered they were early—or at least everyone else was late.[72]

In Saint Petersburg, John Quincy Adams learned about the peace commission only a couple of weeks earlier and was under the logical impression that Clay and Russell would not leave the United States until early April. Adams was still in Russia but started for Sweden immediately after hearing that the commission was assembling there. Meanwhile, Gallatin and Bayard sat comfortably in London mulling British suggestions that the talks be moved to London or somewhere in the Netherlands. Hearing that Clay and Russell were in Gothenburg, they sent a messenger suggesting the change.[73]

The messenger found Clay alone in Gothenburg. Russell had gone to Stockholm, a journey of more than two hundred miles across the Scandinavian peninsula, to present his credentials as U.S. minister. Gothenburg is bathed by the Gulf Stream, making for more moderate temperatures than one would expect in a place facing the North Sea. Clay filled his days exploring the area and examining the Swedish canal network, just the sort of internal improvement he envisioned for America. At night, local dignitaries hosted elaborate dinner parties for the exotic Kentuckian whose sparkling conversation and ready smile fascinated the men and charmed the women. Clay deserted the rustic inn where he and Russell had lodged after first arriving to move into a more comfortable apartment. The weather was wet, but the people were gracious, and he was happily settled in when Gallatin and Bayard's letter arrived. The suggestion that he and Russell pick up and move to another place for the negotiations exasperated him, and he flatly refused to conduct talks in the enemy's capital, an arrangement that could be interpreted as American capitulation. At best he would reluctantly agree to move negotiations to Belgium, a grudging acceptance of Britain's claim that its proximity would speed communication between London and the British commissioners. The town of Ghent—"a most delightful place, in every respect," Kit Hughes reported—was designated for the honor.[74]

The *John Adams* was still in the harbor, but Clay wanted to see something of Europe. He supposed that negotiations might be quickly concluded and he could be home by midsummer, so this would be his only chance to visit storied foreign places steeped in history. He left word for Russell coming back from Stockholm and Adams coming in from Saint Petersburg that he was leaving them the ship to take to Ghent while he and his servant, Washington grocer Frederick Cana, made their way overland soaking up the countryside. It seemed like a good idea at the time—Clay had developed a love of travel that would endure for the rest of his life—but Gothenburg's relatively mild weather soon gave way to the harsher Nordic climes that tested a traveler's fortitude. Clay saw Copenhagen, Hamburg, and Amsterdam on the way to Ghent, where he finally arrived on June 28, and despite the discomfort of the journey, he never regretted it.

Diplomatic protocol required envoys on ceremonial occasions to wear elaborate attire that included a coat adorned with extensive gold braiding. Clay looked quite smart in what would ever afterward be called his "Ghent coat." He had indeed come a long way from the Bluegrass and his Ashland. He was a lifetime away from the Slashes.[75]

BAYARD, ADAMS, AND Russell were already in Ghent, and Gallatin arrived about a week after Clay. Initially they all stayed at the Hotel des Pays-Bas, but they soon rented a house belonging to the Baron de Lovendeghem on the Rue des Champs. They impatiently waited for their British counterparts. Gallatin had told British foreign secretary Lord Castlereagh that the American delegation was heading directly to Ghent, but the five commissioners and their secretaries waited and waited as days turned into weeks with the British failing to appear. The Americans fumed over all the empty talk about a Belgian location speeding communication with London.[76]

In addition, events in Europe had changed everything to their disadvantage. In early April, the alliance led by Britain defeated Napoleon's army, forced him to abdicate his throne, and sent him into exile on the Mediterranean island of Elba. The British people exulted in the victory, but they darkly regarded upstart Yankees who had seemed willing with their distracting war to thwart Bonaparte's defeat. They wanted the British government to punish Americans with a harsh settlement. British tardiness was possibly a tactic, another sign that they intended to press their newfound advantage for a one-sided peace.[77]

The Americans in Ghent also got on each other's nerves. While still at the Hotel des Pays-Bas, the men dined together at 4:00 P.M. every day. Adams groused in his diary about the late hour. After eating, the men lingered at the table to "drink bad wine and smoke cigars, which neither suits my habits nor my health, and absorbs time which I cannot spare." He told them that he would dine alone at 1:00, a schedule he kept only one day because Clay "expressed some regret that I had withdrawn from their table." It was a magnanimous gesture that actually touched Adams, though he would never have shown it to his companions. When writing to his wife, Louisa, however, Adams was different, revealing that behind the mask of the stern, unsmiling Puritan lived a man eager for approval and longing for friendship. Louisa wrote him that she had heard Henry Clay was "one of the most amiable . . . men in the world," and John Quincy wrote her that what she "had heard of the character and temper of Mr. Clay" was entirely accurate. He assured her that he and his fellow commissioners were getting along splendidly. He continued in that vein throughout his time in Ghent, always insisting to Louisa that he and Mr. Clay were the best of friends—a sad and poignant lie, because contrasting temperaments and evolving circumstances would increasingly put them at each other's throats.[78]

Louisa Adams might have been fooled, but the other members of the commission knew the truth of it. Almost from the start, Clay and Adams could barely stand each other's company. They were vastly different in temperament and background, and their habits were a study in contrasts. Clay had been able to sustain professional relations with disparate and disagreeable men, but he had never been forced to live with them day in and day out, had never been compelled constantly to work with them on touchy tasks, and had never found himself confronting someone so persistently humorless and purse-lipped. Clay was by nature cheerful and optimistic; Adams was reflexively pessimistic and gloomy. Adams was well educated, well read, and well traveled; Clay had little formal education and read only when he had to. Clay never missed a party, reveling into the wee hours playing cards and drinking. Adams regarded parties as a waste of time, thought gambling was squalid and ruinous, and verged on teetotalism. He retired early and rose before dawn to read dense books, write in his diary, and pore over his own paperwork. Clay found documents tedious and turned most of them over to his private secretary, Henry Carroll. Adams openly disapproved of Clay's habits as self-indulgent. Clay openly disdained Adams as insufferable and opinionated. And lurking beneath all these differences were dangerous similarities: both were stubborn, always convinced they were right and irritable when told they weren't.

Clay's lifestyle as well as his attitude frayed Adams's nerves. The Kentuckian's room was just next door to Adams's and was often the scene of card games that ended about the time Adams was rising to read his Bible and answer his mail. Jonathan Russell joined in these late-night revels, and Adams resented Clay and Russell's friendship, sourly noting that Russell always followed Clay's lead when the commissioners hashed out disagreements.[79]

John Quincy Adams was officially the head of the delegation, and as they waited for the British, he insisted on keeping everyone busy with regular meetings. These pointless exercises irked Clay. Boredom made everyone testy, but Clay at least appeared cheerful and confident, a merry attitude that Adams found grating. He would have been surprised to discover that Clay was putting up a brave front to hide his own churning anxiety. Clay frequently wrote to his friend Crawford in Paris and confessed that he was pessimistic about America's chances for an acceptable peace.[80]

The British commissioners finally arrived on the evening of August 6. Admiral John James, 1st Baron Gambier, officially headed the delegation, which included Dr. William Adams, a prominent scholar of maritime law, and Henry

Goulburn, undersecretary for war and the colonies, who at thirty was the youngest of the three and, as it turned out, the most active of their number. Historians have painted these men as nonentities, which is unfair. While not blessed with sparkling talent, they were hardly incompetent. Rather, they were second-tier government officials on Lord Castlereagh's very short Foreign Office leash and burdened with his impossible instructions. Impressment was not negotiable. They were to adjust the northern United States border in Canada's favor, to insist on the establishment of an Indian buffer state in the Northwest, and to announce that the United States declaration of war had terminated New England fishing rights off eastern Canada.[81]

Contention between the commissions began right away. Lord Gambier's opening remarks declared the British desire for peace, and Adams responded with a similar statement, but as Henry Goulburn drily and methodically presented Castlereagh's impossible terms, everything slowly unraveled. His presentation left the Americans stunned and silent. Almost every word Goulburn had uttered was completely unacceptable to the United States. After a pause, Bayard broke the silence. He asked what in the world the British meant by an Indian preserve as some sort of buffer state. Affecting an irritating air of self-importance, Goulburn refused to elaborate, and Clay promptly interjected that clarification was completely unnecessary because there was not going to be any Indian buffer state. The American commissioners rose from their seats. They would send a response soon, they said.[82]

Over the next two days, it became clear why Goulburn had been so defensive when Bayard queried him in the first meeting: the British commissioners were not authorized to stray a particle from their instructions, even to the extent of explaining them. Now it appeared that everything was at an impasse, and they awkwardly asked for a delay in the talks. Messengers traveled across the English Channel to the Foreign Office and back, and Gambier finally announced that discussions could resume on August 19.

The impossible instructions had gotten worse. The Indian buffer was not negotiable, period. The British demanded complete military control of the Great Lakes including all shorelines, the continued right to navigate the Mississippi River, and the cession of territory in Maine to facilitate communication between Nova Scotia and Quebec. Britain also wanted to retain possession of American coastal islands they had seized during the war, particularly Moose Island in Passamaquoddy Bay. Capping this incredible list of demands was a warning—delivered with enough menace to make it a threat—that the Americans should not keep London hanging while awaiting instructions from Washington. After a few weeks, the terms might not be so generous. The dazed Americans adjourned to prepare a written response.[83]

Adams believed that as the commission's chief he should be the primary author of any communications to the British, and he drafted a response for his colleagues to review, a sequence that repeatedly occurred throughout the negotiations. Yet the other Americans soon discovered that Adams really wanted only praise for his lofty prose, not recommendations for revisions, and certainly not any criticisms. He sulked and brooded when his drafts came back marked up, with Clay's corrections usually the most pointed and tactlessly blunt. He laughed at Adams's pompous style and pretentious appeals to Providence. He sarcastically disparaged the New Englander's figurative allusions as showy and affected. Gallatin's role as peacekeeper between these antagonistic peacemakers grew. He often interceded to incorporate everyone's views into final drafts and gradually emerged as the delegation's leader despite Adams's official designation as its chief.[84]

Revised instructions from Secretary of State Monroe arrived. These new orders gave the American commissioners more latitude, especially permission to drop objections to impressment, which the end of the European war had made an irrelevant issue. Clay was emboldened by the arrival of these new directives to call what he suspected was Britain's bluff about ramping up its demands. At a dinner party he curtly told Henry Goulburn that if Americans needed instructions from home, they would very well take the time to get them. Warming to this delicious chance to speak plainly, he told Goulburn that British demands were completely unreasonable. London might as well demand that the United States cede New York or Boston. If young Goulburn thought Clay was talking out of school, a note from the American commissioners soon showed otherwise. They rejected the Indian buffer state and British military control of the lakes.[85]

Clay persisted in his belief that the British demands were too incredible not to be an absurd, audacious bluff. Yet even he had to admit that if it was all just a game, Gambier and company were playing it very seriously. On September 5, their sixteen-page manifesto denounced American expansionism, insisted on the Indian buffer, and demanded that the United States take responsibility should the talks collapse. The delegation studied this document in Adams's room. Clay snapped that such impertinence deserved only the briefest response, no more than a half page at most, but Gallatin quietly remarked that duty required an observance of proper procedure. The commissioners began framing an answer, but Clay still fumed and resolved on his own to call this latest British bluff: he asked Goulburn to look into securing him a passport.[86]

The talks were clearly stalled. Social events occasionally brought everyone together, and sporadic, vaguely insulting notes passed between the commissions, but as October passed, no official meetings took place. The Americans sent discouraging reports home about excessive British demands, and the Madison administration released them to the press. Congress, boiling with anger, distributed additional copies as pamphlets. While Americans excoriated the British, shellacking them in a war of words, the British army, no longer preoccupied with Bonaparte and able to turn its full attention to North America, laid plans to shellac the Yankee upstarts and win the war. Very bad news from America was soon on its way to Ghent.[87]

JUST AS GAMBIER was showing a little flexibility about the Indian buffer state and control of the Great Lakes, the American commissioners received news in early October that shattered their hopes for a favorable peace. With talks mired, Clay and Kit Hughes were touring Brussels when word arrived that the British had captured and burned Washington, D.C., on August 24. Insufferable Henry Goulburn wanted Clay to hear about his country's disastrous misfortune as soon as possible. Pretending to be thoughtful by supplying Clay with the latest newspapers, he made sure to include those with news about Washington. Clay was inconsolable over the capital's destruction and somberly contemplated the consequences for the negotiations. When he learned that the British were working on a *projet* (a draft treaty), he insisted on writing the response.[88]

On October 8, the British delivered not a draft treaty but a note that clearly reflected the changed situation. While it softened the demand for an Indian buffer state, it heavily peppered that bit of sugar with insults and other imperious requirements, such as a directive that the United States make peace with the Indians and restore all land they had possessed in 1811. For good measure, the British insinuated that the Louisiana Purchase had been an illegitimate transaction, a gratuitous affront apparently thrown in to keep Goulburn in practice. As a quaint American idiom would have described him, Clay was loaded for bear. He tolerated little editorial counsel from his colleagues as he furiously drafted the response. He defended American territorial expansion, denied an American plan to seize Canada, and snarled that even British insults would not bait him into mentioning (which he proceeded to do) British barbarism and the atrocities of their Indian allies on the American frontier. The inclusion of Indians in a treaty would be unprecedented, Clay said, but he allowed that such an article might be acceptable since Indian conflicts were likely to end in any case when Great Britain and the United States stopped fighting.

Despite the slight British movement on the Indian buffer, the harsh tone of both notes indicated another impasse. In addition, the Canadian border and the question of the fisheries remained unresolved. The British made clear they would not budge on the fisheries. Then on October 21, they proposed *uti possidetis* for the territorial questions, meaning that each would retain the territory they possessed at the time of a treaty signing.[89] The Americans exploded. The October 21 note drove everyone, including Adams, to Clay's angry side. *Uti possidetis* was completely unacceptable! And where, pray tell, was the promised *projet*? The British suggested that the Americans write a *projet* of their own, and in fact Clay and his colleagues were already at work on such a document; but it was not going well.[90]

They quarreled over minor as well as significant questions. A trifling matter concerned how to send a message to Czar Alexander I at the Congress of Vienna. As the great powers were meeting in Austria to arrange post-Napoleonic Europe, Americans in Ghent hoped the czar could persuade the British to soften their terms. When Adams asked how he should send the message, Clay laughed that Adams should fuss over something so trivial. Clay said that dispatching William Shaler might be a logical course since Shaler was the mission's official messenger. Gallatin, however, did not think Shaler's manners were refined enough for an audience with the czar. Adams then proposed to send the letter in the regular mail. Clay erupted in disbelief. The mail! Adams was going to trust a letter to the Czar of all the Russias to the mail! His voiced dripped with sarcasm as he slowly asked if the head of the delegation could not make a simple decision about a messenger. Adams sulked for the remainder of the meeting.[91]

Gallatin worked away on the American *projet,* doing his best to mediate between Adams and Clay, trying his best to balance their demands that their respective regions receive special consideration. Having quashed the Indian buffer state, Clay did not want the British to have unrestricted access to the Mississippi River. The concession, he said, endangered the security of the western United States. Adams insisted that New England retain its fishing rights off the Canadian coast and wanted the islands in Passamaquoddy Bay returned. Gallatin's solution was to let everything remain in place from the Treaty of 1783 and use this new agreement to reconfirm existing arrangements. That meant New England could retain fishing rights, and the British could continue to use the Mississippi. Clay would not have it: How could anyone, he roared, argue that securing the mighty Mississippi River was equal to catching and drying codfish? Gallatin, Bayard, and Adams supported the trade-off, but Clay made clear he would sign neither a note nor a treaty that contained such provisions. The other commissioners paused and considered the need for a united front. Finally Gallatin removed all mention of fish and rivers from the *projet* and instead called for a peace on the basis of the status quo ante bellum, the return of everything to its condition before the war.[92]

Amazingly, circumstances made this particular tactic the most workable, for the British government was already considering a conciliatory stance. The Congress of Vienna stumbled toward dissolution as old prejudices and animosities resurfaced in the absence of the unifying enemy, Napoleon. Disputes over Poland and Saxony were only the latest evidence that Europe was a gaggle of antagonisms barely restrained. And then there was the military situation in America, which had seemed so promising for the British in the early fall but had quickly turned dismal with failures at Baltimore and Plattsburgh. (Clay sent Goulburn the newspapers.) In the wake of these setbacks, the Duke of Wellington, hero of the European war and commander of allied forces occupying France, all but refused to take command in America and advised his government to make peace with the United States. That was the evolving situation as the British commissioners read through the American draft treaty they had received on November 10.[93]

With new instructions from London that addressed the changed circumstances, the British commissioners returned the American *projet* with only marginal notes rather than a counterproposal. With the exception of the Maine islands, they accepted the status quo ante bellum. They rejected the articles on impressment and British confiscations and insisted on an article granting British navigation of the Mississippi. These responses were not perfect, but they were obvious signs of a changed attitude. Yet the American meeting on November 28 to discuss the British remarks was a series of "angry disputes" in which "Clay lost his temper," Adams noted, adding, "as he generally does whenever this right of the British to navigate the Mississippi is discussed." Gallatin calmly pointed out that sacrificing the fisheries would encourage New England Federalists already flirting with disunion. Clay bitterly responded he would not appease disloyal Americans in New England at the expense of patriots in the West.[94]

There matters stood when the Americans invited the British commissioners to meet on December 1, the first official gathering of the delegations since August. The course of this meeting soon reminded them why they had stopped holding them. It was long and unproductive. Clay, however, brought to this discussion his highly developed sense of men at games of chance, and he gradually discerned in the British negotiators what gamblers call a "tell," a sign that reveals otherwise hidden intent and divulges otherwise disguised meanings. The tell in this case was the few British concessions, a sign that they wanted a treaty more than they were letting on. Convinced of this, he resisted his colleagues when they continued to push him to give in on Mississippi navigation rights. He told them he would fight the war for three more years rather than yield, but most of all he stated his conviction that the British "had been playing *brag* with us throughout the entire negotiation." Clay "stalked to and fro across the chamber" and eventually won over his reluctant companions "by outbragging" them. Now that he knew the tell, it was time to play brag with the British. He did. They blinked.

On December 22, the Americans received a message essentially agreeing to a treaty that deferred the Canadian border to arbitration after the war, did not mention the fisheries or the Mississippi River, and abandoned *uti possidetis* for the principle of status quo ante bellum. Everyone assembled on Christmas Eve 1814 at the quarters of the British commission to sign multiple copies of the final document and send them on to London and Washington. The eight diplomats then sat down together for Christmas dinner, a celebration of the Prince of Peace, and raised glasses in civil if not altogether cordial regard. Clay enjoyed himself. He had gambled. And as Lucretia had said, he 'most always won.[95]

ALTHOUGH CLAY WAS not completely pleased with the treaty, he knew it was the best agreement under the circumstances. True, it did not address a single issue pertinent to neutral trade or sailors' rights, but at least Americans had lost "no territory," and "I think no honor." Gallatin reminded everyone that treaties were rarely popular, and Clay took comfort that he had done his best to protect the interests of both his country and his region by blocking needless concessions. As soon as spring promised a more pleasant crossing, he intended to go home to his family and return to Congress. While waiting for spring, he planned a holiday to see a bit of Europe, especially Paris.[96]

It was probably unavoidable that Clay's buoyant mood would have to weather one last fight before the American commissioners left Ghent. For weeks, annoying British antics had accomplished the impossible. They had not only united the Americans but had also constrained them to get along for long spells that all but banished hard words. Even Adams joined the repartee. "Clay remarked that Mr. Goulburn was a man of much *irritation*." Adams responded, "*irritability* . . . is the word Mr. Clay, irritability; and then fixing him with an earnest look, and the tone of voice between seriousness and jest, I added 'like somebody else that I know.' Clay laughed, and said 'Aye, that we do; all know him, and none better than yourself.'" Adams had at last realized that the friction between him and Clay stemmed from their having "the same dogmatical, overbearing manner, the same harshness of look and expression, and the same forgetfulness of the courtesies of society."[97]

Yet at the end of December the Americans fell to arguing about what should be done with the delegation's official papers. Clay wanted them sent to the State Department and persuaded Bayard and Russell to agree with him. Adams believed that the head of the delegation—meaning himself—should keep the papers. He accused Clay of forming a cabal against him. Clay lost his temper and shouted, "You *dare* not, you *cannot,* you SHALL not insinuate that there has been a cabal."[98] It was a silly, pointless argument: Clay calmed down, and Adams won the point. All said their farewells in more or less good humor, and Clay with Bayard left for Paris on January 7, 1815. When Adams later came to Paris, he and Clay went on sightseeing outings.

Clay enjoyed Paris. He had long visits with his friend William Crawford, went to plays, danced at balls, and charmed tablemates at sumptuous dinners. At a soiree in her home, the prominent writer and socialite Madame de Staël asked Clay if he knew that the British had considered sending the Duke of Wellington to fight in America. Clay said it would have been an honor to defeat Napoleon's conqueror, a remark she later repeated to Wellington himself. The general was reported to have said it would have been a great achievement to defeat the brave American people. Upon the backs of such backhanded compliments the world moved on.[99]

Though terribly homesick, Clay traveled to England to assist Albert Gallatin in negotiating a commercial treaty with the British. He delayed his trip to London as long as he could, dreading the prospect of British gloating over their military prowess and deriding American martial incompetence. But then he heard about New Orleans. On January 8, 1815, Andrew Jackson's motley forces of cobbled-together militias and a few regulars had stood on the Rodriguez Canal south of the Crescent City. The seasoned British veterans of the European wars had scornfully called Jackson's men "dirty shirts" before marching resolutely toward a line they knew would break, just as the militia had broken outside Washington. But as the British came across the frozen Chalmette Plain that January morning, the American line did not break. Instead, it hurled cannon shot and musket balls into the advancing Redcoats, winnowing their ranks like a scythe, cutting down their officers and killing their commanding general. In less than a half hour, every contemptible instance of American military failure was avenged, and in Andrew Jackson Americans had a new hero. He became for them the man who won the war that many had thought was lost.

Clay crossed the channel to England with his head high on the news of this heady victory. He held slight hope that the British would agree to a satisfactory commercial treaty, though, and he indulged his reflexive dislike of them. Shortly after arriving he heard that Napoleon had slipped off Elba to return to France and again proclaim himself emperor. Clay cheered, "Wonderful age! wonderful man! wonderful nation!"[100]

Napoleon's return distracted the British and left them little interested in opening commercial negotiations. Clay yearned all the more for home and began searching for an early passage. He attended meetings with British officials, but he was bored and showed it. Gallatin and Adams, who arrived in May as the new American minister to Great Britain, conducted most of the negotiations. In June, after Napoleon's final defeat at Waterloo, Britain suddenly became serious about commercial arrangements, and Clay had no choice but to see the matter through, but not for a minute longer than was necessary. The day after a commercial treaty was signed on July 3, he left for Liverpool to book passage home, envying Crawford and Bayard, who had left for the United States from France two weeks earlier. Bayard had been ill for months, a cause for concern.[101]

Gallatin was not long in joining Clay in Liverpool, and they finally departed aboard the *Lorenzo* on July 23 for an uneventful voyage that ended in New York City on September 1, where sad news awaited them. Bayard was dead. Clay had grown fond of him during their months at Ghent and the jaunt to Paris. News that he had died soon after arriving back in the United States made for a somber homecoming.

And yet there were obligatory celebrations to attend. Prominent New York Republicans and Federalists came out on September 5 for a dinner honoring Clay and Gallatin at Tammany Hall. A multitude of tributes toasted the nation, Clay, Gallatin, and the country's military heroes. Clay's turn came. He rose from his seat, lifted his glass, and shouted, "The eighth of January 1815!" The crowd erupted into lusty cheers.[102]

Clay's toast was a small and expected gesture, no doubt sincere at the time, when the world so long at war was finally at peace and young America had stood its ground against powerful Britain, never more effectively than outside New Orleans behind a stern-faced Tennessean with cold blue eyes and the frontier nickname "Old Hickory," the man, like the wood, who did not bend, did not break. Clay's toast on that evening would be lost in the welter of events and numerous milestones that awaited both him and Andrew Jackson. Clay had returned from Belgium brimming with ambition after ending the war. Jackson, also brimming with ambition, had ended that war with a stunning triumph. On September 5, 1815, Henry Clay lifted his glass to the Hero of New Orleans and no doubt meant it, for the last time.

CHAPTER FIVE

Uncompromising Compromiser

Lucretia had little news from Clay as he traveled abroad. During this time, though, she penned the only letter to her husband that survives. Writing shortly after Clay left Washington, she told him the children missed him and included a brief account of affairs in Washington. She waited for the better traveling conditions of spring before making the long journey home with the children.[1] Back at Ashland, she took Theodore and Thomas out of their boarding school and searched for a tutor for them as well as for Susan, Anne, and little Lucretia. Years earlier, an English housekeeper, Sarah Hall, had joined the family and was a comforting presence at Ashland during these months, as she would be for decades through good times and bad. Even after becoming adults, the children always called her "Nanny" Hall[2]; she remained with the family for more than fifty years.

In May 1814, Lucretia hired Amos Kendall, a young man from Massachusetts, to teach the older children. Kendall had come to Kentucky via Washington, where Clay's friend Senator Jesse Bledsoe had hired him to tutor the Bledsoe children, an arrangement that fell through after Kendall arrived in Lexington. Clay's younger half brother, John Watkins, told Kendall about the Clay children at Ashland, and Lucretia soon hired him at $300 a year plus room and board. Kendall earned every penny, for Thomas and Theodore were rambunctious. But other incentives encouraged him to stay: Kendall aimed to become a lawyer, and Lucretia generously allowed him to use her husband's library.[3]

The two became warm friends. Acting the part of Pygmalion, Lucretia set about softening the sharp edges of Kendall's Yankee manners and easing him into Bluegrass society. She taught him to bow, to enter a room with confidence, and to engage in harmless flirtations, but the social poise that came so easily to her Henry remained elusive for Kendall. He was sincerely grateful for her kindness, though, and came to hold Lucretia Clay in considerable esteem. Even so, he most wanted an introduction to her husband for the doors Clay's influence could open—even more reason to stay at Ashland than Clay's books.[4]

Kendall must have wondered whether it was worth dealing with Theodore and Thomas. Mothers kept delicate daughters under close supervision, and Kendall found the "three fine little girls" delightful. But farm life for boys in the early nineteenth century was the stuff of *Tom Sawyer.* Theodore and Thomas Clay had attended schools where rods were seldom spared, but at Ashland they suffered little, if any, discipline. Kendall tried to persuade Lucretia to take a stronger hand, but she was an indulgent mother by temperament as well as by the customs of the time. Theodore was twelve and Thomas eleven when Kendall took charge of them, or rather they took charge of him. Thomas was prone to abusive tantrums—he once called Kendall a "damned Yankee rascal"—and Theodore could explode into frightening rages. Kendall had to manhandle the boy out of Ashland's kitchen building one afternoon when Theodore threatened a slave with a knife, an ominous sign of things to come.[5]

Kendall's persistence gradually improved the boys at their studies and in their attitude, but he remained an odd, friendless fellow despite Lucretia's guidance. Churning ambition drove Amos Kendall, and others apparently sensed in him what Lucretia could not see: a man very much on the make and therefore not altogether trustworthy. Clay had not yet returned from Europe to give him his references when Kendall became impatient to start his career. In the spring of 1815, he left Ashland for Georgetown, Kentucky, to open a law office and edit a newspaper. That June, he returned to Lexington for court day and fell seriously ill with a "violent bilious fever." Nobody cared enough to tend to him as he writhed sweating in his boardinghouse bed, and he might have died had Lucretia not heard about his condition. She had him rushed to Ashland and for the next month gave him "all the attention which kindness and generosity could bestow." Nursed back to health, Kendall returned to Georgetown just before Clay arrived in Lexington, and a year would pass before they would meet, giving Kendall the chance to ask for favors. Nobody, however, would ever match the kindness already shown Amos Kendall by the quiet, compassionate mistress of Ashland, who had taught him to bow and had saved his life.[6]

FROM NEW YORK, Clay hurried to Lexington and Lucretia by way of Washington, D.C. Seeing the capital's charred buildings was a sobering reminder of the British attack one year before. Clay had been reelected to the House of Representatives by loyal constituents anticipating his return and would be back in Washington soon enough, so he paused only long enough to receive the official proclamation of the city's gratitude and left before a grand celebration in his honor.

After almost two years' absence, he found Lexington much changed with new industries, a growing population, and refinements previously unknown to the region.[7] The town was part of a spectacular economic surge that was especially evident in the West. Cheap land encouraged westward settlement and beckoned European immigrants who swelled a naturally increasing population. The war had ended Indian threats in the Northwest and the South, new roads sped migration into the Ohio Valley, and steamboats began churning upstream on western rivers.

The Clay children had grown considerably. Eliza had been a babe in arms but was now a toddling chatterbox. Henry Jr. had been less than three years old when his father left the country. Now four and a half, he was clever and quick. Much to Clay's surprise, the older boys could now recite Greek, thanks to Kendall.[8]

Clay planned to make his family preeminent in the Bluegrass, with Ashland a showplace using plans supplied by Benjamin Latrobe to add flanking wings to the house. Clay also began importing livestock. He introduced Hereford cattle from England to improve the region's bloodlines.[9] He continued to acquire interests in racehorses, bought expensive merino sheep, and brought jackasses from Europe to breed mules.

Lexington enthusiastically greeted its returning hero. His friends threw him a lavish dinner at Postlethwaite's Tavern, and the city trustees proclaimed their gratitude. When a few complaints surfaced that his election to Congress was illegitimate because he had been in a diplomatic post when it occurred, a special canvass in October yielded another certain victory because nobody saw any use in running against him. People chuckled how Europe must have agreed with Clay because he had finally "gained some flesh" eating rich foreign dishes.[10]

Clay turned over the management of Ashland to his half brother John Watkins, and with Lucretia started for Washington, arriving in early December 1815. When Congress convened on December 4, the House promptly elected him Speaker.[11] Secretary of State James Monroe had conveyed Madison's offer to appoint him minister to Russia, but Clay declined. Clay did not want to serve abroad again. In addition to being politically ambitious, he intended to make the country strong enough to prevent the prospect of having its shores again invaded, its towns terrorized, its capital torched. Many believed that the European peace was but a truce, and Clay meant to prepare the nation for the next war, a job he could accomplish only in Washington, not by smiling at the czar in Saint Petersburg.[12]

President Madison's annual message delighted Clay, for the president's views about the country's economic future precisely matched his own. Madison wanted to keep a relatively large standing army of about ten thousand men, maintain an adequate navy, enhance coastal defenses, and improve the nation's rivers, harbors, and roads. He wanted infant American industry protected from foreign competition and the currency stabilized. As was the president's custom, he drew a broad picture and left the details to the legislature.[13]

Madison benefited from surging nationalism. The United States had fought the world's most powerful empire and emerged relatively unscathed, with its honor (if not all its public buildings) intact. Offsetting the humiliation of seeing Redcoats in Washington, American military victories at Baltimore, Plattsburgh, and most gloriously at New Orleans further convinced Americans that they were no longer untried in a formerly disrespectful community of nations. National pride encouraged national unity and made for considerable political harmony, especially in light of the Federalist Party's decline. Federalist dissent from the war had climaxed at a convention in Hartford, Connecticut, in the closing days of the conflict. There, disgruntled New England Federalists had aired grievances with enough vigor to create the impression of disloyalty. With the Federalists in disarray, it looked like smooth sailing for Speaker Clay as he piloted the president's program through the House.

Yet there were shoals. Republicans clearly dominated Congress, but not all of them found Madison's plans appealing. John Randolph exemplified those wary about large armies, naval construction, and higher taxes. And Republicans more levelheaded than Randolph thought that these matters had been sensible obligations in war but were unreasonable burdens in peace. Those who again embraced small government, low taxes, and a reliance on state militias saw little difference between Madison's proposals and those of arch-Federalist Alexander Hamilton in the 1790s. In that regard, the decline of the Federalists became a problem. William Crawford perceptively observed that the waning of their political opponents could not "fail to relax the bonds by which the Republican party has been hitherto kept together."[14] Beneath the seeming placidity of what would be dubbed the Era of Good Feelings ran currents of conflict that eventually floated the Second American Party System.

Clay noticed the emerging factionalism in his own ranks. He relied on the old War Hawk cadre of the Twelfth and Thirteenth Congresses, men such as John C. Calhoun, William Lowndes, and Peter Porter. Randolph often squawked, but Clay preserved his reputation for fairness in handing out committee appointments and presiding over floor debates. For especially important issues, he carefully chose committee members and their chairmen to yield favorable bills presented to the entire House, but otherwise he appointed broadly to satisfy diverse regional and political interests. Charming and mixing "very much with the members," he was always "affable and engaging in his manners."[15] He needed to be. Pushing through Madison's program required more than parliamentary skill, and only two weeks into the session he joked that he was already "getting rather tired of politics."[16]

The president's nationalist proposals marked a significant revolution in the government's direction, for they were actually the essence of old Federalism. Clay's vision for the country was even more revolutionary. He thought the government was justified in promoting economic prosperity because affluence was essential to national security. A protective tariff to make recently established American industries competitive against cheap foreign imports was key. Regarding the currency and credit, the president had left unspoken how to achieve improvement, but the financial strains of the war had convinced Clay that a national bank was necessary to stabilize the country's money supply and regulate its credit. The war had also revealed the lamentable shortcomings of the country's primitive roads, a flaw that everyone who traveled realized was an impediment to commerce in times of peace, a grave deficiency when at war.

Clay's trusted lieutenants in the House were prepared to help him address these problems. William Lowndes and John C. Calhoun, two South Carolinians who had proven their nationalism before and during the war, had already taken the lead before Clay's arrival to call for a tariff and a bank. To help him realize those goals, Clay appointed Lowndes to head the House Ways and Means Committee considering a protective tariff and made Calhoun the chairman of a select committee on the currency question that would recommend a new national bank.[17]

As these moves progressed, Clay fought those who believed the expansion of federal power would diminish individual liberty and come at the expense of the states.[18] As before, John Randolph emphatically pointed out the dangers of a larger, more powerful federal government. Clay's plan, he bellowed, "*out-Hamiltons* Alexander Hamilton." And as before, he was formidable if often rambling. People could not help but listen to his "shrill, sharp, effeminate voice." He could speak for hours at a time as ideas flew from his mouth as though tumbling from a jumble in his head. Despite Randolph's "astonishing powers of mind," most congressmen consequently viewed him as "a very useless member."[19]

Yet he was an extremely vocal one, railing against the young Republicans' nationalist program. He expressed astonishment that James Madison encouraged it, an observation that gradually alarmed other Republicans as well. This strangely Federalist agenda had them squinting suspiciously as the young men of their party assured them that everything under consideration was constitutional, complete with the imprimatur of "the Father of the U.S. Constitution" himself, James Madison.[20] Whipped to action by Clay's leadership, the Fourteenth Congress moved rapidly through a remarkable assortment of legislation in almost record time, passing bills to maintain an adequate military and improve roads and lighthouses before taking up Madison's two most controversial requests—stabilizing the currency and establishing a protective tariff.[21]

American markets were a rich target for the British after the war. Established British manufacturers could operate at lower costs than their embryonic American counterparts and consequently price goods well below American competitors. Clay and his allies argued that given time to acquire technology and establish a domestic factory system, American manufacturers would be able to compete with any country in the world. A protective tariff—an import tax to raise the price of foreign goods—would make American industry profitable and provide incentives for the creation of a larger, more self-sufficient manufacturing capability. Disregarding the objections of naysayers like John Randolph, most congressmen finally agreed to support a protective tariff when assured it would be temporary. Madison signed into law the country's first import tax designed to regulate trade as well as raise revenue.[22]

Less than a half century earlier, Americans had fought a war with Britain over just such regulatory and revenue policies, but striding away from the American Revolution's purpose paled in comparison to the difficulties of the next part of Clay's project. In consultation with Treasury secretary Alexander J. Dallas, Calhoun's select committee drafted a bill to establish a new Bank of the United States. Built in the image of its predecessor, the planned bank was to be capitalized at $35 million and overseen by a president and twenty-five directors, five of whom the president of the United States would select. Because it would serve as the repository for all public funds and conduct all government transactions, it would be the largest bank in the country, controlling the nation's credit and as well as stabilizing its currency by accepting only sound banknotes. The notes issued by the Bank would be the soundest of all, and its ability to establish branches in the various states ensured that its notes would have the widest circulation.[23]

Clay's support of the measure forced him into a most awkward position. He was pushing for the passage of legislation he had vehemently opposed just five years earlier. His eloquent hostility to a national bank at that time had featured his skewering of the hapless Virginian William Branch Giles, a memorable Clay performance that made his current support of a bank bill not just dubious but embarrassing. On March 9, Clay addressed the House as the Committee of the Whole to explain himself.

The speech of that day does not survive, but a similar oration to his constituents suggests the gist of what Clay told Congress. His speech to the House was a long one, lasting almost four hours and suggesting how uncomfortable his new position made him. In his later speech, he recalled that in 1811 the Kentucky legislature had told him to oppose the Bank. He now said he believed Kentucky wanted a national bank but one that would not abuse its influence by meddling in politics. In 1811, Clay said, he had thought Congress did not have the constitutional authority to create corporations unless it justified invoking the "necessary and proper" clause. Now, in 1816, he argued that the abysmal state of the economy made the Bank a necessary and proper remedy. He candidly admitted that "the Constitution, it is true, never changes," but "fallible persons" could learn from experience.[24]

Clay's most effective plea stemmed from his description of the country's ineffective banking system and the unhealthy fluctuations in the value of paper money. In the end, congressional majorities were persuaded to adopt the Second Bank of the United States (known as the BUS to distinguish it from its predecessor), although the vote in the House was close at 80 to 71. President Madison signed the bill into law, and the Bank began operations on January 1, 1817, with its headquarters in Philadelphia. Its supporters' high hopes of a better managed economy, however, were soon dashed, for the Bank was badly managed in its opening years and did little to control a bloated credit bubble that finally burst in 1819. Many would blame the BUS for the economic panic and serious depression that followed. They would become the foundation of a new political movement dedicated to thwarting Henry Clay's vision for America.

SECRETARY OF STATE James Monroe saw himself as Madison's heir apparent to the presidency, but opposition mounted within the party both to his nomination and the traditional method of bestowing it. Many, including Clay, criticized the congressional caucus system of choosing a presidential nominee, and a sizable faction contemplated nominating Secretary of War William Crawford because he seemed superior to Monroe in both intellect and talent, having "risen entirely by merit."[25] Clay liked both men, and because he did not want to be in the position of supporting one over the other, his problem seemed solved when Crawford withdrew.

As the caucus opened, Clay offered a resolution declaring that it was "inexpedient to nominate candidates," but he was promptly voted down. Possibly Clay was quietly acting on Monroe's behalf, responding to rumors that Crawford's supporters intended to ignore his demurral and nominate him anyway, a possibility that Monroe's backers feared might give Crawford the prize. They wanted to delay the nomination in order to obtain an explicit statement of withdrawal from him.[26] Some even thought Clay supported Crawford, but he voted for Monroe, and the Virginian eked out a 65 to 54 victory. Clay immediately proposed that Monroe and his running mate, New York's Daniel D. Tompkins, be submitted to the people.[27] It had been a close run within his own party, but Monroe was on track to score an overwhelming victory against the hobbled Federalists in the fall, and as the election neared, they were so lackadaisical in their support for their candidate, Rufus King, that the question was only how resounding Monroe's victory would be.

The members of the Fourteenth Congress would not be so fortunate. As they neared the end of their session, they committed a political blunder so colossal that it would cost about two-thirds of them their seats. It began harmlessly enough. In February 1816, Clay's fellow Kentuckian Richard M. Johnson casually remarked that representatives' pay of $6 a day made for longer sessions because it encouraged members to delay adjournment in order to collect the extra money. It was an interesting observation about a practical problem, and Clay appointed Johnson as chair of a select committee to consider a solution. That committee recommended a bill that was officially named the Compensation Act but would infamously become known as "the Salary Grab."[28]

The bill established a flat $1,500 salary for congressmen to replace the $6 per diem, a substantial raise of about $600 per year. Clay stood to gain even more from the change. As Speaker, he drew $12 a day, and under the new arrangement, his salary would increase to $3,000 per year. Most saw nothing wrong with this, because $6 a day could not cover even their most basic expenses. Indeed, it amounted to less than some government clerks earned, which upon reflection seemed hardly proper for the men who managed the affairs of the republic. The paltry per diem was unintentionally undemocratic as well. Clay told the House that the current level of compensation meant that only men of independent means could afford to serve in Congress, making it a body of wealthy elites. A wealthy South Carolina planter who opposed the bill drew Clay's wrath: How dare he block a measure that would provide entrée to congressional service for the ordinary working man? After a round of such self-congratulation for enduring the financial sacrifices of public service for so long, they sent the bill to Madison's desk, and he signed it.[29]

The remarkable insularity of Washington's political class has seldom been so vividly displayed. Blind to the consequences of giving Congress a salary larger than that of almost every voter in the country, they had compounded their seeming avarice with blatant self-interest by awarding themselves this princely sum rather than applying it only to future Congresses. Voters throughout the country exploded and then simmered, counting the hours to election days when they could punish these brigands at the polls. The two-thirds who were not returned for the Fifteenth Congress were either defeated or prudently retired.

When Lexington heard that Clay had voted for the creation of the BUS and the Compensation Act, attorney and state legislator Thomas Barr announced his candidacy for Clay's seat. Barr, however, stepped aside when a meeting of twenty-five militiamen at John Higbee's Mill put forward former United States senator John Pope. Clay tried to discredit Pope's candidacy as the product of an undemocratic and vaguely illegitimate process, but it was soon apparent that he had a stiff fight on his hands.[30] Like Clay, Pope had come to Lexington from Virginia while a young man, a noticeable character owing in part to a physical oddity, having lost an arm in a youthful accident. He considered himself a loyal Republican, but in the Senate he had occasionally shown an exasperating independence from both party and constituents. Unlike Clay, Pope had ignored the legislature's instructions and voted to renew the First Bank of the United States, and he had been the only Kentuckian to vote against declaring war on Great Britain in 1812. Not everyone liked Pope, but precisely because he did not pander for popularity, he was highly respected. Clay's recent votes made Pope's principles even more palpable. When Clay asked an Irish immigrant why he planned to vote for Pope, the man explained in a thick brogue that at least Pope had only one hand with which to raid the Treasury.[31]

Clay defended himself on the stump as best he could, but many thought his change of heart about the Bank bewildering and his vote for his own pay raise indefensible. One anonymous critic claimed to have admired Clay until he put his "foot upon our necks." Clay was a great man only in the mold of "Caesar, Marius, Cromwell; and woe to Rome and England that they were!"[32] Other critics attacked him for taking money from the poor, even using doggerel to mock Clay's greed:

> O! Wont to hear
> What roaring cheer
> Was spent by Johnny Congress O!
> And how so gay
> They doubled their pay
> And doubled the people's taxes O!
> There was Clay in the Chair
> With his flax-coloured hair,

A-signing tax bills cheerily O!
And smiled as the rabble
So lowly did gabble
And the Salary bill was carried O![33]

Finally aware that explanatory orations would not win the day, Clay doubled his efforts. He enlisted family to campaign for him. Porter returned from Louisiana and vouched for his older brother's character. Clay debated Pope at Higbee's on July 31 and traveled the district to kiss babies and pump every voter's hand he could reach. His supporters countered attacks in the press and tarred Pope as a Federalist, but only when Clay finally admitted that he had been terribly wrong about the salary grab, promised to secure its repeal, and begged the voters' forgiveness did they grudgingly return to his camp. He won by a close vote of 2,493 to 1,837 and would later chuckle to his friend Caesar Rodney that his "Constituents had the grace to pardon me."[34]

Before the Clays left for Washington and the last session of the Fourteenth Congress, he made plans to send Theodore and Thomas to a New York boarding school where they would spend the fall and winter terms before rejoining their parents in the capital in February, "much improved." He would place their oldest girl, twelve-year-old Susan, at Mrs. Vail's girls' boarding school in Baltimore.[35] He hired tradesmen to work on Ashland's two wings and began acquiring various plants and fruit trees for the grounds. Lucretia was in the final days of her ninth pregnancy and shortly before they left for Washington presented the family with another daughter, whom they named Laura.[36]

IN LATE AUGUST, Clay received an offer from President Madison to become Secretary of War. Clay's reasons for declining were obvious. As Speaker of the House, he wielded more power and enjoyed greater prominence than he would in the cabinet. In addition, he had been reelected after a hard-fought contest by making promises that he could not keep if he headed off to the War Department. But most of all, Clay had his eye on a bigger prize. With everyone certain of Monroe's election, Clay wanted to be the new administration's secretary of state. Monroe was expected to leave Madison's cabinet intact, but by becoming president he would create a vacancy at State, the most senior and important cabinet post, which had also become a springboard to the presidency. Clay believed his work as Speaker for Madison during the war and his service at Ghent had earned him that honor. He was so confident that the post would be his that he rented a house for his family rather than taking rooms at a boardinghouse.[37]

Clay did not realize, though, that beneath Madison's proffer was an elaborate plan to form a ready-made cabinet for the Monroe administration, a plan that Madison had gone to a fair amount of trouble to make happen. James Monroe had remained at State, but a fair amount of shuffling had occurred in other departments. When Secretary of the Treasury Alexander J. Dallas resigned, the president persuaded William H. Crawford to move from the War Department to Treasury to make way for Clay. Crawford did not want to do this, but he reluctantly agreed with the understanding that Clay would succeed him. When Clay declined the post, Crawford accordingly expected to remain in it, but Madison still moved him to Treasury and offered the War Department to William Lowndes. When Lowndes refused it, Madison left it to Monroe to fill. Crawford felt he had been ill used.[38]

Ultimately Clay would feel that way too. These maneuvers were veiled at the time, but in retrospect they show that in Madison and Monroe's plans, Clay was supposed to be at the War Department and was never considered for the State Department. When Monroe finally formed his cabinet, Clay would not be in it. The new administration would soon have cause to be sorry.

Monroe easily won the election with 183 electoral votes to King's 34, but for the time being the president-elect made no announcements about appointments, and Clay presided over the House of Representatives, assigning sections of President Madison's last annual message to committees. Then suddenly President-elect Monroe, the State Department, even the House of Representatives did not seem in the least important. The Clays' baby was seriously ill.

Laura Clay was only two months old when the family arrived in Washington. She had contracted whooping cough on the journey from Kentucky, and the days that followed became an agonizing vigil for Lucretia, helpless as sleepless nights came and cheerless dawns followed, all hours marked by the baby's continuous, heartrending cough. Lucretia's sister Nancy, soft-spoken Elizabeth Lowndes, and Margaret Bayard Smith were on hand to spell her, but hers was a lonely watch that only the mother of a dying child can know. Henry wore a stricken expression and was given to vacant stares. Margaret would never forget the night in early December when it finally ended. As she cradled Laura in her lap, Clay knelt beside her chair and wept. He stood as if to leave but instead leaned toward the tiny face for a last kiss. "Farewell, my little one," he murmured. The coughing that had tormented the "lovely infant" stopped.

The next day Clay worried that he would be seen as weak and negligent for not presiding over the House. Margaret gave him a talking-to and set him straight. Lucretia was distraught and needed him. He stayed in, planned the small funeral, and sat in silence with Lucretia. When a few days later they received reports from New York that Thomas had been in an accident, they were frantic with worry until they heard from a friend that the boy was not badly injured.[39]

WHEN COPING WITH personal tragedy, Clay buried himself in work. He dutifully spoke for the repeal of the Compensation Act and suggested a more modest adjustment, from $6 to $8 per day, that eventually passed.[40]

Clay also helped to found an association whose work would become an important part of his life. Taking its cue from state organizations like the one in Kentucky, the American Colonization Society held a preliminary meeting at the Davis Hotel in Washington on December 21, 1816, with Clay presiding. The gathering agreed to consider "the expediency and practicability of ameliorating the condition of the Free People of Color . . . by providing a Colonial Retreat," a place that would be eventually fixed on the western coast of Africa.[41]

On New Year's Day in the House of Representatives chamber, the first regular meeting of the society took place, with Clay again presiding. It elected George Washington's nephew, Associate Justice of the Supreme Court Bushrod Washington, president and made Clay an officer. Most founding members were slave owners like Clay, among them John Randolph, who believed that free blacks set a dangerous example by revealing for slaves the possibilities of freedom. Clay too recognized free blacks as a problem, but he also argued that white prejudice would never allow freed slaves the full rights of citizenship. His solution of voluntary colonization was meant to benefit free blacks as much as it was to insulate restive slaves. Nonetheless, he was careful to declare that the society's purpose was not to attack slavery as an institution.[42]

Henry Clay was no longer the young idealist of 1798–99 who had fought for abolition in Kentucky. He owned slaves and continued to buy them. While he was not a relentless pursuer of fugitives, he occasionally took pains to recover them rather than suffer financial loss. Yet he was always ambivalent about the morality of owning people. He helped a former family slave who had gained freedom purchase his brother, and Clay would free a number of his own slaves over the years. Clay spent considerable effort trying to recover Nathaniel Hart's slave, Isham, who had been captured with his master at the River Raisin and then sold by Indians to a Louisiana planter. His labors were intended not to restore a valuable piece of property for the family but to give Isham his freedom.

As a sustaining member and future president of the American Colonization Society, Clay helped people free slaves and encouraged their colonization. And though writers frequently cite a portion of his speech to the Kentucky Colonization Society in 1829 to allege that the real reason for his advocacy of colonization was his inherent racism, only selective quotation supports the charge. Free blacks, he said, were "the most corrupt, depraved, and abandoned" class of people in the nation, but he immediately followed that observation with a statement that is seldom quoted: "It is not so much their fault, as the consequence of their anomalous condition. Place ourselves, place any men, in the like predicament, and similar effects would follow. They are not slaves, and yet they are not free. The laws, it is true, proclaim them free; but prejudices, more powerful than any laws, deny them the privileges of freemen." Clay believed that only colonization would give them a chance to live as free men with dignity.[43]

It was considered an enlightened view at the time, one held by open-minded people in both South and North, Abraham Lincoln included. Yet for all its relative progressivism, the view was deeply flawed. Most free persons of color in the United States did not want to leave what they considered their home. They resented the implication that they were a danger to society. That good-hearted men such as Clay and Lincoln could not grasp this was one of the enduring evils of slavery.[44]

IN HIS LAST annual message, in December 1816, President Madison again mentioned internal improvements, which the Fourteenth Congress had done little to address during its first session. On February 4, Calhoun introduced a measure that would soon be called the Bonus Bill proposing that the $1.5 million received from the Bank of the United States for its charter, along with the Bank's future dividends, be placed in a permanent fund to finance the construction of roads and canals. Calhoun's eloquent appeal explained how improving one part of the country could strengthen the entire nation. Clay agreed and applauded Calhoun for presenting a plan "cementing the union—in facilitating internal trade—in augmenting the wealth and the population of the country."[45]

Many throughout the country were not sure about that. Reflexive resistance met proposals that had the government paying for projects that seemed to benefit only distant regions and local populations. People in Charleston were apt to bristle over paying for a road in New Hampshire, while Granite Staters would grumble about paying for the dredging of Charleston Harbor. In addition to these self-interested objections to internal improvements, many thinking men found them constitutionally troubling, as they empowered the federal government to undertake projects, spend money, and inevitably encroach on states' rights. Given these obstacles, the Bonus Bill would not have stood a chance in Congress had not James Madison urged the legislature to consider the matter. Madison's seeming conversion, along with Thomas Jefferson's, to the idea of limited federal projects convinced enough skeptics that the Constitution's "Necessary and Proper" clause might indeed sanction such enterprises.[46]

Consequently the Bonus Bill passed Congress, though with only a two-vote margin in the House, and was dispatched to Madison in the closing days of his administration. Clay and Calhoun had every reason to believe that surmounting the congressional hurdle meant the difficult part was done, but Madison and Jefferson had suggested that a constitutional amendment might be necessary for the kinds of projects that Clay wanted, which was an ominous portent for the Bonus Bill. On March 2, Calhoun paid a customary courtesy call on the outgoing president and Mrs. Madison at the Octagon House, a wealthy Virginia planter's property that served as the president's residence while the gutted Executive Mansion was being rebuilt. Calhoun chatted politely with the Madisons, wished them well, and prepared to leave. As Calhoun walked toward the door, Madison called to him. The president seemed uncomfortable and clearly had something on his mind as he accompanied Calhoun toward the exit. After a pause, he hesitantly said that he planned to veto the Bonus Bill because he thought it unconstitutional.

The information stunned Calhoun. All of his hard work had been carried out on the assumption that the president wanted a bill authorizing internal improvements, and now with one in hand he was going to strike it down. Calhoun rushed to Henry Clay with this news, and Clay quickly wrote to the president to implore that he not use the veto and instead leave the matter to James Monroe to decide. Madison was not swayed. He vetoed the bill.[47]

His veto message detailed specific objections that were shared by critics of the policy. The bill authorized no specific improvements but merely established an enormous pile of money that all but invited corrupt dealings and tainted trades, what later generations would describe as pork-barrel politics. To judge the constitutionality of an internal improvement bill required weighing specific projects against the "Necessary and Proper" test. He cited the constitutional convention, about which he could speak with more authority than anyone else, to remind Congress that the Framers had drafted the "Necessary and Proper" clause not to give it infinite unrestrained power but as a gauge to measure the worth and consequences of individual initiatives.

Revealing the level of his disappointment in this episode, Clay took the additional extraordinary step of trying to override the veto of his own party's president. Revealing the level of opposition to the very concept of internal improvements, the override failed.[48] A major element of the program that he and Calhoun felt was essential to national progress had been repudiated.

Clay's disappointments mounted in those early days of March 1817. Monroe's cabinet announcements were finally made official, and John Quincy Adams was the new secretary of state. Clay felt humiliated at being passed over, but his embarrassment soon gave way to angry resentment. Being rejected for Adams was especially vexing. During their six months together in Ghent, Clay had concluded that to know Adams was to dislike him, and he sincerely believed that the New Englander's barbed personality was unsuited for the State Department. Worse, Clay did not trust Adams to protect western interests, because he had been so willing to bargain them away at Ghent.

Monroe did not help matters when he offered Clay the War Department, a decidedly inferior cabinet post, especially in peacetime. When Clay turned Monroe down "in the most decided manner," Monroe then made a worse blunder by proposing that Clay replace Adams as minister to Great Britain. Clay hardly thought it a consolation to be offered Adams's leavings.[49]

Because Clay's irritation obscured for him Monroe's perfectly good reasons for his cabinet choices, he could not see that he was being unfair to a man with a complex set of predicaments that had nothing to do with satisfying Henry Clay. Federalists circulated rumors that Monroe had made a deal with Clay for his support in the Republican caucus. For blocking Crawford's nomination, they whispered, Clay was to receive the State Department. No such arrangement existed, but the suggestion of impropriety horrified Monroe. In addition, William Crawford was senior to Clay, with an impressive résumé: he had been in the government longer, had served in Madison's cabinet, had been minister to France, and had been elected president pro tempore of the Senate. Giving the State Department to Clay would have slighted Crawford, who was already annoyed by Madison's shuffling him from War into Treasury. Finally, Monroe wanted a geographically balanced cabinet with one member from the North, one from the South, one from the Mid-Atlantic region, and one from the West. The most qualified loyal Republican from the Northeast was John Quincy Adams, a career diplomat, making him the logical choice for the State Department. Monroe tried to mollify the other two aspirants to State by bringing them into the cabinet as well, which was why he asked Crawford to remain at Treasury and offered Clay the War Department. Crawford said yes; Clay said no, and Monroe sought out another westerner, first considering Andrew Jackson but asking former Kentucky governor Isaac Shelby, who also declined. Ultimately, Monroe settled on John C. Calhoun, a southerner who, with the Georgian Crawford, tilted the quest for sectional balance to the South. But Monroe could console himself that it was not a perfect world.[50]

In fact, imperfections cropped up in the most unexpected places at the start of this "Era of Good Feelings." When nobody consulted Speaker Clay about plans to dress up the House chamber with red plush chairs for Monroe's inauguration, he curtly insisted that the Senate would have to be satisfied with "the furniture of the Hall, such as it is." Because of a quarrel over chairs, James Monroe had the distinction of being the first president sworn in outdoors.[51]

Clay did not attend Monroe's inauguration, which might have been a show of petulance over being denied State, but he did not cut himself off from the administration either. He asked Monroe to appoint friends to federal jobs, and the president usually obliged. Clay kept his disappointment largely to himself, joking with friends about the cabinet and letting Monroe continue to consider him a friend and an adviser. Whether Clay's pique colored his attitude toward the Monroe presidency is uncertain. His disagreements with the administration are often filtered through the lens of John Quincy Adams's diary and consequently seem to have stemmed entirely from Clay's personal displeasure. Clay always claimed, however, that he differed with the administration solely on policy. Perhaps the truth was somewhere in between.[52] In the fall of 1817, he counseled Kit Hughes not to brood over being denied a diplomatic appointment he wanted. He told Hughes "to acquiesce, with a good grace, in what is unalterable . . . to patiently wait a more favorable turn of events." It was good advice. Clay might have taken it himself.[53]

The Clays stayed in the capital during that summer of 1817. Henry had business interests in Washington, his daughter Susan was in school in Baltimore, Lucretia was in the early months of her tenth pregnancy, and the family was installed in a comfortable house. As the days shortened and shadows lengthened with autumn's approach, Washington was a ghost town. Congress was not in session, and legislators as well as members of the cabinet had left for their homes. President Monroe toured New England to cultivate support in that last bastion of Federalism. On November 9, 1817, Lucretia gave birth to her tenth child, their fourth son, James Brown Clay. Unlike Henry Jr., James was frequently ill and gave his parents several anxious months before finally gaining strength.[54]

MEMBERS OF CONGRESS began trickling back into town at the end of November, and Washington came alive again. Once Lucretia regained her strength, the Clays went to parties and hosted their own with broad guest lists that even included John Quincy Adams. Yet Washington was not the same without vivacious Dolley Madison at the head of society. Elizabeth Kortright Monroe was a reserved woman who did not call on wives and with her husband avoided socializing in private homes to prevent the impression that the president had favorites. The Monroes gave parties and held levees, but these lacked the sparkle of Mrs. Madison's events. In any case, the president and his wife were frequently ill during his eight years in office and limited their social calendar. In matters both convivial and political, Monroe's presidency did not measure up to Clay's standards.[55]

Voter anger over the Salary Grab meant that an extraordinary number of the Fifteenth Congress were freshmen, and Clay hoped that he could play on that inexperience to undo Madison's eleventh-hour fit of constitutional caution over internal improvements. He was encouraged that the House overwhelmingly elected him Speaker once again, but his easy victory did not mean the House would automatically do his bidding. Some new members found Clay arrogant and resented his efforts to use them for his purposes. Many lodged the same constitutional objections to federally funded internal improvements as previous Congresses, objections that Monroe, like Madison, shared. As Clay surveyed his opponents, he grew frustrated. Friends in Kentucky proposed running him for governor, and he considered it.[56]

In fact, Clay had contemplated retirement from Congress since spring. The principal reason he did not quit and go home was his desire to steer the United States to support Latin American revolutions fighting for independence from Spain. This issue gave rise to Clay's sharpest disagreements with the Monroe administration. The president tried to mollify Clay, and a formal break never occurred. In addition, many suspected that Clay's fixation on recognizing Latin American republics was just another way for him to embarrass Monroe and Adams. Yet his disgust over the administration's reluctance to support Latin American revolutions was quite sincere, and he had planned before the fall session started to make it a major issue for the Fifteenth Congress.

Clay had early expressed sympathy for Latin American revolutionaries because he saw them as comparable to America's patriots of 1776. He criticized United States neutrality between Spain and its erstwhile colonies as a breach of faith and "came out with great violence against" Monroe's detachment.[57] When Monroe refused to recognize the republics but sent a fact-finding mission to South America instead, Clay acidly contrasted the $30,000 cost of the mission to the mere $18,000 necessary to pay for an official minister to Buenos Aires. He angrily denounced those who said such matters were beyond the province of Congress and spoke passionately over the span of three days in March 1818 urging recognition. He was sorely disappointed at not only losing that vote, but by a resounding margin of 115 to 45 at that. So much for the Spirit of '76.[58]

Monroe actually sympathized with the revolutionaries, but he could not risk a rupture with Spain by seeming to encourage the disintegration of its empire. Secretary of State Adams was negotiating with Spanish minister Don Luis de Onís to acquire Spanish Florida, but the talks were not going well and were beset by troubling events. When pirates and mercenaries overran Amelia Island on the east coast of Spanish Florida, Monroe authorized American military forces to oust the freebooters because they posed a threat to U.S. coastal trade and the southern border. These brigands had vague connections to Latin American revolutions, and Monroe knew that Spain did not want them on Amelia Island any more than he did. Yet he had to be careful, for any American military action against Spanish territory anywhere and for any reason threatened to spoil Adams's work. Even so, Monroe thought another military campaign in Spanish Florida to suppress violence by Seminole Indians on the Florida border was easily justified. The administration sent Major General Andrew Jackson into Florida to chastise those Seminoles, confident that the laws of nations sanctioned the pursuit of enemies across international borders.[59]

WHEN CLAY TOOK his family home after Congress adjourned in the spring, he was only vaguely aware of these developments. In Kentucky, friends applauded his stand on Latin America and his efforts to promote the West, and he stood for reelection to the Sixteenth Congress unopposed. In November, Clay returned to Washington without Lucretia and the children. Laura's fatal illness on the trip the previous year made them cautious, and James's fragile health as he approached his first birthday called for prudence.[60]

As Clay prepared for the trip, he heard troubling rumors about Jackson's campaign in Florida. Old Hickory, it was said, had taken Pensacola, the capital of Spanish West Florida. Clay noted that if this were true, Jackson had committed an unconstitutional act by attacking a foreign power without congressional approval.[61] By the time Clay arrived in Washington in late fall, the capital was buzzing with additional news about the Florida invasion that rapidly pushed every other issue aside. Jackson's actions at Pensacola had been accurately described, which was bad enough, but there was more, much more, and it all spelled troubled for the administration politically and for the country diplomatically.

Jackson had gone into Florida in early 1818 with orders to chastise Seminoles near the United States border. Secretary of War Calhoun included instructions not to molest any Spaniards or attack Spanish forts or settlements. Yet Jackson moved on St. Marks, a small Spanish post, where he demanded the garrison's surrender. At St. Marks, Jackson imprisoned an elderly Scottish trader, a British subject named Alexander Arbuthnot, for befriending the Seminoles. Old Hickory then headed east to scatter Seminole towns near the Suwannee River. There another British subject, a former British Royal Marine captain named Robert Chrystie Ambrister, fell into American hands. Returning to St. Marks, Jackson convened a court of his senior officers to try Arbuthnot and Ambrister for inciting the Seminoles to make war on the United States. The court convicted and sentenced both to die, but Ambrister threw himself on his captors' mercy with such sincerity that they reduced his sentence to a flogging and imprisonment. Jackson, however, had both men executed. He then marched on Pensacola, shelled it into submission, and forced the Spanish provincial governor to sign an instrument of surrender. Leaving an occupying force, Jackson headed home.[62]

Jackson's two-month campaign had cut more than a wide swath in Florida. In addition to chastising Seminoles, which was the sole official purpose of his invasion, Jackson had summarily hanged two unoffending Indians and had murdered two British subjects. The Indians had not even had a trial, but considering the drumhead court-martial of Arbuthnot and Ambrister, it would not have mattered. Jackson obviously intended to ignore rulings if they ran counter to his wishes. He also obviously intended to ignore the orders that prohibited any attack on Spaniards. He had forcibly taken both St. Marks and Pensacola. Jackson's campaign was not just diplomatically inexcusable and domestically impolitic. It was illegal.

When news of these incredible exploits reached Washington, Monroe was in Virginia and the cabinet was scattered. Not until mid-July did the president and his secretaries frantically gather to craft a response that might justify to the British and Spanish embassies Jackson's murdering the former's citizens and assailing the latter's provincial government.[63] Divisions immediately emerged. Calhoun and Crawford wanted Jackson punished for insubordination.[64] Monroe paused short of that plain course of action, however, as did Attorney General William Wirt, who usually formed an opinion only after discovering the president's. John Quincy Adams alone defended Jackson, on the grounds that this show of force could convince Spain that the better course was to sell Florida to the United States instead of having it stolen. Aside from the diplomatic advantage that might result, Jackson was enormously popular with Americans, particularly westerners and southerners, and condemning him was risky. With such arguments, Adams persuaded Monroe and the cabinet to sustain Old Hickory in the face of both foreign outrage and domestic indignation. Calhoun and Crawford were not happy, but they consented to the plan.

The United States was lucky that the British government's outrage was more designed to satisfy British public opinion than to menace America and that Spain was too distracted by its crumbling empire to go to war with anyone over anything. Through George Erving, the U.S. minister in Madrid, Adams told the Spanish government that its failure to control Florida Indians justified Jackson's invasion but that all territory would nonetheless be returned. The British backed away from a confrontation over the elderly Scot and the hapless freebooter, and the Spaniards grudgingly resolved to cut their losses by resuming talks over Florida, quietly grateful that Florida was still theirs to talk about.[65]

Monroe and the cabinet knew that many in Congress would be far more difficult to mollify, and John Quincy Adams especially worried about Henry Clay's reaction.[66] True enough, some congressmen recoiled from attacking the popular Jackson, and others so strongly wanted territorial expansion that they were not fussy about how it was accomplished. But a substantial number in the legislature took congressional prerogatives under the Constitution very seriously, Speaker Clay foremost among them.[67]

To tread lightly around Jackson's popularity while placating Congress on the Florida affair, Monroe took contradictory positions in his annual message of November 16, 1818.[68] He insisted that Andrew Jackson's behavior was justified and worthy of congratulation. Yet he also insisted that Jackson had not been authorized to take Spanish posts, which accordingly would be returned to Spain. This peculiar statement that sustained Jackson in one breath and disowned him in the next left Clay and others both bewildered and unsatisfied. Alabama's territorial governor, the former congressman and senator William W. Bibb, plainly stated these worries: "no man should be permitted in a free country to usurp the whole powers of the whole government and to treat with contempt all authority except that of his own will."[69]

Hoping to preempt Clay's assignment of the president's Florida explanation to its logical place, the unfriendly Committee on Military Affairs, Jackson supporters on December 8 tried to have it placed in the Committee on Foreign Relations, which was inclined toward Jackson. The debate on this purely procedural matter consumed two days and concluded with Military Affairs charged with examining the Florida affair. The debate also gave rise to questions about the constitutionality of Jackson's actions, but Clay reminded the House that the time to debate the war would come when the committees brought in their reports.[70] The two committees went to work as Washington entered the holiday season nervously anticipating what stand Congress would take when it reconvened after the first of the year.

Clay made the rounds of Christmas parties that culminated with the most lavish of them celebrating New Year's. Foreign ministers and cabinet secretaries hosted gatherings at their homes, and "a magnificent ball at the Marine barracks" was followed by "a refulgent dinner at the President's." Concerts, plays, and performances by novelty acts such as magicians enlivened evenings during which everyone in the political establishment traded jests and raised glasses as if the best of friends. Attorney General Wirt cynically noted that there was "so much bowing—so much simpering—so much smiling—so much grinning; such fawning, flattering, duplicity, hypocricy [*sic*]—my head spun—my stomach turned." Clay, on the other hand, not only had the stomach for such socializing, he regarded the politicking that went with it as mother's milk and the events themselves as enjoyable amusements.[71]

The parties gave Clay a chance to discover attitudes about Jackson's actions in unguarded social moments. People were troubled, that much was clear, but Clay could not tell how many had the courage to criticize the Hero of New Orleans. Part of the answer came on January 12, when the Military Affairs Committee issued a majority report condemning Jackson for the trial and execution of Arbuthnot and Ambrister. Yet a minority report by the committee's chairman, Richard Mentor Johnson, endorsed Jackson's comportment as perfectly proper. Clay and Johnson, both Kentuckians and friends, had never disagreed on a political question. Soon, because of Andrew Jackson, they would disagree about almost everything.[72]

Legal, moral, political, and personal motives framed the three-week debate over Jackson's actions. Virginian states' rights advocates, for instance, expressed alarm over growing federal power, and others lamented the seeming congressional indifference to Monroe's constitutional nonchalance if Jackson were not condemned.[73] Clay clearly disapproved of what Jackson had done, but his reasons for pursuing the course he chose during these weeks were subjected to suspicious scrutiny. Clay had met Jackson once a few years before. He had also handled a minor legal matter for Jackson in Kentucky, but all their contact had been through correspondence.[74] Nothing suggests that Clay saw Jackson as a political rival, but as this affair unfolded, Old Hickory's popularity became increasingly evident, and some in retrospect supposed that Clay was delivering a preemptive blow. Others saw Clay as using the debates to undermine the administration, an extension of his other efforts to make Monroe and Adams sorry Clay had not been given State.[75]

Yet if Clay wanted to discomfit Monroe, he could have tied Jackson more effectively to the administration. Instead, as Jackson's passionate followers mounted fervent defenses of him and his actions, Clay's decision to challenge Jackson likely stemmed from motives similar to Calhoun's. If a United States Army officer could make war on his own initiative and execute captives without trial or under the cover of rigged tribunals, the Constitution meant nothing.[76]

Clay planned to come down from the Speaker's chair on January 20 to make a major speech on the Florida invasion. Announced in advance, the address was his most important since returning from Europe and led to a flurry of expectation. The Senate scheduled an adjournment to allow its members to attend, all the foreign ministers came to Capitol Hill, and the ladies of Washington appeared in droves to hear his voice. Observers had never seen such a crowd. The House gallery was packed to overflowing, and extra chairs were placed on the House floor to accommodate ladies. Spectators stood in the lobby and shoved for a place at the chamber door. Awaiting Clay, the assemblage raised a loud din of chatter over which laughter occasionally broke out as congressmen flirted with their female guests. When Clay finally rose to speak, however, "such a silence prevailed that tho' at a considerable distance," Margaret Smith "did not lose a word."[77]

He spoke for three hours. He intended to speak longer, but he started too loud and his voice gave out. Throughout he held his audience spellbound, and even those who disagreed with every word he spoke had to admit that his wit, sarcasm, and sincerity made for a masterful performance. Federalist Louis McLane detested Clay, but he freely conceded that the speech was "the most eloquent one I ever heard."[78]

And yet Clay's address on January 20, 1819, has most often been described as a serious miscalculation, for he not only attacked the popular Andrew Jackson, he also made in the space of three hours an implacable, relentless personal enemy. Clay claimed no personal hostility toward Jackson, but he could not defend behavior he found morally and constitutionally indefensible. Yes, Spain had clearly violated the treaty of 1795 that required it to control Indians within its borders, but that violation did not justify the wrong done by American forces when placed in historical perspective. The 1813–14 war with the Creek Indians had ended with Andrew Jackson's draconian peace that had forced many Indians into Florida, two of whom Jackson executed in this latest foray simply because he had found them. Killing "an unarmed and prostrate captive" was an unpardonable departure from the philosophy that defined Americanism and guided Americans, the culture that made the rule of law supreme over the will of a powerful man. In that regard, Arbuthnot and Ambrister's guilt or innocence was beside the point. More central was the question of whether they had been killed in accordance with the law after having access to due process. Jackson said that because they had allied themselves with Indians, the two were criminals, but where in the laws of nations was such a finding supported?

He addressed the broader implications of Jackson's constitutional transgression. The Constitution placed the power to make war exclusively with Congress, and everyone knew the sound reason for restricting that authority to the representatives of the people. The president clearly did, for he had assured Congress in March 1818 that the campaign against the Seminoles would not involve a foreign power, a statement Monroe believed to be true at the time. Yet on the very day that Monroe had sent Congress that assurance, Jackson was writing to the administration about his plan to take St. Marks, a plan that had Jackson exercising a power only Congress possessed. Jackson then announced that by destroying villages on the Suwannee, he had all but concluded his campaign, but Jackson subsequently interpreted the Spanish governor's protesting the unprovoked attack on Spanish territory as an affront and had marched on Pensacola.

Clay warned that allowing Jackson's behavior "to pass, without a solemn expression of the disapprobation of this House" would repeat the sad histories of Greece, of Rome, and of France. All of those glorious, free nations had relaxed restraints on their militaries and had paid the ultimate price for doing so. Americans had a duty to prevent "a triumph of the military over the civil authority—a triumph over the powers of this house—a triumph over the constitution of the land."[79]

He was done, and the House and galleries exploded in applause and cheers as Clay exited to the lobby. He sipped on a drink as colleagues extended hands, slapped him on the back, and heartily congratulated him on his triumph. It was gratifying, but when his eye settled on Margaret Smith sitting alone at the base of a stairway, he strode over to join her, "throwing himself most gracefully into a recumbent posture." People would remember him there, chatting with Mrs. Smith, occasionally acknowledging the repeated congratulations of passersby with a smiling nod, the toast of the Capitol making it appear perfectly natural to lounge smiling next to an elegant lady on the risers outside the House chamber.[80]

He was the toast of the Capitol at least for that day, but his friends had reason to worry that Clay's stance had done him long-term political injury. Although Clay had taken pains to avoid attacking Monroe or Adams, those supporting Jackson had had their suspicions about Clay's motives confirmed, at least in their own minds, and they tallied his speech as a score to be evened. Old Hickory's arrival in Washington three days after Clay's speech caused a stir among those eager to see matters evened right away. Richard Johnson had predicted that Jackson's temper would cause "a rattling among the dry Bones," but Clay had not meant his remarks as a personal attack, and he promptly called on Jackson to make that clear.[81] Yet for Jackson everything touching upon him was personal, and he was decidedly chilly during Clay's visit. In addition, Jackson regarded the controversy over his Florida campaign as a conspiracy launched by a growing list of enemies. He set his henchmen to the task of smearing the motives of William H. Crawford, whom Jackson suspected of being his chief enemy in the cabinet, and William Lowndes as well as Henry Clay, his enemies in the House. Jackson was intent upon ruining their reputations for daring to criticize him. He threatened to cut off the ears of anyone who spoke against him. He considered challenging Clay to a duel but was waiting for Congress to adjourn, and cooler heads persuaded him to drop it.[82]

Events and Jackson's popularity rather than his bullying threats saved him from formal censure. On February 22, Adams and Onís finally signed a treaty that ceded Florida to the United States. Later dubbed the Transcontinental Treaty because it also established the border between U.S. and Spanish territories all the way to the Pacific Ocean, it deflated Jackson's opponents and energized his supporters, now armed with proof that his Florida foray had paid real expansionist dividends. Richard Johnson and other Jackson men were the minority on the Military Affairs Committee, but they became a majority in the House itself, defeating the report condemning Jackson. In the Senate, a report denouncing Jackson never came to a vote.[83]

As a political controversy, the Florida affair ended unsatisfactorily for everyone. Jackson's opponents grimly surveyed what they perceived as serious constitutional wreckage resulting from the failure to discipline an arrant military leader disdainful of his superiors and contemptuous of the people's tribunals. Jackson was vindicated, but he brooded over criticisms that he snarled were merely the sniping of ingrates and schemers, men he marked as suspect in their love of country because they did not love him. He planned to settle scores eventually and had taken names. Henry Clay topped the list.

EVEN AS THE controversy over Florida blazed, another unexpected domestic crisis emerged. In a way, Clay had planted the seeds for it in December 1818 when he presented a memorial from the Territory of Missouri, in essence a request for admission to the Union. Clay had friends and family in Missouri and was interested in paving the territory's way to statehood. The request was routinely referred to committee, and there the matter remained, ticking. On February 13, 1819, it exploded.[84]

New York congressman James Tallmadge proposed an amendment to the Missouri enabling bill. The Tallmadge amendment said that no more slaves were to be brought into Missouri and provided for the gradual emancipation of children born to slaves already there. The House was in the Committee of the Whole to discuss the enabling bill, and Clay leaped to attack Tallmadge's proposal. Because of the late hour on Saturday, the House adjourned before opinions could be aired. It placed the matter on Monday's calendar. The weekend turned tense over the prospect of a serious quarrel.[85]

At first Clay was curiously blind to Missouri's potential for causing serious trouble. Federally funded internal improvements and the recognition of the

South American republics remained his priorities.[86] Yet southerners considered the Tallmadge amendment a portentous menace to sectional balance. Although in 1788, when the Constitution was adopted, the North and South were roughly even in wealth and population, the passing years saw the North growing richer and more populous, resulting in a growing northern majority in the House of Representatives. Only by maintaining equality in the Senate, where twenty-two free state senators were balanced by twenty-two from the slave states, could southerners hope to foil northern efforts to meddle with slavery. Restricting slavery in Missouri could set a precedent for the rest of the enormous Louisiana Purchase and encourage emancipationists elsewhere, possibly in the South itself.

The House debate on Tallmadge's amendment featured arguments for and against slavery that would become all too familiar in coming years. It also featured Henry Clay at his moral nadir on the slavery issue. He stood firmly with the proslavery side, voicing with seeming conviction arguments that would become a staple of slavery proponents. He compared slaves to northern factory workers to suggest that slaves were materially better off as to food, clothing, and shelter, the closest he ever came to describing the institution as a positive good, and something he would never do again. To his marginal credit, he did at least say that the existence of slavery was regrettable, but he disagreed with Tallmadge's presumption that Congress had the right to dictate slavery's status in any part of the Louisiana Purchase. As it happened, the point was timely because northerners were also seeking to eliminate slavery in the Arkansas Territory. When the vote on Arkansas yielded a dead-even division with 88 for and 88 against slavery, Clay cast his tiebreaking vote to keep slavery unrestricted in the new territory. It was not his finest hour.[87]

Rhetoric became alarming during the second day of debate on the Missouri question. Thomas W. Cobb threatened disunion if Tallmadge did not withdraw his amendment. The New Yorker, said Cobb, was kindling "a fire that all the waters of the ocean cannot put out, which seas of blood can only extinguish." Tallmadge darkly responded, "Let it be so! . . . if civil war . . . must come, . . . let it come!" Under the shadow of such talk, the House narrowly passed the enabling bill with the Tallmadge amendment and sent it to the Senate, where southern strength succeeded in removing slavery restriction. The final session of the Fifteenth Congress ended with the fate of Missouri undetermined, giving the sections time to feed their unique anxieties over the question.[88]

Southerners gradually embraced the unnerving conclusion that northern antislavery rhetoric could incite slaves to rebellion, and northerners suspected that southern vehemence about Missouri signaled a design to spread slavery to all new territories west of the Mississippi. Meetings throughout the North instructed representatives to support the Tallmadge amendment.[89]

This first serious disagreement between the sections on slavery revealed the issue's uncanny ability to affect seemingly unrelated questions. For example, attempts to restrict slavery made southerners consider that expanding federal power wielded by growing northern majorities could lead to nationally mandated abolition. By way of such predictions, even the BUS became an unpopular symbol of an extensive federal reach that could affect slavery.

By 1819, the BUS had enough problems without adding sectional distrust to them. In that year, the first serious financial panic since Washington's presidency struck the nation hard, destroying businesses, closing banks, throwing enormous numbers out of work, and ushering in a lingering economic depression. The causes of this economic calamity were various, but land speculation figured prominently. The western branches of the BUS were deeply involved in these reckless investments, and the BUS in general had encouraged rather than restrained the dizzying credit spiral that resulted throughout the country. People unversed in the arcane formulas of discount rates and the relationships between sound credit and stable currencies knew only that when they lost their homes or saw their local banks driven to failure by called loans, the BUS was the culprit.

Consequently, when the House revived questions about the Bank's constitutionality, Clay was disturbed. He had already suffered a constitutional setback on internal improvements with Madison's veto of the Bonus Bill, and he was greatly relieved when the Supreme Court weighed in favorably on the Bank shortly after the congressional session ended. In the case of *McCulloch v. Maryland,* Chief Justice John Marshall ruled that federal agencies could not be impeded by states, a decision in which he famously declared that "the power to tax is the power to kill," and he also declared the Bank constitutional. Marshall could make the BUS legitimate, but his ruling could not make it popular.[90]

Clay returned home after Congress adjourned with the hope that the economic crisis was not as dire as reported, but what he saw was disheartening. During that spring and early summer, he traveled to New Orleans to see his brother John, purchase sugar to sell in Kentucky, and attend a dinner in his honor. As he returned home aboard the steamboat *Napoleon,* he saw the same suffering along the river that had shadowed his visit to the Crescent City. Bank failures and falling agricultural prices were compounded by a severe drought that left crops withering in the fields. The great Mississippi and Ohio were so shrunken that Clay had to leave the *Napoleon* to travel overland, and he was late in returning to Ashland, thus missing James Monroe, who was on a western tour.[91]

The panic's grim consequences further shaped Clay's strong views on economic development. He was convinced that the inability of the BUS to ward off the crisis was the result of the Bank's mismanagement rather than the Bank itself. More than ever the country needed a central fiscal agent to regulate credit and the currency, and the ouster of the Bank's inept president William Jones in favor of Langdon Cheves encouraged Clay. Thereafter, he took a more vigilant interest in the BUS and in due course managed its legal affairs in the West.[92]

JOHN QUINCY ADAMS claimed that some disgruntled congressmen wanted to prevent Clay's election to the Speakership of the Sixteenth Congress, but he again won the post in a lopsided vote.[93] Clay continued to promote Latin American independence and to protest flaws in the Adams-Onís Treaty.[94]

But his forum was largely preoccupied with what was becoming a perennial crisis, for the Missouri question dominated the session, and Clay finally understood the importance of resolving it. On the most basic level, Missourians were angry at being treated differently from other territories because they happened to own slaves. Led by Thomas Hart Benton's *St. Louis Enquirer,* Missouri's newspapers demanded admission on Missouri's terms. Benton had family connections to Henry Clay. He was named after Lucretia's father, Thomas Hart, who had been Benton's great-uncle. Colorful adventures marked Benton's progress from Tennessee to Missouri, including an alliance with Andrew Jackson that ended when the two tried to kill each other in a Nashville street brawl. That was in 1813, but in Missouri, Benton had risen to prominence as a newspaper editor and politician. He now expected "Harry of the West" to support Missouri's application.[95]

That Clay only gradually focused attention on Missouri actually showed that he was more in touch with the country. For all the heat generated by the question, it remained an issue relatively confined to Washington politics. The territory understandably saw its statehood as the highest national priority, but the rest of the country felt that the economic crisis merited more attention from the government. Congress, however, ignored the rest of the country and took up where it had left off regarding Missouri. When the Maine district, a part of Massachusetts, with the state government's consent, requested admission to the Union as a separate state, southerners howled over the potential of further tilting the sectional balance, but perceptive observers saw in Maine an opportunity for a quid pro quo.

On December 30, 1819, Clay spoke about this to the Committee of the Whole. He had no objection to Maine's admission, but he wanted to know Missouri's fate before casting his vote. He thought it was fundamentally unfair to place restrictions on Missouri and none on new states in the East. He did more than suggest that the vote for Maine should be predicated on the vote for Missouri. Massachusetts congressman John Holmes, a resident of Maine, said that surely Clay's idea "did not extend quite as far as" to trade Maine for the unconditional admission of Missouri. Clay succinctly answered by muttering "Yes, it did," pausing between the words for emphasis, making each loud enough for everyone to hear. He then elaborated: no restrictions on the admission of states could be permitted, no matter their section or their situation. Surprised by the hostile reluctance to connect the New England and western requests, Clay was grateful that Congress had time to overcome it. Massachusetts had not yet worked out the details of Maine's separation, and time could calm tempers and light the proper way.

In this first great compromise of a career whose fame would rest largely on Clay's ability to craft conciliation and resolve contentious questions with mutual concessions, he realized that time was always reason's greatest ally. Given enough time, anything was achievable, the fieriest tempers would cool, the most rigid positions would bend. Wait, he told Holmes, and see. Northern votes passed the Maine enabling bill in the House, but southerners in the Senate had their cue. They insisted on linking Maine's admission to Missouri's.[96]

After a pause, Illinois senator Jesse Thomas stepped up with a plan. A moderate with strong southern ties, Thomas proposed not just the unrestricted admission of both Maine and Missouri but also a demarcation of the Louisiana Purchase at latitude 36° 30', which was the southern border of Missouri. Except for Missouri, all states formed north of that line would be free; any states south of it had the option to choose slavery.

The proposal became famous as the Missouri Compromise, and within Clay's lifetime he would be erroneously credited for having framed it. Possibly the confusion resulted from his remarks suggesting the linkage of Maine and Missouri, but Thomas's plan as proposed in the Senate contained the significant addition of 36° 30', which Clay had nothing to do with. Actually, Clay never publicly spoke for or against the Missouri Compromise, and he was in fact doubtful that it would calm rancor or long quell disunion. One Sunday morning as he left church services, then held in the Capitol, he told John Quincy Adams that within five years the nation would come apart to form three separate confederacies. It was a gloomy long-term forecast. In the short term, he glumly doubted that Thomas's plan could pass the House.[97]

Clay believed that the failure of compromise endangered the Union in a practical way. Sectional political parties would arise, further polarizing the country. When rumors predicted that northern Republicans would nominate one of their own rather than the incumbent James Monroe, he condemned the alleged movement. Despite his differences with Monroe, Clay saw great perils in any effort to unseat him.[98]

The Senate finally passed Thomas's compromise on February 17 and sent it to the House. Clay supported the compromise as the only reasonable solution but remained uncharacteristically pessimistic about its chances. The problem was that both southerners and northerners found different portions of it objectionable for different reasons, but those objections made opponents of the measure into unlikely allies against it. Only moderates like Clay with the strong support of President Monroe could push it through the House, but there weren't enough of them, and they failed.[99] The House stubbornly voted yet again to admit Missouri under the Tallmadge amendment, which the Senate just as obstinately rejected yet again on March 2, sending back a bill admitting Missouri without restrictions and marking 36° 30' in the rest of the Louisiana Purchase. Another House vote would likely have yielded the same insistence on including the Tallmadge amendment had not the implausible majority against it been broken by cleverly separating Missouri from the Missouri Compromise line. Each of these could attract slim majorities, as indeed they did. Neither side was satisfied, but when traversing difficult ground, the best that could be hoped for was that everybody was equally uncomfortable, more often than not the definition of political compromise.[100]

The following morning, however, John Randolph tried to upset the wagon and spill its cargo by demanding a reconsideration of the issue. Clay ruled Randolph out of order. House rules, he said, clearly required the completion of routine matters before any new business could be considered. Randolph unsuccessfully appealed and sat sulking as the House introduced petitions and committee reports. Occasionally Randolph piped up to repeat his motion, but he was each time ruled out of order. Finally, with all old business completed, Randolph offered his motion, but Clay announced that because the clerk of the House had already taken the Missouri bill to the Senate, it could not be reconsidered. Randolph was dumbfounded. He blurted that the clerk had violated a member's prerogative to ask for reconsideration, but his motion of protest was defeated too. Randolph sat fuming. Clay had done it to him again. Through a crafty use of parliamentary procedure, the Speaker made sure that the Missouri Compromise passed Congress.[101]

CLAY SUFFERED FINANCIAL reverses in the economic panic and decided not to place his name on the ballot in the upcoming summer elections. Instead, he would return to Kentucky, practice law, and try to restore his assets. His retirement was not meant to be permanent, but it did make urgent his desire to move on several important issues that had been shoved aside by the economy and Missouri. After the sectional crisis was resolved, Clay had only the remaining two months of this session and the second session in the winter of 1820–21 to promote the initiatives he valued most.[102]

The best Clay could accomplish for the Latin American republics was a narrowly successful resolution (80 to 75) asking the president to consider sending a minister to certain governments. In his impassioned speech for the resolution, Clay on May 10, 1820, first used the expression "American System" to describe not just national economic sovereignty but also the potential for hemispheric solidarity of a New World committed to republican liberty against the corrupt crowns of old Europe. Not until Spain finally concluded its deliberations on the Adams-Onís Treaty and ratified it in the fall of 1820, however, was there a chance for the United States to begin building such camaraderie. Clay's victory on the issue was at best partial.[103]

Clay went home in May. He had not seen his family in more than six months. Many constituents regretted his decision to retire, but Clay was determined to resume his law practice before returning in the fall for his last congressional session. The economic downturn had hit Lexington especially hard. The rapid contraction of credit collapsed the region's manufacturing production and agricultural yields as businesses shuttered their windows and the hemp market shrank. Other towns such as Louisville and Cincinnati on the Ohio River became rivals benefiting from the increasing prevalence of steamboats carrying passengers and hauling cargoes, making Lexington a sleepy outpost that would never recover its former commercial vitality. Clay's investments in the town's now slumbering economy nearly ruined him, and he briefly considered moving the family to New Orleans, where lawyers' fees were higher.[104] He scrounged up business wherever he could, but not until the Bank of the United States hired him to represent it in Ohio and Kentucky was he able to make headway in restoring the Clay family coffers. When the BUS put him on a hefty retainer the following year, he finally began to see financial light at the end of the tunnel.[105]

Hard times had him looking everywhere for assets, especially to help his equally strapped siblings. The Virginia lands that included the plantation Euphraim that Clay's mother and stepfather had sold in innocent violation of John Clay's will were recovered through the efforts of a Virginia cousin, attorney Benjamin Watkins Leigh. The legal achievement was made sweeter by the warm letters between Leigh and Clay, the beginning of a lifelong friendship.[106]

In late October 1820, Clay resigned the Speakership with a letter to the clerk of the House.[107] He arranged for Lucretia to move with the younger children into a house he rented in Lexington. She was in the last months of her eleventh (and last) pregnancy, and Clay wanted her close to her family during his absence. He placed Ashland's operations under an overseer. After celebrating Christmas with the family, Clay started out for Washington.[108]

The congressional session began with a bruising battle to replace him as Speaker, a consequence of lingering rancor over Missouri. Clay had always been elected Speaker on the first ballot, but it took the House twenty-two ballots to elect John W. Taylor of New York to succeed him.

The presidential race for 1824 was also in full swing.[109] In some ways, that contest had been shaping up since Monroe's election in 1816. Given the signal honor of being the last president to run unopposed, Monroe's reelection in 1820 had featured a nearly unanimous vote for him in the Electoral College with only a single elector opposing, keeping George Washington's record intact.[110] At the start of Monroe's second term, presidential aspirants immediately became more obvious in their campaigning. Three members of Monroe's cabinet—Adams, Crawford, and Calhoun—stood at the pinnacle above a number of lesser lights seeking the prize as well. Nobody thought that Clay's leaving the legislature meant his permanent retirement from public life, and the presidency did indeed beckon him. Crawford correctly perceived that "there are but few men who have less relish for retirement than Mr. Clay."[111]

Clay found the House in the midst of reducing the military as part of the political games between Crawford's and Calhoun's congressional supporters. Clay applauded retrenchment during difficult economic times, but it also helped that army reduction would legislate Andrew Jackson out of the military.[112] Most of all, though, Clay hoped at last to compel Monroe to recognize the Latin American republics. He again pushed through a resolution favorable to that course but was exasperated when the Missouri controversy reappeared to disrupt congressional business, this time in another guise.

When the previous session had passed the Missouri Compromise, Congress gave Missouri leave to draft a state constitution, and a convention soon produced a document that called for a law prohibiting free blacks from entering the state. Northerners said the clause plainly violated Article IV, Section 2, of the U.S. Constitution, which states that "citizens of each state shall be entitled to all Privileges and Immunities of citizens of the several states." Because free blacks could be citizens in several northern states as well as Tennessee and North Carolina, barring them from Missouri infringed on their "Privileges and Immunities." A large majority in the House refused to approve Missouri's constitution, and the hard-won compromise of the previous year threatened to unravel.

Missouri already considered itself a state and had sent Thomas Hart Benton and David Barton to the Senate and John Scott, previously the territory's congressional delegate, to the House. The Senate at least seated Benton and Barton, though without voting privileges, and agreed to admit Missouri, leaving it to the courts to rule on the offending part of the state constitution. The northern majority in the House, however, insisted that Missouri change the state constitution as a condition of admission.[113]

The threat that the Republican Party would divide along sectional lines reemerged as southerners again threatened disunion. For a month, Clay worked within the Committee of the Whole and behind the scenes to craft a compromise.[114] He proposed and then chaired a sectionally balanced committee of thirteen to work out a solution. After a week, its majority report recommended Missouri's admission if it promised not to pass any laws discriminating against the citizens of another state. A lengthy debate on February 12 ended with the proposal failing 83 to 80. The following day, with the measure under reconsideration, Clay "alternately reasoned, remonstrated, and entreated" for almost an hour. He managed to bring two additional votes to his side, but several opponents absent for the first vote now swelled the ranks against the bill, and it again failed, 88 to 82.[115]

And there the matter stood when a joint congressional session gathered to count the electoral vote from the fall presidential election. The procedure was more a formality than usual, since Monroe had run unopposed, but the complication of what to do with Missouri set the stage for a dramatic confrontation. Like any other state, Missouri had presidential electors and expected them to be counted. A joint committee chaired by Clay recommended to the House that Missouri be included in the tally unless someone objected, in which case two votes would be taken, one with and one without Missouri. It was an ungainly solution, but the House consented, and the president pro tempore of the Senate, John Gaillard of South Carolina, began calling out the states and their totals.[116]

Everyone grew edgier as Gaillard neared Missouri. When he finally called out the purported state's name, New Hampshire congressman Arthur Livermore leaped up to object that Missouri was not a state and its votes could not be included. John Floyd of Virginia came to his feet just as quickly to shout that Missouri was most certainly a state and its electors most certainly would be counted. Floyd put his sentiment into a motion, and the national legislature dissolved into bedlam as members shouted objections and shook fists. The Senate walked out. The House finally calmed down enough to try to sort matters out, but John Randolph kept debate lively with wild remarks and dire predictions. Clay gained the floor to remind everyone that the House had already decided how to handle any objection. He suggested tabling Floyd's motion to allow the legislature to fulfill its constitutional duty of electing James Monroe. Upon re-flection, that sounded sensible. The Senate reappeared, the tally was completed, and two totals were recorded. The country was fortunate that it did not, in this case, matter what they were.[117]

The Missouri question remained unresolved as ratifications on the Transcon-tinental Treaty were finally exchanged on February 22, but the treaty's conclu-sion calmed northern fears that Texas would serve as an avenue of southern expansion. The prospect of maintaining balance in the Senate weakened objec-tions about Missouri, and on that very day Clay proposed that a joint committee of twenty-three representatives and seven senators craft a solution for Missouri. The resulting proposal echoed that of Clay's House committee on February 12: Missouri would not interpret its constitution as allowing the passage of a law in-fringing on the "Privileges and Immunities" of citizens of other states. Work be-hind the scenes made for an abbreviated debate in the House and a favorable result of 87 to 81 for this final compromise, Henry Clay's principal contribution to resolving the Missouri controversy. Missouri made the required pledge and became a state on August 10, 1821.

As the session closed, Clay thanked Speaker Taylor for presiding with fair-ness during a difficult time, and privately he expressed cautious optimism that "wisdom and prudence may keep us united a long time, I hope for ever."[118] It was not to be forever, for slavery only slumbered, and only for the time being.

AFTER CONGRESS ADJOURNED on March 3, Clay remained in Washington for a couple of weeks to attend to business and argue cases before the Supreme Court. He wanted the government to pay him additional compensation of $4,500 for expenses incurred while he negotiated the commercial treaty with Great Britain, and he applied directly to James Monroe for the sum. Adams vi-olently objected. Not only was Clay seeking the same level of compensation Adams had received as a senior diplomat, he had gone directly to Monroe rather than through Adams at the State Department. Adams told Monroe not to ap-prove the money. Monroe, however, consulted Attorney General William Wirt, who saw nothing untoward about Clay's request. Monroe approved it.[119]

Adams and Clay were thus again at odds when Clay called on him just be-fore leaving for Kentucky. The visit was on the surface a courtesy call, but Clay was obviously checking on the status of his payment. Adams played along, though, and they parted on friendly terms. Later that evening he ruminated in his diary about Henry Clay, a man he would never understand, try as he might. Clay was "an eloquent man, with very popular manners and great political manage-ment," but like so many important men in the country he was "only half educated." Adams thought Clay's "morals public and private, are loose, but he has all the virtues indispensable to a popular man . . . and the sort of generosity which attaches individuals to his person." It was a pensive observation.

A few days later, one of Clay's friends approached Adams to sell him a ticket to a farewell dinner planned in Clay's honor. Adams snapped that he would buy the ticket but could not attend. He later sniffed to his diary that such dinners were not an American practice and accused Clay of importing an obnoxious British custom.[120] Rarely did John Quincy Adams mislead his diary, his closest confidant. He knew very well that such dinners were a fashionable way to pay tribute to prominent men throughout the country. He did not admit to his diary that he had never been treated to one.

Adams also had to entertain the likelihood that Clay was a rival for the presidency. No Speaker before the Civil War would use as effectively the precedents set by Clay to manage the House of Representatives or to wield his level of influence over legislation and policy. As a result, Americans would regard few nineteenth-century Speakers as men of sufficient vision and power to merit consideration for the presidency. Nobody doubted Clay's capacity for broad vision or his ability to wield power, qualities on vivid display as he had presided over the House, qualities that had not dimmed when he took his place on the floor. Nobody doubted that Henry Clay was presidential timber.

CHAPTER SIX

"I Injured Both Him and Myself"

WHEN HE RETURNED home, Henry Clay was again treated to a sumptuous dinner, the type of display that John Quincy Adams regarded as "a triple alliance of flattery, vanity, and egotism."[1] Clay could not have disagreed more. He did not see his exit from politics as permanent, and he regarded these events as encouraging evidence of his persistent popularity. At the dinner, he continued his criticism of the Monroe administration for not recognizing Latin American republics, a fashionable stand to take in liberty-loving Kentucky. When the president finally acknowledged those new nations months later, Clay was vindicated, and Latin Americans would forever look gratefully upon him for being a friend during their early struggles.[2]

When Clay returned home in the spring of 1821, Lexington still suffered from the economic slump, but it sustained its reputation as a cultural center, in part because Transylvania University attracted students from all over the nation. Clay continued to serve on the university's board of trustees during these years, a time in which Andrew Jackson's nephew was a student, as was young Jefferson Davis, the future president of the Confederacy. Yet times were hard in Lexington, and Clay made his situation worse by generously cosigning notes for friends who often left him responsible for their debts. He was fortunate that his reputation as an excellent attorney attracted a brisk business to his practice, and his profitable arrangement with the BUS allowed him to begin retiring his debt fairly quickly. He needed every penny.

While Clay had been away, Ashland had seen some changes. In February, Lucretia delivered their fifth son and last child, John Morrison Clay, named for Clay's father and brother and for his friend James Morrison. Clay secured an appointment for his second son, seventeen-year-old Thomas Hart Clay, to the United States Military Academy, and the boy left for New York during the summer of 1821 to begin an ill-fated adventure. His math skills were so deficient that he lasted only a few months before West Point dismissed him in early 1822, and then he did not show up to meet his father in Washington. Instead he squandered his travel money on a drunken gambling spree in New York City and remained stranded there until Clay managed to get him funds for the trip home. The West Point disaster and the New York romp shook Clay's faith in Thomas, who seemed determined to avoid responsibility and to cultivate debauchery.[3]

In the spring of 1822, a happier if bittersweet event occurred when Susan Hart Clay married Martin Duralde, Jr. The marriage folded Susan into an extended family of Clays in the Crescent City: Martin was the younger brother of Julie Duralde Clay, wife of John Clay, Henry's brother. Later that year, when the newlyweds moved to New Orleans, Anne Clay accompanied them for a visit. It was quite an adventure for Anne, who was fifteen. And it was difficult for Henry and Lucretia to see Susan embark on a new life away from them. She was only seventeen.[4]

Aunt Julie took Anne under her wing, and during the dazzling whirl of parties the girl met James Erwin, an entrepreneur with interests in New Orleans and Tennessee whose father, Andrew, was a prominent Tennessee businessman, politician, and, most notably, an opponent of Andrew Jackson. James had dash and élan, more in fact than Anne or her parents realized, and young Anne's heart didn't stand a chance. The speedy courtship resulted in a wedding the following fall in Lexington, possibly more bittersweet for Henry Clay than Susan's, because clever Anne was always his favorite.[5] As if to compensate for the departure of the girls, Martin and Susan in 1823 gave the Clays their first grandchild, Martin Duralde III.

But indescribable sadness was yet to devastate Ashland in 1823. Early that year, fourteen-year-old Lucretia Hart Clay became ill and grew steadily worse through the spring. Never a strong child, she took a sharp turn for the worse in May, and by June her racking cough and bloody sputum revealed that she was dying of tuberculosis. Clay canceled all long-distance travel and refused cases in Ohio. He and Lucretia were at their little girl's bedside when she died on June 18, 1823, the third of their daughters who would forever be a child.[6]

IN EARLY 1822, Clay argued cases before the U.S. Supreme Court, breezed through the Washington social scene, and visited Richmond, Virginia, as a commissioner for the state of Kentucky in order to resolve a land dispute between Kentucky and Virginia.[7] His arrival in Richmond marked a homecoming and included pleasant reunions with old boyhood friends such as Tom Ritchie, who had become the influential editor of the Richmond *Enquirer.* Clay tried to persuade Ritchie to abandon his allegiance to states' rights and embrace a nationalist program. Ritchie was courteous but unconvinced.

Richmond's hospitality was typically lavish—Clay was treated to a grand parade through the middle of town on his way to the statehouse—and its citizens were appreciative of their guest. An overflowing crowd including many ladies heard Clay's "most impressive" address of three hours in which he laid out Kentucky's case in the land dispute and appealed to Virginians' pride by expressing his delight at sharing their heritage. His suggestion for arbitration came to nothing, however, and he turned his efforts to securing a rehearing of the 1821 Supreme Court ruling against Kentucky in *Green v. Biddle* by drafting an amicus curiae ("friend of the court") brief. Clay's brief was the first such document submitted to the Supreme Court, a groundbreaking gesture that has since become a commonplace in cases before the Court. The justices agreed to revisit the case but again ruled against Kentucky. Rather than closing the matter, however, considerable confusion continued in years to come as Kentucky defied Virginia's attempts to recover title to disputed lands, and not until a statute of limitations came into play was the issue resolved.[8]

Clay almost exhausted himself with his work for the BUS. His friend Langdon Cheves had taken over a bank in crisis with its books full of bad loans and had set about saving the institution by restricting credit for both state banks and individuals. Cheves hired Clay and other attorneys to bring suit to collect delinquent loans. Clay also helped the BUS to recover $100,000 from Ohio, taxes levied in defiance of *McCulloch v. Maryland.*[9]

The debt cases posed a ticklish problem for a man with political ambitions. Clay urged leniency and recommended extensions in many instances, but his association with the Bank during hard times made him unpopular in some circles, even in Kentucky. As in other states, the Kentucky legislature debated whether the state should help debtors, an argument that gave birth to two factions, the Relief and Anti-Relief parties. The Relief Party, advocating moratoriums on foreclosures, suspected Clay because of his association with the BUS. Although Clay tried mightily to stay above this fray, the issue would eventually lose him significant political support and rupture long-standing friendships as well. He needed both because he had decided to return to Congress and was considering a run for the presidency.[10]

The field was crowded. As early as 1822, a dozen aspirants were already testing the presidential waters. Some were long shots, such as Vice President Daniel D. Tompkins, whose alcoholism made his chances slim. New York governor DeWitt Clinton, an avid proponent of internal improvements, had gained luster by shepherding the Erie Canal into construction, and William Lowndes was a respected South Carolina statesman. But Clinton could not shake his regionalism, and Lowndes died before the campaign commenced. In the end, only a few noteworthy contenders actually stood as rivals, chiefly Crawford, Adams, and Calhoun, all members of Monroe's cabinet and consequently powerful because of their patronage. Clay also had to worry over disquieting stories out of Tennessee about Andrew Jackson's plans. A Jackson candidacy could seriously damage Clay's chances in the West.[11]

For the time being, though, the other candidates seemed most formidable. William H. Crawford was not solely a southern candidate, for his national appeal was evident in the coveted support of New York's powerful Albany Regency. When Republican politicians under the leadership of Senator Martin Van Buren had joined to control New York's complex network of factions, local interests, and egocentric personalities, Van Buren was hailed as a miracle worker for magically cobbling together this workable faction, informally called the Bucktails. His decision to back Crawford was a ringing endorsement of the Georgian's electability. Van Buren did not back losers.

John Quincy Adams, peppery and shrewd, had ruled the State Department for six years with a cool head and an unwavering resolve, and there was no question that he was eminently qualified for the presidency. Yet he labored under the handicap that many people did not much like him. Even those who did, after a fashion, could muster little enthusiasm for a man who seldom smiled and often snarled. As the secretary of state, he occupied the post from which both Madison and Monroe had moved seamlessly to the presidency, as much a tradition as anything could be in a government less than four decades old. Despite a feigned indifference to honors and office, Adams was eager to see the tradition continued.

The man who sat across from Crawford and Adams in Monroe's cabinet meetings was an interesting study in talent, industry, and guile. John C. Calhoun had not been Monroe's first choice for the War Department, nor even his second. But he proved himself tireless, diligent, and innovative in that post, and he surmounted the deficit of his youth—he was only forty-one in 1823—with such unremitting competence that others wondered where his ambition would lead him next. Perceptive observers, including Adams, deduced that Calhoun was quietly ruthless and ready to bowl over anyone who stood in his way. The truth of the matter was more complicated than that. Born into middling circumstances in a South Carolina Scots-Irish community, Calhoun rose through hard work and natural aptitude. His family made sacrifices to send him to good schools, first his brother-in-law Moses Waddell's Academy, and then Yale, where Calhoun established himself as something of a prodigy.

He married money. Floride Colhoun, John's first cousin once removed, was eleven years his junior, from the well-to-do side of the family, and fetching in her own right if a bit high-strung. She was an heiress to a fortune that allowed John to pursue politics and afforded them an opulent style of living. Their courtship had been ardent, although the one love poem that John had written to her oddly began every stanza with a lawyerly "Whereas," a portent of his behavior after their marriage, which was always kind but never again passionate. Nonetheless, men envied Calhoun for his beautiful, rich wife and his seemingly charmed political career, and they admired him for his talent as well as his dark and rugged good looks. Yet almost nobody liked him.

It was easy to see why. It was not just the stately house called Oakly (later known as Dumbarton Oaks), which had been purchased for the couple by Floride's mother. Nor was it because of his graceful wife who smelled of verbena and money, or even Calhoun's arresting stare that signaled a first-class mind unwilling to suffer ordinary mortals, let alone the fools among them. It was the impression that Calhoun was both enormously principled and thoroughly insincere, a humorless man who chuckled only when cued by the laughter of those who got the joke. In the fall of 1821, Calhoun promised Crawford his support for the presidency but privately mocked his colleague and characterized his possible election as a national calamity. By the following spring he was openly hostile toward Crawford, and by the summer of 1822 he was disparaging Adams as well.

Ambition did not so much change John Calhoun as it revealed him. Shy by nature, he drove himself to become a successful public man. His candidacy became for him a great religious crusade, a messianic mission to save the country from certain destruction. It was as good an excuse as any for public rectitude and private treachery. Those who saw only the rectitude supported him; those who felt the treachery distrusted him.

Clay thus weighed the weaknesses and the strengths of his rivals. He planned his resumption of public service with a run for the Eighteenth Congress, scheduled to convene in the late fall of 1823. His easy victory in August 1822 gave him more than a year before his return to Washington. He could arrange his affairs and quietly begin the letter-writing campaign to advance his presidential candidacy. In addition to his demanding legal workload, though, he battled chronic health problems. Never physically vigorous, Clay suffered from frequent colds and other infections that were occasionally debilitating. During 1822 and 1823 he was frequently under the care of physicians. Often bedridden, he read irritating reports in newspapers that described him as dying. The rumors hurt his viability as a presidential candidate.[12]

Other events in 1822 also undermined Clay's chances. In January, Congressman John Floyd of Virginia called for President Monroe to release correspondence between the government and the American peace commissioners at Ghent, hoping that it would reveal how Anglo-Indian relations had affected negotiations. Among those papers was Jonathan Russell's letter to Monroe, then secretary of state, alluding to disagreements in the delegation and promising to send another communication with details. That subsequent letter of February 1815 was not in the files, but Russell, now in Congress, obligingly supplied a copy. Russell's copy described John Quincy Adams as willing to sacrifice all western interests, including the navigation of the Mississippi, to retain New England fishing rights.[13]

Clay's friends chortled, confident that Adams could never recover from revelations that would cost him every vote outside New England. Yet Russell's original letter soon turned up and proved to be seriously at odds with Russell's supposedly true copy. Clearly the "copy" was a fabrication to hurt Adams, and many suspected that Clay was the author of the scheme if not the letter. Adams certainly thought so and was prepared to class him with Calhoun as willing to stoop low to achieve the presidency. Clay distanced himself from Russell, and Adams eventually wrote a damning refutation that made Russell look deceitful, which he likely was, and foolish, which he most certainly was.[14] Moreover, Adams's refutation turned the regional tables on Clay by depicting him as advocating only western interests at Ghent. The two briefly pounded each other in the newspapers before dropping the matter, possibly because Clay could see no advantage in challenging the memory of a man who rose hours before dawn to scrawl the minutiae of his life in a diary. This early round went to Adams.[15]

During the summer and fall of 1822 a much greater threat to Clay's candidacy came from the unexpected ambitions of a man completely outside the political establishment. Andrew Jackson, formerly a major general in the U.S. Army, had become a national symbol of all that was right or could be right about America. He was astonishingly popular with the public. Like Calhoun a generation after him, Jackson had risen from the ranks of the poor Scots-Irish of South Carolina, but unlike Calhoun, he had not gone to fine schools and married wealth. Instead, Jackson had gone to Tennessee and married another man's wife. In that coarse western country, lanky, long-faced Jackson carved out a life to mimic the ways of a gentleman by acquiring property and influence until he resembled a gentleman as much as anyone else in his neighborhood did. He was like Clay in that accomplishment. It was on the battlefield, though, that he achieved a celebrity that would have been remarkable for any place or any time. Jackson was a self-taught tactician; by nature he knew how to attack and by canny intuition when to defend. The War of 1812 provided him with the stage to display these talents, which were happily blended with Jackson's prodigious resolve. At New Orleans in January 1815, he validated the judgment of those rag-tag soldiers who had dubbed him "Old Hickory."[16]

Stories about the adulation of a grateful nation immediately became part of American lore. New Orleans began the practice of naming things after him. A tavern keeper in North Carolina, it was said, pulled out an ancient bar tab from Jackson's youthful carousing days and scrawled on it PAID IN FULL AT NEW OR-LEANS. He might as well have spoken for the entire nation, which seemed pre-pared to forgive Jackson not only his debts but all of his lapses as well.

As it happened, there were quite a few lapses. Jackson's bad temper was made doubly dangerous by a touchy sense of personal honor. The result was a life dotted with enough violence to give credence to tales that the Hero of New Orleans was actually a brawling thug unfit for polite society. He was just the man for taking care of marauding Indians or invading Redcoats, but was pre-cisely the man to avoid when the business was taking care of republican govern-ment. As his behavior in Florida showed, Jackson often reacted in ways that confirmed that judgment. Clay's criticism of Jackson in that incident was, in Jackson's eyes, evidence of a Washington cabal, one that included treachery in Monroe's cabinet, where Jackson was certain Crawford was his most deter-mined enemy. When Jackson threatened to slice off the ears of anyone who questioned his judgment, enough bodies and body parts lay in his wake to sug-gest he meant it.

The American people did not care. That kind of popularity sooner or later as-sumes its own dynamic and generates its own magnetism. Some people saw early on that this unlikely man was becoming irresistibly emblematic to the American people. Some of these visionaries were longtime friends, some were political opportunists jumping on an accelerating bandwagon, but they all whis-pered the word "presidency" in Jackson's ear. They became his handlers as well as his supporters, taking on the task of shaping him to match the image the peo-ple had already embraced. In July 1822, his handlers persuaded the Tennessee legislature to nominate him for the presidency, but political observers outside Tennessee interpreted it as a meaningless tribute to an aging hero. Clay even considered the possibility that antiwestern forces had engineered Jackson's nomination in order to divide the region's vote and elect an easterner. Surveying the supposedly empty honor afforded to Jackson, Clay saw the fine hand of John Quincy Adams.

In retrospect they were all curiously blind to what was about to happen, but the ordinarily sagacious political professionals who misread these events could be excused for misinterpreting the signs. Jackson was fifty-six and seemed physically spent from a hardscrabble life. Many thought he would be content to retire to the Hermitage, his home outside Nashville. He himself claimed this was his only desire. Political observers outside Tennessee reassured each other that he was telling the truth. His handlers, however, were only getting started. Jackson remained coy about his candidacy, but his friends were steely-eyed and serious. They next secured Jackson's election to the United States Senate. He would take his seat at the same time Clay returned to the House.[17]

ALTHOUGH CLAY UNDERESTIMATED Jackson, he saw the wisdom in obtaining a state nomination of his own. A nod from Kentucky would not be nearly as important as one from another state, and he spent the summer and fall of 1822 urging friends in Ohio to boost him in the Buckeye legislature. Clay's occasional advocacy of southern interests, such as his ambiguous stand on slavery in the Missouri debates, hurt him in the North, though. A Republican caucus in Ohio endorsed him in January 1823, but it was hardly as ringing as the approval of the entire legislature, and it was only a rump caucus at that.[18]

For the rest of 1822 through 1823, Clay corresponded with supporters in Louisiana, New York, and Missouri to suggest ways to improve his organization. His friends offered advice as well. From New York, Peter Porter urged Clay to court the wily Van Buren away from Crawford. Yet Clay resisted the temptation to make promises he would find awkward to keep. He repeatedly declared his "fixed determination to enter into no arrangements, to make no bargains," to remain "free & unshackled, to pursue the public good" according to his best judgment. He also avoided controversies with rivals. He made no attacks and maintained "a perfectly decorous course." As other candidates were sure to drop away, he wanted his affability to appeal to their uncommitted supporters.[19]

If Jackson did not become a serious candidate, Clay already controlled most of the western vote, but he wanted to be more than a regional candidate. Taking Porter's advice, he tried to improve his standing in New York, where Van Buren and his Bucktail Republicans had made enemies trying to ram Crawford through the legislature.[20] In Virginia, Clay hoped that hailing from the Slashes in Hanover County still counted for something. Just how much was difficult to say. His visit there in 1822 had not been encouraging, for Virginia Republicans suspected that Clay's nationalism would eventually diminish the South's influence. The Richmond Junto, a nebulous group of important Virginia Republicans tied together through kinship and financial alliances, supported Crawford.[21]

Garnering support in the East became more urgent as the likelihood of Jackson's candidacy became more obvious. Old Hickory was certainly acting like a candidate as he corresponded widely to assess the national strength of his rivals.

Clay knew about the letters flying from the Hermitage across the nation, and he struggled to keep up. Shortly after the death of little Lucretia, however, he fell seriously ill. Confined to his bed and able to manage only brief trips into Lexington, Clay's legal practice suffered and his pen faltered. Soon rumors about his future competed with the truth. They said he would not take his seat in the Eighteenth Congress that December. Some said he was dying.[22] He was still dangerously ill when he pulled his gaunt frame from the bed at Ashland to depart for Washington.

CLAY, ADAMS, AND Calhoun counted one another as foes, but at this point in their careers they essentially agreed that the country was best served by coordinated national initiatives ambitiously conceived and broadly executed. Yet the implementation of what Clay began calling the American System proved oddly out of phase with popular attitudes in the 1820s. Many Americans had grown wary of centralization, were increasingly opposed to the Bank of the United States, and were troubled by the prospect of paying for projects that were seen to help only distant locales. Crawford should have benefited from this emerging consensus for decentralization. With the exception of his support for the Bank (and even that was qualified), he opposed the expense and authority inherent in a nationalist agenda. Yet paradoxically, Crawford enjoyed almost no advantage from what should have been popular positions. Instead, many plain folk regarded him as the establishment's candidate because he was the favorite of the discredited Republican congressional caucus, and enemies painted his tenure at Treasury as marred by the corrupt use of patronage to purchase political support. Although he was the marginal favorite for having graciously stepped aside for Monroe in 1816, Crawford's star was partly dimmed by these charges of elitism and dishonesty. Crawford and Clay had been good friends until political rivalry caused them to grow apart. They remained cordial but wary as the campaign season commenced. Then, in the fall of 1823, as Clay lay ill at Ashland, something happened to Crawford that changed the entire dynamic of the upcoming election.[23]

Crawford had good reason to flee Washington, D.C., in the summer of 1823. The fetid swamps around the capital bred sickness in the hot months, and he sought relief from the heat and refuge from disease by traveling to the nearest high ground, the rolling Blue Ridge of western Virginia.[24] By the time Crawford arrived at James Barbour's home, however, he was seriously ill. Barbour anxiously summoned a local doctor who was probably imperfectly skilled. Most doctors were trained rather than educated, serving as apprentices to established practitioners, watching and learning from men who had received their inadequate training the same way. Armed with a deficient medical arsenal, the doctor attending Crawford waded into battle and made a terrible mistake. Thinking Crawford suffered from a heart malady, the doctor administered digitalis, an extract of the poisonous foxglove plant and toxic if incorrectly dosed. In fact, it was an extremely dangerous drug. The measure separating a fruitless from a fatal dose could be less than a drop. The doctor gave Crawford too much. With his heart beating wildly out of control, Crawford suffered a massive stroke and began to die.

Miraculously, he clung tenaciously to the slenderest thread of life. When the initial crisis passed, he was paralyzed and blind, his mouth twisted, his tongue thick and nearly speechless. What had happened was kept secret, and for the most part the effort was successful, though word that something was wrong at the Barbour mansion reached at least one neighbor. In October, the elderly Thomas Jefferson, who no longer left home for much of anything, traveled from nearby Monticello to visit Crawford, rumored to be ill but convalescing. In Crawford's darkened room, Jefferson gazed sadly at the withered form and spoke words of encouragement to the vacant eyes. This was a man dead but for the dying.

In November, a stricken but still breathing Crawford returned to Washington. Working at the Treasury proved too taxing, and he went into seclusion at his home on the corner of Massachusetts Avenue and Fourteenth Street, where he lay motionless, his eyes swollen and crusted shut with a new infection, the room's shutters closed against any light.

A growing din of gossip naturally speculated about Crawford's condition and the presidential contest. His rivals, including Henry Clay, measured the changed landscape and weighed how Crawford's impending death could help their causes.[25]

WHILE CLAY HAD lain ill for so long that summer and fall, family and friends had begun to worry that he might not recover. He took the waters at Olympian Springs, and his physicians put him on "the blue pill" for dyspepsia, but he did not improve. In November, starting toward Washington and certain that he would have to head south for his health soon after reaching it, Clay took matters into his own hands. He purchased a small carriage and a saddle horse and resolved to ignore his doctor's prescriptions and stop all medication. On the journey, he alternated between the carriage, the horse, and hiking, and arrived in Washington in fine fettle. In fact, he would remember that his stamina had never been better, and he was prepared to work like a horse.[26]

Washington was buzzing with rumors about Crawford, but it was also speculating about Andrew Jackson's ability to forgive and forget those who had condemned his conduct in the Seminole War. Jackson's journey from Nashville to Washington resembled a royal progress, with cheering crowds lining the streets of every town and village along the way. Children threw flowers, ladies waved handkerchiefs, and militias paraded with paunchy veterans at their head. Jackson was the picture of dignity, a paragon of calm, for his handlers intended for Old Hickory to make all of his enemies his friends, starting with Henry Clay.

Clay already knew from contacts in Tennessee about Jackson's plans to rehabilitate his image, so he was not surprised when Jackson and Tennessee senator John Eaton invited him to dinner. After a pleasant evening, Jackson and Eaton drove Clay back to his rooms on Ninth Street, where they parted as friends. Clay was not deceived by the show of cordiality, but he played along like a good veteran of such charades.[27]

Jackson's popularity could not touch Adams's in New England, but it undermined Crawford, Calhoun, and Clay in their key strongholds. In addition, Old Hickory's team of tenacious and discerning political operatives proved just as effective on the road as in Tennessee. They not only controlled their candidate but shaped public opinion with a network of newspapers that placed Jackson far ahead of rivals who fashioned their campaigns on outmoded rules and timeworn traditions. Calhoun was an early casualty of the Jackson machine. The South Carolinian hoped to establish national credentials by building support among Pennsylvania's political elite and securing the state's nomination. Jackson's supporters, however, bypassed the party bosses to create an effective grassroots network throughout Pennsylvania. The result was an event that stunned the political world when a convention in Harrisburg endorsed Jackson for president and named Calhoun his running mate. Lacking essential northern support, Calhoun dropped his presidential bid and accepted second place on a Jackson ticket. That Calhoun also appeared on the Adams ticket in some states emphasized his appeal and pointed to the sagacity of Jackson's highly professional organization in claiming him when they could. Their business was to win an election, and there was not an amateur among them.[28]

Many thought the election for Speaker was a reliable indicator of whether Clay or Crawford could attract more significant support, for it pitted Clay against Crawford supporter Philip Barbour. Clay's overwhelming victory seemed proof of Crawford's waning fortunes, but Crawford's adherents insisted it meant no such thing.[29] Worse, Crawford's already abysmal health worsened further in December, and false optimism about his recovery was growing as ineffective as it was tedious. Martin Van Buren consequently decided that the only way to save Crawford's candidacy was to secure the Republican congressional caucus's nomination.[30]

The caucus had not met since 1816 and even then had been criticized as a discredited vestige of elitism. As most states broadened the franchise to attain universal white male suffrage, nominations from state legislatures or conventions became a more desirable alternative, but Crawford's health made that option unlikely. By necessity, the traditional if tarnished caucus became the only way to convince the nation that Crawford was the true Republican candidate.[31]

All the other candidates condemned the caucus, although Clay paused to weigh the possibility that it might choose him instead of Crawford. Finally convinced that it would not, he too denounced it as undemocratic.[32] Crawford's supporters moved ahead, though, and managed to convene something resembling the caucus of old. On the night of February 14, 1824, only 66 of the 216 Republican members of Congress nominated Crawford. Acting as if this meant something, Crawford's people audaciously offered the vice presidency to Clay and then to Adams, but had to settle for Albert Gallatin. The halfhearted belief that Gallatin might possibly deliver his home state of Pennsylvania to the ticket could not cloak this poignantly nostalgic gesture that tried to revive the halcyon days of Jefferson and Madison. In the end, Gallatin did Crawford more harm than good, but it was the caucus nomination that hurt Crawford the most. Opponents quickly tarred him as a creature of the elite.[33]

SPEAKER CLAY KEPT on good terms with everyone by making fair committee assignments and allowing all reasonable debate. He promoted himself as the architect of the American System and was congenial rather than confrontational with the administration. Grateful that Monroe had finally recognized the Latin American republics, he enthusiastically supported the part of the 1823 annual message that became known as the Monroe Doctrine, a warning that the Americas were closed to new European colonialism, a position that complemented Clay's earlier call for hemispheric economic ties and cooperation.[34]

Clay was not so enthusiastic about the section of the message that pledged to limit American involvement in Europe. He shared this concern with others such as Daniel Webster, who offered a resolution calling for American recognition of Greek revolutionaries seeking independence from the Ottoman Empire. Clay thought that Webster's resolution celebrated America's founding principles and revolutionary past, but others did not agree. The resolution failed, and though the administration did not support the Greek Revolution, Clay did not publicly disparage Monroe. The Speaker's goal as candidate was to avoid controversy and maintain a positive attitude.[35]

Privately he grumbled. When Monroe and Adams ignored his recommendation that William Henry Harrison be appointed minister to Mexico, Clay muttered that "favorites, fawners and sycophants" controlled the administration and that he would make no more recommendations.[36] The appointment of his brother-in-law James Brown to head the far more prestigious embassy in France somewhat consoled Clay, though, and Nancy excitedly told Lucretia to send her a wish list of clothes to buy in Paris. Lucretia would need fashionable outfits, laughed Nancy, when she became First Lady. Lucretia could not have cared less.[37]

In the short term, Clay hoped his improved relations with the administration would smooth acceptance of his legislative program. Though he had originated none of the components of what he called the American System during this congressional session, they were increasingly regarded as his program, almost the equivalent of a modern political platform and proof that Clay was more than a regional candidate. An enthusiastic supporter declared that President Clay would take the nation to "the highest pinnacle" with his American System.[38]

To be sure, the Panic of 1819 and the depression that followed increased support for federally funded roads to revive commerce, but Monroe repeatedly vetoed efforts to pass such legislation. The challenge was to fashion a bill that Monroe could deem constitutional. The General Survey Bill of 1824 planned to have the Army Corps of Engineers survey projects to benefit the entire country.[39] In a major speech to the House on January 14, Clay lauded the measure. Some projects, he said, were simply too large and expensive for individual states. If anyone doubted the constitutionality of harbor improvements and interstate roads, the Constitution empowered the government "to establish Post Offices and Post Roads," and Congress obviously had the authority "to build" them.[40]

Strict constructionists like John Randolph countered that expanding the government's power to build roads eventually would give government the power to end slavery, another foreshadowing of how fears over this issue had begun to color southern perceptions of everything. Yet Randolph's mean streak compelled him also to parse Clay's grammar, diction, even pronunciation.[41] Randolph's contempt likely stung Clay, for he was sensitive about his educational deficiencies, but in this setting and at this time it revealed more about Randolph's tin ear than Clay's shortcomings. Clay was able to express regret about his poor education while adding that he had been "born to no proud patrimonial estate." He continued, "From my father I inherited only infancy, ignorance, and indigence. I feel my defects; but, so far as my situation in early life is concerned, I may, without presumption, say they are more my misfortune than my fault." Thus Henry Clay began the myth of his youthful poverty while passively showing John Randolph to be pretentious and petty, besting him again, this time with such finesse that the thin-skinned Virginian did not even feel the spear.[42] And

Clay won the point about the legislation as well. The General Survey Bill passed both houses and also the constitutional scruples of James Monroe, who signed it into law.

The tariff was another matter. Although economic hard times suggested that domestic manufactures and commerce were the keys to American prosperity, Clay faced significant obstacles in his effort to raise tariff schedules. Southerners bristled because the tariff had already raised the price of foreign imports and domestic goods while their agricultural staples, such as cotton, suffered in depressed markets. On the other end of the scale both economically and geographically, northeastern shippers were distressed because of diminishing European imports that the tariff made artificially expensive. They were against anything that worsened that situation.[43]

Clay's advocacy of higher tariffs was informed by his acquaintance with Irish-born Philadelphia publisher Mathew Carey, who wrote extensively about the advantages of a protective system and an integrated economy. Clay corresponded with Carey, whose influence is evident in Clay's major speech to the Committee of the Whole on March 30 and 31.[44] It featured standard appeals to patriotism and described people hit by the recent economic crisis, but it also included a lesson in political economy that made this speech a methodical, logical argument stripped of Clay's customary rhetorical flourishes. Aiming his remarks at "the high-minded, generous, and patriotic South," he explained that protecting American industry would not blight the nation with factories and urban slums but would economically liberate it from Europe. In his conclusion, he prayed that "God, in His infinite mercy," would "conduct us into that path which leads to riches, to greatness, to glory."[45]

The speech was hardly the stuff of schoolroom recitations (though he did use the phrase "American System" in its soon to be famous domestic context for the first time), but it gained wide currency, and Clay used it as a campaign document, distributing it in those states that benefited most from a tariff. His stand on the issue was not just political expediency, though. Clay became fixated on raising the protective tariff. He worked behind the scenes in Congress and buttonholed colleagues at social events. He was "ardent, dogmatical, and overbearing" and talked of little else.[46] The Tariff of 1824 barely passed the House with a five-vote margin, but it passed, and the Senate followed suit after tacking on some harmless amendments. Clay laughingly celebrated like a schoolboy, tossing off a pun about Connecticut congressman Samuel Foot and New York congressman Charles Foote, who had defected from the pro-tariff ranks. "We made a good *stand,*" he quipped, "considering we lost both our *feet.*"[47]

As he had the General Survey Bill, Monroe signed the measure. The nation seemed well advanced toward embracing Henry Clay's American System, and it seemed reasonable to assume that it would soon embrace Henry Clay as well.

AS PRESIDENTIAL CAMPAIGNS almost always do, the campaign of 1824 became nasty. For a year, Illinois senator Ninian Edwards used the pseudonym "A.B." to publish a series of anonymous letters in the *Washington Republican* accusing William Crawford of financial malfeasance. By the time Edwards was revealed as the author, he was on his way to Mexico to become its U.S. minister, but he openly accused Congress of negligence in not investigating his allegations. The House called for documents, and Clay appointed an investigative committee, but he was careful not to burn any bridges. He still had hopes that he could lure Crawford's supporters to his candidacy, and he was more than fair in choosing the committee members. Eventually it would exonerate Crawford— a whitewash, Adams privately complained, but he kept his opinion to himself to avoid alienating Crawford's supporters—but the charges of misconduct were the least of the Georgian's problems. He suffered a relapse that again confined him to his bed and revived rumors that he was dying. As 1824 wore on, he seemed certain to drop out of the presidential contest, one way or another.[48]

Clay did not see the need to engage in macabre calculations about Crawford's viability. He had concluded that no candidate would score a majority in the Electoral College, which meant that under the Twelfth Amendment, the House of Representatives would choose the next president from among the top three finishers. Clay's experience in shaping congressional majorities under ordinary procedures might make his influence in the House's selection of the next president nearly irresistible. After all, under the rules that gave each state one vote, little states with a single congressman wielded as much clout as populous states with large delegations.[49]

Congress adjourned on May 27, 1824, and Clay returned home to direct his presidential efforts from Lexington. He hoped that his legislative successes would strengthen his cause, particularly in the Mid-Atlantic region. He spent that summer and fall trying to determine the states certain to fall in his column balanced against those that were merely possible or at worst unlikely. The varying ways that states chose presidential electors complicated these forecasts. Since 1800, many states had abandoned the seemingly undemocratic practice of having legislatures choose electors. Instead, statewide popular votes or the division of states into electoral districts became prevalent. In the latter instance, electors from different districts could fall to different candidates, making for a mixed outcome rather than the usual winner-take-all result. In states where legislatures still chose electors, the electoral vote could also be split among more

Situated in a part of Hanover County, Virginia, called the Slashes, this modest but comfortable farm called "Clay's Spring" was the birthplace and boyhood home of Henry Clay. *(Engraving from the authors' collection)*

In later years, as part of his political image, Clay's youth was framed on the notion that he had been "The Millboy of the Slashes." The myth became part of the common lore, as this fanciful illustration from a late-nineteenth-century juvenile biography shows. *(From John Frost,* The Millboy of the Slashes: Young Folks' Life of Henry Clay, *1887)*

Dr Sir

By Dick you will receive 9 pieces of Gold & three half bits being the £10 due to Mr Davis, Mr Hay says he cannot pay interest on the claim — the original amount of all accts due from the Directors of the Public Buildings (with the — particular names of the persons to whom they were due) having been settled by the auditor & present to the assembly — who allowed just enough to pay of the principal. — I enclosed the exon agt the Mr Nelsons to you, by Mr Oliver. — — — Yr Obedt Servt

Henry Clay

Jany 9 — 1793.

written when Clay was 16 years old

This 1793 letter from Henry Clay to Peter Tinsley is the earliest surviving document in Clay's handwriting. Written shortly after he began working as a clerk in the Virginia Chancery, it displays a more ornate penmanship than his mature handwriting, but it is hardly the work of an unschooled primitive. *(Courtesy of the Transylvania University Library Special Collections)*

George Wythe was the chancellor of Virginia when Henry Clay became his clerk. A celebrated legal scholar and signer of the Declaration of Independence, Wythe was a kind mentor who helped to transform the boy from the Slashes into a confident young man. *(Detail from "The Signers of the Declaration of Independence" by Ole Erekson, Library of Congress)*

Clay had become a fashionable gentleman by the time he moved to Lexington in the late 1790s. This miniature shows him a year before he vaulted onto the national stage to fill a vacancy in the United States Senate in 1806. *(Engraving by D. Nicholls based on a miniature by Benjamin Trott, from Noah Brooks,* Statesmen, *1893)*

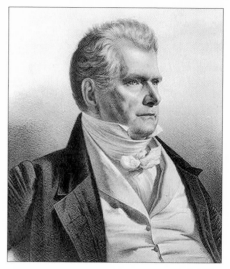

Felix Grundy was an early opponent of Clay's in the Kentucky legislature, but he became a member of Clay's War Hawk faction in the Twelfth Congress. Emblematic of the shifting alliances of politics, Grundy later became a Jacksonian and is shown here while serving as Martin Van Buren's attorney general. *(Library of Congress)*

Former vice president Aaron Burr's shadowy plans in the American West threatened to tarnish Clay's national career at its outset when Clay agreed to defend Burr in a grand jury proceeding. *(Bust by Jacques Jouvenal, U.S. Senate Collection)*

One of Henry and Lucretia Clay's closest friends in Washington was Margaret Bayard Smith, a social maven whose observations of life in the capital provide valuable insight into the political workings of the early republic. *(Library of Congress)*

As a member of the War Hawks, South Carolinian John C. Calhoun was one of Clay's most trusted lieutenants. His nationalism waned in the 1820s, however, and he became a rival and eventually an enemy. *(Library of Congress)*

John Randolph of Roanoke suffered from a malady that kept him beardless and high-voiced for all his tortured adult life. He was a vicious political opponent and early on detested Henry Clay. They eventually fought a notorious duel, but by the time of Randolph's death in 1833, he grudgingly admired Clay. *(Library of Congress)*

Clay liked President James Madison and, as did everyone, he adored Madison's smart and vivacious wife, unofficially "Cousin Dolley" to Clay because she had family connections in Hanover County. Yet Clay ultimately judged Madison as overwhelmed by the demands of the war with Britain and found vexing the president's constitutional reservations over Clay's legislative program. *(Library of Congress)*

Ghent became the site of the negotiations to end the War of 1812. It was little changed when captured in this later photograph. Christopher Hughes described it as "a most delightful place, in every respect." *(Library of Congress)*

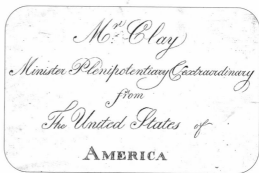

Ornate dress and formal calling cards were part of the official kit for American diplomats abroad. Clay's "Ghent Coat" is a prime example. *(Photograph by Mary Rezny, courtesy of Ashland, The Henry Clay Estate, Lexington, Kentucky)*

Swiss-born Albert Gallatin had served as Thomas Jefferson and James Madison's secretary of the treasury before his appointment to the American Peace Commission. He became indispensible in soothing arguments among his colleagues, especially those between John Quincy Adams and Clay. *(Painting by Rembrandt Peale, courtesy of Independence National Historical Park)*

A century after the signing of the Peace of Ghent, this painting by Amedee Foriestier commemorated the event as "The Hundred Years' Peace." Lord Gambier shakes hands with Adams as Gallatin stands just behind him. Kit Hughes is in the foreground, and Clay is seated behind James Bayard. *(Courtesy of Library Canada)*

The British occupied Washington, D.C., in August 1814 and burned several public buildings including the Executive Mansion and the Capitol, shown here as Clay would have seen it upon his return to Congress in 1815. *(Library of Congress)*

While Clay was in Europe, Lucretia hired New Englander Amos Kendall to tutor the children at Ashland. She was kind to him and even saved his life when he fell gravely ill, but Kendall eventually turned on Clay when the Jacksonians proved more useful associates.
(Library of Congress)

South Carolinian Langdon Cheves was a War Hawk, and succeeded Clay as Speaker when Clay departed for Europe in 1814. Cheves became the president of the Second Bank of the United States in 1819 and eventually employed Clay to represent its legal interests in the western states. *(Library of Congress)*

Clay supported James Monroe for the presidency in 1816 but was disappointed when Monroe offered him what Clay regarded as a minor cabinet post in the new administration. Clay remained in the House of Representatives. *(Library of Congress)*

As revolutions swept across Latin America, Clay supported the efforts of fledgling republics to throw off Spanish rule. His stand earned him Latin America's enduring admiration and gratitude, and he is shown here holding a message of thanks from South American republics. *(Courtesy of the University of Kentucky)*

William H. Crawford had long been a friend of Clay's, but disagreements over the BUS strained their relations. Crawford was also a rival for the presidency in 1824 and incredibly edged Clay out of contention despite being gravely ill. *(Library of Congress)*

Acerbic and proud, John Quincy Adams irritated Clay when they served together at Ghent and irked him by taking the State Department post in Monroe's cabinet. Yet Clay supported Adams over Andrew Jackson in the House vote for the presidency in 1825. When Clay was made secretary of state, Jacksonians immediately labeled the arrangement the "Corrupt Bargain." *(Library of Congress)*

Washington remained a rural village throughout the early nineteenth century, as this view of the Capitol in 1828 shows. Livestock can be seen grazing in the foreground. *(Library of Congress)*

An unrelenting political assault on John Quincy Adams and Clay made Andrew Jackson's election to the presidency a certainty in 1828. Old Hickory would remain Clay's bitter enemy for the rest of his life. *(Library of Congress)*

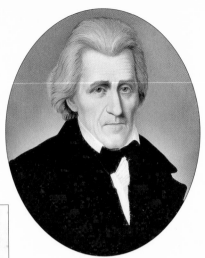

PLAIN SEWING DONE HERE

SYMPTOMS OF A LOCKED JAW

"CLAY
"Might stop a hole, to keep the wind away."

The Jackson-Clay clash provided abundant grist for cartoon mills during the eight years of Jackson's presidency. Titanic battles over the BUS and Nullification as well as Clay's 1832 presidential bid defined the period. *(Library of Congress)*

Martin Van Buren was a master coalition builder who earned the nickname "Little Magician" for fusing factions first in Albany for New York State politics and then across the country as the architect of the Democratic Party. His magic, however, played out when he followed Jackson into the presidency. Through it all, Clay remained a friend despite their deep political disagreements.
(Library of Congress)

Kentuckian Richard M. Johnson was for years Clay's friend until he bolted for the Jacksonian camp in the 1820s. Once a dashing war hero (he was credited with killing Tecumseh during the War of 1812), Johnson had become slovenly and dissolute by the time he served as Van Buren's vice president. *(Library of Congress)*

Francis Preston Blair was yet another Kentuckian who turned on Clay to become an enthusiastic Jacksonian. As editor of the Democrat newspaper *The Washington Globe*, Blair wrote many a venomous editorial condemning Clay and the Whigs in the most scurrilous terms. *(Library of Congress)*

THE GLOBE–MAN

After hearing of the Vote on the Sub-Treasury Bill.

Abolitionist Joshua R. Giddings disagreed with Clay about gradual emancipation, but their abiding cordiality exemplified Clay's talent for keeping personalities out of personal differences. *(Library of Congress)*

Clay's cousin Cassius M. Clay became an ardent opponent of slavery in Kentucky. His calls for immediate emancipation and his talent for poisonous prose ultimately estranged him from his kinsman. *(Library of Congress)*

Only slightly younger than Clay, Aaron Dupuy was one of the slaves at Clay's Spring who was taken to Kentucky by Clay's mother and stepfather. He and his wife, Charlotte, remained with Henry Clay at Ashland for the rest of Clay's life. *(Courtesy of the University of Kentucky)*

Charles Dupuy became Clay's personal servant in place of his father and accompanied him on his extensive travels. The artist John Neagle visited Ashland in 1842 to paint Clay's portrait and produced this sketch of Charles when he was in his mid-thirties. Clay freed Dupuy in December 1844. *(Courtesy of Hugh R. Parrish III)*

New Yorker Thurlow Weed was called the "Wizard of the Lobby" for his remarkable influence over the state legislature in Albany. In a career that spanned four decades, he repeatedly worked to thwart Clay's presidential plans, never more effectively than in the 1840 contest. *(Library of Congress)*

The aging former general William Henry Harrison supplanted Clay as the 1840 Whig nominee because Clay's supporters were outmaneuvered at the Harrisburg Convention. He took the disappointment in stride, but stories later circulated that he had been enraged at being passed over. *(Library of Congress)*

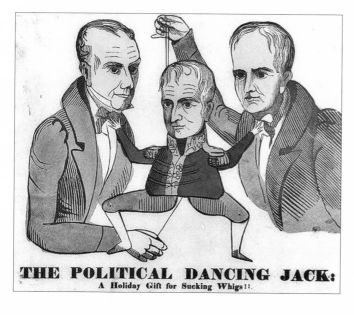

THE POLITICAL DANCING JACK:
A Holiday Gift for Sucking Whigs!!.

Democrats tried to depict Harrison as a puppet of Henry Clay and, in this cartoon, Henry A. Wise. The charge was an exaggeration, but it made Harrison resentful and ultimately worked to turn him against Clay. *(Library of Congress)*

In 1841, quarrels between the new Whig majority and Democrats spun out of control when Clay insulted Alabama senator William R. King. A duel was rumored, but friends arranged a public reconciliation. *(Library of Congress)*

John Tyler became president when Harrison died on April 4, 1841. Tyler had been little more than a ticket balancer and the second half of a catchy slogan until then. He and Clay were on friendly terms at first, but that soon changed. *(Library of Congress)*

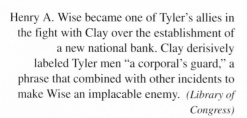

Henry A. Wise became one of Tyler's allies in the fight with Clay over the establishment of a new national bank. Clay derisively labeled Tyler men "a corporal's guard," a phrase that combined with other incidents to make Wise an implacable enemy. *(Library of Congress)*

Although always troubled by some measure of bad health, Clay in the early 1840s was at the height of his powers as he prepared for the 1844 presidential contest. *(Retouched from Brady, courtesy of Henry Clay Simpson, Jr.)*

Whigs and Democrats both employed imagery and symbols left over from the 1840 Harrison candidacy, especially variations on the coonskin cap theme. Clay was referred to as the Old Coon by Whigs proud of his cunning and by Democrats condemning his alleged deviousness. *(Courtesy of Ashland, The Henry Clay Estate, Lexington, Kentucky)*

The Democrat nominee in 1844 was Tennessean James K. Polk. The first "dark horse" candidate proved effective in the campaign, and his shrewd maneuvers along with an extraordinary amount of voter fraud defeated Clay, to almost everyone's astonishment. *(Library of Congress)*

Theodore Frelinghuysen was a distinguished New York reformer who seemed a perfect running mate for Clay in 1844. Democrats distorted his ties to Protestant philanthropic organizations, however, to portray him as an anti-Catholic bigot. *(Library of Congress; campaign ribbon courtesy of Ashland, The Henry Clay Estate, Lexington, Kentucky)*

Leslie Combs was one of Clay's most devoted friends. He called on Clay at Ashland after the 1844 defeat and found him profoundly disappointed but resigned to his loss. *(Frontispiece from* Narrative of the Life of General Leslie Combs, *1852)*

than one candidate. As Clay tallied the possible results in these various settings, the cardinal imperative was not to win but to place among the top three. Crawford's condition more than suggested he would.[50]

By June, William Crawford could not utter a word, and his supporters scrambled to salvage what they could of a deteriorating situation. Expectations of Crawford's death fueled rumors that his camp might turn to Clay or at least put Clay in the vice-presidential slot. If Crawford died before the election, Clay would become their candidate. If Crawford died after winning the election, Clay would become the nation's president-elect. Martin Van Buren asked Thomas Hart Benton to put such a proposal to Clay, mindful that Benton was Lucretia's cousin. The family connection was immaterial to Clay, though, and Van Buren's offer did not interest him. He and Crawford fundamentally disagreed about the role and purpose of government, and nothing could cloak the brazen cynicism of the arrangement Crawford's friends proposed. He also found the prospect of advancing to the presidency over Crawford's dead body vaguely distasteful.[51]

In any case, Clay saw no reason to give up, as Calhoun had, and settle for the vice presidency. In fact, he was likely to land among the finalists in the House. By his reckoning, everything depended on Andrew Jackson in one regard and New York in another. Jackson's popularity in the West had eroded Clay's early strength in the region, and by summer, only Kentucky remained certain. Even in the Bluegrass, Clay's enemies were promoting a Jackson movement, distributing pamphlets in Kentucky and throughout the West extolling Jackson's selfless patriotism while accusing Clay of every moral and political sin imaginable. The message was that Clay was simply unfit for the presidency.[52]

The question of character has always been a staple of presidential elections, but it became an especially prominent issue in 1824 as Jackson's people questioned Clay's and lauded Old Hickory's. The tactic succeeded in planting seeds of doubt about Clay. The country, after all, was in the midst of the Second Great Awakening, a fundamentalist Christian revival of far-reaching political as well as social implications. Clay had earned repute as an effective political broker, but that made it easy to paint him as a backroom dealer. Clay made no secret that he drank spirits, but that made it easy to whisper that he was a drunkard. He was famous for gambling, and that made it easy to depict him as reckless. Adams primly speculated on Clay's excesses, estimating that his losses in 1823 alone amounted to more than twenty thousand dollars—a clear exaggeration, but a perception shared by many. Taken in sum, these opinions about Clay's character made him damaged goods. Typical was the assessment that Clay had served the country well but his bad habits made him unqualified for the highest office in the land.[53] A North Carolina congressman described Clay as a "column that presents so beautiful a Corinthian capital" but "does not rest upon the broad basis of moral confidence."[54] And Congressman Romulus Saunders accused Clay of suffering from a "laxity of principles."[55] William Lenoir, another prominent North Carolinian, flatly declared that "a man who does not conduct himself morally" could not handle the "important business of a Government."[56]

Of course, not everyone thought Henry Clay was a libertine. Responding to vivid stories about the drinking and gambling of his free-spirited youth, friends could rightly claim that he had grown out of such childish intemperance. Fair-minded political opponents liked Clay because they always knew where he stood on issues and admired him because he never concealed his opinions. And yet, for those opponents, fair-minded or not, Clay's oratorical talents presented the vaguely troubling prospect that "the influence and power which his eloquence" could give him as president would make him politically dangerous.[57] Thus was it possible for his rivals to plant doubts about his character, his ambition, his past, and his plans, and even to use his strengths against him. If one did not know Henry Clay well, doubts found fertile ground; if one knew Henry Clay well, he seemed too good to be true, too talented to be trustworthy—a classic case of damned if he did, damned if he didn't.

Given his image problem, Clay should not have neglected the newspapers. The other candidates had partisan presses to churn out plaudits and assail rivals, squelch rumors about their champions and start gossip about opponents, Jackson's being the most effective. But Clay was remarkably indolent about this indispensable facet of a national campaign. In the late summer, his tireless but frustrated operative Josiah Johnston courted editors for Clay in New York and Pennsylvania with some success, but it was too little, too late. "There is one advantage at least you enjoy by having no press," Johnston comforted Clay. "You provoke no hostility."[58]

Most damaging of all, Clay too slowly awakened to Jackson's astonishing popularity and the incredible efficiency and effectiveness of Old Hickory's handlers. They had made everyone else look like rank amateurs, starting with the masterful maneuvers that won Pennsylvania the previous fall. It was both amusing and sad how everyone had scrambled afterward, trying to gain traction as Jackson's people greased additional skids. Poor Crawford was the saddest: once robust, now felled like a dying oak, reduced to showing himself in painful carriage rides around the capital, trying to quiet rumors and wick away the stench of impending death.

Messengers from the Crawford camp approached Clay a second time to repeat the offer of the vice presidency, and again Clay said no. Clay also rejected other attractive bargains that would have helped him in crucial states. He refused to name DeWitt Clinton as his vice president, despite the boost it would have given him in New York. "I can make no promises of office, of any sort, to any one, upon any condition whatever," Clay told Johnston. Others might scramble, but Clay would not. "Whatever support shall be given by me, if any," Clay declared, "must be spontaneous and unbought."[59]

Johnston applauded his friend's scruples, but he likely regarded the sentiment as quaintly antique, especially while he rushed around key states trying to win support with his hooded eyes and courtly voice, all for a man too principled to win except on his own terms. Clay's attitude, in short, was frustrating. Nobody realized it would also prove profoundly ironic.

CLAY HAD TO capture a respectable number of New York's thirty-six electoral votes to land in the top three finalists for the House. To boost his chances, Clay's friends named former New York senator Nathan Sanford as his running mate, and rumors that Adams and Clay forces would join to eliminate Crawford from contention caused Van Buren to renew his attempts yet again to place Clay on Crawford's ticket.[60]

Clay did not reject a temporary alliance with the Adams camp, and, growing nervous about his chances, he paused over Van Buren's offer. Jackson's candidacy had so excited the West that Clay doubted he could win the entire section, and without it, he would need a large eastern state to keep his chances alive. Crawford's grave condition—"a living death," one of Clay's friends told him—meant that if Crawford finished in the top three and Clay got him elected in the House, Clay might be in the White House within only a few months. Van Buren's pitch came with an air of urgency, because as autumn approached, the time for getting Clay on the ballot with Crawford in enough states was short.[61]

In the end, Clay rejected Van Buren's offer. Though it was tempting, it smelled, and Clay refused to hold his nose. Yet he framed his rejection in veiled language about not entering unseemly bargains. Van Buren judged such statements sufficiently ambiguous to warrant dumping Albert Gallatin from the vice-presidential slot on Crawford's ticket, a move that proved indirectly and unexpectedly disastrous for Clay. Gallatin's withdrawal gave the impression that Clay would replace him as vice president and quit the presidential race. His supporters in the West were further discouraged when Jackson partisans circulated reports that Clay had ceased to be a candidate for either office. Believing the stories, many Clay supporters did not vote for a man they believed was not running, thus suppressing Clay's totals.[62]

As the fall elections drew near, Clay outwardly maintained his characteristic optimism. He caught a bug, possibly from Theodore who had recently returned with a serious fever from visiting his sister Susan and uncle John in New Orleans, but he was convalescing when election returns began to form a sketchy picture.[63] With good reason, he was confident about Kentucky, which he easily won, but his expectation of sweeping the upper Midwest grew dim as he prepared to return to Congress. His stand on the Missouri Compromise hurt him with antislavery forces in those states, and his legal work for the BUS alienated debtors in the region. He barely won in Ohio over a surging Jackson but lost in Illinois and Indiana where he had been the early favorite. Opponents had spread exaggerations about his gambling and condemned his owning slaves as a sign of inherent immorality. An Indiana newspaper invented a story that Clay had wagered ten slaves on drawing the longest straw from a stack of rye.[64]

Clay left Ashland in mid-November, bound for Washington and certain that he had not won the election. But he had not expected to. He consoled himself that by his calculations, nobody else had won either. If all of Louisiana and part of New York fell in his column as he projected, he would make it into the final three in the House of Representatives. He correctly deduced that Adams and Jackson would be first and second in the Electoral College, though in which order he did not know, and once in the House, it would not matter. A careful observer made an apt horse racing analogy: "if Clay can be brought on the Turf, he will make sport, be sure of it!!"[65]

Clay journeyed to Washington without Lucretia. He wanted her with him, as always, but she resisted, and he finally let her stay at Ashland. Some have suggested that her reluctance revealed her growing reclusiveness and grief over her dead children. Yet she was likely more assertive about what she wanted after twenty-five years of marriage, and she had never found Washington appealing. In addition, she had a household to run with Eliza, James, and John still young children at eleven, seven, and three years, respectively. Though supposedly grown up, Theodore at twenty-two and Thomas at twenty-one worried her considerably as well. They studied law, but their labors were only intermittent, and both drank too much too often as they took an extraordinary amount of time deciding what to do with their lives. Only Henry Jr., almost fourteen at the end of 1824, exhibited discipline as well as ambition. His father increasingly placed his highest hopes on the boy's slender shoulders.

His most agreeable companion on the trip as Clay crossed into Virginia was the weather. The mildest autumn in anyone's memory had caused farmers to postpone their annual hog killings until the first heavy frosts, and late November continued warm and dry. On November 26, Clay stayed at the Albemarle Hotel, really only a roadside tavern near Charlottesville, and the following day he pulled up at Monticello to pay his respects to Thomas Jefferson. He planned to visit Jefferson and then James Madison at Montpelier for a few days before continuing to Washington.

Clay's visit with Jefferson was doubtless stimulating. The Sage of Monticello at eighty years was surprisingly robust, and his mind was as clear as his house was cluttered, both filled with a lifetime of artifacts, testaments to Jefferson's love of natural science. They would have talked about the objects strewn throughout Monticello's entrance hall, about the strangely warm weather, of course, and of crops and horses, and they likely shared stories about bad health, especially their chronic indigestion. They almost certainly talked about the election, although Clay's visit really was social rather than political.

Jefferson must have wondered what was happening to his country, sentiments that he likely left unspoken. He had been wrong about some things: wrong about using commercial restriction as a cudgel against Britain, wrong about conquering Canada by merely showing up, wrong even about his ideal republic, the one filled with educated yeomen who would come in from their plowing to read Homer at their hearths in the original Greek. Those farmers never had existed as Jefferson had pictured them, but they were spreading across the western landscape in another form, another kind of creature altogether, soon to be called Jacksonians.

Jefferson was depressingly right about other matters, especially slavery, which had caused the Missouri crisis—a "fire bell in the night," he had called it—and the regrettable compromise postponing rather than resolving the issue by drawing a line that Jefferson was sure would increasingly demark two peoples under one flag.[66] Clay had been part of that, and Jefferson's favorite candidate had nearly died at a neighbor's house the year before, likely never to recover to advance Jeffersonian principles of limited government. Jefferson disagreed with Clay's notions about federal power, but he had to marvel that Andrew Jackson, a partially educated backwoodsman who always smelled faintly of bear grease, might ascend to the chair held by Washington, and all because of forty-five minutes' work outside New Orleans on the Chalmette Plain. And though Jefferson was almost certainly too courteous to say that Clay was not his first and probably not even his second choice for the presidency, we might wonder what the Sage of Monticello did say to Henry Clay about who should be the next president and what Henry Clay confided to Thomas Jefferson.[67] Only days after Clay's visit, Daniel Webster visited Monticello and found Jefferson surprisingly animated in his denunciation of Andrew Jackson. "His passions are terrible," exclaimed Jefferson. "He is a *dangerous man.*"[68]

JUST AS CLAY had predicted, the unofficial count in the Electoral College in late November had Jackson in the lead and Adams second, but third place remained in doubt. Clay had been confident that Crawford's illness would ultimately give not only Virginia pause, but New York and Louisiana as well, and that third place would be his. Yet bad news awaited him when he arrived in Washington. By then, the first week of December, unofficial returns had come in for all states except Louisiana. He had lost Virginia, and New York had dealt him a devastating blow.

Circumstances in New York had troubled Clay throughout the fall, and he finally admitted, "I know not the secret springs which have produced such a strange result in N. York. I have moved none of them."[69] The secret springs were, in fact, a bizarre contrivance of shifting balances largely engineered by Adams men in the New York legislature. When that body met in November, enterprising Thurlow Weed and other Adams supporters struck a deal with Clay's faction to split New York's electors in a way favorable to Adams and Clay and at Crawford's expense. As proposed, Adams received 25 electors, Clay 7, and Crawford 4. By taking most of Adams's leavings and cutting Crawford's total, Clay would have placed third in the national canvass.[70]

Yet the deal unraveled when the designated electors met on December 1 to cast their votes for president. Pressure from all sides skewed everything, but there was bad faith as well. Two of Clay's electors simply did not show up, and their absence allowed the other electors to choose Adams men as replacements. One Adams elector then switched to Crawford, and a Clay elector switched to Jackson, rendering a final count of Adams 26, Crawford 5, Clay 4, and Jackson 1. The tally moved Crawford to third nationally.[71]

Surveying the result, Clay had to agree with his supporters that the Adams camp had betrayed him. Thurlow Weed had used Clay's help to obtain the lion's share of New York's vote for the New Englander and, having accomplished his object, had blithely cast off the Kentuckian. Adams, after all, was more likely to defeat the invalid Crawford in the House of Representatives. With Van Buren protecting Crawford's interests and Weed tending to Adams's, Clay's people had been simply bamboozled. It was the first of many sleights of hand for Weed in a career that would span decades. As a boy, he had callused those hands on the family farm and on Hudson River work boats. Now an accomplished politician and newspaper editor at the tender age of twenty-seven, he was already working up calluses on his conscience, a requirement for a politician in Martin Van Buren's state and Andrew Jackson's America.

LOSING NEW YORK meant that Clay had to have all of Louisiana's five electors to move ahead of Crawford, an unlikely feat in a state dazzled by Jackson.
Faithful Josiah Johnston resided in Louisiana, though, and he joined with other
Clay supporters to assure him that they controlled the legislature, where, as in
New York, the state's electors were chosen. Clay was not so sure. Bad news had
begun to roll in with appalling frequency. Opponents had spread the story in Indiana, Illinois, and Ohio that he had allied with Crawford, and the lie gained
enough currency to lose him the first two states while very nearly costing him
the third. Clay heard how rumors describing him at death's door or as having
abruptly withdrawn from the contest had further eroded his support in key areas,
including the all-important Louisiana. A sense of helplessness dampened his
jaunty optimism, and the rebuff of the West injured his ego. Virginia had gone
for Crawford, casting its lot with a blind invalid. Clay was reduced to donning a
jolly manner while grimly waiting for news from the lower Mississippi. When
that news arrived, first as rumor but soon in unofficial but verifiable reports,
Clay knew the worst had happened.[72]

He should have won Louisiana. His friends were perfectly right: he had the
votes in the legislature. But fate and shrewd maneuvers by his opponents denied
him the prize. As for fate, two legislators pledged to Clay suffered a carriage accident on the way to the vote and missed it. Second, the same rumors that had
injured him in Ohio, Indiana, and Illinois had flown to Louisiana as if on wings.
He was to be Crawford's vice president, said one; he was so discouraged that he
had quit the race, said another. Such talk disheartened Clay's supporters, leaving the door open for the other camps to make their move.[73]

His people were bested by yet another set of deals by politically ruthless
men with cold calculation. Andrew Jackson's considerable following in
Louisiana obviously derived from his exploits at New Orleans and the careful
concealment of his opinions, if he had any, about tariffs and other potentially
unpopular subjects. Only a small minority of Louisiana legislators supported
John Quincy Adams, but each man's supporters knew that at the end of the day
their candidates were certain to be among the top three finalists before the
House of Representatives. Events in Louisiana were thereafter steered by a
Jackson-Adams alliance to exclude Henry Clay from the finalists, giving Jackson or Adams—as to which one, they would hash out later—a better chance of
winning the presidency in the House of Representatives. The result was a split
ticket that gave Jackson three Louisiana electors and Adams two. Even though
he had controlled more legislators than either Jackson or Adams, Clay did not
receive a single electoral vote from Louisiana.[74]

With this news, Clay finally knew he had not just lost but had been eliminated. Jackson had 99 electoral votes, Adams 84, Crawford 41, and Clay 37. The 7 votes Clay should have received from New York with the 5 from Louisiana would have pushed Crawford to a relatively distant fourth, and Clay could have worked his magic in the House, the plan he had long envisioned as the only way to become president in the 1824 election.

It was all rather humiliating, especially to lose to an invalid who couldn't read a state paper, sign his name, or speak clearly enough for even close friends to understand him. In Clay's estimation, that described Andrew Jackson too, leaving off the invalid part. And capping the many injuries was an insult to Clay's intelligence. Thurlow Weed later transparently lied by claiming that his behavior in New York was based on a pledge that the agreement with Clay's men would only hold if Clay won in Louisiana. Anyone with a calendar knew that New York had made its decision long before news from Louisiana could have influenced it. Weed intuitively knew that in politics the audacious lie is always the best one.[75]

THE WEEKS THAT followed the news of his defeat gave Clay ample opportunity to salve his wounded pride. As the capital hummed with anticipation about how the House would resolve the inconclusive election, its members overwhelmingly reelected Clay their Speaker, proof that he still wielded considerable power. He threw himself into an unceasing social whirl of parties where pretty girls giggled over his harmless flirtations and, tellingly, friends of Jackson, Adams, and Crawford fetched him drinks and chuckled over his slightest witticisms. Always outwardly jovial, Clay masked his disappointment and became privately amused at this transparent courtship by his former rivals. "I enjoy the rare felicity, whilst alive," he marveled, "which is experienced by the dead." Having lost the contest, but not his influence, he was placed in the extraordinary position of using that influence to choose the next president. He chucked over "hearing every kind of eulogium and panegyric pronounced upon me."[76] He was having an enormously good time.

Meanwhile, the social event of Washington's season loomed when Marie-Joseph Paul Yves Roch du Motier, better known to Americans as the Marquis de Lafayette, arrived in the capital to coincide with the last session of the Eighteenth Congress.[77] Begun the previous summer at Monroe's invitation, Lafayette's American tour everywhere had attracted immense crowds grateful for his service, nostalgic for the virtue of an earlier time, and eager to venerate a disappearing cohort of aging veterans. Lafayette, himself aged and infirm, nonetheless remained a vibrant symbol of the Revolution's idealism, a reminder of the long odds and improbable triumph of a motley people over the world's most powerful empire. He had toured much of the Northeast and had visited Yorktown on the anniversary of the British surrender. Now Washington prepared to honor him in peerless fashion.

Clay had met Lafayette in France almost ten years before and had stayed in touch ever since with fond letters. He greeted the elderly Frenchman warmly on the morning of December 10 for an intimate breakfast and suggested that Lafayette praise past American patriotism in his address to Congress later that day. Congress greeted Lafayette's remarks with more than ovations. It voted to give the old man $200,000 as well as a 24,000-acre township from public lands. Clay was privately aghast at the extravagance, but held his tongue and checked his impulse to oppose the popular gesture. He could not have helped but wonder, though, how many miles of road could have been carved out of the western wilderness with those federal dollars (more than $4 million in today's money), and how many prosperous farms were to be held in abeyance by the marquis's American fiefdom.[78]

The parties in Lafayette's honor were gratifying, though, and Clay basked in the social flurry and courtly lavishness that lit up the city's evenings. These events did not divert attention from the pending decision about the presidency so much as they pleasantly raised anticipation and provided glittering settings for speculation among the partially informed and maneuvering by the candidates' friends. To those not in the know, Henry Clay appeared detached from the issue, poker-faced when obliquely flattered, occasionally teasing the edgy contenders. Everyone realized that much "depends upon Mr. Clay."[79]

Clay's inertia, though, concealed his own quiet maneuvering, if imperfectly. When Kentuckian Robert P. Letcher began dropping in on John Quincy Adams in late December, it was noticed. Letcher's visits were ostensibly to discuss public affairs, especially Kentucky politics, yet he was Clay's friend and roomed at Clay's boardinghouse, an association that troubled supporters of Jackson and Crawford. Actually, up to a point, Letcher's somewhat directionless conversations with Adams were curiously frustrating, but when Letcher expressed concern that the Kentucky legislature might instruct the state's congressional delegation to vote for Jackson, Adams perked up. Now they were getting somewhere.

Letcher casually asked Adams his opinion of Clay. Adams said he felt no ill will toward Henry Clay—a clipped response, not necessarily a lie, but not completely sincere either. Even though Letcher claimed that he was not speaking for Clay, Adams had the growing impression that Clay's friend was trying to discover what could be expected in exchange for Clay's support. If that was indeed the purpose of these visits, it made Adams extremely uncomfortable. Dark-haired and swarthy, Letcher was known as "Black Bob," and the prospect of bargaining for the presidency with such a man repelled Adams. In that regard, Letcher's visits became troubling, especially because Adams could not afford to offend him without risking Kentucky's vote. Then, on New Year's Day, Letcher's series of calls reached their object: Would Adams be willing to have a private meeting with Henry Clay?

Adams said yes.[80]

That evening Martin Van Buren and members of his congressional mess hosted a dinner party for Lafayette at Williamson's Hotel. The reception at the fashionable hostelry saw hundreds gathered, including every prominent man in the city. Henry Clay glided through the assemblage, pausing to drop quips at clusters of notables, laughter trailing after him like the wake of a cruising ship. When he saw Andrew Jackson and John Quincy Adams sitting near the fire with an empty chair between them—almost a cordon sanitaire—he must have laughed at their funereal appearance. Both stared straight ahead, their faces sour. True enough, the expression was natural to Adams even in repose, but Jackson could usually muster pleasantries at these affairs. Perhaps he was ailing, or possibly he had nothing to say (the numerous parties tended to exhaust small talk) and was uncomfortable sitting near his chief rival for the presidency. Clay found the solemn tableau irresistible. He walked across the room and sat down in the empty chair. As he looked back and forth at the two men, a sly smile parted his wide mouth. He pretended to study them. They pretended not to notice him. Finally, he deftly delivered a line aimed more at his audience than at his former adversaries: "Well, gentlemen, since you are both so near the chair, but neither can occupy it, I will slip in between you, and take it myself!" Laughter rippled out across the room, reaching a crescendo as more people got the joke or had it repeated to them. Amid this hilarity Adams sat stone-faced. If reports that Jackson smiled are true, it was certainly a forced smile. Neither he nor Adams thought any of this was a joking matter.[81]

And actually, Clay didn't either. Later in the evening he quietly approached Adams and softly told him that they should speak privately in a few days. Eight days passed before a note from Clay arrived at Adams's home asking permission to call that evening at six. Those eight days had seemed an eternity. Adams immediately replied to come, yes, by all means.[82]

THE FIRST NINE days of January 1825 had been for Henry Clay a postscript to a decision he had made some time before, and if we can believe his later recollection, quite some time before. He later claimed that he began weighing the possibility that he might not finish in the top three even before he had left Ashland in November. The disappointing news from Indiana and Illinois had certainly made that unpleasant prospect more likely, and his optimism about New York did indeed have the sound of cheerful whistling in the dark. In short, and according to Clay, he had considered supporting Adams while still gazing at waving bluegrass. That contemplation became resolve when his defeat became certain, and several friends later confirmed that determination.

We can never be absolutely certain whether this was true or if Clay concocted this story only after everything about what he and Adams decided on that January night went dreadfully wrong. If true, the chronology is a powerful defense against the charge that Clay held out his support for the highest bidder, an auction for which Crawford did not have the assets and Jackson the stomach. But an inescapable logic drove what Clay did, if not how he did it, suggesting that his decision to have Mr. Adams as president was inevitable, regardless of its timing. He certainly would have known at least this before he left Kentucky.[83]

Clay went to Adams's lodgings on January 9 possibly by the lash of his own ambition but certainly by a simple process of elimination. Even if Clay had agreed with Crawford's ideas on government, the Georgian's health made his potential presidency unlikely and probably impossible. Andrew Jackson's temperament made the prospect of his presidency chilling for Clay, who believed Old Hickory exhibited every characteristic that should be avoided in an elected official. Not only was Jackson a "military chieftain" whose Florida exploits had raised the specter of Caesar, he had also demonstrated an appalling disregard for American law during his occupation of New Orleans at the end of the War of 1812, for the laws of nations by attacking Spain, and for basic humanity by killing men without trials. He had displayed an ungovernable temper during his brief stint as territorial governor of Florida. Clay knew his decision would damage his popularity in the pro-Jackson West, especially in Kentucky.[84] Yet he was convinced that Jackson's election "would be a precedent fraught with much danger to the character and security of our institutions." He could not "believe that killing 2500 Englishmen at N. Orleans qualifies for the various, difficult and complicated duties of the Chief Magistry." He would not be a party "to the election of a military chieftain."[85]

Clay sincerely believed that what was now being called *his* American System was the only way to promote the country's domestic welfare and preserve its security from foreign threats. In his mind, that required a legislative program maintaining the Bank, enacting protective tariffs, and authorizing internal improvements, all implausible under the limited-government philosophies of Crawford or Jackson. Even Adams did not completely agree with Clay's legislative vision, but in the balance of the three, he was simply the least of the evils.

For obvious reasons, Clay would have kept his decision to himself until he was certain of his defeat. From accounts by people in whom he confided and from Clay's own words, we have evidence that at least before the New Year, he had decided to support Adams, even before Letcher's visits to Adams had obliquely broached the subject of Clay's possible place in the coming administration. Letcher's primary purpose, in fact, seems to have been the discovery of Adams's views about a wide range of issues in addition to Adams's opinions about Clay. This last was certainly important for more than just personal reasons, though. The recent campaign had been bitter, and Clay knew that Adams suspected him of having encouraged many nasty attacks. Clay never nursed grudges, for he knew that in politics today's enemy was often tomorrow's ally. But others were less philosophical. Adams almost matched Andrew Jackson for prickly pride that had a long memory for slights. If Clay's programs were to prosper during an Adams administration, he needed a personal as well as a political reconciliation with the peppery little man from Massachusetts.[86]

So the eight days between Clay's brief conversation with Adams and the meeting it proposed were undoubtedly a coda to a decision already made. Beginning at six o'clock on the evening of January 9, the two spent about three hours in Adams's study, and most of what was said there would remain forever behind that room's doors, for neither man left a lengthy account of their discussion. Adams perfunctorily noted in his diary that the two talked about the past and the future. They did not, Adams claimed, confer about Clay's possible place in the new administration. Instead, he said, Clay wanted assurances that they were in accord on broad public principles, meaning the American System. Comfortable with Adams's stance on those principles, Clay finally told Adams what more than a few already knew and almost everyone else suspected. Clay gave Adams his support.[87]

Adams certainly understood that he was gaining more than just Clay's vote in the Kentucky delegation. Clay would use his almost irresistible influence in the House to persuade others to vote for Adams as well. It could all be decided on the first ballot, something nobody had thought likely before. This cheerful prospect obscured for the Puritan and the gambler that they were about to make the biggest mistake of their careers.

Snow covered the ground as Clay left his appointment. Much of Washington stayed indoors close to hearths and cozy fires. The wind was arctic and wet. A storm was coming.[88]

BEFORE HE ANNOUNCED his endorsement of Adams, Clay quietly began lining up votes. At such a task, he was at his most skillful, a political manager who could pluck deals out of thin air. Yet his numerous consultations about his plans had virtually revealed his choice of Adams, and Jackson's supporters panicked when Clay's politicking all but confirmed it. The vote in the House would take place on February 9, giving them just one month to stop Henry Clay from making John Quincy Adams president. Despite Jackson's affecting a magisterial aloofness from petty politics, his operatives had been trying to arrange deals themselves. Just days before the Adams-Clay meeting, Jackson sourly speculated that Adams, Crawford, and Clay were in league against him. He was wrong about Crawford.[89]

Clay spent most of two weeks strolling from meeting to meeting. Then word arrived from the Kentucky legislature instructing the state delegation to vote for Jackson. If the news gave Clay pause, he did not show it. Despite being on record that such directives were inviolable, he continued to pressure his Kentucky colleagues as well as other western delegations to vote for Adams. Jackson supporters hoped that Frankfort's instructions rather than Clay's brokering would save the day, but they redoubled efforts to ally with Crawford just to play it safe. When the Kentucky delegation announced on January 24 that they would ignore their state's instructions, gloom settled in over Old Hickory's camp. Clay finally announced for Adams as well, a signal that Prince Hal's work was finished. Only the actual vote on February 9 would show whether it had been effective.[90]

As the day approached, Clay's work certainly seemed to have been successful. With Kentucky came Ohio, and Jackson's people frantically tried to dam the tide. They resorted to thuggish tactics, threatening popular uprisings if the House rejected Old Hickory and mounting a smear campaign against Clay. On January 25, the Philadelphia *Columbian Observer* printed a letter from an anonymous author claiming that Adams and Clay had made a tainted deal. The writer said he had evidence that Adams had promised to make Clay secretary of state in exchange for Clay's help in the House of Representatives. Other papers printed the letter in a crudely conceived operation that would first soil Clay as a power broker in the upcoming election and then make his acceptance of any post in an Adams administration seem proof of the letter's accusation.[91]

Clay met this challenge head-on. When the letter appeared in the Washington *National Intelligencer,* he demanded that his accuser step from the shadows with such vehemence that he all but invited a duel. A few days later, Congressman George Kremer of Pennsylvania came forward, and Clay immediately regretted being a party to what was obviously a sorry mess. Kremer was an embarrassingly doting Jackson supporter, an oafish eccentric whom Clay described as "an old vulgar gross drinking half Dutchman half Irishman." It was doubtful that poor Kremer had written the letter but almost certain that he had been put up to claiming it.[92] His high-pitched, screeching voice had prompted some wag at some point to dub him George "Screamer," a rhyme on "Kremer" that enough people found funny to have the name stick, only one of the many sad aspects of Kremer's indifferent public career. He was too stupid to take seriously, and everyone concluded that his "muddy and contracted mind" could not have concocted the attack on Clay without direction.[93] Clay had no intention of meeting this pathetic Jackson pawn in a duel, but instead asked that Congress investigate the charges. Kremer had no evidence and became a sputtering fount of inconsistencies during the congressional inquiry that ultimately judged his accusations to be groundless. Everyone would remember the accusations, though. Andrew Jackson and his minions would see to that, which was the whole point in the first place.[94]

Clay's character continued to come under attack. He put up a brave front, but he was deeply hurt by some of his critics. He had braced himself for the Jackson camp's spiteful barbs, but many Crawford people were spitting denunciations too, some of them Virginians whom Clay considered old friends. His native state had placed him dead last in its popular vote, and now friends he had known since childhood were accusing him of corruption. Had he ever known them at all?[95]

JOHN RANDOLPH AND Edward Livingston were the only two congressmen present in 1825 who were members of the House of Representatives that had elected Thomas Jefferson in 1801. Speaker Clay consequently wanted a committee to draw up procedures to govern the February 9 vote. Meanwhile, he vigorously lobbied Daniel Pope Cook of Illinois and John Scott of Missouri, each the lone congressman for their states. Illinois had gone for Jackson in the general election, and though Cook wanted to vote for Adams, he was under more than considerable pressure—he was receiving death threats—to vote accordingly. Missouri had voted for Clay, with Jackson second, and Clay battled Thomas Hart Benton over Scott's vote, for Benton had put aside his differences with Jackson to jump on Old Hickory's bandwagon. Clay persuaded Cook to vote his conscience and bested Benton to claim Scott for Adams.[96]

At noon on February 9, representatives and senators assembled in the House chamber. They first heard the tally of votes for vice president declaring John C. Calhoun the winner. As expected, the count of the presidential ballots yielded no majority, and the Senate retired to allow the House to elect the president from the three top candidates. Each state received a box to collect its delegation's ballots and appointed a member to take it to a table where Daniel Webster and John Randolph waited. There they would conduct a count of the twenty-four boxes' contents and record each state's choice. To win, a candidate needed a simple majority of thirteen.[97]

Everyone predicted that of the three candidates, Adams would win the most states on the first ballot but fall short of a majority, despite Clay's work. On a second or third ballot the slightest switch of votes in this or that delegation could then shift momentum, break the contest open, and allow for serious haggling to begin anew. Van Buren expected Adams to win as many as twelve states, a total perilously close to victory, especially because New York was almost evenly split between Crawford and Adams. Van Buren lobbied hard among New York representatives to stop them from putting the New Englander over the top on the first ballot, and he had all but succeeded except for one vacillating holdout.

Stephen Van Rensselaer was one of the wealthiest men in America, the inheritor of enormous landed estates in New York that he had turned into models of productivity and social experimentation. He was in politics entirely because of his civic-mindedness, but he had never distinguished himself, possibly because he was pleasant by temperament and eager to avoid confrontation. Understandably, then, he found the contentious decision of choosing the next president not only daunting but disconcerting, especially when Van Buren explained to him that his vote would likely decide the question. By Van Buren's count, if Van Rensselaer voted for Crawford, New York would be tied, giving Adams only twelve states on the first ballot.[98]

Because Van Buren planned to tout Crawford as a compromise candidate on a second ballot, it was crucial that he persuade Van Rensselaer to make a second ballot necessary. He and Delaware congressman Louis McLane had an advantage in that they lodged and took meals with Van Rensselaer, and their relentless coaxing and prodding finally brought him over to Crawford. By the time Van Rensselaer arrived at the Capitol, though, Clay had discovered Van Buren's plan. Accompanied by Daniel Webster, Clay hustled Van Rensselaer into the little "Speaker's Room."

It was neither Webster's nor Clay's finest moment as they browbeat the confused old man, vividly describing the national turmoil if the House failed to elect the president on the first ballot. Van Rensselaer left the room nearly in tears but committed to do Clay's bidding. Convinced that the good of the country depended on a decisive first ballot, Stephen Van Rensselaer's key vote made John Quincy Adams president by giving him New York.

Martin Van Buren later excused Van Rensselaer's decision by inventing a curious story that endured for many years. As Van Rensselaer prepared to vote, Van Buren said, he prayed for guidance, his head bowed and his eyes closed. Opening his eyes with his head still bowed, he spied on the floor what he took to be a sign from above: an Adams ballot. He placed it in New York's box as his vote, confident that he was doing God's will. The quaint story was a pure fabrication. Van Rensselaer said immediately after the event that he had acted according to his sense of duty to the country.[99]

Initially, all seemed calm in the wake of this surprisingly quick resolution. A congressional delegation took the results to Adams, who received them with an affected air of subdued calm. As always, he revealed his actual sentiments to his diary: "May the blessing of God rest upon the event of this Day!"[100] That night, at a reception hosted by President Monroe, he encountered Jackson. Official Washington held its collective breath, but Old Hickory only bowed courteously and extended his hand to congratulate Adams on his victory.[101]

Jackson's generous gesture did not reflect his true feelings, which were hardly jovial. At first, he and his friends were stunned enough to be civil, but after analyzing the House vote, they became livid. In addition to the seven states Adams had taken in the general election, he had captured six others that rightly belonged to someone else. In the general election, Kentucky, Missouri, and Ohio were Clay's, while Maryland, Louisiana, and Illinois should have been Jackson's.[102] He did not take long to reach the conclusion that Adams and Clay's base intrigue had cost him the election. "Was there ever witnessed," he snarled, "such a bare faced corruption in any country before?"[103] The days of Jackson's smiling congratulations were over.

Adams early planned to offer the State Department to Henry Clay, but Clay always claimed that the post was never a trade for his support. When the offer came, though, he worried about how it looked. He asked friends if Kremer's accusations—proven groundless but still in currency among capital gossips—should prevent him from accepting. Most of those friends told him that the opportunity was too good to refuse. They assured him that with Kremer discredited, talk of corruption and bargains would soon die down.[104] Clay heard what he wanted to, but he also reasoned that not to accept the post in order to avoid criticism would only serve to give even more credence to the rumors. He would not be intimidated by idle gossip.

The announcement that Clay had accepted the post did not merely fuel gossip, however. It set off a firestorm. Andrew Jackson bellowed to a friend that "the *Judas* of the West had closed the contract and will receive the thirty pieces of silver." Jackson ominously added, "His end will be the same."[105] Pro-Jackson newspapers proclaimed that Clay "DIED—*politically,*" on the day of the House vote because "he fell victim to cunning, fraud and intrigue."[106]

Clay and Adams had underestimated Jackson as a candidate, but they had missed the measure of him as an enemy by miles. His extensive network of supporters was never more animated and relentless than when given a specific task with a specific goal. With the same cold calculation that had delivered Pennsylvania to Old Hickory at the Harrisburg convention in the fall of 1823, these Jacksonites resolved to destroy Adams's stillborn administration and crush its midwife, Henry Clay. The "Corrupt Bargain" rapidly became an unshakable label, shorthand to condemn the brigand Clay and his coconspirator Adams. Lost in the clamor over the supposedly tainted deal that had bought the presidency were all the programs Clay believed vital to the nation. Adams was to be at best a caretaker. At the State Department, Clay would nearly kill himself trying to make that otherwise.

Twenty-five years later, he would finally make what he described as a "frank confession." He never doubted that his vote for John Quincy Adams had been the proper thing to do, and he insisted that he had been correct to persuade his friends to do the same. Yet he had made a grievous mistake taking the position at State. "By doing so I injured both him [Adams] and myself," Clay would declare, "and I often painfully felt that I had seriously impaired my own capacity of public usefulness."[107]

The president-elect soon had a sobering illustration of just how wrong things had gone when he and his wife attended the theater shortly after the House vote and were greeted by tepid applause. When the performers spontaneously broke into a rousing rendition of "The Hunters of Kentucky," a song celebrating Andrew Jackson's victory at New Orleans, the audience clapped in time and at its finish erupted into a prolonged fit of stamping, whistling, and cheers. The Adamses sat silent through the impromptu merriment staring straight ahead, their faces ever so slightly revealing a mixture of surprise and pain. This would be emblematic of their lives for the next fifteen hundred days.[108]

It officially began when John Quincy Adams took a carriage to his inauguration on March 4, 1825. He had at last attained the pinnacle his venerable father had always hoped would be his son's, a vindication of his own troubled presidency that had been beset by tribulation and crisis. Adams basked in his father's praise and still held hopes that his intellect and visionary ideas would make his administration historic, memorable as one of his country's finest hours.

Clay was there to watch Adams take the oath of office. He had resigned as Speaker of the House the day before and looked forward to plunging into work at the State Department. He planned to be at his desk early the following morning. First light on the day after the inauguration, however, found him so ill he could not get out of bed. He was diagnosed as having a severe cold, possibly even influenza. He would recover, but he never really felt fit for the next four years.

CHAPTER SEVEN

A Thousand Cuts

HENRY CLAY'S NOMINATION to head the State Department prompted a humiliating challenge in the Senate, the work not only of Jacksonians embittered by the election but also of those who feared Clay would be the dominant force in the new administration. That anxiety at least proved the ignorance of Adams's opponents, for the new president was indomitable, but the combination of anger and unease produced an embarrassing opposition to Clay. In the end, the Senate confirmed him by a comfortable margin, but getting to that end had put him through the wringer, an unpromising way to begin.[1]

The confirmation debates in the Senate were just the beginning of his ordeal. Clay remained physically ill, more or less, for the next four years, and barely a day passed that the cry of "corruption" and "bargain" did not appear in the Jackson press. Jackson's supporters interjected the charge in ordinary conversation, referred to it in every stump speech, and made it a feature of campaigns for constables, commissioners, and congressmen. They ridiculed the president as "Johnny Q." and mocked Clay as a bungling diplomat and despicable conspirator. The treatment wounded Adams, to be sure, but he resolved to ignore it, shielding himself with New England pluck. Henry Clay could not. Western traditions of honor and southern rituals of pride ruled Clay's passions, and he would not ignore assaults on his character. As they were bound to, the Kremer charges resurfaced after the inauguration, and Clay took off his coat and spat on his palms.[2]

Initially he explained himself to Kentuckians through their newspapers, knowing the press throughout the country would reprint his words. He had not betrayed the West by supporting Adams, he said, because he had made no secret of his nationalism before the election. He sincerely believed that after himself, Adams would be the best president. In any case, he could not have endorsed a man he judged manifestly unqualified for the post. Turning to the accusations that he had acted dishonorably, Clay all but said that George Kremer had not written the letter that had sparked the controversy. Instead, he was certain that

Jackson's supporters had duped Kremer into claiming the letter as his creation. Someone close to Jackson had written it, most likely Tennessee senator John Eaton, who had been seen visiting Kremer at the time. Concluding with the observation that Jackson and his followers were being petulant in defeat, Clay insisted that the country as well as the new administration had to move on.[3]

Clay possibly believed his response would "triumph over all the villaney [sic]," yet it only riled John Eaton, who immediately fired off a letter to Clay demanding he retract the accusation about the Kremer letter. Clay said that he would gladly do so if Eaton plainly stated that his "nocturnal interview" with Kremer had not helped to produce Kremer's accusations. Eaton adopted indignation as a defense. He did not have to explain anything to Henry Clay, he huffed, remarking for good measure that Clay had taken a rather long time to answer his demand for an apology. Clay angrily responded the next day. His official duties did not allow him to "mark the hours with the same precision as a gentleman of your presumed leisure," he snapped. Eaton could, Clay observed, avoid the issue all he liked, but all could then draw reasonable conclusions about his role in producing the Kremer letter. Eaton published these exchanges, an act Clay thought "silly" because he believed that Eaton had gotten the worst of it. Clay's temper blinded him to the disagreeable appearance of the new secretary of state, in office barely three weeks, engaging in a petty feud.[4]

Eaton was tireless and Jackson was popular, a bad combination in enemies. Reports soon told of mobs burning Clay in effigy throughout the West. Determined, faceless men, moving like shadows, were poking about in his private affairs, trying to acquire letters proving he had sold his support to Adams. In Washington, angry Jackson partisans snubbed him at parties and whispered slanders behind his back. Clay's friends gently soothed him with kind words. He had acted honorably to prevent a disastrous Jackson presidency, they said, and they assured him that the controversy would fade. But they also began to reckon with great unease the resolve of Clay's enemies. The capacity of those enemies for unrestrained abuse surprised them. It shook Clay.[5]

To make matters worse, much of his work at the State Department was worse than tedious. Deskwork had always bored him, and most of his duties required him to spend twelve hours a day at it, signing patents and answering mail. Routine and interminable meetings with foreign diplomats were taxing enough, but office seekers pushed his patience beyond its limits. The only redeeming feature of his job was the unexpected but pleasant discovery that Adams proved easy to work with. Because of the president's special interest in foreign relations, a natural result of his extensive service abroad, he and Clay had lengthy discussions in which they mostly agreed and usually could compromise when they did not.[6]

Unlike congressional service with its recesses and adjournments, Clay's duties at State would be ongoing and uninterrupted. Trips home would be catch-as-catch-can affairs. Years before, when he had expected to become Monroe's secretary of state, Clay had planned to have Lucretia and the children move to Washington, and now he revived the idea. Shortly after the inauguration, he returned to Kentucky to bring everyone who could come to the capital. He had not seen Lucretia and the children for six months, and he hoped that Susan and Anne would come up from New Orleans to Ashland, bringing their husbands, Martin and James, and Susan's little boys, Martin and Henry Clay Duralde, for a grand reunion. Clay worried how Lucretia would adjust to the responsibilities of a cabinet wife, let alone the demands of Washington's social whirl. It would be nice, he thought, if Anne and James could come along, if only for a while. Lucretia had been "cheerfully" preparing for the trip, a good sign, and Anne smiled in a reassuring letter to her father that Mama was "of that disposition to make friends & sincere ones too wherever she goes."[7]

The prospect of seeing them all took the edge off the stories about his new unpopularity in the West. He crossed the mountains at the end of May without once seeing his effigy ablaze and was pleasantly surprised when Kentuckians greeted his arrival with celebrations and dinners in his honor. Everybody was already in a celebratory mood because Lafayette's American journey had just weeks before brought him through the Bluegrass. Kentucky had received Lafayette with lavish balls and treated him to glowing tributes, a glory that shone on Clay, for the old Frenchman had visited Lucretia at Ashland and stopped at Versailles to deliver an address from the balcony of Watkins Tavern, the inn founded by Clay's mother and stepfather. The reminders of Clay's friendship with this enormously popular hero could not have come at a better time.[8]

It was also fortunate for him that Kentucky politics had tumbled into chaos. The central issue remained how to resolve the respective situations of debtors and creditors. The latter had considerable influence, but the former were more numerous, and for the moment, demographics had the upper hand, making the Relief Party temporarily ascendant. Several of Clay's political friends jumped on the Relief bandwagon, including Amos Kendall, Francis Blair, William T. Barry, and recently elected governor Joseph Desha. The Relief majority in the legislature passed a slew of measures friendly to debtors, and Desha quickly signed them into law. The state court of appeals, however, ruled that much of this legislation was unconstitutional. When the Relief Party settled the confrontation by simply establishing a new court, the old court refused to relinquish its authority, and Kentucky suddenly had two judiciaries, each insisting that the other was illegitimate.

The commotion became all-consuming, extending to matters that seemed quite unrelated. At the end of 1824, Governor Desha's son Isaac had robbed and murdered a traveler, leaving a trail of evidence that assured his conviction and a death sentence. Governor Desha's New Court Party accused the Old Court Party of framing Isaac to ruin his father. Public outcry eventually got Isaac a new trial, but people who had nothing to do with politics could testify to seeing him shortly after the murder in bloodstained clothes, riding the victim's horse, his pocket containing the victim's wallet with a considerable amount of money. Again sentenced to hang, Isaac slit his throat, but the suicide attempt only ruined his trachea, and the gallows still waited. Governor Desha could stand it no longer. He threw caution, not to mention duty, to the wind and pardoned his son.[9]

These lurid doings could not distract Kentucky forever, and Clay gradually noticed a disturbing trend as the storm over the presidential election refused to subside. Instead, it eventually spread and became linked to every other imaginable disagreement. In Kentucky, many Relief Party members were outright Jacksonians or inclined toward him (incongruously, because down at the Hermitage Jackson occasionally took a break from denouncing Henry Clay to denounce debtors), and their agreement over credit and bankruptcy issues had organized them at the head of a numerous voter base. In time, they would turn critical eyes to Clay's support of Adams.[10]

CLAY LEFT KENTUCKY for Washington that summer uncertain about when he would return, at least permanently. He hoped that a two-term Clay administration would follow two for the Adams presidency, an accumulation of years that would see him retiring in 1841. Then he could return to Kentucky forever and live out his days, as Thomas Jefferson had at Monticello, to become the Sage of Ashland. It was all a dream in 1825, of course, but one worth planning. Because buying new furniture and other household necessities would be cheaper than shipping what the family owned, Clay had arranged to sell those items he would not place in storage. Consequently, the procession that lumbered out of Kentucky toward Washington was light on baggage. The Clays in it were numerous, however, if nothing else was. The three oldest boys remained behind, but Henry and Lucretia had young James and John as well as twelve-year-old Eliza, excited by the prospect of adventures waiting in the capital, an infectious enthusiasm that lightened everyone's mood. Anne and James Erwin were also on the journey. Susan and Martin Duralde had not made the trip from New Orleans to Kentucky that summer, but Susan wrote her mother a bright letter full of cheerful optimism. She especially wanted Lucretia to put aside her diffidence and enjoy the sparkling social setting Washington offered.[11]

They traveled slowly, their short baggage train of wagons rumbling along behind them. After the journey up the Ohio River, their slow progress came to an abrupt halt about thirty miles outside Cincinnati near the small town of Lebanon, Ohio, because Eliza was ill and feverish. The little girl had always been the picture of health, so although Henry and Lucretia were worried, they assumed Eliza's excitement had simply gotten the better of her. As they lingered at Lebanon, though, she became no better, even worsening in her frowning parents' estimation. Clay summoned a local physician, but his treatments did little good and possibly some harm. Everyone watched in despair and terror as Eliza slowly sank. Then in early August she rallied, and by August 9, the doctor was certain she was on her way to a full recovery. With laughing relief over this miracle, Henry and Lucretia listened as the doctor reckoned that Eliza was not yet out of the woods. It was best, he told Clay, that she stay put in Lebanon until her recuperation was further along.

Clay was already weeks overdue in the capital and gave in to a compulsive urge to rush to his duties. The family would follow when Eliza was stronger. For ten days, Clay jounced east over rutted roads in a stagecoach. Twenty miles from Washington, the coach stopped at a roadside tavern for breakfast, and Clay spied a copy of the *National Intelligencer.* He glanced at the date on the masthead: August 21, the current issue. He would be up on the latest political and diplomatic news. Then he saw the small item as though it alone remained in focus as the rest of the newspaper dissolved into a blur. Eliza Clay was dead, had been dead since August 11, just two days after he left Lebanon.[12]

The singularly cruel blow was made doubly worse by his guilt, by the impersonal way he discovered the news, by contemplating that for more than a week he had been going farther and farther away from Lucretia. Later that day, as he slid limply out of the stagecoach in Washington, he was physically and mentally shattered. Two days passed before he could write to comfort Lucretia and pour out his grief. He arranged to meet her and the children outside Washington to bring them into town the following weekend. The sad procession was a cortege as it made its way to rented rooms, and Lucretia climbed the stairs of the boardinghouse like an old woman. Her dreams and hopes for her young daughter had become a leaden weight. Eliza would never attend the excellent girls' school in the capital. She would never laugh with her mother in this cheerless, lonely city.[13]

Clay threw himself into his work with such abandon that friends worried about his health, but at least he had something to distract him from unrelenting grief. Misery shadowed Lucretia's days. Social engagements were out of the question. Other than tending to two rambunctious little boys, she whiled away empty hours, her dim world the cramped rooms of the boardinghouse. In early October, Clay moved the family into a large rented house with the hope that changed surroundings could abate some measure of their grief.[14]

In New Orleans, Susan Clay Duralde received the news about Eliza after she had sent her cheerful letter to her parents. Her little sister's death devastated her, and she physically wilted in the days that followed. Weak and listless, she mildly alarmed Martin Duralde, but everyone knew that grief could injure the body as well as the spirit. Though concerned, the family in New Orleans was confident that time would heal the wound. In fact, after a few days, Susan appeared to be recovering. Then a high fever seized her, an all too common malady in southern Louisiana, but a disquieting one that could be serious. It soon became obvious that Susan was not just sad but gravely ill. Doctors came and went while Martin helplessly looked on. The doctors, whispering and grim, were increasingly helpless too. Martin simply ceased functioning, withdrawing in the face of the unfolding and unthinkable horror. Someone, possibly Martin's sister Julie, took the two sons to Susan's bedside for farewells, more for their mother than for them. Little Martin, the older boy, could barely understand what was happening, and his younger brother, Henry Clay Duralde, was still teething. At the end, Susan could hardly speak, but she whispered a final regret: she would never see her parents again. She died on September 18, just five weeks after her sister. Susan was twenty-two.[15]

Martin was inconsolable, irrational, and unable to care for the children. His sisters Louise and Julie Duralde Clay temporarily took them in. Receiving the news in Washington, Henry and Lucretia came near complete collapse. For Lucretia, prayer provided some comfort, but her faith seemed hard put to sustain her. She retreated into a quiet sadness in the months that followed. First losing the infant Laura and then Eliza indelibly associated Washington with dying children. Because of Susan, she now had to bear the death of a child in a far removed place. In France, Nancy ripped open letters from Clay and worried that her sister would "never regain her happiness," that Susan's death had "given the finishing stroke to it." The burden of grief made Clay so ill that he considered resigning as secretary of state. "Out of six daughters," he finally cried, "to be deprived of all but one!"[16]

CLAY DID NOT quit his post. Instead, he hoped that work could distract his mind while time healed his heart. The Jacksonian drumbeat about the Clay-Adams bargain spurred him to work all the harder at the State Department and to help Adams frame a popular domestic program. The new administration had a hard row to hoe. Jackson's supporters wanted four years of mounting administration failures to assure Old Hickory's election in 1828. For that reason, they tried to thwart all of its proposals, but others had reason to challenge administration policies as well. Suspicious of expanding federal power, they jealously guarded states' rights and individual liberty. These two groups were not always mutually exclusive. Support for Jackson often coincided with the exaltation of states' rights. But Jacksonians had the motive of political expediency, aside from any philosophical differences with Henry Clay. For all its rough-and-tumble complexities, the election of 1824 had at least set the stage to clarify a fundamental disagreement. A sharp distinction emerged between those who saw the federal government as the prime mover in domestic affairs and those who believed that localism was best.[17]

When Congress convened in December, Andrew Jackson was not in it. He had resigned from the Senate in October. Almost immediately, the Tennessee legislature nominated him for the presidency in 1828, by design starting the next campaign before people could forget the disappointment of the last one. Almost everything about the business of government quickly focused on electing Jackson in four years. His supporters in Congress pounced at their first opportunity, which was their response to Adams's first annual message.[18]

Clay saw it coming. He knew the perils of crossing an angry legislature, and Adams wisely listened to Clay's advice to tone down or eliminate items sure to provoke such great opposition that they had no chance of success. Jacksonians and states' rights proponents nevertheless condemned even the modified version of the annual message. John Randolph, recently elected to the Senate, was characteristically vocal and caustic. In fact, the volume of personal attacks and pure fabrications hurled at the administration surprised Clay as much as they troubled him. Nothing was beyond the imagination of detractors. Jacksonians even accused Adams and Clay of sending Lafayette home in a ship so leaky it was in constant danger of sinking, revealing their contemptible indifference, their unseemly parsimony.[19]

In the face of such unreasonable attacks, there was little one could do except work hard, hoping success would blunt criticism and win the public's support. Clay intended to help with his foreign policy initiatives. He came to detest the mundane parts of his job, but few secretaries of state have matched Clay's resolve to do every part of the job thoroughly and well. Unfortunately for him as well as the country, resolve would not be enough. The State Department did not allow him to use his talents, which were uniquely suited to the legislature, where few could equal Clay's ability to form majorities, construct compromises, and persuade with dazzling oratory. Instead, he was deskbound, writing reams of instructions to men of varying ability in distant capitals, both he and they frustrated by delay and hemmed in by elaborate protocols.[20]

The administration inherited perennial problems with Great Britain and France, although the problems with Britain were less menacing than usual in that they mainly concerned commerce. Adams and Clay thought the British might be willing to open their West Indies colonies to unrestricted American trade. London had already partially opened the door, though with a consequential limitation. All trade with British colonies had to be direct, meaning American shippers could not carry anything but American goods to those colonies or take from them goods for sale anywhere but the United States. This limited colonial trade was an encouraging breakthrough, though, and Clay hoped it was a sign that the British could be persuaded to lift all restrictions. For that task he needed just the right man, and he entreated veteran diplomat and fellow Ghent commissioner Albert Gallatin to replace the elderly Rufus King, the U.S. minister in London.

Gallatin had doubts about British flexibility, and he resisted Clay for as long as he could before reluctantly accepting the post. He left for London in July 1826, and after arriving there either found his doubts confirmed or was disinclined to exert himself to overcome what he regarded as insurmountable obstacles. Gallatin not only failed to budge the British on the West Indian trade, he could not settle the Canadian boundary or secure American navigation rights on the St. Lawrence River either. Clay began to doubt Gallatin's commitment to his mission, and Gallatin grew increasingly touchy over Clay's constant urging to redouble his efforts. Gallatin's failure in London was a serious blow to Clay's tenure at State, dashing all his initiatives to improve Anglo-American relations.[21]

Franco-American affairs posed a more delicate problem. For years, the United States had insisted that the French should pay damages for attacks on U.S. shipping during the Napoleonic Wars. The matter had gone to arbitration, which confirmed many American claims, but the French government repeatedly delayed payment. Clay believed these postponements amounted to bad faith and justified expropriating French shipping as compensation, an extreme response that Adams overruled. Clay was at least fortunate in that Monroe's minister to Paris continued under Adams, providing both continuity to the American position and perceptive reports about events on the ground there. James Brown, of course, was also Clay's brother-in-law, but that was immaterial to the French, who remained obstinate, just as Brown predicted they would. The matter remained unresolved when Adams and Clay left office, another diplomatic failure. The French finally paid the debt during Andrew Jackson's presidency, making Clay's disappointment even more galling. Jackson would rattle a saber to get the money.[22]

Yet Clay was ready to rattle a saber of his own if the situation merited it. He and Adams suspected that the French planned to test the strength of the Monroe Doctrine by reviving their colonial ventures in Latin America. Spanish Cuba seemed ripe for the taking, for rumors described cash-strapped Spain as unable to protect the Jewel of the Antilles. Contemplating the alarming possibility that Madrid might cede Cuba to France, Clay maintained contact with a confidential agent on the island and closely monitored activity in the Caribbean. When Clay learned that a French fleet of twenty-seven ships had left Martinique for Cuba, his instructions to James Brown amounted to a Clay Codicil to the Monroe Doctrine: just as the United States would not abide the establishment of new colonies in the hemisphere, it would not tolerate the transfer of a colony from one European nation to another. The French perceived that Clay was serious and backed off. They denied having any interest in Cuba.[23]

During his service in the House, Clay's support of Latin American independence had earned him the enduring goodwill of struggling revolutionaries. That relationship and his continued interest in promoting strong hemispheric ties across Latin America boded well for excellent relations between the United States and the new republics to the south. He negotiated commercial treaties with several Latin American governments, but the real opportunity for American leadership came early during Clay's tenure at the State Department. Venezuelan Simón Bolívar, celebrated as the liberator of South America and president of Gran Colombia as well as Peru and Bolivia, called a congress of interested states to meet in Panama in the spring of 1826. Even though the United States was not originally on the invitation list, Mexico and Colombia soon rectified the oversight.[24]

Clay was thrilled. The congress promised an opportunity to promote better trade relations throughout the Americas. Using subtle diplomatic pressure and citing the success of its own example, the United States could encourage greater democracy in the infant republics to the south. President Adams, however, was less excited by these prospects. In fact, he was quite wary of weak Latin American nations ensnaring the United States into military alliances that could plunge the nation into wars unrelated to American interests. Clay convinced Adams that enthusiasm had not blinded him to these realities. He assured the president that U.S. commissioners would have carefully worded instructions preventing them from committing to anything other than commercial compacts. Clay also argued that establishing commercial ties could only increase a salutary exposure to U.S. influence and institutions, leading to solid frameworks of government and the avoidance of risky projects such as trying to seize Cuba from enfeebled Spain. Finally agreeing that the advantages outweighed the hazards, Adams consented to sending delegates to the Panama Congress. Clay began searching for apt candidates.[25]

Hoping to head off criticism, Adams asked the Senate to confirm the diplomats and the House to appropriate funds for their mission, but the gesture proved a mistake. When Clay nominated Kentuckian Richard Anderson, Jr., currently U.S. minister to Colombia, and former Pennsylvania congressman John Sergeant as commissioners, anti-administration senators used the confirmation hearings to attack the entire Panama initiative.[26] They spent several weeks scrutinizing Anderson and Sergeant as though they were under arraignment. The Senate Foreign Relations Committee issued a report criticizing the idea of sending a mission at all, and for weeks afterward, whenever the topic appeared on the Senate's calendar, critics leaped to lodge a variety of arguments against it. Isolationists darkly warned that the mission could entangle the United States in dangerous alliances and surrender the country's autonomy to some sort of Pan-American commission. Southerners nodded, frowned, and raised additional objections, including the fact that Latin American nations that recognized the Haitian government of former slaves would incite similar slave rebellions throughout the South. While Jacksonians in Congress kept pounding the idea, Vice President John C. Calhoun lurked around the edges of the argument in exasperating ways. The caprice of American electoral procedures in 1824 had made Calhoun the vice president despite his disdain for John Quincy Adams and his allegiance to Andrew Jackson. Working behind the scenes, Calhoun accordingly played spoiler to block Clay-Adams initiatives, including participation in the Panama Congress. Clay wanted this badly, though, and spent the political capital necessary to obtain it. He used his influence in Congress to counter the partisan bickering over confirmations in the Senate and funding in the House. In the end, he got both the delegates and the money.[27]

Yet it took him a precious long time to do so, and ultimately time became Clay's biggest enemy. When the American commissioners finally started out for Central America, the Panama Congress was already in session. They had detailed instructions from Clay, but his labors were wasted, for neither Anderson nor Sergeant had a chance to act on them. Traveling from Colombia, Anderson fell ill and died en route. In the meantime, the congress adjourned to reconvene in Tacubaya, Mexico, making Sergeant's trip to Panama pointless. Adams and Clay hastily replaced Anderson with Joel Poinsett, U.S. minister to Mexico, but by the time he and Sergeant arrived at Tacubaya, the meeting had adjourned again. All the administration's efforts came to nothing. Worse, British envoys to the Latin American congress were able to point smugly to the conspicuous absence of U.S. participants as evidence of U.S. indifference, tarnishing Clay's otherwise sterling relationships with the new republics. Clay had handed the president another failure, and the administration's critics crowed like roosters.[28]

The lack of U.S. participation at the Panama Congress meant problems for the country in the long term as many Latin American countries began to jettison their republican governments, falling prey to barracks rebellions and into the clutches of military strongmen. Clay even became suspicious that Simon Bolívar's fame had turned the Great Liberator's head. Clay used unofficial channels to dissuade the shift to authoritarianism, and he instructed diplomats like Poinsett to use their influence to encourage democratic rule, but he could do little to reverse these disturbing trends. In Mexico, Poinsett exemplified the problem while exacerbating it. Ineffectual on almost every level, he could not diminish British influence in Mexico City, and he obnoxiously injected himself into Mexico's domestic affairs, making him useless in fulfilling Clay's hope of purchasing portions of northern Mexico, most important Texas. In the end, Poinsett could not even conclude a simple trade agreement with Mexico. Under Clay's guidance, the State Department actually established more trade treaties than his predecessors had, but Poinsett's failure in Mexico was a blot that many unfairly recalled as emblematic of Clay's commercial diplomacy, consequently perceiving all his efforts as disappointing.[29]

JOHN RANDOLPH WAS having the time of his life assailing John Quincy Adams and Henry Clay. Week after week of vicious attacks finally led even John Eaton to complain that the Senate did nothing other than listen to Randolph brand the administration a gaggle of "money changers" and use every debate "to torture" the president and secretary of state.[30] Randolph's behavior was no less exasperating because it was in character, and Clay could bear only so much of it. On March 30, 1826, Randolph's invective finally crossed the line. It was a long and meandering speech even for Randolph, but it contained a clever literary reference to characters in Henry Fielding's novel *Tom Jones* that set the capital to buzzing and Clay to fuming. Randolph spoke of "the coalition of Blifil and Black George—by the combination unheard of till then, of the puritan with the black-leg."[31] Fielding's Blifil was an outwardly pious man consumed with greed, and Black George was a lovable though inherently dishonest servant. Randolph clearly meant these two fictional characters to represent Adams and Clay, but he also cast subtlety aside to make sure everyone understood the insult. Adams was the puritan and Clay the blackleg, slang for a card cheat. Clay intended to kill John Randolph for that remark.

The day after Randolph's speech, Clay summoned his friend the U.S. Army Quartermaster General Thomas S. Jesup to his office with a note for Randolph that cited his "unprovoked attack on my character, in the Senate of the United States, on yesterday." Clay insisted that he had "no other alternative than that of demanding personal satisfaction." Jesup was dismayed. He tried to talk Clay out of sending this challenge, but Clay responded that "no public station, no, not even life, is worth holding, if coupled with dishonor." He insisted that Jesup deliver the note and asked him to serve as his second in the duel.[32]

When it came to threatening violence, Randolph had few equals, but unlike Clay, who almost never threatened violence, Randolph's public life had not featured a single instance of gunplay. In 1807, he had refused a challenge from General James Wilkinson with the contemptuous response, "I cannot descend to your level." Now he had a note from the secretary of state calling him out, and to his credit, he was greatly troubled by it. Randolph went to Thomas Hart Benton's room at Brown's Hotel and asked about his family connection to Lucretia Clay. Benton said he was a blood relative. The news saddened Randolph; he had wanted his friend to be his second. He told Benton that he would ask Congressman Edward F. Tattnall of Georgia to be his second, but he also swore Benton to secrecy. Randolph felt he had no choice but to accept Clay's challenge, to preserve both his honor and the inviolability of Senate debates. And yet Randolph paused; he then looked levelly at Thomas Hart Benton and told him not to worry.[33]

Jesup and Tattnall unhappily made the final arrangements, neither wanting to see the duel happen but neither able to stop it. Nevertheless, they and Benton spent much of the next week trying to work out an agreement that could allow Randolph to say that everyone had misconstrued him and allow Clay to cancel the meeting honorably. Randolph, however, stood firm on the principle he had declared to Benton. No one had the right to demand an explanation for remarks in the Senate, least of all a member of the executive branch.[34]

Randolph had the choice of weapons. It was to be pistols. The seconds outlined additional terms. Ten paces, a distance of about thirty feet, would separate Clay and Randolph. They were to point their pistols toward the ground until hearing the command "Fire!" A measured count of "one—two—three" would frame the time when each could discharge his weapon before hearing the word "Stop!" The seconds selected a spot in Virginia across the Potomac from Georgetown and set the afternoon of April 8 as the date.

On the evening of April 7, Benton called on Clay and found other visitors at the house. His eyes lingered on his cousin. Lucretia sat in the parlor, silent and sad. Since the deaths of Eliza and Susan, Benton had not seen her display the slightest trace of happiness. Five-year-old John slumbered on the sofa, and Benton had the distinct impression that Lucretia, shut away from the world, knew nothing about the duel planned for the following day, but he could have been wrong. Suky Price had supposed the same thing about her calm sister during the Humphrey Marshall duel seventeen years earlier. Benton stayed put when Clay's company left and Lucretia took John up to bed. He wanted to stop this madness, but he could tell it was no use. Instead, he told Clay that their political differences were of no consequence under the shadow of the morrow. He wished him the best. Clay thanked him. They walked to the door, and Benton paused to look at Clay before leaving. It was almost midnight.[35]

First thing the next morning, Benton rushed to Randolph's rooms to implore him to stop this madness. Randolph listened impassively as Benton described the Clay family as he had found them the night before, Lucretia already stricken by grief over losing her daughters, the child curled on the sofa. Randolph again quietly said that Benton should not worry. Randolph sadly told Benton that fighting a duel on his native soil of Virginia was a hard choice aside from breaking Virginia's law prohibiting it, but Randolph also said, strangely, that he would not dishonor the state by doing so. Then he made a promise: at the end of the day, Lucretia Clay would not be a widow or her children orphans. Benton now fully understood their first conversation about this affair. Randolph had never intended to shoot Henry Clay. Nobody would ever be able to revile him for wounding that frail, kind woman, or accuse him of hurting her innocent children. He would not violate Virginia's law or disgrace its ground, because he would not fight back, and if Clay killed him, Randolph could think of no better place to die.[36]

That afternoon, both parties set out for the rendezvous. The day was strange for the second week of April, spitting snow in the morning and turning to a dreary rain as the hours passed. In addition to Jesup, Clay's close friend Senator Josiah Johnston of Louisiana accompanied him. Randolph crossed the Potomac with Tattnall and Congressman James Hamilton of South Carolina. Benton came too, trailing the Randolph party in the hope of saving his friend's life. He found Randolph still in his carriage, exhibiting a disturbing turn of mind, cryptically explaining that circumstances had altered his earlier resolution. Benton could not account for it. He did not know that Randolph had learned that Clay was complaining that the short count for taking aim was insufficient. Clay was not a very good shot, and Randolph interpreted his adversary's concern as a sign he meant to kill him. Randolph simply told Benton that he now planned to shoot Clay in the leg. He swept out of his carriage, strangely attired in a flowing white dressing gown. Benton's eyes followed him. It was madness.[37]

Everyone gathered on the open field. The seconds handed the antagonists their weapons and were reciting the rules a final time when Randolph absent-mindedly pulled the hair trigger on his pistol. It discharged into the ground, the report startling everyone and causing confusion over the broken protocol. The seconds retreated to mull over the matter. Should they count this inadvertent shot to give Clay free aim at Randolph? Clay finally shouted at them from a distance, "It was an accident—I saw it—the shot is near his foot."[38]

The two men took their positions and prepared to exchange fire. At the signal, Randolph's ball sent wood chips flying out of a stump behind Clay, an indication that he was deliberately firing low. Clay's shot tore through Randolph's trouser leg, missing flesh. Benton spoke up. Surely this was enough. There was no need for a second shot. Both men waved him off. With pistols reloaded, they stood ready for the second round. At the command to fire, Clay carefully raised his pistol and pulled the trigger. The ball hurtled toward Randolph, pierced his billowing clothing, and miraculously passed harmlessly on. Randolph pointed his pistol up and shouted, "I do not fire at you, Mr. Clay." He pulled the trigger to send a sharp, harmless report skyward before striding forward with his hand outstretched. Clay met him halfway and exclaimed, "I trust in God, my dear sir, you are untouched: after what has occurred I would not have harmed you for a thousand worlds."

Randolph said solemnly, "You owe me a coat, Mr. Clay."

Clay replied, "I am glad the debt is not greater."[39]

Despite this happy conclusion, the spectacle of the American secretary of state and a United States senator shooting at each other in an open field struck many as inexcusably barbaric and became "the subject of very general animadversion in the publick prints." One editorial asked, "Will not the President dismiss the duelling Secretary?"[40] In addition to the indignity of the event, Clay and Randolph in its aftermath did not even become friendly opponents. Instead, they soon reverted to their old antagonisms, mainly because Randolph could not control his combative reflexes. He resumed his attacks on Clay and Adams, refusing to stop even after he left Congress in 1828. By then, he was a complete Jacksonian.

THE 1828 PRESIDENTIAL campaign commenced the moment Adams won the vote in the House of Representatives. Ordinarily the Clay-Randolph duel would have given the opposition additional grenades to lob at the administration, but Andrew Jackson's adherents reviewed their man's record and wisely concluded that the less said about shooting people the better. They had plenty of other charges to level at Messrs. Adams and Clay. For their part, in only months, Adams and Clay had heard quite enough about their moral shortcomings.[41]

The result was arguably the most vicious presidential election in the history of American politics. Both sides played the political theater, clucking over their opponent's mild peccadillo here, gasping in outrage over his inexcusable moral delinquency there. Some minor transgressions were true (Adams was aloof, Clay drank and gambled, Jackson had a bad temper), but the astonishing stories were apt to be complete fabrications. For the Jacksonians, the "Corrupt Bargain" took center stage in their campaign.

Jackson maintained a dignified silence for the public, but he was actually working behind the scenes with angry resolve to spoil administration policies. Most of all, though, he wanted to gather proof he hoped to "wield to [Clay's] political, & perhaps, to his actual destruction." For Andrew Jackson, the events of early 1825 were as personal as political, perhaps more so, because Jackson possessed a startling capacity for self-absorption and a feral instinct for survival. He plotted Clay's destruction because he was certain that Clay, the "meanest, [*sic*] scoundrel, that ever disgraced the image of his god," was plotting just as assiduously against him. Because Jackson was certain that Clay would use any means to his end—there was, Jackson thought, "nothing too mean or low for him to condescend to"—Jackson felt justified in doing the same.[42]

Actually, Clay was too often ill and always too busy at the State Department to engage in anything nefarious. When rumors surfaced in Washington that Jackson finally had proof of the "Corrupt Bargain," Clay was troubled that the issue was being given new life, but he was also confident that the facts could only vindicate him. This first serious attempt to produce proof of the Adams-Clay bargain involved assertions that a congressman had approached Jackson in the weeks before the House vote to tell Old Hickory that Henry Clay would support him, for a price. If Jackson would promise not to appoint Adams secretary of state, Clay would make Jackson president. The implication, of course, was that Clay was angling for the post. The conclusion of this tale not only tarnished Clay as a schemer but also burnished Jackson's reputation for integrity and plain dealing. It described him as indignantly snapping that he would make no pledges to buy the presidency. The unspoken but clear message was that Adams had.[43]

The story was not altogether a lie, which was the problem with it. The congressman was an unnamed mystery man in the earliest versions of the story, but

Pennsylvanian James Buchanan had in fact approached Andrew Jackson. He had done so on his own, however, not at Clay's request. The facts of this episode therefore provided no proof of Clay's treachery, and that was why the story did not surface for more than a year. After Jackson left Washington in the spring of 1825, he exchanged friendly letters with Buchanan that contained no mention of their interview and certainly no mention of Clay's having instigated it. Not until the summer and fall of 1826 did this tale appear, and by then it included the missing ingredient of Clay as the mastermind. Missourian Duff Green, a Calhoun partisan, had come to Washington in 1825 to buy and edit the *United States Telegraph,* a pro-Jackson paper partly financed by Old Hickory. In mid-1826, Green began claiming that a certain congressman had acted as Clay's intermediary to Jackson in January 1825. Clay supporters branded Green a liar and demanded to know the identity of this congressman, left nameless in Green's accounts. When the editor asked Buchanan to substantiate the story, the Pennsylvanian to his horror found himself thrust to the center of a very ugly controversy. Buchanan, of course, knew that he had acted on his own in approaching Jackson. It had been nothing more than a foolish attempt by a young congressman to become a Washington power broker with a ploy as brazen as it was immature. Now Jackson and his lieutenants wanted him to lie about it, to make it into something much more, something to destroy Henry Clay.[44]

At first Buchanan stalled while he weighed the risks of flatly denying Green's story, for he did not want to offend Jackson. Buchanan bought time by asking Green for more information, but he hoped that logic alone would show him to be a useless witness. After all, he had never been close to Clay and would have been an unlikely messenger for Clay to trust with a delicate mission. Buchanan for a time resorted to a plea of ignorance, but in the end he explicitly denied that he had acted as Clay's agent in the meeting with Jackson. When the matter seemed to disappear at the end of 1826 with his name still left out of it, Buchanan breathed a sigh of relief. The Jacksonians, though, were only taking a breather.[45]

In the spring of 1827, Jackson told Virginian Carter Beverley about the Buchanan interview, but now Jackson himself said he had believed at the time that Buchanan was doing Clay's bidding. This was an extraordinary claim for several reasons. Aside from its coming more than two years after the event, a time during which he had never breathed a whisper about Clay's using Buchanan, Jackson had to know that Buchanan flatly contradicted this version. But instead of the story's collapsing under the weight of Buchanan's denial, Jackson's earnest recitation of it persuaded Beverley that it had to be true. He started spreading it around, in part to provoke a reaction from Clay, who at first dismissed the mounting clamor as just more mudslinging. Clay did not believe that Jackson would tell an outright lie.[46]

By late June 1827, though, Clay knew that Jackson had done exactly that, this time by writing a letter to Beverley repeating the charge against Clay. Beverley was only waiting for Clay to deny the story before making public the name of the mysterious congressman who had approached Jackson for Clay in 1825. By now, Clay was more than eager to know the identity of this intermediary himself. He published in the Lexington *Kentucky Reporter* a letter not only denying a connection to any such person but demanding that his accusers produce him.[47]

James Buchanan watched this controversy reemerge with growing dread. He had understood all too well Duff Green's disconcerting invitation to lie, and now he anxiously waited for Jackson's response to Clay's public demand. The mail soon brought to Buchanan his worst nightmare, a letter from Andrew Jackson insisting that he corroborate Jackson's version of the event. Jackson even had helpful suggestions to avoid the squeamish discomfort of telling an utter lie. Buchanan, Jackson said, did not have to say that he came directly from Clay. Instead, he could simply name one of Clay's friends as having recruited him. Close upon the dispatch of this letter, Jackson unveiled Buchanan as Clay's agent. Pressed to the wall by this audacious and preemptive tactic, Buchanan found his spine, after a fashion, by publicly and privately denying that he had been an intermediary for Clay or anyone else in 1825. Buchanan also strongly reasserted his unalloyed loyalty to Jackson, even though he had in the same breath essentially branded Andrew Jackson a liar.[48]

Jackson's brazen habit of claiming the moral high ground while stooping very, very low continued to surprise Clay, however, and sure enough, Old Hickory and his followers were soon boldly rebounding from the setback to insist that despite Buchanan's clear declaration, their lie about his actions was true. Meanwhile, Clay had another of the alarming signs that there were plenty of scoundrels practicing the political art and more than enough fools to believe them. Rather than turning out his detractors, the 1826 elections for the Twentieth Congress had increased their number, giving Jacksonians a majority for the session that convened in December 1826. Especially mortifying for Clay, Jacksonians formed the bulk of the Kentucky delegation. It was on this solid political foundation that audacious men heedless of contradiction and dismissive of evidence constructed the attack on him. By 1827, it was a towering edifice of lies so rapidly built that Clay could not take the measure of it. The most he could fathom was how hurtful and disheartening baseless charges could be when coming from the mouths of former friends.[49]

In addition to occasionally checking on Ashland, Clay visited Kentucky during the summers to shore up political support. Kentucky also had a restorative effect on his fragile health. Old friends boosted his sagging confidence, family gatherings at his mother's home placed him among loved ones, and breathing Kentucky's air lifted his spirits, all giving him strength to withstand the dispiriting quarrels in the capital. When he returned to Washington from his summer 1827 visit, however, Kentucky rather than the capital became the source of a barrage of attacks against him. They first hurt and then infuriated him.

Clay knew that some of his friends preferred Jackson and disapproved of his support for Adams. Many had joined the Kentucky Relief faction, but he had tried to keep these differences from disaffecting anyone. Francis Preston Blair and Amos Kendall were among this group. Both men saw rising fervor for Jackson as shaping the future of American politics, and eventually they led efforts in Kentucky to elect Jackson in 1828. As secretary of state, Clay awarded printers in each state lucrative contracts to publish federal documents and legislation, and Kendall counted on that plum in Kentucky. By 1826, however, Kendall was using his *Argus of Western America* to attack the Adams administration as well as to campaign for Andrew Jackson. Clay canceled the contracts.[50]

This act merely completed a break long in the making, for Clay had outlived his usefulness for Amos Kendall. When he had asked Clay for a federal job at the end of 1825, pegging his salary needs at $1,500 annually, Clay could only offer a post that paid $1,000. Kendall refused it with an ominous grumble. In addition, Kendall owed Clay $1,500, an act of generosity on Clay's part that became a fertile seedbed for resentment for Kendall, especially when he could not pay back the loan. Meanwhile, Jacksonians throughout the West saw Kendall's newspaper as a valuable medium to disseminate pro-Jackson propaganda and anti-Adams attacks in the region. Kendall's Kentucky friends arranged to repay Clay with a loan obtained from Martin Van Buren, who had also jumped on the Jackson bandwagon. Many of Clay's friends had never liked Kendall, and almost none of them trusted him, one describing him as "a famished wolf," and he now validated their worst suspicions. He mounted a merciless attack on Clay in the *Argus,* its central charge being that Clay had supported Adams only because Jackson refused to bargain.[51]

A lie repeated long enough becomes the truth, and Kendall's accusation coming on the heels of Buchanan's embarrassing denials was no coincidence. He asserted that he knew of letters written by Clay in early 1825 outlining his plans to make a deal with Adams, a clever claim that placed an impossible burden of proof on the accused. Clay, after all, could not definitively show that no such letters existed. Kendall demanded that every Clay correspondent release for publication all his letters. A political enemy even recruited neighborhood children to steal Clay's letters from John J. Crittenden's home. Kendall in the meantime thought he had stumbled on a much more promising lead. In the fall of 1827, he began focusing on the correspondence between Clay and Francis Preston Blair. At the time of the 1824 election, Clay and Blair had been close and regularly exchanged candid, often lighthearted letters on a variety of subjects. In the wake of the election, political differences had pushed them apart, though they remained cordial. Kendall wanted to see those letters.[52]

Clay wrote one of his letters to Blair on January 8, 1825, just one day before his meeting with Adams. Clay had said nothing that even hinted at a deal between him and Adams, but he had made embarrassing remarks in jest, such as describing his decision to support Adams instead of Jackson as "a choice of evils," a reference likely to strain his relationship with the president, possibly so far as to require his resignation.[53] To Clay's relief, Blair refused to release the letter, citing the sanctity of private correspondence. Keeping the letter private, though, only fueled speculation that Clay had something harmful to hide. As the controversy became death by a thousand cuts, Clay concluded that the only way to stop the bleeding was to publish a massive body of irrefutable evidence. He began assembling it during the summer of 1827, and by the end of the year had numerous affidavits attesting to his determination to support Adams long before their January 9, 1825, meeting. He also had testimony that he had used no undue influence on any fellow congressmen and had insisted that every man vote his conscience. He released this *Address to the Public* in December 1827.[54]

Friends assured Clay that the *Address* was a masterful creation certain to end all accusations of a "corrupt bargain," but that thinking was beyond wishful. It was deluded. Clay's publication did nothing to stop the attacks, and his exasperated friends in Kentucky took a step that actually made matters worse. Without his knowledge, Clay's allies in the state legislature introduced a resolution declaring him innocent of all charges that he had entered a "corrupt bargain." Rather than helping Clay, the resolution gave his enemies an opening to insist that the resolution required a thorough investigation of those charges. Clay later referred to it as his "trial" before the Kentucky legislature. It certainly resembled a criminal proceeding as witness after witness gave testimony, none of it pointing to anything shady but much of it crafted to achieve the most embarrassing effect. The legislature ultimately cleared Clay, but the hearings thoroughly aired all the unfounded accusations of wrongdoing, and their appearance in newspapers throughout the country gave them credibility. Proving guilt by omission is a legal impossibility in a court of law, but for public opinion it is the line of least resistance. Clay tried to make light of "the extraordinary proceeding," quipping that "if I am to be hung," he hoped he would "be duly notified of the time and place that I may present myself, in due form, to my executioner."[55]

Clay fought back best he could, publishing a supplement to his pamphlet in the summer of 1828, but as the presidential election neared, the sheer quantity and rising volume of accusations became overwhelming. Kendall was unyielding in his insistence that Blair and Clay publish the January 8 letter, and Clay's friends began to suspect that Blair's resistance had nothing to do with scruples but was instead a way to keep the issue before the public. Clay suggested that trustworthy individuals read the letter and attest to its contents, but Kendall twisted that plan by at last discovering what the letter said and blatantly misquoting it to support his accusations. Kendall even turned his request for a high-paying government job against Clay, saying that it had been an attempt by Clay to buy his silence. It did not matter that Clay could prove Kendall had importuned him for the job and had refused it not on principle but from greed. The only people who believed Clay were the ones he did not need to convince.[56]

IN THE SPRING of 1827, Clay moved the family to the large and comfortable Decatur House on the northwest corner of President's Park (now Lafayette Square). He leased the dwelling from Susan Decatur, the widow of the naval hero Stephen Decatur. In making the move, Clay started a brief tradition. Until 1833, Decatur House would be the unofficial residence of the secretary of state, chiefly for the same reason Clay had moved into it. The house's spacious, cheerful rooms made entertaining easier. When Congress was in session, the administration held a Wednesday levee, and the Clays at Decatur House alternated weeks with John Quincy and Louisa Catherine Adams at the White House. Clay also wanted roomier accommodations for visiting family. Henry and Lucretia had endured much suffering, and they were never happier than when surrounded by their extended family. He often urged his son-in-law James Erwin to bring Anne to Washington for extended visits. Anne always cheered him up.[57]

Clay needed cheering up. He organized Adams's reelection effort for 1828, an election that one perceptive observer remarked would result in "great personal heart burnings." Although he was convinced that presenting the American System to the people in a positive way would render Jackson's invective irrelevant, the constant attacks on his and the president's character kept the administration on the defensive. The campaign quickly descended to the lowest of

political practices. Character assassination and fabricated smears became common coin in the newspapers and on speakers' platforms.[58]

Because the accusations against Adams had virtually no basis in fact, they
were oddly more difficult to answer. Jacksonians snarled that Adams had raided
the treasury to transform the Executive Mansion into a sumptuous palace, even
purchasing a billiard table to indulge his hypocritical craving for low amusements like gambling. The part about the billiard table at least was accurate, for
Adams did purchase one. He fastidiously reimbursed the government out of his
own pocket, though, and he certainly did not turn the White House into a den of
pool sharks. The fabrications against this impeccably moral man reached their
nadir when New Hampshire journalist Isaac Hill spread the story that while U.S.
minister to Russia, Adams had procured an American virgin for the carnal pleasure of Czar Alexander I.[59]

When Jacksonians were not derogating Adams's and Clay's characters, they
found fault with the administration's failures, cloaking the fact that their obstructionism had foreordained those failures. Their stance nonetheless had the
appearance of a program, even if only dimly ascertained as something other
than the program of John Quincy Adams. By 1828, most voters were convinced
that the Jacksonian program would be better, whatever it was.

Throughout his long career in politics and despite his considerable skill at
framing issues, Clay never understood how this evolving dynamic worked. In
1828, he still believed a man's qualifications for office were a supremely important issue, making Jackson's fitness for the presidency a perfectly legitimate
question; but Clay labored under the mistaken belief that telling the truth about
Jackson would suffice. He encouraged his supporters to remind the country
that Jackson was a "military chieftain," code words for a man inclined to
Caesarism. Jackson himself had made the claim plausible by overstepping his
authority in New Orleans and during the Seminole War, but the heat of the
campaign caused his opponents to do some overstepping themselves. The most
controversial instance of that was the "Coffin Handbill," a widely circulated
broadsheet that excoriated Jackson for executing militiamen during the War of
1812 and killing Arbuthnot and Ambrister in Florida. Black coffins representing each of Jackson's victims bordered the handbill.[60]

Denouncing him for murderous rampages was not the worst of it, though.
The nastiest charges against Jackson were salacious and regrettably involved his
wife. The claim that he had married Rachel Donelson Robards before her divorce from her first husband had set tongues to wagging for years. Those foolish enough to snigger that he was an adulterer and she a bigamist took a very
great risk indeed, for if Jackson could find them, he ruined them. One he had

killed. In the campaign of 1828, however, the talk gained such wide currency that killing the gossips was impractical and trying to suppress the gossip impossible. The Adams press shamefully gloried in the story's shabbiest features, neglecting to mention any extenuating circumstances such as Jackson's mistaken belief that the divorce was final or that Rachel's first husband was abusive. Instead, coarse newspapermen with ink-stained fingers and cluttered offices put the elderly Rachel Jackson into the middle of a fight she little understood. Devout to the point of extreme piety, she shrank in shock as her name repeatedly appeared in public print, a violation of the rule about a proper lady being mentioned only at her birth, her marriage, and her death.

No evidence links Clay to these attacks. In fact, he apparently disapproved of them, but that hardly pardoned his silence when they appeared. His friend Charles Hammond, a Cincinnati newspaper editor, was one of Rachel Jackson's most vocal critics, and Clay did not try to stop Hammond nor did he condemn his columns. It was unfair that Jackson held Clay solely responsible for the defamation of his wife and family, and it is unlikely that Clay could have reined in heated partisans, but his inaction made him passively complicit in their actions. His silence was hardly golden.[61]

Jackson never shed his anger over this disreputable aspect of the 1828 campaign, and he never forgave Henry Clay for his supposed role in it. At the time, the potential for Jackson to lose his temper and convince the nation he was unqualified by temperament to be president greatly alarmed his friends. They strained to keep him calm while persuading him that reacting to the attacks would only encourage more, inviting the opposite of his desired result. They kept Jackson under wraps at the Hermitage and portrayed him as a virtuous patriot above the political fray. Henry Clay and his partner in crime John Quincy Adams were the sleazy wheeler-dealers willing to do or say anything to retain their ill-gotten power.[62]

Controlling Jackson was just one sign of a highly efficient political organization that had already shown its shrewdness in 1824. Jacksonians were better organized, controlled more newspapers, and had a keener understanding of what worked and what failed in rough-and-tumble campaigns. Everyone still called himself a Republican in these years, but the Adams wing began to distinguish itself from Jacksonians by adopting the label National Republicans. Many of these nationalists thought themselves clever in branding Jacksonians "democrats," but it indicated their blinkered vision. For them the word was a pejorative summoning the specter of unruly mobs, but in light of the country's rising egalitarianism, it eventually became a badge of honor, and Jacksonians eventually called themselves "the Democracy" or "Democrats," with a capital D.

Delaware and South Carolina were the only remaining states in which the legislature chose presidential electors, and Jacksonian state organizations were ready for the electoral revolution that portended. The new politics required reaching down to the local level and mobilizing one-gallused farmers, prosperous merchants, and local bankers, all wanting easy credit (not a big central bank curbing it) and upward mobility. Jackson clubs sprang up in this fertile ground of localism to throw barbecues, sponsor stump speeches, and promote politicians the voters knew and trusted.[63]

New York senator Martin Van Buren joined the Jacksonian movement, a sure sign of its vitality and appeal. Van Buren was an organizational genius, a "Little Magician" when it came to putting together invincible coalitions. He had strong political ties in the North, where he ran New York's powerful Albany Regency, and in the South, where many were still grateful for his supporting Georgian William H. Crawford, for whom Van Buren had tried to fashion a national organization in 1824. Four years later, his ability to forge an alliance between North and South made him invaluable to the Jacksonian movement. For his part, Van Buren saw in Andrew Jackson a man whose colossal popularity could transcend sectional concerns and regional differences, popularity that had politics' fabled coattails, making election victories inevitable and ensuring majorities that could endure for years. Van Buren's dream was to establish a muscular national political party that would be dominant for decades, possibly forever—or at least until the next election, the closest thing to forever in politics.[64]

The Adams campaign was a pathetic, withered creature in comparison, not just bloodied but bowed by the relentless accusations of swaggering Jacksonians. Rather than cultivating its own grass roots, Adams and Clay conducted themselves according to the quiet rituals of the past. The administration's friends wrote many letters, but mainly to one another, swapping information and cheering on political elites in states essential for victory—what are now called battleground states. Virginia, Clay's birthplace, was one of those states, and he tried to energize his extensive network there to counter Jackson's almost irresistible allure. Yet Clay aimed at a select group of prominent Adams supporters rather than at common voters. A plan to persuade former presidents James Madison and James Monroe to appear on the Virginia ballot as Adams electors, in essence securing their endorsements, fell through. Neither believed Andrew Jackson was fit for the presidency, but both also believed their obligations to that office prohibited them from demeaning it with ordinary politicking. Clay's disappointment was palpable, but he most certainly understood and later, upon reflection, he would applaud their reserve.[65]

For Jacksonians, the dignity of the presidency was something to employ rather than to preserve. They claimed to have the support of another former president from Virginia, more easily secured because he was dead. Thomas Jefferson had passed away on July 4, 1826, but his son-in-law Thomas Mann Randolph published an account of Jefferson's last days claiming that on his deathbed the Sage of Monticello had admitted to never trusting Henry Clay because of his bad character. Furthermore, Randolph said that Jefferson had declared his admiration for Andrew Jackson, who he said should be the next president. Over the course of twenty years, Randolph had become increasingly irrational, often to the point of derangement, making life at Monticello grim and edgy, especially for his wife, Jefferson's beloved daughter Martha. Randolph flew into a rage when Clay expressed doubt that Jefferson had disapproved of him as a person. Randolph set out for Washington to kill Clay, madly racing partway before he cooled down.

In short, he was a demented special pleader whose story about Jefferson's sentiments was dubious on its face. Anyone who knew the family was aware that Jefferson could hardly bring himself to exchange "good mornings" with his son-in-law, let alone open his mind to him on significant political issues. By the time Jackson's people in Virginia had taken up this wretched man's story to brandish it as the Jeffersonian gospel on the election of 1828, Randolph too had died. His widow, Martha, their eldest son, Thomas Jefferson Randolph, and friends of the family knew the tale to be a lie. Jeff Randolph privately told Clay that he was certain his grandfather had neither denounced Clay nor endorsed Jackson. Yet he also implored Clay to spare the family the shame of publically repudiating the deceased Randolph. Clay agreed and braced for the devastating blow this Jacksonian tactic dealt the administration in Virginia. More important than politics, after all, was protecting Thomas Jefferson's heirs, good people impoverished by their patriarch's spendthrift ways, left only with their pride. Clay's choice to leave that pride intact required his silence. This time, it was golden.[66]

THE LAST PIECE of the campaign puzzle for Jacksonians was to deal the administration a devastating legislative blow. During the 1827–28 session of the Twentieth Congress, they launched a plan to dismantle the one advantage the administration had in important manufacturing states: its adherence to a protective tariff. In July 1827, a pro-tariff convention had met at Harrisburg, Pennsylvania, essentially a gathering of Clay supporters that some suspected the administration had instigated to show support for higher duties. When manufacturers clamored for Congress to shield American goods from foreign competition with a more robust protective tariff, the House Committee on Manufactures accordingly reported a bill in March 1828. Designed to placate factory owners in Ohio, Pennsylvania, and New York, the bill was mostly the work of Jacksonians marshaled by Van Buren, who had devised a way for them to have their legislative cake and eat it too. The bill deliberately ignored the interests of New England, where Jackson expected to receive few votes. The Jacksonian plan called for southerners to block all efforts to appease New England, aware that southern opposition to tariffs in general would join with Yankee anger over this one in particular to kill it in a final vote. Jacksonians would nevertheless be able to point to their attempt to help Ohio, Pennsylvania, and New York while basking in the approval of the South and pointing to Adams's stronghold of New England as the principal culprit in defeating the bill.[67]

The plan played out perfectly in the House of Representatives, where all amendments were rejected and the bill passed in a narrow vote. It then went to the Senate, but there the unexpected happened. The plan's architect, Martin Van Buren, shifted course, threw southerners overboard, and allowed amendments that secured New England's support. The combination of Mid-Atlantic manufacturing states, the West, and New England easily passed the amended tariff in both the Senate and the House, and Adams signed it on May 19.

Regarding it as grievously injurious to their regional economy, southerners called the Tariff of 1828 the "Tariff of Abominations," a warning about weighty repercussions in the future. At the time, though, the Little Magician had never been more adroit in pulling off this legislative sleight of hand. Van Buren hoped to diminish the administration's appeal in the West by showing that Jacksonians would literally protect the region's interests. As for the South, Van Buren knew that just as New England would vote *against* Jackson as much as *for* Adams, the South would vote *against* Adams as much as *for* Jackson. Southerners, in short, had no other place to go, and Van Buren was not above selling them out while whispering assurances that the Jackson administration would set matters right. That they believed him bore out the masterful strategy of having Jackson be all things to all people.[68]

Henry Clay watched Van Buren's magic with ambivalence. Before Congress convened, he had heard rumors that the Jacksonians planned to hatch this scheme, but he was at a loss about how to counter it. Instructing administration supporters to oppose the measure would undermine the basic principle of protectionism, a significant element of the American System. That left him little choice but to support the Tariff of 1828, but he did so quietly and tepidly, as though swept up in an irresistible tide. Van Buren had never been more agile.[69]

And Henry Clay had seldom been sicker. Every winter he suffered from colds or influenza, sometimes both, and his chronic digestive problems sometimes laid him low. Grief had apparently begun to afflict Lucretia with a fragile stomach as well. Clay frequently visited mineral springs in Virginia and Kentucky to take the waters as well as dose himself with something stronger. (A resort's 1827–28 register at Virginia's White Sulphur Springs still listed in 1911 Clay's unpaid charge of twelve cents for a mint julep.) He went home during summers, hoping to restore his strength, but he never really rested on these trips, for he had become desperate over the election. He used his travels to meet with groups, however small, to make speeches, however repetitive, and to dispatch letters, however futile, to every corner of the country. By the spring of 1828, unrelenting toil and his usual physical ailments convinced Clay that he was dying.[70]

His changed appearance shocked a friend who had not recently seen him. He was "miserable; care-worn, wrinkled, haggard, and wearing out."[71] A numbness in his left leg gradually moved toward his hip, baffling physicians as to its cause. Disregarding their warnings, Clay continued his grueling pace, a stooped figure whose noticeable limp made him seem decades older than his fifty years. Meeting with his secretary of state now always made Adams sad, for Clay's ashen face and sunken body were scarred monuments to the remorseless "obloquy, slander, and persecution" of the previous three years.[72] In April, Clay finally surrendered to his declining health. Announcing that "he must go home and die or get better," he tried to resign, but Adams urged him to consult other physicians. Clay traveled to Philadelphia to see the renowned doctors Philip Physick and Nathaniel Chapman. They tapped, prodded, stared, and finally concluded what was wrong with him.

He was not dying, they said. Instead, as Adams had suspected, Clay was suffering from nervous exhaustion. He listened with lighthearted relief to the diagnosis and its cure: a better diet, prescribed medicines, regular exercise, and above all, rest.[73] His friends had been more than concerned, and when Clay returned to Washington, Josiah Johnston was typical in laughing aloud when he heard the news. If Jackson "should be elected," he chuckled to Clay, "he will unintentionally do for you what your friends Can not advise—He will save your life by relieving you from the Cares of State."[74]

As much as he could in the home stretch of the campaign, Clay followed his doctors' orders. He went to Kentucky, campaigning along the way, but then vacationed at the Virginia Springs. He continued his remarkable level of correspondence, sending Adams a steady stream of advice in letters made urgent by Clay's discovery of treachery within the administration. The situation was the result of Adams's quaint attitude about federal patronage. Jacksonians repeatedly charged that Adams regularly fired qualified officeholders to replace them with political hacks, yet Adams had actually been more than scrupulous about appointments. Though swamped by supporters wanting jobs, Adams never weighed political loyalty when making appointments. Correspondingly, he felt it was inappropriate to remove someone from his post simply because he differed with the administration.

Clay had always thought Adams's scruples about this matter were ill judged. The overarching tolerance of dissent within the administration weakened its policies and made it vulnerable in elections. Postmaster General John McLean was a steadfast partisan of John C. Calhoun, who was running for reelection to the vice presidency on Jackson's ticket. McLean had been openly using the Post Office's extensive patronage to place Jacksonians in positions of influence throughout the country, and Clay's travels uncovered for him that many federal officials not only differed with the administration but were actively working to defeat it. Clay urged Adams to fire McLean, but Adams refused.[75]

Clay would have dreaded returning to Washington, except for the anticipation of rejoining his family. Decatur House was full of family. Anne and James had come to Washington that spring with their two children. Julia Duralde Erwin, named for John Clay's wife, was two and a half, a Christmas Eve baby. Little Henry Clay Erwin, born the previous June, met his grandparents for the first time. Anne had always claimed a special place in Clay's heart, and now that she was his only daughter, he particularly doted on her. Something about Anne, the tilt of her head, the arch of an eyebrow, her laughter, her turn of phrase, all made her a grand companion. She was much like him in her unshakable optimism and ready wit, but nothing narcissistic tinged his regard for her, because in truth he regarded her as a better version of himself. Anne had his humor, but she also had her mother's gentleness and her aunt Nancy's sparkle, an appropriate gift from her namesake. Not only Clay noticed that rooms brightened when Anne entered them, and one could always find Anne at parties by following the laughter. As Clay traveled for his health, she wrote him letters full of funny stories and clever anecdotes.[76]

Clay was still at White Sulphur Springs when he received the troubling news that Anne's little girl, Julia, was sick with a fever. Other members of the family, including Lucretia and James, also became ill, but as they recovered, Julia faded away. Always a frail child, she did not have enough fight in her and died that August. Clay tried to console Anne and James, but he knew words were of little use. He diverged from his travel plans to meet them along the road when they started for their home in Tennessee early that fall, a somber reunion and sad farewell. Clay returned to a Decatur House still subdued by Julia's death, a sharp contrast to Washington's jittery excitement over the looming election.[77]

Clay had worked tirelessly for more than three years to reelect John Quincy Adams, but his efforts had fallen short of what successful campaigning now required. He had persisted in the misguided conviction that if Adams used the patronage properly (Adams had ignored the advice) or chose the right running mate (Clay volunteered), the people would elect the aloof Puritan over the popular general. When Clay returned to Washington from his summer trip, his optimism had waned under the obvious signs of Jackson's inevitability. Adams had accepted his fate months before. At last, Clay was resigned to it.[78]

Kentucky elected Adams supporter Thomas Metcalfe governor, but it gave both houses of the legislature to Jacksonian majorities and went for Jackson in the presidential contest, a result worse than anyone could have imagined and especially mortifying to Clay. Nationally, Jackson won almost 56 percent of the popular vote and amassed an Electoral College margin of 178 to 83 over Adams.[79]

Clay firmly believed that the Jacksonian smears had been the deciding factor in the election, but it was understandable that he would exaggerate that aspect of the campaign.[80] The relentless program of defamation had obviously hurt Adams and Clay, but much of the country simply balked at the prospect of the economic nationalism that Clay and Adams espoused, and Clay found it hard to fathom that reluctance. He always would. On the other hand, Jackson's victory filled Clay with a smoldering dread. He believed that the worst said about this man was all too true. Jackson had not only lied but had been caught in that lie, and the great majority of voters had not cared. "No greater calamity [than Jackson's election] has fallen to our lot since we were a free people," he said with great sadness. Something beyond politics, beyond elections, beyond speeches and policies, was terribly wrong with the country. Clay trembled for it.[81]

He allowed himself a brief interlude of self-pity and anger before resolving to banish both. He set himself to jollying dejected friends out of their dark moods as well, for Clay likened sadness to sickness, and the only effective treatment was a smart joke and a bright outlook. He told Frank Brooke not to be discouraged, that they all should embrace "hope and fortitude," that the country would survive.[82] When Hezekiah Niles, the editor of the influential *Niles' Weekly Register,* named his newborn son Henry Clay Niles, Clay said with mock solemnity that the name was not a good indication "of your discretion at this time."[83] He assured friends that he would continue to fight for those principles to which he had "dedicated my public life," just not right away. The prospect of going home for an extended stay was more than appealing. Lucretia would be there with him as always, and his Ashland would become an oasis. In the weeks after the election, as his friends had laughingly predicted, Clay's health improved.[84]

Over the next three months, he wrapped up business in the State Department and prepared to go home, while Adams did the same in the White House. Adams offered Clay a seat on the Supreme Court, but he had no taste for the bench, and it was likely fortunate that he declined in any case. At Clay's suggestion, Adams nominated Clay's protégé John J. Crittenden, but the Senate mulishly refused to consider confirmation until the new Congress convened. The Senate then let the nomination die.[85]

The final session of the Twentieth Congress at least meant parties would liven up the capital, and the administration gamely resumed the Wednesday levees at Decatur House and Executive Mansion on alternating weeks. The Clays also hosted lively dinners, giving him a chance to gauge people's views about the incoming administration. He was already contemplating the best way to oppose the radical changes that Jackson and his compliant congressional majorities were sure to enact. His friends assumed that Clay would lead the opposition to the administration, even if he had to do so from Kentucky.[86]

The impending arrival of the president-elect from Tennessee filled Washington with considerable anticipation that only increased when news arrived that Rachel Jackson was dead, a victim, it was said, of her being dragged through the newspapers during the campaign, rough treatment that had broken her heart at the time and had finally stopped it. Jackson now had even more reason to wade into his political enemies, smiting them with biblical vengeance for killing his wife. On less conspicuous levels, many government workers nervously looked for other employment.[87]

Biblical retribution, in fact, seemed the order of the day in Washington, a Babylon of corruption according to Jacksonians. Adams and his cabinet took violently ill. Some secretaries could not leave their houses for days, and the Clays became shut-ins, Lucretia falling sick as well. Margaret Bayard Smith came calling one evening to judge their recuperation and found Lucretia sitting quietly in a chair watching over her sleeping husband on the sofa. When Clay blinked awake, he found both women sitting quietly, gazing at him. Margaret thought he looked very ill and very sad. This close friend suddenly realized she had been allowed to see something extraordinary, something only the Clay family, and possibly only Lucretia, knew as the truth. Like people of a later time who discovered that the laughing Abraham Lincoln was actually a man of deep melancholy, Margaret Bayard Smith had a revelation. When Henry Clay turned his face to the world, he wore a "mask of smiles."[88]

The last administration levee occurred at the Clays', and he donned an especially cheerful mask for the occasion. Jackson had already arrived in town, and as office seekers crowded his rooms at the National Hotel, rumors flew around town about his cabinet selections. The attendees at the Clays' party, all Adams and Clay supporters, gossiped the night away about the abysmal choices Old Hickory was sure to make.[89] As usual, Clay enlivened the gathering, moving from group to group, laughing as if lighthearted. Always "free and easy in his conversation," Clay could put even strangers at ease to "discuss topics with as much freedom as if he were an old acquaintance."[90] Lucretia stood smiling, graciously receiving her guests, though still so ailing "she could scarcely stand."[91] She had reason to smile, though, for the prospect of going home made her so cheerful that she had stopped wearing mourning clothes and instead wore the fashionable Parisian gowns that Nancy had insisted on sending in the darkest days of her sister's grief.[92]

Margaret Smith attended this last official gathering with regret. She dreaded the prospect of her two dear friends leaving the capital, and she pondered the possibility that she would never see them again. During their friendship of more than twenty years, she had developed an enduring admiration for Henry Clay, and his fate seemed terribly unfair. She studied him as he mingled smiling among his guests, "so courteous and gracious, and agreeable, that every one remarked it and remarked he was determined we should regret him" (that is, miss him). Her eyes blurred with tears, and she moved to a quiet corner to compose herself. Clay was suddenly at her side asking what was wrong. She was just sad to see them go, she said. With her hand "pressed in his without speaking, his eyes filled with tears and with an effort he said, 'We must not think of this, or talk of such things *now.*'" He put his handkerchief to his eyes before turning back to the crowd of people. As he walked away from Margaret, he was again wearing his mask of smiles.[93]

THE CABINET DECIDED not to attend Jackson's inauguration, a choice that suited Adams and Clay just fine. They saw no reason to give their symbolic imprimatur to a man who had called them corrupt political schemers. With the exception of Clay's replacement, Martin Van Buren, Jackson's cabinet choices were a singularly undistinguished group of political cronies with few qualifications for office. They all had contempt for Henry Clay, though, and that raised them in Jackson's estimation. Jackson named Clay's former protégé William T. Barry as postmaster general, an appointment that was particularly insulting. A political ally described Barry as "not fit for any station which require[d] great intellectual force or moral firmness," but he had lost against Metcalfe in the Kentucky governor's race and was made postmaster general as a reward for supporting Jackson in Kentucky.[94]

Jackson's selection of his close friend John H. Eaton as secretary of war caused the most gossip. Eaton's qualifications were suspect, but his recent marriage to Margaret O'Neal Timberlake was the real cause of the parlor chatter that gripped the capital. The former Mrs. Timberlake had married Eaton on New Year's Day 1829, only a few months after the suicide of her husband. Many believed that she had been Eaton's mistress before Timberlake's death, and ribald as well as scatological jokes at the Eatons' expense were soon making the rounds. Marrying the Timberlake widow, said one, was like using a chamber pot and then putting it on one's head. The ladies of Washington, however, found the marriage no laughing matter. When Floride Calhoun and cabinet members' wives refused to socialize with Mrs. Eaton, they clashed with Andrew Jackson, who so vociferously defended Margaret Eaton that he allowed "the Eaton malaria" to become "the Peggy Eaton Affair" and disrupt the first two years of his administration. Jackson reflexively blamed Clay for all the trouble, even though the women doing the snubbing were married to Clay's political enemies. After Clay left town, Jackson cast around for someone else to blame, finally settling his wrath on his vice president, Floride Calhoun's husband. Clay's supporters found it all highly amusing.[95]

Clay would have found it amusing as well, but another family crisis had him and Lucretia racked with worry: Thomas Hart Clay was in a Philadelphia jail because of his bad debts in the city. The situation humiliated them while branding Thomas as completely dissolute, possibly beyond redemption. He was almost twenty-six, but neither the study of law nor the opening of his practice had steadied him. He drank heavily, squandered money gambling, and now had seemingly hit bottom. Clay tried to handle the situation from Washington, but neither he nor Lucretia could sleep as they churned with worry over their wretched son and cringed over the shame he was bringing on the family. After some difficulty in tracking down all the debts and fines his son had incurred, Clay paid them and arranged to have Thomas conveyed to Lexington. The prospect of having to deal with him at Ashland made the idea of their homecoming less cheery.[96]

Clay and Adams said their farewells the day before Jackson's inauguration, Clay observing the formality of tendering his resignation during the courtesy call. Considering their rocky start in Ghent fifteen years earlier, they had worked well together, and Clay expressed his hope that they could stay in touch in retirement.[97]

Neither of them was present the next day when Washington saw an unparalleled spectacle as Andrew Jackson became the seventh president of the United States. Thousands upon thousands of Old Hickoryites, those one-gallused farmers, prosperous merchants, and shade tree bankers among them, had flooded the town to celebrate the inauguration, and they descended on the presidential "Palace" to sample the delicacies prepared for the elite of Washington society. The "majesty of the people" in all its rambunctious and boisterous enthusiasm shocked an official Washington accustomed to the staid dignity of Madison and Monroe and the taciturn reserve of John Quincy Adams. While official Washington frowned, the crowds roared, and Henry Clay could whisper, *Told you so.*[98]

Instead of attending the inauguration, Clay was busy with yet another family crisis. As with Thomas's ordeal, this one was embarrassing. When they moved their household in 1825, the Clays had brought the house slaves Aaron and Charlotte Dupuy to Washington. Aaron was slightly younger than Clay and had been with him from the time of his youth in the Slashes of Hanover County. Elizabeth and Hal Watkins took Aaron Dupuy with them to Kentucky, and subsequently Clay made Aaron his manservant. The two usually traveled together. Lottie, as everyone called her, had been born on the Eastern Shore of Maryland, where one James Condon, a tailor by trade, had purchased her in Cambridge, Maryland, while she was still a child. Condon took her to Kentucky, where she eventually met and married Aaron, who enlisted Lucretia to persuade Clay to buy her. Clay did so in 1806, even though Condon apparently took advantage of the situation to demand a high price. Lucretia brought Lottie into the house at Ashland to help with the children. She and Aaron along the way had two children of their own, Charles and Mary Anne.[99]

While they were in Washington, Clay twice allowed Lottie to visit her family on the Eastern Shore, and he later suspected that these trips were the root of all the subsequent trouble. As the family prepared to return to Kentucky after the election of 1828, Lottie announced that she would not go. Insisting that she was free, she filed a petition on February 19, 1829, in the U.S. Circuit Court for the District of Columbia. The deed shocked and angered Clay. Though he had remained active in the American Colonization Society, Lottie's stance called into question his sincerity about gradual emancipation. Clay actually had worked to obtain the freedom of a number of slaves and had been instrumental in freeing and repatriating the African prince Abd Rahman Ibrahima, sold into slavery after his capture in battle. Now he was convinced that Lottie had become the pawn of his political enemies, who even in victory were leaving no stone unturned in their quest to discredit him. True enough, Lottie Dupuy's suit obviously had not been filed in a vacuum, and it did damage to Clay's reputation as a benevolent master.[100]

Nevertheless, Clay decided to fight the court battle. Lottie and the people supporting her suit had made him angry, and he was concerned that the suit would encourage other political opponents to adopt the same tactics in order to embarrass their adversaries. Whether his enemies were in fact behind Lottie's legal action never became known, but if embarrassing him was their aim, they succeeded. He appeared petty and vindictive as he retained lawyers on the Eastern Shore and in Washington to gather depositions and refute Lottie's claims.

Clay believed those claims were groundless. Lottie's suit cited two reasons for granting her freedom. She stated that her mother in Maryland had been free, thus making her free as well. Clay easily proved that Lottie's mother had not been freed until years after Lottie's birth. The other reason stemmed from a promise by James Condon to free her after she had put in years of faithful service, a pledge that Lottie said should now be honored because she had fulfilled her part of the bargain. The court ultimately dismissed that claim as well, ruling that Condon had canceled his pledge by selling Lottie without any conditions.

Adjudicating these questions took time, and under instructions from the court, Clay left Lottie at Decatur House when the family left Washington for Ashland. His attorneys handled the case to its conclusion while Lottie worked as a domestic servant for the new secretary of state, who was also the new tenant of Decatur House, Martin Van Buren. After Lottie lost her bid for freedom, Clay placed her in Anne Erwin's home in New Orleans to help with her children before bringing her back to Ashland. She seems to have borne him no ill will and instead resumed her role in the Clay family without complaint, suggesting that his suspicions about the real authors of this controversy were true. He bore her no ill will either. In 1840, Clay freed Lottie and her daughter Mary Anne in gratitude for her devoted care of his children and grandchildren. She apparently remained at Ashland with Aaron, who had by then turned over his duties as Clay's servant to their son, Charles Dupuy.[101]

In addition to the embarrassing complications posed by Thomas and Lottie, parting from friends in Washington saddened Clay and Lucretia as much as the prospect of returning home gladdened them. The possible consequences of the election also continued to worry Clay. At a farewell dinner at the Mansion Hotel, Clay warned the assembled crowd about the potential for tyranny arising in this new administration. He cited the example of Latin American republics succumbing to military dictatorship as a somber warning of what could happen under Andrew Jackson. He also praised the five hundred thousand citizens who had voted for Adams, evidence "of virtue, of intelligence, of religion, and of genuine patriotism . . . unsurpassed . . . in this or any other country."[102] It sounded like a campaign speech.

It was.

CHAPTER EIGHT

Losing the Bank, Saving the Union

THEIR RETURN TO Ashland was bittersweet. Almost four years as a rental property had left the house and grounds in some disrepair, and Clay threw himself into refurbishing the buildings and reviving the farm. Lucretia purchased new furniture for the mansion, and Clay tended to livestock and planting. Friends urged him to return to politics, but he refused. His health needed restoring as much as his home did. For a while, personal affairs became his exclusive focus.

For the rest of his life, he spoke with pride about his accomplishments at Ashland, the most stunning of which was Ashland itself. Visitors described the farm as comprising "the most highly cultivated grounds in all Kentucky."[1] In addition to growing hemp and grains, Clay continued to breed fine livestock, especially top-quality racehorses. Often in partnership with others, he bought blooded mares and stud horses to make Ashland a renowned source of prized bloodlines, and the place's reputation for producing fast horseflesh spread throughout the country. One of his studs, Stamboul, was ungainly in appearance but earned $2,650 in one year alone.[2]

Clay placed twelve-year-old James and eight-year-old John in a Lexington school. He did not know what to do with Theodore and Thomas, who had floundered from one career to another. Law, farming, or manufacturing variously engrossed them, but their zest for anything always waned. He and Lucretia loved them to the point of distraction, which made their capacity to disappoint so distracting. "Oh!" Clay once howled, "no language can describe . . . the pain that I have suffered on account of these two boys." As the recent caper in Philadelphia had shown, Thomas was a bounder. Nobody suspected, however, what was in store for Theodore.[3]

Clay consoled himself that James and John could still amount to something, but his dreams for young Henry placed a heavy burden on the boy. "If you too disappoint my anxious hopes," Clay told him, "a constitution never good, and now almost exhausted, would sink beneath the pressure." Young Henry became, in short, "the pride and hope of your family."[4] Under such pressure, the boy fed on worry, almost choking on the possibility that any failure would diminish him in Papa's eyes. Henry once timidly ventured that possibly his intellectual abilities were "not above mediocrity," but Clay would have none of that. He continually insisted to Henry that he was smart and clever and naturally could succeed at anything. Clay's certainty did not so much reassure the boy as it stirred his doubts and added additional links to his invisible chain of worry. Papa was always offering advice and pushing him to work harder, to do better, to improve. Henry should read more, Clay said, and should learn the "dead languages." Clay had always regretted not learning Latin and Greek, and when he urged his son to correct that deficiency in himself, Henry suddenly had another burden, another way to disappoint, another way to fail.[5]

He entered the United States Military Academy in 1827 and excelled, much to his father's delight. The challenges at West Point amplified his serious, diligent qualities.[6] Anne saw him in Washington during the summer of 1828 and joked to her father that Henry was at the age when young men are "obliged to put on a very sage and serious air to remind one of" their dignity. Eliza Johnston, wife of Clay's friend Josiah Johnston, had a similar impression while visiting Henry Jr. in Philadelphia, a meeting that left her "surprised to see how grave he has grown." Henry was seventeen, brimming with anxiety.[7]

He was also increasingly uncertain about his career path and gradually had doubts about the army. He even asked for his father's approval to withdraw from the Academy, but Clay was mindful of youthful whimsies, even in his overly serious son, and counseled against a rash decision. Henry obeyed. Henry always obeyed. After the election of 1828, however, Clay agreed that his son's chances in an army under President Jackson had considerably dimmed, particularly because he was Henry Clay, Jr. They both deliberated over alternative careers, the boy always anxious to have Papa's approval. West Point had trained him to be an engineer, and Henry rather enjoyed the work, the clear precision of mathematics appealing to his temperament. Yet when Papa expressed a preference for the law, Henry agreed that perhaps the law would be best.

Occasionally Clay realized what he was doing to this boy and sometimes told Henry to take his counsel as suggestions rather than instructions. Henry, however, was instinctively dutiful. He insisted that he "must consider them as commands doubly binding for they proceed from one so vastly my superior in all respects and to whom I am under such great obligations that the mere intimation of an opinion will be sufficient to govern my conduct."[8] From anyone else, that mouthful would have been suspiciously obsequious; but with good reason,

Papa never doubted his son's sincerity. When Henry graduated second in his class in 1831, Henry wrongly suspected that by falling short of first he had disappointed Papa. Brimming with anxiety, he resolved to try harder and after a year resigned his commission—to study law.

After Eliza and Susan died, Clay doted on Anne, and not just because she was his only surviving daughter. He openly admitted that she was "one of the few sources which I have of real happiness," but both her vivacious temperament and the fact that Clay treated her as a friend rather than a project kept her from feeling, as Henry did, that her papa's devotion was too great not to be disappointed.[9] Clay was never able to make his sons his friends, not even after they married and had children of their own. With Anne, everything was different. Her letters were playful and informative, full of puns and amusing stories about her, James, and the children. James Jr., she said, was "becoming quite a beauty, at least for his opportunities, not having any to inherit from either side of the house."[10] Clay constantly urged James Erwin to bring her to Ashland for lengthy visits, and they did come often, usually between Anne's pregnancies, which meant their arrival always filled the house with chattering children and Anne's laughter.[11] In 1831, Erwin bought the Woodlands, a house near Ashland, and planned for the family to spend a large part of every year in Lexington. Clay was jubilant.

Lucretia thrived on the grandchildren. Susan's boys, Martin Duralde III and Henry Clay Duralde, spent much of their childhood at Ashland or traveling with the Clays. The lads spoke only French at first, but Lucretia organized a program for the whole family of English instruction disguised as a game, and soon her little Creoles were speaking, reading, and writing like Kentuckians. Clay sent them to private schools, and they grew up surrounded by family, which in some ways was a mixed blessing. John Morrison Clay was only two years older than young Martin and three years older than Henry Duralde, and he could be overbearing and sometimes cruel in the manner of a spiteful older brother rather than a loving uncle.[12]

Life continued to pepper the family with losses. Some were expected, but no less sad. In the fall of 1829, Hal Watkins collapsed one afternoon and never again rose from his bed. His death marked the passing of more than a kind cousin, for Hal was the only father Henry Clay had ever known. Clay had often visited his parents at their farm outside Versailles and often wrote to his mother, Elizabeth, when in Washington, though she apparently did not save any of his letters. She wrote her only surviving letter to him while he was at the State Department, but she mentioned his letters as always welcome. She had a clear hand, her penmanship not unlike her famous son's, but her phrasing was stilted and studied, and her letters were likely rare. Elizabeth had been failing for years, and Hal's death deprived her of both his loving companionship and his care. When Clay went to the farm to help bury Hal, he gently told the feeble, grieving woman to come home to Ashland where she would want for nothing and would have everything money and love could provide. No, she said, she would stay in Versailles with Clay's half sister, her daughter, Patsy Blackburn. Only ten days after Hal's death, she died too and was placed next to him in the quiet country graveyard outside Versailles. Three years later, when Lucretia lost her elderly mother, Susannah Hart, apparently the victim of a stroke, the Clays buried the last of their parents.[13]

Just days after he had buried Hal and Elizabeth, Clay received news that his brother John had died aboard a steamboat while returning to New Orleans from St. Louis, the distance from his home requiring his burial in the Arkansas Territory. Also in 1829, Clay's brother Porter lost his wife, Sophia.[14]

The worst blow, however, was the fate of Nancy Brown. Before their return from France, James had reported that Lucretia's sister was gravely ill. She had discovered a lump in her breast and was experiencing a mysterious numbness in her face that puzzled all her doctors. The family read the grim reports and began to expect the worst. As they anxiously awaited the Browns' return, specks of cheerful news during the summer and fall of 1829 gave them hope that Nancy was becoming her old self again, but clearly she had breast cancer, and the brief rally only disguised its rapid spread. When Nancy died suddenly of an internal hemorrhage in the fall of 1830, Henry and Lucretia were stunned. James Brown dissolved in grief and never really recovered. Nancy's laughter and lilting voice had made unthinkable that anything bad could happen to her, and her death pushed the world askew on its axis. Clay found his brother-in-law inconsolable and took on the sad duty of settling Nancy's estate.[15]

BEFORE THE ELECTION of 1828, Jacksonian editor Duff Green had made a prediction. "Mr. Clay will not die without a struggle," he warned Kentuckian Richard M. Johnson, who was also moving into Jackson's camp. "The poison will still remain in his fangs; and so vindictive is he that those who have stood in his way need expect no mercy at his hand." Jackson's election, said Green, would only briefly dispirit Clay, who would then immediately "organize an opposition."[16]

Green understood the man and knew what drove him. Though ostensibly retired from public life, Clay remained a public figure, delivering the occasional speech and maintaining a wide correspondence with numerous friends throughout the country. He lamented that "the course of the new administration is so far

worse than its worst enemies could have anticipated," because a "deluded people" had not only elected "a most incompetent but vindictive" president as
well.[17] Clay was reacting to stories about Jackson's turning out federal office-
holders. A few years later, New York Democrat senator William Marcy famously remarked, "To the victor belong the spoils of the enemy," and gave the
colloquial label "Spoils System" to what Jacksonians preferred to gussy up as
"rotation in office." By any name, however, it amounted to the rewarding of political supporters with public appointments, a system successfully employed by
political machines in New York and Pennsylvania to sustain support through the
public payroll. To some extent, each administration from Jefferson onward had
replaced officeholders, but the tradition had persisted from the colonial era that
only bad behavior, and certainly not political affiliation, merited removal from
office. Adams, much to Clay's chagrin, had resisted removing even open turn-
coats, such as McLean. In that respect, the advent of Jackson's presidency did
mark an acute change. Jackson claimed he was cleansing corruption, but some
of the rogues he rewarded hardly provided convincing proof of his regard for
honest government. Old Hickory's spontaneous inclination to punish opponents
and Van Buren's appreciation for the power of patronage helped to magnify as
well as systemize the Spoils System.

McLean landed on the Supreme Court for supporting Old Hickory, but he
nervously predicted that the administration's ruthless system of replacement
would soon fill "the vials of wrath" among Jackson's foes. Kentuckian William
T. Barry, once Clay's friend but now Jackson's postmaster general, also worried
that the wholesale dismissals could cause unrest not just among the opposition
but of a general sort.[18] Most, however, shouldered up to the trough. The previous winter, Amos Kendall took special delight in conveying Kentucky's Electoral College vote to Washington, and he soon met with Jackson to emerge from
the interview as the new fourth auditor of the Treasury with an annual salary of
$3,000, double what he had unsuccessfully tried to pry from Clay. In this bid-
ding war, Andrew Jackson knew the value of a man who bought ink by the barrel and let his pen freely slip the leash of conscience.[19]

The Jacksonian axe also fell closer to home. John Speed Smith replaced
Clay's friend Crittenden as district attorney for the District of Kentucky, and
John M. McCalla was in as the state's marshal.[20] McCalla, at least, would soon
be sorry for crossing Henry Clay.

Clay had not planned to resume his legal practice, but after his return to Kentucky, circumstances compelled him to participate in a notorious case that also
gave him an opportunity to spear his Bluegrass political opponents. Thomas R.
Benning, the young editor of the Lexington *Gazette,* was a pro-Jackson populist

who opposed Robert Wickliffe's candidacy for the Kentucky legislature and during the 1828 campaign published anonymous attacks on him. Benning did not write them. Instead, Wickliffe's opponent McCalla did, under the pen name of "Dentatus." Wickliffe wisely chose to ignore the insults, but his son Charles found them so offensive that he demanded the name of their author. On March 9, Benning was in his *Gazette* office when the angry young man confronted him. Charles Wickliffe claimed that Benning menaced him with a walking stick, causing Charles to pull his pistol and fatally wound the editor. A grand jury concluded that evidence merited a reduced charge of manslaughter, but Kentucky's Jacksonians thought it should have been murder. That sentiment as well as the political overtones surrounding the case made it most likely that a jury would convict Wickliffe. The elder Wickliffe entreated his friend and neighbor Henry Clay to join a defense team that included John J. Crittenden and Richard H. Chinn.[21]

Clay's participation was slight until the trial's end, when he characteristically relied on emotional appeals to sway the jury, and his treatment of McCalla provided the trial's most dramatic moment. McCalla had reluctantly admitted during the proceeding that he had written the offending articles, and accounts of the slaying described him as lurking at its edges. Clay was determined to paint him as the real villain of the piece, the instigator who had done the insulting while skulking behind a Roman pseudonym. "Who is this redoubtable *'Dentatus'*?" he asked as he surveyed the courtroom. He posed the question again, quizzically gazing at the jury as though truly perplexed, his voice dramatically pitched as though sincerely reflective. He mused that the way the unfortunate Benning had reacted when Wickliffe asked him that question the day of the shooting suggested that Dentatus was "a Hercules in prowess, and a Caesar in valor." Clay whirled and asked yet again, "Who is *'Dentatus'*?" Standing now directly before the jury, Clay seemed to shrink by pulling his arms close to his body, hunching his shoulders around his neck, and bending his knees to diminish his height; he raised his baritone several octaves: "Why, gentlemen, *it is nobody but little Johnny M'Calla!*" The judge's gavel repeatedly rapped amid the din of laughter and surprised chatter, and everyone soon noticed that McCalla had slunk silently from the courtroom during Clay's performance. McCalla never forgave him. Clay did not care. On June 13, the jury deliberated all of seven minutes before returning the verdict of not guilty.[22]

WHEN ANDREW JACKSON took the oath of office in 1829, some believed the gaunt old man would not live to complete his first term, and most doubted he would seek a second. Clay's supporters urged him to enter the contest for 1832 early to steal a march on any Democratic opponent. The Jacksonians meant "to assail and destroy You in every way in their power—This object is never lost for a moment," a friend wrote to Clay, a sign that of all possible candidates, Jacksonians feared him most. Clay had already planned a winter trip to New Orleans to visit the Erwins, and that was certainly a prime purpose for the visit; but he could also use his time in Louisiana to mend political fences and make new friends.[23]

In fact, Clay's January 1830 New Orleans trip signaled the start of his 1832 presidential campaign. In addition to stumping for André Roman and Josiah Johnston, Clay consulted about how best to oppose Jackson's policies and extol the American System, a strategy that filled the next two years of his supposed retirement from public life. Clay was not alone in looking toward 1832. Other candidates also organized their followers, formed alliances, and undermined opponents. Everyone anxiously measured the moods of the old man in the White House, who was apparently pondering his plans as much as observers were, among them his vice president, John C. Calhoun.[24] He too hoped to succeed Old Hickory, but Calhoun's place in the administration required that he be exceedingly careful not to show too much ambition. He had rivals in Jackson's official family and among his unofficial advisers, the group critics dubbed the "Kitchen Cabinet." The most dangerous was Secretary of State Martin Van Buren, who had Jackson's ear because he was willing to flatter and fawn, poses Calhoun found repellent. During Jackson's first year as president, his relations with Calhoun soured as they clashed over Mrs. Eaton's social status. Some speculated that Calhoun's own sinking fortunes would drive him into the arms of administration opponents, a prospect that caused Van Buren to beam.[25]

During these months, William H. Crawford's unexpected reemergence on the political scene was a surprise. He was still in very bad health, but his friends saw him as a good southern alternative to Calhoun, whose ties to southern extremism increasingly and unattractively defined him. Crawford was game but hardly able. Returning to Congress meant the world would hear his thick tongue and see his faltering step and palsied hands. Even Jackson, in comparison, would look nimble. Crawford consequently sought the presidency from the shadows, first by proposing an incredible scheme to Henry Clay. If Jackson did not run, he said, Van Buren and Calhoun were sure to, and a field that also included himself and Clay would splinter the Electoral College to prevent a majority. Crawford suggested that Clay drop out and throw his support to Crawford, who pledged a payoff in victory. He would not only put Clay in the cabinet but also formally designate him as his successor. Crawford's letter "indicates some want of self possession," Clay told Frank Brooke, and as he read and reread it in Ashland's shaded study, he became pensive and sad. His friends worried about all comers and wanted to use the letter to discredit Crawford once and for all, but Clay told them to forget the entire matter. He admitted that his old friendship with Crawford, though buffeted by events, yet haunted him. Clay folded closed the letter with the implausible plan and scratched on it, "Never answered."[26]

Crawford explored another tactic to wreck another rival with a scheme just as mischievous; indeed, it bordered on malice. That spring he informed Jackson that in 1818 Calhoun had recommended Jackson's censure and punishment for disobeying orders in Florida. Although Calhoun's sentiments about Jackson's invasion had been noised about for years, Crawford's revealing the particulars of cabinet discussions was an extraordinary breach of trust. Clay had charitably judged Crawford as having lost his way, but this act of treachery toward James Monroe and his former colleagues, particularly John C. Calhoun, confirmed something darker. Because of rampant rumors, Jackson had suspected something like what Crawford was now telling him, but Old Hickory nevertheless feigned outrage. By now, he and Calhoun were completely estranged, and Jackson cited the Crawford leak as an additional reason to ruin his vice president. Calhoun was in the process of learning what it was like to be Henry Clay.

Calhoun despised Crawford for a sneaky informer, but he blamed Van Buren for making the wretched invalid a cat's-paw in a plot to turn Jackson against him. Calhoun simmered and finally steered a course completely at variance with his customary caution. In early 1831, he published a pamphlet of his correspondence with Jackson and included documents to show the truth of the matter and defend himself against charges of disloyalty. Clay had done much the same thing three years earlier to refute the Corrupt Bargain charges. Clay could have told Calhoun not to waste his time.[27]

THE CRAGGY-FACED man from South Carolina had been destined for greatness but was beginning to retreat into truculence, and for reasons that had more to do with Henry Clay than Andrew Jackson. Calhoun's philosophy of government had undergone a dramatic transformation in the years after the War of 1812. As a nationalist War Hawk, he had matched Clay's enthusiasm for protective tariffs, internal improvements, and a national bank. His alliance with Jacksonians in the 1820s abruptly forced him to oppose all such policies, in part because Henry Clay and John Quincy Adams promoted them. Yet there was more to it than that. South Carolina's growing opposition to the American System also tugged Calhoun away from nationalism. He especially denounced the protective tariff because like many southerners he believed it favored the

North's manufacturing economy at the expense of the agricultural South. The nationalists' attempt to grow and consolidate power in the federal government genuinely alarmed Calhoun, and he branded the tariff as another unconstitutional manifestation of those efforts.[28]

That sort of attitude could make a man a hero at home but a political outsider everywhere else. Calhoun knew this as he eyed the presidency, weighed Van Buren's plots, and secretly caviled at Clay's protectionism. In fact, he had already cast his lot with sectionalists. He had just not yet admitted it. In 1828, his complaints jelled in his anonymous composition, *The South Carolina Exposition and Protest.* The pamphlet essentially outlined a way to block national initiatives with state interposition or nullification. Calhoun built on the work of Jefferson and Madison in their Virginia and Kentucky Resolutions of 1798–99 by adding his own views on the nature of the Union. Because the states had been sovereign before they ratified the Constitution, the reasoning went, their individual sovereignty took precedence over the country they formed. In fact, Calhoun did not recognize the United States as a nation at all but rather saw it as a compact of states, each with the power to judge the constitutionality of federal laws. A state had the right to nullify a federal law it deemed unconstitutional by refusing to enforce it. In response, the federal government could amend the Constitution, after which the state had the option of submitting to the nation's judgment or withdrawing from the Union.[29]

In January 1830, the country saw an attempt to make nullification a viable doctrine rather than a regional eccentricity. Western senators furiously protested northeastern efforts to restrict land sales, and South Carolinian Robert Y. Hayne pointed out how the "Tariff of Abominations" had similarly victimized the South to benefit the Northeast. He suggested nullification as a way to protect minority interests in both the West and the South. The majestic Daniel Webster ("the Godlike Dan'l" was among his nicknames) was appalled, and his reply to Hayne commenced a nine-day debate that ranks as one of the most famous exchanges in American political history. Webster came closest to matching Henry Clay in oratorical ability, and more than a few said he exceeded him, but the two were different kinds of speakers, each peerless as a type. Webster was physically imposing, a big man with a prominent brow, piercing black eyes to match his hair ("Black Dan" was another moniker), and a voice that could make water shiver in tumblers. He now aimed that voice like artillery at nullification, which, he thundered, would destroy the Union. To allow each of the twenty-four states to obey or reject federal laws as it pleased would reduce the Union to "a rope of sand." Hayne often gave as good as he got in these exchanges, but the Godlike Dan'l in the end was spectacular, his concluding statement bringing men to their feet and providing generations of American schoolchildren with words to recite from memory: "Liberty and Union, now and forever, one and inseparable!"[30]

Tying nullification to disunion was a masterful stroke. Calhoun's growing isolation in the administration gave him reasons beyond ideology to fall in line with South Carolina's radicals, but it was a move sure to widen an already yawning breach with Jackson. Old Hickory did not comment on the Webster-Hayne debate, but nobody would be allowed to challenge the government and imperil the Union on his watch. By April, Van Buren had told him that Calhoun was the anonymous author of the *Exposition and Protest.* At that month's Jefferson Birthday Dinner, angry toasts flew between them, Jackson snarling "Our Federal Union—it must be preserved!" and Calhoun responding "The Union: next to our liberty, most dear!" Their break complete, Jackson summoned Francis Preston Blair from Kentucky to establish the Washington *Globe.* It immediately replaced Duff Green's *United States Telegraph* as the administration's official newspaper.[31]

In Kentucky, Clay watched these developments with considerable interest. Like Webster, whom Clay congratulated for his masterful defense of the Union, he thought nullification preposterous. He echoed the New Englander's nationalism: "If a minority could at any time rise up, on any subject and in any part of the Union, and by threats of its dissolution control the majority, that Union would not be worth preserving."[32] Clay found Nullifiers more nonsensical than disturbing, a noisy few trying to bully the nation into meeting their demands, but as their bluster became rash and their actions reckless, he grew concerned. The obvious assault on the protective principle, one of the three mainstays of the American System, signaled trouble, but Clay also concluded that the very concept of nullification threatened to raise serious political storms. Nullification would lead "to immediate disorder and disunion," a result that should "fill every patriot bosom with the most awful apprehensions."[33] Although Calhoun's coming untethered nationally provided an opportunity for Clay's faction to court him, Clay warned against the fallacy of judging the enemy of your enemy to be your friend. Already in 1831, the odor of disunion, though faint, was clinging to John C. Calhoun. Clay could not stomach it.[34]

CLAY INTENDED TO present to the American people a positive program of economic growth and general prosperity. He remained convinced that his American System would best tie the country together economically by making the sections interdependent for their individual welfare as well as the common good. The American System could eventually lower prices for manufactured goods, provide a stable currency and reasonable credit for economic growth, and promote thriving commerce along modern roads and canals. It would make rivers and harbors navigable with innovative engineering techniques and systematic dredging. Economic interdependence would make disunion not only unlikely but unthinkable.

He reluctantly agreed that taking this message to the people required him to alter his campaign methods to fit changing political times. The early Republic considered courting votes vulgar and frowned on electioneering, which replaced calm deliberation with "the worst passions." Political practices in the 1820s rapidly changed that attitude, in large part because many states were allowing more people to vote. Clay found it necessary to mingle with more people. He attended barbecues and began embellishing his modest upbringing as exceedingly humble, a practice rapidly emerging as obligatory and one that eventually created the myth of Clay as "the Millboy of the Slashes." He never completely mastered this new political trade, because he remained uncomfortable plying it. Until the end of his days, he avoided the appearance of his travels as politically motivated, instead always insisting that personal or financial reasons required trips, during which he just happened to make speeches.[35]

More than just distaste for cheap theatrics or discomfort over exaggerating his experiences as a youth restrained him. The demands of the new politics transformed Henry Clay into a truly strange amalgam. On the one hand, he exemplified the political past because of his preference for the staid traditions of Madison and Monroe's time. Yet he also foreshadowed the future by extolling the virtue of planned progress, the idea that the government was not only empowered but obligated to perform economic functions that individuals could not or that private corporations would not.

This strange combination of past and future made him curiously out of place in his time, the Jacksonian period of the early nineteenth century that invoked the People as a mystical entity and insisted that the unbuilt road and the silted-up harbor did not hurt commerce. Clay steered a middle course that made him seem a basket of contradictions. The Progressive movement of the late nineteenth century that promoted moral uplift and active government would seem to be his legacy. Yet Clay opposed coerced morality and recoiled from regulating private economic behavior. A moderate on many issues, Clay was doctrinaire on certain matters, such as the inviolability of the Union and the role of economic progress in preserving it. Dubbed the Great Compromiser, he was not naturally prone to compromise, and instead became, as one perceptive historian has said, "an ideologue of the Center."[36]

Clay's entry into the 1832 presidential sweepstakes became increasingly purposeful because the administration began attacking the American System, or at least parts of it. Jackson, in fact, usually treated internal improvements as political plums and consequently signed more bills to fund them than any one of his predecessors. Yet in May 1830, he suddenly announced a constitutional objection to the Maysville Road and vetoed the bill funding it. The Maysville Road was really an extension of the National Road through Kentucky to the Natchez Trace, a project that would have facilitated travel between the Ohio and Tennessee rivers. Despite the obviously national aspect of the Maysville Road, its length fell entirely in Kentucky, and Jackson described it as a purely local venture that benefited only one state at the expense of the others.

Some laud Jackson's Maysville Road veto as a courageous state paper, but it was actually an expedient political gesture. Posing as the nation's protector, Jackson walloped Henry Clay by injuring Kentucky. Secretary of State Martin Van Buren used it to soothe southern states' rights men anxious about growing federal power that could threaten slavery while satisfying flinty northeasterners who had financed many of their own internal improvements and objected to paying for those in other states. Jackson ran a relatively low risk of permanently alienating westerners with the veto, and he gained allies elsewhere. He was able, for instance, to erode southern support for South Carolina Nullifiers.[37]

The Maysville Road veto infuriated Henry Clay, of course, but it also angered other Kentuckians, who sensed that Jackson was singling them out for punishment. It also exasperated Kentucky's neighbors, who would have profited from an increase in commercial traffic. Clay suggested that Congress draft a constitutional amendment to allow simple majorities to override vetoes, a recurring idea for him that perfectly expressed his belief in legislative supremacy. Jackson's popularity made the plan impractical, however. Indeed, Jackson's popularity seemed to sweep all before it; but he was also careful not to take chances. It was apparent that he had carefully timed his Maysville veto to avoid antagonizing congressmen he needed to pass one of the major initiatives of his first term, Indian removal. He waited until that had narrowly passed, and not until the following day did he issue his Maysville veto.[38]

Like most westerners, Clay had never been a champion of Indian rights, and privately he expressed doubts that Indians could assimilate into or peacefully coexist with white culture. At first, then, his dissent from Jackson's Indian removal policy appeared more opportunistic than sincere, a gesture to exploit the Indian Removal Act's unpopularity in the Northeast. Yet in the years that followed, as dubious treaties filled with counterfeit pledges uprooted entire tribes in the Southeast, he changed. The government's promise to the Indians of protected and provisioned passage to new homes in the Arkansas or Indian territories west of the Mississippi proved empty as hunger, illness, and weather plagued their journeys. Countless Indians perished, most infamously on "the Trail of Tears," and many Americans watched the unfolding horrors with growing dismay. Clay was among them. From the letters of clergymen and humanitarians, Clay followed the plight of displaced Indians and denounced from heartfelt conviction the administration's behavior as dishonest and inhumane. When Clay returned to the Senate, he met with Indian leaders to advise them about avoiding this calamity to their people. Indian removal came to disgust him as it did other National Republicans, and their revulsion informed the stand of the new political party Clay founded in the 1830s. The barbarity of Jackson's policy in its implementation was impossible for him to countenance, and what had begun as a political opportunity to oppose Andrew Jackson became for him another compelling reason to unseat Jacksonians.[39]

SEVERAL EVENTS IN early 1831 convinced the Clay faithful that it was time for him to end his so-called retirement in a formal way and return to the national stage. First, the administration put to rest all doubt regarding a second term, ruling out other Democrat contenders. With only two candidates in the running, Clay's supporters reckoned he stood a better chance. Clay's victory, chortled one, would likely kill Jackson, or at least irritate Old Hickory's famous and chronic digestive problems. "His diarrhea will be brought on," went the joke.[40]

Another event that gave Clay supporters hope was the disintegration of Jackson's cabinet in the spring of 1831. The turmoil over Margaret Eaton had not abated, but it had boosted the fortunes of widower Martin Van Buren, the only man in the cabinet who could offer Mrs. Eaton his arm and not worry about an ugly scene later at home. Jackson consequently judged Van Buren the only gentleman among a cadre of cads and was willing to embrace Van Buren's solution to the crisis. He and Eaton would resign their posts and put pressure on the rest of the cabinet members to follow suit. The plan appears more plausible from a modern perspective than it did at the time, because the idea of the cabinet as completely subservient to the will of the president was hardly a fixed principle in the 1830s. Instead, many saw the cabinet as a relatively autonomous arm of the executive, something akin to a privy council whose collective wisdom helped frame executive responses to legislative policies. The other secretaries did not eagerly prepare to jump Jackson's ship simply because he, let alone Martin Van Buren, wanted them to. It took a few heated scenes that created considerable and lingering animosity, but the other secretaries were ultimately persuaded to resign.

Cleaning out the cabinet to get rid of John Eaton and to punish those who had snubbed John Eaton's wife caused a stir in Washington. As Jackson's official family was being browbeaten to resign, National Republicans hoped the overbearing executive behavior would brand Jackson as an incipient tyrant and the resulting chaos would convince voters of his incompetence.[41] Thus did the opposition try to attach deeper meaning to an otherwise shallow series of events that had oddly preoccupied the executive branch of the United States government for two years. As the Eatons left Washington for Tennessee, Clay kept his perspective. Parodying Domitius Enobarbus's tribute to Cleopatra in Shakespeare's *Antony and Cleopatra,* he said of Margaret that "age cannot wither nor time stale her infinite virginity."[42]

As they chuckled over Democrat contretemps, National Republicans were verging on a schism of their own. A new political party emerging in their traditional strongholds threatened to take voters away from Clay's candidacy. Antimasonry had first appeared in Upstate New York and then spread south to the Mid-Atlantic and north into New England. It condemned the secretive Masonic Order as an elite league that dominated local, state, and national politics at the expense of outsiders. In 1826 William Morgan, a disaffected Mason in New York, had threatened to publish the order's secret rites. Morgan was abducted and efforts to find him and his kidnappers were fruitless, apparently because Masons interfered with the investigation. Morgan never turned up, but a badly decomposed and unidentifiable body found months later confirmed for many the wickedness of the Masons. The Morgan affair transformed what had been a social reaction against special privilege into a full-fledged political movement.[43]

This new party stood to cause Clay considerable trouble. An Antimasonic candidate would poach more National Republican than Democrat voters, but the fact that Clay himself was a Mason spelled problems. His association with the order likely resulted from his efforts to gain status after first arriving in Lexington, and he had been active into the early 1820s, holding important positions in the Grand Lodge of Kentucky. By the late 1820s, however, he was too busy to remain an active Mason, aside from being aware of the political damage it could cause.[44]

Clay at first underestimated the fervor of the Antimasons and took false comfort in the fact that Andrew Jackson was also a Mason. All else being equal, Clay expected that the candidate best promoting their economic interests would claim the Antimasons' votes. Clay gradually became worried, however, that Antimason rabble-rousers were stirring up the masses for selfish political purposes, and in the summer of 1831 he finally realized the threat Antimasonry posed to his candidacy. Still refusing to disavow the Masonic order, he remained baffled over what pertinence any of this had for politics.[45]

In September 1831, the Antimasons held a national nominating convention in Baltimore. Although of a regional character, the convention was historic in the sense that it was the first to choose a presidential candidate. Delegates considered a panoply of prominent political figures, including former president John Quincy Adams, a choice that would have understandably astonished Clay. The convention flabbergasted him just as thoroughly, though, when it nominated his old friend and fellow National Republican, William Wirt, who inexplicably accepted. Although Wirt opposed Jackson's policies just as strongly as did Clay, friends had convinced him that Clay could not defeat Jackson. Perhaps Wirt could, they mused, by seeking fusion with National Republicans. The hope that boosting Wirt to prominence would persuade National Republicans to pick him at their December convention indicated the foolish reveries of the Antimasons. The Antimasons could never be anything but spoilers in a political fight, and Wirt's sad role was made sadder by the likelihood that he was not emotionally stable at the time. Earlier that year, his sixteen-year-old daughter Agnes had died suddenly, and Wirt remained consumed by grief. As for the 1832 election, numerous attempts to join National Republicans and Antimasons failed, but a dispassionate assessment would have informed the rankest political amateur that Wirt could never defeat Jackson. On the other hand, dividing National Republicans dashed any hope of victory at all.[46]

The Wirt candidacy shook Clay to the point of prompting him to consider withdrawing and allowing the party to nominate someone else. He was hardly a rank amateur, but he claimed he was unable to gauge his own chances for victory, and he asked for friends' advice. Those friends read between the lines to discern that he was really asking for their support, and their encouragement was quick and heartfelt. Instead of quitting, they said, Clay should return to public life to become more nationally noticeable.[47] They suggested a return to the Senate, but Clay was reluctant.

He was reluctant in part because he was greatly preoccupied in the summer and fall of 1831 with something other than politics. Theodore had fallen into serious trouble. As a boy, this oldest son could be fearfully unpredictable and prone to violent tantrums, some of them menacing. The family blamed the head injury Theodore had suffered as a child, a conclusion that possibly had merit. That Amos Kendall had had to snatch away a knife Theodore was brandishing at a slave indicated something far more serious than a spoiled, high-strung child, and shadowy, oblique references to similar outbursts over the years point to an ongoing problem that the Clay family coped with rather than addressed. Clay always hoped that the boy would grow out of his short-tempered ways, but mostly he just wanted Theodore to grow up. He brought Theodore to Washington in 1824 "in the hope of reforming him of his indolence and dissipation" but soon had to send him home when Theodore began sneaking off to drink and gamble, once losing $500 he could never hope to pay. Thomas drank excessively and gambled too, but he remained relatively jovial while doing the one and was usually penitent about the other. Thomas got drunk, but Theodore could get ugly. His behavior and moods embarrassed his father. "This is a delicate and painful subject," Clay conceded in 1828, "which parents will know how to appreciate."[48]

During Theodore's periods of calm and stability, which could be lengthy and encouraging, Clay hoped for the best. Just as Theodore could be angry and brooding, when in good humor he could be witty and charming, clever with a phrase, quick to laugh, tenderly sympathetic, impossible not to love.[49] During these good times, Clay entrusted Theodore with important tasks, almost as rewards for correct behavior. The young man explored his father's extensive land holdings on the Kentucky River, traipsing through ten thousand acres of wilderness before returning to Ashland with a healthful tan and a sense of achievement. Though Clay prudently hired managers to run Ashland while he was away, he always asked Theodore to keep an eye on the place. Clay employed Theodore as a State Department courier to take messages to Joel Poinsett in Mexico and to the commissioners at the Panama Congress at Tacubaya. He was hopeful when Theodore showed an interest in the law, and when the young man proved a quick study, Clay was relieved that at last his son might have found his way.[50]

Theodore, however, either lost interest in a legal career or lacked the mental focus to run a practice. In 1830, something more alarming than usual began happening to his mind. He left Kentucky that summer and by early September was in St. Louis. The reason for his trip is unclear, but it seems to have been an argument with Anne. He referred to disagreements with her that he hoped neither she nor James Erwin would hold against him. Possibly Anne had tried to give Theodore a talking-to about nearing thirty with no purpose in life. Her brother had visited New Orleans, apparently in search of opportunities, but disdained all that Erwin sent his way. Theodore's trip to Missouri had the appearance for a time of being a permanent move. He liked St. Louis, he told his mother, and "should I remain here, I perceive a tolerable chance of getting through my journey of life with pleasure."[51]

He soon returned to Kentucky, though, for he had fallen in love with a daughter of the prominent Brand family in Lexington. She did not love Theodore, and his disappointment unhinged him. He became delusional, explaining to himself that her family's disapproval, not the girl's indifference, was responsible for her rejecting him. In the fall of 1831, just as his father was considering his return to the Senate, Theodore charged into the girl's home and held the Brand family at gunpoint. After defusing that dangerous situation, the Brands promptly swore out a complaint. The court summoned a jury, which heard witnesses regarding Theodore's sanity, for the Brand family graciously asserted that his menacing behavior was the impetuous act of a helpless man. It was unfortunately by then the kindest explanation for Theodore's erratic actions, and the Clays cooperated with rather than resisted the sad drama playing out in the Fayette County courthouse that October. Henry Clay and James Erwin testified before a jury of prominent citizens that included Clay's oldest friends, Richard Chinn, Leslie Combs, Robert Wickliffe, and John Postlethwaite among them. They pronounced Theodore insane—a "lunatic" in the legal parlance of the day—and the court committed him to the Eastern Kentucky Insane Asylum.[52]

Thus Henry Clay's oldest son passed into the land of shadows. To the end of their days, Henry and Lucretia hoped Theodore's condition was temporary, and at first they had promising signs of recovery, even to an extent that allowed him brief visits to Ashland. The periods of lucidity were all the more heartbreaking, though, for their increasing brevity. The possibility that the next incident when Theodore was irrational and armed would end tragically compelled Henry and Lucretia to harden their hearts and stop their ears to Theodore's frequent entreaties for release from the asylum, to ignore his unrealistic plans for starting over somewhere else. Days faded into months and months into years, and the pleas gradually lessened until they ceased altogether as Theodore slipped away. When he had been in St. Louis in the summer of 1830 he had told his mother, "I am charmed with this place, and I sincerely hope that I am not throwing away my time."[53] Now Theodore had nothing but time, and his plans and dreams were a knife in Lucretia's heart, another wound as she thought about her boy confined just miles from Ashland but drifting away from her. Eventually he did not recognize any of them, but his days stretched across the decades beyond the passing of his parents and all his siblings save two. Only Thomas, the brotherly playmate of his childhood, and baby brother John remained to bury Theodore Wythe Clay in 1870.

CLAY'S BID TO regain national prominence was best served by succeeding John Rowan in the U.S. Senate. The state legislature had tried to fill the vacancy in the winter of 1830–31, but no candidate could secure a majority. Clay's friend John J. Crittenden came closest, but he was a member of the legislature and would have had to vote for himself to win, which he refused to do. The legislature postponed another vote until late in the summer of 1831, hoping that by then state elections would clarify matters. In those contests, Clay's supporters won a clear majority, and Crittenden was persuaded to step aside. Clay remained reluctant but consented to serve. He defeated Richard M. Johnson, the Jacksonian candidate, 73 to 64. After almost three years, Henry and Lucretia were to go back to Washington. All the children were either grown or in school, and the Clays took with them only their little grandson Henry Clay Duralde.[54]

What everybody would most remember about that winter in the capital was the cold. The ice on the Potomac was three inches thick and stopped all steamboat traffic. Lucretia was miserable. Margaret Smith greeted her affectionately, but Lucretia missed her children, was distraught about Theodore, and was often physically ill. She and Henry Duralde shivered away their days in a small rented house, where their chief amusement consisted of his English lessons. Soon she wished she had not come to Washington at all, as she hungered for news from home. Some of it was mercifully cheerful.

Henry Jr. managed the farm at Ashland when he was not heading up to Louisville to visit pretty seventeen-year-old Julia Prather. They were well suited, her good cheer a nice counterweight to his subdued nature. By the summer of 1832, Henry was deeply in love. Julia was too, seeing in the quiet, serious suitor something grand. On October 10, they married, making Henry the first of the sons to wed.[55]

Lucretia was unhappy in Washington, but the return to the capital placed her husband "in his very element,—in the very vortex of political warfare."[56] Meanwhile, the National Republican convention in Baltimore placed him again in contention for the presidency. Speculation stemming from Antimasons about another candidate came to nothing, and delegates in Baltimore never seriously considered Wirt. Consequently, Clay's was the only name before the convention, and its decision surprised no one. The convention named Pennsylvanian John Sergeant to be Clay's running mate and issued a statement of purpose, the forerunner of the modern party platform, which condemned Jackson's veto of the Maysville Road, his use of government patronage, and his criticism of the Bank of the United States.[57]

Although political parties were still in their infancy, Clay's nomination placed him at the head of those styling themselves National Republicans. He intended to lead the opposition to the administration when he entered the Senate, but his expectations about party discipline were unrealistic. Despite Jackson's setbacks with the cabinet, he remained a political colossus. Clay found the National Republicans to be fractious as well as cautious about crossing an enormously popular president. Those congressional attitudes made realizing his policies to promote economic growth all the more difficult, and, worse, it revealed a remarkable erosion of the principle of legislative supremacy. Clay was astonished at how far "King Andrew" had extended executive power, but he was equally uneasy about the apparent awe this president caused in Congress. Clay intended to do something about that.[58]

Many dismissed Henry Clay's challenge of Andrew Jackson as a mere clash of egos, but behind the fireworks was Clay's principal purpose of reestablishing Congress as the "first wheel of government." His arrival in Washington in 1831 presented Andrew Jackson with a foe unlike any he had ever encountered, for the decorous rules of the State Department no longer hamstrung Senator Clay. Unlike the professorial Calhoun, Clay was agile in debate, dexterous in controversy, and extremely quick in impromptu exchanges. Jackson's supporters, who had been having their way fairly unimpeded for three years, quickly learned to tread lightly around Henry Clay. There were "hundreds, perhaps thousands, of men in the United States, who exceed Henry Clay, in information on all subjects," said a friend, "but his superiority consists in the power and adroitness with which he brings his information to bear."[59]

It was not enough to repeat the old saw that when Clay spoke, people listened, for Clay rising from his desk in the Senate was comparable to the curtain going up in a first-rate theater. He used props for stage business, such as the little silver snuffbox that he absentmindedly rolled from one hand to the other, creating a near hypnotic spell while he spoke. He pulled his snow-white handkerchief from his coat with a flourish and polished his spectacles as though lost in thought, the pause lengthening and listeners' expectations swelling until he again broke the silence with "his unequalled voice, which was equally distinct and clear, whether at its highest key or lowest whisper—rich, musical, captivating." Like any accomplished trial lawyer, Clay commanded attention with tricks to distract the audience when others were speaking. He looked bored and stared at the distance while "eating sticks of striped peppermint candy." Foes and friends reacted accordingly. Clay was "very imperious" and showed "bad temper in debate,"[60] or he displayed "a most courteous and conciliatory deportment to all his great political opponents."[61]

Clay's erstwhile friend Francis Preston Blair prudently adopted the maxim not to demagogue in private when he warned his Jacksonian cronies that Clay was formidable because he "never deserted a friend." Other men had political allies, Blair said, but Clay had friends for whom he showed real and enduring affection.[62] Edward Bates, who became Abraham Lincoln's attorney general, described Clay's charisma as "a winning fascination in his manner that will suffer none to be his enemies who operate with him." "His manly & bold countenance" gave rise to "an emotion little short of enthusiasm in his cause, and nothing short of absolute detestation & contempt for the cowardly" people who opposed him. Henry Clay was "a great man," said Ned Bates, "one of nature's nobles."[63]

CLAY'S IMMEDIATE TASKS in the Senate were to protect the American System and to get himself elected president. Protecting the American System became a significant challenge because South Carolina's protests about the Tariff of Abominations were in full roar, and the state's Nullifiers were readying to move on its polls. Eager to avert a crisis, Congress wavered on protection as National Republicans lost their nerve. Clay warned that to give in to threats only invited more demands, and he worked to isolate both Nullifiers and antitariff southerners angling to form a western alliance by supporting lower land prices.[64]

He first thought he could accomplish this with an alternative tariff, but others doubted the plan would work. The day after Christmas, Clay called on another "junior" member of Congress, Representative John Quincy Adams, who had broken the tradition of former presidents living in quiet retirement. Since leaving office, Adams had been chilly toward Clay.[65] That previous summer, Clay had written to Adams after hearing of James Monroe's death, but his light tone put off the New Englander. Clay noted that Adams's father, Thomas Jefferson, and now James Monroe had all died on July 4, making it "very unfashionable" for former presidents to die on any other day. Every July 5, a former president would know that he had at least another year to live. Clay closed with warm wishes "that *your* fourth may be far distant." Adams was not amused.[66]

In fact, Adams wore annoyance like a frock coat. Meeting with him that December afternoon, Clay tried another joke. He asked how Adams "felt upon turning boy again to go into the House of Representatives." Adams's response was tart: he did not know yet, since the House had done little business. Clay abandoned apparently useless pleasantries and turned to the tariff. His real purpose for the visit, after all, was to generate support for his idea. He assured Adams that southern agitation was merely a bluff that would soon die down, but Adams thought that South Carolina was far from bluffing. "Here is one great error of Mr. Clay," Adams told his diary.[67]

Days later, National Republicans caucused in Massachusetts congressman Edward Everett's rooms to hear Clay explain his plan. In addition to the threat of possible cooperation between the South and the West to kill protection, Clay feared that the administration would adopt an antitariff stance simply to oppose him. Jackson's annual message promised to eliminate the national debt by the end of his first term, in March 1833. It was a laudable goal, but Clay worried about its ramifications for the tariff. A Treasury surplus would make significant tariff revenues unnecessary. Clay's bill would have done away with duties on imports such as tea, coffee, and spices while reducing them on other items. Otherwise, Clay planned to sustain high duties on products still in need of protection from foreign competition. Reducing or eliminating duties, he explained, would prevent a large surplus and require a tariff to produce revenue. Clay was pleasant during his presentation, though Adams also found him somewhat overbearing, an impression that might have resulted from the New Englander's jealousy over Clay's rising fortunes. The two also had a sharp exchange. Adams said they should not defy the president's plan to pay off the debt, but Clay growled that "he would defy the South, the President, and the devil" to preserve the American System. His efforts to jolly Adams were at an end.[68]

Calhoun led the administration's other antagonists in Congress, and had it not been for that faction's extreme opposition to the tariff, Clay might have been able to fold it into a formidable coalition. The two groups grasped what they perceived was a splendid opportunity to act on their shared hostility to Andrew Jackson when his nomination of Martin Van Buren as minister to Great Britain came before the Senate for confirmation. Van Buren's solution to the Margaret Eaton muddle had left him unemployed, and Jackson rewarded him with the diplomatic assignment to Great Britain. The recess appointment meant that Van Buren had already sailed for London when Congress began considering his confirmation, and Calhoun was excited about doubly embarrassing the Little Magician by compelling his recall.[69]

Van Buren's tenure at State made him more than qualified to represent the United States at the Court of Saint James, but Jackson's enemies wanted to make clear that Congress had not become the administration's rubber stamp. That resolve was made easier because Van Buren's climb to power had left behind it a wake of ill will. Senators spoke of his role in engineering the widespread dismissals and in causing the rupture between Calhoun and Jackson. Van Buren had managed to usher in excellent Anglo-American relations and had finally persuaded the British to open their West Indian colonies to American trade, securing an agreement that had eluded Clay. Yet more than sour grapes motivated Clay's opposition to Van Buren's appointment to London. Clay was livid that Van Buren had ingratiated himself with the British by criticizing the Adams administration, a gesture that had prostrated and degraded "the American eagle before the British lion."[70]

Opposition forces arranged for the vote to end in a tie, giving Calhoun the honor of breaking it to defeat Van Buren's confirmation. Afterward, Calhoun was reportedly giddy: "It will kill him dead, sir, kill him dead. He will never kick, sir, never kick."[71] Van Buren did not need to kick. Humiliating him only made Van Buren a martyr in many people's eyes, a victim of partisan bickering. His rejection by the Senate would bring him home, but hardly in disgrace. Instead, he would again be at Jackson's side, accelerating the plan for him to replace Calhoun on Jackson's 1832 ticket.[72]

Van Buren had drawn Clay's and Calhoun's supporters together, but the session's tariff debates drove them apart. Jackson's secretary of the Treasury, Louis McLane, was working with the House Committee on Manufactures (chaired by Adams) to draft a tariff satisfactory to the South while sustaining at least the principle of protection. Clay did not like the looks of that development, for the last thing he wanted was for the administration to be able to claim credit for solving this crisis as the election neared. As the House committee worked on the McLane-Adams bill, Clay wrote his own to present to the Senate on January 11, 1832. Administration men immediately attacked Clay's plan as insufficient in its reductions, punitive toward the South, and harmful to the market. Clay grew openly irritable and tenacious, "prepared for anything to advance his own views," possibly even strike a "bargain with the devil."[73]

As far as Clay was concerned, that was precisely what John Quincy Adams had done. His cooperation with the Jacksonians was galling, particularly when they began branding Clay a Federalist in comparison.[74] Meanwhile, senators fearful of a confrontation with South Carolina Nullifiers preferred the more moderate Adams-McLane tariff, and Clay's impatience boiled over in a speech that spanned three days in February. He provided a long look at the history of tariffs in the United States. Not so long ago, he said reflectively while staring at Calhoun, almost everyone acknowledged the wisdom of the protective tariff. The year 1816 came to mind when a majority that included the current vice president had approved the tariff and had embraced the American System as the best way to ensure American prosperity.[75] Clay was amazed at the mistaken idea that free trade would solve all the world's economic problems. He shouted, "Free trade! Free trade! The call for free trade, is as unavailing as the cry of a spoiled child, in its nurse's arms, for the moon or the stars that glitter in the firmament of heaven. It never existed; it never will exist." Instead of liberating American commerce, free trade would only place the nation "under the commercial dominion of Great Britain."[76]

Clay's seemingly interminable blizzard of words was an exhaustive treatment of the subject as well as simply exhausting, for both him and his listeners. He was tired, and many he had wanted to persuade remained unconvinced, which set the mood for confrontation. The old War of 1812 veteran Samuel Smith came unsteadily to his feet, unaware that he was about to be figuratively knocked off them. Smith confessed to having been among those Clay had mentioned who formerly supported protective tariffs but now opposed them. He simply doubted the need for Clay's higher duties. Clay derisively turned on Smith. What this old relic and Jacksonian toady was really saying, Clay thundered, was that he no longer cared about American manufacturers. He recited an insulting rhyme: "Old politicians chew on wisdom past / And *totter* on in business to the last." Smith took the bait. Leaping to his feet, he snarled that "the last allusion is unworthy of the gentleman," and shouted, "Totter, sir? I totter! Though some twenty years older than the gentleman, I can yet stand firm, and am yet able to correct his errors. I could take a view of the gentleman's course which would show how inconsistent he has been." Clay shouted back, "Take it, sir, take it—I dare you." Cries of "Order!" rang through the chamber as Smith bellowed over the din, "No, Sir, I will not take it. I will not so far disregard what is due to the dignity of the Senate." The Senate quickly adjourned for the day.[77]

Jacksonian newspapers universally condemned Clay's treatment of Smith. Francis Preston Blair's *Globe* played on the issue of age with an editorial headlined "Mr. Clay's Senility," ignoring that the seventy-nine-year-old Marylander had actually shaved five years off his age in comparing himself to Clay.[78] The feisty performance, however, energized National Republicans heartened to see someone rearing up on his hind legs at imperious Jacksonians. Clay during his audacious days in the House had never been better, they thought, and even those who disagreed with him "admired his splendid talents, his bold, chivalrous & manly bearing" and "his fearless & uncompromising spirit in what he deemed to be right."[79]

Better yet, Clay seemed to be winning. His resolution was sent to the Committee on Manufactures, of which he was a member and likely to dominate its discussions. Yet opponents had a plan to turn westerners against Clay. To distract the committee from rapid deliberations on Clay's bill, Thomas Hart Benton managed to get an administration initiative referred to the Committee on Manufactures as well, even though it obviously had nothing to do with manufacturing. Benton's bill instead proposed to lower land prices through a complicated system of distributing proceeds to the states. The measure was popular with westerners, and Clay's opposition to it risked his western support in the coming election. He did not believe in artificially high land prices, but he refused to let Benton and the Jacksonians bully him to win votes. In addition, Clay worried that extremely low land prices on the western frontier would depress property values in the settled areas while removing land revenues as a source of income for the government. Securing funds for internal improvements would then become all but impossible.[80]

Clay knew that southerners were likely to support any proposal that committed the West to oppose a tariff, and before such an irresistible majority took shape, he moved to supplant the administration's land policy with one of his own. His alternative was similar to Benton's, but its differences, while key, allowed Clay to portray it as a compromise. As in the administration plan, the government would distribute proceeds to the states for explicit purposes such as internal improvements, education, debt retirement, or colonizing freed slaves. Yet Benton had proposed selling the lands directly to the states, while Clay wanted the federal government to retain possession and sell to individuals or private consortia to ensure top dollar for the tracts. As enticement for the West, Clay proposed that a state would receive 10 percent of revenue from the sale of public lands within its borders. The Treasury would divide the balance among all the other states in sums based on population. Keeping land prices relatively high would please easterners worried that cheap land would lure their citizens westward, and the government would be forced to rely on a tariff for operating funds. Though proponents of lower land prices were not happy with Clay's plan, it was a shrewd interweaving of specific interests for a common good, and it attracted enough support from the Northeast and more populous Western states to pass in the Senate. Clay foiled Benton's ploy to make him appear an enemy of western interests, but his bill died in the House.[81]

Clay's tariff fared no better. He had the votes to bring it out of the Committee on Manufactures, but many of his colleagues still believed the Adams-McLane proposal was a less confrontational compromise. The House's tariff did not abandon protection, which was the only reason Clay found it marginally acceptable, but it drastically reduced many duties to 1824 levels. Clay labored to raise rates with amendments, but the House rejected the changes, and rather than risk a crisis with South Carolina, the Senate finally conceded. Protectionist circles at least credited Clay with preserving their principles. The bill that ultimately passed both houses in July 1832 little resembled Clay's but was essentially the one Adams and Secretary McLane had originally proposed. Jackson signed it, and many hailed it as a laudable and satisfactory compromise. South Carolina Nullifiers could not have disagreed more.[82]

IN ADDITION TO debating a new tariff and land policy, Congress also considered renewing the charter for the Second Bank of the United States. The bank's current charter would not expire until 1836, but BUS president Nicholas Biddle hoped that holding the renewal debate in an election year would compel Jackson to sign off on what had become a popular institution largely responsible for a thriving economy.

The move was risky, however, because Jackson disapproved of the BUS.

Shortly after his inauguration in 1829, he told Biddle he disapproved of all banks, which was something of an exaggeration, although Jackson's own financial problems thirty years earlier had indeed created in him an enduring distrust of paper money. Like many westerners, he held the BUS responsible for the Panic of 1819 and the resulting financial crisis. He believed that loans in bank-notes that exceeded an institution's actual holdings were inherently dishonest, and he inclined toward using only specie for financial transactions. Biddle's steady leadership of the BUS since 1823 had inspired growing support for the Bank, even in Jackson's cabinet, but Jackson remained unconvinced that it served the financial interests of the country so much as it fattened the wallets of its wealthy investors.

Left unspoken, of course, were less lofty reasons for disliking the BUS, such as its independence from the executive, making it a patronage engine the administration could not control. Jacksonian constituencies, local bankers among them, chafed under Biddle's ability to control credit, always on the restrictive side to their thinking. Biddle did not realize how deep those resentments ran or how determined Jacksonian politicos were to transfer patronage privileges to the U.S. Treasury. Rather, he hoped he could change Jackson's mind before the BUS charter expired. From the day of Jackson's inauguration, Biddle used diplomacy and gentle persuasion to convert Old Hickory, but the BUS president rubbed the U.S. president the wrong way from the start. Biddle's belonging to one of Philadelphia's most patrician families, his sterling education, and his diplomatic service abroad made him seem aloof. His immersion in the complex world of national finance made him seem arrogant. He was an excellent financier but as it turned out a poor politician and an ineffective pleader. Biddle occasionally overcame these deficiencies with questionable practices, such as putting prominent politicians on the BUS payroll, a move that laid him and the Bank open to charges of corruption. In 1829, he had sealed for Jackson the impression of suspect dealing. Biddle proposed early recharter in exchange for the BUS assuming the national debt, pledging to pay it off by 1833 as Jackson wanted. That interview with the president went quite badly, because Jackson bristled at Biddle's transparent attempt to buy support for recharter by taking on one of Jackson's pet projects. He never trusted Biddle again, and he instantly hardened against the Bank. He made clear in his first annual message that he was opposed to its recharter.[83]

The following year, Biddle considered asking for early renewal anyway, hoping the Bank's popularity and the good economy would induce Jackson to consent. Credit was stable, and the Bank's notes circulated nationally as sound currency. Biddle asked Clay's advice, but the former BUS attorney counseled caution. If Jackson vetoed a renewal bill, Bank supporters could not muster the two-thirds majority to override it. Biddle decided to wait.[84]

His decision to ask the Twenty-second Congress for early renewal at the end of 1831 seems to have been coincidental with Clay's return to the Senate, not because of it. Evidence indicates that Biddle's course was his own, taken entirely independently of advice from Clay. It so happened that Clay by then agreed with Biddle that the time for recharter had arrived. Jackson's December 1831 annual message indicated a softening position on the Bank, and everyone knew that Secretary of the Treasury McLane supported recharter and might take the lead on a bill allaying Jackson's remaining objections. In addition, Biddle judged that Jackson was more likely to sign a recharter before rather than after the 1832 presidential election. He would not want to alienate Mid-Atlantic states, where the Bank was especially popular, and thereby put his reelection bid at risk. Clay saw the wisdom in Biddle's calculation, though he was not as confident that Jackson would sign the recharter. On the other hand, Clay had done some calculating of his own. A Jackson veto was likely to throw those valuable Mid-Atlantic votes into Clay's column.[85]

Congress took up recharter in January 1832, but an investigation into the Bank's alleged misconduct delayed substantive debate until May when the charges were finally declared groundless. The ensuing discussion, however, was odd in that the Bank's proponents made little effort to dispute objections to it. This passivity immediately raised speculation that Clay and the National Republicans actually wanted a Jackson veto in order to create an important campaign issue. Only circumstantial evidence supported that conclusion, but the evidence was nonetheless convincing. For example, Clay confided to friends that he expected a veto and that it would cost Old Hickory Pennsylvania at the very least. In addition, orchestrated moves to produce a formal rather than a "pocket" veto indicate that the National Republicans did not want recharter so much as they wanted to force Jackson's hand.

The Constitution provides two ways for a bill to become law. One is straightforward: Congress passes the bill and the executive signs it. The other is indirect: if the president does not sign the bill within ten days, it becomes law without his signature—but only if Congress is still in session. Otherwise, the bill dies. If Congress does not adjourn within those ten days, a president wishing to kill a bill must formally veto it and return it to the legislature with an explanation. Traditionally, presidents had wielded the veto only when they believed a bill to be unconstitutional, meaning that the will of Congress as the voice of the people trumped policy differences. In any case, the veto message provided a point of departure for Congress either to override the veto with an extraordinary majority of two-thirds, or to tailor the bill to the president's satisfaction. On the other hand, if Congress adjourns within the ten days and the bill expires without the president's signature, the resulting "pocket veto" requires no message, in part because Congress cannot debate an override if it is not in session.

The Senate passed the bank recharter on June 11, 1832, but the House did not vote until July 3, a mere six days before scheduled adjournment. Clay worked with Webster to postpone the close of the session until July 16, forcing Jackson to provide a formal veto message. Clay clearly intended to run on this issue because he believed a presidential veto would prove immensely unpopular.[86]

Just as there was little doubt that Congress would pass the bill, there was little doubt that Jackson would veto it. Most of his cabinet, including his Treasury secretary, supported recharter, but Jackson would have died rather than sign a bill he correctly assessed as meant to embarrass him. Van Buren was at his side when the bill came to the White House on July 4, and Jackson snarled, "The bank is trying to kill me, Mr. Van Buren, but I will kill it." Ignoring his official counselors, Jackson turned to his Kitchen Cabinet, which included men such as Amos Kendall and Francis Preston Blair. The clear, articulate prose in the veto message was certainly not Jackson's, although it perfectly conveyed his attitudes. The primary authors were probably Amos Kendall; Jackson's nephew and secretary, Andrew Jackson Donelson; and his attorney general, Roger B. Taney, the one member of the cabinet who approved of Jackson's stand on the Bank. Because Kendall was so heavily involved, the veto was accordingly short on constitutional principles and long on populist propaganda.[87]

The Bank, said the message, was unconstitutional because Jackson said it was. It dismissed Chief Justice John Marshall's decision in *McCulloch v. Maryland* by insisting that the president was the equal and possibly the superior of the judiciary in weighing the constitutionality of legislation. The message took some pains to show how precedent was largely immaterial in making such determinations, implying behind the thinnest veneer of legal reasoning that the president's personal preference, a sort of constitutional intuition, was most important. As an effective political statement rather than a sound legal argument, the veto excelled. It condemned the Bank as a tool of plutocrats, a dangerous monopoly, an anti-American establishment that relied on foreigners, particularly Britons, to form a substantial number of its stockholders. Jackson's constitutional objections were half-baked, and his populist attack was patently unfair and relied on shameless distortions of a well-run, efficient financial institution, but that did not matter. The veto portrayed him as a champion of the common folk, ever vigilant as their protector against privilege and predatory interests. In that regard, it was a political masterpiece. It also clearly implied that the members of Congress who wanted recharter were not just enemies of the people's interests, but enemies of the people. Although he had gotten what he wanted, the implication that supporters of the BUS were cynical and corrupt made Henry Clay hopping mad.[88]

The veto itself also left him greatly alarmed. When the Senate began debating it on July 11, Webster took the lead for the BUS by presenting a lengthy history of the Bank's usefulness in promoting a healthy economy and the case for its constitutionality, but the following day, Clay raised the larger issue of executive responsibility and legislative supremacy. Jackson, he said, had used the veto in a way the Framers never envisioned. Clay was quite correct in assessing Jackson's veto message as a momentous expansion of presidential power. In more than forty years of constitutional government, presidents had vetoed legislation on only ten occasions, and each of those had derived almost entirely from questions of constitutionality. Jackson had referred to the Constitution in his message, but he essentially objected to the recharter of the Bank because he found the Bank personally objectionable. This was a vast assumption of executive prerogative. Jackson effectively amplified the president's power to the equivalent of two-thirds of Congress and made the executive branch of government an entity with potentially imperial authority over both the legislature and the courts.

Clay warned the Senate. Jackson's presumption that his constitutional judgment was superior to that of Congress amounted to a treacherous act of executive usurpation, the sort of overreach Americans had found despicable in a king and should find no less appalling in a president. Those legislators who had voted for the Bank's original charter and had voted to recharter were the people's representatives, subject to the people's approval or rejection, and were consequently far more qualified than Jackson to make those judgments. How dare Andrew Jackson, Clay thundered, question the motives of any duly elected member of Congress for supporting the Bank?[89]

The next day, Thomas Hart Benton responded for the administration and was particularly provocative in taking Clay to task for making remarks "wanting in courtesy, indecorous, and disrespectful to the Chief Magistrate." Clay slowly rose from his seat and demanded the floor to dispute Benton's remarks and especially to answer his personal criticism, which was the part of Clay's reply that everyone would recall.[90] He could not allow Benton to instruct him "in etiquette and courtesy," Clay said with mock innocence, because, after all, he was not sure which of Benton's opinions about the president to adopt. Should it be the one in which Benton "complained of the President beating" his brother "after he was prostrated and lying apparently lifeless," or the one when Benton predicted that if Jackson were elected, congressmen would have to arm themselves?[91]

Benton took the floor. He admitted to an earlier "personal conflict" with Jackson, but they had fought as men. He denied ever making the statement that Jackson's election would require congressmen to carry weapons. Clay whirled. He drew the words out slowly in a measured cadence: "Can the Senator throw his eyes on me—will he look in my face and assert that he never used language similar to that imputed to him?" Benton, "after a pause," shook his finger at Clay and said, "He could—he could." Clay's eyes narrowed as he said, again slowly, "Can the Senator look me in the face and say he did not make use of such language?" Benton repeated that he had not. Clay asked a third time. Benton for a third time said no. Clay abruptly sat down, but Benton kept talking, quickly working himself into a stew. He would pin this "atrocious calumny" to Clay's sleeve, he shouted, and "it would stick, stick, stick there, and there he wished it to remain."

Clay sprang from his chair and raised his voice too, shouting that "he returned the charge of calumny to the senator from Missouri." Jacksonian senator Littleton Waller Tazewell of Virginia, temporarily presiding, ruled the debate out of order and told Clay to sit down. Clay protested that he wanted to explain his remarks. Tazewell insisted that "no further explanation will be heard from the gentleman from Kentucky." Clay demanded to know on what grounds he was being ruled out of order. His inappropriate language, said Tazewell. Clay sputtered that Benton's language had been just as objectionable. Very well, said Benton, and he promptly apologized to the Senate, admitting that his language had been out of order. Clay gave up. He wearily offered a similar apology to the Senate but added, "For the Senator from Missouri I have none."[92]

The Senate did not override the veto. The date of the vote, Friday, July 13, might have struck some as a significant indicator of the legislature's luck. Jackson was on his way to striking down twelve congressional enactments, more than all his predecessors combined. The stroke of a pen had effectively demoted Congress to a potentially subordinate role in the lawmaking process, depending on the whim of the president, a change that would have profound repercussions for constitutional government, as Clay warned.

The capital, however, was too preoccupied with the current drama staged by Benton and Clay to worry much about such abstractions. For days following their angry exchange, rumors swirled that they would fight a duel, and not until the two headed home did the gossiping stop.[93]

———

THESE QUARRELS EXHAUSTED Clay. The battles over the tariff and the Bank had taxed his failing stamina to the breaking point, and he longed to be at Ashland. On the way home from Washington, he, Lucretia, and little Henry Duralde stopped at White Sulphur Springs for a brief rest. The Clay caravan was "a strange medley," as he described it, consisting of "four servants, two carriages, six horses, a Jack ass [recently purchased for his mule-breeding business], and a Shepherds dog." The resort's owner, James Caldwell, a close friend and political supporter, had gladly prepared comfortable accommodations for everyone, for Clay was a regular guest. He had visited the Kentucky or Virginia springs during the hot summer months for years, because they were on cooler high ground. Sometimes called simply the Virginia Springs, White Sulphur was not luxurious, but it did provide a pleasant, rustic setting nestled in mountains for congenial groups to gather. During this stay, Clay impressed the son of Washington architect Benjamin Latrobe as "certainly the most pleasant man I ever was in company with."[94]

The override vote was a symbolic gesture at most, a ploy by National Republicans to emphasize Jackson's stand on the Bank, which they expected voters to punish with telling and possibly decisive disapproval. Biddle thought the veto displayed "all the fury of a chained panther biting the bars of his cage," and Clay believed it would certainly damage the president with the business and manufacturing communities. He was likely correct that more Americans approved of the BUS than actively loathed it, but he never understood how Jackson's veto message resonated with the common voter and how successful Jackson had been tying the National Republicans to special interests and painting them with the brush of corruption.[95]

Ever the optimist, he hoped that from the sanctuary of Ashland he could direct a successful campaign based on a popular appeal to the American System. If he could convince New England, hold the Mid-Atlantic, and make inroads in the West, he thought that he just possibly had a chance.[96] He nevertheless needed the Antimasons to abandon their independent campaign and join National Republicans if he were to have any hope of defeating Jackson. He told his operatives to refrain from criticizing Wirt. Instead, he sought to find common ground and show the Antimasons that only unity could lead them to victory. Wirt finally came to his senses to promote fusion. Although efforts in New York gained some ground, most Antimasons remained wary of National Republicans, who they suspected were under Masonic control.[97]

Even had these fractured factions united, they could never have matched the effectiveness of the Jacksonians. Van Buren had built the Democrat House, and operatives like Kendall ran it. The vulpine Kendall directed the central Hickory

Club in Washington that disseminated information to local counterparts throughout the country. Clay was well aware of the deficiencies in the National Republican organization, such as it was, and he tried to persuade friends to get out his message and work to turn out voters, but all efforts were too little as well as too late.[98] Meanwhile, he was barely able to keep up with the Jacksonian press's relentless smears. Blair's *Globe* invented a story that in 1809, after Clay's duel with Humphrey Marshall, he had recovered from his wound at a friend's home, where he had repaid his host's kindness by fleecing him at brag, merrily taking money the man could not afford to lose. Clay refuted the story in the *National Intelligencer* and for good measure branded as a lie the *Globe*'s claim that the bullet recently removed from Jackson's left arm was from a wound he had suffered in the service of the country. Jackson, said Clay, had actually taken that bullet in the infamous Nashville street brawl with the Bentons in 1813.[99]

The early news from state elections in the late summer did not bode well for Clay. The Kentucky governor's race set a dismal pattern of defeat. Fraud abounded as Jacksonians came into southern Kentucky from Tennessee to stuff ballot boxes, sometimes so exuberantly that tallies in several counties exceeded the number of eligible voters. Clay had no solution for such brazen tactics, and he was reduced to urging his friends to work all the harder for the main contest in the fall. He seems to have realized, though, that no amount of work would make a difference. As the campaign neared its end, he had to quash a new wave of rumors spread by Blair's operatives in Kentucky that he had withdrawn from the race. It seemed they never slept.[100]

Returns from the presidential canvass at the end of October quickly revealed that he had lost the election; the only hope that remained was that Antimasons would be as much a spoiler for Jackson as for Clay, preventing a majority in the Electoral College, but that was a slim possibility at best. Adding to the unhappy prospect of inevitable defeat, erstwhile supporters asked Clay to withdraw in favor of Wirt should Jackson fail to receive a majority of the electoral votes. That humiliation proved unnecessary, though the request certainly wounded Clay's feelings.[101]

Jackson's popular vote percentage declined 1.8 percent from his margin over Adams in 1828, but his victory in the Electoral College was devastating. A coalition of National Republicans and Antimasons would not have made the slightest difference. Jackson won walking away. Clay took only Kentucky, Maryland, Delaware, Massachusetts, Rhode Island, and Connecticut, giving him a mere 49 electoral votes. Jackson had 219.[102] Depressed and humiliated, Clay seriously considered resigning from the Senate to make way for John J.

Crittenden, but Crittenden persuaded him to reconsider. As Clay prepared to travel to Washington, he was nonetheless sick at heart.[103]

Clay regretted Jackson's victory more bitterly than he did his own defeat. During the campaign, he had fearfully weighed the prospect of another four years under Jackson and concluded that "a real crisis in our Republic has arrived."[104] He regarded "the reign of Jackson" as just that: a tenure marked by the growing supremacy of the executive, "the reign of corruption & demoralization." In the process, shuddered Clay, Andrew Jackson had "put a pick axe at the base of every pillar that supports every department and every valuable institution in the Country." He could not comprehend why the country abided it, could not fathom why the people had confirmed it.[105] "The dark cloud," Clay said, ". . . has become more dense, more menacing[,] more alarming."[106]

THOUGH NOT FOR lack of trying, Clay would never win the presidency. Instead, he remained in the Senate for the next ten years, went into retirement for seven years, and returned to the Senate in the final days of his life. The Senate became his political home, and he left his mark indelibly on it. He served on, and often chaired, virtually every standing committee. He brought finely honed parliamentary talents to bear, employed charm, used sarcasm, and hurled invective to wield a level of influence that made him peerless in the annals of the upper house of the national legislature. He sincerely believed that restraint and cooperation would best secure the country and promote its welfare, and he came to abhor extremism. Intelligent, informed men could always reach an agreement in Clay's political world, as long as they negotiated in good faith. That was the reason he found the changes wrought by Jacksonian politics so disturbing. Physical intimidation and character assassination were not the stuff of reason; they were not the marks of good faith.[107]

As he returned to Washington in December, he was therefore troubled to his very core. Fifteen-year-old James Brown Clay was his only companion, for Lucretia did not make the trip. Racked by guilt over leaving Theodore, she refused to suffer that gloom again in dreary, contentious Washington. Clay planned to send James on to Boston to learn the workings of a mercantile firm, leaving Clay alone in the capital during the bleak winter.[108] He tried to remain cheerful and labored to put the best face on the election. He felt "entitled to your congratulations for our recent political defeat," he told a friend. "Jackson had so completely put every thing into disorder, that we should have found it very difficult to mend fences and repair injuries."[109] His lighthearted manner was more than ever a mask of smiles.

In fact, his response to a major emerging crisis threatening the Union revealed the level of his disenchantment and disengagement. Late that fall, just after the election, South Carolina nullified the tariffs of 1828 and 1832. Many had assumed the nationalism exhibited by congressional majorities would cow South Carolina radicals, but it had only enraged them. South Carolinians trooped to the polls to approve a convention, and on November 24, 1832, it passed an ordinance nullifying the tariffs and setting February 1, 1833, as the day collections would end in South Carolina. John C. Calhoun resigned from the vice presidency, and the South Carolina legislature promptly held a special election to place him in Robert Y. Hayne's Senate seat, vacated when Hayne was elected governor, signs that the Nullifiers were running things in the Palmetto State and that Calhoun had finally, irrevocably transformed into a sectionalist.[110]

Andrew Jackson's initial response to South Carolina's defiance puzzled Clay. On December 4, the president's annual message contained a relatively mild endorsement of states' rights as a principle, which hardly seemed appropriate in light of what had just happened. Clay was made no happier, though, when six days later Jackson issued a crackling proclamation threatening force if South Carolina did not rescind nullification. Clay suspected that Jackson's belligerence would only cause South Carolina to dig in its heels, and he was not alone in fearing that the crisis could bring on civil war, a brushfire that could spread beyond South Carolina to unite the entire South and destroy the Union. Noting the geography involved in coercing South Carolina with a federal military force, one Nullifier boasted, "To reach us, the dagger must pass through others."[111]

Clay initially stood apart from the dispute. In fact, he left Washington as it was heating up, ostensibly to start James on his way to Boston. After sending James to Massachusetts, Clay tarried in Philadelphia at the home of friends. His absence from the capital was distressing to his allies. Many believed only Henry Clay could avert a clash between Jackson and the Nullifiers. As the days passed, Clay's protectiveness of the protectionist principle began to reemerge, and he finally resolved that South Carolina could not be allowed to bully the rest of the country, and Jackson must not be goaded into destroying it. He slowly roused himself to do something to save it. He was still in Philadelphia when he began drafting a modified tariff.[112]

When Clay returned to Washington, a sharp reduction of the tariff was already under debate in the House. Gulian Verplanck, chair of the House Ways and Means Committee, was its principal author. Verplanck, a New York intellectual descended from Dutch patroons, dabbled in literary criticism and displayed fierce political independence. He had broken with Jackson over the Bank, but the administration's desire to resolve the crisis with South Carolina had forced it to swallow hard and back Verplanck's tariff proposal. That bill would have reduced tariff rates immediately and within a year all but eliminated them as a protective measure for domestic manufactures. Not only would this have been a decisive blow to the American System, Clay feared it would cause manufacturing regions to consider disunion. He also believed the carrot of tariff reduction significantly weakened the stick of threatened force, an incongruity that confirmed rather than discredited nullification. Indeed, Jackson was tending toward wild contradictions with his policies that tried to balance states' rights, overawe Nullifiers, and placate Indian removal proponents. At the same time that the president was threatening to quash nullification with the army, he was supporting Georgia's defiance of the Supreme Court in its efforts to expel Cherokee Indians from the state. Given this muddled situation, Clay found it sensible to propose his own tariff. He did not like the Verplanck bill because it undermined protection, but it also had administration support, causing him to oppose it from reflex. The Nullification Crisis presented him with an opportunity to renew his opposition to the Jackson administration and to earn praise for saving the Union. He marshaled his allies.[113]

Jackson asked Congress to pass a Force Bill giving him authority to coerce tariff collection in South Carolina. Nullifiers were sporting revolutionary cockades and oiling firearms, but calmer South Carolinians were taking pause over the possibility of Charleston in ruins and federal soldiers in charge. The state indefinitely extended its February 1, 1833, deadline for abolishing the tariff, a major conciliation that showed a real desire for a compromise solution. In Washington, however, debates over the Force Bill brought tempers to such a pitch that many began to doubt that there was a solution to prevent Jackson's irresistible force from catastrophically meeting nullification's immovable object. Clay hastily weighed the chances for compromise, especially one undertaken against the active opposition of the administration. He did not have the votes.[114]

Worse, the emergency was making otherwise reliable friends behave unpredictably. Clay's longtime ally Daniel Webster was suddenly attending dinners at the White House, supporting the provocative Force Bill, and joining manufacturing-state legislators to oppose tariff reductions. As Clay frantically sought allies in the deteriorating situation, the emergency also had the effect of finally forming a coalition of the most unlikely bedfellows. Henry Clay and the nationalists joined with John C. Calhoun and his extreme states' rights faction. Although Calhoun's people much preferred the Verplanck tariff to anything Clay might propose, the administration's support of it made them reject it out of hand, for Calhoun was intent on depriving Jackson of any credit for solving this crisis. Webster's rebuff forced Clay's agents into conversations with Calhoun to arrange a meeting that some called Clay's "great leap across the Potomac." At odds for years and openly estranged since 1824, Clay and Calhoun at first sat in stilted silence, and once begun, their discussion proceeded in fits and starts. The possibility of federal bayonets flashing in Carolina, however, was a terrific incentive to let bygones, for a time, be bygones, and soon the two were making progress. Clay emerged from these discussions at last prepared to propose a compromise, because he was confident that Calhoun would support it. Clay could only pray that Calhoun would be enough.[115]

Meetings between moderate states' rights men and moderate tariff proponents worked out the details, and Clay took the measure of his odd assortment of allies to compose a bill. On February 11, as the Senate braced for another long and contentious debate over the Force Bill, Clay gained the floor and stood stock-still as the murmuring chatter in the chamber fell to a hush. He announced that he would present a formal compromise proposal the following day. He sat down. Debate proceeded, but there was a palpable change in the chamber, a sense of many releasing a nervous sigh, eyes closed, whispering to themselves, *At last.*

Clay opened the day's business on February 12. His proposal was decidedly different and far more drastic than the one he had begun drafting in Philadelphia in December. His earlier plan had been to leave all current duties in place until 1840. After that year, tariffs would have ceased their protective function and only generated revenue. Clay explained this new plan for several hours. He would lower duties beginning in 1834. The rates currently over 20 percent would be gradually reduced over the next six years to bring all down to a 20 percent ceiling by 1840. They and any rates below the 20 percent cap would remain frozen for two additional years. After 1842, the tariff would exclusively raise revenue. Rather than the Verplanck bill's immediate reduction, gradual declines would allow manufacturers to prepare for disappearing protection.[116]

As Clay finished his presentation and asked "leave" to present his bill formally, administration supporters prepared to pounce, if only to keep Clay from gaining plaudits for breaking the impasse. Senator John Forsyth of Georgia objected to giving Clay "leave" to do anything, and Samuel Smith ground his axe from the clash the previous spring to lodge an objection as well. John Holmes of Maine exclaimed in frustration that never in his Senate career had he "heard an objection made to a motion of leave." Jacksonian senators glowered across the aisle, ready to gain the floor and join the orchestrated plan to block Clay at the outset, but the chair recognized Calhoun. The gallery watched the South Carolinian rise from his desk. Clay's eyes were on him, and the chamber fell suddenly silent, like a church in prayer. Calhoun slowly but firmly declared that he supported Clay's motion. Spectators in the gallery were not aware that the two had made an arrangement. Now, as Calhoun spoke, they heard his words in amazement and immediately exploded into loud cheers, stamping, whistling, and raising such a noise that only the threat of eviction caused the celebration to end. Clay had seized the momentum from the administration. As Calhoun took his seat, Clay's eyes were upon him.[117]

The work on compromise then began in earnest, and just as Clay suspected, the easy part of the process, while pleasantly dramatic, was over, and the difficult business of addressing specifics was just beginning. Clay was agreeably surprised that President Pro Tempore Hugh Lawson White appointed a congenial select committee to write the bill, made Clay its chairman, and resisted White House pressure to load it with administration supporters. Jackson and White were friends as well as fellow Tennesseans, but White was also highly principled and extremely alarmed over South Carolina's defiance and Jackson's promise of force. Not only did White ignore Jackson's directive, he appointed staunch Clay ally John Clayton and Clay's unexpected ally Calhoun to the committee. Jackson would never forgive White for this, but freed from exasperating obstructionism, the committee worked both swiftly and productively. It had to, because the Twenty-second Congress was due to adjourn on March 2.

Then Clayton tried to insert home valuation into the bill, and everything threatened to fall apart. Clayton wanted the value of imports to be set upon arrival in American ports rather than the usual practice of having valuation occur at the point of export. The change would not only give American customs officials control over the process, it would also mean higher tariff collections. Calhoun flatly said home valuation was unacceptable because it would raise the price of imports. He threatened to withdraw his support from the entire compromise, but Clayton was unyielding. Home valuation, he insisted, was the least Congress could do for manufacturers. Home valuation, insisted Calhoun, placed southern farmers in an even greater bind by jacking up prices in an overly protected market. Clayton lost the battle, for Calhoun was too valuable to be crossed, and the bill came out of committee without the offending proposal.[118]

Jackson refused to endorse the bill, but neither did he try to block it. In the end, he realized that Clay had lured all opponents, including him, into a game of brag in resolving this dispute. The apparent alliance between Clay and Calhoun, however fragile and opportunistic, also worried him. The most he could wring as a concession from Congress was the Force Bill, which Jackson insisted upon as the quid pro quo for Clay's tariff. Clay shrank from placing that power in the president's hands, but he also knew there was no point in cornering Andrew Jackson. Removing the tariff as a source of friction with South Carolina would eliminate the need for coercion, making the Force Bill wholly symbolic. Upon that rationale, Clay did not object to it as part of a compromise package.[119]

In the meantime, other predicaments arose quite unexpectedly. When the constitutional requirement that revenue measures must originate in the House troubled some senators, Clay coordinated a bit of procedural cunning that recalled his days as Speaker. He had the bill rushed over to Kentucky congressman Bob Letcher, who promptly gained the floor, ostensibly to propose an amendment to the Verplanck bill but actually to recommend replacing it with Clay's compromise. The House was sick of debating its bill and was visibly relieved to pass Clay's with a 119 to 85 vote. The bill hurtled back to the Senate. By then, night sessions had become the only way to complete the work, and it was late when the Force Bill came up for a vote. Clay rarely attended night sessions because the fumes from the Senate's oil lamps made it difficult to breathe, but other reasons probably had more to do with his absence during the Force Bill vote. He was always able to make the truthful, if technical, claim that he had supported the compromise tariff without actually voting for the Force Bill.

Clay thus emerged from the crisis as a friend to the South by reducing the tariff and not voting for the Force Bill. Calhoun had reason to dispute Clay's allegiance to southern interests, however. During the debates, Clay had waited for just the right moment to restore home valuation by way of an amendment. Calhoun sat smoldering, realizing that the wily Kentuckian had also lured him into a game of brag by waiting until the last minute to spring this change. Calhoun could either accept home valuation or scuttle the compromise and risk federal force in South Carolina. He ultimately voted for the tariff. As for Jackson, he signed both bills, though he made a point of signing the Force Bill first. Many southerners would never forget that bit of symbolism, and it immediately drove some from Jackson's camp. Time and circumstance would place them in Clay's, where they did not really belong philosophically and where they would eventually cause a great deal of confusion and trouble.[120]

Jackson did not sign a third piece of legislation from that congressional session. Clay had reintroduced his land revenue distribution bill in the Senate. As before, it proposed dividing revenue from the sale of public lands among the states according to population. In addition to providing money for state funding of internal improvements, Clay's distribution plan would have prevented surpluses in the federal Treasury, making a tariff indispensable in generating needed revenue. The measure again passed the Senate, and this time around, the House as well. The roughly simultaneous passage of distribution and the Compromise of 1833 made the former erroneously seem a third element, along with the tariff and the Force Bill, of the legislative parcel. More than a few consequently thought that Jackson was obligated to sign the distribution bill in return for the Force Bill, and Congress wearily adjourned the day after sending him the bills. Jackson signed the tariff and the Force Bill. He pocket vetoed distribution.[121]

It was a small victory for Old Hickory, but Clay's overall triumph was spectacular. Only four months earlier, he had lost the presidency in a humiliating landslide. Now he was being hailed as the nation's savior. A few die-hard protectionists were bitter about his compromise tariff, but he could counter that Verplanck's would have been worse. Jackson's support of the Verplanck tariff indicated a willingness to abandon protection and alienate voters in manufacturing regions. Clay's success also revived National Republican fortunes, while Jackson's behavior left many southerners disenchanted with him and distrustful of his presidential power. A strange and loose coalition of Jackson's old enemies and former friends grew out of the clashes over banking, the tariff, states' rights, Indian removal, and nullification. Divergent interests saw something larger than a mere broker in Henry Clay as he fashioned the Compromise of 1833. Collaboration rather than quarrels could succeed in preventing bloodshed and preserving the Union. It was not the final time the Union in crisis would nervously wait for him to take the floor, listen to him with eyes closed, and sigh in relief, *At last.*[122]

ONE DAY IN mid-January, Clay had tried to lighten the mood in the Senate by introducing a petition from two fellow Kentuckians, Leonard Jones and Henry Banta. They were asking for a federal land grant "to extend and propagate their discovery" of eternal life. Jones and Banta, in fact, claimed they were living proof of that discovery. The Senate was already laughing as Clay admitted that he was presenting this petition to avoid risking its authors' "endless enmity," but as his colleagues and the gallery gradually realized his joke, the hilarity swelled, and even Clay's opponents had to shake their heads, smiling. He could pull off that sort of thing with a flawless delivery, the sonority of his voice making the absurd sound plausible.[123]

Possibly John Randolph was there that day in the gallery. If so, he would have enjoyed the amusing scene. The years intervening between his duel with Clay and the winter of 1833 had been unkind to Randolph. In 1829, Old Hickory had sent him to Russia as U.S. minister, but his health soon forced him to come home. Dissipation and devolution became his principal companions as his incipient lunacy led to frequent episodes of outright madness. He was elected to the House of Representatives in 1833, but he was in wretched health. If Randolph saw the amusing scene about everlasting life, it would have been ironic. He was dying.

Friends on at least one occasion did bring Randolph to the Senate gallery, which in those days was situated on the Senate floor just behind the members' desks. Randolph looked ghastly and could only walk while grasping the arms of companions. He had resolved to leave Washington for England to restore his health, but he wanted to visit the Senate to "hear that voice once again." He was talking about Henry Clay.

Randolph had his companions prop him up so that he could see Clay as well as hear him. When Clay finished speaking, he walked from the rows of desks into the gallery and stood next to Randolph's chair. He quietly asked about Randolph's health, and Randolph squeaked that he was "a dying man." Clay laughed gently. The response was something of a Randolph trademark, a reply that for years had been his spontaneous retort to routine greetings. Randolph looked up at Clay and wheezed that he had come to the Senate just to see him, to hear him, one last time. Clay sat beside him and they spoke in low tones until Randolph motioned that he was tired and wanted to go. Clay took his hand. They did not need to say farewell to know it was good-bye.

Andrew Jackson's plan to coerce South Carolina appalled John Randolph because he saw it as infringing on states' rights. "There is one man, and one man only, who can save the Union—that man is Henry Clay," John Randolph said.[124] The irreversible descent continued as he traveled to Philadelphia. He talked of his famous duel with Clay, repeating that he would never have done anything to cause Lucretia or her children pain. On the other hand, Randolph sadly noted that nobody would have particularly cared if Clay had killed him, a sentiment he had brooded over for years. That April night before the duel in 1826, James Hamilton had listened to John Randolph say he could not bear to think of Lucretia and the children crying over Clay's grave, "but when the sod of Virginia rests on my bosom, there is not one in this wide world, not one individual, to pay this tribute upon mine."[125]

John Randolph died in Philadelphia on May 24, 1833. There were no heirs. His physical deformity would have made them out of the question even if he had ever found someone to marry him. His principal legacy consequently consisted of a handful of colorful quotations, an eccentric allegiance to antique Republicanism, a reputation for mad dissipation and relentless self-destruction, and a vacated plantation with a darkened tumbledown house, its fields full of weeds, its slaves emancipated by a will that also funded their passage to the free states. In a way, a less obvious but no less important legacy was Henry Clay, the only man John Randolph believed could save the Union. Because Randolph had held his pistol skyward that April afternoon seven years earlier, the Western Star lived. Lucretia Clay and her children had not suffered. The Union was safe. That was something worth remembering, something noble and good to cherish, as Randolph heard "that voice" one last time.

CHAPTER NINE

Whig

CLAY'S RETURN TO Ashland in early April 1833 came not a moment too soon. He was emotionally and physically drained. Despite his fatigue, after only days he was thinking about a summer trip. Travel always invigorated him, and a northern journey would allow him to escape Lexington's summer heat. It would also afford the opportunity to visit political friends, though as always Clay wished to avoid the appearance of politicking. Instead, he framed his plans as recreational and intended to include as much family as could accompany him. Their destination was to be Boston to see James, who at sixteen and far from home was lonely. Yet Clay would quietly court support there for another effort to recharter the Bank in the upcoming Congress. The BUS had three years remaining on its charter, after all, which seemed plenty of time to change enough minds to make Jackson's objections immaterial.[1]

That spring, however, cholera came to Kentucky and altered his plans. Called Asiatic cholera because of its origins on the Indian subcontinent, it began its inexorable spread in the early nineteenth century along trade routes to Russia, Western Europe, and England, achieving a global and deadly reach as a pandemic that claimed millions of lives a year. By 1832, it was in North America.[2]

Kentucky had been spared so far, but deaths in more populous places such as New Orleans and New York were sufficiently numerous to terrify the country. Jackson opposed an effort to set aside a day for "general humiliation and prayer" because he said it violated the separation of church and state, but most suspected that Clay rather than the Constitution was behind Jackson's stance. The Kentuckian had successfully promoted the move in the Senate.[3]

In 1833, cholera found Lexington, and many residents fled what quickly became a ghost town. Those who remained stopped venturing out. Stores closed, and larders went bare. Newspapers ceased publication, isolating Lexington from news of the outside world except for what could trickle in through the post office. The Erwins moved from the Woodlands to Ashland, where the entire family gathered as though under a medieval siege. In the first three days, fifty people died in Lexington. After two weeks, that number had swelled to 350, and by the time the epidemic ended, the town had lost almost 10 percent of its population. Ashland weathered the siege, fortunate in its relative isolation and access to untainted water. No one at Ashland, black or white, got sick.[4]

That spring, Clay did lose a dear friend, though not to cholera. At 5:00 A.M. on May 19, the *Lioness,* a Red River steamboat, was forty miles above Alexandria, Louisiana, when crewmembers in the hold accidentally touched off a cargo of gunpowder with a candle. The explosion blew the boat apart and killed fifteen people, seven of them passengers. Josiah Johnston was traveling with his son on the *Lioness* to visit family, and though the boy survived, his father did not. Clay could hardly believe the news. Johnston had been a staunch friend from their earliest days in the House of Representatives, informally managing important aspects of Clay's 1824 bid for the presidency and loyally standing by him in its aftermath to become an invaluable supporter in the Senate. As one of Clay's "truest and best of friends," Johnston had been that rare entity in politics, the person who never wavered, was always sincere, and was invariably reliable.[5]

Clay fretted about the fate of Johnston's widow, Eliza, a Washington belle noted for her "bewitching grace & dignity." Eliza had not made the trip with her husband, having just given birth to another son, Josiah Stoddert Johnston, Jr. For years, she had been mildly infatuated with Henry Clay, feelings he had always inferred but had treated as nothing more than the eye-batting flirtations common among coquettes at parties and in innocuous letters. Others were not so sure. Bob Letcher once remarked that if Clay were to die, Eliza Johnston would go into deep mourning. "She would most certainly devote the residue of her life to grief and melancholy," Letcher said, only half joking. For his part, Clay traded harmless verbal trifles with Eliza as he did with other belles such as Olivia Walton LeVert, some of them strikingly beautiful. It did not matter if they were pretty, though, for Clay enjoyed the game of gallantry in itself. He liked the company of women and personified the description of the gentleman as the man who winks at a homely girl. Winking at young widows, however, invited unseemly talk, and after offering traditional expressions of condolence, he had little contact with Eliza. Two years later, she moved into the enemy camp by marrying a confirmed Democrat, becoming Mrs. Henry D. Gilpin, her new husband destined to serve as Martin Van Buren's attorney general.[6]

THE LENGTHY QUARANTINE at Ashland canceled Clay's plans for his trip, and by the time he could again consider it, other events prevented the family from accompanying him. Both Anne Clay Erwin and Julia Prather Clay were expecting, and Lucretia wanted to be with them when the babies came. Clay understood, and he put off his departure until she could go with him. On July 20, Julia gave birth to Henry Clay III; but Clay must have been able to persuade Lucretia to leave before Anne's lying-in, because she, Johnny, and Henry Clay Duralde accompanied him when he left Ashland on September 26. Anne had still not delivered her baby, but if Clay intended to enjoy any political benefits from the trip, so often postponed, he had to get started. While Clay was trapped at Ashland, Jackson had spent the first part of the summer touring New England to court support in a National Republican stronghold. A few communities mildly protested the Bank veto, but mostly Jackson enjoyed a cordial reception. He was warmly greeted in Massachusetts, and Harvard made him an honorary doctor of laws, much to the chagrin of John Quincy Adams. More than ever, Clay believed his trip to the region was necessary.[7]

Both Clay and Lucretia likely regretted leaving when they did, however. Anne gave birth to a boy on October 2, but the baby died so quickly that he was never named. The traveling Clays did not receive the news until they were en route from Baltimore to Philadelphia, and their grief over the loss was mingled with relief when James Erwin reported that Anne was sad but safe. Clay was pleased that she would remain at the Woodlands rather than return to New Orleans for the winter.[8]

Political observers were mindful of the large, enthusiastic crowds Clay attracted throughout the journey to New England and were not in the least deceived by his insistence that he was merely on vacation. John Quincy Adams, already sour over ovations given to Jackson, grumbled that "the fashion of peddling for popularity . . . is growing into high fashion." He acidly noted in his diary that "Mr. Clay has mounted that hobby often, and rides him very hard," but Adams routinely disparaged the success of others. Any objective assessment would have judged the trip a popular triumph.[9]

It was also productive. Clay met privately with influential people and mended some political fences. Rancorous relations had marred his association with Josiah Quincy for years, but Clay called on him anyway. Quincy, who as Harvard's president had been given the impossible task of reconciling Adams to Jackson's honorary degree, was intimately acquainted with Massachusetts' political establishment. Clay was charming and Quincy cordial throughout their meeting. On the other hand, Daniel Webster's absence during Clay's visit to Massachusetts caused talk of an irreparable rift, which had some merit. The two had recently exchanged friendly letters, but their sharp words during the tariff debate would forever place a wall between them.[10]

As he left New England for the opening of Congress, Clay could mark the undertaking as an overall success. Admirers on every leg of the trip had presented the Clays with gifts ranging from simple tokens to expensive livestock. Citizens of Newark, New Jersey, gave Clay a handsome carriage that became one of his most prized possessions. (It still resides in the carriage house at Ashland.) When the Clays arrived in Washington, however, news from Lexington was mildly distressing. Thomas had returned from a failed farming venture in Indiana and was drinking again. The asylum had tried to release Theodore for longer periods as a test of his stability, but Henry and Anne finally found their brother's moods too unpredictable and became apprehensive enough to arrange his renewed detention. The Clays rented a small house in Washington, and he tried to handle the crises through the mail, with limited success. He was also concerned about Lucretia. That winter, she always seemed to be ill, barely recovering from one ailment before falling prey to another. Already spare by nature, she began to lose weight, and his concern gradually gave way to alarm.[11]

AS THE TWENTY-THIRD Congress opened, National Republicans tried to counter another attack by President Jackson on the American System. Jackson correctly judged that BUS supporters were still aiming to renew its charter. Angry about Clay's receiving credit for the compromise tariff, especially in the South, Jackson intended to destroy the Bank before Clay had a chance to use that political capital to pass a new bank bill. The result was a series of events that continued the contentiousness of the veto, an episode known as the Bank War.[12]

Suspecting that Biddle would resort to anything to stave off the Bank's impending demise, even manipulating credit to the country's detriment, Jackson looked for ways to hobble the Bank and settled on removing its federal deposits. At first, he considered stopping deposits while steadily reducing government money held in BUS vaults by using it to discharge the government's routine expenses. Slowly drawing off the government's funds would not only debilitate the bank's power, it would guarantee its end when its charter expired in 1836. The plan was long in the hatching, and Jackson began discussing it with Vice President Van Buren, his cabinet, and other advisers shortly after his second inauguration. He dismissed out of hand the recent congressional investigation that pronounced the Bank a sound, efficient financial institution. Amos Kendall had always been able to read the signs that indicated Jackson was closing his mind on an issue. "Little is gained by attempting to manage the old man," he once said. This was one of those times.[13]

If anything, Kendall and Francis Preston Blair urged an immediate rather than a gradual withdrawal of federal funds. Van Buren, however, persisted in the recommendation that any such move be measured, fearing that cornering Biddle would self-fulfill Jackson's prophecy by goading him into contracting credit. In any case, removing the deposits was easier said than done. The BUS charter stipulated that only the Treasury secretary had authority to withdraw money from the bank, and Louis McLane doubted that doing so was legal before the charter expired. When Jackson appointed McLane secretary of state, it was a fortunate move for him, because his opinion would have put him at odds with the president, never a prudent position for someone in Jackson's cabinet. Jackson chose William Duane to succeed McLane at Treasury in part because he was a vocal critic of the Bank and presumably agreeable to the removal of federal deposits, but Jackson made the irritating discovery that Duane had the same reservations as McLane. By the time he returned from New England that summer, Jackson had decided on immediate withdrawal and wanted the process completed before Congress convened in early December. When Duane resisted, Jackson asked for his resignation. Duane refused, his defiance resting on the traditional view of cabinet ministers as more councilors than subalterns. Jackson promptly fired him. Attorney General Roger B. Taney, a staunch opponent of the Bank and among those eager to remove its federal money, became the new Treasury secretary. Federal funds from that time forward were placed in several dozen state institutions, soon dubbed "Pet Banks" by administration critics because they were apparently being rewarded for supporting Jackson. Biddle soon fired back. Losing the federal deposits forced him to retrench, but he gratuitously called in such a large number of loans that he inadvertently validated the Jacksonian denunciation of the BUS as too powerful and hopelessly corrupt.[14]

National Republicans were livid over these developments, but the drastic steps shocked many Democrats as well. Clay came into the Senate in December spoiling for a fight and soon got several. Not only was Jackson destroying the BUS, he launched an attack on distribution with a blistering denunciation of Clay's land bill that he had pocket vetoed the previous spring. Clay was undeterred on both fronts. He planned to reintroduce distribution and began organizing opponents of the administration to counter its policy on federal deposits. His most innovative tactic in that regard was the fight to wrest from Vice President Martin Van Buren the authority to appoint Senate committee members and designate their chairmen. By a 22 to 18 vote, the Senate changed its rule to allow members to select committees. That the administration was stripped of this seminal power did not bode well for Jackson's policies in the Senate.[15]

Clay immediately used his growing momentum to challenge the administration's assault on the BUS. A rumor that in September 1833 Jackson had read a justification for removing the deposits to his cabinet caused a stir, and Clay demanded that the president produce that document. Jackson sternly refused, claiming executive privilege. Clay had expected as much and would have moved more quickly to his next tactic except that he wanted to wait for a few absent senators to arrive in Washington. He was also worried that Webster's misplaced loyalties on display in the previous Congress might still be in force to make him friendly toward the administration. By Christmas, his worries over Webster were allayed. Not only was "the Godlike Dan'l" repelled by Jackson's executive overreach, Biddle had put him on an Olympian retainer. Webster's loyalties were misplaced no more.[16]

Clay was careful but also bold, for he intended to pursue an audacious course. On December 26, he stood in the Senate to read a series of startling resolutions. They urged the censure of Jackson for exceeding his authority and the reprimand of Taney for removing the deposits. Clay's concern over the economic consequences of Jackson's actions was second only to his dismay over the broader issue of executive usurpation. He regarded Jackson's effort to destroy a congressionally sanctioned agency as disgraceful and dangerous, regardless of when that agency's charter would expire. He also disputed Jackson's right to fire a Senate-confirmed department head simply because that man had refused to break the law.[17] Jackson's use of the veto, his corruption of the civil service with the Spoils System, and his attempt to grasp all government money imperiled "the very existence of Liberty."[18]

Clay spoke on these issues for two full days in late December, exploring in every possible way how Jackson had seized power, violated the Constitution, and trampled the laws of the nation. He compared Jackson to Caesar and Duane to the tribune Metellus, whom that earlier despot had also dismissed simply for enforcing the law. He warned that if this new despotism took root in their equally vulnerable republic, Congress would "die—ignobly die," its members reduced to "base, mean, abject slaves." They would earn "the scorn and contempt of mankind" and would die "unpitied, unwept, unmourned!" Spectators in the gallery hung on every word as Clay's baritone drew each word in a steady cadence and rose in a dramatic crescendo. Instantly upon his last syllable, they erupted into such loud cheers and applause that Van Buren ordered them removed. The censure fight was on, however, to consume the next three months with arguments, counterarguments, and much invective. Clay became a dynamo of debate, speaking more than sixty times to defend his resolutions and repeat his warnings. Friends cautioned that Jackson partisans might physically assault him. "The scoundrels dare not approach me," he growled. "Their assassination is of character, not of persons."[19]

Administration men such as Benton and Felix Grundy defended Jackson's actions, and Jacksonian newspapers ginned up popular prejudice against the patrician Biddle and his hydra-headed monster of corruption. Clay and his allies presented petitions from citizens begging for a return of the deposits and the recharter of the Bank. Each side accused the other of causing the country's growing economic distress, but neither offered real solutions. Everyone preferred to make speeches.[20]

Jacksonians had a majority in the House, but Clay had the votes in the Senate, where members who were not pro-Bank deemed Jackson's removal of the deposits irresponsible. There, all Jackson's minions could do about censure was delay it. After defending Jackson's conduct proved ineffective, they resorted to technicalities, arguing that the Constitution did not give the Senate power to censure the executive. If National Republicans thought that Jackson had broken the law, they should introduce articles of impeachment in the House. Clay would not take that bait. The last place he wanted to pass judgment on Jackson's conduct was the pro-Jackson House of Representatives. He continued to push for a vote in the Senate.[21]

On March 7, Webster endorsed a petition from Philadelphia mechanics decrying the failing economy, and Clay concurred. Obviously playing to the gallery, he made a dramatic appeal to Van Buren, who sat placidly presiding at the front of the Senate. Clay turned toward the vice president and affected an air of anxiety. "If I shall have been successful in touching your heart, and exciting in you a glow of patriotism, I shall be most happy," Clay entreated. "You can prevail upon the President to abandon his ruinous course, and, if you will exert the influence which you possess, you will command the thanks and plaudits of a grateful people." Clay sat down, and the chamber fell into a surprised hush as Van Buren rose from the dais, stepped down, and slowly walked toward Clay's desk. The Little Magician nonchalantly asked him if he might have a pinch of Clay's fine snuff. Clay nodded; his half smile revealed that he, and possibly he alone, understood Van Buren's gamesmanship. The vice president helped himself and wandered slowly back to his chair.[22]

As the Senate neared the moment of decision on censure, Clay's relations with the vice president took on an uncharacteristically serious tone. Van Buren proposed a wager of "a suit of clothes" on the New York and Virginia state elections. Clay replied that if those states approved of Jackson's behavior at the polls, it would mean "that our experiment of free government had failed; that he [Van Buren] would probably be elected the successor of Jackson; that he would introduce a system of intrigue and corruption that would enable him to designate his successor; and that after a few years," the government would "end in dissolution of the Union or in despotism." Van Buren cackled at what he called a preposterously "morbid" set of predictions, but Clay was quite serious. He "replied, with good nature" that he "deliberately and sincerely believed" what he had said.[23]

On March 28, the Senate voted 26 to 20 to censure Jackson for exceeding his authority in removing the deposits and 28 to 18 to condemn Taney for doing Jackson's bidding without appropriate cause.[24] The longest debate in the Senate up to that time accomplished nothing but Andrew Jackson's embarrassment. The censure did nothing to restore the deposits, and later resolutions instructing Jackson to put them back were useless. Clay won this battle, but Jackson won the war.

Rather than saving the BUS, Clay made Jackson's behavior an issue to unite Jackson's opponents. Accomplishing that goal, if only temporarily, was no small achievement. Many who voted to censure Jackson would never vote to recharter the BUS or support Clay's American System, but they could at least agree that Andrew Jackson was dangerous. In a speech to the Senate on April 14, 1834, Clay likened the opposition to Jackson to British Whigs' opposing the dictatorial policies of their king.[25] Clay was not the first to call Jackson's antagonists Whigs, but his use of the label in this speech struck a chord because of the growing impression that the Democrat Old Hickory was becoming "King Andrew." This loose coalition of allies would henceforth be called Whigs.

Calling themselves Whigs instead of National Republicans made it easier to attract southerners to their ranks. National Republicans were associated with northeastern business interests, but Whigs could claim a pedigree that stretched back to the American Revolution to describe patriots fighting the abuses of the British crown. A few southern states' righters had already compared their resistance to growing federal power under Jackson to that revolutionary struggle and had begun calling themselves Whigs. Southern and northern opponents of the administration thus achieved unity under this newest old appellation. The second American party system was aborning.[26]

Clay and Martin Van Buren had always gotten along and often traded good-natured banter at social occasions. One story had Van Buren presiding over a state dinner attended by foreign diplomats and members of Congress. In the course of the lively conversation, everyone agreed that British Tory governments could be more flexible toward the United States because, unlike Whigs, Tories did not have to dodge accusations that republics beguiled them. Clay turned quickly to Van Buren and asked permission to propose a toast. Van Buren told all to charge their glasses. Clay stood, his wineglass raised, and called out, "Tory ministries in England and France, and a *Whig ministry* in the U[nited]

States." Everyone laughed, but Van Buren appeared ill at ease. Clay later recalled that poor Van Buren "had no tact in warding off a sally or joke."[27]

THE CENSURE ENRAGED Jackson. He fired off protests to the Senate, claiming that it, rather than he, had violated the Constitution by presuming the power to censure the president. Clay was dizzy over his victory and chortled that Jackson should quite literally have his head examined: he suggested that Jackson consult with phrenologists (so-called scientists who claimed the shape of the head revealed character traits) who would "find the organ of destructiveness prominently developed." Clay's tongue carried him so far as to have him injudiciously declare that the president's protest would be "the last stroke upon the last nail driven into the coffin," and then he realized what he was saying and stopped himself to add quickly, "not of Jackson, may he live a thousand years!—but of Jacksonism." The Senate voted 27 to 16 to reject Jackson's protest. For the next two years, vindication was the principal goal of the administration. Jackson was resolved that he would not be denied it.[28]

Congress adjourned not a moment too soon, for Clay had grown tired and testy, even with his friends. One night he had Benjamin Watkins Leigh, Robert Letcher, and John M. Clayton to his rooms to discuss a draft of a distribution bill. A nice supper, a bottle of wine, and a crackling fire soon had his guests nodding off while Clay read the bill aloud. He continued, oblivious to his dozing audience until Letcher started snoring. Clay's voice boomed in an expletive-laden reproach that awoke everybody. "Old Jackson himself was never in a greater passion," chuckled Clayton, "nor ever stormed louder."[29]

Clay was alone at the close of the session because he sent Lucretia to White Sulphur Springs in the hope that the waters would restore her health. Lucretia was obviously cheerful about leaving Washington, but everybody could see that there was something physically wrong with her. Clay had watched her waste away over the winter as her appetite vanished and she had shed so many pounds that her slight frame had become skin and bones.[30]

The stay at the Springs made no difference, and Lucretia became so weak after returning to Ashland that Clay feared she would die. He did not travel that summer because he refused to "separate myself from her." No doctor could make a credible diagnosis, and no treatment could revive her appetite. Then in late summer she showed a gradually improving interest in food and began taking nourishment. In the fall, her weight loss stabilized and then reversed itself. A flood of relief swept over the entire family, especially Lucretia's husband. Nobody could ever say what was wrong with Lucretia Clay for most of 1834, but her chronic dyspepsia and appetite loss suggest that she of the calm demeanor but turbulent heart had worried herself into an ulcer. At the haven of Ashland, she mended and was soon herself again.

As things returned to normal at Ashland, Clay arranged to send thirteen-year-old John Morrison Clay to a college preparatory school at Princeton, New Jersey, an establishment he found promising enough to warrant the enrollment of the Duralde boys the following year. James, who had come home to go back to school, soon proved an indolent student, however, and decided a radical change was in order. Clay reluctantly consented to his plan to become a farmer in Missouri. Clay provided the land, but he suspected the venture was an ill-advised project for an eighteen-year-old who had so far shown little direction or purpose in life.[31]

RESULTS FROM ELECTIONS held in late summer and early fall were mixed. Whigs made gains in western states such as Kentucky and Ohio and in parts of the South, and Jackson had to exert pressure even in Tennessee to bring followers into line. But Whigs were disappointed by Pennsylvania and New Jersey. Clay rightly worried that his new coalition was still too fragmented. An apparent alliance with extreme states' righters like Calhoun was brittle at best. They recoiled from the American System. Calhoun never saw himself as a Whig.[32]

The shaky coalition meant that Clay could never count on a reliable base to support his programs, and for the rest of Jackson's presidency he was on the defensive. The victory scored with the censure proved fleeting. Senators might oppose Jackson on any number of issues, but they did not necessarily agree with Clay. He strained to produce a compromise that would satisfy nationalists and states' righters, hoping his plan to distribute federal land revenues to the states would be sufficient for nationalists and palatable to southerners. Yet even his friends showed little enthusiasm for the idea.[33]

In addition, it seemed that Jackson was on the verge of going to war with France over its delinquent depredation claims. As chairman of the Senate Foreign Relations Committee, Clay took under advisement the part of the president's annual message that dealt with deteriorating Franco-American relations.[34] He knew the particulars of the dispute all too well, for it had troubled his tenure at State, one of the several unresolved problems he had handed off to Van Buren. Unlike the British trade issue, the French nut remained impossible to crack. Arbitrators had declared that France owed the United States money, and France had signed a treaty agreeing to pay, but the French dithered and then hinted that they might just forget the entire matter. Jackson's impatience turning to anger bubbled up in his annual message with threatened reprisals against French property and a request for additional discretionary funds to beef up the military. The implication was clear.[35]

Clay criticized Jackson's belligerence and opposed giving him any money, but the stand seemed more partisan than scrupulous. As secretary of state, Clay had made similarly aggressive recommendations to Adams, who had prudently disregarded them. To Clay's relief, much of the Senate, including many Democrats, chose to respond with similar caution to Jackson's rattling saber.[36] Instead of endorsing Jackson's call for reprisals, Clay's committee recommended a policy of wait-and-see. If the French continued their noncooperation, then would be the time to consider retaliation. Later in the session, Clay used his influence in the House of Representatives to kill a measure that would have given Jackson $3 million in discretionary funds. Aside from the unprecedented grant of unfettered money, Clay argued that giving it to Jackson would make it appear as though the country were preparing for war. In his experience, he observed with unintended irony, such preparations often caused a rush to war.[37] When Congress adjourned, Clay hoped Jackson would be unable "to goad his party into war" before it met again.[38]

CLAY HAD LITTLE desire to return to Congress that fall.[39] The prospect of renewed arguments about France, the fight over distribution, the unflagging Democrat effort to expunge the 1834 Senate censure, all made him weary. As the presidential election year of 1836 loomed, Whigs appeared in complete disarray as they tried to choose a candidate to run against Jackson's handpicked successor, Martin Van Buren. Clay also had personal reasons for delaying his departure for Washington. On November 2, Anne gave birth to her fourth son, Charles Edward Erwin, at the Woodlands. It marked the end of her eighth pregnancy in twelve years of marriage, but something was different about this one. The baby was healthy, but she was not. Instead of bouncing back quickly as she had always done in the past, she became quite ill and could not leave her bed. Her condition did not improve in the days after the baby's birth, and everyone soon became desperate with worry. Clay had planned to travel to Princeton to visit John and the Duralde boys at their boarding school, a detour that would require an early departure if he were to arrive in Washington in time for the opening of Congress. He nevertheless delayed his trip while Anne remained in any danger. By mid-November, though, she was clearly mending, and the scare passed. Clay began his trip on November 18, but he had forebodings. The next day he wrote Lucretia from Maysville that he felt "very uneasy about our dear daughter."[40]

Clay swung through New Jersey to visit the boys and then made his way to

Washington, arriving with a bad cold in the second week of December. His friend John J. Crittenden was joining him in the Senate for the Twenty-fourth Congress and had left Kentucky later than Clay. Crittenden reassured him that the doctors had declared Anne out of danger. Clay remained uneasy, however, and confided as much to Lucretia. She was the only person to whom he could unburden himself, and across the miles, he revealed his deepest fear: "Our only daughter, and so good a daughter—there is no event that would so entirely overwhelm us as that of her loss." The next day he begged James Erwin for the latest news. A letter in Anne's own hand telling him she was better would be best. Despite his premonitions, Clay received a steady stream of good news from home, and gradually he relaxed enough to turn his attention to politics.[41]

It was late in the afternoon of December 18. The Senate had adjourned for the day, and Clay lounged at his desk in the chamber laughing and talking with several friends. A clerk brought in the day's mail. Clay shuffled through his stack looking for letters from home. There were two. He lit up while reading the first, a cheerful account of Anne's steady improvement. Her recovery was advancing so rapidly, in fact, that she planned to return with James to New Orleans in only a few weeks. Clay picked up the other letter. It was from Kentucky's Episcopal bishop, Benjamin Bosworth Smith. Clay's friends, talking among themselves, were startled to hear him seem to choke. His face had turned ashen. He tried to stand, but the room whirled and his legs buckled. His colleagues caught him as dead weight. As he opened his eyes, he quietly murmured, "Every tie to life is broken." Anne had died suddenly on December 10.[42]

Clay went into seclusion at his boardinghouse. He poured out his grief in a letter to Lucretia: "Alas! my dear wife, the great Destroyer has come." He "would have submitted, cheerfully submitted, to a thousand deaths to have saved this dear child. She was so good, so beloving, and so beloved, so happy, and so deserving to be happy . . . the last of six dear daughters." He could never recover from this loss. "One of the strongest tyes [*sic*] that bound me to Earth is broken—forever broken. My heart will bleed as long as it palpitates. Never, never can its wounds be healed." He could not stop weeping. "This dear child was so entwined around my heart; I looked forward to so many days of comfort and happiness in her company." He begged Lucretia to "kiss my dear grandchildren for your affectionate and afflicted husband."[43]

Losing Anne gutted Henry Clay. Indeed, losing Anne devastated every Clay from Princeton to Missouri. James Erwin could not bear to remain at places that reminded him of her, and he fled the Woodlands immediately after her funeral. He took the two older boys with him, but the younger children, including the baby, remained with Lucretia. James Clay was in Missouri starting his farm when he received the sad letter announcing the death of his "last sister." Henry Jr. had taken Julia and the children on a European tour and for a long time remained blissfully unaware of Anne's death. Fourteen-year-old John at school in New Jersey wrote poignant letters to his mother that also turned out to be prophetic. Reflecting on "how much the death of my poor sister should humble us all," he told his mother to be kind but firm with Anne's children, certain from his own experience that the kindness would be abundant, the firmness only occasional.[44]

"Borne down by the severest affliction with which Providence has ever been pleased to visit" him, Clay stayed in his rooms until he nearly went mad. He finally returned to the Senate—he reintroduced his distribution bill—but everyone was startled at how broken he was. Otherwise, he kept to himself and wrote home frequently. He confided in Lucretia about his crushed spirit; he admonished Thomas not to add to her burdens. She was certainly busy caring for three small children, one an infant, her little girl's last laughing gift to the world. In their small faces, Lucretia could see Anne.[45]

ONLY SUPERHUMAN WILL saw Henry Clay through the weeks that followed. He became fixated on passing the distribution bill, particularly because he saw its success as tied to the humanitarian project of colonizing freed slaves. Slave states could use the money to implement a different sort of internal improvement. Rather than building roads, they could fund gradual emancipation. Clay remained convinced that only that process could persuade slaveholders to eradicate the institution, and colonization would shield freed slaves from mistreatment. On this issue too he embraced the center, publicly declaring the immorality of slavery while trying to find the compromise that would appeal to fellow moderates. He did not believe that the federal government had the constitutional authority to interfere with slavery in the states, but he recognized Congress's right to abolish slavery in Washington, D.C., and federal territories, though he did not believe it should do so. To his thinking, the Missouri Compromise had settled the territorial issue. Because Maryland had ceded the land for the District of Columbia, to abolish slavery there without the consent of Maryland, as well as bordering Virginia, would be inappropriate. Washington's citizens should also have a say in the matter.[46]

Extremism on slavery alarmed Clay. Calhoun had actually begun a crusade to have the Senate automatically table any petition requesting the abolition of slavery in the District of Columbia, a move that ultimately resulted in the derisively labeled "Gag Rule." Calhoun also wanted to prevent the post office from delivering abolitionist material in the South. Both initiatives disgusted Clay as obviously counter to constitutional protections regarding the right of redress and free speech. Agitation for or against slavery sharpened sectional differences to a cutting edge capable of cleaving the Union while making moderate solutions increasingly unlikely. Abolitionists generally denounced colonization, and southern proslavery advocates were wary of it, but Clay continued to insist that it was the only reasonable way to end slavery. He supported the American Colonization Society and became its president in 1836.[47]

In the spring of 1836, Texas won its independence from Mexico. American immigrants in Texas had staged the revolution, and it was rather a foregone conclusion among them that American annexation would automatically follow Texas independence. Despite his satisfaction with the event, Jackson paused in his response. The administration was in the midst of a dispute with Mexico over American claims, but more important, Americans were deeply divided over the wisdom of adding the vast slave domain of Texas to the Union. Jackson even preferred to leave to Congress the decision about recognizing Texas as a sovereign republic. In the early summer of 1836, Congress debated that question and laid bare northern qualms about recognition as a step toward annexation.[48]

Clay presented the Senate Foreign Relations Committee's report in June 1836 that recommended recognizing Texas when the president judged its government to be stable.[49] On the other hand, southern agitation for annexation—an obvious ploy to add new slave territory to the Union and increase the South's political clout—disturbed Clay. Not until the end of his term did Jackson recognize Texas. Old Hickory left it up to a future administration to decide about annexation.[50]

DURING THE WINTER of 1835–36, politics increasingly revolved around the upcoming presidential election. Democrats had already held a convention the previous spring to rubber-stamp Jackson's choice of Martin Van Buren. Democrats appeared to be united behind Van Buren, but significant issues—such as monetary policy—actually divided them. When a group of New York laborers who opposed the Pet Banks' inflationary policies tried to air grievances at a Democratic meeting in Tammany Hall on October 29, 1835, conservatives shut down the gaslights, hoping that darkness would silence the protests. Instead, the dissidents continued the meeting by striking matches called "loco focos." Whigs soon began calling all Democrats "Locofocos." The label had a nicely disparaging ring to it.[51]

Democrat disunity, however, paled compared to Whig disarray, a symptom of that loose coalition so worrisome to Clay. Unable to unite on issues or on a single candidate, Whigs had resorted to running three regional candidates in an effort to appeal to distinctive constituencies. Clay initially thought the plan laughable. If every faction of a party insisted that a candidate perfectly fit its principles, "there can be no union or harmony."[52] Yet that is what had happened. Northeastern Whigs supported Daniel Webster, northwestern Whigs supported William Henry Harrison, and southern Whigs supported the former Jacksonian Hugh Lawson White. In the midst of this willy-nilly stumble, Clay was occasionally urged by his friends to run, but even before Anne's death he had had no heart for the race and certainly had none for it after December 1835. The best the Whigs could hope for was that the multicandidate approach would fragment the Electoral College and throw the question into the House of Representatives.[53]

Clay attempted to remain aloof from the election while nevertheless supporting the Whig cause. He preferred Webster for best exemplifying Whig principles. Despite Clay's patronage of William Henry Harrison during the military hero's early political career, he had come to see Harrison as vain, posturing, dim-witted, and unqualified for the presidency. Clay liked Hugh Lawson White but accurately assessed him as more inclined toward states' rights than a nationalist program. To his consternation, though, it gradually became apparent that Harrison was the most popular and consequently the most electable of the three.[54]

Because he so wanted to see the Democrats defeated, Clay set aside his low opinion of Harrison and endorsed him. Ordinarily Harrison's flaws would have made more compelling the entreaties from Clay's friends that he should enter the contest. Yet Clay was unmovable. Even had Anne lived, the humiliation from 1832 was still too fresh for him to risk another such embarrassment this soon. He insisted that he could not accept a nomination unless he was certain that the people wanted him. There did not appear to be such a groundswell for his candidacy.[55]

By removing himself from the contest, this consummate political animal appeared to have lost interest in not just politics but life. He certainly hoped Whigs would prevail and had forebodings for the country should Van Buren win, but his old fire was gone, his heart a fading ember.

His overwhelming grief over Anne's death never really subsided, and other concerns mounted as well. In New Jersey, John was miserable—neither the prep school nor Princeton had agreed with him—and wanted to come home. He also became quite ill with typhoid fever while visiting Clay in Washington during the late spring of 1836. For two weeks, Clay and Charles Dupuy took shifts to watch over John each night, and a female nurse spelled them during the day while Clay was in the Senate. Henry Jr. arrived from Europe and immediately pitched in as well, and to everyone's relief, John began to improve. He gradually recovered from his dangerous illness, but he wanted to be at Ashland. Lucretia, discovering how dangerously ill her youngest child had been at the worst of his ordeal, never again wanted him far from her side. She soon had her baby boy home.[56]

CLAY FINALLY DECIDED to retire from public life and dedicate his remaining years to his family and farm. His letters were steeped in resignation and inclined to despair. All his efforts to stop Jackson from destroying the American System had been futile. The conflict with France still hung fire, and Clay suspected that Jackson wanted war if for no other reason than to spend the growing surplus and doom Clay's hope of distributing it to the states. He was pleasantly surprised to be wrong about this at least. Jackson never apologized for his earlier belligerence, but he did declare that when he had threatened France, he had not meant to threaten France. The French realized that that was as good as it was going to get with Andrew Jackson and paid the claims. There was no war, and the surplus was preserved.[57]

Clay still hoped to distribute that money to the states for internal improvements and colonization. Widespread support for distribution included some Democrats under political pressure from constituents eager to receive the money. Yet western senators persisted in their wish to reduce the price of federal lands, a move sure to endanger the surplus, and Clay had to fight them at every turn. Even worse in his view were the growing instances in which people simply expropriated public lands by showing up in advance of government surveyors. At the end of March 1836, he stoutly opposed Robert J. Walker's plan to reduce land prices for people who had settled on public property. Walker wanted to grant them "preemption," which meant exclusive rights to purchase land at bottom dollar. Clay called these people squatters, a term Walker found objectionable when applied to those he claimed were the backbone of the nation, the very men who had fought under Jackson at New Orleans. Walker exclaimed that if the men Clay derided as squatters had been in Washington in 1814, they would have saved the city from the British torch. The gallery loved this sort of talk, and it greeted Walker's tribute to patriotic American yeomanry with loud applause. Clay waited for everyone to settle down. He innocently claimed no disrespect to squatters but impishly added that he "hardly thought they would have saved the Capitol unless they had given up their habits of squatting."[58]

Calhoun and Clay worked together to push a distribution plan through Congress. They described the money being divided among the states as a loan in order to satisfy the constitutional qualms of opponents, but this transparently semantic dodge fooled nobody. The states would never pay back the money. In addition, the Deposit-Distribution Act, as its name indicated, required the initial deposit of money in state banks before distribution to state governments. Even worse from Clay's perspective, the bill provided for only a single act of distribution and did not tie the policy permanently to the sale of federal lands. Most expected Jackson to veto it, but to everyone's surprise he signed the bill into law. Old Hickory judged the large majorities that had favored the bill as veto-proof, and he was careful to avoid hurting Van Buren's election in the fall by opposing a popular measure.[59]

Jackson instead tried to offset the impact of distribution by reducing federal revenues from land sales. His plan was to announce a new Treasury policy by way of the Specie Circular, a change recommended to him by Thomas Hart Benton, whose preference for hard money gained him the alliterative nickname of "Bullion" Benton. The Treasury would accept only specie rather than banknotes for land sales. The administration meant for the Specie Circular to be a crafty method of lowering western land prices by discouraging speculation. Instead, ordinary investors inferred that Jackson's pronouncement meant the government had no confidence in the nation's banks, and they began to pull their money from dubious and healthy banks alike. As depositors scrambled to withdraw gold and silver, banks nervously curtailed loans in order to sustain their reserves. Meanwhile, wealthy speculators continued to dominate the land market because only they had specie on hand or the necessary credit to obtain it. The alarming rate of withdrawals, the removal of federal funds under the Deposit-Distribution Act, and the arbitrary demand for specie to purchase land made for an extremely unstable fiscal situation. By spring 1837, major Pet Banks in the Northeast, once flush with government deposits, had seen their specie reserve depleted by two-thirds. The state of affairs verged on financial catastrophe.[60]

Meanwhile, the Whig hope that the presidential election would go to the House proved unfounded. Van Buren took a majority in the Electoral College with 170 votes to 124 for the other candidates. Harrison, however, finished with a respectable 73 electoral votes, even with the divided Whig field, showing strength in the West, Mid-Atlantic, and Upper South. Some in the party started thinking about Harrison and 1840.

More immediately, the rapid glide toward an economic Niagara continued as Congress opened its session in December 1836. Clay led the Whigs to assail Jackson's lack of judgment, but he also offered a practical compromise. The government should stop transactions with unhealthy banks and accept banknotes exclusively from reputable institutions, meaning only those that had sufficient specie reserves to back their paper. Clay warned that if Jackson's specie policy remained in place, not only would American businesses suffer, but the American people would have a first-class panic and lingering depression on their hands. A bill containing most of Clay's plan passed Congress near the end of the session, but Jackson pocket vetoed it. The rapid glide continued.[61]

Clay had only reluctantly returned to Washington. Van Buren's victory had deeply depressed him, and the unrelenting battles with Jackson had left him exhausted. He had all but decided to quit after his term, but when the Jacksonians commenced what he regarded as the most contemptible gesture in American political history, they sealed his decision. From the moment the Senate in 1834 had censured the president for removing the deposits, Jacksonians had worked to have it expunged from the legislature's official records. For Old Hickory, this drive for vindication became all-consuming and summoned the worst of his vindictive enthusiasms. He and his lieutenants exerted pressure on legislators in Democrat-controlled states to pass resolutions instructing their senators to vote for an expunging resolution. In states evenly divided between Whigs and Democrats, Jacksonians worked tirelessly to elect Democrat majorities.[62]

The authority of state legislatures to instruct House and Senate members had always been as controversial as it was uncertain. In 1811, Senator Henry Clay had cited the Kentucky legislature's instructions as a prime reason for his opposing the renewal of the first Bank of the United States, yet in 1825, Representative Henry Clay had disregarded the legislature's instructions to vote for Andrew Jackson. Clay was not alone in obeying or ignoring such directives according to circumstances, and clearly the case rather than any firm principle guided most members of Congress. Those who steadfastly held that state legislatures had the right to instruct congressional delegations drew a line between senators and representatives. Legislatures elected senators to represent the entire state, while voters divided into districts elected House members. Yet the notion of senators serving in Washington as essentially ambassadors from their states and consequently subject to state control was nevertheless vague. When a Jacksonian majority gained control of the Virginia legislature, it told Senators John Tyler and Benjamin Watkins Leigh to vote for expunging the censure. Tyler resigned rather than comply; Leigh refused to vote to expunge, but he kept his seat, at least until the end of the session, when he resigned for personal reasons.[63]

By the final congressional session of Jackson's presidency, the unflinching labors of his supporters had produced the necessary votes in the Senate for his vindication, and a weakened opposition could only delay the inevitable. In this task as in others, Thomas Hart Benton piloted the administration's project by proposing the resolution to expunge the censure.

During debates over previous resolutions of this sort, Clay had always said little. In this debate, he remained silent until the final day, and because common knowledge had it that he planned to speak, the gallery was packed. He rose from his desk, and the crowded chamber went silent. He reminded everyone that he was the author of the censure and thus felt compelled to oppose Benton's effort to erase it from the Senate's official records. His silence in all previous debates on this measure had rested on the assumption that nobody could seriously have expected the Senate to mutilate its own annals—but, he added sarcastically, the Jacksonian majority was apparently capable of anything. Clay refrained from rehashing his reasons for the censure but emphatically declared that everything contained in it was true. Obliterating it would not change what had actually happened.[64]

It was a caustic speech, and Clay showed more than his usual contempt for the administration and those senators doing its bidding. As he prepared to conclude, he asked, "What patriotic purpose is to be accomplished by this expunging resolution? Is it to appease the wrath and to heal the wounded pride of the Chief Magistrate?" He mocked Benton's resolution for directing that "Black lines!" be physically drawn through the censure. Clay wanted the pen used to draw those lines to go to Democrats as a tainted trophy. He recommended that they create a new mark of American aristocracy to commemorate their "noble work." They could style it "the Knight of the Black lines." He whirled on his colleagues and roared for them to go to their homes and tell their constituents "that, henceforward, no matter what daring or outrageous act any President may perform, you have forever hermetically sealed the mouth of the Senate."[65]

The vote to expunge passed 24 to 19. As the Senate secretary pulled the journal out to draw the black lines, Clay and opposition members stalked out of the chamber. The secretary marked out the censure and scratched into the journal the words "Expunged by order of the Senate, this 16th day of January 1837." Spectators in the gallery hissed and booed, and the presiding officer, Senator William King of Alabama, was about to have them evicted when Benton began to have qualms: the sergeant-at-arms, he suggested, should remove only "ruffians" who objected to the Senate's vote, the implication being that the majority of spectators approved of it. The men who had redressed the supposed wrong done to Jackson brazened it through, for they had little choice. Clay's sarcasm became reality. They presented the pen that had drawn the black lines to Jackson, who promised to preserve it as one of his "precious relics." Irony was lost on the old man.[66]

———

IN THE AFTERMATH of this event, Clay all but ceased participating in Senate debates. The expunging resolution had been for him the final blow to degrade Congress and demoralize the country. He liked Van Buren personally but doubted he would markedly differ from the man who had handpicked him for the presidency.[67] Clay told Frank Brooke that he would leave the Senate "with the same pleasure that one would fly from a charnel-house." His next birthday would be his sixtieth, and he had never felt so old, so tired.[68]

Inauguration day was sunny and mild. The Senate assembled to see the new vice president, Richard Johnson, sworn in before moving to the East Portico for Van Buren's oath and address. Visitors mingled with senators as they awaited the official party. Clay spied Thomas Ritchie, the editor of the Richmond *Enquirer*. The two had been close when they had first met as teenagers in Richmond but had grown apart after the War of 1812, primarily because of Ritchie's disapproval of the American System. They remained cordial until Clay's decision to support Adams in the House vote of 1825 completely estranged the editor. Ritchie's *Enquirer* became a relentless critic of Clay and everything he advocated. They had not seen each other in over a decade. Francis Preston Blair had said that Clay never abandoned a friend, and that inauguration day, he proved it by crossing the chamber with his hand outstretched. Clay was willing to risk the rebuff, and Ritchie was unwilling to exact it. He took Clay's hand and genially remarked "that Time had laid his hands so gently upon" the Kentuckian. Clay laughed and lifted his hands as if to hold something back. He promised that he would "keep the Old Fellow off as long as" he could. They continued laughing and reminiscing until Van Buren and Jackson entered arm in arm and the spell was broken. Henry Clay and Thomas Ritchie would not say a single word to each other for another thirteen years.[69]

Van Buren's day was festive, although not as raucously celebratory as his predecessor's. Clay gauged the crowd descending on Washington from Van Buren's New York as being "as great as it was from Scotland, when James [VI] ascended to the throne of England."[70] The country, at peace and apparently prosperous, witnessed another quiet passing of power, the end of Jackson as president if not of Jackson as a force within the great party engine the new president had created. Van Buren's inaugural address promised to keep the country at peace and pledged its continued prosperity. He lauded moderation, especially regarding slavery. He pointedly deprecated the growing agitation by abolitionists to ban slavery in Washington, D.C., which was his first misstep as president.[71] It would not be his last, for with that remark he made instant enemies of abolitionists on the first day of his administration. Relations with Britain proved more fragile than anyone realized. Worst of all, the rapid glide to economic disaster had almost reached the steep falls, perversely waiting until the Little Magician became president, an office that seemingly robbed him of his wand.

Late that spring, the economic current plunged the country over the brink. Banks began to fail, and major businesses that relied on credit to operate began to close their doors. Banks that survived suspended specie payments on their notes and called in loans, some good, some bad, all increasingly uncollectable. The Panic of 1837 had many causes, some related to the ill-judged policies of Jackson's administration, some completely beyond the control of any president or any government. True enough, banks were short of gold and silver because of the Specie Circular and because of Jackson's insistence on paying off the national debt (much of it held by foreigners) in specie. Yet great and silent forces beyond anyone's power were also in play. In the early 1830s, abundant Mexican silver inflated prices and lubricated the machinery of global trade, as promoted by British banks and British firms, especially as it reached around the world to the Orient. After 1835, however, the Texas Revolution and U.S. claims against Mexico dramatically diminished the supply of Mexican silver. While that was happening, the value of American cotton failed to keep pace with the rising prices of European goods, and those British firms that customarily extended credit to southern planters and cotton brokers abruptly halted the practice as they surveyed the weakening world economy. Under pressure to loosen credit domestically, British bankers confronted the costs of an abysmal grain harvest that forced Britain to stave off famine by importing significant amounts of European wheat. Not only did those British bankers stop southern credit, they called in loans from American banks, whether good or bad, and some of these too went uncollected. These accumulating events reached a critical mass in early 1837, just as Van Buren was being sworn in. Panic shot through American financial markets, shattering the banking system and throwing the general population into disarray as a tide of business failures swept over the country. By summer, America had simply stopped working, and forlorn crowds of hollow-eyed men clustered at the doors of more and more banks, trying to get their money, wandering away dazed as those doors closed early, the vaults empty, their contents vanished.[72]

At first, the crisis seemed to paralyze Van Buren. Earlier financial downturns had never been so thorough and smashing, and earlier nostrums of government inaction had seemed sensible. Jackson told Van Buren to let the markets sort themselves out, but the deepening disaster gave rise to demands for some sort of government intervention. Finally, Van Buren felt he had no choice. He concluded that banks were the fundamental problem, especially the Pet Banks so long favored with federal deposits and now deprived of them. Actually, Van

Buren was in error. Most banks, even the Pet Banks, had behaved responsibly, had not heedlessly extended credit, and had maintained healthy reserves. That Van Buren and his advisers erroneously blamed banks for the financial catastrophe goaded them into hastily formulating a plan of action. They especially wanted to act before annoying Whigs could raise the specter of the BUS. Van Buren summoned a special session of Congress for September 1837. He planned to present to it a proposal for a "Subtreasury" or "Independent Treasury." It was to be a "divorce," as the president portentously called it, of all government funds from private banks.[73]

AS THE ECONOMY imploded, Clay spent the spring and summer at Ashland, far from the tumult. He had planned a trip to St. Louis to inspect his Missouri lands and visit James, but Van Buren's call for a special session intervened. As Clay tracked the financial crash through newspapers and correspondence, he was certain that Jackson's policies had caused it. Hearing the rumor that Van Buren intended to cut all connections between the government and the nation's banking system, Clay was horrified. The move, he warned, would further diminish confidence in banks and worsen bad policies that had already gone far toward destroying the country's financial structure. The only hope rested in that summer's state elections giving Whigs a congressional majority. They could then reverse the madness, block any additional folly, and enact a sensible program to restore credit and repair the economy. Clay prepared for the worst, however. He made plain that he could at least acquiesce in a reasonable administration plan to relieve the country's suffering, but he left home in August very doubtful that one would materialize. In fact, reports that Jackson in Nashville was behind Van Buren's rash plan to abandon the banking system disheartened him.[74]

Van Buren wanted not only a "divorce" of federal funds from the banking system but also the issuance of specie and federal notes backed by the Treasury. Yet critics pointed out that federal notes competing with banknotes could only depreciate the value of the latter, further damaging the banks themselves. Whigs criticized the plan as a very messy divorce indeed, one certain to deepen the chaos in American commercial centers. They also saw a sinister political result in devaluing banknotes: the party that controlled the Treasury would control the monetary system.[75]

Several factors hobbled Whig efforts to block the proposal, however. The most damaging was John C. Calhoun's defection to the administration, a move that stunned Clay and Webster. They judged it a treacherous betrayal that confirmed Calhoun's lack of principle and his shameless intention to further his own political fortunes by whatever means at hand. Just at that moment, Martin Van Buren seemed to be the handiest way for Calhoun to rise, and the strange alliance between the two—between the president and the man who had chortled over killing him "dead" in a Senate confirmation proceeding—substantiated all the unseemly features of the new politics.

Confronting the administration's formidable phalanx, Clay put up a stout fight in the Senate, but the numbers were clearly against him. When he repeated that only the American System's promotion of strong banking could revive collapsed markets, everyone might have noted he was going blue in the face. He nevertheless pointed out the inconsistency of Van Buren's establishing a government bank by any name—"Independent Treasury" seemed the most fashionable at the moment—while blaming banks for causing the disaster. He derisively compared the proposal to blaming the bullet rather than the trigger-man for killing the victim. The administration nevertheless had the votes in the Senate, especially because of Calhoun, and the Subtreasury plan passed. The House of Representatives, however, turned thumbs down, and witnesses reported Clay as shouting "Hurrah!" when he heard the news. The special session closed. Neither executive nor Congress had realized a single accomplishment to alleviate the country's distress or solve the government's economic plight.[76]

The futile special session left Clay little time to visit Ashland before he had to return to Washington for the regular session in December. Lucretia stayed behind. Nobody knows whether she made a flat declaration of her intention never to return to Washington or it simply worked out that way, but she never set foot in the capital again. Her absence gave rise to stories about her being an eccentric recluse, tales that created the impression that she was withered and desolate, a shade wandering the halls of Ashland like a timid cat, silent and with lowered eyes. Eventually, people would forget that she had ever come to Washington and would even claim that she never had. They would not recall the quiet woman whom fashionable Margaret Bayard Smith had for years valued as a dear friend, the two in a carriage making calls, tending each other's children, mingling at the Wednesday levees at Decatur House. In Washington, Lucretia had loved to play the piano with the children dancing around it, and she still played, only never again in Washington. Far from being a shrouded mansion, Ashland rang with Lucretia's music, her motherless grandchildren now the dancers, her friends from her church her companions, the activities of the community and the work of her dairy filling her days.

In short, Lucretia Clay was too busy to bother with nonsense in Washington. The Duralde boys mostly lived at Ashland when not in school, and Anne's younger children were a constant presence as James Erwin traveled on business.

Theodore was just miles away, of course, and Henry with his dear Julia and their growing family frequently visited, requiring rooms to be readied and treats to be prepared for the little ones. John loved Ashland and was off to its stables first thing in the morning to tend to the swift horses he found both fascinating and friendly. They apparently returned the feeling.

Thomas had worried his parents sick, but he gradually found his way by finding a girl. In storybook fashion, she lived next door and had grown up with him and his siblings. Her parents were the French immigrants Augustus and Charlotte Mentelle, who operated a boarding school across the road from Ashland where most of the Clay children had received their earliest education with other local youngsters, including little Mary Todd, future wife of Abraham Lincoln. Clay was away at the special session, but Thomas had not postponed his plans to take Mary Mentelle for his wife that fall. The Clays were delighted to have her join the family. She had been a fixture at Ashland as a small child, one of those people who grows up on the edge of a family as a sort of mascot, and now she had agreed to be Thomas's lucky charm. Bright and cheerful, she chattered in person and bubbled in letters, and Clay adored her for loving his boy, once lost, now found.[77]

Coming just weeks after the wedding, Ashland's Christmas that year was happier than it had been in quite some time. Yuletide celebrations were different in those days, but the day still held special significance for family. Children laughed and danced at cheerful parties, such as one at the Wickliffes' where Clays and Mentelles joined other guests to feast on roasted turkey. Henry and Julia's family rounded out the complement along with Aunt Suky and her daughter, Nanette Price. Lucretia with Julia, and Mary with her mother Charlotte, staged large family dinners of their own, complete with mince pies, cakes, and candy. "Your Ma," Mary wrote to James, and then corrected herself to say, "our Ma is not lonely, as there are [sic] always someones [sic] comfort to look after."[78]

Lucretia had her little Creoles and the Erwin youngsters charging about excitedly, but she missed James, who was away in Missouri trying to get started as a farmer, and she worried about him. He was lonely and confessed to his mother that he was a little lovesick over not being in love. "You said you wanted a woman," little Martin Duralde bluntly wrote him. "Why there are lots of them." Apparently there were not any of them where James was, though, and Lucretia worried about him alone during the holidays. She found his flute and sent it to him, enclosing fifty dollars in the package. She claimed to have found it tucked among his things at Ashland, but this was obviously money from her dairy business. It was Christmas.[79]

Lucretia missed her husband as well, since he was gone this Christmas as he had been for so many others, a casualty of the legislative calendar that always saw Congress in session during December. Two years earlier, when Anne had been ill but seemingly recovering, Clay had left for Washington with such reluctance that he had committed to retirement. He had told Lucretia that he hoped "that this is the last separation, upon earth, that will take place, for any length of time, between us."[80] Then Anne died, and his world collapsed.

Everything paled in the wake of that loss, but as it darkened his life, it had the oddly compensatory effect of putting everything else, including politics, into perspective. The immutable law that all things change and the certainty that the passing of enough time will partly restore the spirit, if one is willing, partly lifted the veil. But it was the economic panic, which suddenly made the Whigs relevant and made possible their becoming a coherent party, that sent breath across the fading ember in his heart. Whig victories all over the country in the summer and fall elections partly lifted the veil too. For the first time since Anne's death, Henry Clay gradually came into focus. He squared his shoulders and set his jaw. He would not retire. It was time "to see the Goths expelled [from] the Capitol." There was work to do.[81]

CHAPTER TEN

"I Had Rather Be Right than Be President"

WHEN THE STEAMBOAT *Detroit* hit a snag and foundered on the Ohio River in late summer 1838, the newspapers reported that Clay and John J. Crittenden were on board. They were not, instead having booked passage on the *Buffalo,* which rescued the *Detroit*'s stranded passengers. "Whig boats do not founder," Clay joked to a friend concerned by the news. He told of taking on some "Locofocos" from the wreck and added, "We shall I hope soon have to relieve others of them from the more important wreck they have made of the Administration."[1]

Indeed, the lingering effects of the financial panic and the Democrats' inability to offset them pointed to an all but certain Whig victory in 1840. Nevertheless Clay cautioned that they still had a lot of work to do. "The adversary is in possession of the field," he noted. As Van Buren's continuing frustration over the Subtreasury stalemate increased public dissatisfaction, even Clay's caution dropped away. "If we do not beat him," he said, "we deserve to be gibbeted."[2]

Although Clay was the undisputed leader of the party in Congress, the prospect of his candidacy for 1840 did not stir universal enthusiasm among Whigs, and their qualms annoyed him. The objection that he would unite the Democrats like no other Whig was especially exasperating. "I do not like to be run down by other Candidates or would be Candidates on our own side," he grumbled. He scoffed at fears over provoking Jackson and Van Buren supporters: "as if that party were to elect a *Whig* Presdt.!"[3]

One of the Whig contenders from 1836, Hugh Lawson White, decided not to try again and in the end supported Clay, but Daniel Webster and William Henry Harrison were obviously in the hunt. Daniel Webster's poor showing in 1836 had not blunted his ambition nor slowed his plans, and though Clay was aware of Harrison's appeal, he believed Webster was the stronger opponent. Discerning Whigs, he thought, would eventually realize that Harrison was a shallow vessel. Webster was anything but shallow, and at first it appeared as though Clay had reason to be worried. Webster remained bitter over the Harrison and White candidacies in 1836, and he sustained toward Clay a special resentment for not supporting him in that contest. Webster accordingly resolved shortly after Van Buren's inauguration to proceed toward the nomination, this time with more finesse.

He could never match Clay's influence in the Senate, so he aimed at attracting rich business interests in Massachusetts, New York, and Philadelphia, especially the last, where Nicholas Biddle's bank kept him on handsome retainers that were barely concealed bribes.[4] His extensive connections in New York City included Whig clubs and the editors of influential newspapers, and he hoped their support would set into motion an irresistible momentum. Because the South detested him, he need not worry about alienating southerners, which made the task of satisfying northerners easier.[5]

In May 1837, the Godlike Dan'l traveled through the West, a ploy to drum up support and counter Harrison's popularity in the region. By then the economic panic had presented him with a new issue, and he laid into Van Buren's ineffectiveness, excoriated Benton's hard-money stand, and blamed the Specie Circular for destroying the economy. His handsome second wife, Caroline, fifteen years his junior, and his bashful, pretty nineteen-year-old daughter, Julia, accompanied him on the trip, helping to offset his reputation as something of a rake. The family also came overland from Maysville for a weeklong visit at Ashland. Clay's generous hospitality included lavish dinners, continuously filled glasses, exciting outings to horse races, and sparkling repartee. By the time the Websters departed, a casual observer would have supposed that he and Clay were close friends rather than wary competitors. Clay marveled over Webster's "defective judgment in what concerns himself and his prospects," but the large and apparently adoring crowds the New Englander attracted in places like Louisville gave the Kentuckian pause. He insisted that these demonstrations for Webster were only "homage to his ability" and certainly not enthusiasm for his potential candidacy.[6] Webster's popularity worried him, though, and by that summer Clay was criticizing his rival's "shocking" ambition that threatened to divide Whigs and lose them the 1840 election.

In the months that followed, they shouldered at each other, sometimes in silly ways. When Webster initiated a move to repeal the Specie Circular, Clay used some legislative trickery to preempt the measure with one of his own, boosting his prestige with the business community. Clay claimed that the maneuver was not meant to antagonize Webster, but he nonetheless grumbled about the effort to give Webster credit for the proposal. "This competition about the resolution," he admitted, "was unworthy of either of us." Webster remarked in exasperation, "So the world goes!"[7]

Despite the large crowds he had attracted in the West, Webster's success on his 1837 tour was more show than real, and Clay had discerned that. He was nervous about Webster's strength in New York, though. As it happened, that too proved illusory, because Thurlow Weed believed Webster's ties to Biddle were as toxic as was his early career as a Federalist. But even so, Clay's New York supporters worked to quash the Webster boomlet in their all-important state by insisting that any nominee be chosen by a national Whig convention.[8]

The idea for the convention did not originate with Clay—early that summer, William Henry Harrison's Ohio supporters were urging one to nominate their man—but Clay approved of it as a way to fend off Webster.[9] The idea made political sense, because it was the best way to avoid the chaotic multiple candidacies of 1836. Yet by striking down Webster with this tactic, Clay courted peril, for the timing of the convention was crucial to his chances in it. With the economy in ruin, Clay's popularity instantly rose as his dire warnings about the Democrats' fiscal policy seemed confirmed by events. Suddenly his prescriptions for putting things right through government intervention, especially by reviving the Bank, seemed sensible, and because Clay was their principal advocate, his candidacy looked popular and politically logical. The sooner he could be placed before a convention the better, since improving financial conditions would likely dim the people's enthusiasm for his program and diminish for Whigs his attractiveness as a candidate.

The Whigs, however, quarreled over when to hold their convention. Harrison's supporters wanted it to occur in May 1838, but everyone else thought that was much too early. Clay was among them, although mistakenly, because an early convention at the height of the country's economic misery would have been to his greatest advantage. Hugh Lawson White advised that Clay's best chance was to have the nomination made in the summer of 1839 at the latest. Clay, however, began to take a dim view of the convention altogether. By the spring of 1838, his suspicions about Harrison's maneuvers were growing. Harrison's people had first proposed the convention, Clay noted, and eventually he thought he could see their reasoning. Harrison could not secure a national endorsement (meaning one that included the South, where he was weak) in any other fashion.[10] Southern and southwestern Whigs were repelled by the idea of a convention because they saw it as emulating the process that had produced Van Buren's candidacy. Clay held a considerable advantage in the South, and if these Whigs refused to attend, it would deal Clay a serious blow and boost Harrison's odds.[11]

But Clay had already agreed to accept a convention's decision by the time he entertained these doubts. And though he finally realized that an early date would be to his advantage, the goals of state leaders determined when the party would make its nomination. They did not want a presidential nominee complicating their local elections, contests in which Whig victories were otherwise assured. Consequently, in April 1838 a Whig caucus in Washington put out the word that the convention would be held in Harrisburg, Pennsylvania, a full year and a half later. Clay agreed to this, and though doing so was in retrospect a mistake, he had no choice.[12]

Meanwhile, his conviction that Webster was his most dangerous opponent persisted into the spring of 1838, and he finally decided to confront the problem directly. He met with Webster on June 13 for a lengthy conversation in which he candidly assessed Webster's chances as less than slim. He should step aside and avoid dividing the party, Clay said. The meeting was friendly, but Clay left it convinced that Webster would continue his quest for the nomination. "He will be control[led] by his friends," Clay concluded, "or will submit to the force of circumstances." And while Clay believed that Webster's friends would eventually persuade him to quit, he also thought Webster would do so "slowly and sullenly."[13]

Clay was right about Webster's reluctance to withdraw, but he did not seem to realize the perverse pleasure Webster took in remaining a candidate solely to obstruct him. In part, Webster was motivated by revenge for Clay's endorsement of Harrison in 1836. The Massachusetts legislature had already returned him to the Senate, but he began avoiding controversial votes in the third session of the Twenty-fifth Congress, as though it mattered. "Mr. Webster has been here several weeks," Clay mused, "& wraps himself up, so far as I know, in perfect silence."[14] Yet Webster clearly did not have a chance—Clay was right about that too, and Weed plainly told Webster that he would not be the nominee—but he remained a putative candidate even after he left the country for an extended sojourn in England in 1839. Not until that June did he formally withdraw, in a letter dispatched from London. Webster did not recommend anyone in his stead, but that omission too spoke volumes. By then, though, Clay knew who his real rival was for the nomination.[15]

AS EARLY AS 1837, many Whigs were gravitating toward William Henry Harrison, especially in Upstate New York where leaders like Thurlow Weed and William Seward thought him more electable than either Clay or Webster. Harrison had the support of Antimasons in Pennsylvania led by the mordant Thaddeus Stevens. Harrison was also quite strong in Ohio, where he resided, and in Indiana, where he had solid ties from the beginning of his public career. The old general (he was nearing sixty-eight), along with his unofficial campaign manager, Charles Todd, kept in touch with veterans nationwide, men who fondly recalled serving under him and who were sure to give him their votes in 1840 just as they had in 1836. In July 1837, Whigs in Ohio got the ball rolling by nominating him—a surprise to Clay, who had thought he could wrest the state from Harrison.[16]

Even after the Ohio nomination, Clay continued to underestimate Harrison's strength. An observer described as mere "pertinacity" Harrison's reading of his strong showing in 1836 "as an indication of his strength and popularity." "Never was a man more deceived," Clay's correspondent assured him.[17] Events would prove that judgment quite incorrect, but for a time Clay seemed well justified in accepting it. He had earlier concluded that the western part of New York was for him, as was New England, including Massachusetts, despite Webster's obstinacy. South Carolina hated Webster and was averse to Harrison, and after Calhoun, preferred Clay, described as "a noble creature" and "the only opposition man who has the slightest chance."[18] North Carolina, Louisiana, and Georgia were strongly in his column. Even Tennessee looked to be his, much to Andrew Jackson's chagrin. Old Hickory's followers made speeches throughout the state imploring Tennesseans to spare him the insult of having his enemy vindicated while the Old Hero still breathed. John Bell chuckled that if Tennessee went for Clay, Jackson would "burst [a] blood vessel & expire."[19]

At first Clay thought that resolutions in the Kentucky legislature recommending him for president were too early and displayed "more zeal than discretion," but as winter gave way to spring in 1838, his political star was so ascendant that he brimmed with confidence. The Ohio and New York state elections the previous fall had handed Whig candidates impressive victories, returns that Clay interpreted as an overpowering trend.[20]

Yet sustaining his strength meant walking a fine line to avoid alienating the northern and southern wings of the party. Hard times made that easier in one respect. Although Calhoun routinely denounced the American System as "the source of all our oppression, disorder, and corruption," he hardly spoke for the South.[21] Southern Whigs, in fact, were not altogether averse to Clay's economic ideas, for many elite planters had come to realize that a better transportation system could mean brisker commerce for southern agricultural staples as well as northern manufactured goods. They also recognized the commercial benefits of stable credit and a sound currency. In addition, Clay carefully tempered his views on these matters to avoid appearing doctrinaire. He was flexible about the Bank. He still insisted that the country needed a national bank, for he truly believed that only a central agency could establish and maintain a sound currency, but he admitted its resurrection was not politically feasible in the absence of widespread popular acceptance, which he acknowledged did not exist. He softened his views on the tariff, stating his continued support for the lower duties of the Compromise of 1833, and he gauged state expenditures on internal improvements as sufficiently funded by land revenue distribution, making federal funding unnecessary. When Clay repeated these sentiments to northern audiences, Edward Everett deduced that they signaled "a gentle edging over to Southern ground."[22]

Handling the slavery controversy was not so simple, especially when Calhoun tried to make mischief with it during the already contentious Twenty-fifth Congress. The South Carolinian's break with the Whigs and his alliance with Van Buren were partly opportunistic, but he also was motivated by his growing belief that Clay was as soft on abolitionism as Webster was hard against slavery.[23] Moreover, while most southerners preferred to let the sleeping dog of slavery lie, Calhoun roused it to rally his section and force northern accommodation. He introduced six resolutions in the Senate on December 27, 1837, four of them markedly provocative. Two of the resolutions repeated Calhoun's view of the Union as a mere compact of sovereign states in which each exercised complete control of its internal affairs, an obvious way to protect slavery from outside interference. That much the Senate could swallow. The remaining resolutions, however, stuck in the majority's throat. Calhoun insisted that the federal government not just refrain from interfering with slavery but actively protect it. For good measure, he capped his demands with an assertion that blocking Texas annexation on the basis of slavery was not only unfair to the South but unconstitutional.[24]

The initiative marked the beginning of Calhoun's blatant proslavery crusade, thereafter the defining theme of his career, but it was also a way of forcing Henry Clay's hand on the issue. Along with others, Clay recognized that with the slavery issue, Calhoun's "real aim [was] to advance the political interest of the mover and to affect mine."[25] He countered with several speeches in the Senate in January and February 1838, his manner "easy and graceful, but imperious and commanding."[26] He criticized Calhoun's confrontational tone and his agitation of issues such as Texas annexation, an initiative that would only embolden abolitionists and panic southerners. The injury done to the Union would be incalculable. Clay insisted that Calhoun's menacing approach was not an effective way to protect the rights of slaveholders. Moreover, Clay claimed that his amiable and conciliatory tone was no less firm and much more productive. In addition, he could not "believe that it is prudent or wise to be so often alluding to the separation of the Union. We ought not to be perpetually exclaiming, wolf, wolf, wolf." He then launched into an effective metaphor:

> We are too much in the habit of speaking of divorces, separation, disunion. In private life, if a wife pouts, and frets, and scolds, what would be thought of the good sense or discretion of the husband who should threaten her with separation, divorce, or disunion? Who should use those terrible words upon every petty disagreement in domestic life? No man, who has a heart or right feelings, would employ such idle menaces. He would approach the lady with kind and conciliatory language, and apply those natural and more agreeable remedies, which never fail to restore domestic harmony.[27]

The passage was classic Clay, illustrating the fundamental difference between his and Calhoun's temperament, the one whimsical and humorous, the other reflexively dour and dark. When Clay applied this technique, he could draw in followers, charm listeners, and inspire emulation, even by an essentially melancholy man like Abraham Lincoln, who like Clay learned to dress his points in comic garb to make them more appealing. The Senate broke into prolonged laughter over Clay's domestic allusion. Calhoun glowered.

Clay proposed six resolutions of his own to offset Calhoun's. Slavery should be exclusively controlled by the states, and petitions to abolish slavery in them should be rejected because they requested Congress to act beyond its authority. On the other hand, Congress could indeed abolish slavery where it exercised jurisdiction, as in the District of Columbia or federal territories, and should accordingly receive any petitions about those areas. He was on record as being adamantly opposed to a general policy that ignored petitions, for it would endanger the fundamental right to seek redress. Instead, he wanted a system to separate the mischievous work of fanatics from the reasonable requests of citizens. Until slavery touched on this issue, Calhoun had agreed that the right to petition was "guaranteed by the Constitution" and that it was a "duty" of Congress to receive them. By 1838, protecting slavery had altered the South Carolinian's perception of constitutional propriety but not the Kentuckian's.[28]

A lengthy debate ensued and the final votes, after much talk, were mixed, but Clay was at least able to persuade the Senate to reject Calhoun's most intemperate language. Instead, his colleagues agreed that the government should neither protect nor interfere with slavery and that abolitionism was bad because it imperiled the Union. When it was all over, Clay felt that he had deftly stepped around Calhoun's slavery snare.

The cut-and-thrust matches with Calhoun, though, spilled over into other matters and other arguments. Their exchanges grew testy, even belligerent, and on February 19, 1838, during the debate on the perennial Democrat effort to create the Subtreasury, Clay delivered a blistering four-hour address in which he accused Calhoun of being a Nullifier and, worse, of allying with Van Buren for base political advantage. Both charges visibly stung the South Carolinian, and some thought Clay had gone too far.[29] Calhoun struck back in a speech that took him all of three weeks to prepare. It included a less than oblique reference to the Corrupt Bargain as a more pertinent example of politics trumping principle.[30] Despite being ill, Clay immediately answered. He did not need "two or three weeks to prepare" his response to Calhoun, he roared, and he then commenced a full-scale attack on the South Carolinian that traced their work together over the course of three decades. He ultimately described Calhoun as a changeling on significant issues. They had worked together and had agreed for years on most important policy measures, but "we concur now in nothing," Clay announced. "We separate forever."[31]

Ever since the 1824 campaign, their relations had been tinged with suspicion and sometimes marred by outright mistrust, a state of affairs worsened by the Nullification Crisis, but a shared aversion to Jackson and his policies had drawn them together. Calhoun's allegiance to the Whigs was never solid, though, just as his allegiance to Van Buren proved equally fragile. And though his increasingly inflexible sectional response to all national problems would eventually have caused a breach with Clay in any case, Calhoun's abrupt desertion of the Whigs and his support for the Van Buren administration surprised everyone. His and Clay's final break in early 1838 was particularly unpleasant because it featured clashing egos as much as opposing ideas. Referring to his performance in the Senate on February 19, Clay could gloat that he had "handled Calhoun without gloves," and the impressive debates (Webster also participated with a spirited defense of Clay that flattened Calhoun with sarcasm) have long been deemed among the most brilliant in the Senate's history.[32] Yet Clay upon reflection gave way to foreboding.

He thought Calhoun's behavior "most extraordinary" and was troubled by what he perceived as the effort to promote disunion. He grimly assessed his erstwhile friend's little clique that made up for its small size with relentless activity. Its aim was to persuade southerners that the federal government from its very start had been injuring the South to benefit the North. "I believe in private life he is irreproachable," Clay concluded, "but I believe he will die a traitor or a madman."[33]

Calhoun freely confessed, "I don't like Henry Clay." He was "a bad man, an impostor, a creator of wicked schemes." Calhoun swore he "wouldn't speak to" Clay. "But, by God," Calhoun blurted out in the same breath, "I love him."[34]

LUCRETIA REMAINED BUSY with the grandchildren, her church, Ashland's dairy, and Lexington's community activities. As always, she was self-sufficient and frugal, and Clay worried that she kept it from him when she ran short of funds. Her days at Ashland were mottled with everyday aches and pains, sometimes requiring the attention of Lexington doctor Thomas P. Satterwhite or W. W. Whitney. She was feeling her age and having to resort to small treatments and prescriptions more than she had before. Sometimes she indulged herself with little pleasures, which pleased Clay. She was fond of "good fresh Macaroni," and he was glad to ask Julie Duralde Clay to send some up from New Orleans.[35]

Life at Ashland during these years was often enlivened by a houseful of grandchildren, causing Clay to report cheerfully that the place had "all the animation which it exhibited twenty years ago."[36] Anne's boys, Eugene and Edward, "as fat as seals," often stayed at Ashland, and her daughter, Lucretia Clay Erwin, had started school but was having a hard time "fixing her attention on her studies." Clay wanted Thomas to consult with Lucretia about where to send the Duralde children to school. Clay preferred that they board with Thomas and Mary and offered to pay a generous allowance to offset the boys' expenses. The suggestion was a sign of the salutary effect Mary was having on his son.[37]

"During a long life," he wrote to the children of a friend, expressing what was surely his wish for his children's children, "I have observed that those are the most happy who love, honor, and obey their parents; who avoid idleness and dissipation, and employ their time in constant labor, both of body and mind; and who perform, with regular and scrupulous attention, all their duties to our Maker, and his only Son, our blessed Saviour."[38] In sum, it was a clear statement of the millennial spirit that fueled the exuberant reformist ideas of Whigdom. The world could be made better through hard, careful work and obedience to a higher authority, whether vested in one's parents or in God. Speaking from experience and "much observation," he had come to the conclusion that anyone "who is addicted to play loses money, time, sleep, health and character."[39]

Despite the didactic tone he often took with his children and grandchildren, Clay believed that everyone must find his own moral way as an exercise of free will. Whig philosophy lauded temperance and Whig reformers promoted it, but Clay believed it a worthy cause only so long as it used "mild measures":

The misfortune in human affairs is that we convince ourselves of what we suppose to be right, and then we endeavor, as we ought to do, to persuade others; but if we fail to convince them, we then resort to force. Hence, religious intolerance, proscription, the stake &c. Now, it is generally admitted among us, that in Religion, the greatest of all our interests, every man should be left free to follow any or none, as he pleases. But if we may not compel men to be religious have we a right to oblige them to be sober? Have we a right to constrain them to eat or not to eat, to drink or not to drink, not as they please, but as we choose to think it best for them?"[40]

With uncanny foresight he predicted that temperance would "destroy itself whenever it resorts to coercion, or mixes in the politics of the Country." When Massachusetts Whigs passed a law that required all liquor sales to be a minimum of fifteen gallons (to suppress the trade by mandating a high quantity), Clay called it "indefensible." Temperance was creditable only as moral suasion, not legislative coercion. "No man likes to have, or ought to have, cold water or brandy, separately or in combination, put in or kept out of his throat upon any other will than his own."[41]

His determination to see his grandchildren well educated stemmed partly from a mixture of Enlightenment rationalism and millennial liberalism. But it also resulted from his awareness of his own deficiencies in formal schooling, which he often lamented. It is inaccurate, however, to take at face value contemporary assessments of him as indifferent to books and uninterested in abstract thoughts. Possibly Clay understood the maxim summed up in the couplet "Good rule of thumb / In politics, too smart is dumb" and accordingly cultivated the image of a practical man with useful ideas rather than an intellectual like Hugh Swinton Legaré or even, for that matter, Daniel Webster or John C. Calhoun. But occasionally he let slip that he was an astute political philosopher and a confident intellectual. When Francis Lieber asked him to read his book on legal and political hermeneutics, Clay made perceptive suggestions for its improvement, some as arcane as the distinction between transcendent and extravagant construction and some as practical as a greater emphasis on the legislature's obligation to adhere to constitutional prescriptions. Lieber thought enough of Clay's remarks to incorporate the changes into a subsequent edition.[42]

Clay's suggestions to James for broadening himself with a reading program reveal what Clay regarded as essential historical knowledge. He recommended a thorough grounding in Greco-Roman traditions by studying histories of ancient Greece, Plutarch's writings, and Edward Gibbon's *Decline and Fall of the Roman Empire.* He also recommended David Hume's history of England, William Russell's study of modern Europe, Henry Hallam's multivolume history of the Middle Ages, William Robertson's three-volume history of the reign of Charles V, John Marshall's five-volume biography of Washington, and Carlo Botta's history of the American Revolution. "You should adopt some systematic course, as to time," he told James, "that is to read so many hours out of the 24."[43]

He worried about James, whose move to Missouri was not working out. Clay repeatedly urged him to try to be happy and stay busy despite his being "loansome," and the reading program was apparently designed in part to give the boy something to do. Clay above all feared that James would fall into dissolute habits and follow the twisted path of Thomas (only recently rescued by Mary Mentelle) and John, who drank too much and whom Clay suspected of feigning illness at Princeton to get out of his studies.[44]

"I have feared your solitary condition might prompt you into it [dissipation]," he warned James, and he urged the young man to consider "any arrangement by which you can come back to Kentucky and live in the midst of your friends." As the boy's loneliness fed his gloom, Clay sent money and advice: Stay busy! In fact, "constant employment" was "the great secret of human happiness." James should court a girl, marry her, start a family. "I have been looking out for a wife for you," Clay said, "but I suppose you will have to select [one] for yourself." In any case, he begged James not to keep to himself too much. When the boy admitted that he wanted to get out more but then reported that he hadn't, his father anxiously wanted to know why and then thought he had hit on the reason. "Do you want clothes?" he asked, possibly recalling his own boyhood awkwardness so many years before at the Chancery in Richmond, and he offered to supply money for a new wardrobe.[45] But most of all, he wanted his son to come home to Ashland. As it happened, Clay's political plans would unite him with his son sooner than he had expected.

LIKE THE REST of the country, Lexington felt the effects of the panic, and investment capital rapidly dried up.[46] Transylvania University also felt the sting of harsh conditions. Clay actually owed the university $10,000 that he had borrowed from his friend James Morrison's bequest to the school, which required a $600 annual payment, and he owed $1,200 a year on a $20,000 loan from John Jacob Astor. Yet his prospects remained sound despite the economic downturn. He made $72,000 in 1838 and owned property in Lexington assessed at $13,000 in 1837, which increased to $14,000 in 1838 and to $16,000 in 1839. His property in Fayette County, including Ashland, where forty-eight slaves toiled, was valued at $43,790. In addition to other out-of-state holdings, he owned land at the confluence of the Grand and Missouri rivers, near Brunswick.[47]

That January, Clay showed a dark temper in clashes with colleagues. He again attacked Mississippi senator Robert J. Walker's attempt to legislate preemption into federal land policy as a way to reward squatters at the expense of the federal Treasury. Learning from earlier experience, Clay was at first careful to distinguish between a bad policy and its potential beneficiaries by tempering his description of squatters as having "many worthy and excellent men among them," but in the debate that followed he lost his temper. He heatedly asked why it was proper for those squatters "to seize upon and rob the United States of their possessions?" When Indiana's John Tipton objected to Clay's defaming his constituents, Clay heedlessly characterized squatters as a "lawless rabble."[48] His vote against preemption hurt him in Arkansas and Missouri, but everybody could respect him for voting "the way he believed was right."[49] His reckless remark, however, would come back to haunt him.

That spring he also snapped at nephew John S. Hart for delaying the manufacture of Ashland's hemp while he attended to that of another uncle. It was not the first time the Harts had let him down. Hart's brother Thomas had behaved similarly, and Clay's patience was at an end. He was "disappointed and mortified" and vowed that unless John Hart fulfilled the bargain, their business relationship would end. "I will not be trifled with again," Clay warned. He soon had cause to regret his edginess in this episode as well, for Hart was killed by a lightning strike that summer.[50]

Otherwise, Clay lived well and had much to be grateful for. He stocked Ashland with imported wines, including a superior Madeira brought from Portugal at no small expense (almost $400 per pipe, the equivalent of 126 gallons). He wanted to give up snuff but was unable "to discontinue the use of that stimulant" and was appreciative when Kit Hughes sent him some boxes as a gift. While in Washington, he picked up the tab for posh dinner parties at the celebrated American & French Restaurant where good food and copious drink were the standard fare, along with card games. Clay still found the capital's society, if not its politicians, sparkling. He boarded at Mrs. Hill's, conveniently situated near Gadsby's. His congenial fellow lodgers included John J. Crittenden, his closest friend. Samuel Southard could be morose—his marriage to an unstable hypochondriac made him more than miserable—but Tom Corwin was a genuine wag with a wicked sense of humor.[51]

When another boarder at Mrs. Hill's, Representative William J. Graves, a fellow Kentuckian and friend of Clay's, killed Maine representative Jonathan Cilley in a duel on February 24, 1838, the affair caused a national scandal that touched on Clay. Graves and Cilley had been quarreling over the character of James Watson Webb, the Whig editor of the New York *Courier and Enquirer,* whom the Democrat Cilley criticized and the Whig Graves defended. In the duel that resulted, Henry Wise acted as Graves's second and was present as the an-

tagonists squared off at eighty yards and fired three rounds at each other with rifles, the last killing Cilley. The capital was outraged by the unique barbarity of
the encounter—using rifles had obviously meant a fight to the death—and the
Supreme Court refused to attend Cilley's funeral in symbolic protest just as
Congress opened a lengthy debate on anti-dueling legislation. Later, after he
and Clay had become enemies, Wise claimed that Clay had encouraged the affair by revising Graves's challenge, but Clay convincingly explained that he was
merely trying to soften the language in the hope of effecting a reconciliation. At
the time, though, even Clay's peripheral involvement in the incident had repercussions. A correspondent from Maine said it was hurting his presidential
prospects with New Englanders repelled by dueling. He wanted Clay to make
clear that he had tried to prevent the Graves-Cilley duel in particular and that he
opposed the practice on principle. Clay obliged, explaining that he had tried to
stop Graves and Cilley from meeting, even going so far as to involve the authorities, but unsuccessfully. Clay found the entire matter sad, sordid, and distasteful, and he insisted that he wrote privately and definitely not for publication. He
had learned the hard way not to dignify with denials unfounded charges against
him.[52]

IN THE FALL of 1838, Clay asked Nicholas Biddle for a loan of $5,000 to
$10,000 to help him purchase a stud horse in England. Biddle quickly approved
the loan—he always took care of his bank's friends—and lightheartedly wrote
to Clay about arranging "the visit of the illustrious stranger whom you propose
to invite over." Biddle insisted that Clay did not need a cosigner. Ashland alone
would cover the loan, and in any case, Biddle said, Clay had "a very fair
prospect of an addition . . . of $25000 a year" to his income. That was the salary
of the president of the United States.[53]

Clay's questionable political strength in the North remained a problem,
though. In New York, the abolitionists had sufficient numbers in all counties
west of Albany to influence if not decide elections, and Thurlow Weed doubted
Clay's ability to surmount their opposition. Weed was also worried about the
Antimasons' disapproval of Clay, a situation mirroring that of Pennsylvania,
where Thaddeus Stevens and newly elected governor Joseph Ritner led that sizable faction of the Whig Party. Clay always doubted that Antimasonry would
become a broad or comprehensive political movement attracting support across
the Union, but in the quest for the 1840 nomination, it didn't have to be. The Antimasons' sway in Pennsylvania and key parts of New York were enough to
cause him a great deal of trouble.[54]

Clay has been described as trying to improve his standing with Upstate

New Yorkers by taking an anti-British stance in the wake of a violent Anglo-American clash along the Canadian border. In 1837, a small minority of Canadians staged an uprising against British colonial rule, and quick-tempered Americans got mixed up in it because it offered a chance to twist the British lion's tail. On December 29, 1837, the British captured and burned the American steamer *Caroline,* which had been supplying Canadian rebels across the Niagara, unfortunately staging the raid on the New York side of the river. The invasion of American soil was bad enough, but garish American accounts described the burning vessel as loaded with screaming victims while plunging over Niagara Falls. Actually, only one American was killed, and the *Caroline* had run aground well short of the falls.[55]

On January 4, 1838, Van Buren received the news while hosting a gathering of Whigs at the White House, Clay among them. The president pulled General Winfield Scott aside and quietly told him, "Blood has been shed; you must go with all speed to the Niagara frontier."[56] At first Clay took a measured tone and counseled against American anger. It was a stand consistent with his earlier attitudes.[57] Yet on January 9, he told the Senate that the British action was an "outrage. . . wholly unjustifiable, and not in the slightest degree palliated by any thing which preceded it."[58] His shift in this regard was probably his reaction to the shocking and erroneous stories of the *Caroline*'s fate rather than an opportunistic tactic to curry New York's favor.

Winfield Scott, who calmly and firmly managed the aftermath of the *Caroline* incident, gained luster in the Empire State because of these events. Thurlow Weed and William Seward actually turned to Scott as an alternative to Harrison. Similarly, Scott's deft handling of riled tempers in Maine during the Anglo-American quarrel over ownership of the Aroostook Valley further increased his standing and gradually made him another serious rival for northern support.

The gravest injury to Clay's candidacy resulted from a rebounding economy that caused state and local elections in the fall of 1838 to go badly for Whigs throughout the country, almost erasing their gains from the previous year. These results bewildered him. He scrutinized Ohio and wondered about the activities of the crafty Amos Kendall, who had been in Columbus a week prior to the election. "For what purpose?" Clay asked. "How easy was it for him to issue orders to his deputies and to render them effectual by appropriate means, throughout the State?"[59] Yet Whig failures could not be blamed exclusively on cunning politicos like Kendall or even the animosity of abolitionists. Something else was clearly wrong, and Whigs began to wonder if it was Henry Clay.

Clay's appeal stemmed from the belief that his prescriptions for the economy promised improvement. If the economy did not need his correctives,

Whigs feared that Clay would only unite Van Buren Democrats and push away undecided voters. When the Antimasons nominated Harrison on November 13, 1838, Clay's luck seemed at low ebb. The meeting was held in Philadelphia, and though it professed to reflect the will of Antimasons nationally (or at least the six states that sent delegations), it was most telling for what it revealed about Pennsylvania. That state's Antimasons had controlled the convention and were obviously committed to blocking Clay in order to promote Harrison.[60] That Antimasons now constituted a strong faction of Pennsylvania Whigs did not augur well for Clay's chances with the state party.

By that November, Whigs fretted that Clay, Harrison, and Van Buren might divide the Electoral College to throw the election into the House, and the situation looked so grim that Clay thought about withdrawing from the contest.[61] The small Whig victories in New York and Virginia provided the only bright news. In both states, Clay had been courting Democrats disaffected by Van Buren's hard money policies, the group that styled itself conservative Democrats and included the Virginian William Cabell Rives and New Yorker Nathaniel P. Tallmadge. Achieving a combination between those elements and Clay Whigs in Virginia and New York could set up an irresistible momentum that might put him over at the Whig convention.[62] In addition, Clay's New York operatives tried to charm Weed by supporting Weed lieutenant William Seward for governor. That maneuver was risky and ultimately proved fruitless when Weed remained skeptical about Clay's chances. Ironically, the Kentuckian's support of Seward further alienated New York Antimasons.[63]

Nor was this Clay's only problem in New York. Webster's supporters contrived a scheme of "triangular correspondence." Men pretending to be Clay's supporters in solid Clay counties wrote letters to others living in his firmest enclaves entreating hard work on his behalf because he was unexpectedly weak where they lived. Everyone was misled into believing that Clay was slipping in places where he was actually strong, an impression that stalled his momentum statewide. Evidence indicates that this technique was also applied in Ohio.[64]

Clay's plan to attract Virginia's conservative Democrats proved unproductive as well. The plan focused on supporting Rives in his 1839 Senate reelection bid, a strategy that required blocking his Whig opponent, John Tyler. Neither party nor personal loyalty figured into this scheme, for Clay simply needed Rives's people to secure the endorsement of the Virginia legislature; he otherwise liked and respected Tyler. Virginia's robust states' rights faction, dubbed the "Impracticables," despised Rives, and the result was a yearlong stalemate between the "Practicable" Whigs supporting the Democrat Rives and the Impracticable Whigs supporting Tyler. Bad feelings festered and grudges grew.

Clay was deprived of backing from Richmond when it would have most counted, and Tyler's candidacy badly divided Virginia's Whigs over Clay's plans, party allegiance, and states' rights.[65]

Most exasperating of all were persistent claims in the North and South that routinely misrepresented Clay's positions on slavery. "He ought to have seen," Calhoun said acidly, "that it was impossible for him to take middle ground on the abolition question."[66] On February 7, 1839, Clay delivered a major address to the Senate that was mainly an effort to quell charges from Calhoun's quarter that he was a closet abolitionist but also addressed accusations from Van Buren's followers and northern Whigs that he was too ardent a defender of slavery.[67] To placate the latter, Clay reprised his opinion that slavery was a moral bane on both chattel and master. He appreciated why abolitionists opposed it, he said, for they were understandably embracing an admirable moral imperative. These were not ideas of the moment, but views he had held for some time.[68]

He tempered this praise with an emphatic disapproval of abolitionists for their impracticality, something he also had stated before. They proposed to end slavery but had no plans for dealing with the economic devastation that emancipation would inflict on the nation, let alone planters, a cost he reckoned at more than a billion dollars.[69] In addition, the unfeasible aims of abolitionists provided no solution to the racial imbalance that would result in those parts of the South with large slave populations. Faced with losing the strictures of social control that slavery afforded, southerners would certainly choose secession over coerced emancipation, and from that, Clay concluded that abolitionism was fomenting disunion. In fact, Clay thought that the abolitionists' rejection of gradual compensated emancipation and colonization delayed positive steps rather than hastened them and endangered national harmony to the point of jeopardizing the country's existence.[70]

Clay's attitudes in 1839 represented a balance between moderate northern opinion, as represented by men like Abraham Lincoln, and the anxiety of southern Whigs. Clay's position helped to soothe the latter by reassuring them of his rightness on slavery. He continued to regard slavery as indefensible in the abstract, but he also insisted that it was anything but an abstraction. Given the choice, he would never have placed it "amongst us," but that choice was not available. Slavery was in place and required practical solutions, not idealistic visions.[71] Abolitionists who proclaimed that the Constitution should not stand in the way of abolishing slavery left Clay aghast: "If any citizens of the United States, who object to a particular part of the constitution, may elude and disregard it, other citizens, dissatisfied with other parts, have an equal right to violate them; and a universal nullification of the sacred instrument would be the necessary consequence."[72] Instead, Clay grounded his approach in the Jeffersonian tradition of trusting in time, a benign Providence, the "chapter of accidents," and adherence to the rule of law to solve the problem.[73]

Clay's attack on the abolitionists drew grudging praise from Calhoun. "I heard the Senator from Kentucky with pleasure," he admitted, but privately he muttered that Clay "had no choice" but to make such a speech. Calhoun assessed it as "far from being sound on many points" and doubted it would strengthen Clay's candidacy.[74] The sour South Carolinian was not alone, for even Clay's friends worried that the speech was too candid and would provide opportunities for both northern and southern extremists to dog his heels. He ran it by William C. Preston a few days before delivering it, and Preston warned him about its impolitic tone. Preston said that Clay emphatically responded, "I trust the sentiments and opinions are correct; I had rather be right than be President."[75]

The remark achieved wide currency and met with considerable acclaim. It seemed especially admirable when compared to the political cynicism of spoilsmen brazenly scrambling for office and patronage. Yet both friendly and critical biographers have doubted that Clay actually said it, or that if he did, he was sincere.[76] The suspicion that at best he fashioned the statement for political effect, however, does not seem to have occurred to his contemporaries. On the contrary, everyone at the time seems to have accepted it as something Clay would say. Many, in fact, firmly believed that he was too principled to be elected president, insisting that he would never abandon his core beliefs "to gain popularity. He will do right—let consequences be what they may."[77] His behavior in this slavery debate confirmed his earnestness. His stand did prove costly with abolitionists, a bloc that for a time had actually preferred Clay to Van Buren because of "the infamous pledge" Van Buren made in his inaugural about not touching slavery in the District of Columbia.[78] Yet these same men grew disenchanted with Clay when he refused to set an example by freeing his own slaves.[79] He was still the president of the American Colonization Society, whose plans to relocate freed slaves to Africa repelled abolitionists who thought them motivated by antiblack prejudice. Clay's February 7 speech completed the estrangement, but he had grown as impatient with abolitionists as they were with him.[80]

Northern Whigs held little truck with abolitionists, but Clay's description of slavery as a practical problem amounted to a defense of the status quo that discomfited them. On the other side, southern extremists objected to his denunciation of slavery as a moral stain. It would take more than twenty years of sectional strife and coalescing opinions before a man holding these deftly balanced attitudes could stand a chance of winning the presidency, and then it would crack the country apart. In that regard, Clay certainly knew that his expression of those opinions in 1839 carried considerable political risk.[81]

We might take him at his word, then, that he meant what he said, not only in his February 7 speech but also in his response to Preston's warning about it. He had repeatedly stated that the presidency "never possessed any charms in my sight which could induce me to seek it by unworthy means, or to desire it but as the spontaneous grant of those who might alone bestow it."[82] Just as he did not want to become president in the absence of popular approval, he did not want to become president by being wrong. That is what he told William C. Preston.

IN EARLY 1839, as Clay seemed in eclipse, his enemies sniped at him about matters great and small. When Thomas Hart Benton pushed for "graduation" (meaning the gradual lowering of federal land prices on tracts left unsold), the debate gave Clay's detractors a chance to revisit his criticism of squatters as a lawless rabble during the preemption debate of January 1838. The effort to depict Clay as an enemy of new states and their inhabitants brought Crittenden to his feet in defense of his friend. He insisted that Clay's remarks were being distorted, but Illinois senator Richard M. Young cited John Tipton as his authority. Possibly Clay did not remember denouncing squatters in such derogatory terms. He had been ill and irritated in early 1838, the debate was animated, and he confided to friends that he "very seldom read any Speech made in Congress—not even my own."[83] But the evidence fairly well proved that he had indeed called squatters a "lawless rabble." Francis Preston Blair's Washington *Globe* at the time noted that Clay used this phrase, and the *Congressional Globe* reported the exact words as having been spoken by him on January 27, 1838. Nevertheless Clay persisted in his denials. The charge, after all, could have seriously injured him in the West. He insisted that Richard Young had vindicated him, for Young had indeed exhibited an admirable sense of fairness by admitting that he might have inferred Clay's language from the tone of his remarks rather than their precise substance. Young's admission was a fairly weak reed, though, and the "lawless rabble" remark became another cudgel Clay himself had rashly put into the hands of his enemies.[84]

It was not the West but the North, and especially New York, that most worried him that spring. The spontaneous grant of approval Clay said he required might have been welling up there if he could believe encouraging reports from Upstate residents like Tallmadge and Peter Porter. But just to be sure, Clay decided to take a summer tour through the western portion of the state, where heavy Antimason and abolitionist numbers threatened to make him weakest. He was favoring a leg injured when a horse kicked him in late April, missing his kneecap by inches, and his determination to make the trip in any event reveals how important he thought it was. Because he wanted to avoid the unseemly appearance of electioneering, he worried about how the trip would be perceived, yet he was also genuinely excited about the chance to see the Great Lakes, Canada, and Niagara Falls, none of which he had ever visited. Best of all, his son James agreed to accompany him.[85]

In New York, Clay's resolve to avoid the appearance of electioneering vanished when he became aware that Winfield Scott was the favorite of influential upstate politicians like Thurlow Weed and William Seward. Clay promptly headed for Buffalo, the informal headquarters of both New York abolitionists and Antimasons. There he delivered a speech on July 17 in which he praised the region's natural splendor, thanked New Yorkers for supporting his stand against Britain in the War of 1812 (a way to make a passing allusion to the need for British atonement in the *Caroline* affair), and promoted the cause of protective tariffs by reminding the audience of his role in the Compromise of 1833 and how it had saved the Union. Pointing out the value of internal improvements to the state's commerce, he called for projects to be funded by the distribution of land revenues to the states.[86]

The speech was designed to present him as a logical and attractive alternative to Harrison, who was at best vague on specifics of any sort of program, and to Scott, hence Clay's allusion to his stand in 1812 and the recent British violations of the border as a way to blunt the praise lavished on Scott's calming of the *Caroline* incident. He also meant to appeal to New York's conservative Democrats, such as Tallmadge, and by showing himself in the heart of Antimasonry and abolitionism, to allay the reservation of these groups.

Clay and James continued their journey, passing through Lockport, Rochester, Canandaigua, and Oswego in the days that followed. In late July, they crossed the border to tour Montreal and Quebec, a side trip that allowed Vermont supporters to intercept him on his return and persuade him to visit Burlington. As Clay boarded the steamboat at Port Kent, he accidentally encountered William Seward, who barely concealed his discomfort over the chance meeting. Seward had been carefully avoiding Clay in the hope that he would not have to reveal his support of Winfield Scott, but the two were thrown together long enough for an awkward conversation on the ride down Lake Champlain. Seward told Clay that New York abolitionists would not abide him, but Clay politely disagreed. After all, he had evidence from his journey that New Yorkers of all stripes were more than enthusiastic about him.[87]

By the time he and James arrived at the United States Hotel in Saratoga— a holiday there being the ostensible reason for the entire trip—Clay was quite pleased with his undertaking, despite his uncomfortable conversation with Seward. Large, spirited crowds had turned out everywhere he went, and his arrival at Saratoga on August 9 was marked by a spectacular welcome. A sizable committee and numerous citizens met him on the outskirts of town. He climbed into a new barouche drawn by four gray horses and started for the resort as a band struck up a lively march. The parade that trailed him stretched for more than a mile. Artillery barked from the hills, cheering crowds choked the streets, and the large piazza in front of the hotel was filled with ladies, there by exclusive reservation. The day had started out stormy, but the sun was shining by the time John Taylor greeted Saratoga's famous guest. Clay responded with an hour-long speech that Philip Hone thought could have been shorter and less political, but the crowd shouted its approval and women wildly waved their handkerchiefs. That evening a glittering reception for him was attended by eight hundred people, many of them among the nation's most distinguished citizens.[88]

Clay's visit to Saratoga coincided with the zenith of the social season. "All the world is here," noted Hone. "Politicians and dandies; cabinet ministers and ministers of the gospel; office-holders and office-seekers; hum-buggers and humbugged; fortune-hunters and hunters of woodcock; anxious mothers and lovely daughters: the ruddy cheek mantling with saucy health, and the flickering lamp almost extinguished beneath the rude breath of dissipation."[89] Winfield Scott, whose star was "fast rising," was also at Saratoga that August, as was President Van Buren, staying on the same floor as Clay. Everyone was good-natured. The president sent Lucretia greetings, "as he always does," said Clay, and the two had a comical encounter in a packed corridor. "I hope I do not obstruct your way," said Van Buren. "Not here, certainly," laughed Clay.[90] He, Scott, and Van Buren all appeared in the grand saloon of the United States Hotel one evening to trade quips with one another while gallantly mingling with the "fair ladies."[91]

Clay's time at Saratoga was thus an unbroken series of pleasantries marred only briefly by James's taking a tumble from a horse that then stepped on his ankle. Clay assured Lucretia that James was only injured "a little" and was healing nicely, so even that event was a minor distraction.[92]

And then Thurlow Weed arrived. The Albany lobbyist had tried to get Horace Greeley to travel to Saratoga and convey New York's reservations about Clay's presidential aspirations, but the editor got only as far as Albany before the prospect of an unpleasant interview caused him to abort the errand. Weed then took on the job himself and had a meeting with Clay that he later remembered as "something of an ordeal."[93] He told Clay that he should withdraw from the contest because his considerable political liabilities jeopardized Whig success on both national and state levels. Too many voters, said Weed, were repelled by his support of the BUS, by his ties to the Masons, by his slaves at Ashland, by his recent attack on abolitionists. That very month, returns from Indiana, North Carolina, and Tennessee had signaled dismaying Whig defeats, clearly demonstrating that something was wrong. Weed said that it was Clay.

Clay countered that the cheering crowds throughout Upstate New York refuted this grim assessment. He even thought that abolitionists had warmed to him. He refused to withdraw, but now he at least knew clearly where the New York political establishment stood, a confirmation of his suspicions raised by his meeting with Seward, an encounter the governor made plain would not be repeated. Seward always claimed that his differences with Clay were only political, but the simple fact of the matter was that he did not like "Harry of the West."[94]

At the end of August, Clay concluded his tour with a visit to New York City, arriving from Newburgh aboard the steamer *James Madison* on August 21. A grand procession escorted him up Broadway to the steps of City Hall, where dignitaries greeted him with appropriate remarks. Clay replied with a speech that Philip Hone this time found suitably shorter, although the brevity was less a stylistic decision than a physical necessity, for Clay was nearly exhausted. He took rooms at the Astor House, and an endless parade of visitors began consuming his three-day stay while his evenings included trips to the theater. Audiences broke into spontaneous applause upon his appearance and spent performances hardly looking at the stage, instead craning their necks to glimpse him in his box. Weighing the official accolades and surveying the popular approbation, Philip Hone likened it to the treatment afforded Lafayette. Clay was sure to win the presidency, he thought, except that the Whigs were "the most untractable, unreliable party which ever stood up against corruption and bad government."[95]

Democrats viewed Clay's progress as warily as did New York's Whig leaders. James Gordon Bennett's *Herald* chronicled Clay's movements with a mixture of grudging admiration and mocking humor. Bennett was no admirer of Van Buren, and the *Herald* told of the enormous crowd that accompanied Clay to the wharf on Liberty Street for his departure. A man reportedly grabbed Clay's hand and squarely met his eye, exclaiming, "Look here, old Harry, God bless you!" Clay was used to this sort of thing, of course, but it was a stirring close to the trip. The man kept Clay's hand clasped and shouted, "If you don't beat that d—d Kinderhook poney, you're a gone sucker, and no mistake."[96]

Clay had no intention of being a gone sucker. That September, as he and James headed home through Baltimore and Philadelphia, Whigs in Virginia assembled in Staunton, endorsed him for president, and named Nathaniel P. Tallmadge as his running mate, putting Virginia in Clay's camp with an incentive for New York to follow. In addition, the meeting appointed Clay's friends James Barbour and Benjamin Watkins Leigh to the delegation for the Harrisburg convention.[97] More than ever, Seward's and Weed's warnings seemed easy to dismiss.

CLAY HAD HARDLY returned to Ashland before his candidacy began to unravel. In Indiana his enemies revived the Corrupt Bargain charge and insisted that only Harrison could take the state from Van Buren. Rumors in New York told of his quitting the race. He sent a chilly letter to Seward asking him to quash them, but he began to sense that he was facing an overwhelming tide. Supporters in North Carolina continued to pledge their support, but they concluded that Harrison was more "available," which was the word at the time to describe a candidate as electable. Continuing Whig reverses in state contests depressed him. "The elections everywhere this year," he said with uncharacteristic melancholy, "indicate unexpected success on the part of the Administration."[98]

In one sense, Clay was quite correct to characterize Democrat victories as unexpected, though his discernment was not evident at the time. The economic recovery that had been dimming his chances since 1838 turned out to be unsustainable in the face of financial setbacks overseas, and when British lenders called loans in October 1839, more than eight hundred American banks were forced to suspend specie payments. The depression that ensued ran even deeper than the one caused by the Panic of 1837, but its consequences also spread throughout the country more slowly. Not until the following spring and summer did it become apparent that economic woes had returned with a vengeance, and by then the Whigs had chosen their nominee. Working from the erroneous belief that the economy was sound, they concluded that Clay could not win, unaware of the renewed financial catastrophe that would engulf Van Buren and finally do him in. Anyone could have been elected over Martin Van Buren in 1840.[99]

That "anyone" was not to be Clay, however. In the fall of 1839, as the economic downturn was occurring but not yet being felt, Weed and Seward were determined to nominate Winfield Scott. The string of Whig defeats beginning in the fall of 1838 and continuing through 1839 convinced them that Harrison was no better than Clay, because Harrison had been the front-runner when Democrats rebounded. Harrison tried to counter this perception by highlighting his attractiveness with wavering Democrats, Antimasons, and legions of veterans. He was also careful not to antagonize anyone. He assured Clay that he never viewed Clay's trip through Ohio as poaching on his turf, and he claimed to be embarrassed that he was contending against Clay for the nomination, a situation he oddly described as having been forced on him by "fate." Harrison's noncommittal stance did not deceive Clay. He was instead more convinced than ever that Harrison was pursuing and fully expected to receive the nomination.[100]

Events in Pennsylvania also took a troubling turn for Clay that fall. A group of former Antimasons, now Whigs, led by Thaddeus Stevens, withdrew from the state Whig convention over Clay's candidacy and under the disingenuous banner of "Harmony" endorsed Harrison. Stevens's motives were partly mercenary: he hoped for a cabinet post in a Harrison administration. Born into poverty, Stevens had clawed his way to affluence with a relentless program of self-promotion. He wore an unsightly wig that accentuated his bald pate and had an awkward gait because of a clubfoot. Such defects in any other man would have stirred pity, but Thaddeus Stevens was so exceedingly disagreeable that he rarely aroused compassion. Nobody could recall his ever smiling. Though not a delegate to the national convention in Harrisburg, Stevens would control those from Pennsylvania who were committed to Harrison. Thurlow Weed had hopes that the two Pennsylvania delegations, one for Clay and the other for Harrison, would cancel each other out and boost Winfield Scott's chances as a compromise alternative.[101]

OFFICIALLY LABELED THE Democratic Whig National Convention, the gathering opened proceedings at Harrisburg on December 4, 1839, in the Old Zion Lutheran Church on Fourth Street. It was a historic assemblage, for it would actually nominate a presidential candidate rather than ratify a decision already made somewhere else. As a consequence, a great deal of uncharted ground lay before the delegates, and the prize was accordingly destined to fall to those who were most organized and able to map their way. As much as Clay had anything resembling an organization, it was based on promoting the American System. Clay supporters recruited followers based on their adherence to that program and their commitment to its advancement. That tie was supposed to bind them to Henry Clay, the American System's most constant advocate, making issues the dominant theme of the campaign. Moreover, Clay's strategy appealed to state and local leaders, confident that the rank and file would follow.

Yet it was a dubious political approach in 1839. With the exception of Clay's New York tour the previous summer, his calls to action went out to lieutenants in the Whig leadership. Enthusiasm at the grass roots was presumably just supposed to happen, like the currents of a river cutting a new channel according to the laws of nature. In part this certainty arose from Clay's belief that sensible people would find his program sensible, but it was also a result of his distaste for electioneering, something he briefly overcame that summer, but only after much soul-searching, after protests that he was not really campaigning, and finally after the realization of a compelling need to make his case with the people, at least in Upstate New York. Clay's reluctance gave the impression that he was aloof and lacked the common touch at a time when Jacksonian Democrats had made the common touch an essential part of popular politics.

It was not true, of course, that Clay was aloof. Rather, he represented a different time and a more sedate sort of election politics. He was never able to understand, in any case, how it was possible for men like Weed to say that the people did not want him, when clearly the people were keen about him. It was rather the state leadership who opposed him, and he thought it incredible, exasperating, and undemocratic that while "eight or nine tenths of the Whigs" in New York preferred him, Weed and his ilk "preferred to make a nomination in conformity with the wishes of the one or two tenths."[102]

Even if men like Weed had found Clay politically appealing (and they did not), they would have regarded him as damaged goods because they did not believe in much of anything beyond victory at the polls. Clay's approach had already failed in 1832. A campaign based on issues had revealed itself to be nothing more than a sure way to lose elections.[103] Weed could claim that he wanted to reject Clay to spare him the "mortification" of certain defeat, but he was really more interested in not losing the opportunity for certain victory against an unpopular president. Like Stevens, Weed was not a delegate, but also like Stevens, he attended sessions in Harrisburg as a ubiquitous presence. He tirelessly promoted Winfield Scott, just as Stevens did William Henry Harrison. Given a level playing field, these two, acting too clever by half, could have maneuvered themselves and their champions out of the picture. Yet they made sure the field was anything but level, and each in a different way exerted considerable control through disciplined organizations. The evidence of their cunning was their ability to block Clay, whose candidacy was actually quite hardy when the gavel first came down and the convention began establishing its rules.

Clay's candidacy was strongest, but it was also beset by difficulties. His support was most solid in the South, but southerners were underrepresented in the convention because Georgia, South Carolina, and Tennessee did not send delegations, for the reasons that Clay had feared, and the delegate from Arkansas was too late in arriving.[104] Clay's most serious problem, though, arose from the torpor of his operatives, who let the convention spin away from them by agreeing to incredibly damaging compromises and rules. Resolving Pennsylvania's confused situation resulted in an agreement that nullified Clay's significant minority support in the Keystone State. The Chambersburg (Clay) delegation was combined with the more numerous "Harmony" (Harrison) delegation, making the latter the majority and giving Thaddeus Stevens control of Pennsylvania's vote.

But the method of balloting that the convention adopted dealt Clay's chances the worst blow. Harrison delegates from Massachusetts—Webster's former but no less spiteful partisans were at work—cooperated with Pennsylvanian Charles Penrose (Stevens's lieutenant) to install what amounted to a unit rule for counting state ballots. Employing a convoluted process of secret votes polled through committees, a state's majority would count as a winner-take-all result. The procedure instantly made Clay's numerous minority votes in New York, Pennsylvania, and Ohio immaterial, votes that otherwise would have helped advance him toward the nomination in a straightforward poll. Clay supporters did not realize how they had been bested until it was too late, and when Clay's cousin Cassius Clay tried before the decisive final ballot to have all the delegates polled and Maryland supporter Reverdy Johnson tried to restore individual balloting, they were summarily slammed down. Thomas Hart Benton later called these shrewd maneuvers by Weed, Stevens, and others a mixture of "algebra and alchemy" and correctly concluded that they had meant the "political death of Mr. Clay."[105]

Yet not right away. Clay even led on the first ballot with 103 votes to Harrison's 91 and Scott's 57, but that plurality was as close as he ever got to the majority of 128 necessary for the nomination. Weed immediately went to work to seize the momentum by persuading anyone who would listen that Clay's slender numbers revealed he could not win the general election. He managed to peel Connecticut away from Clay and to end a deadlock in the Michigan delegation, throwing both states into Scott's column. The result was that Clay slipped on the second ballot to 95 while Scott's numbers increased to 68. Harrison held steady at 91. Thaddeus Stevens then made his move. Scott's momentum could have been decisive at this point, and Weed was preparing to approach the Virginia delegation to persuade it to make the switch from Clay. But Stevens was just as diligent and even more devious than Weed. The grim Pennsylvanian limped frowning among the delegates, seemingly without purpose, but his object was to drop a piece of paper, seemingly by accident, in the midst of the Virginians, who promptly examined it. The document shocked them. It was a letter from Winfield Scott to New Yorker Francis Granger currying favor with New York antislavery forces. Nobody ever discovered how Stevens came by the letter, but the Virginians immediately announced that they would never support Scott, which meant an ebbing Clay would make Harrison the nominee.[106]

Virginia's declaration in fact broke the dam. Weed was stunned at first, but he quickly realized that without the South, Scott didn't stand a chance. He moved just as quickly to swing the Scott votes he controlled into line with Harrison to prevent Clay from scooping them up. The proverbial bandwagon now came into play as more and more Scott delegates scrambled aboard for Harrison. Even a handful of Clay supporters joined them. The third and final ballot gave Harrison the nomination with 148 votes, 20 more than he needed. Clay had dropped to 90, and poor Scott, who would never learn his lesson about writing foolish letters, stood at a mere 16. While the manipulations of northerners like Weed and Stevens were the most apparent causes of Clay's defeat, it was ironically southerners who really lost him the nomination: those who would have voted for him didn't show up, and those who did show up made the avowal that wrecked Scott, whose numbers went to Harrison.[107]

The choice of Harrison flabbergasted those southerners, and Clay stalwarts, regardless of section, were livid over what they regarded as a contemptible intrigue. Although the choice was eventually unanimous, thanks in large part to Henry Clay, Thurlow Weed nervously surveyed Clay's angry supporters and gauged the unity as "anything but cordial."[108] The convention now strained to conciliate southerners and Clay's friends by selecting a southerner who was also a friend of Clay's for the vice presidency. The ballot nominating Harrison occurred near midnight on Friday, December 6, and urgent negotiations by the Weed-Stevens organizations to complete the ticket continued into the wee hours of Saturday. Yet finding an avowed Clay supporter who was willing to run with Harrison proved easier said than done. Reverdy Johnson announced that neither he nor John M. Clayton, who was not at Harrisburg, would accept. Benjamin Watkins Leigh also refused. Thurlow Weed was possibly telling the truth that the inability to find a Clay southerner finally compelled the choice of at least some southerner willing to accept, and that turned out to be John Tyler. Many believed at the time that Tyler was a Clay southerner, for he had been committed to Clay during the convention and was described by Greeley as weeping over his defeat. Whether Tyler cried that Friday night or not, he cheerfully and eagerly accepted the convention's nearly unanimous nomination the next day. Leigh announced that Virginia would refrain from voting for one of its own members. Possibly the Old Dominion's delegation did act from a sense of "delicacy," as Leigh tactfully explained.[109]

The convention adjourned without declaring any fixed principles, an omission that, along with their issueless but appealing nominee, contributed to the myth that the Whigs did not actually stand for anything. Nobody seems to have given any additional thought to the selection of John Tyler. His task was merely "to be," that is to say, to balance the ticket and, as some thought, to placate Clay by the simple fact of being placed on it. The Virginia delegation's behavior, however, was an early warning sign. Tyler was an honorable man, but his mild demeanor disguised obstinacy and pride, which his fellow Virginians had glimpsed before. His resignation in 1836 over the Expunging Resolution struck some as grandstanding, and it had made Benjamin Watkins Leigh appear indecisive. The protracted contest with Rives over the Senate seat had also created ill will. Yet, as the delegates finished up at Harrisburg, nobody seemed to have given any additional thoughts, cheerful or foreboding, to the selection of John Tyler.[110]

When it was all over, Clay certainly had a right to be bitter, because his friends' inactivity as much as his enemies' machinations had cost him the nomination. More than three decades later, Henry A. Wise described Clay's reaction to the selection of Harrison in colorful but extremely unflattering terms. Wise said that Clay on the evening of December 6 had been drinking heavily and upon hearing the news from Harrisburg exploded into a drunken, profane rage. Stalking back and forth, he reportedly shouted, "My friends are not worth the powder and shot it would take to kill them!" Wise said that he and friends had tried to calm Clay, but he would not be stopped: "It is a diabolical intrigue, I know now, which has betrayed me. I am the most unfortunate man in the history of parties: always run by my friends when sure to be defeated, and now betrayed for a nomination when I, or anyone, would be sure of an election." Wise also recalled that from that moment until February 1844, Clay "was excessively intemperate in his habits, and more intemperate in exacerbation of temper and in his political conduct." Wise cited an alleged confrontation with Winfield Scott at a reception in Boulanger's restaurant as well as Clay's irritable conduct in the Senate to indicate that in disappointment, the Kentuckian had become a mean drunk.[111]

Wise's account and reproachful observations did not appear until 1872, and though they contained references to others witnessing Clay's embarrassing behavior, Wise was the only person ever to recall it. It soon became part of the Clay lore, however. In 1887, Lucius P. Little published a lengthy and admiring biography of Kentuckian Ben Hardin, a political opponent of Clay's, that drew freely on the reminiscences of Wise and other Clay adversaries. John Pope, for example, was said to have been relieved by the result at Harrisburg because of Clay's overweening ambition. "We should have witnessed in America all the extravagancies of the Bonaparte dynasty, and hazarded all the calamities it brought upon France," Pope was alleged to have said, leaving one to wonder what on earth he was talking about. Lucius Little also elaborated on Clay's encounter with Scott that was supposed to have occurred at a Washington banquet Scott gave for Harrison after the Harrisburg convention. "I am happy to meet you, Mr. Clay," Scott said with his hand extended. "I'll be d—d if you are, General Scott," Clay supposedly replied. Recall that the previous summer they had both been at Saratoga at the United States Hotel. At the time, Clay knew that Weed and Seward were supporting Scott but nevertheless remained on jovial terms with him.[112]

Clay's biographers have always repeated these anecdotes, sometimes with the caveat that Wise became Clay's unswerving foe in the early 1840s. One of Tyler's biographers, however, discounted much of what Wise said as having been supplied "by a vivid imagination," and the editors of Clay's papers simply dismiss the Virginian's account as a fabrication.[113] Too often these stories have been given too much credence. Not until their appearance in the 1870s and 1880s did a single report describe Clay's response to the Harrisburg convention in this way. At the time, anti-Clay newspapers only said, also without evidence, that he was disappointed over being "politically dead" or lampooned his generous replies to Whig testimonials.[114]

The documentary evidence supplies a completely different picture. Weeks before Whigs gathered at Harrisburg, Clay on November 20, 1839, supplied Kentucky delegates to the convention with a letter in which he said that if he were not chosen, "the nomination will have my best wishes, and receive my cordial support." Leslie Combs read this letter to the convention on December 7, and it did much to relieve a tense situation. In addition, Clay partisan Reverdy Johnson, angry about the manipulations of Weed and Stevens but obeying Clay's call for unity, proposed that the Harrison and Tyler nominations be made unanimous.[115] Clay wrote to his son Thomas within days of Harrison's nomination to say that "I should be sorry that you or any of my friends or connexions should display any irritation or dissatisfaction about it." He told Henry Jr. exactly the same thing.[116] When Whig delegates from eighteen of the twenty-two states at the convention attended a testimonial dinner for Clay at Brown's Hotel in Washington on December 11, 1839, twenty-four speakers praised him for his high-mindedness, and he responded with a glowing testimonial to Harrison. Clay insisted that the upcoming election was not about himself or Webster or Scott. "Vote heartily," he told them, "vote heartily, as I shall, for the nomination which has been made." He concluded to lusty applause that "not men, but principles, are our rules of action."[117] Harrison later thanked him for "the magnanimity of your conduct towards me in relation to the nomination for the Presidency."[118]

In addition to these public and private statements, Clay actively campaigned for the ticket by delivering almost a dozen major addresses in 1840, most notably during a tour in Virginia, a large rally at Baltimore, and a visit to

Nashville, Tennessee. To those who wavered and found little good in Harrison's candidacy, Clay was insistent that "with Harrison there is hope, much hope, with V. Buren there is no hope whatever."[119]

Rather than nursing a grudge, he felt like "a free man, at liberty to pursue my own inclinations, and unembarrassed by 10 or 12 months of turmoil." At least part of him apparently agreed with the correspondent who also found a silver lining in the failed bid for the nomination by observing that to contend for the presidency, "a man has to give up his own self respect or every hour give offense to some pedagogue that stands over him with uplifted rod."[120]

DEMOCRATS GATHERED AT Baltimore and halfheartedly nominated Van Buren for another run, despite his connection to the country's financial distress, again in full sway by early 1839. They were accustomed to Jackson's popularity winning the White House, even for his successor, and they now faced the prospect of having the tactic turned on them.[121]

The Whigs called the president "Martin Van Ruin" and set about making their aging nominee into a reasonable Whig facsimile of Old Hickory. They referred to Harrison as "Tippecanoe" or "Old Tip" to revive memories of his victory at Prophetstown on Tippecanoe Creek in 1811. He insisted that he was still strong and vigorous. Throughout the campaign, he repeated, as if by rote, that his "bodily health" was "actually better than it has been for ten years."[122]

Nationally, the lack of a platform helped Whigs avoid inconvenient pledges that might have alienated this or that faction within the party. They instead concentrated on elevating Old Tip to the presidency with songs and symbols. Shortly after the Harrisburg convention, a dim-witted Democrat journalist accidentally gave them the most potent of those symbols. Asked by a disappointed Clay supporter how to persuade Harrison to withdraw in Clay's favor, the reporter scoffed that Harrison would be content with a pension, a log cabin, and a barrel of hard cider.[123]

Within weeks, Whigs had merrily adopted the hard cider barrel and rude log cabin as badges of honor. On January 20, 1840, a couple of enterprising Pennsylvanians came up with the idea of projecting a large transparency on a wall. The picture purported to show Harrison's cabin complete with coonskin cup and cider barrel. Armed with these rousing symbols, the campaign took on the air of a religious revival.[124] Harrison was peddled as the plain but virtuous Ohio farmer, reluctant but willing to answer his country's call and toss out crooked Democrat spoilsmen. Of course, candidate Harrison bore little resemblance to the real Harrison, who was not of lowly birth but hailed from a prominent Virginia family. He did not live in humble poverty, did not sleep in a one-room log cabin, and preferred whiskey to hard cider. In fact, putting Harrison over as a man of modest origins was a remarkable feat. Far from residing in a simple log cabin, he lived in a sixteen-room mansion on a farm that stretched across three thousand acres near North Bend, Ohio.

Even more remarkably, Whigs distorted the public's perception of Martin Van Buren. His youth had been truly impoverished, but Whigs branded him a pompous blue blood. They called him "Sweet Sandy Whiskers," claiming that he perfumed his muttonchops, wore corsets, and preferred sissified French cuisine over hearty American fare. Worst of all, they erroneously reported him as turning the White House into an opulent palace at public expense. Old Tip wore simple homespun and swigged hard cider, Whigs boasted, while Little Van donned ruffled shirts and sipped champagne, a frivolous fop, a contemptible squirt.[125]

Enormous Whig rallies and long lines of Whigs marched while chanting slogans emphasizing the failure of Van Buren's financial policies. Entrepreneurs hawked log cabin symbolism in every way imaginable. Yet by far the most memorable device of the campaign was the Whig slogan "Tippecanoe and Tyler Too," which combined Harrison's bona fides as a military hero with alliteration on his running mate's name, a phrase that the aristocratic Philip Hone sniffed provided "rhyme, but no reason."[126] Inspired by the campaign's official beverage, cider-guzzling Whigs howled the slogan as they pushed large balls through towns and villages to represent the snowballing majority for Harrison. Such hogwash seemed to substitute for serious discussion, and ever since, most historians have insisted that hullabaloo and flummery dominated the 1840 campaign.

Democrats and Whigs, however, held different beliefs and promoted different positions, and the people were quite aware of those differences and the choices available to them. Whigs existed for other reasons than opposing Andrew Jackson, and despite their diversity they developed a coherent political philosophy and became a rational ideological movement. True enough, differences among party members presented a bundle of contradictions: the party was a home for Masons (like Clay) and Antimasons (like Thaddeus Stevens), supporters of the tariff, proponents of free trade, planters with slaves, northern abolitionists, national bank advocates, national bank opponents, devotees of the American System, foes of the American System. Yet Democrats presented just as many contradictions. Jacksonians claimed to exalt individual liberty and ferociously condemned anything that smacked of "privilege," but they enforced party discipline by punishing individualism and rewarding conformity with a patronage system that nurtured the very privilege they decried. They had, grumbled Clay, "without the smallest pretense of right to the denomination, erroneously assumed the name of Democrats, and . . . under color of that name, they have made rapid and fearful progress in consolidating an elective monarchy." They had denounced the BUS while trying to create a government bank and had denounced internal improvements while funding expensive projects under other labels. In fact, Jacksonians were not opposed to a national bank but were specifically opposed to Biddle's bank because it posed as a huge pool of patronage beyond their control. The attitude, as one economic historian has noted, threw them into wild inconsistencies.[127]

Though Democrats claimed to represent the common people and characterized the Whigs as elites, both parties attracted Americans from all classes and sections. The widely diverse membership was healthy because it encouraged compromise and kept factions from adopting extreme positions or pushing for drastic measures. Party strength throughout the nation also delayed the formation of sectional political blocs, such as an inflexible southern one defending slavery or a northern one assaulting it, though that day was coming. For the time being, most Democrats and Whigs avoided the slavery controversy because it divided their northern and southern wings and jeopardized their chances in national elections. When Calhoun notably abandoned this prudence to adopt a take-no-prisoners approach in late 1838, he offered a revealing glimpse of Democrat objections to other aspects of the Whig program. For example, Democrat hostility to internal improvements stemmed as much from the desire to protect slavery as from constitutional scruples. At a time when southerners were committed to preserving the status quo, an economy transformed by a market revolution promised diversity and all the unwelcome changes that came with it. In addition, a government capable of central planning would also have the power in theory to abolish slavery.[128]

Americans were conscious of the differences between the parties, even when those differences took the form of general abstractions. Because Democrats said that the native intelligence of good, sturdy Americans would embrace and protect liberty as a natural exercise, they saw publicly funded schools as unnecessary. Whigs believed that ignorance was the path to tyranny and that only an educated citizenry could preserve its liberty. Democrats were suspicious of social reformers; Whigs promoted moral reform, especially temperance, despite the hard cider symbolism of 1840. Moreover, Whigs saw society as naturally harmonious, regarded community as an engine of progress, and believed government should promote economic growth and national development, while Democrats fiercely protected states' rights and insisted on keeping federal involvement in social and economic matters at the barest minimum. As Van Buren had shown in response to the panic, Democrats believed that allowing matters to sort themselves out was the best way to handle economic distress. Whigs wanted the government to establish a national bank to stabilize the currency, wanted protective tariffs to promote American industry, wanted internal improvements to facilitate American commerce. Democrats wanted an expanding, expansive "agricultural empire" and consequently pushed for Texas annexation and later fought a war to acquire California. Whigs wanted economic improvement through internal improvements and recoiled from expansionism. Clay thought the country was large enough and should focus on developing what it had, especially since acquiring new territory always caused harmful arguments over slavery. Webster even envisioned a partitioning of North America into three republics, with the United States controlling the East, Texas the Southwest, and California the West.[129]

Whigs were a motley bunch, but they did have a vision for the country that they expressed in concrete terms. Democrats wrote a platform at the Baltimore convention, but their positions more resembled a bundle of attitudes than they did a consistent ideology. They exalted local control of affairs and sought to preserve it through strict party loyalty. The Whigs did not care for political parties and formed one only because, as Clay pointed out, it proved impossible to win elections without it. Political parties "can only . . . be extinguished," he conceded, "by extinguishing their cause, free Government, a free press, and freedom of opinion."[130]

On the national stage, Clay himself addressed specifics of the Whig agenda during his New York tour in the summer of 1839 and then during his campaign speeches for Harrison in early 1840. The party did not believe it could elect Henry Clay in 1840, but that did not mean it did not stand for anything. As a first principle, Whigs were committed to ending petty and palpable corruptions in government institutionalized by the Spoils System and by disgraceful political tactics to keep incumbents in power. Clay thought such practices simply "demoralizing."

> Misrepresentation, falsehood, bribery, forgery, perjury, corruption of the Ballot boxes, have all been established upon members of that [Democrat] party. When one party employs such means, sooner or later, in self defense and from necessity, the other party will be tempted to appeal to the same arts. And the corruption of the whole mass will quickly follow. Then, farewell to Liberty.[131]

For Whigs, protecting American liberty was a paramount obligation and just as important as repairing the economy. By running for office on a party ticket, a candidate necessarily pledged to carry out the party's program if elected. The people rightly expected it. The people would have known precisely what they were getting with Henry Clay. At the time of the Harrisburg convention, however, William Henry Harrison's most appealing feature for shrewd Whig politicos was that his views on issues were at best vaguely apprehended. He was attractive precisely because he had no issues to harm him and no enemies to assail him. But he too understood his responsibility to stand with the people who worked for his election and at least not block their way after victory. "I have made promises of great *amendments* in the administration of public affairs," Tom Corwin declared, "& I do not wish to be made out a liar & fool both, by the history of the first six months of the *new era.*"[132]

As Whigs marched on the campaign trail in 1840, they had assurances from Harrison himself that in victory he would not frustrate them, would not make them appear to be liars and fools. He did not come out explicitly for a new national bank, for instance, but he made clear that if Congress felt one was needed, he would not stand in the way.[133] It was a reassuring endorsement of legislative supremacy, another first principle for Whigs, and such statements by Harrison comforted Clay and his friends.

Nobody seems to have given much thought to John Tyler's opinions on the matter.

CHAPTER ELEVEN

Three Campaigns

THERE IS AN old saying that troubles come in threes. In the years following Clay's disappointment at the Harrisburg convention, he would be a living illustration of it. During that time, he waged three campaigns, all interconnected but each having different objectives. One was the immediate effort to get Harrison elected. Concurrent with that effort was Clay's own bid to follow Harrison in the presidency in 1844. He planned to begin staking his claim for Whig loyalty with selfless and energetic exertions for the party and Old Tip. He counted on Harrison's pledge that he would serve only one term and looked beyond the old man to other possible rivals.[1]

The third campaign was economic, and involved reviving the national bank to stabilize the currency, sustaining a protective tariff to promote industry, and distributing land revenues to the states that in turn would be used to fund internal improvements. Clay was reasonably confident that the realization of the Whig program would be relatively easy. He was certain that he could persuade Whig majorities in Congress to pass it, and that he could rely on Harrison's assurance of executive passivity to sign it into law.

The third campaign, though, proved the adage about troubles coming in threes. A development that shocked the country was the cause, although Clay himself had both dreaded and expected its occurrence. No foresight or preemptive action could have prevented what happened—the devastation of the Whig program and the near destruction of the party—and nothing but Clay's abject surrender to circumstance would have prevented many from settling on him almost all the blame for what happened. Yet the die setting up the debacle had been cast by other hands in another place long before. It had been cast at Harrisburg by men who had wanted to win the election at all costs. When it all went wrong, it was easier to blame Clay.

CLAY AND HIS slave Charles Dupuy moved into Mrs. Denny's boardinghouse on Third Street for the first session of the Twenty-sixth Congress, but later moved to rooms at Mrs. Arguelles's.[2] Even with the glowing accolades of the Brown's Hotel banquet still in his ears, Clay was uncharacteristically melancholy that winter. He had a nagging cold, and the weather was bitter as an occluded front dropped enormous amounts of snow on the capital. John had traveled to Missouri and wound up "entirely dissatisfied with it," as Clay had expected, but now as John headed back to Ashland "in the dead of winter," Clay was uneasy until he knew that the boy had reached home. "This is the last winter that I shall be separated from you, whilst we both live," he promised Lucretia, and likely he meant it, at the time.[3]

In Washington, drafty rooms resisted the efforts of even the most cheerful fires to warm them, and going anywhere outdoors became an exasperating ordeal. Such winters made "small folks still smaller," said one Virginian. "It chills the blood and makes us irritable which makes us disagreeable to others as well as ourselves." Little wonder then that Clay's work in the Senate was marked by increasing irritability. The House of Representatives reminded Clay's grandson Martin Duralde "of a parcel of schoolboys," but Clay had grown weary of many colleagues in the upper chamber as well, often finding them dim or venal, sometimes both. The discovery that members were abusing their mileage allowance calculations and engaging in small corruptions with the franking privilege and with printing, fuel, and stationery allowances appalled Clay. He promoted efforts to clean this up by limiting benefits such as the stationery allowance to $20.[4]

But it was the larger and recurring issues that summoned his fiercest responses. In mid-January, Democrats led by New Yorker Silas Wright, the chairman of the Senate Finance Committee, brought up the Subtreasury bill for debate yet again. Clay was on fairly civil terms with Wright, but he regarded these dogs with their Subtreasury bone increasingly tedious, and he now so vehemently clashed with the finance chair that it briefly brought the Senate to a standstill. Wright was overmatched. "His voice is not melodious," admitted a friendly description, "though after listening to it a short time it becomes not unpleasing." It was hardly a qualification for going into verbal battle with Henry Clay. He also squabbled with Mississippi senator Robert Walker—"little Walker," in Clay's estimation—whom he reported to Lucretia that he had "scornfully repelled. My friends said that I annihilated him."[5]

Calhoun was also involved in this debate, though, and that spelled trouble. Calhoun had hoped that Clay or Webster would carp about Harrison's nomination in order to divide the Whigs and leave an opening for him to run, but Whig unity had forced the South Carolinian to continue his rapprochement with Van

Buren. He attended the president's New Year's Day reception at the White House, where the two whispered plans for a private meeting. The result was the revival of the president's darling, the Subtreasury, this time with Calhoun's influential support. Clay wearily went unto the breach. He voiced the same objections and advanced the same arguments he had spoken in the seemingly countless previous debates on this question, but Van Buren was obviously determined to have this victory, Pyrrhic though it might be. As the bill assumed the shape of an idée fixe, at least for the Democrats supporting it, Clay angrily deduced that he was fighting a determination to continue voting on this measure until Congress got it right, at least by the administration's lights. Calhoun's trimming and turning especially annoyed him, and the Democrat press complained that Clay repeatedly singled out the South Carolinian as "the special object of his wrath this winter."[6]

Clay lost his temper as he hoarsely ran through the now familiar litany of Jacksonian transgressions, including the Spoils System that corrupted the public service and the excessive executive authority that threatened to make the president a despot. Van Buren had perpetuated these ills, Clay growled, and his cronies had sullied government while wrecking the economy. There was, he shouted, "a day of reckoning at hand."[7]

On January 23, 1840, Van Buren finally saw his Subtreasury plan pass the Senate with a slim six-vote majority, thanks to his alliance with Calhoun. The work to secure passage in the House would be more difficult and consume six additional months of debate and maneuver, but this latest fight only made Clay more determined to put aside his distaste for campaigning and help elect Harrison. He exhorted Whigs to "tell your constituents of the nomination—of a bleeding Constitution—of the Executive power against which we are waging a war of extermination—of executive machinery and executive favor—of one President nominating his successor and that successor his successor. Tell them to put forth all the energies they possess to relieve the land from the curse which rests upon it."[8]

In February, as Clay prepared for a campaign trip to Richmond, he wrote to Henry Jr., who had taken his father's loss of the Harrisburg nomination particularly hard. Henry Jr. looked at the whole world somberly, an inescapable consequence of his temperament, but Clay was happy that Julia Prather, pretty, clever, and lighthearted, had found his son. She tempered his brown studies and was in the process of filling his life with little Clays, though that too was cause for concern because childbearing had not been easy for her, with two daughters, Matilda and Martha, dying in infancy. They were expecting a new arrival any day, though, and Clay was eager for news. Soon he learned that Thomas Julian Clay (always "Tommy" to the family) had come into the world.[9]

Days later, however, another letter arrived from Henry with the terrible news that Julia was dead. Complications from Tommy's birth were the cause. Clay spent a sleepless night before writing to his son the next morning—the news "was so sudden and appalling," he said—and the distraught tone of Henry Jr.'s letter that revealed a man quite overwhelmed by grief worried him. Clay gently reminded his son that Julia had left him "tender & responsible duties to perform towards the children of your mutual love and affection." Clay could not help but remember in vivid detail the wretchedness of that cruel December five years earlier when Anne had died, and in the same way as Julia, her fate also marking a time both of birth and of death. "I beg therefore, on my account, as well as that of my dear Grand children," Clay said to his shattered boy, "you will take care of yourself."[10]

CLAY'S HEART WAS out of the Richmond trip, but so many extensive arrangements had been made that he decided to go.[11] He left for Richmond with Henry A. Wise, who was ailing with a severe sore throat that made speaking difficult. A large crowd awaited their arrival at the city's railroad depot and escorted them to the Powhattan House, where Benjamin Watkins Leigh introduced him to a gathered throng. People had come from all over the state for the Whig rally, some even braving horrid roads. William Bolling, a friend from Clay's youth, was among them. Clay was consoled by these companions, and Bolling found his old friend at Leigh's residence for tea. Frank Brooke was there too, and the group talked well into the night before returning to the Powhattan. In many ways it was just what Clay needed, and he was soon glad that he had made the trip.[12] The next day, a grand dinner was held in honor of their famous guest, an event touted as "the greatest ever given in Richmond, or perhaps in the United States" and so largely attended that it had to be held in an enormous warehouse. William Bolling came in through the door set aside for invited guests and thus managed to sit near Clay and hear "the *greatest Orator,* & the *greatest man & patriot* now living in these United States."[13]

Clay used this speech to enlarge the revision of his early history for current political circumstances, consciously adding to the creation of the boy who never was, an image of "a lank, lean youth of twenty, with sandy hair and ruddy complexion, fatherless, homeless, friendless, and penniless" who had left Richmond those many years ago "to seek his fortune in the 'far West.'"[14] The audience was both captured by the fiction and captivated by his telling of it, including those whose personal recollections of young Clay, even if dim, were most certainly and decidedly different from this new account. It did not matter. The huge gathering was pin-drop silent, which made the frequent eruptions of thunderous applause echoing through the warehouse all the more deafening.[15]

John Tyler was there, arriving after everyone had already begun eating, but he was immediately introduced by Benjamin Watkins Leigh and spoke very briefly, insisting that he had merely come to honor Clay, whom he lavishly praised. Interestingly, though, "he avoided political allusions as improper in consideration of his position at this time."[16]

The journey coming so close to the news of Julia's death put Clay in a reflective frame of mind, and his swing through Hanover County on the way back to Washington only increased his pensiveness. The stop at the Slashes was bittersweet. He had not been there for almost fifty years, and he found everything so changed as to be unrecognizable. His maternal grandparents' and his father's graves were not only without markers but also under a wheat field. A row of cherry trees partly remained, but he noted that like him, they were aged and frail. The hickory tree that had produced "the finest fruit of that kind which I ever tasted" was down and rotting. The house once called Clay's Spring still stood but had been considerably altered, though Clay identified the room where he had been born. He met only one person he remembered from the old days, an elderly woman of eighty, a cousin of his mother's and "evidently not long for this world." He visited the church where he had first attended school, but it too "was in a decayed condition which indicated that we should probably both tumble down about the same time."[17] Lucretia must have read his account of visiting the Slashes with a sense of wistfulness as well, hearing about a time before he had known her and detecting an uncharacteristic sadness in his words. In the wisdom of the times, a man's sixty-third year was the pivotal age that ordained great changes in health, the beginning of physical devolution. Clay soon noted that his birthday would mark his grand climacteric, and he said plainly to Lucretia, "I should be glad to be spared a few years longer until I see the Country through its difficulties, and get over my own."[18]

Observers judged the trip a success in what it meant not only for Whig unity and Harrison's candidacy, but for Clay's reputation. "There is usually much hollowness in such things," remarked James Barbour, but "the pageant of Mr. Clay's reception" pointed to the fact that "justice awaits the real patriot." The sentiment and his obvious popularity were not lost on Clay's friends, or even those who at present found it prudent to be his friends. Even before the Harrisburg convention, Harrison and Scott supporters had whispered assurances that either of their presidencies would be directed by Henry Clay. It was a deliberately flattering concession at the time. Later, though, for Harrison's supporters as well as Harrison himself, not to mention his running mate, it prepared the ground for a toxic suspicion that others would nurture.[19]

HENRY JR. ARRIVED in Washington soon after his father's return from Virginia. Clay judged him "in pretty good health, but still in very bad spirits."[20] He likely counseled Henry to follow his favored form of therapy in coping with grief, which was to travel and above all stay busy, for Henry did both in the months to come. By summer he was back in Kentucky and deeply involved in promoting Harrison's candidacy. He also announced himself the Whig candidate for lieutenant governor. Disappointed in that bid, he challenged Thomas F. Marshall for the Lexington district's congressional seat, though he ultimately withdrew in the interest of Whig unity.[21] He would never really recover from losing Julia, and there would never be the suggestion of his marrying again, an odd path for a young widower with children. Clay at first worried that the children would add to Lucretia's already heavy responsibilities, a burden (Lucretia would have bristled at the word) in addition to that imposed by the Erwin and Duralde broods, often in residence at Ashland. But Henry III, Nannie, and Tommy were largely raised by Henry Jr.'s first cousin, Nanette Price Smith, Lucretia's niece. It was plain that their father would never love anyone else, and he evidently would not marry without love. He became a living monument to Julia's memory and continued as such even after he found something he believed worth doing with his life, even if his father did not approve of it.[22]

On May 4, Clay participated in a grand procession of the Young Whig Men at Baltimore to ratify the Harrisburg ticket. At the Canton Race Track, he addressed a teeming crowd, and if there had been any lingering doubts about his purpose in the coming contest, he allayed them to the cheers of his audience. "This is no time to argue," he shouted. "The time for discussion is passed. . . . We are all Whigs—we are all Harrison men. We are *united*. We must triumph."[23]

It was a rousing performance, but it also disclosed an ominous discovery. He found that addressing large groups in the open air worked "a tremendous exertion of the lungs," and the parade and speech left him exhausted and slow to rebound. This was a new and sobering infirmity for a man who had earned his fame as well as his political fortune with a compelling baritone that could be musical in small settings and, up until now, reliably stentorian outdoors. Because he did not feel up to it, he declined to attend "an old fashioned Virginia Barbecue" even though its sponsors offered to schedule it for his convenience.

In addition, the affair at Baltimore had been raucous, celebratory, and for Clay probably the first full-blown example of the ballyhoo that defined the 1840 campaign. He seems to have found it distasteful. He turned down an invitation to attend a Fourth of July celebration planned by Whigs in Philadelphia. "I think self-respect requires," he said after Baltimore, "that I should not convert myself into an itinerant Lecturer or Stump orator to advance the cause of a successful competitor."[24]

Despite this resolve, Clay accepted an invitation to a public dinner for him in Hanover County in late June. The event provided him with the irresistible opportunity to return again to the Slashes as a proud native, but it also gave him a forum to declare Whig principles and outline a Whig program. That this should be done more forcefully had become a special concern for him. In late May he expressed regret that the Harrisburg convention had issued no platform, an omission that allowed Democrats to say that the Whigs had no program and to disparage Harrison as "General Mum." Although he was aware that many of his fellow party members thought it better to say nothing and avoid the possibility of words being twisted, he disagreed. He wanted someone to put out a statement explaining what a Whig administration would accomplish.

While Clay was stating the Whig case, the House of Representatives finally passed the Subtreasury bill on June 30 by a vote of 124 to 107, the result of the unyielding efforts of Calhoun's lieutenants and administration operatives. Van Buren delayed signing it into law until July 4. It was a symbolic gesture that Andrew Jackson believed would improve the Little Magician's reelection chances just as Jackson's Bank veto in 1832 had boosted his. Yet Van Buren was not Jackson, and the Subtreasury had become as divisive for Democrats as it was distasteful for Whigs. The nearly four-year fight to put it in place had damaged the party in New York and Virginia, and in retrospect quite needlessly, because Treasury secretary Levi Woodbury had been shifting money from state banks to the Treasury for three years under the terms of the Deposit-Distribution Act, in essence a de facto subtreasury. By the time Van Buren received the bill, the economy was again in shambles, finally showing the ill effects of the renewed economic slump, and many voters were ready for the change that the Whig economic program promised.[25]

"FOR SEVERAL MONTHS I have been afflicted with constant colds and hoarseness," Clay wrote Lucretia shortly after returning from his two-day stay in Hanover County. He described a troubling routine for July: "Two or three times I have put on and taken off my flannels. I have begun again to rub the surface of my body every morning with Spirits and Salt." Under instructions from his Washington physician, William Thomas, Clay became a steady customer of apothecaries C. H. James and R. S. Patterson. He told Lucretia, "I must find some relief, or I cannot survive." That was unlike Clay, and it was also unlike him to leave Congress early for home. Not only sick but exhausted, he departed Washington on Sunday, July 12, eight days before the first session adjourned. The rivers were navigable, allowing him to take the Wheeling route, and he was at Ashland in a little over a week.[26]

He was determined to get some rest and catch up with the family, whom he had not seen for more than eight months. He received four to five invitations a day to speak at rallies and meetings, but he turned them all down.[27] Yet his resolve to rest wavered when he was given the chance to speak at a large Whig convention to be held at Nashville in mid-August. In part, bearding Old Hickory in his own den was more than appealing, especially since Jackson had been misbehaving, to Clay's way of thinking. Jackson had published a letter in the Nashville *Union* endorsing Van Buren and lashing out at Harrison's record as an officer and statesman, a violation of the tradition that former presidents should not act as political partisans.

The convention soon became "one of the most immense gatherings ever convened in the South-western States." At least thirty thousand enthusiastic Whigs showed up, took over the city, and hurrahed for Harrison and Tyler as they went to dinners so massively attended that at one there was room for only one thousand of the ladies present to sit down while they ate.[28] On August 17, Clay made the principal speech to the gathering. He had been worried about his voice, but it did not fail him, and the cheering, stamping throng frequently stood rapt as he defended his actions resolving the 1825 election, assailed Van Buren, and praised Harrison and Tyler. That much was expected, but some unpredicted portions of the speech particularly elated the audience. One of Clay's remarks seemed spontaneously witty. When he brought up Felix Grundy, someone called out that Grundy was in East Tennessee campaigning for Van Buren. Clay immediately retorted, "Ah! . . . at his old occupation, defending criminals!"[29] The witticism had actually occurred to Clay shortly after arriving in Nashville. He had asked if Grundy was in town, and when told about the state speaking tour, the retort about "defending criminals" occurred to him a full two days before the convention speech. Like any seasoned performer, Clay had it handy for a seemingly off-the-cuff reference.[30]

He was also ready for an apparently spontaneous jab at Van Buren in comparison to Harrison. Responding to Democrat scoffing over Old Tip's scant military achievements, Clay shouted that Harrison had fought more battles without suffering a defeat than any other American general. Democrats claimed Harrison was not a statesman? Clay countered that Harrison had held numerous posts of public trust. Then someone in the crowd shouted for Clay to tell of Van Buren's "battles." Clay flashed his wide smile, and the crowd tittered. "Ah," he said. "I will have to use my colleague's language, and tell you of Mr. Van Buren's three great battles! He says that he fought general commerce, and conquered him; that he fought general currency, and conquered him; and that with his Cuba allies, he fought the Seminoles, and got conquered!"[31] The multitude roared.

Clay naturally mentioned Andrew Jackson in the speech, and it was these remarks that later caused the most fireworks. Although Clay's initial reference was gracious—he told the crowd that he had "no unkind feelings" for "the industrious captain in this neighborhood"—he also criticized Jackson for reneging on a host of promises and for appointing Edward Livingston secretary of state at a time when Livingston's financial embarrassments were as obvious as they were significant. Jackson was already livid over Clay's visit, but the disparagement of his administration was more than he could stand. Just two days after Clay's speech, Jackson published a letter spitting with fury in the Nashville *Union* denouncing Clay for criticizing Livingston after Clay had accepted the State Department in a crooked bargain. "Under such circumstances," Jackson ranted, "how contemptible does this demagogue appear, when he descends from his high place in the Senate and roams over the country, retailing slanders against the living and the dead."[32]

Clay responded the very next day with a lengthy reprise of the events he had described in his speech and concluding: "With regard to the insinuations, and gross epithets contained in Genl. Jackson's note, alike impotent, malevolent, and derogatory from the dignity of a man who has filled the highest office in the Universe, respect for the public and for myself allow me only to say that, like other similar missiles, they have fallen harmless at my feet, exciting no other sensation than that of scorn and contempt."[33] This, of course, was not true, for Clay was every bit as angry as Jackson. He had traveled to Old Hickory's backyard and had roused a teeming crowd, but he had also prodded an aging lion who never slumbered and who, once resolved to hatred, never relented. Clay's peculiar aptitude for making powerful and relentless enemies did not diminish as he aged. At Nashville in the summer of 1840, he reminded the most powerful and most relentless of all his enemies why he was and always would be one.[34]

WILLIAM HENRY HARRISON won the election of 1840 by less than 120,000 popular votes out of some 2.3 million (1,274,624 to 1,127,781), but he stacked up a crushing victory of 234 to 60 in the Electoral College. The election also overturned Congress to install Whig majorities in both houses. These victories resulted from hard economic times, as many across the country resolved to throw out those perceived as having caused the financial mess and refusing to do anything to correct it. Silas Wright groused that considering the kind of campaign that had been waged, the only mandate was to raze the Capitol and replace it with a log cabin, but his wry observation actually reflected deep frustration among Democrats.[35]

They were in fact more than a little puzzled. Democrats could grumble all they wanted that they had merely been outshouted, but Whigs throughout the country had made plain their plans, and the people gave evidence with their votes of their intention to embrace those plans. Clay clearly outlined Whig intentions in widely reported speeches at Taylorsville, Nashville, and Shelbyville, and others did the same in pamphlets and newspaper editorials. Understanding that the American people understood what the election was supposed to accomplish is key to comprehending what happened in its wake.

The man the Whigs had chosen to run instead of Henry Clay was a pleasant person who basked in good company and was rewarded for his even temper with affection from his family and loyalty from his friends. Yet Harrison's imposing bearing and unruffled demeanor could not disguise the fact that up until his winning the presidency, his career had been undistinguished. Worse, he had occasionally displayed an unseemly ambition, seeking and sometimes seeming to grovel for public appointments and comfortable sinecures. His talents were modest, and by the time he became president, his health was fragile.[36] Discerning Whigs more than suspected his limitations. "Harrison was not the man I most desired to see fill the Presidential chair, but Clay or Webster," wrote one. "My motto is in my president and in my preacher an aristocracy of mind with commanding intellectual acquirements."[37] Others were less charitable. Andrew Jackson predictably railed that Harrison had played "the part of the Ohio Black Smith [*sic*]" and found his behavior as president-elect so "disgraceful" as to confirm that Harrison had no "common sense." States' rights men such as Beverley Tucker took comfort that Harrison's shortcomings would weaken the presidency. "The throne is too high," Tucker said shortly after the Harrisburg nomination, "and it may be well to place a man upon it who will degrade it by his embicility [*sic*]."[38]

Clay disagreed to the extent that he knew Harrison was not contemptibly stupid. He thoughtfully evaluated the president-elect, judging his strengths as "honesty, patriotism, a good education, some experience in public affairs, and a lively sensibility to the good opinion of the virtuous and intelligent." Yet Harrison, thought Clay, was also prone to "vanity & egotism. And the problem to be solved is whether the former can afford protection against the sinister influences to which the latter expose him."[39] Even before the election, Clay had troubling signs that Harrison's pride might complicate matters. "I should be much gratified to see you on your way home," Harrison had written to Clay in June, "but the meeting must appear to be accidental. Can you arrange such a one?"[40]

They had not met then, nor did they meet during the campaign season, accidentally or otherwise. Then after his victory, Harrison traveled to Kentucky to meet with Charles A. Wickliffe, ostensibly on business about his purchasing Harrison's Kentucky land claims. At first, Harrison said he wanted to meet with Clay as well, but he abruptly changed his mind because it "might give rise to speculation & even jealousies which it might be well to avoid." Harrison suggested that instead he could meet with an intermediary who could relay Clay's views and suggestions about the impending administration.[41]

Harrison's trip was clearly more related to politics than land parcels, and for that reason alone he should not have made it. Twenty years later, when Abraham Lincoln was elected president, Thurlow Weed suggested that Lincoln travel to New York to visit William Seward, who had been his chief rival for the nomination. Weed cited Harrison's November 1840 visit to Kentucky as precedent, but Lincoln ignored the suggestion, "wisely" in the judgment of one historian.[42]

In Harrison's case, the visit was a bad miscue for several reasons. It revealed his sensitivity over continuing reports that Clay would be the "Mayor of the Palace" in the new administration, directing all activities from patronage appointments to legislative initiatives. In reacting this way, Harrison was playing into the hands of mischief-making opponents, for these predictions either appeared in Democrat newspapers, or they were the work of resentful Whigs jockeying for position by fouling the well for Clay.[43]

Trying to prove he was his own man and would be the master of his administration, Harrison unnecessarily placed himself amid the divisive quarrels of Kentucky's Whigs. Sixty-two-year-old Charles Wickliffe was a Whig, but he had always chafed under the ascendancy of Henry Clay, who was his superior in debate. A Wickliffe kinsman candidly likened Charles's weak oratory to trying to explode "a powder magazine . . . by throwing snow-balls at it."[44] Well-spoken or not, Wickliffe disagreed with Clay about almost everything. As a member of the Kentucky congressional delegation in 1825, he had voted for Andrew Jackson, and in the intervening years he had staunchly opposed Clay on issues ranging from gradual emancipation to revenue distribution. With his older brother Robert, who happened to be a Jacksonian Democrat, Wickliffe was poised to mount a serious challenge to Clay's dominance of Kentucky politics. Their mother had been a Hardin, tying them to influential Ben Hardin, another Bluegrass foe of Clay's, who had given Robert the nickname "Duke," now "the Old Duke" as he neared sixty-six, because he was the wealthiest and most imperious man in Kentucky. The Wickliffes had a long reach in matters political, social, and even matrimonial: Robert Wickliffe's youngest daughter, Margaret, was to marry William Preston, a Whig and a friend of Clay's, just days after Harrison's visit.[45]

Harrison's plan to meet with a member of this family greatly troubled Clay, for it likely meant a Wickliffe association with the new administration that would damage his standing not only in Kentucky but in Washington as well. Moreover, throwing this meeting in Clay's face just days after the election was both impolitic and churlish on Harrison's part because Clay was the acknowledged leader of the party in Congress and had worked hard for Old Tip's victory. In short, it was a costly and ill-conceived way for Harrison to show his independence.

Clay did not stand on ceremony when Harrison arrived in Frankfort on November 21. Instead, he rushed there to head off the Wickliffes. They intended to have Harrison install Robert Wickliffe, Jr., as his private secretary, giving the family the president's ear, and Charles A. Wickliffe as postmaster general, giving the clan access to vast patronage power. Clay thus swallowed his pride because his political self-preservation required it. He graciously invited Harrison to Ashland. Old Tip accepted, though reluctantly, making it seem he had been dragooned into Lexington.

Clay had him alone, though, and was free with advice. In several conversations, including one on November 25 during Ashland's midafternoon dinner, Clay discussed cabinet appointments. Harrison offered Clay the State Department, but he turned it down. Peter Porter advised him not only to avoid serving in the cabinet but also to seek a diplomatic post, possibly as minister to England, to be "detached from the political squabbles of the next four years," but Clay had no intention of detaching himself from the exciting prospects that a Whig president with Whig congressional majorities promised. Taking Harrison at his word about believing in legislative supremacy, Clay looked forward to returning to Congress for the first time in years.[46]

Sensibly weighing the reality that Webster could not be overlooked by a Whig president, he said that Webster's appointment to a suitable post would not vex him. He suggested the State Department. In fact, anything but Treasury, because he claimed to believe Webster had no talent for finance. Although Clay was precisely correct about his impecunious rival, his primary concern was the large patronage pool Webster would have at Treasury. He also made an effort to solidify his influence in the cabinet by putting forward the names of friends, especially Crittenden for attorney general.[47]

Clay viewed these conversations as successful in that they preserved his influence and promoted a positive relationship with the executive branch. For his

By the 1840s, Ashland had become a prosperous farm as well as a showplace. It was also Clay's refuge from the world. In the engraving above, he is seated in the foreground. The engraving below depicts the pleasant landscape that greeted the many visitors who traveled to the estate as if to a shrine. *(Courtesy of Ashland, The Henry Clay Estate, Lexington, Kentucky; Library of Congress)*

Clay was an expert horseman who began riding as a youth in the Slashes. Through the years, he owned outright, or as a member of syndicates, champion racehorses. *(Courtesy of Ashland, The Henry Clay Estate, Lexington, Kentucky)*

HENRY CLAY.

THE FARMER OF ASHLAND.

Lith. & Pub. by N. Currier, Spruce St N.Y.

Foremost among the many artifacts that Clay prized at Ashland was a cracked goblet that George Washington used during the American Revolution. It is still displayed at the estate. *(Courtesy of Ashland, The Henry Clay Estate, Lexington, Kentucky)*

The artist George P. A. Healy
(Library of Congress)

Clay circa 1842. The renowned artist George P. A. Healy was commissioned by Louis-Philippe of France to paint portraits of American statesmen from life. Healy visited Ashland in 1845 and produced several studies as well as the full portrait to the right. The engraving above suggests that some of Clay's family were partly correct that Healy had failed to capture Clay accurately. Yet among the many likenesses of her husband, Lucretia thought Healy's was the best. *(Library of Congress)*

Copy of Healy's Henry Clay by Maurie W. Clark *(Courtesy of Ashland, The Henry Clay Estate, Lexington, Kentucky)*

Lucretia Hart Clay was an intensely private woman married to an intensely public man, but she was far from a timid recluse. There are not many portraits of her, and this one by Oliver Frazier likely took some license to soften her features. *(Courtesy of Dr. Bill Kenner)*

Henry and Lucretia's second son, Thomas Hart Clay, caused his parents many anxious moments. Expelled from West Point after one term and prone to drunken binges, Thomas finally found his way through the love of a good woman, neighbor Mary Mentelle. *(Courtesy of Dr. Bill Kenner)*

Raised within sight of Ashland, Mary Mentelle was a childhood playmate of the Clay children. Her marriage to Thomas Hart Clay brought her formally into a family that already adored her. *(Courtesy of Dr. Bill Kenner)*

Henry and Lucretia's third son was his father's namesake, Henry Clay, Jr., and became the young man for whom Clay had the highest hopes. *(Courtesy of Ashland, The Henry Clay Estate, Lexington, Kentucky)*

The death of Henry Clay, Jr., in combat during the Mexican War broke his parents' hearts and contributed to Henry Clay's religious conversion. *(Library of Congress)*

Julia Prather's marriage to Henry Clay, Jr., brought great joy into the life of an overly serious young man. Her tragic death in 1840 devastated the family and sank young Henry into perpetual mourning from which he never recovered. *(Courtesy of Ashland, The Henry Clay Estate, Lexington, Kentucky)*

Henry and Lucretia's tenth child, James Brown Clay, tried several careers before settling on the law and practicing briefly with his father. Clay obtained a diplomatic appointment for James in 1849, and he served one term in Congress in the late 1850s. He sided with the Confederacy during the Civil War. *(Courtesy of Ned Boyajian)*

James B. Clay's marriage to Susan Jacob brought another beloved daughter-in-law into the Clay family. Susan greatly admired her father-in-law and took it upon herself to preserve many of his papers after his death. *(Courtesy of Ned Boyajian)*

John Morrison Clay was the youngest of Clay's eleven children. He struggled with alcohol in his youth and later displayed signs of the mental disorder that afflicted his oldest brother, Theodore Wythe Clay. His life was transformed by the discovery of his talent for breeding champion racehorses. *(Courtesy of Ashland, The Henry Clay Estate, Lexington, Kentucky)*

The Illustrious Guest by James Henry Beard

Despite his lengthy retirement from office and his failed presidential bids, Clay remained one of the country's most popular and recognizable people, as this previously unpublished painting shows. In 1847, New York artist James Henry Beard captured the essence of that celebrity in *The Illustrious Guest,* in which Clay nonchalantly reads a newspaper while locals gather to stare at their famous visitor. Beard had a sense of humor to match that of his subject, as the detail of the tavern's guest register shows. The artist has placed his name on it along with Clay's signature. *(Private collection)*

The Capitol as it appeared during the Mexican War and the debates over what would become the Compromise of 1850. *(Library of Congress)*

Henry and Lucretia Clay posed stiffly to commemorate their fiftieth wedding anniversary, both clearly showing the emotional scars of the many family tragedies that plagued their five decades together. Clay was also struggling with a serious cough that he rightly suspected was tuberculosis. *(Courtesy of Ashland, The Henry Clay Estate, Lexington, Kentucky)*

James K. Polk's pledge not to run for a second term in 1848 offered Clay and the Whigs an excellent chance to capture the White House. Clay's hopes were dashed when General Zachary Taylor won the Whig nomination. *(Library of Congress)*

Horace Greeley, the eccentric editor of the New York *Tribune,* was Clay's unofficial campaign manager in the final bid for the presidency. By the time of the Whig National Convention, Greeley knew that Clay's chances were less than slim. *(Library of Congress)*

Kentuckian John Jordan Crittenden had been Clay's most cherished friend for years, but Clay's discovery that Crittenden was working behind the scenes for Taylor in 1848 estranged them. *(Library of Congress)*

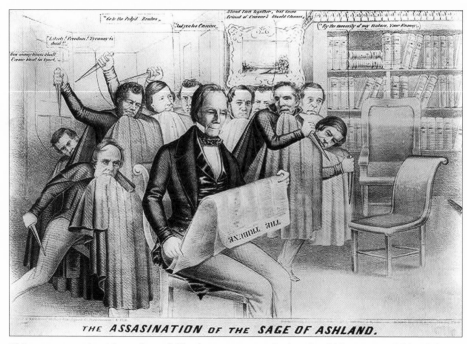

THE ASSASINATION OF THE SAGE OF ASHLAND.

This cartoon took a blunt view of Clay's treatment at the hands of his supposed friends in 1848, comparing their furtive desertion of him for Taylor to Caesar's assassins. *(Library of Congress)*

Although increasingly ill by the time he sat for this photograph, Henry Clay still displayed some of the spark, especially in his eyes, that made him a charismatic leader for a half century. *(Library of Congress)*

A fellow Whig and often a fierce rival, Daniel Webster cooperated with Clay when it mattered most during the compromise debates in 1850. *(Library of Congress)*

By the time this photograph was taken of John C. Calhoun, he and Clay no longer spoke socially. Calhoun was now near death and had become a radical sectionalist who reflexively opposed any measure put forth by Clay. Nevertheless, the two met one last time when Clay visited Calhoun as he lay dying. *(Library of Congress)*

New York senator William Seward was a protégé of Thurlow Weed and no friend of Clay's. Seward opposed Clay's compromise plan in 1850 and provocatively told the Senate that there was a "higher law" than the Constitution. *(Library of Congress)*

Pennsylvanian James Buchanan was a Senate colleague for many years and frequently bantered with Clay during proceedings. He was among those who marveled over Clay's return to the Senate in 1849. *(Library of Congress)*

A self-made man much like Henry Clay, Millard Fillmore became president when Zachary Taylor suddenly died. Clay admired Fillmore's honesty and candor, rare traits in career politicians, and was grateful for the new president's support in the fight for the Compromise of 1850. *(Library of Congress)*

Illinois senator Stephen A. Douglas ultimately became the principal architect behind the Compromise of 1850, but he expressed open admiration for Clay's efforts and praised his patriotism. *(Library of Congress)*

In one of the most famous depictions of Henry Clay, he addresses the Senate during the debates on his compromise proposals in 1850. *(Library of Congress)*

Although a Whig ally, Maryland senator James A. Pearce accidentally destroyed Clay's complex plans just prior to the Senate vote on the compromise package at the end of July 1850. *(Library of Congress)*

In this 1860 reproduction of an 1852 lithograph depicting the important statesmen who had saved the Union in 1850, the engraver made a significant change. Clay remains prominent at just left of center, holding his customary cane. Daniel Webster stands to the right with his hand resting on the scroll. Yet John C. Calhoun, the third member of the Great Triumvirate, has been replaced by Abraham Lincoln in the middle, despite the fact that Lincoln was out of office from 1848 until his election to the presidency in 1860. *(Library of Congress)*

Lucretia Clay's cousin, Thomas Hart Benton, began his political career as a staunch ally of Henry Clay but ultimately became a Jacksonian, making him Clay's bitter enemy. In the end, though, Benton conceded that the "Corrupt Bargain" charge had been trumped up for political purposes.
(Library of Congress)

Artist Robert Weir's painting captures Clay's final communion as administered by Senate chaplain Charles M. Butler and witnessed by Clay's servant James Marshall. Thomas Hart Clay arrived shortly afterward to take his father home from Washington, and though Clay briefly rallied, he never left his rooms again. *(Courtesy of the Kentucky Historical Society Collections)*

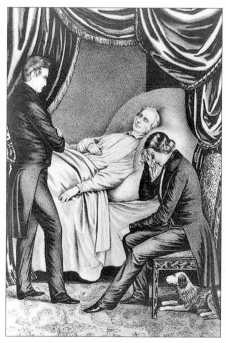

Clay died on June 29, 1852, with Tennessee senator James C. Jones and Thomas Hart Clay at his bedside. *(Library of Congress)*

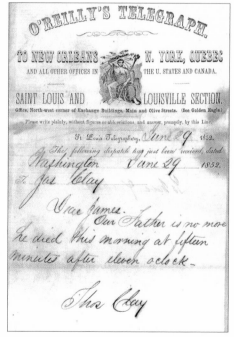

Thomas Hart Clay dispatched this telegram to his brother James shortly after their father died in Washington. *(Library of Congress)*

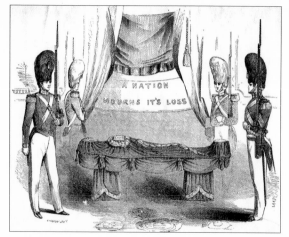

Henry Clay lay in state in his unusual human-shaped coffin at numerous stops on the funeral journey back to Lexington. The plate covering his face could be removed for viewing, but the practice was discontinued after the early part of the trip. *(Courtesy of Ashland, The Henry Clay Estate, Lexington, Kentucky)*

Clay's funeral in Lexington featured a spectacular and lengthy procession from Ashland to the Lexington Cemetery. Thousands crowded into the town to view the ornate hearse drawn by impressive horses and tended by liveried groomsmen. *(Courtesy of the University of Kentucky)*

FUNERAL PROCESSION OF THE HON. HENRY CLAY, IN NEW YORK.

New York was one of the many cities that held elaborate funeral ceremonies for Clay weeks after he had been laid to rest in Lexington. The urn in the funeral carriage symbolized Clay's presence in the New York ceremony where thousands lined the route to pay their respects. *(Courtesy of the New York State Library)* part, Harrison in the aftermath appeared warmly inclined to Clay. Just before his inauguration, Harrison spoke publicly of Clay as "my firm personal and political friend" and went on to say, "I consider his judgment superior to that of any man living, for . . . I have never differed with him on any important subject that I did not afterwards become convinced that *he was right and I was wrong.*"[48]

Weighing those encouraging words, Clay took comfort that he had blocked the Wickliffes' drive to supplant him. Robert Wickliffe, Jr., did not become Harrison's private secretary (though he did trail him to Washington as part of the new president's entourage), and Charles A. Wickliffe did not become postmaster general.

Two things did worry Clay, though. One was that Harrison might remain "apprehensive that the new Administration may not be regarded as *his* but mine." Clay was concerned that "artful men for sinister purposes will endeavor to foster this jealousy," and he was determined to dispel any reason for it.[49] The second matter that concerned him was Harrison's health. Despite Old Tip's repeated claims of vigor, Clay was not so sure. Others also noticed that something was not quite right with the old fellow. After a public reception during the Kentucky trip, one person in attendance thought that Harrison appeared "pretty well worn out."[50] Clay was even more plainspoken. "I think the strength of his mind is unabated," he said, "but his body is a good deal shattered." He repeated the observation using the same word, "shattered," to John Quincy Adams a couple of weeks later in Washington, a sign that the state of Harrison's health was much on his mind.[51]

AS CLAY PREPARED to leave for Congress, James abandoned his Missouri farming experiment and returned to Ashland. A year earlier, he had made a prolonged visit to Natchez, where Clay suspected that he had "gotten involved in some love affair," but no girl was ever mentioned, and James returned to Kentucky alone. Clay was relieved to have him back in any case, since he trusted James to handle business at Ashland while Thomas was occupied with starting up his hemp and bagging business. Thomas had high hopes for success, although he was finding it difficult to secure capital during hard times, and Clay began staking him with hefty advances, generosity that would prove to be a serious mistake.[52]

Clay and his slave Charles Dupuy left Ashland on November 26 for Washington. Reaching the capital on December 6, he settled into his rooms at Mrs. Arguelles's and began catching up on his correspondence, a sign that the first of his three campaigns having succeeded—the one to elect Harrison—it was time to commence the other two, promoting his candidacy for the presidency in 1844 and enacting the Whig program. He called on Van Buren at the White House and received John Quincy Adams for a friendly chat. These were not merely cordial rituals but had the purpose of surveying the ground and reading political prospects. Disappointed Democrats would be up to no good, he concluded, and he mentioned the need for a special session of Congress.[53]

Van Buren's humiliating defeat led John C. Calhoun to believe that he could be the Democrat nominee in 1844. He itched to run against Henry Clay, who he suspected had obtained Harrison's blessing as his successor, and like the Kentuckian, he began laying the foundation for his bid early. On December 15, 1840, he walked into the Senate chamber and heard Clay arguing for the immediate repeal of the Subtreasury, just a half year into its existence. Calhoun countered with what amounted to a stump speech not only defending the Subtreasury but exalting Jeffersonian principles of limited government. Clay knew what this was about. Calhoun was giving notice that he would lead the opposition against the Whig majority with every weapon at his disposal.[54]

Clay soon left Washington for New York, the professed purpose of the trip being to visit three of his grandsons (James Erwin, Jr., Henry Clay Erwin, and Henry Clay Duralde) at their private school on Long Island. When Clay and Charles Dupuy checked in to the Astor House in Manhattan, most people realized that politics would also play an important part in this visit. Editor James Gordon Bennett quipped that the boys on Long Island were "not the only grandchildren that brought Mr. Clay to New York." Bennett listed every prominent Whig in the city as eagerly seeking Clay's favor, and indeed many did call on Clay, hoping that he could use his influence to gain them a place in the new administration.[55]

Clay and Charles left New York on Tuesday, three days before Christmas. They also left the boys and their classmates in the care of Peter Porter, who treated them over Christmas to the circus and a tour of the Bowery.[56] As for Clay, he boarded the Jersey City ferry to catch the train for Philadelphia and found himself in the company of Caroline Webster and Congressman Edward Curtis's wife. They were on their way to Washington to join their husbands. He "greeted them with great cordiality, and expressed his delight in having their company to the capitol [*sic*]."[57] That was likely true, if incredible, or at least it was a deceptive gesture of instinctual gallantry: Clay knew that Webster was going to prove a troublesome rival in his bid for the presidency, and Clay would soon have cause to loathe Edward Curtis. But in the brisk breezes that buffeted the Jersey ferry that December day, Clay was chivalrous and charming. At least by all appearances, the trio made for delightful company, but it was perhaps an omen that by the time he had reached Wilmington, he had become so ill with his nagging cold that he was in his bed for almost two days and otherwise confined to a room until he felt well enough again to travel, which was not until December 30.[58]

He arrived in Washington in time to attend Martin Van Buren's final New Year's Day reception, an event he would not have missed for the world. The weather was stormy and miserable, sleet mixing with snow to pelt people as they arrived, and attendance was thin as a result. John Quincy Adams heard Clay tell Van Buren "that nothing but devotion to *him* could have induced him to come out from his lodgings on a day such as this." Adams interpreted the remark as an example of the Kentuckian's sarcasm. "Clay," he sniffed, "crows too much over a fallen foe."[59] Yet there was plenty of evidence to indicate that Clay was sincere. His relations with Van Buren had always been civil and often quite affable. Even the Democrat press had noticed how Clay "was inspired with the greatest respect for the *man,* though he detested the *magistrate.*"[60] Clay likely felt sorry for the political antagonist he also regarded as a personal friend, a man sniggered at as Sweet Sandy Whiskers and unfairly maligned for turning the White House into a sumptuous palace. Now at Van Buren's final grand levee, the falseness of the latter charge was laid bare. The place was in shambles, the East Room's wallpaper peeling, its large carpet threadbare, and the satin damask nearly worn off the seats of the chairs.[61] Henry Clay stood at the center of the East Room amid a glittering array of bejeweled women impatient to catch his eye and laughing men eager to shake his hand, a cluster of people larger than that around Van Buren. Clay did not feel well, and rather than crowing, he was likely sincere in what he said to the little man who at the end had been forced to rely on John C. Calhoun, of all people, for political sustenance. This last party, ruined by the weather, lightly attended by Washington society, and lacking even meager refreshments, was no occasion for gloating. It all just seemed rather sad.[62]

IN THE JANUARY term of the Supreme Court, Clay joined Charles L. Jones and Daniel Webster to represent Robert Slaughter in the case of *Groves v. Slaughter,* a complicated dispute involving slavery, the state of Mississippi, and the validity of promissory notes. In fact, *Groves v. Slaughter* was about two legal disputes. One concerned Robert Slaughter, a slave trader who was demanding payment for slaves he had sold into Mississippi in 1836. Groves, who had endorsed a promissory note for the purchaser, claimed that the transaction violated the part of the Mississippi constitution prohibiting the introduction of slaves into the state "as merchandize" after May 1833, a move designed to prevent the drain of capital from the state. Groves insisted that because the transaction was illegal, he was under no obligation to pay Slaughter, who then sued him in the federal Circuit Court of the Eastern District of Louisiana. When the circuit court upheld Slaughter's claim, Groves petitioned the Supreme Court.[63]

Clay, Webster, and Jones were in part interested in recovering the money owed to Slaughter, despite its unsavory nature, because a promissory note was still a legal contract that could not be disregarded without imperiling all commercial transactions. Yet a more significant issue than debt collection arose from the possibility that Mississippi had violated the U.S. Constitution by presuming to regulate interstate commerce, a power reserved to Congress. Because the interstate commerce in question had been in slaves, the case became a sensitive test of the balance between federal and state power and had the potential to affect the institution of slavery itself. As John Quincy Adams succinctly discerned, "The question is whether a State of the Union can constitutionally prohibit the importation within her borders of slaves as merchandise."[64] The implications were therefore staggering. In determining the validity of Slaughter's promissory note, the Court could have been forced in 1841 to delve into a titanic issue: the legal status of slaves as property and as people. Doing so would have had the same sort of impact on the slavery controversy that the Dred Scott decision did sixteen years later. In short, such a decision could have accelerated an already angry debate over slavery, possibly to a violent conclusion.

That was why a case that seemingly involved only the sordid business of slave trading and the mundane matter of an unpaid bill featured celebrated and high-powered legal talent on both sides. In addition to Clay and Webster, Slaughter's team included Walter Jones, a legal genius renowned for his encyclopedic knowledge and something of an eccentric in dress and speech. Despite a high, thin voice so hushed as to give the impression that he was nodding off during his arguments, he had "piercing" eyes and an exceptional talent for lodging brief, pointed presentations.[65] Representing the State of Mississippi were Henry D. Gilpin, the U.S. attorney general (and second husband of Clay's old friend Eliza Johnston), and Mississippi senator Robert J. Walker.

Oral arguments began on February 12, 1841, a Friday, and continued until the following Friday, drawing large numbers of "distinguished counselors . . . and scores of men eminent in other professions" to the Court's chamber on the ground floor of the Capitol's north wing, both to see the celebrity lawyers at work and because of the case's possible significance. The presence of Clay and Webster accounted for "the ladies [who] occupied all the vacant seats of the Court-room and crowded everyone but the Judges and counsel out of the bar."[66]

As was his custom in the Senate, Clay did not speak from a prepared text but relied on brief sentences to serve as cues. He spoke for about three hours, and the spectators remained attentive throughout his lengthy remarks. He pointed out the economic repercussions that would result from allowing Groves to ignore the debt, for the precedent would not only affect Slaughter but would also involve "more than $3,000,000, due by citizens of the state of Mississippi, to citizens of Virginia, Maryland, Kentucky and other slave states." He assessed the legal implications of canceling the contracts that promissory notes represented and provided a detailed analysis of the Mississippi constitution's intent and the Mississippi legislature's actions to show that not until 1837, the year following Slaughter's transaction, did the legislature pass a law enforcing the prohibition.

The easiest way to win the case was to argue that Mississippi had overreached its authority and therefore could not have made the Slaughter transaction unlawful. Yet Clay was troubled by the possibility of invoking the interstate commerce clause to curb a state's right to control its own affairs, especially regarding slavery. Doing that could trigger a dire response throughout the South. In his notes, he insisted that "Congress has neither the power to disturb the existing institution [of slavery] or to establish it within a State" and "Congress cannot therefore do what the Abolitionists seek." If congressional control over interstate commerce could be used as Adams had mused—that is, to regulate or otherwise impinge upon the institution of slavery—it would become a powerful weapon in the abolitionist arsenal and might spur southerners to a calamitous reaction. Indeed, Robert Walker "threatened tremendous consequences" if the states were brought to heel in this way.[67]

As it turned out, the justices were also apprehensive about tackling the sobering issues of slavery and states' rights, and when they handed down their decision on March 10, a majority managed to dodge those questions by essentially agreeing with Clay. Because there had been no legislative statute enforcing Mississippi's constitutional prohibition on importing slaves, the Court ruled that the prohibition had not been in effect at the time of Slaughter's transaction. Upholding the circuit court's decision made it "unnecessary to inquire whether this article in the constitution of Mississippi is repugnant to the constitution of the United States."[68] Chief Justice Roger Taney even went so far as to say that the issue of exclusive federal control over such a matter was "little more than an abstract question which the court may never be called on to decide."[69]

That, of course, turned out to be a stunningly mistaken prophecy, as Clay feared. Taney could not have imagined that eventually the political system would bring something very much like this question to the Court and that he himself would see it as more than an abstraction. Sixteen years later, Taney would feel compelled to decide the question, come hell or high water. In due course, just as Clay had feared, both hell and high water came with a vengeance.

HARRISON OFFERED WEBSTER a place in the cabinet, as Clay recommended, but he gave him the choice of Treasury or State, against Clay's advice. Clay did not know about this, because Webster chose State, but it indicated that Harrison was inclined to give only lip service to his counsel, and in other appointments he soon gave Clay reason to be concerned. Though his friends were prominent in the new administration, with Crittenden appointed attorney general and John Bell secretary of war, it was disconcerting to learn that Tom Ewing was moved from postmaster general to Treasury to make a place for Frank Granger. That was Webster's doing, and the change was the first sign that the New Englander might be able to exert more influence from within the administration than Clay could from outside it.

The appointment that Clay most wanted was that of his friend John Clayton. Clay had wanted Clayton at Treasury, but with that taken, he was prepared to settle for secretary of the navy. When Harrison balked, Clay pressed the matter, unwisely ignoring his own advice about not exciting Harrison's sensitivity over who was really in charge. In late February, Harrison traveled to Richmond for a rest before the inauguration and visited attorney James Lyons, a staunch supporter who was the president of Richmond's Tippecanoe Club. According to Lyons, Harrison was quite agitated about Clay's behavior, which he described as violent and overbearing to the point where Harrison had barked: "Mr. Clay, you forget that I am the President!"[70]

Possibly Harrison's sharp remark was caused by the dispute over Clayton, but it is also possible that Harrison never said it. Lyons, like John Tyler, was a former Jacksonian Democrat who had become a Whig when repelled by Andrew Jackson's overbearing manner. Yet Lyons had never really deserted fundamental Democrat principles, and his most notable contribution to the 1840 campaign was a states' rights manifesto called the Whig Address, which incongruously repudiated Whig principles by denouncing the protective tariff and declaring a national bank unconstitutional. Moreover, Lyons had asserted that Harrison condemned the Bank too.[71] Clearly Lyons was no friend of Clay's. In addition to being the only source describing Harrison and Clay as at loggerheads before Old Tip's inauguration, Lyons did not make the claim until almost forty years later in a letter to the New York *World,* a struggling New York daily (Joseph Pulitzer would purchase it in 1883). As we shall see, there are other reasons to suspect both Lyons and the statements in his 1880 letter.

When Harrison gave Navy to North Carolinian George E. Badger, Clay put the best face on it, hoping that Clayton's rejection was "the result of perhaps rather an imp[r]udent rule adopted by Genl Harrison, in respect to the geographical distribution of the members of his cabinet" rather than any intentional slight directed at him. Nevertheless, the president-elect's intransigence hurt Clay's feelings, and he forlornly told Clayton, "Your disappointment will be far less than my own."[72]

By far, however, Clay's most telling disappointment concerned the collector of customs for New York, a position that many regarded as second only to the presidency in the vast patronage it commanded. Clay wanted his supporter Robert C. Wetmore to receive the appointment, but rumor had it that Harrison intended to select Edward Curtis, a former Antimason whom Peter Porter described as "a shrewd and managing man." Clay had little reason to support someone who had worked hard to defeat his nomination at Harrisburg.[73]

Curtis had Weed and Seward in his corner, however, and he had long been a Webster man, so he had a self-interested advocate in Harrison's inner circle.[74] Having Webster's supporter in the collector's post where he could spread the patronage wealth for the New Englander was a chilling prospect. New York Whig leaders apparently realized this might be the main obstacle to obtaining Clay's consent, and Thurlow Weed met with Peter Porter to hint that if Clay withdrew his objections, Curtis would support him in 1844. Clay was not persuaded. If anything, he was all the more suspicious of a man so willing, as he had put it, to row one way and look the other. "How can such a man as Curtis be trusted?" he asked. "My determination not to cooperate in his appointment is irrevocable."[75]

It soon became apparent that his cooperation was immaterial, and in reaction to the slight, Clay lowered his head and resigned himself to the inevitable. Curtis received his appointment after Harrison's inauguration, and Clay's public pose was an obvious attempt to preserve his dignity. He was determined not to let the setbacks over Clayton and Curtis ruin the opportunity presented by a Whig Congress with a Whig president. "We must support this administration," he said, "or rather, I should say, we must not fall out with it because precisely the friends we could wish had not in every instance been called to the cabinet. I have strong fears & strong hopes. And sometimes the one & sometimes the other predominate."[76]

The weather in Washington was gray and raw on March 4, but it did not dampen the enthusiasm of the large crowds in the capital for Harrison's swearing in. A special session of the new Senate came to order at 10:00 A.M., adopted a resolution electing Alabama's William R. King president pro tem for the ceremonies of the day, and appointed Henry Clay to administer the oath to him.

At 11:00 the diplomatic corps and Supreme Court justices entered the chamber, and thirty minutes later, King in turn administered the oath to John Tyler, who delivered "an eloquent and able address."[77] At least Tyler's speech was brief, something everyone would remember with a measure of gratitude later that afternoon. Harrison entered the Senate chamber at a quarter past noon to be escorted to the East Portico of the Capitol, his arrival there greeted by a thunderous ovation and prolonged cheers from the crowd below before everyone settled down. As it happened, they had to settle in, for Harrison commenced an interminable inaugural address of more than eight thousand words, going on for nearly two hours, to this day the longest in presidential history. Webster had tried to tidy it up with careful cuts, but Harrison was intent on showing both his erudition and his stamina, forgetting the connection between brevity and wit, and disregarding the fact that even a young man, bareheaded and lightly clad, should not stand outside in the snow for two hours.

When Roger Taney was finally able to administer the oath, the cheers and applause that followed were likely as much an expression of gushing relief as a tribute to Tippecanoe. Cannon fired from Capitol Hill, echoed by others in remote parts of the city, "and the crowd dispersed." After the ordeal, it most certainly did.[78]

The new Senate of the Twenty-seventh Congress returned to its chamber and was about to adjourn when Willie Mangum gained the floor to introduce a resolution to be taken up the following day. It was a move to fire Democrats Francis Preston Blair and John C. Rives as printers to the Senate. Clay was behind this. On February 19, he had stoutly opposed the dying Democrat majority's effort to reappoint Blair and Rives and thereby saddle the incoming Whig Congress with men "utterly odious to those who were in a few days to succeed to the possession of the Government."[79] Mangum's resolution dismissing them was to be the first initiative undertaken by the Whig majority, and it set off a lengthy and acrimonious debate that stretched over several days and ultimately got out of hand. Democrats cried foul over the Whig effort to break a two-year contract made in good faith with Blair and Rives. Clay countered that the appointment of these men had been an imperious "act of power—pure, naked unqualified power," but moreover he insisted that they should be fired because of Blair's "notoriously bad character."[80]

The move was personal for Clay, because his break with Blair had been ugly in the way that only a rupture between old friends could be, veined with traces of betrayal and deceit. Yet Whigs who had no personal history with Blair felt equally outraged at the prospect of keeping "men in their employ whose only language toward them has been that of contumely and insult."[81] Clay was therefore not alone in condemning the Washington *Globe* and its pugnacious editor. For years Blair had alternated between vicious language and a mocking sneer to mount ferocious attacks on Andrew Jackson's opponents in general and Clay in

particular. In the days when Calhoun was friendly to Whigs, even he had described the *Globe* as "filthy and mendacious," and it was understandable that the
Whig majority would not want to subsidize that press with a lucrative printing
contract.[82]

On March 9, Clay watched in growing anger as Connecticut's Perry Smith
accused him of implying that all senators who had supported Blair were also
"infamous." Then Alabamian William R. King reminded everyone of Clay's
personal friendship with Blair before their break and insisted that the editor's
character would compare favorably with Clay's. The likes of Perry Smith
did not merit his notice, Clay hotly responded, but King, "who considers himself *responsible,*" was quite another matter. King, in fact, had "gone one step
further . . . to *classify* me with the partisan Editor of the Globe." These remarks
by King, Clay shouted, were "false, untrue, and cowardly."

Whispered talk had long painted King as a homosexual, although the only
evidence for the insinuation was a tendency to dandified dress and his close
friendship with another confirmed bachelor, James Buchanan, with whom he
lodged at Mrs. Ironsides's on Tenth and F streets.[83] The rumors, along with the
heightened sense of pride common among southerners, made King touchy, as
John Randolph had been, and Clay's words brought him to his feet amid a raucous clamor that rapidly died away. The dark look on King's face clearly indicated that Clay's remarks, "short and intemperate" in the estimation of John
Quincy Adams, had crossed a line. "Mr. President," King said in measured, terse
tones, "I have no reply to make—none whatever." He sat down. Nobody moved.
The chamber was slipping into reflective silence when Perry Smith piped up to
ask if he really was beneath Clay's notice. "Not at all," Clay snapped. Smith
paused to digest the disdain and then embarked on an embarrassing ramble of
self-pity and awkward sarcasm, but nobody was likely listening to him. The entire body of senators sat as though dealt a hard blow. Clay's words—"false,"
"untrue," and worst of all, "cowardly"—hung in the air like an unpleasant odor.
William Preston rose to say that it was regrettable "that any thing should have
occurred that should have driven honorable Senators to do any thing inconsistent with parliamentary decorum," but the observation at this point was a remarkable understatement. In fact, King had taken the time during the exchanges
following his remark to scribble a note. He motioned for Lewis Linn of Missouri to accompany him from the chamber, and after adjournment, Linn appeared before Clay with a piece of paper, apparently King's note.[84]

That evening rumors raced through the capital that King had challenged
Clay to a duel. Reports also told of their being arrested, but actually only King
was briefly detained for fear that he would do something rash. Both men posted

bonds with D.C. justices of the peace as surety that they would not assault each other.[85]

Bennett's *Herald* had great fun with this set-to, suggesting that sending King and Clay on a journey together over New York's wretched roads to Albany would make them "meek and gentle as new-born kittens," but the incident was unseemly and embarrassing for everyone, most of all for Clay, who had lost his temper and behaved badly. The Senate dismissed Blair and Rives on a 26 to 18 vote, but the affair meanwhile gave rise to wild stories and rising invective throughout the country. In New England, newspapers reported that a duel had killed Clay and left King mortally wounded. Democrat papers branded Clay a "blackleg and demagogue" and ridiculed his pledge not to fight as that of a man "who calls on his friend to hold him by the coat tail, to keep him from striking his antagonist."[86]

Linn, acting for King, and Clay's friends William Archer and Preston worked together to orchestrate a public reconciliation on March 14 near the close of the special session. Preston rose in the Senate to describe the affair as a misunderstanding, which opened the way for Clay to admit that he had been wrong in his interpretation of King's remarks and therefore wrong to lose his temper. He apologized. King followed suit, assuring the Senate that he had meant no offense to his friend from Kentucky. As King was concluding his remarks, Clay was already on his feet, striding across the chamber with his hand out. King took it, and a smattering of applause grew into a thunderous ovation from their colleagues, spectators in the gallery joining in.[87]

The happy conclusion to this incident could not disguise the fact, however, that everyone was on edge in this new arrangement where Democrats, accustomed to being a majority, and Whigs, eager to act like one, were bound to clash. But Clay's overreaction suggested that larger problems were nagging him. The quarrel with Democrats over printers was irritating, but his disagreements with William Henry Harrison had become exasperating. To his thinking, those differences threatened to squander the victory of 1840.

CLAY HOPED THAT the close of the brief special session of the Twenty-seventh Congress would be quickly followed by another "at the earliest convenient & practicable day" to begin enacting elements of the Whig program. He had begun floating the idea shortly after the election, and in early 1841 he openly stated that to oppose the extra session was to favor "the continuation of Mr. V. B'[s] Admon [*sic*] 12 or 18 months after its constitutional termination." As Tom Corwin had said, to win the election and do nothing threatened to make liars of them all.[88]

But Harrison dithered, and soon enough it was easy to see why. His cabinet was evenly divided on the issue, but Webster's negative vote most influenced the president. From their first interview to discuss Webster's joining the administration, Dan'l had been anything but godlike, adopting instead a submissive demeanor toward Harrison that first ingratiated him to the president-elect and then gave him increasing clout with the president. That Harrison, a proud stylist, had consulted Webster on his inaugural address was one sign of that growing power, the selection of Curtis and Granger was another, and the president's attitude about the extra session yet another. Webster's motives were mixed, but his plans for the presidential contest in 1844 were certainly foremost. Blocking the extra session meant that Clay would have no reason to remain in Washington, and Webster could solidify his position with Harrison to guide the administration for eight months unchallenged. Deprived of a forum until December, Clay's tactics for 1844 would suffer a serious setback.[89]

Reasons other than a desire to keep pace with Webster, or even an obligation to address the needs of the people, must have filled Clay with a sense of urgency over the extra session. Given everyone's observations about Harrison's health, there was the distinct possibility that the new president could become ill enough to elevate John Tyler to an acting presidency, at least temporarily. Clay had never said a word to anyone about John Tyler, for it would have been most imprudent to do so, but he had to be concerned that Tyler's attitudes about Whig principles did not necessarily mesh with his own, or Harrison's for that matter. During the campaign, there had been troubling signs. For instance, Pittsburgh Democrats, in a ploy to embarrass Tyler, had requested that he write a letter spelling out his true opinions on the Whig program. Tyler complied, but at the last minute he had congressional Whigs vet the communication. To a man, they said not to publish it.[90] Clay would have known about this cynical maneuver to disguise what Tyler actually believed. It was unsettling.

On March 13, Clay took the liberty to write to Harrison about the need for an extra session and even enclosed a draft proclamation for Harrison to use in calling one. It was a risky move, to be sure, and that Clay was willing to chance it indicates how anxious he was to have Congress get to work as soon as possible. But it immediately proved to be a dreadful mistake. Already testy about what he perceived as Clay's meddling over appointments, Harrison bristled. There was to be a state dinner that evening where Clay and Harrison could have conversed, but the president was angry and instead dashed off a note to Clay that began with a prickly "My dear friend" and went on from there: "You use the privilege of a friend to lecture me & I will take the same liberty with you—You are too impetuous."[91]

Newspaper reporter Nathan Sargent claimed that Harrison's note enraged Clay not only because of its tone but because it all but instructed him to communicate in the future with the administration only in writing. "And it has come to this!" Clay was said to have shouted, though Sargent is the only source for this scene. Despite not feeling very well, Clay kept his dinner engagement at the White House that evening, which was a large party attended by scores of prominent men. In the wake of his and Harrison's exchange, it must have been at best an awkward event for Clay.[92] In any case, he bitterly realized that he was not only beaten on this issue but was also confronting a nearly total triumph by Webster to control the administration. Clay swallowed his pride to repair the damage. He wrote to the president to confess that he was "mortified" by the suggestion that he was dictating to him. "There is danger of the fears, that I intimated to you at Frankfort, of my enemies poisoning your mind towards me." He rather helplessly felt the need to revisit the controversy over Curtis: he claimed that he had not said Curtis should not be appointed, which was not altogether true, but he hedged by explaining that he had merely stated his opinion that Curtis was unworthy of the post. If expressing his opinion meant that Clay could be accused of dictating, there was little he could do about it. He told Harrison not to trouble with answering.[93]

When Harrison did not respond, the silence from the White House sent a clear message, and two days later Clay left Washington for home. He had gotten only as far as Baltimore when he became seriously ill. It has never been clear what was wrong with him, but he later described the malady as an "attack . . . more severe than I was aware of at the time."[94] His ailment was serious enough to stop his trip and confine him to a room at Barnum's Hotel for almost a week. Very likely the repeated humiliations, many of them now embarrassingly public, were finally taking their toll.[95]

On the very day that Clay left Washington, Harrison abruptly relented and issued a call for the extra session, although a disturbing consultation with his cabinet over the plummeting economy, not Clay's influence, was the reason he changed his mind. Biddle's United States Bank of Philadelphia had suspended specie payments, western state treasuries were empty and their governments on the verge of debt repudiation, and Treasury secretary Ewing brought in figures that showed the federal government's already substantial deficit would soon be bloated by more than 11 million additional dollars. The imperative of an appropriations bill and finding the money to fund it compelled the administration to summon Congress, the sooner the better. At this point, even Webster agreed. Harrison called for Congress to meet on May 31.[96]

A week after issuing the proclamation, Harrison came down with a chill and quickly developed pneumonia. Office seekers and official functions had dogged his days, and his rash decision to deliver his lengthy inaugural address in bad weather further weakened his already fragile constitution. The exhausted old man died on April 4, only four weeks into his term, the shortest presidency in American history.

Tippecanoe was dead, and Tyler Too was now the president. Andrew Jackson was ecstatic. Harrison, he said, did not have the energy to withstand office seekers. Jackson speculated that Old Tip had been resorting to "stimulants" to keep pace. His death was the work of a "divine . . . Providence," according to Jackson, a heavenly decree to kill this president in order to save the Union and the republican system.[97]

Jackson's attitude was distasteful and unbecoming, but for the Whigs it was even worse; it was never good for them when Andrew Jackson was happy.

STILL WEAK FROM his illness in Baltimore, Clay had only just arrived at Ashland in early April when he received word that Harrison was dead. "It is greatly to be deplored," he said, though he did not think the news surprising. "I told some of his Cabinet that, unless he changed his habits, he could not live long."[98]

Given Clay's deteriorating relationship with Harrison, John Tyler's succession at first glance should have meant an improvement in harmony between the Whig congressional leadership and the president. Yet considerable uncertainty resulted from the unprecedented event of the president's dying in office and the vice president's assuming his place. Beyond the constitutional prescription of succession, almost everything about it was uncharted, including the minor quandary of what to call John Tyler. John Quincy Adams insisted that at most he should be addressed as the acting president, and Clay continued to refer to him as vice president because he thought that Tyler's "administration will be in the nature of a regency."[99]

He was a pleasant man with kind eyes and manners to match them. Soft-spoken and courtly, Tyler was only fifty-one years old in 1841 but was graying and had a dignified bearing with a sedate air. His sloping forehead, prominent nose, firm mouth, and strong chin made for a fetching face, which some said resembled a statue from the Greco-Roman world. His reserve gave the impression that he was self-effacing, and his affability, warmth, and humor had always made him a gracious friend and cordial opponent, traits that tended to mislead enemies and allies about Tyler's character. Blair had a low opinion of him. Expecting him to become Clay's "pliant tool," he called the new president "a poor weeping willow of a creature," a reference to stories about Tyler's tears over Clay's defeat at Harrisburg. Amos Kendall also judged Tyler as diffident and "not *man enough* for his position," while Clay weighed him as honest, patriotic, and having "ability quite equal to his predecessor" but with the "defect" of lacking "moral firmness." If from different perspectives Blair, Kendall, and Clay concluded that John Tyler was weak-willed, they had considerably missed the measure of the man, for beneath his seeming diffidence, Tyler was proud to the point of preening and principled to the point of obstinacy. "I believe that Tyler is a friend of Clay," said Willie Mangum, adding with discernment, "yet men change as we have recently seen."[100]

Like most outwardly unassuming but inwardly prideful men, Tyler could also be thin-skinned. For example, he was sensitive about his title because he correctly read into it the nature of his identity as chief executive. He did not plan to be a placeholder. Two days after Harrison's funeral, he issued a statement to the people in which he referred to "my administration," an expression Whigs found jarring. Sometimes referred to as Tyler's "inaugural address," on the surface it contained nothing that should have unduly alarmed his fellow Whigs. The new president agreed with Clay that the executive and legislative functions should be completely separate. Tyler's concerns over growing executive power had been one of the reasons he opposed Jackson and broke with the Democrats, and in his April 9 statement he gave indications of supporting the concept of legislative supremacy, at least to a point. But in reaching that point, Tyler also contradicted Harrison by omission. He did not disclaim a second term, for instance, and he implied a more liberal use of the veto in regard to measures he thought were unconstitutional.[101] The language and sentiments troubled many Whigs who had eagerly anticipated the restoration of legislative supremacy in which Congress would set policy under the guidance of their congressional leaders, Clay foremost among them.

Despite the April 9 message, Clay masked his worries about Tyler by claiming to believe that he would "contribute to carrying out the principles and policy of the Whigs."[102] He repeated the sentiment throughout April, but he was not as certain as he pretended. Clay confessed, "I believe—I shall rather say, hope that he will interpose no obstacle to the success of the Whig measures, including a Bank of the U.S."[103] Buoyed by his characteristic optimism, Clay at least claimed that a national bank was all but certain, and he sketched out the desirable features of it in letters to friends. One of those friends happened to be Treasury secretary Ewing, whom Clay expected would have a bill ready for the extra session. He wanted Congress to focus exclusively on the economy and avoid other issues that could distract it.[104]

Although Tyler would come to regret it, his determination to keep Harrison's cabinet calmed the party's fears at the time. Whigs regarded the cabinet's chief responsibility as exercising a high level of control over executive actions. In fact, the cabinet was supposed to act as a committee in which the president participated in discussions rather than presided over them, an arrangement that orthodox Whigs like Attorney General John J. Crittenden endorsed. To their way of thinking, Harrison's councilors would ensure the continuation of Harrison's attitudes in the new administration.[105]

Before Clay left Kentucky, however, he received a candid letter from John Tyler in which the new president said he thought the special session should only repeal the Subtreasury and attend to seacoast defenses. He expressed reservations about establishing a national bank and cited his reasons: the public would be wary of it, and capitalists would be cautious about investing in something that, as Jackson demonstrated, could easily be destroyed. But most ominously, Tyler related his constitutional misgivings over such a bank, remarks that gave Clay pause.[106] Shortly after receiving Tyler's troubling note, Clay had a letter from Ewing, who had obviously taken the measure of Tyler's qualms. The information that Tyler "would wish if possible to avoid the question at the special session" did not reassure, although Ewing did predict that Tyler would comply with the will of Congress. That and the guarantee that Tyler spoke of Clay "with the utmost kindness" and that Clay could count on Tyler's "strong & unabated" friendship were at least slender threads to hold on to.[107]

All too soon, though, those threads would snap. Tyler's defenders later insisted that everyone had known about his opposition to the Bank as well as other Whig projects and that nobody had the right to feign surprise over his opposition to them once he became president.[108] Yet as events unfolded, Whigs were not so much surprised as exasperated. The indication that Tyler intended to devise policy from the White House rather than comply with congressional initiatives overturned the basic principle of legislative supremacy in the first place, but it also undermined the Whig agenda that the country had voted for in 1840. In the wake of a Whig victory largely based on turning back executive usurpation, his claim that he would judge the constitutionality of congressional enactments courted ruin.[109]

Tyler should never have accepted the vice-presidential nomination of a party with which he fundamentally disagreed, for in the end his elevation to the presidency presented him, the Whig Party, and the country with an impossible situation. The nationalist wing was the Whig Party's most dominant, and as its leader, Henry Clay could exercise more influence than Tyler, the sectional advocate. On the other hand, Tyler as president had the powerful weapon of patronage, and more, he had the veto. The clash that resulted was a disaster for the Whig Party and its program, but it was also a debacle for John Tyler, the choice of the cynical Harrisburg delegates who had not taken into account that after all was said and done, he was at heart a Democrat.

IN THE SENATE, Clay quickly moved to establish a select committee to study the abysmal state of the currency and suggest a remedy. Responding to a question about the nature of that remedy, Clay laid his cards on the table. "A national bank," he said, despite Tyler's insistence in his message to the session that he would strike down legislation for any fiscal agent he thought unconstitutional. Clay got his committee, however, with himself as chairman. On June 2, Clay also wrote to Ewing in rather a state of pique. He had repeatedly tried to see him, but the secretary was never available. Clay flatly stated, "I wished to know whether you have made any, and, if any, what progress in the draft of a Bank Charter?"[110] And the following day, he forged ahead to begin the repeal of the Independent Treasury Act, fending off delaying tactics by Calhoun and others who tried to impede any consideration of a bank.

Clay was not alone in believing that the terrible state of the economy was cause for great haste. The refusal of banks to pay specie had dried it up rapidly, and day-to-day transactions were being conducted in banknotes of small denominations, beaten-up foreign currency, even tokens, and a complex web of credit speculation, promissory notes, and discounts. Foreign money remained the most prevalent currency in many areas of the country (and would continue so until Congress changed the system in 1857), with Americans still speaking of money in terms of pounds, shillings, and pence. Bringing order to this chaos was imperative to restoring financial health, and more than a few Americans believed the cure was a national bank. The board of trade in New York City sent Clay a petition signed by some twenty thousand citizens calling for a bank. Produced on a continuous sheaf, the petition was 250 feet long, and Clay dramatically presented it to the Senate by unrolling it with a flourish to show that it stretched from the secretary's table to beyond Clay's desk. Armed with that sort of support from all over the country, he bluntly responded to anyone who proposed alternatives to a bank, "I am tired of experiments."[111]

Getting the kind of bank he wanted would prove more than difficult. Five days after his impatient query to Ewing, Clay presented a comprehensive program to the Senate in which he charged the Whig majority in the House of Representatives with addressing revenue problems by means of loans and a higher tariff to replace the expiring one of 1833. He also urged his Senate colleagues to repeal the Independent Treasury, approve distribution, and revive the Bank.[112] Many saw Clay's agenda as a direct repudiation of Tyler's message.

On June 12, Ewing finally sent over the administration's bank bill. It landed in the Senate like a bomb. Tyler insisted that in establishing a fiscal agent Congress could act only as the District of Columbia's local legislature to charter a bank there. Furthermore, states could refuse branches of that bank by denying permission to create them.[113] Clay and his friends were dumbfounded. Without the branching power, the Bank could not hope to attract investors, hobbling it from the outset. "What a Bank that would be!" Clay marveled. Worse, allowing a state to block a federal agency amounted to a states' right fetish bordering on nullification. "We are in a crisis, as a party," Clay muttered. He now had the first tangible signal that Tyler might "throw himself upon Calhoun, Duff Green, &c &c and detach himself from the great body of the Whig party."[114]

As for Clay, Democrats began decrying his egotism and impatience. "He is much more imperious and arrogant with his friends than I have ever known him," Silas Wright told Van Buren. Blair's *Globe* accused him of being a dictator, and Democrats in the Senate took up the refrain. He was aware of the impression. When Clay tried to counter Democrat delays by changing Senate procedural rules on subjects for debate, he said he would "dictate a modification, though I do not like to be a dictator in any sense." Buchanan chirped, "You do it so well, you ought to like it," and Silas Wright grumbled, "That's fair," causing other Democrats to chime their agreement.[115]

The Whigs referred Ewing's bill to Clay's select committee, ostensibly to discuss it but actually to buy time for the Senate Whig caucus to draft an alternative. That group held lengthy daily meetings for the better part of a week. Sensitive to claims that he was being too dictatorial with friends as well as foes, Clay held his tongue, but the result was nevertheless a bill of his devising. On June 23, he brought it before the Senate. Clay's bill corrected the most obnoxious part of Ewing's proposal as far as Whigs were concerned. In the caucus's adaptation, Congress was competent to establish a national bank with the power to set up branches in the states without obtaining their approval.[116]

A majority of Whigs supported Clay's overt challenge to Tyler, but the subsequent debate over the bank bill pushed some in the party to side with the president. In the House, Henry A. Wise became his fellow Virginian's most steadfast supporter, and Democrat William Cabell Rives ("Little Billy Gold Spoons" to his enemies) followed suit, a portent of Tyler's eventual popularity with Democrats eager to make mischief among Whigs. A so-called Virginia Cabal became unofficial advisers to Tyler, and over the summer Tyler's real cabinet gradually lost influence to this shadow group. The prospect that a slew of presidential vetoes could scrap not only the centerpiece of the Whig program but also distribution and the tariff increases to fund it agitated Tyler's official family. Tom Ewing, it was said, had taken to his bed. Webster began an all-out drive to salvage the situation, first by trying to forge a compromise on Ewing's bill.[117]

Whigs in Congress, Clay included, were just as fearful of a veto. Consequently, while Webster worked on a compromise from his end, Clay reached out to the administration by meeting with Tom Ewing and apparently with Tyler himself. The only account of the interview between Clay and the president relates that it ended stormily with Tyler exploding: "Then, sir, I wish you to understand this—that you and I were born in the same district; that we have fed upon the same food, and breathed the same natal air. Go you now, then, Mr. Clay, to your end of the avenue, where stands the Capitol, and there perform your duty to the country as you shall think proper. So help me God, I shall do mine at this end of it as I think proper." Possibly this meeting occurred and in just this way, but like so much else in this episode, the account comes from a single source, John Tyler's son, who has rather surprisingly been regarded as a perfectly objective chronicler, despite the fact that he never produced a shred of documentary evidence for his account, was not born until twelve years after the event, and was only nine when his father died.[118]

Yet presuming that the president and Clay did have this angry interview, nobody should have blamed the latter for repairing to Congress and performing his duty there as he thought proper. John Tyler had told him to.

AS JUNE GAVE way to July, Clay's bill suffered eroding support as Webster wooed states' rights Whigs and lured the wavering with promises of patronage. Boiling temperatures made all irritable as they worked in the steamy Capitol for seven hours a day. When the Senate considered a resolution to begin the day at eleven rather than ten, Clay was disgusted by the prospect of prolonging debate with shorter sessions. If anything, they should start the day earlier! He recommended his regimen: he went to bed no later than ten and rose no later than five. He exercised by riding for at least an hour, sometimes more, then performed his ablutions, ate breakfast, scanned the newspapers, and went to work. He promised that anyone adhering to this course would be healthy and offered to pay their doctor's bills as a guarantee. The Senate decided to keep to its schedule, but Clay was not being altogether honest about his health. John, who had come with Clay to Washington, reported home that "Papa is at present much debilitated & even exhausted."[119]

It showed. He tired of the Democrats helping to block initiatives and compromises by casting votes with either the president's faction or his to intensify Whig differences. On July 17, a series of Democrat amendments to the extra session's loan bill finally exhausted Clay's patience, and Buchanan smugly said he was sorry to see Clay so angry.

"Not at all," said Clay, "not at all. I wish I had a more lady-like manner of expressing myself."

It was a clear and unkind reference to the rumors about Buchanan's sexuality. Buchanan responded: "I am afraid the Senator will lose the proper intonation of his voice if he pitches it on so high a key."

Clay shot back: "Not unlikely, as you can put my voice so often in requisition. . . . [I will] modulate [my] voice to suit the delicate ear of the Senator from Pennsylvania."

A couple of weeks later, it was Buchanan's turn to lose patience. He snapped that he would not want to be one of Clay's slaves because he was certainly "a severe master."

"Ask Charles," Clay retorted, "if I'm not a kind master." Buchanan said he was mightily sick of hearing about the fabled Charles Dupuy, whose numerous mentions on the Senate floor by Clay had made him "almost as notorious as his master."[120]

Clay's fighting trim could not stem Whig defections from his plan, and by the end of July it was clear that only a compromise reconciling his and Ewing's bills could pass Congress and avoid Tyler's veto. To break the impasse, Clay agreed to strike the branching power from the bank bill and require the consent of states, though within a specified time, after which the Bank could interpret silence as permission. This was a difficult compromise to swallow as it was, but Clay also added an amendment claiming the Bank had power to establish branches even without the states' permission if Congress deemed that the Constitution gave it such power.

On Saturday, August 7, the bill was presented to Tyler in the presence of his cabinet. He had everyone note the time (it was 1:20 P.M.), an ominous point of procedure. Tyler made plain that Clay's compromise was unacceptable, but days passed with no word from the White House, giving rise to speculation about Tyler's plans and the hope that he would let the deadline pass, thus allowing Whigs in Congress to have their way. It was all wishful thinking. On the morning of August 16, Ewing found Tyler putting the last touches on the veto message. He explained that if his objections spelled out in his message were met, Congress could have its bank in three days. As Congress awaited the veto that everyone now knew was coming, Clay received a note from Crittenden confiding that Tyler primarily objected to the proposed bank's power to compete with local institutions in making loans. The information renewed hope among congressional Whigs that a compromise with the White House was possible. On the face of it, they needed only to limit national bank branches to commercial activities such as promoting interstate transactions, a role that would boost local economies without infringing on local lending institutions.[121]

When John Tyler, Jr., appeared outside the Senate, the chamber fell silent as he "with some difficulty" made his way through the crowd gathered at the door to deliver his father's veto message. As it was read, spectators in the gallery began hissing, and Thomas Hart Benton angrily demanded that the sergeant-at-arms turn these people out. Clay watched in silence, unmoved by the commotion but obviously irritated by Tyler's message, which described the branching power in Clay's bill as unconstitutional and rebuked his compromise on state consent as "irrational." That tone colored the entire message and hardly indicated a conciliatory posture on the part of the president.[122]

Indeed, the veto outraged Whigs. That evening, a mob staged a protest outside the White House and the next night returned to burn Tyler in effigy. For his part, Clay regarded Tyler's stance as an act of executive usurpation rivaling those of Jackson and Van Buren. In addition, the veto convinced him that there was no dealing with this president, never mind Crittenden's assurances that removing local discounts would assure Tyler's approval of a bank. As it turned out, Clay was correct, for Tyler had little reason to meet him even partway on this issue. From the moment John Tyler became president, the real issue had not been about a bank or the tariff or distribution. In fact, Tyler's August 16 veto revealed that the bank issue was actually secondary to a larger question: Who was to be the leader of the Whig Party? Giving Clay a bank would certainly have answered that question, but the answer would not have been pleasing to John Tyler. The moment he became president, Tyler decided that he would be a candidate in 1844. The Whig Party was no longer big enough for both him and Henry Clay.[123]

Tyler's behavior after his veto would have provided additional proof of that, had Whigs not been so eager to look the other way, placate him, and prevent a break between their congressional majority and the White House. No one seems to have considered, for instance, that Tyler's objection to local discounts had surfaced quite unexpectedly, for he had not pointed to it in Ewing's original bill as a problem, suggesting that his hostility to the function was a contrivance.[124] The Whigs persevered as Clay became more passive in this renewed effort to pacify the president, not only because he rightly suspected that his involvement would impair real progress, but also because he doubted that real progress was achievable. "If our friends betray us," Wade Hampton ruefully noted, "what can we expect from our opponents."[125] After all, on the night of the veto, a delegation of Democrats that included Calhoun and William R. King visited Tyler to extend praise and congratulation. Tyler had a busy day.

Nevertheless, on the afternoon of the veto (before the mob assembled and the Democrats showed up), Virginia Whig congressman Alexander H. H. Stuart called on Tyler at the White House to propose a bank bill without local discounts. According to Stuart, Tyler leaped at the suggestion, saying that if Congress would send him such a bill he would "sign it in twenty-four hours." And though he instructed Stuart to avoid giving the impression that he was "dictating" to Congress, Tyler told his cabinet that all would be well.[126]

Whigs were excited by what they saw as a major breakthrough. The Whig caucus swung into action, albeit without Clay but with the assurance from Willie Mangum that Clay would pose no obstacle to the new plans. Just to make sure there was no misunderstanding, Senator John M. Berrien and Representative John Sergeant also called on Tyler the next day. Although they noticed that he was not as enthusiastic as Stuart had reported, they inferred that his reticence was to prevent the charge that he was meddling in Congress. They were wrong. That afternoon Tyler told John Bell that he was not certain he could accept any sort of bank at all, and that evening, he gave the cabinet the troubling news that he wanted the question postponed altogether. Unfortunately for him, the hasty work of the Whig caucus, acting on his request for speed and unaware that he had completely changed his mind in the space of forty-eight hours, made a postponement impossible. Its members had written the bill he said he wanted, even to the point of calling its object a "Fiscal Corporation" to avoid even mentioning a bank. They had the votes in both houses to put it on his desk as soon as possible.[127]

As these events were unfolding, Clay held his tongue and even delayed a symbolic attempt to override Tyler's veto. With that restraint, he allowed the Whig caucus to proceed with its plans. On Thursday, August 19, the caucus's amended bank bill was brought before the House of Representatives, while across the Capitol in the Senate chamber, Clay finally broke his silence. He spoke for about ninety minutes, attacking the language of the veto message as "harsh, if not reproachful." He all but accused Tyler of bad faith and concluded that the president would not have signed even Ewing's bill, presumably the administration's measure. Clay also fumed over Tyler's increasing reliance on a Kitchen Cabinet, a group he dubbed "a corporal's guard," a label that stuck in the public's memory as well as John Tyler's. Clay predicted that this group intended to use the presidency to form a third party committed to extreme states' rights. Other Whig critics were less restrained in their criticism of Tyler, derisively referring to the president as "Captain Tyler," a disparaging reference to Tyler's service in the Virginia militia. It became easy to blame Clay's speech and these other critics for alienating Tyler, but that conclusion ignores the president's growing reluctance to support the new bank bill two days before Clay spoke in the Senate.[128]

"The Whigs present the image of a body with its head cut off," said Clay as he became convinced that the breach with Tyler was irreparable.[129] The cabinet gloomily weighed the deteriorating situation. Another veto would compel it to resign, and all of them dreaded the prospect of leaving lucrative employment during hard economic times. One last effort to patch things up seemed in order, and Crittenden took the lead in organizing it. On Saturday night, August 28, he opened his house for a large party of about one hundred guests. His wife graciously arranged for the food and drink and sent invitations to key people, including Henry Clay and John Tyler. Senator Clay showed up smiling, but Tyler was nowhere to be seen. Without the president, the gathering was pointless.

Several congressmen went from Crittenden's to the White House and found its windows dark and doors locked. They banged away until Tyler appeared, and they more or less forced him to come out with them. Back at Crittenden's, Henry Clay answered the door with a broad smile. "Well, Mr. President," he said, "what are you for, Kentucky whiskey or champagne?" Tyler appeared shy and a bit confused, but Clay said, "Lets [*sic*] go take a glass," and the two went to the sideboard. "Come, Mr. Pres[ident]," Clay laughed, "what do you take[?] Show your hand." Tyler always preferred champagne to whiskey, and Clay poured him a glass. Tyler found his voice, and said he had come "for a frolick [*sic*]," although John Quincy Adams thought that he showed more "frolicsome agony" than sincere jolliness.[130]

Possibly Tyler was actually willing to make merry at least for that night, and Crittenden could have judged the event a success. A few days later, at a garden party on Capitol Hill, Clay approached Robert Tyler, shook his hand warmly, and said, "I am very glad to see you. I hope your father is well."[131] Clay was under no illusions, though. Other influences were obviously working their will on the president, and the debate on the Fiscal Corporation took place under "the general belief that he will veto the new bank bill."[132] Accordingly, Clay considered the process futile and resorted to sarcasm and angry invective, satirizing the "Loco Focos" for their August 16 visit to Tyler, evoking roars of laughter among senators and spectators.[133] The Whigs were deadly serious, however, and Clay did not need to say or do anything in this latest tilt with Tyler to rile them up. They were furious that their own president, in depriving them of their program, was likely to hand Democrats victories in the upcoming fall elections. They were grim and determined as they rammed the Fiscal Corporation through both houses and slammed it on Tyler's desk. On September 9, he vetoed it.

Because of the way the bill had come to life, this second veto presented the strange spectacle of a president essentially striking down his own initiative. Two days after the veto, Clay exhibited Whig frustration when he essentially asked: What on earth did Tyler want? The president had asked for the repeal of the Sub-treasury *and* for the creation of a "Fiscal Corporation." He approved the repeal of the Independent Treasury but had twice rejected its sensible replacement. The president had constitutional scruples? Clay pointed to the intolerable constitutional situation that Tyler had created. The president now had power over both the military *and* the Treasury, power over both sword and purse![134]

Even as Clay was speaking these words, Tyler sat at his desk, his son John at his side, and glumly watched as letters of resignation arrived from his cabinet. The first came in at half past noon, and the last appeared five hours later. John Jr. bleakly noted the exact time of arrival for each, a habit of his father's. Packing his papers in the attorney general's office, Crittenden was bitter. "In my present mood perhaps I could not do justice & therefore ought not to trust myself to speak of the President," he told a friend. Yet he did anyway. Tyler's conduct was reprehensible, muttered Crittenden; he had betrayed the people who had put him in office.[135]

CLAY'S ENEMIES—DEMOCRATS, states' rights Whigs, rivals with axes to grind—blamed him for the rupture, claiming that he was driven by ego to challenge the president for supremacy in the party and was spurred by ambition to cast aside an inconvenient incumbent in his way for 1844. Both of those goals required intransigence and imperiousness to the point of provocation, and consequently Clay was being unreasonable, inflexible, and provocative in a deliberate plan to drive Tyler from the Whig Party. This description became a formula for destroying Clay's reputation as a statesman at the time, reducing him to a petty politician with a pretty voice, but a petty politician all the same. Thus a man noted for his joviality was portrayed as overbearing with his friends and a "dictator" who would have everything his way or no way at all.

This theme of Clay's ego and ambition destroying the Whig Party persisted beyond his and Tyler's time, in part because of the Jacksonian lesson that persuasion was nine-tenths relentless repetition, in part because Clay's enemies were numerous and tireless. Rather than the often repeated adage that the victors write the history of an event, the story of anything is actually determined by the unswerving adoption of one version of it, and the telling of that version by a determined cadre of writers. In time, the version with the most persistent adherents becomes the "truth." Thus propaganda becomes history. The version of the Clay-Tyler clash that blamed everything on Clay was exclusively the product of his enemies, both in and out of the Whig Party. Just as Jacksonians were able to represent the routine political arrangement of 1825 as treachery on the order of Judas's betrayal of Christ, Clay's enemies in 1841 were able to render the image of an embittered man attacking an honorable president while smashing his political party in the process. As the years passed, a counter to that image gradually vanished. Enemies solidified it, fixed it as plausible, and gradually gained its acceptance without challenge.

After the Civil War, the publication of Henry Wise's memoir in the 1870s (dedicated to Tyler), Lucian Little's friendly account of Clay's Kentucky adversary Ben Hardin in 1887, and Lyon G. Tyler's two-volume tribute to his father in the 1890s furthered the process. These works appeared when nostalgic southerners, embracing the "Lost Cause," tended to remember many of the events preceding and during the war as missed opportunities. Virginians added a possessive protectiveness of the Old Dominion's sons, including Robert E. Lee and others such as John Tyler, often praising them by disparaging people from someplace else. Lee lost at Gettysburg because of his non-Virginian subordinates. Tyler had his presidency ruined because of the selfish aspirations of Henry Clay. In the midst of all this, James Lyons of Richmond published his damaging recollections in the New York *World* of August 31, 1880. There was Clay described as "violent" toward Harrison and arrogantly announcing early in the extra session that "Tyler dare not resist; I will drive him before me," the very picture, drawn four decades after the event, of the dictatorial and arrogant schemer.[136]

In the wake of these widely accepted accounts, the definition of "balance" became assigning at least some share of the blame to Tyler, but only to emphasize that there was plenty of blame to go around. Mostly, though, even objective or friendly biographers have been apt to cast Clay in the role of spoiler in 1841 and mark his behavior as lamentable. Less friendly writers condemn it as deplorable, even going so far as to say that Clay did not really want a bank at all but merely used Tyler's well-known opposition to it as a way to alienate him from the party.[137]

Yet Clay alone could not have challenged John Tyler without the unwavering support of his congressional colleagues, who were equally incensed by a putative Whig president acting like a Democrat. Tyler defended his inflexibility as a defense of the Constitution, claiming that Clay wanted to make the president a tool of the legislature, but Clay did not want to diminish Tyler's independence in those areas where it was constitutionally clear. Congress had no authority, Clay insisted on one occasion, to question the president's placement of U.S. military forces in war or peace, and any attempt to impinge on that executive prerogative was perilous. "In a crisis," Clay said, "when all depended upon secrecy and celerity in military operations, the plans of the commander might be thwarted by the interference of the legislative branch of the Government."[138]

"In what sense is Mr. Clay a *dictator*?" a Whig newspaper finally asked. "He has no offices to bestow—no patronage—no power. . . . The men who concur with him in opinion do so as his equals and his friends."[139] Political allies and objective observers apparently agreed. One pointed out that the label of "dictator" had been settled on Clay by the "locos" and that it was more appropriate to call him "the great Statesman of the West."[140] Later, after Clay had retired from the Senate, another joked about it, bemoaning the tendency of Congress to dally and speechify in the absence of a real leader and wishing for someone to impose a measure of legislative discipline: "If we had the Dictator, he could do it, like a soldier."[141]

In the fall of 1841, after the bruising fight, when everything had gone to ruin, Clay's enemies were in full voice, and they circulated the story that he had engineered the cabinet resignations to discredit Tyler's administration and ruin Tyler politically. Some pinned the story on Webster, and men who knew better characterized it as a baseless slander, especially when Ewing, Badger, and Bell explained themselves in lengthy letters to the newspapers. But the tale would not die. Two years later, its persistence exasperated Tom Ewing. Webster, he said, knew very well that nobody had consulted with Clay but had acted out of honor, had responded in the only way they could to a man who turned his back on his friends to embrace their enemies.[142]

At the time, Whigs dismissed out of hand such attempts to slander Clay. He emerged from the veto fights stronger than ever, and numerous Whig newspapers throughout the country that fall were already plumping him for president. He had not gotten his bank, but he had won the battle for political supremacy.[143] The gulf between the Whigs and Tyler immediately widened to complete rupture. Two days after the cabinet resignations, Whig congressional delegations convened in a garden near the Capitol and expelled the president from the party. In the months to come, Daniel Webster seemed to court the same fate. For on that Saturday of mass resignations, when it appeared that Tyler was indeed to be sunk by the desertions from his administration, Webster had not sent him a letter. Instead, Webster had come to Tyler's office to say that he would like to stay. Hearing these words, Tyler was giddy. "Give me your hand on that," he cried, "and now I will say to you that Henry Clay is a doomed man."[144]

CHAPTER TWELVE

Four Letters

"HENRY CLAY INSANE!" screamed the headline. "We should not be surprised to hear that he should attempt the assassination of Tyler, and all who oppose a Bank." "Like a whale stranded on a mudflat," Clay "lashed and spouted filth all around."[1] One Democrat newspaper in Ohio reported that rancor against Tyler had turned murderous. Clay's brother Porter—"a preacher of the gospel," it sniffed—had exclaimed on learning of the second veto, *"I wish somebody would assassinate him."* And another Whig was said to have pledged *"one hundred specie dollars to any one who will kill him."*[2] Not much of this was true, of course. Clay was not crazy, and Porter Clay most certainly had not wished Tyler dead. Yet some people apparently did. The president had in fact received death threats.

Even with all the acrimony during the extra session, some things had been accomplished. A new bankruptcy law was a sound measure, but in trying to help debtors, it incongruously seemed to favor wealthy spendthrifts. It was so unpopular that Whigs and Democrats alike began lobbying for its repeal the following year. A loan for $12 million to cover an anticipated budget deficit simply continued the Van Buren administration's practice of floating the Treasury with bond issues, but nobody much trusted the government's solvency after the quarrel over the Bank, and the loan did not begin to solve the revenue crisis. Raising the tariff proved equally difficult and in the end yielded disappointing and ineffective rates that produced insufficient returns.[3]

Land policy suffered as well, mainly because it became inextricably linked to the tariff. Without high duties, the government needed revenue from its only other asset, the public lands, a situation that required maintaining relatively high land prices, which the East favored but the West protested. Democrats had always opposed the distribution of land sale proceeds, favoring instead low land prices resulting from graduation (the gradual lowering of land prices) and preemption (preferential treatment for squatters). Clay could not persuade western members of his party to take the political risk of disowning preemption, because the policy was popular with their land-hungry constituents.

The compromise necessary to pass a Whig land law consequently produced a most unsatisfactory bill from Clay's perspective. By including a preemption policy, the legislation became a clear Democrat triumph. Preemption also diminished the funds available for distribution and, if that were not enough, Democrats peeled away enough Whigs to tack on an amendment tying distribution to the tariff as well. The instant that tariff duties climbed above 20 percent, distribution would cease. The irony was that Clay, with a Whig majority and an ostensible Whig president, had been able to realize only a fraction of the Whig program, while Democrats, in the minority for the first time in over a decade, were scoring gains that had eluded them during all the years they controlled Congress and occupied the White House.

In sum, the extra session dealt a serious blow to the Whigs. Despite having "passed in Congress all our great measures," as Clay somewhat inaccurately put it, lingering bad feelings about the Bank cast a pall over everything. Having repealed the Subtreasury, the Whigs put nothing in its place, leaving the Treasury to operate much as it had under Van Buren. More in sorrow than anger, Clay lamented, "If the President had been cordial with us, what a glorious summer this of 1841 would be!"[4]

Too late in moving toward conciliation, Tyler's second veto message was relatively timorous in tone compared to his first, and he plaintively inventoried the loan, the bankruptcy law, the tariff, and land policy as evidence that he could work with congressional Whigs. He even promised to reconsider a new fiscal agent when Congress met in regular session at the end of the year. But these were, after all, just words, and Tyler's actions spoke much louder. Before the second veto, Clay had been certain that the president would never join the Locofocos: "The soil of Virginia is too pure to produce traitors." By mid-September, he was not so sure. "Tyler is on his way to the Democratic camp," he predicted to the Whig caucus. "They may give him lodgings in some outhouse, but they will never trust him."[5]

It appeared that Tyler had wanted his cabinet to resign all along, for he was obviously ready with replacements when it did. His new cabinet contained several men whose primary qualifications were their allegiance to states' rights or their opposition to Henry Clay. At least they were all Whigs, although they were also, like Tyler, former Democrats. Clay described them warily as "a curious" lot. "If they work well together," he said, "it will be against all the laws of union and harmony; for a more incongruous collection of gentlemen could hardly have been got together."[6]

And then there was Daniel Webster. Tyler's jubilant exclamation to Webster that the two of them would doom Clay laid bare his belief that an alliance with the New Englander was imperative to salvaging his presidency, not to mention sustaining his quest to establish dominance in the party. Webster's motives for staying in the cabinet and risking his standing among Whigs were mixed. He plausibly explained to Massachusetts Whigs that duty required him to continue at the State Department while relations with Britain remained unsettled. New York had indicted one of the men allegedly responsible for torching the *Caroline* and was trying him for arson and murder, a proceeding that London warned would mean war if the trial ended with a conviction and death sentence. Weighing Webster's responsibilities, Clay accepted his reasoning, but he also gave Webster fair warning that if he were staying on to take Tyler's part, Whigs would condemn him.[7]

Clay's warning in the fall of 1841 did not sit well with Webster. He seems to have sincerely believed that Clay was behind the cabinet resignations, suspecting that the episode was engineered to injure him as much as to embarrass Tyler. Perceptive observers believed that Webster's decision to stay in the cabinet stemmed from his plans for 1844. Yet Clay found Webster's strategy hard to follow, especially if he thought he could exert any influence over Tyler. Clay knew that the president's intimates habitually spoke of Webster with contempt while flattering Tyler with visions of a third party and a second term. As for Webster's credibility with fellow Whigs, it had been seriously damaged when he acted as liaison on the second bank bill, assuring Congress that Tyler was on board. It was difficult to see how he could recover from the taint of Tyler's bad faith.[8]

Congress adjourned on September 13, a rainy Monday, and that night, the Whig caucus gathered for its farewell meeting. Everyone was somber, "like the weather and the night, dark and gloomy." Chairman Nathan F. Dixon, a Rhode Islander, had a puckish sense of humor despite his imposing appearance. At sixty-seven, he was "of the old school of gentlemen" and dressed accordingly, his snow-white hair in a cue that almost reached his waist. His gray eyes peered from behind spectacles at the doleful tableau the Whigs presented, but then he saw Clay, "tall and majestic," rising from his chair, beaming a broad smile, a cheerful lilt to his voice that perked everyone up.

"This is a dark night," Clay said, but he urged his fellow Whigs to take heart. "We, Senators, will soon pass away, but our principles will live while our glorious Union shall exist. Let our hearts be cheerful."[9] And as Clay continued, they did become cheerful in spite of themselves, in spite of John Tyler. Clay outlined the ordeals of the session and spoke in specifics about a program all knew by heart—bank, tariff, currency—but his insistence that those principles would not perish made them feel they were hearing it all fresh and for the first time. Like Dixon, they were looking intently at Henry Clay as he spoke. As they listened to his confident speech, they knew they were looking at the future of their party, and as their glimmering optimism grew, they saw the future of their country as well, at least if they had anything to say about it.

Clay castigated Tyler, of course. That sort of flourish had become automatic with all of them. But his close was a lighthearted tribute to Dixon's "manner . . . which . . . by a single look, kept order at our meetings." To a growing chorus of chuckles, Clay said that "the most excited, the most boisterous, has been quieted at once, and brought into lamb-like docility." He concluded by wishing that "the whole civilized world" had seen such a deft and good-natured chairman at work.

Dixon rose to the occasion. He said he considered himself Clay's superior as a presiding officer for he had kept "order among the most disorderly body that was ever assembled." By now, everyone was laughing, both surprised and relieved that the wake had been unexpectedly transformed into a celebration. Dixon continued: some might have suspected that Clay "was not in full earnest" in his praise of the chair's parliamentary skills, he solemnly intoned. But they should always "give [Clay] full credit for sincerity, for any remarks he may make before ten o'clock at night"—Dixon theatrically paused—"after that there may be some doubts."[10] The room erupted into applause and roars of laughter.

It was almost midnight before everyone parted, and the next day they began their journeys home. They left Washington buoyed by the cheerful words, jovial banter, and infectious optimism of Clay. "Remember," he would say throughout an otherwise depressing autumn, "that we have a fine Country."[11]

They intended to make him the future of it.

BACK IN LEXINGTON, Clay attended to Ashland's enterprises, including the financial health of the farm, the care and feeding of his horses, and producing that year's brood of pigs. Clay preferred Berkshires. He bred them in the first week of December in order to have piglets in April. In the second week of May, when the pigs could crack corn, the boars were neutered and the sows spayed for meat in the fall. He held out enough boars and sows for reproduction, segregating them until early December to begin the process anew. He always fed them well. Clay believed that "starving never succeeds with man or beast."[12]

He saw that mules were delivered to a buyer and arranged for an auction of some forty blooded cattle, selected horses, several asses, and about thirty additional mules. Clay was not merely winnowing his inventory of livestock. He needed money as the economic emergency afflicting the country finally began to hit close to home. James Erwin's finances remained a worry, not just because of the grandchildren but also because Erwin's business was in part linked to Clay through endorsed notes and loans.[13]

Clay's primary source of anxiety was Thomas's rope and bagging business that had been founded in partnership with Mary's brother Waldemar Mentelle. James Brown Clay participated briefly in the venture, though only in a limited way, and Clay was always its primary backer. Begun with high hopes in 1839, the business was troubled from the start by fluctuating prices, unexpected expenses, bad weather, and the normal difficulties of starting up any venture in hard times. Thomas turned out to be at best a marginal businessman, and Waldemar wasn't appreciably better. Bad reports followed upon bad reports with distressing frequency, and that fall, matters began to unravel. To keep Thomas afloat, Clay endorsed notes and dispatched bank drafts. Despite his encouragement and advice, he suspected the Clay-Mentelle rope and bagging venture was sinking.[14]

As for himself, he felt he had little choice, quite literally throwing good money after bad as he doggedly continued his assistance, indebting himself and pledging to cover Thomas's debts for tens of thousands of dollars. The business lasted only into the following summer, but by then Clay had sunk almost $30,000 into it, a massive liability that forced him to pledge Ashland as collateral. He began the unpleasant task of calling in loans with minor success, as he scrupulously avoided dunning debtors. He also sold off assets it had taken him a lifetime to accumulate. Unless his fortunes improved, Clay confronted the possibility of losing everything, including Ashland. He put on a brave face. "The times are gloomy enough," he told Lucretia, "but we must all try to preserve our spirits, and not sink beneath their pressure."[15]

While this depressing state of affairs began unfolding, the fall state elections added to the gloom. Skillful patronage appointments kept John Tyler's political fortunes alive by sacrificing Whig unity and, worse, by confusing voters. The result was, as Clay had predicted, a rout by Democrats in state after state. In just one year, all the gains of 1840 vanished, because Whig voters did. Across the country, they stayed away from the polls in droves. Clay said candidates should have expected it. Tyler had betrayed them all. Why would people remain loyal to a party led by a treacherous man?[16]

The catastrophe convinced most Whigs that they had to rally around a leader with unquestioned allegiance to the party's agenda. Obviously, that was not John Tyler, and because of his continuing association with Tyler, it was not Daniel Webster. Some were touting "that Peacock Genl. Scott," but his support was at best slight. Only Henry Clay, the man they had cast aside in 1839 for the electable Harrison, now carried the magical prestige described by nodding politicos as "availability." Southern Whigs came to the conclusion fairly early and were important in boosting Clay's popularity. To them, Tyler's first veto had been an understandable, if not agreeable, expression of his constitutional principles, but many regarded his second veto as simply spiteful. One North Carolinian thought that Whigs "should hoist the Clay flag forthwith," and Willie Mangum was soon exhorting his neighbors in the Old North State to take the lead, "nominate Mr. Clay for the presidency, *unconditionally,*" and quash all maneuvering and double-dealing at the national convention.[17]

With his political fortunes on the rise, Clay arrived in Washington on Sunday, December 5, for the regular session of the Twenty-seventh Congress with a miserable cold. He never completely recovered his health throughout the session. In January, he was diagnosed with a severe case of pleurisy, which laid him low for days. Clay was consequently not the leading cause of Tyler's continuing problems with the legislature during these weeks. Instead, Whigs on their own made the president's life miserable. Convinced that reconciliation with the administration was futile, they mounted a full-bore attack to block Tyler's initiatives in the House while the Senate refused to confirm many of his appointees.[18]

In the void left by the repeal of the Subtreasury and his vetoes of a bank, Tyler tried to satisfy both Whigs and Democrats with a fiscal agency he dubbed the Exchequer, but nobody in either party much cared for the ungainly creature. Additional restrictions designed to allay Tyler's obvious distaste for a real national bank did not help. In fact, the Exchequer bill did not stand a chance of being adopted, and when Tyler stubbornly insisted that the country supported his plan, Clay shook his head: "Poor deluded man!"[19]

Finally, in the last week of December, Clay was well enough for a time to resume his Senate seat, and he immediately took up the fight against the Exchequer with parliamentary maneuvers that sent the proposal to a committee that in turn refused to bring it to a vote. Meanwhile, on December 29, he proposed constitutional amendments to curtail executive power. Foremost in his plan was the restriction of the hated veto. He always claimed that it was not Tyler's behavior that prompted him to oppose the veto power (after all, he had made similar proposals during Jackson's presidency), but rather, sound principles of republican government led him to do so. Unchecked veto authority, he said, gave the president despotic power to control the course of legislation. He could hamper and usually kill congressional initiatives merely by intimating that he would veto them. At the very least, Clay said, an override should require only a simple majority, and eventually he deprecated every instance of a veto, from the great George Washington to the miserable "Captain" Tyler, as an abuse of power, a thwarting of the people's apparent will in their elected representatives.[20]

Clay also wanted to institutionalize Harrison's pledge to reduce the president's control over the Treasury by giving Congress authority to appoint its secretary. To prevent patronage abuse bordering on bribery, Clay proposed to bar members of Congress from accepting presidential appointments during their terms. Finally, he declared his support for an amendment to limit the presidency to one term.[21] Clay's amendments proposed radical changes, and though he was quite serious about them, he could not even persuade his friendly colleagues to give them any more than passing attention. In the end they became more symbolic than realistic proposals, at best emphasizing the dangers of executive usurpation. None ever came to a vote, and all quietly disappeared in March 1842.

Clay remained ill and irritable, and Senate debates brought out the worst in him as he fell into the habit of lashing out at the slightest provocation. During the debate on repeal of the Bankruptcy Act, Clay butted heads with Thomas Hart Benton when Benton began imperiously hectoring Whigs who held the floor, adding to the insult by haughtily lounging in his chair. When Benton began shouting "False, false" during Nathaniel P. Tallmadge's remarks, Clay rose to insist that the senator from Missouri was out of order. Benton shouted at him. Clay whirled, his face a thundercloud. "The Senator shall not address *me* in his seat," he spat, "and if he does, it shall be followed by language corresponding to such conduct."[22]

Three days after his irate exchange with Benton, Clay suffered a back seizure so severe that he would have fallen if friends had not caught him. He called it "lumbago," one of those picturesque terms the nineteenth century used for lower back pain, and he soon reported it as a passing malady. Yet it was clear that his work was beginning to impose a high toll on him.[23]

To make matters worse, relations with Tyler reached their lowest ebb, for the president gave as bad as he got. Anyone even suspected of supporting Clay was politically punished, and his most distant acquaintances found themselves frozen out of the patronage. The "President is moreover jealous, envious, embittered towards me," Clay said glumly as he assessed their irretrievable relationship, and he caviled at suggestions he was mainly at fault. "He has power; I have none."[24]

That February, Clay's mail contained a letter from Carter Beverley, the author of the infamous 1827 letter that had given new life to the charges of the Corrupt Bargain by giving Jackson the chance to say that Clay's friends had put the presidency up for bids. Clay had always regarded Beverley as simply another Jackson pawn and was certain his letter had been prompted by Jackson in the same way and for the same reason George Kremer's wretched accusation had. Now, Clay had to be surprised as he read Beverley's lengthy note. The Virginian said he was certain that the timeworn allegations against Clay would be resurrected for the 1844 election, and he therefore wanted to repair the damage he had done in 1827. He recanted his earlier accusations. It had taken fifteen years for him to say so, but Beverley now declared that he had concluded "long ago" that "the very greatest injustice was done you in the charge made." To allay suspicions that this latest statement was arranged for political effect, Beverley pledged that he and Clay had had no contact for more than a decade.[25]

From the tone of his response, it seems Clay was scarcely impressed by Beverley's soul-searching and the confession it produced. The entire affair, he said, "has been of late very rarely thought of by me," and he claimed that only after rereading the 1827 letter was he reminded of Beverley's role in the affair. Neither of these statements was truthful, of course, for hardly a day went by that Henry Clay did not smart under the ancient charge that he was a corrupt schemer. All could not be forgotten nor any of his tormentors forgiven for the years of irreparable damage just because they were now willing to admit they were wrong. At most, he could register a cool gratitude. "I am thankful for the justice your letter has done me," he said, "which is creditable to your heart." As for the admission, Clay assured Beverley that he did not need it for *his* conscience but would act on Beverley's permission to publish it to prove as baseless "the calumny of which I have been the object." Beverley was exultant, as if Clay's chilly note were an absolution.[26]

Carter Beverley's conscience was clear and his mood lighthearted as a result, but Clay had lived with this cloud over his head for so many years that he knew Beverley's prediction was unrealistic. Sure enough, in his campaign for governor of Tennessee the following year, James K. Polk began talking about Clay's "Corrupt Bargain" with references so casual as to indicate they had become a reflexive routine with Democrats, like inquiring about one's health or mentioning the weather. It had become over the years a kind of verbal tic. As 1844 approached, they again resorted to the charge as if to fill the air while thinking of something else to say. Clay knew that as long as a single supporter of Andrew Jackson walked the earth, the phrase "Corrupt Bargain" would never die.[27]

OF COURSE OTHER attacks were made. In February, Clay's role in the 1838 duel between William Graves and Jonathan Cilley again became a point of dispute. Because Tyler partisan Henry A. Wise was at the center of this latest controversy, Clay suspected that dredging up the episode had as much to do with assaulting his character as with getting the facts straight.[28]

As the regular session of the Twenty-seventh Congress wore on, the government had to address the looming financial crisis caused by the failure of Treasury bonds to attract investors. Making the situation worse, the first of two tariff reductions mandated by the Compromise Tariff of 1833 had already occurred in January, and the second was to take place in the summer. Worried that a strapped Treasury would not be able to fund basic operations, even the military, Tyler and the Whig majority clashed on how best to solve the problem. He wanted to stop distribution, but Whigs wanted to postpone tariff reduction. On February 15, Clay introduced a plan in eleven sprawling resolutions, which he described as a comprehensive project to restore the country's prosperity and stabilize its economy. Government solvency and the restoration of confidence were crucial. In fact, Washington should lead by example through retrenchment that embraced the strictest economies, cutting departmental budgets in the executive branch as well as the judicial. Nothing, not even the franking privilege, should escape scrutiny. He condemned the recent practice of raising revenue with loans and Treasury notes. Instead, the tariff should be increased, and the linking of distribution to tariff levels repealed. Distribution was a pledge to states already suffering dire financial embarrassments, and breaking that promise would not only mean dishonor but would discourage renewed confidence in the government. Learning that Alabama Democrats had pushed the state to take the lead in refusing on principle to accept its portion of distribution proceeds, Clay was dismayed. Any state's refusal to do so was resistance to federal law, he said, and merely applied the doctrine of nullification by "sneaking and cowardly" means rather than "the bold and daring ones" of South Carolina in 1832.[29]

Having spelled out the Whig economic vision in elaborate detail, within twenty-four hours Clay wrote to the Kentucky legislature to resign from the Senate effective March 31. He had accepted the seat with the likelihood that he would not serve the entire six-year term, and as early as the previous fall he had been intimating that he would not remain beyond another session of Congress and was likely to leave before it concluded. Washington, he said, "has ceased or is ceasing to have any charms for me."[30] Doubtless that was true, but two other factors were the leading causes for the decision's timing. He wanted to quit while the Kentucky legislature was in session and could choose his replacement (the Kentucky General Assembly unanimously selected his friend and lieutenant Crittenden, as it happened), but his presidential plans mostly determined his timing. His stated reason—that he was resigning to remove a source of strain between Congress and the White House—was obviously a pretext and deceived nobody.[31]

Instead, his departure on March 31 would come just prior to the Whig convention in North Carolina, scheduled for April 4 and urged by Mangum and others to nominate Clay. The Tarheel endorsement would consequently occur after his official retirement in order to avoid any suggestion that he was using his place in Congress to politick for the presidency. Freed from that restraint, he could begin consolidating his national support in the third and last of his campaigns, heading off rivals like Webster, who was doing himself in with Tyler, and Winfield Scott, who was attractive at most as a running mate on a Clay ticket. Appearance in these political games was everything, and despite his obvious intentions, Clay was careful to continue the ruse of reluctance, insisting that he had not yet decided "to consent to the use of my name."[32] That sort of statement didn't fool anybody either.

Clay so wanted a vote on his eleven resolutions before his retirement that he overexerted himself, defending his program in late March with a speech of three hours. Observers noted that his performance was disjointed and rambling, and the next day he suffered "an excrutiating [*sic*] stricture" on the left side of his chest. His physician cupped and purged him, but the signs pointed to something a great deal more serious than a cold or rheumatism. It is very likely that on March 24, Clay suffered a heart attack. He had ruefully predicted that his retirement would not satisfy his enemies. "Death only can accomplish" that, he said, "or the total loss of public confidence." As the doctor applied the red-hot glasses to blister out the supposed toxins and dosed him with emetics, Clay almost gave them their first wish.[33]

He was on his feet, however, just a week later to deliver his farewell address to the Senate, denying his enemies his death, and with an emotional performance proving that he could still command public confidence. He traced his history with the Senate to laud it as "this noble theatre of my public service," and he recalled the many friends with whom he had served. He expressed regret over the disappointments of this and the extra session, but he was certain that reflection and time would put matters right. He could not overlook, though, how "a recent epithet . . . has been applied to me," that "I have been held up to the country as a dictator!" He bristled:

> If I have been a dictator, I think those who apply the epithet to me must
> at least admit two things: In the first place, that my dictatorship has been
> distinguished by no cruel executions, stained by no deeds of blood,

soiled by no act of dishonor. And they must no less acknowledge, in the second place . . . that if I have been invested with, or have usurped the dictatorship, I have at least voluntarily surrendered the power within a shorter period than was assigned by the Roman laws for its continuance.

Having gotten that out of his system, he continued in a more reflective, pleasant tone, and finally, after presenting John J. Crittenden's credentials, he closed:

May the blessings of Heaven rest upon the heads of the whole Senate, and every member of it; and may every member of it advance still more in fame, and when they shall retire to the bosoms of their respective constituencies, may they all meet there that most joyous and grateful of all human rewards, the exclamation of their countrymen, "well done thou good and faithful servants." Mr. President, and Messieurs Senators, I bid you, one and all, a long, a last, a friendly farewell.[34]

Crittenden ceremoniously took his seat, and it was done. A prolonged ovation along with whistles, shouts, and even tears greeted Clay as he ambled through the chamber, shaking hands and receiving in that moment sincere, unalloyed affection from both Whigs and Democrats crowding around him. Calhoun made his way through the throng of senators, finally coming face-to-face with the man he had come to call an enemy. They had not spoken socially since 1837, their oblique and sometimes searing references to each other coming exclusively in often angry debates on the Senate floor. They did not speak now in the raucous din that kept on and on as each stood staring into the other's eyes. They had begun together so many years before, boarding in the War Mess, when the new country was on the verge of challenging Britain over honor as much as commerce. They had stared without blinking at the most powerful empire on earth, the talented boy from the Carolina Upcountry and the magnetic one from the Virginia Slashes, a good team. Then they had been immortal. Now they were old men, sicker than they knew, like the country, and divided over slavery and sectionalism, like the country. Calhoun's passions, so relentlessly suppressed under his didactic manner, had begun to act as forge and anvil on the rugged good looks of his youth, making everything about this iron man stark, severe, metallic, even his eyes, which he often fixed in an angry stare. But now they stared at Henry Clay to see the end of an era, and even the iron man could not help himself as he welled up. Calhoun extended his hand. Clay opened his arms.[35]

Their embrace stirred an even greater volume of cheers and applause, but more important for them, it washed away the venom for a brief moment, the best medicine in the world for Henry Clay's injured heart, more than good for what ailed him.

HENRY CLAY HAD every reason to believe that he had closed a chapter of his life with his retirement from the Senate. His ten years there seemed in symmetry with his career in the national legislature, a fitting counterpart for his groundbreaking service as Speaker of the House, and his achievements in many contentious sessions, while meager in number, were significant. His defeats were profoundly disappointing, but mostly people would remember his victories, especially his successful work to defuse crises that threatened the Union. He had mastered the workaday routines of the Senate and occasionally chided much younger colleagues who found legislative schedules too arduous; but his real talent was in the magic of his personality. Whether he was mesmerizing his colleagues and the gallery from the floor, or producing improbable majorities through casual conversations at parties and careful negotiations in committees, Clay walked the capital as a giant. When he said his farewell to deafening applause and John C. Calhoun's sad stare, it indeed marked the end of an era. Most such conclusions emerge as important only in retrospect, but all who witnessed Clay retire from the Senate knew they had seen something extraordinary. For the rest of their lives those men and women would tell of that occasion, ending with the simple declaration: "I was there."

Clay quit the Senate but did not immediately leave for home. Instead, he remained in Washington for most of April to attend a round of parties in his honor. His lingering in Washington was not just social but political, as Democrat newspapers resentfully noted. "Henry Clay is *eating* and *dancing* his way to the Presidency," one grumbled, obviously put off by evidence of his swelling popularity and signs of increasing Whig unity behind him. As expected, North Carolina did its part to launch his presidential bid when the Whig convention in Raleigh gave him a ringing endorsement. A delegate reported that "the very mention of his name appears to brighten the countenance of every member and inspire him with fresh and increased zeal."[36]

Feted in Washington and celebrated across the country, Clay triumphantly returned to Kentucky where the mild winter had given way to a glorious spring. Although on the day of his arrival, May 2, the weather had turned gray and drizzly, it didn't matter. As he approached Lexington, thousands on horseback and mules and ladies in countless carriages streamed out to greet him at the Five Mile Bridge, the procession stretching more than a mile. Lexington's bells pealed as a band stood outside the Dudley House blasting out favorites such as

"Jenny Get Your Hoe Cake Done" and "Rosin the Bow." In due course, Clay reached Ashland and Lucretia. He had been longing to see both.[37]

Of all his many callers that spring, Clay was most eager to have Martin Van Buren visit him at Ashland. He extended a hearty invitation for Van Buren to make the house his "headquarters," and the ex-president gratefully accepted the hospitality. He arrived on May 20 and remained at Ashland for almost a week. Van Buren was in good health, a plump 172 pounds (not such a "little" magician anymore), and thoroughly enjoyed his time with his host. Unlike Jackson and Calhoun, who took political disagreement as a personal affront, these two could put aside differences to share stories, trade jests, gossip, and lay wagers, and they apparently did just that and little else during Van Buren's stay. In fact, Clay remarked after Van Buren departed that they had spoken about many things but had not discussed political affairs.[38]

It seems unlikely that these two political animals could spend days together and not talk politics, especially in light of what happened in 1844. Clay would later visit Van Buren's New York home, "Lindenwald," where they "talked over old scenes without reserve." These visits became objects of deep suspicion, suggesting to some cooperation beyond cordiality. Yet possibly their time together was in fact only spent in telling jokes and recalling "old scenes." Just as everyone expected Clay to be the Whig nominee in 1844, Van Buren became a foregone conclusion for the Democrats. His southern journey was, after all, a political trip thinly disguised as a sightseeing jaunt, the custom of the time. Possibly they both had been cagey, at most feeling each other out with indirect remarks, preserving the good humor that was so elusive for their supporters. "Thus do the sensible leaders of the two parties," James Gordon Bennett mused, "while away the lovely spring afternoon in Ashland, with a glass of cool claret between them—the birds singing over their heads—the heavens bright and blue above—and their respective partisans throughout the country, abusing, fighting, and disgracing themselves like so many fiends, in the conflict that is about [to take] place."[39]

Lexington held a grand barbecue in Clay's honor on June 9. It was the perfect occasion for him to launch his campaign, and he looked forward to it with "excitement." On the appointed day, about twenty thousand people gathered outside of town at Maxwell's Spring, a lush bluegrass pasture hemmed by stately trees. There would have been more people from distant locales, but bad weather during the previous two days had discouraged travel. Great piles of meat and vegetables were put on tables at one o'clock, and after the food and the customary toasts and tributes, Clay rose to speak. For more than two hours before a cheering crowd, he turned in a characteristically masterful performance.[40]

After a brief biographical sketch in which he once more exaggerated the poverty of his youth (a staple of American politics by now) and again explained his actions in 1825 (a staple of Clay's political life by now), he hit his stride to smite Democrats hip and thigh. He cataloged the financial dislocations of the 1830s and what had caused them, particularly Jackson's and Van Buren's mishandling of the currency, land policy, and the banking establishment. That was only the start, though, and he delved deeper to condemn nullification, the admission of territories without proper procedures, and state election frauds perpetrated to secure Democratic majorities.

Where he was lengthy and methodical with his denunciation of Democrats, he dismissed John Tyler as unworthy of notice. Calling Whigs to action in his final paragraph, he shouted at its close, "As for Captain Tyler, he is a mere snap—a flash in the pan—pick your Whig flints and try your Rifles again."[41] The crowd rollicked and rolled in delight at this sharp, succinct barb, just as Clay knew it would, but others, including his son James, winced over it. "Perhaps your criticism . . . is just," Clay later admitted to a friend who gently chided him for the remark, especially its reference to firearms. Clay rather lamely defended himself with humor by reminding critics that he was talking to a Kentucky audience, some of whom, being hunters of Kentucky, were "accustomed to the rifle." Yet on reflection he was sorry to have been caught up in the moment, a trap that often snared the habitually extemporaneous speaker. "After all," he finally sighed to a critic, "you may be right."[42]

"All our friends here," wrote Crittenden from Washington, "would be flattered by your correspondence, & you must task yourself a little to please them." Yet Bob Letcher, who had been impressed by Clay at the barbecue, at least up to a point, was wary of ruining a sure thing. "The old Prince is taking a pretty considerable rise everywhere, I can tell you," he wrote to Crittenden. "I guess he now begins to see the good of leaving the Senate,—of *getting off* a while merely to *get on* better." Yet Letcher worried about Clay's tendency to talk himself into trouble, not just in speeches like the one at the barbecue with the imprudent crack about Tyler, but with impolitic letters. "He must hereafter remain a little quiet and *hold his jaw*," Black Bob counseled. "In fact, he must be *caged*—that's the point, *cage him*! He swears by all the gods, he will keep cool and stay at home. I think he will be prudent, though I have some occasional fears that he may write too many letters."[43]

Nobody could have imagined in that sunny spring of Clay's western star rising that Letcher was more right than even he knew. He had reason to be worried about Clay's travels and especially about Clay's letters. Henry Clay was an indefatigable letter writer and could churn out a half dozen to the hour. More than a few Whigs feared that Clay's volubility would eventually spoil everything. "If St. Paul had been a candidate for the Presidency," one fretted, "I should have advised him to cut the Corinthians and not to let the Hebrews even see his autograph."[44]

DURING THAT SUMMER in 1842, Kentucky's grand weather produced abundant yields, and Clay was busy with "extensive preparations to Water rot Hemp," a new process for him because he had always before used the process of dew rotting. Meanwhile, his lieutenants in Washington kept him abreast of events, and taking to heart Crittenden's advice, he was not timid about counseling them on strategy. A series of deft maneuvers made Willie P. Mangum president pro tem over Tyler's choice of Richard H. Bayard. The defeat wounded the White House because it was another sign of Tyler's declining influence in Congress.[45]

Despite that success, Whigs had the same problem in 1842 as in the previous year. Clay's program was just as certain to invite Tyler's veto then as before. Whigs delayed passing legislation as a tactic, throwing bills on Tyler's desk amid the gravest financial distress in the hope that it would make him reluctant to strike them down. Consequently, it was not until late in June that Congress voted to postpone to August 1 the second tariff reduction and distribution. Tyler did not hesitate in the least. He promptly vetoed it on the grounds that distribution was prohibited as long as tariff duties remained above 20 percent.[46]

From one perspective, Tyler could argue that Congress had linked the 20 percent duty rate with distribution, but Whigs could counter that he was no longer applying the maxim that he would veto bills only on constitutional grounds and was now doing so when he simply disagreed with a measure. His insistence that he knew best was alone enough to fan Whig anger. Crittenden looked for the silver lining. With every veto, he told Clay, "Tyler is one of your *best friends.*" Clay, however, took little pleasure in the continued thwarting of the party's agenda. Not to stand for anything other than winning elections and holding on to office was repellent. Government under that formula became merely a grubby scramble for power and privilege. Tyler might think he was doing right, but Clay was finding it hard to continue giving him that much credit. "We could get along with a man who was only a fool or knave, or mad," he muttered, "but the extraordinary occurrence of all three of those qualities combined in one person is intolerable."[47]

After this latest setback, the Whigs decided to use the tariff to bait a trap. Instead of reducing duties below 20 percent, they raised them so steeply that Tyler would not be able to stomach them. For good measure, they again included distribution in defiance of his most recent veto, clearly to provoke another one.

Either the Treasury would dry up or the Whigs would have their tariff. Clay was more direct. The party, he declared, had "bearded the old Lion [Jackson] amidst his loudest roars. Surely it will not give way, or suffer itself to be frightened by the pranks of a Monkey."[48]

As expected, Tyler vetoed this new bill on August 9, and as planned, Whigs embarked on a determined effort to drive him from the party once and for all. Even though they had already expelled him, Tyler continued to call himself a Whig.

The Whigs finally succeeded in forcing John Tyler to make plain his opposition to almost everything they stood for, and his repeated use of the veto gave validity to their accusations of executive usurpation. Yet Whigs also skewered themselves with this strategy. The country was in no mood for squabbling and symbolism while the government faced default and bankruptcy. Congress had to provide a source of revenue, and that obligation ultimately forced Whigs to strip distribution from a tariff bill. Doing so further divided them because many would not support a tariff without distribution. Only by cracking the whip did Whig managers manage to ram the bill through, and Tyler clenched his teeth to sign it. The government simply had to have the money, distasteful as this was to almost everyone as a means to get it.

By almost every measure the extra and second sessions of the Twenty-seventh Congress were disastrous for the Whig Party. Flush with victory in 1840, two years later all they had to show for it was a petulant president, a re-tired statesman, a slightly higher tariff obtained only by sacrificing distribution, and an unsatisfactory land policy achieved only by their swallowing preemption. Their legislative program aside, the real catastrophes for the party lay in elections. Just as in 1841, the fall elections of 1842 held grim portents, only this time they included congressional off-year contests that turned out enough Whigs in the House to install a Democrat majority.

The likely prospect of Tyler moving toward the Democrats or stealing away wavering Whigs with a third party movement completed the wretched picture. Only Clay's growing popularity gave them hope. Perfect strangers not only felt a connection, they did not refrain from telling him so. A man from Clayton, New York, spoke for many: "I have never had the honor of a personal acquaintance with you, but Still I love you," he told Clay that spring. "Strange as it may seem:—I have communed with your mind, and the name Henry Clay is endeared by 10,000 recollections." In the bright light of such adulation, his candidacy seemed irresistible, his victory in 1844 inevitable. Georgia Whigs nominated him, and New York Whigs would not hear of any other candidate. "Clay is going ahead like a *locomotive*," Crittenden marveled. Tyler could not challenge him, nor, it seemed, could any real Whig. Winfield Scott's fortunes in Pennsylvania were illustrative. A brief Keystone boomlet for him that summer quickly fizzled. Scott knew the truth of it. "He is a good Whig & a good fellow," Crittenden nodded, certain that Scott would support Clay when the time came. They all would.[49]

BY THE 1840S, no campaign was complete without heartwarming stories highlighting a candidate's rapport with ordinary people. One making the rounds about Clay had him stopping at an exclusive hotel in Virginia. The clerk did not recognize Clay and after surveying his dusty clothes concluded he was a farmer who had fetched up far above his place and far beyond his pocketbook. There were no private rooms, the clerk sniffed, but he could allow Clay to bunk in with several other lodgers of his sort. Clay said that would be fine and trudged up four flights of stairs to a room full of snoring tradesmen. The next morning as they all dressed for breakfast he quickly made these fellows his friends with his easygoing manner and wealth of funny stories. Downstairs, they asked who the "funny old cock" was, but the staff did not know. Their roommate soon appeared in the dining room, and a well-dressed, courtly gentleman quickly rose from his chair to greet "Senator Clay." The tradesmen swallowed hard, and the clerk was in a cold sweat as he quietly ordered the best room in the place prepared, the one reserved for the president of the United States. He then timidly approached Clay to offer a stumbling apology and inform him his room was ready. "Never mind, sir," Clay said, "your *rooms are all occupied,* [and] I am perfectly satisfied with my present accommodations."[50]

Another story told of a blacksmith approaching Clay in Blue Lick Springs, Kentucky, and wanting to shake his hand. Clay heartily took the "honest hand" that forged iron with one that forged laws while chuckling that they both "had to strike while the iron was hot." The blacksmith said admiringly, "My blows only make the anvil tremble, whilst yours shake empires." The Louisville *Journal* nodded approvingly, "This was well said."[51]

Clay actually never pandered to the poor, however, even in election seasons. When Ohio Democrat William Allen tried to abolish the tariff on salt by arguing that it would benefit the poor, Clay called the effort highly offensive because "any attempt to select certain classes for taxation was absurd." When Thomas Hart Benton also tried to use the poor as a political stalking horse by claiming that blankets should be on the free list because poor people used them, Clay branded the reasoning as twaddle. Such a move, he said, would not warm a single pauper but would instead create a British monopoly on blanket manufacturing.[52]

Nevertheless, these principled stands could not escape the new political realities imposed by an expanding franchise. Ideally a candidate would be able to claim that he had been born into poverty and had grown up in humble surroundings, the humbler the better, a log cabin the most current fashion thanks to the Whig strategy in 1840 that made Harrison into a cider-swilling, raccoon-skin-capped man of the people. The coonskin symbolism endured, turning Whigs into "Coons" even after the election, and they accordingly became nickname-happy, tagging everyone they could with folksy monikers. In addition to being the Old Chieftain, Harry of the West, and Prince Hal, Clay was now dubbed "the Old Coon," derisively by Democrats for being a schemer, admiringly by Whigs for being an agile, clever champion. Cartoonists began attaching Clay's face to raccoon bodies to show him treed by the opposition or outsmarting it, depending on the press.[53]

Whig strategists set about rewriting Clay's early years to create a new set of symbols tailored especially for him. "The *Mill Boy of the Slashes* is to be honored in every Whig procession by a string of the honest yeomen of the country," predicted the Alexandria *Gazette*. They would be "mounted on tackeys [ponies] with switch tails, with a meal bag over the shoulder, just as *Harry* used to ride (when he was a poor fatherless boy) through the slashes of Hanover to carry home to his mother bread for her dinner."[54] The writer probably got away with ignoring the presence of Hal Watkins and the relative prosperity of Clay's Spring, but perceptive readers might have scratched their heads over young Clay not just fetching flour but kneading it into dough and baking it to boot, all while riding home on horseback.

Clay had dabbled in this political art before, working to depict his youth as poor and put upon, but after he retired from the Senate and began his undistracted quest for the presidency, it was time for the professionals to take up the task. Enjoined by one correspondent to trust exclusively in God to deliver the country, Clay said he thought prayer was certainly a creditable idea but not to exempt human exertion: God helped those who helped themselves.[55] Accordingly, the newspaper editor and successful dramatist Epes Sargent was recruited to write Clay's campaign biography, and Philadelphia publisher Grigg & Elliott put out an almanac featuring another brief biography of Clay written by Nathan Sargent (no relation to Epes), with laudatory songs, anecdotes, and poems integrated into the calendar pages. Nathan Sargent was careful to include more on Clay's tribulations as an orphan than had ever before appeared. The print run was significant: fifty thousand copies to sell for $15 or $20 per thousand, whatever the traffic would bear. These pamphlets became so ubiquitous that it was said a vendor approached Daniel Webster as he was leaving the Astor House in

New York City to ask, "Take the life of Henry Clay?" Webster was supposed to have replied, "I cannot take the life of so eminent a citizen."[56]

Epes Sargent took his task seriously and tried to obtain personal information for authenticity. "I never kept a diary," Clay confessed. "I never thought the events of my life worthy of such a record." He did send Sargent some memoranda drawn entirely from memory. If they were useful, said Clay, "I can send you more of such trash."[57] The Whig editor Calvin Colton, a former clergyman turned journalist, had more luck as he worked on his campaign biography of Clay, and from this kernel came the first full account of his life (published in 1846), a two-volume work informed by personal papers and family letters, some of which Colton never returned, much to the Clay family's eventual dismay. In any case, putting together these tracts made Clay vaguely uncomfortable. He was not being falsely modest when he wished that Epes Sargent "had a better subject for his pen." At the same time, Clay thought that Colton was producing something too striking and interesting. After reviewing an early draft, he noted "a few inaccuracies, and too much commendation and panegyric." A credulous public would indelibly etch the inaccuracies into the historical record.[58]

Harrison had broken the tradition of a candidate's passivity during the 1840 campaign to overcome Democrats' disparagement of him as "General Mum," and Clay soon thought himself impelled by necessity and circumstance to embark on campaign trips far more numerous and extensive than anyone had undertaken before. "Henry Clay is very busy in the west," the New York *Herald* observed in the fall of 1842. Indeed he was. The immediate draw was the Ohio Whig convention gathering in Dayton on September 29. With an entourage that included Crittenden, Thomas Metcalfe, and Charles Morehead, Clay headed north for this event through Maysville and Louisville, crossing the Ohio at Cincinnati where twenty thousand people awaited his arrival. Along the way, he delivered seemingly impromptu addresses, but he actually had carefully constructed them to detail the Whig program in precise and unwavering language. He repeated virtually the same address to the thronging masses that descended on Dayton for the Whig convention. Their numbers staggered even those who had seen the enthusiasm of Harrison's 1840 campaign, with some estimates counting two hundred thousand. Whether the fervor was for Henry Clay or for the ideas he espoused did not matter at this point. If these popular outpourings meant anything, Democrats had reason to be worried.[59]

When Clay left Dayton for a series of appearances in Indiana, however, an incident marred the trip, although at the time many scored it a triumph. It occurred in Richmond on October 1 and pointed to the growing and disruptive role the slavery controversy was to play in elections. Indiana's antislavery movement was relatively new but vital and animated. A reformist faction of the Quaker community was at its core, and it was finding voice by attracting recruits and organizing into activist groups such as the Liberty Party and the Indiana Anti-Slavery Society. In anticipation of Clay's visit, the latter organization circulated a petition entreating him to free his slaves. The plan was to force it on him in Richmond. The petition reportedly had about two thousand signatures.

The gesture had the look of a stunt designed to embarrass Richmond's guest, and local Whigs were quite agitated by the time Clay arrived, but events suggest that his hosts had developed a plan to turn the abolitionists' ploy against them. That Saturday afternoon, about ten thousand Hoosiers stood in the bright Indiana sun to hear Clay deliver his stock address lauding the Whig program and denouncing Democrat corruption. After he finished and the cheers at last died away, Whig congressman James Rariden did not ignore the abolitionists as they signaled for his attention. Instead, he invited them to approach the dais to present their petition, a peculiar indulgence that at least some of them suspected was a baited trap. Nevertheless, Hiram Mendenhall, a strapping fellow, shouldered his way through the unfriendly crowd, ignoring its muttered growls, and held out the sheaf of papers to Clay, who refused to touch them. Rariden took the petition and read it aloud as the crowd's mood turned increasingly ugly.

Clay raised his hands to call for calm and implored everyone to show Mendenhall "no disrespect, no indignity, no violence, in word or deed." Clay had good reason to be sincerely earnest about this. Just seven years before in Alton, Illinois, a confrontation between a raging mob and the abolitionist editor Elijah Lovejoy had ended with his murder. Clay could not have been blind to the risk Mendenhall was taking nor to the considerable harm an incident like the one in Alton could mean for the Whigs' cause. He therefore walked a very fine line as he proceeded to dissect the unfortunate Quaker who soon found himself shamed, not for being an abolitionist but for being rude.

Clay asked why Mendenhall would present this petition in this way. It was clearly nothing more than a symbolic gesture to embarrass him, and consequently it had made all of Indiana appear churlish. Suppose, Clay asked, that Mendenhall were to visit Kentucky only to be greeted by Clay with a petition demanding that he give up his farm? Clay then turned to his audience and explained slavery's relation to states' rights. He made particular reference to the health of his slaves (the obligatory mention of Charles Dupuy occurred here, the sort of thing that irked Buchanan in the Senate) and described the cruelty of liberating the helpless and infirm, which was only one of abolition's dangers, the most dire being the possibility of race war. He ended by turning back to Mendenhall, who had stood self-consciously frozen during Clay's remarks.

Hiram Mendenhall should mind his own business, Clay declared, and if he were charitably inclined, he should attend to the needs of widows and orphans.[60]

Judging from the reaction of the crowd at the moment and the newspapers in the weeks to come, it was a successful performance, if hardly a laudable one. Aside from the staged spontaneity—shabby political theater that was beneath Clay—at Richmond he laid bare his discomfiting accommodation of slavery's fundamental immorality, despite his singing the praises of Quaker tenderness. Clay said that slavery was wicked, just as he always did, but he also rationalized it under a blizzard of words that recounted the historical record but actually revealed the limits of his conscience when confronted by the realities of property. Standing off the dais, waiting obediently and silently, Charles Dupuy heard Clay say these words. A visitor to Ashland just weeks later referred to him as "Black 'Charles' of Mendenhall Memory" who was "a happy fellow & is a Chesterfieldian in all the rules of etiquette of highlife."[61] One can only wonder if Charles Dupuy was happy and full of Chesterfieldian equanimity that sunny day in Richmond, Indiana, when he heard Henry Clay compare his worth as a human being to that of a farm.

CLAY COMPLETED His western tour by delivering another major address to a teeming audience in Indianapolis, and he had no reason to think that anything untoward awaited him when he arrived at Columbus, Indiana, several days later. Appearing on the steps of the courthouse, he listened in stunned disbelief as former Whig congressman William Herod introduced him. Herod had served under Andrew Jackson and the lingering attachment to Old Hickory got the better of him, prompting him to begin his introduction by shouting "Hurra for Jackson!" Clay was livid, and immediately shouted, "Hurra for Jackson, you say. Where is your country? I say hurra for my country, and the man that says hurra for Jackson, deserves not the name of a freeman, but he ought to be a subject of the autocrat of Russia, and have the yoke of tyranny placed upon his neck till he was bowed down; down to the very dust."[62] It was obviously time for Clay to go home.

His outburst was not at all characteristic during these months, because he did his best to keep the peace in the party and mollify all who could lodge any objections against him for past positions and future policies. He patiently explained to one correspondent that he opposed direct taxes except in time of war, favoring instead a tariff sufficient to raise revenue and protect American industry. He opposed free trade because all other countries imposed restrictions on American commerce. Mindful of the ire of Antimasons that had cost him so dearly in 1839, he explained to another query that he had become a Mason many years before because of "youthful curiosity and a social disposition." He recalled the Masonic goals as "charitable and benevolent," their work resembling that of a social club. In any case, he saw no reason to support or oppose anyone because he was a Mason but instead looked upon the Constitution and the law as a proper guide for judging a man's worth to the country.[63]

Keeping peace in the party was no small task. Ambitious challengers such as Winfield Scott, John McLean, and Daniel Webster disregarded the signs that pointed to Clay's inevitability and began agitating for a national convention where they hoped to repeat 1839 and broker him out of the nomination. Clay buried any residual bitterness he felt over what had happened at Harrisburg and counseled others to do the same. Sometimes, he said, it was necessary to throw "a veil on the past for the sake of the future." At the same time, however, he insisted that he would not accept the nomination from a convention unless he was sure that it reflected the people's will, which was a way for him to oppose a convention without seeming to. When the congressional Whig caucus nevertheless announced in early 1843 that the party would hold a national nominating convention the following year, Clay acceded because he had little choice.[64]

He also realized that a convention could relieve him of the touchy task of selecting a vice-presidential nominee, a decision certain to alienate this or that Whig faction. As it became clearer that Clay would be the nominee, numerous aspirants for the second slot on the ticket began popping up. Clay was prudent in refraining from publicly endorsing anyone in particular, but in private he obliquely inclined toward Millard Fillmore. Others agreed that the New Yorker could best mollify abolitionists and Antimasons and, if Clay died, would not be obnoxious like Tyler. "I think Mr. Fillmore deserves the high estimate in which he was held by the Whigs of the last Congress," Clay said. "I think him able, faithful, and with uncommon business habits."[65] It was the closest he came to supporting anyone.

On the other hand, Clay actively quashed the suggestion that he consider Daniel Webster. On September 30, 1842, Webster delivered an extraordinary speech at Boston's Faneuil Hall, and though the bulk of it addressed his negotiations with Britain over the Maine boundary, he mounted an ill-judged defense of John Tyler and, in a badly disguised attempt to challenge Clay's mounting ascendancy in the party, made some roundabout attacks on the Kentuckian. He laid the blame for Whig failures in Congress and at the polls at the feet of those ultras who refused to work with the president (meaning Clay), and he denounced the battles over the Bank and the tariff as unnecessary (meaning they were contrivances of Clay). He criticized the recent Massachusetts Whig convention for having read Tyler out of the party, but it was obvious that his real aim was to condemn its endorsement of Clay.[66]

"Was ever man so fallen as Mr. Webster?" Clay bitterly asked. He never completely trusted "Black Dan" for remaining in the cabinet, and now he was "shocked and afflicted" by his behavior. Webster had dramatically asked in his speech, "Where am I to go?" Clay indignantly commented, "I confess, with pain & regret, that I have not since seen where he has gone."[67]

The following year, when it was clear Clay would be the nominee, intermediaries urged him and Webster to reconcile, hoping that Webster could land on Clay's ticket. Clay was adamant in his opposition and fired off a series of letters to his friends and Webster's advocates explaining why. He pointed out that he had done nothing to alienate Webster. He had defended him during his confirmation as secretary of state. On the contrary, Webster had done the alienating by allying with Tyler. Clay angrily noted how Webster's latest project seemed to be promoting John McLean for the nomination, and that he had even heard that Webster had considered supporting Calhoun! To suggest reconciliation with a view to Webster's becoming Clay's vice president was absurd. Clay did not think there was "the remotest probability" that a national convention would consent to placing Webster on the ticket. In any case, Clay flatly stated he would make no bargain for the presidency—words carefully chosen to resonate. These letters finally satisfied even Webster's supporters that Clay was serious, and they dropped the bid for the vice presidency.[68]

Clay spent the winter social season of 1842–43 in New Orleans where as many as fifty thousand people awaited his arrival on December 23, and the city held extensive programs to entertain and honor him. The purpose of the visit was more business than politics, however, for Clay was now laboring fully under the shadow of Thomas's business failure, an unmitigated financial disaster that made the trip rather "cheerless and uncomfortable" despite the nonstop gaiety. He was to argue a case before the Louisiana Supreme Court in late January, but with Ashland mortgaged, he feverishly tried to collect debts and to sell the hemp stacked in warehouses, enjoying little success in either endeavor. Then, as if to cap the clouded nature of his visit, on January 3, as Clay appeared at the Louisiana Supreme Court, a deranged man fired a pistol at the ceiling of the courtroom. "You may hear that it was fired at me," Clay told Lucretia. "It is possible that my presence may have occasioned it; but I do not believe that the man had any design against any body."[69]

If not firearms, the weather seemed pitted against him. Clay left New Orleans on January 30 aboard the *Creole* bound for Mobile. The following day a terrifying storm over the Gulf of Mexico buffeted the boat with towering waves and gale force winds, and when it did not arrive in Mobile on time, the steamer and all on board were presumed lost. At the end of February, a steam packet arrived in Memphis with the news that Henry Clay was dead. Of course, it was not true, as he quickly reported to Lucretia. It had been "a very boisterous passage," he said, but "we were not in fact in any danger." Not until early March did reports begin to circulate that the *Creole* was safe and Clay was "yet in the land of the living." By then he was also back at Ashland, "like an old stag which has been long coursed by the hunters and the hounds."

"I am not sure that I shall leave home at all before winter," he said, and for once, he meant it.[70]

JAMES BROWN CLAY returned permanently to Lexington and at last settled on a career as a lawyer, much to his father's relief. Clay tracked James at his studies and assured him that at twenty-five he was young enough to gain distinction if he were "industrious & diligent." Clay repeated to his capricious son, "Very industrious and diligent." By the time Clay returned from New Orleans, James had opened an office, and Clay set himself up in it with the threefold purpose of helping James get started, taking fees to offset part of his mounting debt, and making himself accessible to political visitors.[71]

Most pleasing to him was another sign that the young man was not just settling in but settling down. He met, fell in love with, and married Susan Jacob, daughter of wealthy John J. Jacob of Louisville. While her father did not entirely approve of the match, Susan did not care. Henry and Lucretia could not have been happier, though, and Susan returned their affection with warm devotion. She never lost her awe of the master of Ashland. Her seventeen-year-old brother likely described her feelings best when he wrote to her, "It is said by persons when first treading upon the classic shores of Greece and Rome," that "they feel a turn of mind of a very romantic and poetic nature. . . . You are standing upon the same soil and breathing the same air in which Homer & Virgil lived. Why should not a similar sensation be experienced by one when arriving at Ashland, it too has a great and illustrious possessor."[72]

United behind Ashland's illustrious owner, Whigs reached a zenith of confidence in the fall of 1843, though considering their persistently uninspiring showing at the polls, it was hard to see why. From their commanding majority in the House of Representatives during 1841 (133 Whigs to 102 Democrats), they suffered a significant reverse in the 1842 elections to give the Democrats a majority of 142 to 79. Surveying this development, Clay worried that Whig certainty was not so much deluded as it was breeding overconfidence and complacency. State elections over the summer of 1843 were mixed at best and included some unpleasant surprises. Indiana's palpable enthusiasm for Clay during his visit earlier in the year made the result of the state's August 7 election as unexpected as it was shattering. Democrats emerged with majorities in both houses of the state legislature. These trends alarmed Clay, and he renewed his calls for the Whigs to establish a system of general organization with a central committee for the nation, subsidiary ones for each state, and local ones for counties and towns, all of them to mount an active correspondence. His counsel in this regard had become a repetitive refrain, but there was no certainty that Whigs would ever cast off the tendency to trust that their program alone was attractive enough to persuade the people, making extraordinary exertions by the party organization unnecessary.[73]

It was in the midst of these unfolding events that Clay decided to plan an extended trip for the spring of 1844, this time through the southern states. He had an invitation from a North Carolina committee in Raleigh that reminded him of his 1842 promise to visit the state, and it seemed fitting that he would go to the place that had been the first to endorse his presidential bid. Getting to Raleigh would give him the excuse for a circuitous path through Alabama, Georgia, and South Carolina. He could continue from North Carolina into Virginia and finally arrive in Washington. Clay loved to travel. He confessed as if in a reverie that there were two places in the country he wanted to see more than any other, Nantucket Island and the Eastern Shore of Virginia, because in those isolated locales one could observe the perfectly preserved manners and customs of old Europe as they existed from the days of the earliest immigrants. Much of his planned southern tour, he noted with a kind of boyish enthusiasm, would take him "on ground which I never trod before." In addition to the exciting prospect of seeing new places, undertaking the journey in the spring of 1844 seemed an ideal way to show himself to a part of the country indispensable to his victory the following November. He weighed the risks. "Will these Southern trips create any jealousy at the North?" he asked Peter Porter. In the end, wanderlust won out. "You know," he said, "I have never been in those States."[74]

WHILE WHIGS WERE growing in confidence despite their election setbacks, the Democrats sank into malaise despite their successes. Philosophical and personal divisions were pulling Democrats in various directions, and the added stress of sectional differences threatened to pull their party apart at the seams. Van Buren's candidacy had a measure of fervent support, but it also revived equally passionate complaints about his lackluster showing in 1840, although nobody could agree on the reasons. Some said his economic policies had made him the victim of soft-money conservative Democrats like Tallmadge and Rives, while others insisted that relentlessly repeated Whig lies had simply smeared him into defeat. John C. Calhoun briefly sought to supplant the Little Magician, and Clay relished the prospect of running against a man who would "theorize" the country "to death." Calhoun's individual effort sputtered from the start, though, and in 1844 was replaced with a general sectional demand that the Democrat nominee be proslavery, ideally a southerner.[75]

John Tyler might have been just the man to satisfy the Calhoun wing. He certainly wanted to be, and his aggressive use of patronage ultimately revealed a bold and radical plan to rearrange the political landscape by forming an entirely new party out of Democrats disgruntled with Van Buren and Whigs alienated by Clay. If Tyler's third party gambit were dynamic enough, it might even subsume the Democrat Party and give him its nomination. In any case, Tylerites planned to hold a convention at the same time the Democrats did in May 1844. The prospect that everything could blow up because of these two conflicting, simultaneous meetings was quite real. Van Buren's people were more than troubled by the possibility.[76]

These developments naturally delighted Whigs. They were certain that Captain Tyler's audacious plan would founder, but not before doing Van Buren considerable harm. They looked forward to putting Clay's vision as well as Clay's person against Sweet Sandy Whiskers and his failed economic policies. They were certain that the contrast would again awaken voters to the sensible course just as it had in 1840. Only this time, death and betrayal would not force the Whigs to stray from the sensible course. They would beat Van Buren again, and they cheerfully dusted off the complaints and revved up the attacks from four years earlier.

As the serious campaign season began, Whigs committed themselves to strategic emphasis on their best issues, the tariff foremost among them. The party tended to divide along sectional lines on the wisdom of a new bank, but it showed remarkable unity in insisting that the Tariff of 1842 had been successful in resuscitating the country's melancholy financial state. True enough, the duties that Tyler had grudgingly accepted in 1842 had made the Treasury flush while retiring the deficit. That happy condition had encouraged agricultural and manufacturing markets to perk up. As 1844 dawned, the Whig press and Whig candidates hailed the protective tariff as the country's savior, and with the economy on the verge of achieving a satisfying hum, everyone, Democrats included, expected Whigs to show up at the polls in force in November.[77]

If the Whigs had been able to hold on to that issue and otherwise limit the election to economic concerns, they likely would have won. They were alert to the dangers posed by the country's growing nativist movement, a reaction to surging immigration, especially an influx of Irish Catholics in northern cities. Wages already depressed by hard times fell further as immigrants were willing to work for almost nothing. In addition, the belief that Catholicism was an alien culture controlled by Rome and subversive to American values was beginning to find expression in political organizations such as the American Republican Party in New York, the forerunner of the Native American Party that appeared shortly after the election of 1844.

These antiforeign elements troubled Clay even more than the Antimasons. Their attempt to gain credibility and influence by allying with Whigs was most disturbing. The electoral implications were significant because Irish Catholics gravitated toward a welcoming Democrat Party that organized them into voting blocs rather than trying to reform them with temperance lectures. In the three weeks before the election of 1844, as many as five thousand immigrants in New York City alone were naturalized so they could vote. Whigs, with their reform policies and reliance on a strong Protestant base, found it all but impossible to attract these new arrivals, and complaints that many immigrants were hastily naturalized or were allowed to vote even when not citizens further cemented their bond with Democrats. Clay consequently approached the issues of immigration and naturalization gingerly. Neither he nor the Whig Party opposed immigration and naturalization, he insisted, especially that of Irish Catholics. He pointed to his long record of supporting Spanish American independence and voting for land grants to French and Polish immigrants. Yet he also insisted that the government should enforce naturalization. Otherwise voter fraud would make elections meaningless and destroy the people's faith in democracy. There was a reason, after all, that felons who were citizens were not allowed to vote. Like felons, residents who were not citizens were more likely to sell their votes to the highest bidder, polluting the franchise and soiling the very concept of civic virtue. "I am in favor of American industry, American institutions, American order, American liberty," Clay proclaimed, but he added, "I wish our Country, forever, to remain a sacred asylum for all unfortunate and oppressed men whether from religious or political causes."[78]

Most damaging for Whigs was the Texas question that came to the forefront in late 1843 and 1844, because it would prove Clay's undoing. Texas quickly displaced the economy as the primary concern of the voters, in part because the improving economy made it a less compelling point of dispute, but primarily because it intermingled that generation's two greatest points of political contention: territorial expansion and slavery.[79]

Ever since gaining its independence in 1836, Texas had been wobbly, stalked by debt and threatened by hazards. Mexico regarded the Lone Star Republic as a rebellious province that one day would be repatriated, through conquest if necessary. The Mexican government made menacing gestures at the mere suggestion that the United States might become involved in this dispute, but the prospect of Texas reviving arguments over slavery expansion stayed Washington's hand more than did the threat of Mexican hostilities. Jackson and Van Buren had accordingly rebuffed Texan overtures to join the Union.

Meanwhile, Texas had to maintain an expensive army in the expectation that a much larger Mexico would strike again. Peril rather than choice prompted Texas to open negotiations with England and France with the aim of possibly becoming a protectorate. The best Texas could manage by 1840, however, was commercial treaties with France, Holland, and Belgium.

That did not mean Britain was indifferent about Texas. On the contrary, the British government was more than eager to see Texas remain independent in order to block American expansion into the Southwest. Ideally, Texas would become a marionette with London pulling the strings, possibly even contriving a disagreement that would give the Royal Navy and Redcoats a chance to dismantle Monroe's impudent doctrine. British merchants also saw in Texas a large market that would allow them to bypass the American tariff and promote free trade. British textile manufacturers eyed Texas cotton that would lessen their dependence on exports from the American South. The French were no less calculating, hopeful that Texas could be the key to their colonial resurgence in the western hemisphere.

For the United States, these were troubling aspects of the Texas problem, to be sure, but it was the noise being made by British abolitionists that most alarmed southerners. The British antislavery movement was industriously trying to establish a grip on Texas in the hope that abolition there might ignite abolition in America's Cotton Kingdom. The prospect terrified slave-owning southerners.

Clay was slow to realize the explosive potential of this issue, but he was aware of the sectional passions it was sure to arouse. As early as the spring of 1843, he refused to issue a public statement opposing Texas annexation. The pronouncement would have improved his image in New England, but it was also certain to injure him in the South. It was an intensely sectional issue, with almost all support for annexation coming from the South and almost all in opposition coming from the North. Clay danced around this conundrum by saying he did not think a significant number of citizens favored annexation, and he claimed that he had heard no mention of it during his recent visit to New Orleans. Even if that were true, which was doubtful, and even if he believed it,

which was also doubtful, he unwisely disregarded a looming storm on slim frag-
ments of personal experience and anecdotal evidence. In contrast, he was much
more forthcoming when queried about American expansion into Oregon. The
move risked a confrontation with the British, who were on the ground there, and
promised to rile southerners, who bristled at the prospect of so much nonslave
territory coming into the Union. Clay, however, carefully worded his reason for
opposing Oregon. In addition to the region's being too remote and thus too expensive to protect, he said, time and demographics were on America's side. Oregon was, after all, even more remote and costly for the British. In both instances,
though for different reasons, Clay counseled prudence and delay.[80]

In the months that followed, because of John Tyler, it became more difficult
to dismiss the issue. Unlike his predecessors, Tyler was more than ready to risk
a sectional firestorm over Texas annexation. For him, Texas became a cudgel to
use against his enemies and a cause with which to attract southern friends. The
president's plans became more apparent after Webster resigned in May 1843.
Tyler's fellow Virginian Abel Upshur became secretary of state. Upshur shared
Tyler's enthusiasm for annexation and was equally heedless of its consequences. The two worked behind the scenes to persuade Texas to sign a treaty,
a task made more difficult because Washington's previous snubs made the Lone
Star government wary. Meanwhile, Tyler sent Duff Green to London as a special envoy, and Green reported to the administration that the British planned to
fund compensated emancipation in Texas, a story later proved false. At the time,
though, it sent Tyler into a mild panic.

In December, Clay's friends warned him that Tyler's exertions were making
Texas annexation a controversial issue in the North, but he remained outwardly
unconcerned. Tyler could plan all he wanted, and the world, including the
North, could judge his motives accordingly. The president was only revealing
his impotence, Clay said, for annexation could occur only through a treaty, and
the administration could not muster the two-thirds of the Senate necessary to
ratify it. In fact, Clay was certain that "such a recommendation would be the last
desperate move of a despicable traitor."[81]

Nevertheless, Texas began to cause Clay twinges of worry. He recalled a letter he had written confidentially to William Ellery Channing years earlier, a letter in which he had adamantly opposed annexation. Channing was dead now,
but Clay asked friends, if possible, to obtain the letter from Channing's heirs. He
remained cagey about his reasons. "I do not wish to make or encourage new issues, as I regard this to be," he explained, "but, and in the progress of events, it
may become necessary for me to make some public expression of my opinions
on this project, in which case I should prefer availing myself of that letter."[82]

Yet it was hardly a new issue by the end of 1843, and he was well aware of that, as a letter he wrote the following day to Crittenden shows. He had been giving Texas a great deal of thought, and he was framing up a response to the annexation controversy to test on his friends. Clay believed that the United States should concentrate on developing what it already owned, especially when any new territory would cause unhealthy arguments. Any annexation treaty, he said, could not be ratified, and the southern hope that Texas would make the slave states dominant in national politics was misguided. The North would simply offset the South's gain, possibly by annexing Canada. (He was wrong only about the place, which actually would be Oregon.) In addition, annexation would dishonor the United States in the eyes of the civilized world by revealing that the country intended to spread slavery rather than pursue a sensible plan to end it.

Tyler's annual message provided indirect notice of the administration's intent to enter into negotiations with Texas for annexation. Although Clay was convinced that Tyler's aggressive stance on annexation was designed to create discord among Whigs and distract the nation from his failures, he still maintained for the time being that silence was best. Yet he also intended to be ready with an answer should the time come for the question. By the end of February, Upshur almost had a treaty. Clay was just beginning his southern tour. For months, he had insisted that the question of what to do about Texas was irrelevant. Thanks to John Tyler, that question was suddenly to be on the entire country's lips.[83]

CLAY ARRIVED IN New Orleans on December 23 with plans to remain in the area for two months before embarking on his southern tour. He was again feted at numerous events in the city. The simple fact of the trip and all the activity surrounding it filled Democrats with suspicion and resentment, and their public prints commenced a sniping attack on almost every aspect of Clay's doings that continued unabated through the spring and summer. Amos Kendall revived stories about Clay's excessive gambling and drinking, and others took up the refrain. Most of these attacks he wisely ignored, but when Democrats began a vigorous effort to breathe new life into the Corrupt Bargain story, he could not remain silent. Andrew Jackson wrote to the editors of the Nashville *Union* on May 3, 1844, to declare that he still firmly believed Adams and Clay had befouled the presidency with their arrangement in 1825. Blair reprinted the letter in the Washington *Globe* of May 18. Clay said he could hardly believe this ancient history was again in currency, and he responded as he always did, by amassing testimony to refute the charge, a strategy that his enemies smiled at and his friends, rightly judging it ineffective, had come to find tedious.[84]

Nothing Clay did was exempt from scrutiny or criticism. In New Orleans, when he participated in the Eighth of January parade commemorating the Battle of New Orleans, Democrats branded him a hypocrite for denigrating Jackson's achievement while trying to claim for himself its luster. He electioneered in several Louisiana parishes where beautiful weather, parties, and balls marked his progress. Someone Clay had met almost twenty years earlier called on him that February in New Orleans and thought him much changed: "He seems to have shrunk in size, and his manners, though most kind, urbane, and cheerful, have no longer the vivacity and great animal spirits that then accompanied them." Age was clearly reshaping Clay physically, but his acquaintance likely misjudged the cause of Clay's subdued manner. He was suffering from another of his chronic colds.[85]

Clay left New Orleans for Mobile on February 24. The Alabama port greeted him warmly, and he visited friends Henry and Octavia LeVert for about a week. John joined him as he traveled north through the Alabama Black Belt to Montgomery and then east to Columbus, Georgia, all new sights for him. Large and appreciative crowds turned out along the way, and many cheered his stock campaign address touting Whig programs and blaming Democrats for the country's predicaments, although just as many fell silent when he talked of a protective tariff. By the time he reached Milledgeville on March 19, he had adjusted the message. He delivered his speech from a large platform built especially for the occasion. Seats for dignitaries were arranged on it, and Clay's place had him facing directly into the sun, a situation an organizer tried to correct by suggesting that he move to the south side of the platform. Clay quipped that he "wished to be on all sides," and there was a burst of laughter. Possibly nobody remembered the remark when he later claimed in his speech that what he really favored was a revenue tariff that would provide merely incidental protection to manufacturers as it supplied the government with sufficient money to allow the distribution of land revenues to the states. That seemed to sit better, and he was able afterward to say truthfully that the tariff, as he now framed it, excited no great animosity in the South. He did not say that judging from the deplorable state of Georgia's roads, the state could use all the distribution it could get.[86]

A deft old master at the give-and-take of such appearances, Clay was having fun. He was leaving Milledgeville when a spring thunderstorm opened up the skies and a farmer ran after his coach in the pouring rain. The farmer implored Clay to come up the hill to his house. His wife wanted to meet Clay but was too ill to come out. Clay paused and then said that he was too old to risk traipsing about in a soaking rain. The farmer was offering Clay his coat when a boy appeared running down the hill and shouting, "Daddy, daddy, Mammy says you must get Mr. Clay to name the b-a-b-y! if he won't come!"

That he could do, said Clay, asking whether it was a girl or a boy. A girl, said the farmer. "Then tell your good lady to call it *Lucretia,* after my wife." The farmer beamed. Clay asked the name of the farmer's wife. "Louisa." Clay beamed. He promised that he would return the honor by naming his next daughter after her. The farmer stared before cackling and repeatedly slapping his knee as Clay's carriage pulled away.[87]

Much of the trip was like that, a mixture of serious politics and silly fun, a combination Clay liked best. His reputation for jokes as well as his considerable celebrity preceded him, and people turned out to see a famous, likable personage as much as to hear a political speech. In Augusta, a newspaper correspondent studied him closely as he mingled among the crowd gathered at the Masonic Hall. "There's something about him that draws one to him, and makes one feel perfectly familiar," said the reporter. Clay began his speech, and the reporter noted how he was "monstrous ugly if you go to siferin' out his features like yould common people's." Then as the voice filled the hall, Henry Clay became "the best looking man I ever saw. His mouth is like an overseer's wages, extending from one year's end to tother, but when he speaks, you wouldn't have it any smaller if you could."[88]

Traveling by way of Savannah, Columbia, and Charleston, Clay finally reached Raleigh on April 12, his birthday. He sustained the pretense that this was not a political trip but a sightseeing tour, though he had made enough speeches to become hoarse. His friend Benjamin Watkins Leigh traveled down from Virginia to see Clay's reception and found him "in fine spirits, and in the best humour." Clay made "an excellent speech," Leigh told Mangum, all the better because the old master had learned not to attack Tyler too energetically in the Deep South and continued the tack as he headed north. "The very slightness of the allusion marked his contempt more strongly than the most laboured invective could have done."[89]

On the very day that Clay arrived in Raleigh, John Tyler's administration concluded a treaty with the republic of Texas consenting to its annexation by the United States. It was the work of Calhoun, ironically enough, as though the fates were determined to unite Clay's most implacable foes against him. In late February, an accidental cannon explosion aboard a warship during a gathering of Washington politicos had killed Abel Upshur, and Tyler appointed the South Carolinian to head the State Department. Calhoun pursued Texas annexation just as tirelessly as his deceased predecessor had but with the added motive of emphasizing its expansion of slavery. He hoped to force Van Buren's hand on the matter, provoking open opposition to annexation that would cause southern Democrats to abandon the New Yorker. To remove any doubt about the proslavery aspect of Texas, Calhoun wrote an inflammatory letter to British minister Richard Pakenham praising slavery as a positive good and casting annexation as a way to thwart British abolitionism. Calhoun meant to be provocative, and the political conflagration that resulted fulfilled his wishes. Tyler sent the treaty and accompanying documents, including the Pakenham letter, to the Senate on April 22 with a request for closed deliberations, but antislavery senators refused to keep anything confidential. Benjamin Tappan of Ohio gave everything to the press on April 27.

While these events were occurring in Washington, Clay made a fateful decision in Raleigh. The news of the treaty convinced him that he could no longer delay his statement and that in fact he might have waited too long. If Van Buren preceded him in opposing annexation, Clay's following suit would make him appear expedient rather than principled. Consequently, on April 17 he wrote a lengthy letter for publication in the *National Intelligencer* opposing immediate annexation generally and Tyler's treaty particularly. Several of his friends agreed it was his duty to make his views public, so Clay sent the letter to Crittenden. He was confident that it was a sound declaration, but he wanted Crittenden and others to review it as well. He also left it to his friend in consultation with other Whigs to determine the timing of its publication.[90]

Later known as the Raleigh Letter, this communication filled Crittenden with considerable foreboding. Apprehensive that Clay had seriously misjudged southern sentiment, he strongly advised against its publication, but Clay's worries over losing the North to Van Buren made him insist. Crittenden finally relented. The Raleigh letter appeared in the *National Intelligencer* on April 27, the same day as Tappan's release of Tyler's treaty. Nor was this all, for on that same day, a statement from Martin Van Buren opposing annexation also appeared in the Democrat Washington *Globe*. Clay had been correct at least in the presumption that he and Van Buren were on "common ground" and that something on the issue was imminent from the Little Magician. The timing, however, amounted to a coincidence so incredible and spectacular that almost nobody believed it to be a coincidence at all. Instead, many jumped to the conclusion that Van Buren and Clay had cynically colluded to avoid a controversial issue that could disrupt their respective campaigns.[91]

That most certainly was not the case. For years, Clay and Van Buren had opposed annexation on principle, and for much the same reason: slavery expansion endangered the Union. By 1844, the rapid push for Texas annexation directly threatened it, forcing the two men to break their silence. That they had done so simultaneously was an accident that had everything to do with their friends and nothing to do with them. Van Buren wrote his letter on April 20, three days after Clay's. It was a response to Mississippi congressman William H. Hammett in which Van Buren simply showed that he was no longer willing to placate the South by avoiding Texas. In the days that followed, Silas Wright gauged northern anger over Tyler's treaty among his Senate colleagues and became worried that Van Buren supporters might alienate the North by unwittingly supporting annexation. Wright decided on April 27 to publish Van Buren's response to Hammett in the *Globe* to set the record straight. Only by chance did Crittenden on that same day at last yield to Clay's demands that the Raleigh letter be published. Speculation that Clay and Van Buren had struck a deal, possibly during Van Buren's visit to Ashland two years earlier, is groundless for at least two reasons. The Texas controversy was not the foremost issue in 1842, nor did anybody conceive that it would be in 1844; and even if they had been gifted with such foresight, both Clay and Van Buren were too prudent to make such a bargain two years before the election.[92]

Just as Crittenden feared, southerners squinted at Clay's statement and grumbled. For the time being, though, they did nothing more. The Whig convention met in Baltimore just days after the appearance of the Raleigh letter, and Clay's stand on Texas did not injure his standing among the delegates. Many southern Whigs agreed with Alexander Stephens that Texas annexation was "a miserable humbug" that Tyler and Calhoun had contrived "to divide and distract the Whig party at the South." The convention unanimously committed to Henry Clay, ignored Texas altogether, and bickered only about the best candidate for vice president, a decision that Clay left to the delegates. They finally chose Theodore Frelinghuysen of New Jersey.[93]

Van Buren became an immediate victim of his opposition to annexation. "The southern portion of the *Democracy* are furious at Van Buren's letter," noted the abolitionist *Liberator.* "There is considerable chance that he will be dropped, and Tyler, Cass, or Calhoun, taken up." Southern Democrats flatly declared that they would not abide Van Buren as their nominee, giving other Democrats opposed to Van Buren the excuse to push him aside and ultimately nominate Tennessean James K. Polk, a choice that showed Andrew Jackson's continuing and weighty influence in the party. Livid over Van Buren's opposition to Tyler's treaty, Jackson essentially read his former protégé out of the party, threw his support to his fellow Tennessean, and linked annexation with patriotism. Jackson reflected mainstream Democrat attitudes about territorial expansion that saw sectional disharmony as a surmountable obstacle, a mere

matter of horse-trading to remove northern objections. The Democrats consequently adopted an unequivocally expansionist platform that placated antislavery objections over Texas with a promise to balance it by acquiring a free "All
Oregon" from Britain.[94]

In stark contrast, the Whigs did not even mention Texas in their platform.

CLAY ARRIVED BACK at Ashland only days before the Democrats discarded
Van Buren at Baltimore. A torchlight parade greeted him, "music filled the air,
and ever and anon the boom of the 'big gun' wound up the chorus." An observer
claimed to see on Clay's face a solemn expression as "he thought of the high office he will soon accept from the hands of an admiring people. Let him have it."
Democrats, however, were soon spreading a story describing how he received
the news of their nomination. One of his sons, it was said, burst in on him at
Ashland and asked him to guess the Democrat nominee. "Why Matty, of
course," Clay was reported as saying. Told no, he seemed puzzled. He guessed
Lewis Cass, then Buchanan. Finally informed that it was Polk, Clay purportedly
jumped from his chair and exclaimed, "Beat again, by God!" The opposition
took great delight in this preposterous fabrication. They soon were tweaking it
a bit to have Clay shout, "Beat again, by hell!" which struck many as better. Its
colorful nature got the story repeated even by people who did not believe it.
Then gradually, as is the case with any recurring lie, the story began to seem
possible, then plausible, and finally it acquired the trappings of truth. By September, Clay was hearing from correspondents wanting him to refute it, a sure
sign that doing so was pointless.[95]

Clay was surprised that the Democrats had dumped Van Buren, but actually
his opinion about Democrat disarray was strengthened when they did so. "I do
not think I ever witnessed such a state of utter disorder, confusion and decom-
position as that which the Democratic Party now presents," he had observed in
early May, and as far as he could see, nothing had changed. He was confident
that he would defeat Polk. The Tylerite convention in Baltimore nominated the
president and adopted a pro-annexation platform, thus putting forth a candidate
unlikely to succeed but liable to hurt Polk by splintering the annexationist vote.
Whigs seemingly had nothing to worry about.[96]

Yet over the summer, Clay's grand advantage gradually disappeared. James
K. Polk was responsible for some of that. Whigs mocked him as an undistinguished nonentity, but he had been in national politics for years, including a
stint as Speaker of the House. In fact, he was a better candidate than even the
Democrats at first believed. They had nominated him as a "dark horse," a racing
term here used for the first time in politics to denote a winner that comes out of

nowhere. Once the standard-bearer, he proved effective in wooing back disgruntled Van Burenites and cementing the loyalties of Calhoun's faction. Democrats called him "Young Hickory" and chortled over the return of their glory days. They also courted John Tyler with pledges that the new administration would protect his appointments, promote his expansionist policies, and cease attacks on him in the Democrat press, especially Blair's *Globe*. By late August, the promise of a diplomatic post abroad, possibly an appointment by Polk as minister to Great Britain, clinched the deal. "So Tyler has withdrawn!" Clay exclaimed. "And that upon the promise of a Mission, made by our opponents!" He could console himself that "there were suitable equivalents in that bargain; for nothing was given and nothing will be received," and indeed, no appointment occurred, but that would be cold comfort later. As the election loomed, the implications of Tyler's joining forces with the Democrats were simply profound.[97]

Democrats were also able to make the Whig convention's selection of Theodore Frelinghuysen as the vice-presidential nominee seem a serious mistake. Whig versifiers licked their pencils to come up with such gems as "Hurrah, Hurrah, the country's risin' / for Harry Clay and Frelinghuysen" (sung to the tune of the all-purpose "Dan Tucker"), but Democrats licked their chops at the prospect of branding Clay's running mate a bigot. The charge was a contemptible smear, for Theodore Frelinghuysen was a fine man, even extraordinary, with impeccable credentials that included service in the United States Senate and work with benevolent moral reform movements. Yet these admirable civic activities proved his Achilles' heel, for his religious work had put him in the orbit of anti-Catholic elements in Protestant churches. All the moral advantage of Frelinghuysen's spotless and spiritual life evaporated as Democrats roared that his nomination revealed a secret Whig plan to erect a Protestant theocracy. They whispered to Catholics, especially Irish immigrants teeming in urban wards, that Frelinghuysen's work with the American Missionary Society and the American Tract Society proved not just his prejudice but the intolerance of all Whigs. These tactics were effective and, for Whigs, maddening. The Democrats had it both ways, excoriating Clay for being a libertine and tarring Frelinghuysen for being devout.[98]

As Democrat attacks became more vicious, Whig unity began to fray at the edges. Instead of defending Frelinghuysen against the outrages, they blamed him for hurting the ticket. The most troubling fissures in Whig unity, however, had to do with Texas annexation. The Democrats began aggressively promoting their plan to extend America into both Oregon and Texas, linking immediate annexation to patriotism and tarring its opponents as abolitionists. As that strategy gained ground in the South, the Whig stand on Texas as defined by Clay's

Raleigh letter became increasingly difficult to defend. Clay watched his strength in the South ebb and Polk's grow. At the end of June, the Whig situation had become critical. Georgia Whigs, for example, were confident that Clay could still win, except "the only difficulty we have, is the Texas question."[99]

On July 1, Clay sent a letter to Stephen Miller for publication in Miller's Tuscaloosa *Monitor*. It was a relatively brief note that later became known as the First Alabama Letter (Clay would unfortunately feel the need to write another later in the month). His purpose, he said, was to deny in the plainest terms that his Raleigh letter had been a ploy to court the abolitionist vote. Instead, he opposed *immediate* annexation because he thought it sure to arouse sufficient northern anger to endanger the Union. Saying that much, at least, gave no grounds for a charge of inconsistency. That Clay also felt obliged to say "Personally, I could have no objection to the annexation of Texas" did not even indicate a shift in his thinking, for he had told Alexander Stephens before writing the Raleigh letter that he would not oppose annexation if it could be accomplished without harming the Union.[100]

More troubling, the first Alabama letter indicated a potentially disastrous shift in his political approach to the issue, one he recklessly completed on July 27 with another letter, this time to the editors of the Tuscumbia *North Alabamian*. The Second Alabama Letter committed the serious mistakes of insisting that slavery did not really enter into the question of Texas annexation, which made him look foolish, and of intimating that as president he might find it advantageous to annex Texas himself, which made his Raleigh letter appear craven. One could cite his insistence that he would only accept Texas if it could be done without dishonoring the nation, risking war, or disturbing sectional harmony as evidence that Clay had indeed sustained a principled consistency over the course of the Raleigh and Alabama letters; but political inferences in the midst of a campaign are never so subtle. Instead, the Alabama letters were nothing short of devastating.[101]

The Democrats focused unremittingly on the supposed inconsistencies and concessions, and Clay was finally compelled to write yet another letter because, as he said in a massive understatement, "my two Alabama letters have created some unfavorable impressions in particular localities." Posted to the *National Intelligencer* on September 23, his lengthy explanation was closely argued and perfectly sensible in pointing out his unfailing caveat that only if it did not hurt the Union could he support Texas annexation. Yet the very fact that he had felt it necessary to write this lengthy clarification showed that it was unlikely to do any good. In sum, his letters about Texas annexation had totaled three, another proof of the maxim about trouble. Clay tried to break the hex with a fourth. It did not work.[102]

Meanwhile, Democrats pursued other avenues of attack, leaving no stone unturned. They unearthed the ancient charge that Clay had been too young to serve in the Senate in 1806 and that he had perjured himself in taking the oath, a way to launch additional attacks that irregularities had always mottled his career. Clay clubs throughout the nation nervously sought evidence to clear him of the Corrupt Bargain charge, while Democrat campaigns in the North painted him as a staunch defender of slavery and in the South as an abolitionist. These tactics received exasperating help from Clay's cousin Cassius, who published an impolitic letter at this crucial stage of the contest describing Clay as friendly to abolition. The gesture further hurt him in the South and did him little good in the North, and Clay had to renounce it, which then hurt him in the North and began his estrangement from his kinsman.[103]

As the decision approached, excitement mounted, newspapers became more frenzied in their attacks and defenses, and voters laid wagers and made plans. Many Whigs were still so certain of Clay's triumph that they were scheduling journeys to Washington for the inauguration. In Lexington, people were already calling him "the 'President.' " And finally, the prolonged tensions of the lengthy campaign began to wear thin, and more than a few people wanted to see the thing done. "Of politics, that all absorbing theme," said one Whig, "I am heartily sick and tired, yet here it is the only topic of conversation—business—pleasure everything yields to it."[104]

It is customary to speak of the elections during this period in the singular, as in "the election of 1844," but actually what occurred in the fall of 1844 was a series of elections that decided state contests as well as national ones, including the presidency. These were not held on the same day throughout the nation but were scattered events, and state elections that fell during the late summer were always taken as portents. As those state returns came in, Clay was outwardly confident but privately worried. Democrat turnout was surprisingly high in his home state of Kentucky and his strongholds of Virginia, Tennessee, Georgia, Louisiana, and North Carolina. In addition to the Democrats' throwing everything they could lay hands on at him, he had injured himself in the North with his stand on Texas and the late repudiation of Cassius Clay's statements. The smearing of Frelinghuysen had driven immigrants into the Democrat fold while diminishing his grand moral standing as a counter to questions about Clay's character. Clay's stand on slavery had been misrepresented in such ways as to alienate northerners while making southerners suspicious.

Thus in the first two weeks of November, the issue played out in the shadow of Whig disadvantages that combined to become ultimately inescapable. On November 13, Clay knew the result. "The intelligence brought to us this morning has terminated all our hopes, our suspense & our anxieties in respect to the Presidential election," Crittenden wrote him. "We now know the worst—Polk is elected, & your friends have sustained the heaviest blow that could have befallen them." The defeat was all the more excruciating because victory had been so close. Polk defeated Clay in the popular vote by a margin of only 38,000 (1,339,368 to 1,300,687) out of the extraordinarily high turnout of 2.7 million (including Liberty Party votes), a number representing 78.9 percent of eligible voters. The count in the Electoral College was similarly close, with Polk at 170 and Clay at 105, New York's 36 votes being the difference.

Analyses of this result have pointed to myriad causes ranging from the fateful mistake of the Alabama letters to the emergence of the vital Liberty Party in New York that siphoned significant antislavery votes from Clay, votes that would not have gone to Polk but that Clay needed to overcome Polk's advantage on annexation. As stunned Whigs surveyed the wreckage, they quickly saw that the key to the election had in fact been New York, where the Liberty Party's impact, combined with an extraordinary amount of voter fraud in the immigrant population, had tilted the scale and given Polk the prize.[105]

Clay, the savvy head counter, had known all along that New York was the key to the contest, and when he received the news about the state returns, he knew their significance. Some reports had him in tears throwing himself into Lucretia's arms, and Cassius Clay would later describe Clay in a blistering tantrum, but the former stories were apparently fabrications, and Cousin Cassius's account came after their rift. Susan Jacob Clay always insisted that nothing frantic or highly emotional occurred at Ashland the day Clay learned of his defeat, but rather that her father-in-law accepted it sadly but with resignation. Frelinghuysen wrote to recommend that they both take succor in "the promises & consolations of the Gospel of our Saviour," but whatever his demeanor at the time, Clay remained profoundly troubled by the outcome of this election. He quietly admitted that he had "fearful forebodings" about the fate of the country. He could only hope that they "may, in the sequel, be found to be groundless."[106]

Everyone had believed that 1844 was to be Clay's time. He had believed that too, and for most of the campaign season, his certainty of victory had been an unshakable expectation, akin to certainty that the sun would rise at dawn or the stars would run their nightly courses. It was supposed to be a triumph that would vindicate him as well as Whig policies. Even as the chance for victory slipped away over the summer, the reality of Clay's inevitable victory gradually transforming into Clay's inescapable defeat had been impossible to grasp, and even the jarring fact, finally laid bare in the second week of November, that 1844 was to be yet another missed opportunity was difficult to absorb. As Clay slowly did so, however, the blow was certainly crushing, but it was also strangely cathartic.

Ashland's routines were restorative, and Clay now had time to reflect on many matters beyond the quest that had consumed virtually every particle of his attention for the last four years. He wrote more sparingly in the days after the defeat, mainly to answer notes consoling him on the loss. On the morning of December 9, he went to his desk and briefly answered a circular asking him to endorse Reverdy Johnson for the U.S. Senate (Clay declined, saying it would be "indelicate and improper" to meddle in Maryland's affairs), then turned his attention to drafting another document.[107]

On that December morning in 1844, that document's brevity as well as its legal formality imparted a cold, lifeless character to its words. Yet as Clay framed them, the words were as golden as anything he had ever produced in his loftiest flights of oratory. Clay dipped the fine-pointed nib of his pen and scratched "H. Clay" at the bottom of the paper, a deed of emancipation.

Charles Dupuy was free.[108]

CHAPTER THIRTEEN

"Death, Ruthless Death"

ELECTION POSTMORTEMS DEEPENED Whig despondency. Stories of rampant fraud came in from all over the country. Louisiana had been lost because the Democrats cheated in places like Plaquemines Parish, where they managed a 970-vote majority even though the parish had never tallied more than 340 votes in previous elections.[1] New York, however, had decided the election, and there the fraud was simply unbridled. Democrats had openly baited Roman Catholics, immigrants, and abolitionists, but their secret operations in voter fraud had been no less obvious. The Central Clay Committee in New York City spent $5,000 investigating the matter, but nothing came of it.[2] The thousands of illegal votes were those of immigrants, impossible to trace and, given the slip-shod records and loose checks of the time, impossible to invalidate. Clay was thus "*cheated* out of his election by vote fraud," wailed Leslie Combs.[3]

On December 4, Combs came to Ashland as one of Kentucky's twelve presidential electors. The day before in Frankfort they had unanimously cast their votes for Clay and Frelinghuysen and now had come to Lexington to pay respects to Clay. Governor William Owsley and citizens of the town accompanied the group to Ashland. The electors gathered at the base of the house's front steps, and Clay slowly emerged through the large front door. Joseph Underwood read prepared remarks lauding Clay and Whig principles while lamenting his loss, bitterly denouncing it as "fraud upon the election franchise." Clay was gracious in his response. Their gesture touched him deeply, he said, and he was equally grateful for the privilege of living in Kentucky, now for more than forty years. He flatly stated he would not condemn the Polk administration and was silent on the issue of election fraud. Instead, he expressed confidence that Whig principles would endure, just as the country would, although both temporarily faced discouraging prospects. "I have the high satisfaction to know that I have escaped a great and fearful responsibility," he said, and he spoke of the "peace and tranquility" he looked forward to in retirement.[4] His voice was still strong and rich, but he looked very old and very tired. Some of the electors pulled out handkerchiefs as he spoke. Clay was clearly exhausted, and his visitors now had confirmed what they had suspected. He was saying good-bye.

Even from a distance the scene was affecting. In Washington, John J. Crittenden confessed that newspaper accounts of it made him "quite melancholy."[5] When Clay told him that he merely wanted to spend "the remnant of my days, in peace and retirement" at Ashland, Crittenden at last believed that he meant it.[6] Possibly at the time Clay believed he meant it too.

They both should have known better.

EVEN IF CLAY really intended to retreat for good from public life, the public would not retreat from him. Accolades from his admirers never ceased, and the material proof of their affection arrived almost daily at Ashland. In Philadelphia, a hat made especially for Clay from the finest Rocky Mountain beaver was put on display and became a tourist attraction before its dispatch to Kentucky. And while many of the gifts were small and charming, some were so generous they were discomfiting. Lucretia, for example, received "a brilliant bracelet studded with diamonds" that Clay gratefully acknowledged but she would seldom if ever wear.[7]

Yet it was Clay who received a series of spectacular gifts during the spring and summer of 1845 that left him speechless. He faced a grave crisis in his financial affairs; in fact, his money woes eroded his customary optimism more than his political disappointments ever had. For almost a decade, the gradual depletion of his assets had been more than alarming, reducing his net worth by more than half since 1839. He had trouble paying his 1844 taxes. Helping Thomas absorb the failure of his hemp and bagging business saddled Clay with an unexpected $20,000 obligation. Added to that were the costs associated with closing his friend John Morrison's estate. In addition, there was the loan from John Jacob Astor, making the sum of Clay's total indebtedness a staggering $40,000 (more than a million dollars in today's money). He tried to reduce that figure by selling off lands he owned in Missouri and Kentucky, but he could barely manage to keep up with the interest, let alone shrink the principal. At the beginning of 1845, his financial emergency reached a critical point. Clay had offered his beloved Ashland as collateral to save Thomas from bankruptcy. Now he was certain to lose it.

Then in mid-February, Clay received a letter from John Tilford, the president of the Northern Bank of Kentucky, which held the bulk of his notes. Tilford had peculiar news: the bank had received from donors, who wished to remain anonymous, $5,000 to apply to Clay's debt. They wanted, Tilford reported, "to render your remaining years free from pecuniary cares." Furthermore, they felt their gesture repaid "only part of a debt they owe you for your long and valued Services in the cause of our country and its institutions."[8] A few days later, Clay received another note from Tilford informing him that an additional $5,000 had arrived. Clay was at first astonished. Then he was embarrassed. Although Tilford never revealed the benefactors' identities, Clay could readily guess their names. He sought to explain directly to a few how he had become so insolvent, candidly citing Thomas's troubles as the primary cause.[9] But most of all, Clay was profoundly touched. Tilford's strange but happy role as go-between for these singular acts of generosity continued, and through him Clay profusely thanked his nameless friends for their kindness, especially for "the delicate manner in which it has been rendered." He hoped that it had not caused anyone the slightest financial hardship, and he wanted all to know that if the situation had been reversed, he too would have rushed to their aid.[10]

The money continued to pour in from Boston, New York, Philadelphia, and New Orleans and was deposited in varying but substantial sums over the course of March and April. In short order, every penny Henry Clay owed the Northern Bank of Kentucky was paid off. Then in the months that followed, his friends began paying off his Astor loan as well. Clay protested that this was really too much, but he was gently told not to worry. It was, said William N. Mercer, the least his friends could do.[11] Yet Clay insisted. Continuing the pretense of ignorance, he told Tilford, who continued to execute the group's financial wishes, to inform his friends they had done more than enough. He would repay Astor on his own; they should send no more money.[12] "I am not rich," Clay told a correspondent who was unaware of his financial rescue and was writing to offer help, "but I am now nearly free from debt, and I possess a competency to enable me, to live in comfort during the remnant of my days, and to fulfill some of the duties of hospitality."[13]

The matter was handled quite deftly and kept as private as possible, but the story was too good to remain undisclosed for long. Newspapers soon reported it, and eventually imparted to the episode a more theatrical flair: Clay, the story went, appeared at the Northern Bank to make a payment when the cashier handed him the note and told him it was entirely settled. Clay was said to have wept. None of this happened. Clay clearly first learned of his friends' generosity from Tilford's letter.[14]

Unencumbered by debt for the first time in years, Clay flourished. His estate did too. Visitors admired its "profusion of venerable forest trees, evergreens and shrubbery" that adorned the main grounds, a nucleus of fifty acres surrounded by the larger working farm. A winding carriage road snaked through a shady grove to the house from which radiated an abundance of walking trails lined with dogwoods, periwinkles, and redbuds. Mockingbirds and whip-poor-wills filled the trees. The house was equally inviting, modestly but comfortably furnished and containing "many choice and valuable evidences of the respect of his countrymen."[15] Ashland had become the showplace Clay had always imagined. Lucretia's dairy thrived and boasted cheese and butter houses constructed of cool, insulating stone. There were also chicken coops, dovecotes, barns, and sheds, all trim and well maintained. The stables housed handsome horses, increasingly the focus of John's life. Lucretia, who also cultivated ornamentals in a spacious greenhouse, supervised a four-acre fruit and vegetable garden. Beyond this prosperous farm, Ashland became a sprawling six-hundred-acre plantation of cultivated fields devoted to wheat, rye, corn, and hemp. Pastures of fabled bluegrass fattened lowing cows and pedigreed sheep. All fences were in good repair, and weeds were regularly hoed down in their corners as well as amid the crops those fences protected.

The routines of the estate were pleasantly consistent. Lucretia rose early to organize the day's work in her gardens and the dairy and to see to the sale of her butter and cheese to Lexington markets and households. The "milk and egg" money that resulted was hardly a trifle; her enterprise brought in about $1,500 a year. She would also make certain that any guests in the mansion were comfortable. "Mrs. Clay is one of the best hearted women I have ever known," reported one. "She is all attention to my wants."[16]

Clay rose early too and usually dressed plainly in clothes of American manufacture. He might attend to some improvement to the main house—he raised the roof line at the dining room during these months, for instance—and nurture the array of plants he had carefully situated over the years for the best aesthetic effect.[17] Shortly after his retirement in 1842, he had resumed practicing law, both to deal with his debt—"I am not at all unwilling to receive liberal fees," he joked[18]—and to help James establish himself at the bar. After his debts were no longer an issue, he still spent several hours a day at the office, a plain establishment with "no cushioned chairs, carpeted floors, mahogany book cases and desks."[19] He strode through Lexington swinging a gold-headed cane and puffing on a cigar. A little girl established a charming ritual with Clay: she placed her sunbonnet on the counter of her father's store, and Clay would drop a silver ten-cent piece in it as payment for a kiss on his cheek. He might stop by to see Leslie Combs or go to the courthouse to trade yarns with young attorneys. On Saturday evenings, he often visited the market in downtown Lexington, where crowds gathered around him at vegetable stalls to shake his hand or discuss the weather. "I believe he really is," said one visitor, "one of the happiest men on earth."[20]

His greatest delight came from watching his land blossom and his livestock fatten. Clay was always a serious farmer. His goal was to make Ashland a model of husbandry boasting the best and most improved stock breeds.[21] He was an early advocate of scientific agriculture and experimental breeding. He varied his crops and saw to their methodical rotation to prevent soil exhaustion. He also replenished his fields with liberal applications of natural fertilizers and planted nitrogen-fixing legumes. His work with hemp growing earned him renown, and he published articles describing successful methods for cultivating and harvesting the plants; his discourses on the methods of rotting hemp fiber from stalks filled pages.[22] He dug a large canal, a quarter of a mile long, three feet wide at the bottom and six feet wide at the top, and two and a half feet deep, to drain the low ground, and built vats to water rot his hemp. Convinced that properly prepared American hemp was the equal of its Russian counterpart, he boasted he would rig the sailing ships of the entire U.S. navy with cordage made from Ashland's crop.[23] Meanwhile, his work as a stockman gained him notice for pioneering efforts to improve the bloodlines of cattle, sheep, and horses. He bought animals in Europe, sparing little expense when he found a promising prospect to develop a superior breed.[24]

OUT OF PUBLIC office since 1842 and defeated in 1844, Clay remained in the public eye through his work as an attorney. He was involved in two of Kentucky's most notable courtroom dramas during these years. The first was the murder trial of Lafayette Shelby, son of James Shelby and grandson of Isaac Shelby, the scion of one of the state's most prominent families. Young Shelby, hotheaded and touchy, knew Henry M. Horine only as a fellow lodger at a Lexington hotel, but on January 10, 1846, he took Horine's customary chair at dinner and then took exception to Horine's objections. Shelby accosted Horine in the street for his impertinence, tried to provoke a fight, and then shot him dead. Shelby was held without bail, and the family appealed to Clay, who took the case.[25] "It is a very hard case," Clay remarked in considerable understatement, for his client had clearly murdered the man, "but for the sake of his numerous and highly respectable connections, I hope to be able to secure his acquittal."[26] As the trial commenced at the end of June, Shelby was in such despair that he wanted to kill himself, but his "highly respectable connections" as well as Clay's dramatic courtroom presence befuddled the jury to indecision.[27] Shelby's defense rested in part on his being provoked by Horine's insolent stare in the dining room. Years later, Judge R. A. Buckner recalled how Clay showed that a mere look could be more offensive than words by forming "such an expression to his countenance of withering contempt and hate that all confessed that it was more insulting than any other form of expression."[28]

The news of the hung jury caused a small riot in Lexington, where a mob, incensed by the obvious favor shown to Shelby, burned judge, jurors, and Clay in effigy.[29] Clay was slated to defend Shelby in a second trial scheduled for September 1848, but the defendant was not willing to press his luck and fled to Texas. He did not return until 1862, and by then the Civil War had made him and the murder old news. He never answered for killing Horine.

The Shelby affair was Henry Clay's last criminal case, but his last notable court appearance was in a civil trial over a contested will. The case involved the enormous estate of Mary Bullitt, known as Polly, the daughter of Alexander and Mary Bullitt. Both had children by previous marriages, representatives of Kentucky's most important families whose blood and marriage ties broadly linked them to other prominent families in the state, including the Clays. Polly's mother was a Churchill (of Louisville's Churchill Downs), and Mary Churchill's first husband, Richard Prather, was a distant relation of Henry Clay, Jr.'s late wife. Their daughter, Eliza Prather, married James Guthrie, a wealthy Louisville businessman, leader of the state Democratic Party, and railroad promoter.

It was into this web of interlocking families that Polly Bullitt was born, and that would be the cause of all the trouble later on. Alexander and Mary had two other children together, but it was soon clear that Polly was severely retarded, and they consequently arranged a considerable inheritance for her care.[30] When the Bullitts both died in 1816, Polly was only eight, and her half sister, Eliza Guthrie, as her guardian, sent her to the Sisters of Charity of Nazareth, a Catholic convent near Bardstown. Polly lived with the nuns until she was nineteen and then lived in James Guthrie's home. Failing health and increasing mental debility eventually required her to live at the St. Vincent Infirmary, and there her brief, sad life ended in 1843 at age thirty-five. Yet it was claimed that she had dictated a will bequeathing her entire Bullitt fortune to her Guthrie nieces, James and Eliza's children, Mary, Augusta, and Sarah. The Bullitt children by Alexander's first marriage immediately challenged this will, charging that Polly, unable to count, unteachable, and irritable to the point of tantrums, had not been mentally capable of crafting such a document. They accordingly claimed that the will was a transparent manufacture of the Guthries.[31] When the court upheld the will, the Bullitts appealed and hired Henry Clay to represent them. The case was heard again in 1849 and instantly became sensational theater for the same reasons it would be for any time: it featured prominent, affluent families in dispute, it had at its center a mentally disabled child and at its periphery a Catholic convent with nuns attesting to Polly's competency, and it offered the prospect of loving nieces being rewarded and rightful heirs being cheated. And it showcased Henry Clay, a lion in winter to be sure, but a lion nonetheless.

The complaint against the will hinged on Polly's fitness to make it, and Clay consequently attacked those who defended her competency, which required him to challenge the priests and nuns, especially Catherine Spalding, the formidable mother superior of the Sisters of Charity of Nazareth. Clay knew the order well—he had handed out diplomas at Nazareth's first commencement—but he was unrelenting in cross-examination and characteristically biting in his demeanor.[32] Over the course of a week in late April and early May, he performed for a courtroom packed with "the most distinguished ladies" of Louisville.[33] His final appearance drew an outsized crowd of women, young and old, who began to arrive at eight in the morning, hours before he was to speak. The judge ordered one bench cleared to accommodate the ladies, then another, and another, until the only males remaining were the lawyers, the jury, and a little boy curled up on a windowsill who refused to budge lest he lose the chance to hear Clay. One lady sat in Clay's chair as soon as he rose to speak, and others squeezed into the jury box. Clay wore a black suit and a white cravat, "stood as erect as a flagpole, spoke with great deliberation and distinctness, and held spellbound the attention of the judge, bar, and jury, as well as the crowded court-room." They listened as he swelled his rich baritone to emphasize a point or occasionally mutter in mock resignation under his breath, though quite audibly, "Guthries, Guthries, Guthries—always there are Guthries."[34]

Finally handed the case, the jury deliberated for three hours before notifying the court that it could not reach a verdict. As in the trial of Lafayette Shelby, Clay had managed to plant enough doubt to cause a jury to stall in indecision, but in this instance, it meant a defeat for his clients. The previous ruling upholding the will was allowed to stand. Yet nobody would ever forget Henry Clay striding and gesturing before that court, befuddling one witness into doubting his own signature, causing fits of hilarity to rock the assembly, his biting sarcasm delivered with a smile, the judge himself quietly shaking with laughter before reluctantly gaveling the proceedings back to order. Nobody would ever forget that they had seen a lion, impressive in any season, making the mundane memorable, winning the crowd if not the case.[35]

"I AM ENDEAVORING to separate myself as much as I can from this world," Clay told a friend in early 1845, "but, in spite of all my wishes for seclusion, great numbers call to see me at this place." He did not have the heart to turn them away.[36] In fact, Ashland hummed as a center of warm hospitality. Visitors showed up out of the blue, and sometimes as many as a half dozen people, strangers to each other as well as to Clay, would appear on his doorstep, always expecting him to do most of the talking and saying virtually nothing themselves.[37]

One of the visitors to Ashland that summer attracted wide notice. George Peter Alexander Healy, a gifted young American artist who had been studying in Europe, came with a special commission from "Louis-Philippe, the king of the French," as he styled himself to denote his distance from monarchical pretense. Louis-Philippe fondly recalled his four years of residence in the United States during the turmoil of the French Revolution, and he dispatched Healy to paint portraits of America's aging statesmen, including Andrew Jackson, John Quincy Adams, Daniel Webster, and Henry Clay. In May 1845, Healy arrived in Boston aboard the steamer *Hibernia* and hurried first to Nashville because reports accurately told of Andrew Jackson's imminent death. The artist then traveled north to Ashland, bringing with him the Jackson portrait, which he had only just completed before Old Hickory's demise. If Clay regarded this as some sort of portent, he didn't say so, although as he sat for Healy—"a most unpleasant occupation," he complained—he wasn't feeling very well, nor was Lucretia. Yet both liked what Healy was doing, and Clay judged him "an artiste of real talent."[38]

Everyone, including Clay, had commented on the apparent inability of even the most practiced artists to capture a decent likeness of him. Portraits of Clay were like the "body without the Soul—the Head without the mind." In short, his features required animation to make them express his personality. "*Clay in calm repose,*" a friend concluded, "was not Clay *at all.*"[39]

Many artists did try to capture the fire that animated Clay's features, and some came close. Matthew Jouett painted several portraits of him. Several years before Healy's visit, the Philadelphia artist John Neagle had come to Ashland to paint one of the most famous likenesses of Clay ever produced, a full-length portrait that Neagle boasted broke from the tradition of simply sticking a head on a prepainted body. It was instead actually a full representation of Henry Clay.

Healy's labors, however, were of a different class, and the portrait that resulted was a testament to his skill. Clay was shown full-faced and gazed steadily with his mouth set in what appeared to be the start of a smile. His features were less sharp and his eyes were softer. Some family members would recall that Healy had considerable difficulty getting the eyes right, and not all of them liked the result. Not only did he not capture the color (a very pale blue), he "failed absolutely to get the expression or the fire," they said.[40] It was always Lucretia's favorite likeness, however. Healy presented a copy to her as a gift, and she had it framed and mounted at Ashland. When admirers proposed to take it to Frankfort, she would not "part from it."[41]

Extended family was a constant presence at Ashland. Grandchildren often filled the house with chatter and laughter, eager to see Grandmama and Grandpapa, who were generous with treats and hugs.[42] In addition to Henry and Lucretia, John remained in residence, and while their houses were being built, Thomas and James with their families lived at Ashland too. Even after the older sons moved their families to their new houses, they remained nearby, and social routines kept the house full. Thomas and Mary always came to dinner on Sunday afternoons, for example, as did Henry Jr.'s children, Nannie and Tommy.[43] Henry Jr. remained in Louisville, but he often came to visit the children, who were living in Lexington with cousin Nanette while going to school. Clay repeatedly tried to get Henry to move back to Lexington, even to live at Ashland, but he would not. Henry was hard to make cheerful. Julia had been dead for five years, but for the young widower, her passing might have happened only yesterday.[44]

Clay hovered over his children when they were near him and clung to them when they were distant. When he traveled, he wanted regular letters and complained when they were not forthcoming. It was important to him that everyone stay in touch, and Clay thought it odd when others did not. When, during his extended stay at Ashland, artist John Neagle did not receive any letters, Clay observed, according to Neagle, that "my family did not seem to care for me."[45]

When Clay was in ready proximity to his children, he could be smothering. Losing all his daughters filled him with dread about the children who survived. In addition, he had always treated his girls differently. For them he had always been full of praise and encouragement, an attitude that extended to his daughters-in-law as well. James's wife, Susan, became Clay's confidante and informally his private secretary, the keeper of the documents and, according to conjecture, destroyer of same if they were potentially unflattering. "I never knew a man more loved—adored in his family than Henry Clay," Susan Jacob Clay would remember. "I never heard him speak an unkind nor even a hasty word to any member of his household."[46] That sort of reverence could be endearing, but it also emphasized for his sons that their father cast a long shadow.

Because they had been allowed to grow up largely undisciplined and at considerable liberty—a custom of the times as well as a result of their parents' indulgence—all of the boys came uncertainly and unevenly to the burdens of adulthood. Theodore's insanity placed extra expectations on his brothers. They naturally chafed under them, which prompted even more hectoring from their father. Clay could never shake off his inclination to run things and manage people, and his sons never fully escaped his watchful eye nor were spared his advice in matters great and small. Henry Jr. stubbornly remained in Louisville, but when he considered running for Congress from that district, his father was ready with counsel as well as encouragement. He was soon suggesting that Henry Jr. move in at Ashland to save money and be near his children, possibly to go into business with Thomas. Henry Jr. would have none of it.[47]

Thomas and James were often unhappy as they and their families lodged at Ashland waiting for their houses to be finished. James was practicing law, but his father showed up frequently at the office with suggestions for improving this brief or that argument. Clay had advice about how to raise and educate his grandchildren too.

These boys became young men under the nearly impossible circumstance of being the sons of a great man of considerable renown and achievement. Living up to that standard was daunting enough without its exemplar's constantly, reflexively offering guidance. Worse, what Clay considered fatherly devotion could be stifling and was sometimes hurtful. Thomas was under no illusion that his father always regarded Henry Jr., serious and talented and bookish, as the most capable of the sons. Thomas was solemn enough all right, but he was never quite able to manage a success. He had launched his hemp and bagging business with high hopes and his father's generous capitalization, but the hopes had been dashed and his father nearly ruined when the business failed. In debt to his father for $20,000 (an obligation never repaid and finally forgiven in Clay's will), Thomas eventually embarked upon another business, a sawmill, but the equipment was second-rate, and he had to depend on his father again to come up with the $600 necessary to improve it. Thomas lived at Ashland, cheerless and irritable, eager to move in to his own house, even if it was only minutes away. He quarreled with John frequently, and the arguments could be heated enough to send one or the other stomping out. The subsequent truces were awkward and halfhearted.[48]

The arguments were usually John's fault. As the baby of the family, a child who came to Henry and Lucretia after so much loss and heartbreak, he was terribly spoiled by his parents and so petted by Lucretia that John's brothers tended to be jealous of him and mildly resentful of her. "I think you do your mother[']s heart wrong in supposing it engrossed by John," Clay admonished James, adding what he knew to be true: "I believe that she affectionately feels for all her children. Her manner does not always truly indicate the intensity of her actual feelings."[49] Nevertheless John's brothers had a point, for Lucretia was doggedly blind to the boy's faults.[50] He could be petulant and temperamental. Any good behavior on his part was such an unexpected treat that his parents were apt to characterize it as exemplary.

"John looks very serious," Clay reported to Lucretia when he and his son were on their way to enroll him at Princeton in 1837, "but has conducted himself well." In only a few months, though, John's experiment at college went awry. "John has lately given me great pain," Clay admitted, "and I almost despair of him." After John visited Ashland in the spring of his freshman year, the boy's level mood and good conduct encouraged his father, but upon returning to Princeton, John began disappearing for days at a time on drunken sprees in New York and Philadelphia. It was clear that when far from home, he could not resist indulging "his frailties" of strong drink and careless gambling. In March 1839, Clay himself requested that Princeton expel John from the junior class. The college was more than happy to oblige.[51]

And so it went. Clay next enrolled John in Washington College in Washington, Pennsylvania, with his grandson, Henry Clay Duralde, hopeful that a relative's companionship and the watchful eye of the headmaster would settle both boys down (Henry Duralde had his own problems). Clay confidentially informed the headmaster that John lacked "the will to study," a shortcoming he had cheerfully admitted to his father. "He has a high and irascible temper," Clay warned the school, but added that he was "easily acted upon by kindness and persuasion."[52]

John's hair-trigger temper continued to be a problem, but in the spring of 1845, his demeanor took an ominous turn. Over the course of several weeks his behavior grew increasingly unpredictable. By early April, Clay openly worried that John was becoming "more and more deranged" and at last broached the unthinkable: Would his youngest son, like his oldest, have to be committed?[53] As with Theodore—hardly a comforting comparison—the ostensible cause was a girl: "His passion for Miss J——revived," Clay explained, "and yesterday [April 4] he attempted to see her, but she, being advised of his situation, properly declined to receive him." Unrequited, John roamed the woods into the wee hours and became "wild and boisterous in his language," even "incoherent." At least he, unlike Theodore, had not threatened anyone—yet. After John's failed attempt to see the girl, Clay made the arrangements, and John went "quietly to the Hospital, without any resistance." Lucretia was heartsick.[54]

A week passed, but John was no better. If anything, he was worse. "I am afraid," Clay sadly confessed, "that John's case is hopeless." He was even more unhinged than Theodore had been when they first put him away. Clay found the state of affairs unbearable. He tried to comfort himself by making certain that Theodore and John, suddenly unexpected roommates, were as comfortable as possible in a building full of lunatics. He stationed a family servant in their room to see to their needs. But the matter preyed on his mind, especially because John retained enough rationality to suffer from his confinement but not enough to justify his freedom. Theodore at least had slipped into a catatonic state that shielded him from his hopelessness. (Fanciful stories that described Theodore as thinking he was George Washington and holding presidential levees for the other inmates at the asylum were complete fabrications.[55]) John's slender thread of lucidity, however, also gave Clay hope that his son could possibly come home. By the end of April, Clay was considering just such an experiment, and in early May, John finally returned to Ashland. He seemed better—in fact, better than his old self—but neither Clay nor Lucretia would ever again be easy about the boy. When John traveled alone and did not stay in touch, his parents always worried.[56]

John eventually found himself, and found a girl (if an unlikely one). For decades John remained a bachelor horse breeder. Hearing that his nephew Eugene Erwin, Anne's third son, had been killed while serving as a Confederate colonel at Vicksburg, he wrote to console Eugene's young widow, Josephine Russell Erwin. Their letters eventually assumed a warm, tender tone, and Josephine came to Lexington with her three daughters. John and Josephine married, with the result that Anne's little brother would raise her grandchildren as his own children. Thus would John eventually find his place as a stockman and breeder of horse racing champions and father to his little nieces. John would be all right. He even came to affectionate terms with Thomas. "You cannot imagine how much I was gratified at hearing of your visiting at Thomas's and talking kindly together as brothers," Clay wrote to John.[57] When he penned that letter, Henry Clay was in Washington, dying, still worrying about them all.

JOHN'S PLIGHT WAS only one source of family trouble for the Clays during these years. James and Susan's little girl was born in 1844 with a spinal defect so severe that everyone feared she would die, or at least be unable to walk. Lucy survived and turned out to be a cheerful child despite the chronic problems that filled her life with doctors and painful braces. It hurt her grandfather's heart, and he was always eager to pet and spoil his brave little Lucy. He often picked and peeled figs for her breakfast, arranging them on a tray with a freshly cut rose.[58]

Contemplating the situation of his beloved Anne's children also made Clay sad. Anne's widowed husband, James Erwin, remarried in 1843, taking as his second wife Mary Margaret Johnson, niece of Clay's old friend and nemesis Richard M. Johnson. When he married, Erwin left behind a trail of financial irregularities in New Orleans. He died in 1851, having had two more children with his second wife. He also left no will. The picture of James Erwin that afterward emerged was indistinct but unsettling. He had pretended affluence or poverty for best effect, depending on the situation. Family had served as particularly easy marks. Anne's nephews, the Duralde boys, were left flat broke by Erwin's frauds.[59]

It was cold comfort that Erwin had treated his and Anne's children just as shabbily. He had squandered their share of Anne's inheritance and died owing them $37,000, not counting years of interest—money that none of them would see, since the second Mrs. Erwin proved tenacious in claiming her and her children's share of the meager leavings.[60]

Under these shadows, the Erwin children remained a troubled lot. James Erwin, Jr., died of a self-inflicted gunshot wound in New Orleans. Henry Clay Erwin died in 1859 at the Galt House in Louisville of tuberculosis. Andrew Eugene, always "Eugene" to the family, was placed in a mercantile house in New York by his grandfather, but the work did not agree with the boy, and he soon went to California. He did well there and married Josephine Russell, whose widowhood would later throw her together with Eugene's uncle John. More or less cast adrift by her brothers and father, Lucretia Clay Erwin married Frederick Cowles, a "very poor, altho' a very good person," according to her grandfather.[61]

In similar fashion, the Duralde grandchildren presented an unbroken chronicle of misfortune. Martin and Henry Clay Duralde seemed to enjoy visiting Lexington, but as he grew older, Henry Clay Duralde bounced from one private academy to another before retreating to his native New Orleans. He emptied his already meager purse and neglected his family, including his grandfather, whom he ignored during Clay's visits to the city. Finally Henry Duralde fled to California on the *St. Mary*, a schooner that rounded Cape Horn and paused at Valparaiso, where he wrote his grandfather a long apology confessing his profligacy and vowing to turn over a new leaf once he reached the West. In less than a year Clay received word that his grandson had drowned in the Sacramento River.[62]

And then there was Martin, the little boy who had come wide-eyed to Lexington after his mother's death, able to speak only a few words of English. Martin became a midshipman in the navy and in spring 1839 was slated to sail on the *Constitution* to the Pacific. He was ill, however, and the navy was wary about sending him. Martin's complaint was respiratory and real, but Clay wondered if the illness was actually the result of Martin's reluctance to go so far from home. After all, said Clay, his grandson had no ancestral history of consumption. And with this first mention of that time's dreaded word for tuberculosis, Clay acknowledged the possibility that something might be irremediably

wrong with his grandson. Clay suggested another ship to a more salubrious destination, perhaps the Mediterranean, and Martin did eventually sail on the
Brandywine to that duty station. But the signs were on him, and soon there was
no denying that he was very ill.[63]

Returning to the States, Martin was clearly unable to continue in the navy. In
late 1844 he suffered a serious hemorrhage and began a sad descent, wandering
in search of a place to breathe better and cough less. He went to Cuba before returning to Ashland in early 1846, but soon he left for the sulphur springs in Virginia that summer. In early July 1846 he paused at Blue Sulphur Springs, which
catered to consumptive invalids. By this time, the stout boy whom Clay had
once helped outfit with a new wardrobe was almost a skeleton. Martin tried to
ride in the mornings before breakfast and said hopefully that the waters were
helping.[64]

His optimism was fleeting. He moved to Red Sulphur Springs, but upon reflection, he judged it as only a place where consumptives came to die. On July
18, he left for the resort spa at White Sulphur Springs, not to take the waters—
he was finally convinced they did no good—but to find a more cheerful setting
to "let Nature pursue its own course." Martin told his grandfather, "I have become a confirmed case of consumption and can only hope to linger out a life of
much suffering."[65]

And suffer he did. Seeking warmth, he moved through Richmond on his way
to Old Point Comfort in Hampton, Virginia. He told his grandfather that he
would continue to write as long as he could, but there were only a few more letters from him, and then nothing until word came from a doctor in Philadelphia.
Martin, he said, had died on September 17, 1846, at the Columbia Hotel. His
possessions included a pocket watch and a trunk with some clothes. His wallet
contained $143 in southern banknotes, a deposit slip for $1,300 on a New Orleans bank, and a lottery ticket. Clay asked that the money be used to bury Martin and pledged to supply any additional funds that were necessary. "Death,
ruthless death," he bitterly mourned, ". . . has now commenced his work of destruction, with my descendants, in the second generation."[66]

Clay had not even known that Martin was in Philadelphia. He had wanted
the boy to return to Ashland for his last days, but Martin had declined. So
Susan's boy, aged twenty-three years, died in a hotel room surrounded by
strangers and flanked by his small possessions. He had hoped even at the end
that his luck could still change. He had bought a lottery ticket.

"YOU ASK ME if I am happy?" Clay wrote a friend in the months after the election of 1844. "Ah! my dear friend, who on earth is happy? Very few, I appre-

hend, if any."[67] Certainly he had reason to be discouraged by the course the Polk administration had pledged to plot in both domestic and foreign policy, but in the meantime he watched the closing days of the Tyler presidency with growing dismay. The annexation of Texas had become an obsession for John Tyler, and his efforts to accomplish it remained stalled by the impasse of slavery. The annexation forces simply did not have the two-thirds majority in the Senate to ratify a treaty with Texas, but Tyler and Secretary of State John C. Calhoun contrived the idea of bypassing that constitutional procedure with a joint congressional resolution, which required only simple majorities in both houses. Clay was bitterly amused by these doctrinaire interpreters of strict constitutional construction essentially disregarding constitutional rules. When the House of Representatives fell in line with Tyler to give his resolution a 22-vote majority, Clay cried, "God save the Commonwealth!"[68] The Senate was not quite as pliable, but the unrelenting persistence of annexationists finally delivered the goods in that chamber too. The clock was ticking away the final hours of Tyler's presidency when he finally signed the resolution annexing Texas, but sign it he did, the crowning achievement, in his estimation, of an otherwise failed administration.[69]

It was, in a way, a gift to the incoming Polk administration. It at least spared Polk the political brawl that annexation threatened, which would have been a blemish on the traditional honeymoon with the legislature. But the gesture hardly guided Polk out of the territorial woods, and in some respects it blocked his path even more. The Mexican government, livid about what it described as the simple theft of its property, broke off diplomatic relations. Furthermore, Texas had never established its southern border with Mexico, claiming it to be the Rio Grande, while Mexico insisted it was fifty miles farther north, on the Nueces River, which had been the provincial Texan border when it was indisputably Mexican territory. The Rio Grande/Nueces disagreement made slight difference on its eastern end, but the western portion was quite another matter. There, as the Rio Grande snaked northward a good five hundred miles farther to the west, it would give a considerable part of New Mexico to Texas, and there Mexico drew the line—or more accurately, Mexico refused to let Texas draw any such line. Polk supported Texas's claim and thus created yet another point of contention with Mexico City.

Polk also inherited another territorial dispute that the Tyler administration had not been able to resolve in the slightest, and it had the potential to be very serious because it put the United States at odds with Great Britain, which many correctly noted was definitely not Mexico in terms of military power and international influence. The argument was over the vast Oregon country, a region in the Pacific Northwest that dwarfed even Texas in its expansive potential. Polk came into office, of course, saddled with a Democrat expansionist impulse that would find expression in the absurdly belligerent slogan "Fifty-four Forty or Fight," a fetchingly alliterative phrase fraught with grave diplomatic consequences. Would James K. Polk really clench the country's fists to secure the bulk of western Canada, despite Britain's impeccable territorial claims to much of the region? Antislavery advocates certainly wanted him to, for a larger (free) Oregon coming to the United States served as a counterweight to (slave) Texas, and Polk found himself caught between angry abolitionists who did not trust him and the thigh-thumping, gallus-popping expansionists who formed the core of his political support. Watching all this unfold from Ashland, Clay was more alarmed for the country than amused by Polk's dilemma. The former War Hawk now judged the prospect of hostilities with Britain a "calamity"; the erstwhile expansionist who had eyed the plum of eastern Canada now deemed its western regions "a territory so distant from them both [America and Britain], and at present so unimportant to either."[70]

Efforts to negotiate an Oregon boundary proved fruitless, and when Polk gave the required one-year notice that he intended to end the Anglo-American joint tenancy arrangement in the Oregon country, a pact in force since 1818, Clay was dismayed.[71] Yet he should not have been. Irresistible forces fated the peaceful resolution of the Oregon controversy. "I do not think," predicted a sagacious observer, "nor have I thought from the first that we will have war with England."[72] Fighting was in neither country's best interest, and a treaty ultimately settled the boundary at the 49th parallel, considerably south of the 54° purportedly worth fighting for—an American concession, but far enough north to give the United States possession of the Columbia River, a British compromise of some note.

Antislavery men howled over the perceived surrender, but Polk had good reason to embrace the arrangement. Great Britain, after all, was not Mexico. The latter was a much more attractive and likely prospect for a war of conquest, which by the time the Oregon Treaty was signed had already started.

Polk wanted the grand bay at San Francisco in order to promote American interests in the Pacific, and a considerable number of Americans imbued with a sense of "Manifest Destiny" felt foreordained to extend their dominion from sea to shining sea. To that end, Polk tried to compel Mexico to negotiate by making the border dispute with Texas the center of all controversies. He ordered General Zachary Taylor to march south of the Nueces River and plant the flag in the disputed region, and he sent an envoy to Mexico City to purchase California. Taylor's move was provocative, the envoy's cause was hopeless, and the Mexican government was provoked by the one and intractable with the other. Inevitably there was an incident on the border, and Polk used it to ask Congress for war. Hectored and goaded by the administration's claims that American blood had been spilled by an invader on American soil, Congress agreed on May 11, 1846, to make war on Mexico. Fourteen Whigs in the House voted against the declaration of war. Eventually they would be lionized as "the Immortal Fourteen."

Congress called for fifty thousand volunteers to join Taylor's forces, and the country responded. Within a week a mass meeting in Lexington produced two organized companies of mounted infantry, and Governor William Owsley's May 17 proclamation exhorting Kentuckians to form volunteer companies drew responses from all over the state, including the Louisville Legion, which became the 1st Kentucky volunteer infantry. Private citizens were already doing their part. Henry Clay, Jr., cheered the Louisville *Courier*, "can raise in an hour as noble and brave a band as ever shouldered a musket or thrashed an enemy."[73] In only five days, Kentucky had filled its requisition of troops. Everyone's blood was up regardless of political affiliation or partisan policies. Daniel Webster's youngest son, Edward, helped to raise a regiment in Boston. And Henry Clay's namesake became second-in-command of the 2nd Kentucky volunteer infantry.[74]

Clay did not want his son to go to war in Mexico. His opposition was not because the duty was sure to be dangerous; he regretted that the war itself was not "more reconcilable with the dictates of conscience."[75] Clay's was a widespread Whig sentiment. "Who would be glad at this time," asked the Lexington *Virginian*, "when the war clouds are gathering around the horizon, to see HENRY CLAY at the head of affairs?"[76]

Meanwhile, Henry Clay, Jr., helped to drill his regiment in Louisville. His decision to join the fight in Mexico was complicated, but it essentially distilled to several essential and inescapable motives. He had lacked purpose ever since Julia's death, and his return to his military commission at this moment offered not only direction but meaning to what had become an aimless life unfulfilled by legal briefs, unsuccessful runs for Congress, or dithering about in the state legislature at Frankfort. True enough, he volunteered in defiance of his father's wishes—the only time he had ever disregarded his father's wishes about an important matter—but in that defiance he was ironically adhering to the most basic lesson learned from his father: the love of country expressed not just in words but deeds. So he donned a uniform and spent the scant days before he and his men left for Zachary Taylor's army teaching them the rudiments of army life. He showed them how to fight as a unit and how to behave like soldiers, things he had learned at West Point years earlier but had never practiced himself in the field.

In June, the Kentucky volunteers began departing from Louisville by steamboat, first to Memphis, then overland to Little Rock, Arkansas, and on from there through Texas to the Rio Grande. They followed Taylor's tracks into Mexico to swell his army along with the legions of volunteers from other states.[77] Henry managed to write often because Taylor's invasion was uneventful after a victory at Monterrey in September, a fight the Kentucky volunteers had missed while making their way overland. By early 1847, Taylor had moved his army farther south from Monterrey, camping it some twenty miles south of Saltillo at Agua Nueva, about a hundred miles from the Rio Grande. There it had little to do but drill and get into trouble, the small number of regulars doing most of the former and the volunteers almost all of the latter. Henry assured his father that reports about undisciplined antics by the 2nd Kentucky, especially its unbridled drunkenness, were exaggerated. It was true, he admitted, that his immediate superior, Colonel William R. McKee, could be lax with the men and drank himself, sometimes to excess. But everyone was bored, and Henry found himself in the unenviable position of taking up the slack with the regiment. He longed for the carefree life of a private, but mostly "for a battle that it may have an end."[78]

The prospect for a decisive engagement seemed less likely because Taylor's army was shrinking. In fact, it was already a greatly changed force by the time the Kentucky volunteers joined it. President Polk was angry about Taylor's handling of the victory at Monterrey—the general had made a bargain that allowed defeated Mexican forces to retreat unmolested—and he was troubled that Taylor's growing popularity would make him a political enemy with influence. The president decided to redirect operations in Mexico by stopping Taylor's campaign and promoting another invasion led by Winfield Scott, who would land at Vera Cruz and march from there on Mexico City. Scott's operation drew off all available men, including those in Taylor's army, who were being sent to join the new American force assembling at Tampico. "Taylor is very sore about late proceedings in Washington," Henry observed at Agua Nueva. "He was not mentioned in the President's message and has been supplanted in command by Scott in a very cavalier manner." Furthermore, Henry confided to his father, Taylor "was not free from ambition" regarding the presidency.[79]

Taylor was, however, lacking a force of regulars. He sat exposed in a forward position with a diminished army composed almost exclusively of untested volunteer regiments. He brooded over slights and prepared to do whatever was necessary to save a reputation obviously under attack by political forces at home.

When newspapers reported that he had quarreled with his staff at Monterrey, he worked to counter the rumors, young Clay joining the effort to declare that "none but the most amiable relations have existed" between the general and his subordinates.[80] Young Henry was "in bad spirits" at Agua Nueva, his father told the family, "owing to his having no prospect of active service."[81] The absence of the prospect suited the elder Clay just fine. Shortly after arriving in Mexico, Henry had injured his right arm, either by dislocating or breaking it, according to various accounts, and had been assigned to Taylor's staff while on the mend. The news was mixed when Henry told them his health was fine and he was returning to the 2nd Kentucky, his arm still in a sling. Then in mid-February, one of his letters casually mentioned in a postscript that Santa Anna was rumored to be approaching their position with twenty thousand men.[82]

For a time, particularly as his son marched to join Taylor, Clay was caught up in the patriotic fervor of the war himself. On an extended visit to New Orleans at the end of 1846, he dined with the New England Society of Louisiana, where some members were preparing to embark for Scott's expedition. "I felt half inclined to ask for some little nook or corner in the army," Clay told the gathering, "in which I might serve in avenging the wrongs to my country." Perhaps it was the wine that made him say this. Possibly the burst of enthusiastic applause that greeted this incredible statement prompted Clay to go on: "I have thought that I might yet be able to capture or to slay a Mexican," he said to another appreciative ovation. The assembly loved the sentiments, and Clay basked in his customary ability to say just the right thing to the right group. His old friend Christopher Hughes, however, read about Clay's remarks and cringed.[83]

HENRY JR. LEFT his two youngest children in place at Nanette Smith's home in Lexington, but he deposited his oldest, Henry III, with James and Susan Clay, who had trouble with the boy from the start. This youngest Henry Clay had concerned his father for a long time. He took his mother's death understandably hard and developed a withdrawn and sullen attitude that was simultaneously passive and defiant. Modern adolescents have perfected to a near science the art of facing the world with a mixture of contempt and indifference, but such behavior was novel for Henry Clay III's time, and though everyone could understand its likely cause, everyone found it increasingly tedious. His father had tried to offer guidance, but he inevitably slipped into the habits of his own father in doing so, his words framing lectures and his approach chiding.[84] Away in Mexico, he continued his efforts. "Nothing gives me more pleasure than to learn that my children are happy," he wrote young Henry from the camp at Agua

Nueva. "True happiness consists not a little in the discharge of duties."[85] The boy's grandpapa would not have said it any differently.

Henry III was under gentle but firm instructions to mind his Uncle James and Aunt Susan, but they had their hands full with their difficult, insolent charge. "The faults which Henry Clay displays with you, he had developed at Ashland," Clay explained to his daughter-in-law. After Julia's death it had been impossible to take a firm hand with the grieving boy, and the result was now plainly unfortunate. Clay regretted it. "We must do the best we can with him . . . until his father returns, which I suppose will be next summer, when I hope he will take some decisive course with him."[86]

Clay commiserated with Susan from New Orleans, where he was visiting with William Mercer, as was his custom during the winter, and this first one of the war was no different.[87] He was preparing to return to Ashland when he heard that Zachary Taylor had fought a large battle and suffered heavy losses. Some reports had the casualty figures as high as two thousand men, but Clay hastened to reassure Lucretia that he doubted the fight was as big as that.[88] He did have to assume, however, that whatever had taken place near Agua Nueva that February had involved Henry. There was his son's troubling postscript, after all, about Santa Anna and tens of thousands of men.

On March 29, Clay returned to Ashland and found the farm running smoothly, in better shape actually than he had expected it to be. The weather was glorious with the air full of lovely fragrances and warmed by a soft spring sun. It was good to be home, and Clay spent the next day settling back into his routine. At midafternoon, the families gathered in Ashland's dining room for a welcome home dinner, chattering and laughing, the children eager to hear of Grandpapa's adventures on his trip. James entered the room, and everyone paused because he had a peculiar, drawn look. He told them the news.[89]

IT WOULD BE hailed as a great victory and its author, Zachary Taylor, would be lauded as a staunch patriot and stalwart soldier, the man who had faced incredible odds to hand Americans a victory as unlikely and as significant as Andrew Jackson's at New Orleans. It would instantly make Taylor a national champion and a political prospect of the first order. Yet the fight at the hacienda of Buena Vista was a meaningless battle that Taylor had recklessly invited to happen and had bungled at its start by depending on terrain to make up for his paltry numbers. The Mexican army commanded by Antonio López de Santa Anna numbered at least twenty thousand men, likely more. Zachary Taylor did not have five thousand men. He had only one organized brigade and a motley collection of untested volunteer units. Taylor's withdrawal to Buena Vista as the Mexicans entered Agua Nueva puzzled Santa Anna, who finally concluded that Taylor was in panicked retreat and decided to attack with his vastly superior numbers despite their fatigue from a forced march. Taylor was not in retreat. He wanted this fight to reclaim his reputation. He had deployed his men on a series of fingerlike plateaus that extended from a steep mountain face. The fifty-foot-deep arroyos that separated these plateaus made it hard for the Mexicans to mount an attack. They also made it nearly impossible for the forward units of Taylor's army to execute a retreat.[90]

Lieutenant Colonel Henry Clay, Jr., and the 2nd Kentucky volunteer infantry were part of these forward positions, and when the Mexican attack began in earnest on February 23, they bore the full force of it. The fighting became confused and vicious, "the hardest fight that has been fought in Mexico," according to one soldier. "We lost a great many officers."[91] The 2nd Kentucky soon found itself isolated when other regiments began retreating. As some four thousand Mexican lancers hurtled toward them to cut off any additional escape, the Kentuckians plunged into "a deep ravine . . . with rugged banks to climb."[92] Trapped, they suffered terrible casualties as Mexican artillery winnowed their ranks. Colonel McKee staggered to the ground where Mexican bayonets would finish him. Lieutenant Colonel Clay hit the ground with a serious wound too, but his men appeared out of the smoke and whistling shells to bear him up and carry him to the rear. They had gone only a short distance before a burst of Mexican grapeshot knocked three of them down dead and tore additional wounds in Henry. The noise was horrible, deafening, confusing, concussive, but Henry was shouting at his men and managed to raise his voice above the din, commanding them to leave him and save themselves. They looked at his broken body. They ran. Shortly the Mexican assault reached where he lay, and Santa Anna's soldiers repeatedly speared him with their lances until he was lifeless.[93]

Americans deeper in the rear, near Buena Vista, finally stood firm, and upon them the Mexican army broke its will. As Santa Anna retreated toward Agua Nueva and from there to Mexico City, Taylor's army gathered its dead from the barren countryside. There were no trees, so burial parties broke up wagons for makeshift coffins and crude grave markers. The Kentucky dead, Henry Clay, Jr., among them, were buried near Saltillo. One of Henry's comrades snipped a lock of his hair and sent it to Ashland with the assurance that Henry would not be left in Mexico. When the war was over, he would be brought home for burial.[94]

It was only one of many letters that began to arrive at Ashland "from every quarter, in every form, and in the most touching and feeling manner," Zachary Taylor wrote from Agua Nueva.[95] "He gave every assurance that in the hour of need I could lean with confidence upon his support," he said, professing that "to your son I felt bound by the strongest ties of private regard."[96] The many expressions of sympathy helped a bit, but not much, especially when detailed reports of Henry's last minutes reached Ashland. "We have been tortured," Clay said, "by account after account, coming to us, as to the manner of his death, and the possible outrages committed upon his body, by the enemy, whilst he had temporary possession of it."[97]

In the weeks that followed, Clay pondered the solace that Lucretia found in her faith. The compassionate attention from the Christ Church congregation and the kind words of the Reverend Berkeley were surely supportive, as were the comforting rituals of worship. But for Lucretia there was obviously more to it than that. She was both devastated and at peace, blasted by grief and placidly reconciled to it, salved by a spiritual grace that was mysterious and appealing, a fortress of faith, a gift. For years Clay had wondered at Lucretia's resilience as it was repeatedly tested by tragedy, but after this latest calamity he suddenly wanted sanctuary in that fortress too. From within it he might better bear the memories of the dead daughters, the slain son, even see without tears the crooked back and awkward gait of brave little Lucy, her twisted spine no longer a mockery but part of a meaningful plan in which suffering and sorrow cloaked something else, something glorious, everlasting.

Clay had never been irreligious, but he had avoided joining a church, even Lucretia's, which he had helped found forty years earlier. Yet he had always believed in a higher power, and he often explained times of baffling hardship as the work of a benign Providence. Confronting tragedy or disappointment, he sought solace and meaning by studying theological works and occasionally queried clerics about sin and salvation. A prominent Methodist minister recalled that Clay had been "a good deal concerned on the subject of personal, *experimental* religion."[98] Besides the fact that Clay was nearing the end of his life, Henry's death gave him even greater reason to see meaning and comfort in a formal declaration of faith. Sincerity was crucial to his entering any church. Clay was raised in a Baptist home, his father a preacher and his mother devout, and a staple of their religious belief was that an insincere conversion was a grievous sin. It stained with pretense a powerfully private matter between God and man, usually for base public effect. Clay could have joined a church dozens of times over the years when it would have done him political good, but he could never bring himself to wear in his soul that stain. His actions after Henry's death were heartfelt in the truest sense, and even writers inclined to view his behavior with skepticism do not think his embrace of Christ Church at this critical moment in his life was anything but genuine.[99]

On June 22, 1847, the Reverend Berkeley read the ritual of baptism in the parlor at Ashland, dipping his hands into an enormous cut-glass vase to flick the consecrated water onto Henry Clay's brow.[100] Lucretia looked on as her husband laid aside the prayer book to respond to the ritual from memory—he had been studying. Mary Mentelle Clay and her children joined him in receiving the sacrament, their knees also bent and bodies bowed, the huge portrait of Washington and his family forming the backdrop for Clay and his family as they entered the community of Christ. Two weeks later, Clay received communion at the Chapel of Transylvania University for the first time, Lucretia with him, her mighty fortress large enough to shelter all the world, but for now enough to shelter her family, particularly for her two Henrys, for the son who had perished so far from home and for the husband next to her, a gift.[101]

On Tuesday, July 20, Clay took Henry III, Nannie, and Tommy to Frankfort to join the twenty thousand people who had gathered for the burial of Kentucky's fallen heroes, among them his son, their father, who had all been brought home by Kentucky's emissaries. The ceremonies included a speech by John C. Breckinridge, a service by the Reverend John H. Brown, a 21-gun salute, and an impressive tribute by the Masons. But all of this was eclipsed by what happened after the caskets were lowered into the ground. The surviving Kentucky volunteers formed behind Colonel Humphrey Marshall and marched slowly by the graves, not to a dirge or a muffled drum, but in absolute, mesmerizing silence, an unplanned, impulsive, unexpected homage. Inspired by the scene, twenty-seven-year-old Theodore O'Hara, himself among those volunteers, penned a requiem he entitled "The Bivouac of the Dead," a poem that achieved such widespread fame that it would be etched into monuments years later to honor the dead of another war, one that Henry Clay dreaded as much as he loathed the one that had killed his boy.[102]

Despite the comfort of his faith, Clay remained bitter about a war he excoriated as "calamitous, as well as unjust and unnecessary."[103] And despite his firm belief that God could heal the wound of his loss, he suddenly found Ashland's blossoming glories profoundly depressing. Everything about it was "associated with the memory of the lost one. The very trees which his hands assisted me to plant, served to remind me of my loss."[104] He could not bear it. Four days after the funeral in Frankfort, he fled his home for White Sulphur Springs with plans to travel on to Cape May with William Mercer.[105] Lucretia remained at Ashland, of course, as did his other sons and their families. Clay salved his wound with prayer, but he ultimately resorted to his habit of travel as therapy.

His poor troubled grandchildren had suffered terrible, indescribable tragedies in the deaths of their mother and now their father. Under the terms of

Henry Jr.'s will, which he had prudently drafted just weeks after leaving Louisville on the way to Mexico, he made official and permanent his informal arrangements for those children: Nannie and Tommy remained with Nanette Smith, in whom he reposed "much confidence and love" with good reason, for the two Clay children embraced this kind, smiling guardian and called her mother; James was to raise Henry III.[106] Nannie wept over her father's memory and explained best how they could all make their way. "Yes we have lost our dear Father," she told her brother. "Now we are poor little orphans indeed and must love one another with all our hearts."[107] Nannie was only nine. Her grandpapa at seventy would not have said it any differently.

CHAPTER FOURTEEN

The Last Gamble

MILK WAGON HORSES could never be retired and remain modes of conveyance. Even with their wagons unhitched, they would stubbornly follow their customary routes, pausing at each stop along the way, unable to break habits so deeply ingrained that they had become unconsciously natural. By the 1840s, Henry Clay was such an animal, retired from public life but persistently drawn to it. The quadrennial presidential contest was a scheduled stop along the route of his existence, and he would react accordingly, even if the Whig Party unhitched its wagon from him.

The Whigs came out of the defeat of 1844 deeply divided and despondent. The party was a shattered machine, broken in spirit and falling apart. While some insisted that only a leader of Clay's stature could take the party to triumph, many were no longer sure. The 1844 results seemed to point to the hopelessness of a Clay candidacy. If he could not win at those odds, he could not win.[1]

Trounced in local elections, many Whigs became convinced that only an overwhelmingly popular candidate could save their political futures, someone able to draw in untethered voters and disaffected Democrats, an attitude that dimmed Clay's chances. Young Whigs were especially tired of disappointments and resolutely committed to such a strategy. This youthful movement in the party had a barely concealed contempt for the exhausted banners of Whigdom that proclaimed the Bank, the tariff, and the road and rail network as the reasons to hold office. Everybody who had come of age in the Jacksonian era knew that the reason to hold office was to dispense patronage, ensure incumbency, and build a movement with influence and interest. Upon such pillars, a party could enact its policies from positions of strength.

These hard-eyed, hardheaded young men with lean looks and keen aspirations were perfectly correct, of course. After 1844, they early committed to the principle of Anybody But Clay. At stake, as it turned out, was the soul of the party, its viability as a political creature, its very existence as a sustainable entity. The young Whigs were not going to let Clay ruin the party any longer. They were going to do that themselves.

The pull of practicality was almost irresistible for those Whigs who were tired of losing and eager to put their noses in the patronage trough. A considerable portion of the party, however, insisted that 1848 should again be a contest of principles, and their call was bolstered by Whig victories in the autumn elections of 1846, a reflection of discontent with Democratic economic policies. Suddenly the young Whigs' disenchantment with their party's credo seemed overwrought, even wrongheaded. Principles again held sway, and Clay was the one national figure of unquestioned fealty to Whig principles, his closest challenger in that regard being Webster, who was truly detested in the South. All else being equal and unchanged, Clay's political fortunes were ascendant, at least on the surface. At Ashland, the old dray horse put up his ears.[2]

Clay's interest in another run for the presidency had never really abated, despite his seeming farewell to the Kentucky electors in December 1844. Much of the Whig press did not long take seriously his declaration of final retirement either. One story told of his leaving the Lexington market on a Saturday evening in late 1845 when a stout stranger bluntly said, "This must be Henry Clay." The two shook hands as the stranger stared evenly at Clay and said, "I have never before seen you, sir, but I voted for you; and in '48 I *shall* vote for you again: my home is Indiana—God bless you, sir."[3]

Despite such encouragement, Clay remained guarded. He watched other aspirants carefully. In addition to Webster, a fixture in these quests, Ohio's Thomas E. Corwin rode a brief boomlet, and the transparently ambitious Associate Justice John McLean put out feelers and was considered a tempting alternative who could subordinate principles and broaden the party's appeal. Military heroes were also mentioned, especially Winfield Scott and Zachary Taylor.

Meanwhile, Clay criticized all talk of 1848 as premature. He chided Webster for proposing to lower the tariff, a criticism meant to appeal to Pennsylvania's manufacturing interests. Scott had a following (even Crittenden was leaning toward Scott in light of Clay's apparent indifference), and between him and Taylor, Clay judged Scott the more serious adversary and consequently described Taylor as the "most sincere and honest man." Clay, however, reflexively opposed a military-minded man's aspirations to civic office. He believed that Taylor was the most military-minded man ever considered for the presidency, more so than Jackson or Harrison, really politicians who had once been soldiers.[4]

Yet events upended Clay's cautious approach when suddenly in the spring of 1847 the Anybody But Clay movement received an unforeseen boost. Clay was correct about Winfield Scott's fading star, but he completely misjudged the explosive appeal of Zachary Taylor. In two early engagements of the Mexican War, Taylor had scored victories at Palo Alto and Resaca de la Palma that caught the country's notice. When he crossed the Rio Grande, he began to resemble a war hero on the order of Andrew Jackson. Leading Whigs began a courtship to deprive the Democrats of claiming this popular champion by branding him as one of their own. A political unknown, Taylor was nominally a Whig whose growing enthusiasm for the party stemmed from his anger at James K. Polk. But Taylor's ties to the Whigs were quite tenuous, and his popularity rested with the waning recollection of his early successes in Mexico, victories that were certain to be superseded by Scott's exploits on the march to Mexico City. By all the evidence, Zachary Taylor was a spent force in early 1847, his army dwindling as he fell further out of favor with his civilian superiors, men intent on diminishing if not wrecking his reputation. Then he won at Buena Vista and became a popular hero of startling power. "If truth, honesty, and tallents [sic] deserve to be honored," marveled one Whig, "God knows Taylor does."[5]

Buena Vista was the wild card, the unexpected and unforeseen event that elevated Taylor to become Henry Clay's principal rival for the Whig nomination—an irony in that it was the event that had killed Henry Clay's son. It immediately became clear as Whigs gravitated toward Taylor that Clay had seriously underestimated him.[6] Worse were the even more telling signs that the party was slipping away from its Old Chieftain, despite his shrewd perception and sense of survival. Many people mirrored the attitude of the Alabama Whig who admitted that little was known about Taylor's principles and that "Mars was not competent to occupy Jupiter's place," but that Taylor was the most electable man. "It is with me a rule," he concluded, "ever if I can not get the best [to] take the next best I can get."[7]

The Taylor boom was put together by seasoned professionals scarred by countless campaigns, and it was given energy by young men tired of losing elections. Handlers played up Taylor's strengths for southern Whigs by emphasizing his fealty to slavery. Taylor's ties to slavery were a weakness in the North, but supporters diminished the importance of that disadvantage by reminding northern Whigs that Clay was a three-time loser. Taylor was electable, they cooed, because he alone could unify the party and draw in enough non-Whig voters to ensure victory. Even in the absence of a rival like Taylor, with the laurels of Buena Vista on him, Whigs in the Senate had concluded that Clay was "out of the question." Instead, they believed that Clay should promptly support Taylor or face the prospect of looking small and petulant.[8]

Calls for uniting behind Taylor were quite seductive. In Kentucky, Clay's

Whig enemies naturally embraced Taylor, but more ominous was the desertion of his friends. Such defections were understandable to a point, for Clay did not seem to be interested in the nomination, and his supporters consequently felt no disloyalty in supporting other candidates. Crittenden had taken Clay at his word about retirement and had become a Scott man, but like other Kentucky Whigs he began actively working for Taylor in early 1847. There were ties between the two beyond political affinity. Taylor had lived many years in Kentucky, Crittenden's first wife had been a relation, and his son was on Taylor's staff in Mexico.

Yet Crittenden was troubled by his central role in this episode. His coaxing and encouragement were the deciding factors in Taylor's resolve to seek the Whig nomination, and Crittenden's efforts for Taylor became so enthusiastic that he became the general's unofficial campaign manager. He was also drawn into close concert with Clay's enemies from the Tyler breach who were naturally supporting Taylor—men like John Pope, Tom Marshall, the Wickliffes, and Ben Hardin.[9] Worse, Crittenden was furtive as he worked for Taylor's candidacy in Kentucky and beyond. It became a worrisome game of who knew what, who had revealed what they knew, and how much such disclosures exposed his desertion of Clay. "All I ever believed," a fellow Taylor supporter assured him, "was what you said without reserve. Not that you did not prefer Mr. Clay to all other men, but that you did not believe he could be elected, & you did believe Genl. Taylor could." With such ramblings of negatives piled upon negatives and twisted into soothing rationalizations, Taylor's men salved the qualms of their Brutus for a decision he had made long before. A higher duty to the party, they said, required disinterested action, and thus personal disloyalty to its aging chief was rationalized. They hoped that Crittenden and Robert P. Letcher, acting as Clay's friends, would persuade him to step aside for Taylor. Those who urged Clay to do otherwise were dismissed as "sycophants."[10]

Clay did not know for many months that his closest friend was covertly working with his bitterest enemies, that he was leading other friends into alliances whose secrecy would, when revealed, make them look treacherous and stain their architect with the appearance of betrayal.[11] Clay was aware of the Taylor boom taking shape in Kentucky, a movement that understandably caused him "some mortification," but he did not have any hard evidence of Crittenden's role in it until returning to Ashland from a northern trip in September 1847. He received a letter from a New York acquaintance named Joseph L. White who had become aware of disquieting, possibly even treacherous deeds by Clay's friends. White was especially disappointed by Crittenden's labors for Taylor, and he asked if Crittenden were acting with Clay's approval.[12] Clay later claimed, given his own prolonged uncertainty about his candidacy, that he could not blame any of his friends for throwing in with Taylor, but the news about Crittenden was different. At first, he answered White to defend his old friend: "I am not aware that Mr. Crittenden has done any thing inconsistent with his friendship for me," Clay flatly declared.[13] But the very next day, Clay also wrote to Crittenden about White's letter, which he enclosed, suggesting that it probably should be given no more weight than the unfounded rumor it was. "I think it due to our mutual friendship & the candour & confidence which have existed between us," Clay said, "that it should afford you an opportunity of perusing the enclosed letter."[14] Crittenden's response is lost to us—Clay sent it to White, who apparently did not keep it—but his old friend evidently confirmed his loyalty for Clay who assured Crittenden that "I thought I understood you." He added with relief, "I find I did."[15]

But Clay did not understand Crittenden at all. Crittenden had every right to support Taylor, of course, and even had good reason to judge Taylor as more electable than Clay, but given the opportunity to reveal those opinions, he flinched.[16] Clay's maneuvers to secure the Whig nomination would not have been fundamentally altered had he known about Crittenden's actual attitude, but at least he would have known that the long friendship and the personal assurances of a man he counted as unswerving were meaningless. He would have known that Crittenden was in fact going into the camp of the enemy, playing Brutus to Wickliffe's Cassius, and he would have been spared the foolish gesture of defending his friend to a New York correspondent. Being duped by someone he implicitly trusted most wounded him. When Crittenden's behavior finally revealed his actual sentiments, Clay's true friends were dismayed. Leslie Combs bluntly told Crittenden, "I am very—*very* sorry for your course."[17]

ASTUTE OBSERVERS, ESPECIALLY Clay's foes, began speculating about his intentions as soon as the election of 1844 was over. John Tyler marveled as early as the summer of 1845, "Can it be that he looks to '48[?] Is the fire of ambition never to be extinguished[?]"[18] A year later, Clay's purpose had become even more obvious, if not overt, and the Wickliffes were certain that "the old hoss *Hal* is for the Presidency & no mistake." They scoffed at what they perceived as calculated tactics to improve his image with the voters. Wickliffe dismissed Clay's entering the Episcopal communion as "his infant Baptism," and the abolitionist press reckoned it to be a cynical move to dispel "those ugly qualms" about his character.[19]

Yet Clay remained noncommittal, always insisting that he would be a candidate only if the Whigs united behind him (a caveat made somewhat doubtful by Taylor's popularity) and if his health remained sound. Even more than Taylor's high status with Whigs, the question of Clay's health was a paramount obstacle he had to overcome if he hoped to attract reluctant Whigs as well as convince his friends he was up to the demands of a campaign and of the presidency that would follow. The reality of the matter partially absolved those friends who doubted his viability, for Clay was not altogether candid about the state of his health as 1848 loomed.

His physical condition was sure to be an issue if only because of his advanced age. Wide reports of his lack of stamina during the latter part of the 1844 campaign worked against him. Many people recollected him as aged and stooped, a tired old man who lost elections. "How does Mr. Clay bear his defeat?" asked one concerned Whig. "It was rumored the very day of the decisive bad news was received that he was very ill with scarlet fever. But I am in hopes that it was a mistake."[20] It was an erroneous report, but Clay actually had something else wrong with him. Much of his political effort during the months that followed his defeat in 1844 was devoted to concealing this fact. In that effort, he was remarkably successful, and even careful biographers have been inclined to marvel at the extraordinary, if brief, Indian summer Henry Clay enjoyed in his autumn years. He toured extensively, not just to indulge his love of travel, but to keep himself in the public eye and generate reports in friendly Whig newspapers that described him as the picture of youth and vitality. "Time has laid but a sparing hand upon the great American statesman," observed one account. "I never saw him look better or happier, his step is elastic, his faculties appear fresh and vigorous, and the chances are that he will live to witness the election of several Presidents."[21]

His journey to White Sulphur Springs and then to Cape May in the summer of 1847 took him through Baltimore and Philadelphia, where he repeatedly insisted that he only wanted to escape the painful reminders at Ashland of Henry Jr. and that this was not a political trip, but he attracted large crowds nonetheless and was occasionally induced to speak.[22] The newspapers talked of his bounding energy that would be the envy of a man decades younger, and at Cape May he conspicuously took sea baths amid pretty girls who begged for kisses and giggled as though he were a dashing beau instead of a wizened grandpa. "There is a deep feeling still abiding towards me," he proudly reported to Lucretia, "and a hope in regard to the future, in which I do not allow myself much to indulge."[23]

This gadding about created the impression that Clay's seventy years were of no consequence and hid that he was ill beyond the chronic complaints that had bothered him for years. His dental problems and dyspepsia, even his tendency for nagging respiratory infections like bad colds and bronchitis, differed from what was happening to him now, and he must have known that, for there were glimpses of his real condition scattered among the radiant reports. At White Sulphur Springs in the summer of 1845, John Tyler thought that Clay was "much changed, I think, since I saw him. He is as old as his gait indicates."[24] While traveling the following winter, Clay had a bad cold that was still troubling him more than two months later. During his stay in New Orleans that winter, he tried to book passage to Cuba but was prevented from making the trip because the steamboat was no longer running. Grandson Martin Duralde was at that very instant in Cuba because the warm climate was thought to relieve symptoms of tuberculosis.[25]

It is difficult to know with certainty just how sick Clay was during these years, for he took considerable pains to conceal his true condition from his family and friends as well as the public. When he traveled to New Orleans that winter of 1846–47, he insisted that it was not to regain his health "but to retain what I have," which he said was excellent. In the meantime, Clay did not travel to Mobile as he planned, apparently because he did not feel up to it.[26] When he dictated a letter, he defensively explained that the handwriting was his son John's but quickly added that he was not using him as an amanuensis because of ill health.[27] He went to Cape May "where I desire to enjoy a Sea bath, which I have never in my life before had the opportunity of doing." But again he was quick to explain, "you must not however infer that my health is bad. It is on the contrary very good."[28] His repeated avowals of good health were, in short, a case of protesting too much.

The people of Clay's time called tuberculosis "consumption" because of its wasting assault on the body. By any name the disease was still the same slow but relentless killer, so contagious at certain stages of infection that it was the stuff of epidemics, so lethal as to be the primary cause of death in Europe and North America throughout the nineteenth century. Tuberculosis made no distinctions of age or gender and was just as likely to ravage upper-class households as dreary tenements. It killed Keats, Goethe, and Chopin, and it moved through the Brontë family like a scythe. It would fell John C. Calhoun and is strongly suspected of killing John Breckinridge, Clay's early Kentucky mentor. Kit Hughes's wife died of tuberculosis. It tortured and then took off Martin Duralde, who was at Ashland possibly at the height of his contagiousness, though it is impossible to know whether Martin infected his grandfather. Indeed, Clay might already have had the disease, for it was feasible to carry it in a dormant state for years before it began its attack on the body in earnest. As early as the 1830s, he found night sessions in the Senate disagreeable because the lamps fouled the air and made it difficult for him to breathe. He could have contracted it from anyone at any time during his long public career and many associations, for the bacillus was everywhere, an extraordinarily robust organism able to defy all but the most determined disinfection. People in Clay's time did not know any of this, of course, and only a few eccentrics even speculated that consumption might be contagious. The prevailing opinion placed its cause as heredity or dissolute habits. Clay, for example, had doubted Martin's initial diagnosis because there was no family history of adult consumption.[29]

Infection occurred when a victim coughed or sneezed, launching tubercle bacilli into the air where healthy people inhaled them. Usually nothing happened. Healthy people's immune cells quickly isolated the bacilli by encasing them into hard little knots. Yet some people, compromised by some other illness or simply too young or too old to put up an effective fight, were not so lucky. In these people the bacilli multiplied, as they were only partially encased by immune cells. Respiratory function gradually ebbed, a development that accelerated in the final stages of the disease. Tuberculosis victims lost weight, suffered from increasing exhaustion, and were plagued by a racking cough that eventually brought up blood as well as sputum, evidence that open lesions were forming. In time those lesions promoted infection, high fevers, and soaking perspiration, especially at night, ruining any chance for sleep. Finally, breathing became labored, and exhaustion levied its own physical tax, often the concluding one. The best that could be done in those hopeless final days was to make the patient as comfortable as possible, usually with liberal doses of opiates.

As Clay ended the presidential campaign of 1844, it is probable that he was in an early stage of tuberculosis, either from a recent contraction or from a flareup of a dormant strain he had previously contracted, possibly years earlier. On occasion he could still summon remarkable reserves of energy, but his bad days would begin to rival in number the good ones, and his already fragile health was bent, not yet to the point of breaking, but to points where rebounds were less heartening and thorough. He knew the symptoms—everyone did—and knew the fate they foretold. He watched Martin suffer and wander, establishing a family history to explain for Clay his own plight, and Martin's wretched chronicle foreshadowed Clay's own end, one approaching in only a handful of years at best. Confronting that reality with characteristic optimism, Henry Clay, like Martin, bought a sort of lottery ticket of his own.[30] It was his bid for the presidency, one last time.

AFTER BUENA VISTA, Taylor's popularity gave him an aura of political invincibility, but his boosters actually had their work cut out for them. As "Old Rough and Ready"—the gruff no-nonsense general loved by his troops for his frank, uncomplicated manner—Zachary Taylor was likable. Henry Jr. had found him engaging, even inspiring, during the long weeks at Agua Nueva, but he had also noted Taylor's ambition regarding the presidency.[31] Neither Henry nor his father knew that those ambitions were being stoked by Crittenden and others, and nobody knew that those efforts would summon forth the least attractive aspects of Taylor's personality.

What emerged was a man both egotistical and obtuse. Although he claimed no capacity for politics and repeatedly insisted that he was not interested in the presidency, that he did "not care a fig about the office," he nevertheless believed promoters who hailed his sagacity and wisdom.[32] Worse, he took to posturing in letters meant to display that sagacity and wisdom for the country. In the weeks following Buena Vista, these letters from Mexico rattled Whigs and nearly ruined Taylor's political career before it got started. Most disturbing were his declarations that he was above the squabbles of party, that he was neither Whig nor Democrat, and that he had no firm commitments regarding political issues except to serve the American people. The meaning of such muddleheaded statements was anybody's guess, but Whigs were understandably troubled. "If Taylor keeps writing letters," one drily observed, "Clay will be nominated."[33]

Taylor's newly found conviction that he best understood the real workings of politics and how to manage them coincided with his inflated belief that his principles were superior to those of a corrupt political cohort in both the Whig and Democratic parties. He relied on his military service to establish his patriotic bona fides and bristled when anyone scrutinized or questioned his positions or motives. He had a tin ear, was both opinionated and instinctively wrong, and tended to make the worst political decisions with a certainty that increasingly exasperated the men who were trying to put him over. His core supporters embraced him because they thought he could win, not because he shared their political philosophy, for he was essentially uninterested in promoting specific programs, Whig or otherwise. He accordingly suspected that their good wishes only masked a nefarious plan to keep him away from the Democrats until they could dump him for Clay.[34]

"I think it impossible that the General should maintain silence as to his principles," Clay said in early August 1847. "He must make some public avowal of them, in other words he must say whether he is a Whig or Democrat."[35] In late September, Clay told Crittenden that he wanted no conflict between his and Taylor's supporters. Clay said that if such a thing occurred, "it will not be my fault."[36] The following day he wrote to Taylor, who was still in Mexico, to say as much as well as to inquire directly about the general's plans. Meanwhile, Clay's friends worked to correct the impression that Taylor had the unqualified support of Kentucky's Whigs. In October, a committee headed by George

Robertson and including Leslie Combs drafted a confidential letter to circulate among Whig organizations throughout the country. The circular declared that the Taylor movement in Kentucky did not represent the state's actual Whig sentiment.[37] This letter did not remain confidential for long, of course, and Taylor men were livid over it. Told by Crittenden and Letcher that Clay would not stand in their way, Taylor's supporters now had evidence very much to the contrary. Indeed, Crittenden's problems were complicated by the possibility that Clay was in the hunt, and he sought to counteract the baleful effect of the circular by arranging a deal with Taylor men in Kentucky to prevent overt displays of support such as an endorsement of Taylor by the legislature or even his nomination by the state Whig convention. Crittenden insisted that such restraint was necessary to avoid embarrassing Clay; it also would keep masked Crittenden's involvement with the Taylor movement, possibly until Clay had in fact decided to withdraw.[38]

In the ensuing months, however, reining in the Taylor movement became increasingly difficult, especially after November 13, 1847, when Clay went far in removing doubts about his pursuit of the nomination. On that day, he delivered a major policy speech in Lexington in which he registered his strongest opposition yet to the Mexican War and flatly rejected the possibility of gaining territory from it. His opening was dramatic, a lament about the gloomy day that he said reflected the condition of the country as it was saddled with an illegitimate war of aggression, a product of Polk's dishonesty and the imprudent annexation of Texas. Clay proposed solutions for the resultant problems confronting the country, the most important being his recommendations that Congress take an active role in setting the war's aim and manner of its prosecution, that the government establish a proper boundary for Texas, and that the administration pledge not to acquire any territory to expand slavery.[39]

Although Clay remained noncommittal about being a candidate, the Lexington speech was the all but formal launch of his campaign for the nomination and the initiation of a drive to bolster the Whig Party for the expected battles over the expansion of slavery. "Party lines are broken down," one Whig had exulted upon the emergence of the seemingly apolitical Zachary Taylor, "and the distinction between Wiggery [*sic*] and democracy confounded."[40] Yet even Taylor realized the deep differences that separated Whigs and Democrats on the usual issues of "Banks, Tariffs, internal improvements, Wilmot Proviso . . . to raise up some, & break down others."[41] The most profound difference, though, concerned what to do with any Mexican territory gained during the war. In this, the contrast between Whigs and Democrats was stark: expansionist Democrats wanted all the land they could get—some even wanted all of Mexico—and

Whigs did not want any land at all. The Democrats said a Mexican cession would compensate the country for the expense of the war. Whigs viewed the war as a tainted project, an act of naked aggression against a weak neighbor undertaken precisely to effect a land grab.[42] They adopted a position succinctly articulated as "No Territory."

The Whig position was most striking because it allowed southerners and northerners to avoid arguing about slavery, and at this point in the controversy, simply not talking about slavery was the best way to promote sectional harmony. If there was no territory to squabble over, its status as slave or free became irrelevant. In addition to taking the threat of slave expansion off the table for edgy northerners, the "No Territory" stance removed for southerners the specter that the deserts of New Mexico, so obviously inhospitable to slavery, would tilt the slave-free sectional imbalance further in the North's favor.

Yet if Whigs had stumbled on the best way to steer clear of disruptive slavery debates, the country was not so fortunate. Polk's primary purpose in going to war was to acquire the Pacific coast and the Southwest, a goal that necessarily meant the Democratic Party was committed to obtaining new lands. This coincided with the reality that of all the issues that threatened to disrupt politics in the election of 1848, slavery loomed largest, even worse than in 1844 when the Texas question had become so contentious. Certainly slavery made earlier arguments over the national bank, trade, and federally funded roads seem mild disagreements in comparison. This was particularly evident in the prolonged and angry quarrels over Representative David Wilmot's proposal regarding any territory that might be gained from Mexico. Shortly after the war started in 1846, President Polk asked Congress to appropriate $2 million in the hope that he could use it to persuade Mexico to sell its western provinces and prevent any additional hostilities. Wilmot, a Pennsylvania Democrat, tried to tie the money to a pledge that slavery would never exist in any territory taken from Mexico. Angry southerners doggedly fought the measure, but it twice passed the House. Although southerners were able to block the Wilmot Proviso in the Senate, they soon discovered that it had become an unrelenting antislavery position taken up by an increasing number of northerners. The proviso assumed a life of its own, a talismanic symbol for antislavery men, a menacing insult to southerners. An open sore in political debates resulted, and one's position on the proviso became a test of sectional loyalty. All but one free state legislature endorsed it, and southern states passionately condemned it. Worse, it undeniably blurred party lines and truly confounded the differences between Whigs and Democrats, a development that was hardly the stuff of glad tidings, for it forced the sections into politically untenable and inflexible unity regardless of party. As the proviso threatened to collapse parties as national organizations, compromise became less likely and violent overreaction became more probable.

The speech in Lexington was Clay's overt bid for northern support in the coming contest, a staking of the ground that separated his declared position on the Wilmot Proviso from that of the ambiguous General Taylor. Careful that everything he said would be accurately reported, he asked the journalists not to take notes at the event, promising instead to provide them with a written version. He told Horace Greeley that he expected the speech to establish him "as a Western man (I protest against being considered as a *Southern* man) with Northern principles."[43] It certainly seemed to persuade Greeley that Clay was the best candidate. The eccentric editor of the New York *Tribune* had been inclining to Corwin, but by the end of the month, he was giving Clay advice and chortling over plans by Whigs in New York City "to hold a great public demonstration in response to your Lexington Speech."[44] This relationship with Greeley was natural in a way, for they shared the same vision for the Whig Party, and the editor soon became Clay's unofficial eastern campaign manager.

Yet Greeley's loyalty to Clay has been questioned, if for no other reason than he was a member of Thurlow Weed's faction of New York politics, the so-called junior partner in the triumvirate that included Weed and Seward, men who were at best lukewarm and occasionally hostile to a Clay candidacy. Greeley pushed Clay to choose Seward as his vice president, and his other activities, especially late in the day, suggested other goals. Possibly his maneuvers were calculated to dim the chances of the leading candidate, whoever that was at any given time, to keep a deft balance between all rivals, deadlock a convention, and have Seward emerge as the Whig dark horse in the manner of the Democrat Polk in 1844.[45] In that estimation, Clay was a way to stop Taylor, nothing more. Possibly that was the way it was—a game within a game, a snarl of complexities in which nothing was really as it seemed, and nobody said what was true, whether Crittenden or Letcher or Greeley.

Or Zachary Taylor, for that matter. In early November, Taylor responded to Clay's September 27 letter with an answer that on its face was more than cordial and perfectly candid. Nothing could come between him and Clay, he said, and most important, he declared that he had recently told a mutual friend about his willingness "to stand aside, if you or any other whig were the choice of the party."[46] The mutual friend was Crittenden, and what Taylor told Clay was true: he had told Crittenden he would defer to Clay. But he had also told Crittenden that numerous correspondents were telling him that the Whig Party would never support Clay's candidacy.[47] That bit of intelligence Old Rough and Ready chose to keep from the Old Chieftain.

If Taylor's willingness in November to stand down in deference to Clay was sincere at the time, it became less so as time wore on. From his home in Baton Rouge, he again assured Clay of his friendship, but he declined an invitation to visit Ashland and ominously declared that letters from Kentucky "intended to produce unkind feelings on my part towards you" had failed to do so.[48] Clay surely wondered, What letters? What Kentuckians? Only a few days later, Taylor told Crittenden that he had no intention of formally withdrawing from the presidential contest.[49] That much, at least, was true. By the spring of 1848, Taylor had convinced himself and was busily convincing others that he had never promised Clay he would step aside. "I did not then, nor do I now believe, that Mr. Clay could be elected if he was the only Whig candidate in the field," Taylor said, adding that Clay had obviously misunderstood him.[50]

Crittenden was in hot water with Taylor's Louisiana supporters, who were angry about the confidential circular letter and displeased by reports that Crittenden had guaranteed Clay his loyalty. "I have no recollection of saying to Mr. Clay what he supposed me to have said, and what I think I did not say," Crittenden assured wealthy New Orleans businessman Albert T. Burnley in a letter that Crittenden told him to keep secret. Burnley was among those Taylor men who wanted the Clay matter settled once and for all, but Crittenden could only offer what he described as a "true and candid statement" of the situation: Clay was on his way to Washington, Crittenden said, where nobody "would desire and advise him to become a candidate under present circumstances."[51] Clearly Crittenden wanted everyone to wait just a while longer and was praying that Clay's reception in Washington would finally convince him to retire to Ashland.[52]

THE MORE WHIGS got to know Taylor, the less they liked him. The memory of the pluperfect mess John Tyler had created was still fresh, and Taylor's reputation noticeably dimmed in the North. "Taylor seems still to be declining," John McLean observed in Ohio, and Thurlow Weed believed that Old Rough and Ready was finished in New York. Weed even predicted that Clay would be the nominee with William Seward as his running mate.[53]

All was not well with Clay, however. His Lexington speech had produced mixed results at best. Because American soldiers were still in the field, its emphatic denunciation of the war struck some people as vaguely unpatriotic. There was nothing vague about its reception in the South, though, where it alienated many Whigs and spurred Democrats to proclaim that Clay would sell them all out to northern abolitionists.[54] Clay had not endorsed the Wilmot Proviso, but he had essentially adopted its spirit by vowing to resist slavery expansion in the West, and too many southerners regarded that position as rank apostasy. Northern Whigs responded more positively, but it remained to be seen if their enthusiasm would overcome their reservations about Clay's age, his awful record as a presidential contender, and his uncanny ability to unify otherwise discordant Democrats against him. Clay himself was disappointed, for the varied reactions were definitely not the groundswell of support he had always said was necessary to justify another run for the presidency.

In any case, his efforts left many establishment Whigs unmoved. In Congress, Taylor picked up enough support to merit the formation of an official organization that arose from a core of seven Whig junior congressmen picturesquely labeled the "Young Indians." They were indeed relatively youthful. One of them was Abraham Lincoln, who was just turning forty. Lincoln, who had been in Lexington visiting his in-laws, the Todds, had heard Clay's November 13 speech and apparently liked its message, considering his resolute opposition to the war. Clay had always been Lincoln's ideal as a statesman, but he became a Young Indian nonetheless, a sign of Clay's limited appeal in the North. Most of the Young Indians were southerners, but their commitment to Taylor emerged before Clay's Lexington speech and had less to do with slavery than with their desire to discard old men who specialized in losing elections. They were just as averse to Webster as to Clay. The Virginians in their ranks actually wanted to reshape the Whig Party on a nostalgic model drawn from James Monroe's time, one presumably without partisan rancor, a new coalition that would partner issueless Whigs and disaffected Democrats to rid the government of corrupt patronage and inaugurate a new era of patrician republicanism.[55] Taylor's talk of soaring above party politics and governing as an American made him seem just the man to accomplish that goal, and Virginia's Young Indians warmed to their work of getting him nominated by state conventions rather than taking their chances at a national one that was likely to fall under the influence of the old guard—or, as Taylor called them, the "wire pullers." "General Taylor *cannot be nominated in a Whig National Convention*," Greeley emphatically predicted. Worse, a national convention was likely to do something foolish like declare a set of principles and thus push away wavering Democrats necessary for victory in the general election.[56]

This situation presented Clay with a clear imperative. He knew after the Lexington speech that many state conventions in the South would likely be unfriendly to him, and he was alarmed that in the absence of a national convention the Whig Party might make its bid for the presidency by jettisoning its principles, or more precisely, by nominating a man who had no demonstrable Whig principles at all. He recognized at last that the party was drifting from him at its political hub in Washington, whence congressional Whigs radiated spokes of influence to the courthouses and crossroads of the country. As much as he moved decisively on anything during these months of pondering and hesitancy, he moved decisively on this front.

It was brutally cold in Kentucky that December, and foot-deep snow blanketed the ground as Clay left Ashland for Washington the day after Christmas. He was "to attend to some professional engagement," it was said (he actually planned to argue cases before the Supreme Court), but the sagacious suspected he was going to take "a survey of the ground," after which "he will no doubt be better prepared to decide upon his future course."[57] Clay arrived in Washington on January 10, when mounting northern anger over southern ultimatums concerning Taylor was reaching its peak.

The capital, despite being cold and dreary, worked its old magic on him as always, and Clay began returning the favor, to the amazement of his friends and consternation of his enemies. Charming, vigorous, and clever, he appeared at parties to enchant stout matrons and nubile girls, who, regardless of age, giggled at his jests and blushed when he winked. The matrons prized his gloves as keepsakes, the girls greeted him with kisses, and Crittenden and Clayton were "in great distress." For Clay did more than grace social salons. He quietly visited the lodgings of influential Whig leaders, always "calm, & in the best temper & frame of mind," to speak of Whig programs and Whig honor, to ask after wives and children, to remind men of venerable friendships, to tell jokes and reminisce about past campaigns, to speak of future hopes. He ranged from the capital on a couple of long weekends to visit friends in Baltimore, and he spent a week in Berkeley County, Virginia. He was an honored guest at the marriage of Thomas Hart Benton's daughter to Susan Jacob Clay's brother, and the next day he marched into the House chamber, which had been temporarily turned over to the American Colonization Society, to deliver a lengthy speech as its president, an event that highlighted for northerners his lifelong commitment to gradual emancipation. The Benton affair had the side effect of proving he could be on civil terms with Democrats, as did a couple of visits to James and Sarah Polk at the White House where he traded quips with Mrs. Polk. She was no more immune to Clay's charm than the other ladies of Washington: in a large company, she told him that if a Whig were destined to succeed her husband, she would prefer it to be Clay.[58]

William Seward watched all of this with a mixture of fascination and disgust. Clay, incredibly, single-handedly, was turning back the Taylor tide, achieving in only days for himself what a legion of operatives had labored for months to accomplish for Old Rough and Ready. Meanwhile, Clay found it increasingly difficult to resist the coaxing of friends who were themselves enthralled by this

remarkably sleek political animal, social lion, tireless promoter of Whig principles, and real danger to Democrat aspirations. Taylor men continued to grumble
that Clay could not win, but as January gave way to February, they were shaken
and showed it.[59] Clay supporters, gloomy for so long, were suddenly energized
by the Old Chieftain, and they now told him that he was the only man standing
between Taylor and the presidency, the only man who could sustain Whig principles. Friends noted that he was "apparently in fine & vigorous health, feeling
beyond all doubt that he is quite able to take upon himself the burthens of office."[60]

If we are to believe his frequently repeated statements to family and friends,
Clay had left Ashland determined to announce that he would not seek the presidency, but possibly that was just a way for him to avoid the embarrassment of
being cast aside. After a few weeks in Washington, however, he decided not to
decide, at least not right away. He had always maintained that he would not
make a definitive announcement until the spring, and now he resolved not to
make any statement of his intentions until he returned home.[61] After all, his
being cast aside appeared less likely as northern Whigs transformed caution
over Taylor into outright anger over aggressive plans to make him the nominee
with southern state endorsements. Finally those northerners had had enough and
emphatically insisted that the Whig candidate would have to be the product of a
national convention. Taylor men tried to get their way by threatening to support
him even if the Whigs nominated someone else, but they seriously overesti-
mated their strength and their man's appeal. A few wary southerners joined
northern Whigs in Congress to demand a national convention. It was scheduled
for June 7 in Philadelphia.[62]

Even the Young Indians, with all their pretensions to savvy political maneuvering and claims of knowledge about how best to win elections, had to admit
that it had been a remarkable couple of months, for them a sobering lesson in the
power of personality and the art of professional politicking. There was, after all,
a reason he was called the Old Coon, the Old Chieftain, Prince Hal, Great Harry
of the West, the Sage of Ashland. Those nicknames marked identities created
over a lifetime of achievements and disappointments. All were melded into Mr.
Clay, who returned to Washington in early 1848 and showed the town how politics was done.[63]

ON FEBRUARY 21, 1848, John Quincy Adams suffered a massive stroke and
collapsed on the floor of the House of Representatives. He died two days later.
Clay was still in Washington when Adams was stricken, but by the time Adams
died, Clay had left for Philadelphia. The departure had been long scheduled, but

it made Clay appear indifferent to Adams's fate and disrespectful of his memory, and his enemies made as much as they could of it. Worse, his itinerary roughly coincided with that of Adams's funeral cortege as it proceeded through Philadelphia on its way to Massachusetts, suggesting that Clay was persisting in a tasteless disregard for the former president. Clay had been loyal to Adams while serving as his secretary of state, and he had occasionally tried to sustain friendly contact with "Old Man Eloquent," but he had never really liked the prickly New Englander. Now that Adams was dead, Clay made clear that he intended no impertinence. In Philadelphia he appeared in Independence Hall on February 26 to deliver a short eulogy in which he described Adams as "a great patriot." He did not hide from close friends, however, a fatalistic resignation that indicated he was essentially unmoved by the old man's passing. Clay was an old man himself. "So we go!" he told Kit Hughes, another old man who had been with Adams and Clay at Ghent more than forty years earlier.[64]

The criticisms of his behavior were bitter in some quarters, but they did him no lasting harm. If anything, he seemed to be leading a charmed life. While staying at Mayor John Swift's residence, Clay went to bed as his servant, unaccustomed to the gas lighting, simply blew out the flame without turning off the jet. Swift awoke just before dawn to the strong odor of gas. He rushed to Clay's bedroom, opened the door, and was almost knocked down by the fumes. As Swift frantically raised a window, he looked with terror at the bed, almost certain that his guest had been asphyxiated. "Mr. Clay," he called out, "Mr. Clay, are you alive?" The bedclothes stirred. "Never felt better," said Clay.[65]

He left Philadelphia on March 7 bound for New York City, where enormous crowds heard him speak at Castle Garden. Several weeks earlier, a huge meeting had attracted some ten thousand cheering supporters and was matched by a statement of support from the Whig caucus in Albany. Clay met with Martin Van Buren, building speculation that his and the Little Magician's friends would be collaborating in the state. He also met with Albert Gallatin, effecting a reconciliation with the old man, now in his late eighties and still lively but with only a year and a half to live. In some of this, Clay was likely just mending fences and tidying up personal loose ends, but these travels and speeches and meetings struck many as having much deeper meanings.[66]

By the time Clay reached Ashland on March 30, he had every reason to feel a high sense of accomplishment. However, the success of his trip was already fleeting. While Clay received the acclaim of northern crowds, events moved decisively against him. As he left Washington, the Polk administration received a treaty ending the war with Mexico and detailing a massive cession of Mexican territory to the United States, including California and all the territory to its east stretching to Texas. On March 10, the Senate ratified the Treaty of Guadalupe Hidalgo. The three months between the treaty's ratification and the meeting of the Whig convention in Philadelphia obscured the towering impact of this event on Clay's candidacy, but it would be revealed in due course.[67]

More immediately evident was a setback he suffered in late February at the Virginia Whig convention. Whig meetings were also held in Kentucky and North Carolina on the same day as Virginia's, February 22, which coincidentally happened to be both George Washington's birthday and the first anniversary of Taylor's triumph at Buena Vista. The outcome in Kentucky was of considerable importance to both Clay and Taylor, but the event itself greatly troubled those of Clay's former friends who faced the prospect of at last revealing where they stood. For months Crittenden and Letcher had sustained an uneasy truce with Taylor men that had kept Kentucky from endorsing either the general or Clay. As the convention loomed, the plan to have it adjourn without pledging delegates to anyone was the best they could do for Clay, and they salved their consciences by insisting it was really a kindness to shield him from a humiliating defeat by Taylor, or to save him from the physical ordeal of a campaign, which they were sure would mean defeat for the Whigs in November.

Taylor's supporters had been bristling over stories about Clay's triumphant trip to Washington, and as the local convention neared, they suspected that the agreement to send uncommitted delegates to Philadelphia was a trick. They threatened to cancel the arrangement. "If the Ball opens with an angry discussion," warned Letcher, "the fat is in the fire." Clay's former friends frantically tried to keep that from happening. They put in writing assurances that he would eventually withdraw. "Great G–d," wailed Black Bob, "if he could have foreseen the predicament in which he had placed us friends and his party in this country [Kentucky], it [*sic*] could not have hesitated a moment about declining."[68] Clay's former friends were only just barely able to persuade the Kentucky Whig convention in Frankfort on February 22 to stick to the arrangement and send uncommitted delegates to the national convention. That very result, however, had the ironic consequence of making the pledge of his withdrawal less valid, because true Clay supporters believed his position was growing stronger.

Furious Taylor men promptly strode into a Taylor rally already under way in Frankfort to join in an endorsement of Old Zach. Telegraph dispatches from Frankfort did not distinguish the regular Whig state convention from the Taylor rally, and Whigs across the country mistakenly concluded that the latter reflected the will of the state party. Later that very day at a crucial point in the Virginia Whig convention, Taylor men used that confusion to announce that the telegraph had brought news that Kentucky had nominated their candidate. The report caused the Virginians to pause, and all it then took to shove them over to Taylor was an outright lie: North Carolina had endorsed Taylor as well, Old Zach's supporters proclaimed. Virginia followed suit. Everyone had counted Virginia in Clay's column, and with good reason. Only through confusion and misrepresentation was the Old Dominion handed to Taylor, because North Carolina, like Kentucky, had not pledged its delegates to anyone. Clay, not Taylor, was the favorite of North Carolina Whigs, but the convention that met in Raleigh that same Tuesday was not certain about the Old Chieftain's intentions and had decided to keep its delegates uncommitted.[69]

Despite this good fortune, Taylor seemed bent on self-destruction. In the first weeks of 1848, he slipped his letter writing leash and sent out a series of rambling communications that revived the worst of Whig fears. Stubbornly cultivating his image as a man beholden to no party, he accepted any nomination that came his way, including those of the Native American Party and the People's Party. Taylor boasted about his independence and basked in his broad appeal, but Whigs were worried that he was risking the election, not to mention what his attitudes might mean regarding distributing patronage. The publication of Taylor's views, starting in February 1848 when his supporters were laboring mightily for him in the state conventions, finally drove party leaders to reconsider their allegiance to a man with no apparent allegiance to them. Unwavering Taylor supporters strained to repair the damage by begging him to declare his fidelity to Whig principles, but he mulishly refused and made matters worse by again depicting himself as above politics. He even said that if the Whigs did not nominate him, he would run as an independent.[70]

Taylor's missteps obscured the injury done to Clay by the state conventions in late February, and Clay still could hear the gushing praise of friends and the cheering of crowds as he finally decided not to withdraw. Virginia was not his any longer, but Kentucky and North Carolina were uncommitted. He received good reports from Georgia, and even glimmers of encouragement from Louisiana, Taylor's home state, where Clay could possibly return the favor done to him by Old Zach's Kentucky operatives. Clay's northern support seemed stronger than ever, and Ohio governor William Bebb finally gave up on Tom Corwin and all but promised Clay that the Ohio delegation would be his in Philadelphia.[71]

Clay's decision came late and after months of his former friends' whispered promises that he would not run. Despite their better judgment, Taylor men had believed that Clay was on the verge of declaring that he would be content to retire forever to Ashland.[72] To stop that speculation, he issued a formal statement announcing his intention to place his name before the convention in Philadelphia. Dated April 10, Clay's statement appeared in the Lexington press on April 12, his seventy-first birthday, and was nationally published in the days that followed.[73]

Considering the need to quell false tales about his withdrawal, the announcement was an understandable gesture, but it was also a serious mistake. It shattered a venerated tradition of American presidential politics. Candidates were not supposed to be striving politicians but reluctant recruits finally answering the people's call. Clay's announcement was unprecedented, and it alienated many Whigs because they thought it haughty and presumptuous. In New York, upstate Whig Washington Hunt called the announcement "a clear case" of political suicide. Clay had "evidently treasured up all the clever things said to him by flatterers and parasites during his recent tour," grumbled Hunt. "I consider him out of the question."[74]

Yet others thought "it was high time" Clay made his intentions known and were delighted that he had.[75] The Whig establishment might have been outraged, but the people did not seem to have found his gesture irredeemably offensive. "Mr. Clay has not five friends of his nomination in both branches of Congress," observed the Georgia Whig Robert Toombs, "but eight-tenths of them are afraid to open their lips upon the subject to the public."[76] Nevertheless, Clay was surprised by the reaction to his announcement, and he resolved to keep quiet in the weeks after it. When he was told that only his clear opposition to slavery expansion would ensure Ohio for him, he insisted that he had said all he intended to say about the matter. He was determined to adhere to a promise he had made to Greeley months before to keep mum.[77]

The Old Chieftain was now on record as wanting the nomination, an intention that at last exposed for Clay the true sentiments of John J. Crittenden. On the day he drafted his announcement, Clay sent Crittenden a copy of it, with the aim of enlisting him in his effort. Crittenden responded in early May. "I hope it may turn out for the best," was all Crittenden could offer Henry Clay. He insisted that Clay had known all along his "opinions & apprehensions on the subject," which were, Crittenden said, that Clay could not be elected and thus should not be put forward as a candidate. Crittenden rather helplessly observed that the presidential election was "becoming more & more perplexed."[78]

Clay now knew that Crittenden had deserted him. Clay did not respond. Crittenden would never write to him again.

Now that Clay had declared, all of Taylor's pompous talk about being above politics and his practice of accepting nominations from other parties had to not only come to a stop but be disavowed. In Washington, even before he had responded to Clay's April 10 announcement, John J. Crittenden consulted with his fellow lodgers Alexander Stephens and Robert Toombs and drafted a letter for Taylor's signature that would unequivocally vow allegiance to Whig principles. Some have claimed that after Clay's April announcement, Crittenden stopped working for Taylor, but that was not true. Crittenden took a central role in saving Taylor's candidacy well after Clay's statement of intent.[79] In the letter—he was working on it two weeks after Clay had declared himself—Crittenden sought to have it appear that Taylor plainly endorsed the idea of a passive executive and that he would be respectful of the congressional agenda on tariffs, the economy, and internal improvements. Crittenden took a swipe at "ultra" Whigs (meaning Clay, a particularly nasty touch coming from Crittenden's pen), but he also had Taylor promise that he would use the veto only to strike down clearly unconstitutional legislation, a jab at the veto-happy Tyler.[80] Crittenden and his colleagues hoped that this statement would repair all the damage Taylor had been doing to himself—never mind that much in the letter would be as much a surprise to Zachary Taylor as it would be soothing to Whig sensibilities.

In fact, saving Taylor from himself made for a considerable amount of heavy political lifting. Even as Crittenden was crafting his letter, Taylor was reacting to Clay's announcement by writing a letter of his own. Dated April 20, 1848, the letter went to the Richmond *Whig* and declared that he would accept the Whig nomination only if the convention did not bind him with pledges. Worse, he claimed he had always intended to be a candidate for the presidency regardless of what the Whigs or the Democrats did. These statements were completely at variance with those Crittenden had devised for him. When Crittenden's creation arrived in Baton Rouge, Taylor's handlers promptly sat him down to transcribe it, sign it, and immediately send it to his brother-in-law John S. Allison. Soon to be known as "the Allison Letter," it went to the Baton Rouge newspapers on April 22. The telegraph transmitted it across the nation. Taylor's supporters, Crittenden foremost among them, hoped with all their hearts that the Allison letter would at least cancel out the potentially lethal effect of Taylor's Richmond *Whig* blunder.

At the end of April, Zachary Taylor wrote Clay a sugared letter oozing with false modesty (Clay possibly knew more about the mood of the people, Taylor said), false flattery ("you were my first choice," Taylor said), and false statements (he never wanted to be president, he said). But mainly Taylor dealt with the problem of his promise in November 1847 to step aside if Clay wanted to run. Taylor had actually stated the pledge to Crittenden as well as Clay, and the general was at first under the impression that it had come to light because of Crittenden. In late March, Taylor told Crittenden that he could not remember ever having written to him about the matter.[81] After Clay's April 10 announce-ment, Taylor concluded that his withdrawal promise had been exposed by his November 4, 1847, letter to Clay. He now told Clay that the matter was in the hands of the people, who had registered their preference in several state conven-tions. Taylor said he could not in good conscience now withdraw after receiving such sincere demonstrations of esteem.[82]

Clay was not overly troubled by any of these developments. After the reve-lations about Crittenden, nothing could surprise him, and if anything, he became even more hopeful that his supporters could deliver him the nomination in Philadelphia.[83] Several weeks would pass before Whig delegates assembled in Philadelphia to choose the candidate, plenty of time for Taylor to write more let-ters.

It was Taylor's turn, though, to lead the charmed life. Whigs did not care that he obviously had not written the Allison letter, because "fools build houses— & wise men live in 'em."[84] Most important was that the letter went far in calm-ing Taylor's shaken supporters.[85] But something had already happened that was far more damaging to Clay's chances than any of Taylor's impolitic letters were to his, even if Old Zach continued to write foolish things to the newspapers. The early opposition of important Whig groups such as the Young Indians and the desertion of his own friends certainly dimmed Clay's chances in 1848, but his bid for the nomination fell victim to forces beyond his control. Beginning with his Lexington speech of November 1847, Clay staked everything on opposing the Mexican War. From that position, he sought to placate northern hostility to slavery expansion and soothe southern honor by flatly rejecting any potential territorial gains from the war. Thus he could make the Wilmot Proviso both un-necessary and irrelevant.

After the Senate ratified the Treaty of Guadalupe Hidalgo on March 10, however, there was no war to oppose, and the territorial gains were an accom-plished fact. A month before he made his formal declaration and long before the Philadelphia convention, Clay and the Whigs who supported him lost the only issue that made him an appealing candidate, someone other than an establish-ment figure who lost elections. The end of the war created a new set of circum-stances that gradually made his positions disagreeable both to the North and to the South. The question of whether the new western territories would be slave or free revived the Wilmot Proviso as a northern cause. It also renewed it as a threat to the South. Because he would not support Wilmot, Clay disappointed northern Whigs indispensable to his candidacy, hence the pleas from Ohio for him to make a plain declaration about the matter. Clay would not; he could not without completely losing the South. The consequences in the North were not clear until everyone gathered in Philadelphia, but northern Whigs had been quietly looking for alternatives to Clay for weeks. Winfield Scott was often suggested. Ultimately, however, they resigned themselves to Old Zach's nomination. Taylor's role in the Mexican War became less objectionable to them because the war was over, and his purported electability tipped the balance for those eager to drink from patronage troughs. On the other hand, Clay's Lexington speech opposing slavery expansion in the West made him unacceptable to southern Whigs and cemented their initial inclination to become Taylor men.[86]

The Treaty of Guadalupe Hidalgo smashed every reason that the Whig Party had, other than sentiment, to make Henry Clay its presidential candidate. He sat at Ashland counting the days until the Philadelphia convention, but his numbers in this last lottery had already come up weeks before. They were losers.

THE DEMOCRATIC PARTY'S convention met in Baltimore on May 27, also with the chore of addressing the changed situation regarding the Mexican Cession. Democrats were just as divided as Whigs over slavery in the new territories, and an outright endorsement of the Wilmot Proviso promised to alienate the southern wing of the party. Consequently, Democrats adopted a policy they called popular sovereignty, which had all the political advantages of seeming to do something while actually doing nothing at all. Under popular sovereignty, the inhabitants of the territory would decide whether they were to have slavery or not, a gesture that the Democrats saw as perfectly compatible with their notions of decentralized, limited government, in essence the ultimate expression of Jacksonian states' rights. As in everything, popular sovereignty's devil was in the details, such as when exactly the settlers would make their fateful decision, which was vitally important since the presence of even a single slave made less likely the exclusion of slavery as an institution. But addressing specifics ruined the beauty of popular sovereignty's indecisive ambiguity, the very feature that made it a workable dodge of the slavery issue. No specifics were therefore confronted. Instead, Democrats nominated Lewis Cass, an old Michigan moderate with a distinguished record and a reputation for deliberation so ingrained that Lincoln likened him to an ox—what Clay called "irresolution and want of decision." But at the time, bovine apathy seemed precisely the way to deal with the difficult sectional problem of slavery. The Whigs had lost their No Territory policy when the Mexican War ended to include an enormous western land cession. The Democrats adopted a No Decision policy in its stead.[87]

Whig delegates assembled in Philadelphia during the first week of June. Northerners were fragmented, and southerners insisted that nominating Taylor was absolutely necessary, both bad signs for Clay. Taylor's forces were extremely well organized, having expanded the Young Indians into a much larger Palo Alto Club to include growing numbers of Whig congressmen. As delegates bound for Philadelphia paused in Washington, Palo Alto members buttonholed them on train station platforms to persuade them that only Taylor could win in November. Leading Clay supporters, including Greeley, were exceedingly despondent but soldiered on.[88] They set up Clay's headquarters at Mayor Swift's office and held nightly meetings in which Greeley, Leslie Combs, and John Minor Botts planned strategy. Surveying the dismal prospects, they concluded that Winfield Scott as a running mate for Clay was their best hope of stemming the Taylor tide. Scott had a deadly habit of writing letters even more foolish than Taylor's, and he had sunk his own candidacy as a result, but teamed with Clay he could possibly help unify northern delegates and stop the southern momentum for Taylor. Scott, as it happened, was agreeable to the idea and was apparently approached by Clay operatives. Yet for some reason, Scott's availability as well as his willingness to go on the ticket with Clay was never revealed to the delegates at Philadelphia. In addition, he was bedridden with severe diarrhea (a souvenir of his Mexican campaign) and could not contact the convention personally. Instead, rumors exaggerated his illness to make him unappealing as a candidate of any kind, and Taylor forces were able to suppress Clay's last best chance to overtake their man.[89]

On Thursday, June 8, Zachary Taylor, Henry Clay, Daniel Webster, Winfield Scott, John Clayton, and John McLean (whose support was so paltry his friends promptly withdrew him) were placed in nomination. Everyone expected Clay to lead on the first ballot, but everyone knew that he would also fall short of the 140 votes required to secure the nomination. His managers, in fact, had estimated his first ballot total would be 115 votes, and from that figure they hoped to consolidate with Scott's supporters to attract the little more than two dozen delegates necessary for the prize.

When the balloting ended, however, the convention was shocked by the result. Taylor, not Clay, led with 111 votes, and Clay had fallen far short of his benchmark with only 97. Just one Ohio delegate voted for him, revealing a serious disintegration of northern opposition to Taylor, but Kentucky's delegation was the momentum shifter that broke Clay's back. Only 5 of his own state's 12 delegates remained loyal to the Old Chieftain.[90]

Clay's candidacy never recovered. In two subsequent ballots that evening he continued to lose ground, and even a recess could not stem the tide. The next day, June 9, the dam broke on the fourth ballot. Taylor's total climbed to 171 votes, well beyond the number necessary to win, while Clay sank to a dismal 35, falling to third place behind Winfield Scott. Only James Harlan of the Kentucky delegation had remained steadfast until the end. It was over. Henry Clay would never become president of the United States.

The convention nominated Millard Fillmore as Taylor's running mate, something of an olive branch extended to the Clay wing. Clay liked Fillmore, and he was a rival of Seward's, but his selection was clearly a sop, and the party adjourned to do battle with the Democrats amid considerable self-congratulation that was all the more hearty because the convention had elected not to adopt a platform of any kind. The Democrats had decided with popular sovereignty to let sleeping dogs lie, but the Whigs had spinelessly resolved not to get a dog at all.

Despite his insistence otherwise, the Whigs' rebuke embittered Clay, and as he gave the matter more thought, the behavior of his "friends" enraged him. According to family tradition, he went so far as to draft an angry narrative that described Crittenden's treachery, excoriating him and the Kentucky delegation for their betrayal. James, however, persuaded him not to publish it until he had taken time to reflect. Clay cooled down and was said to have torn the letter to pieces, but James's wife, Susan (the keeper of the documents), gathered up the pieces and put them away. They were last seen—or at least their contents were last heard—when read to a historian of the Whig Party in 1920 by Susan's son George H. Clay. The document afterward vanished.[91]

That is the family tradition, and as far as it goes, it corroborates Clay's apparent decision to keep his own counsel regarding Crittenden. He did not utter a word about Crittenden's candidacy for Kentucky governor, which in a way spoke volumes as a refusal to endorse the person who had been his closest friend. In fact, it was reported that James was the Clay in eruption, not his father. It was also said that the Crittendens had no compunction about speaking ill of Henry Clay.[92]

For his part, Crittenden did not write to Clay after the convention, nor did he try to call when he visited Lexington during the summer of 1848. What Clay thought of all this can only be conjectured. Observers insisted that he never discussed his friend's disloyalty, even within his own family. Indeed, as Whig divisions had mounted during the spring and early summer of 1848, to the extent that they threatened to lose the election in the fall, Crittenden had been mentioned as a compromise candidate to supplant both Clay and Taylor. Clay, it was later said, had not objected.[93]

In the wake of the disappointment, he simply retreated to Ashland, and his loyal friends brooded.[94] Clay never again felt any great affection for the Whig Party. Three years after these events, he had resigned himself to all that had happened—at least, he said so. He evinced little interest in hearing additional details about double-dealing in Philadelphia, and he claimed that Taylor's nomination had "now no other than an historical interest" for him. "The thing is passed," he said, "and no one has more quietly submitted to the event than I have."[95]

EVEN THOUGH HE was now armed with the Whig nomination, Taylor again began insisting that he was above party. The attitude exasperated Whigs and delighted Democrats, who lampooned Taylor as a political Hamlet soliloquizing, "Independent or a Whig—that is the question. Whether 'tis better for my chance to suffer the slings and arrows of outrageous Clayites or to come forth at once a thorough Whig and by surrendering end them."[96]

The parody was too close to the truth for Whigs.[97] A serious move materialized to challenge Taylor, and in the first week of September a mass meeting in New York City's Vauxhall Garden actually named Clay-Fillmore electors. Clay quashed this spontaneous, quixotic, and tardy show of support, however, by emphatically repeating to numerous correspondents and to the newspapers that he would not run as an independent.[98]

Ironically it was Cass who suffered the consequences of a splintered party when the Democrats' "No Decision" dodge of popular sovereignty alienated antislavery elements of the party. During the summer, New York Barnburners joined with remnants of the old Liberty Party to establish a national organization based on the alliterative exhortation, "Free Soil, Free Speech, Free Labor, and Free Men." The Free-Soil Party held its convention in August 1848 in Buffalo, New York, and became a haven for disaffected antislavery Whigs as well as Democrats, nominating Martin Van Buren with Charles Francis Adams as his running mate. The Van Buren candidacy pulled just enough votes away from Cass to give Taylor the victory in November.[99] By then, Taylor had been firmly brought to heel by Whig leaders weary of his disastrous letters and political pretentiousness. In September, they forced him to sign yet another Allison letter that even more firmly stated his allegiance to Whig principles.

Whigs tried to use Clay as an example of party unity, but the effect was at best mixed. Much was made of the fact that Clay voted a straight Whig ticket in the Kentucky state elections that August, in which he had even cast a ballot for Crittenden as governor.[100] But Clay would not give Taylor his blessing. Instead he privately castigated Taylor and provided correspondents with warnings about why they should not support him.[101] In November, he simply did not vote. He was ill, it was reported, and confined to his bed, which evidently was true. It spared him a difficult decision.[102]

The outcome of the November election "was the triumph of General Taylor, not our principles," Horace Greeley later observed. "It showed that a majority preferred General Taylor to General Cass for President: that was all." Clay agreed that the contest was one of men, not ideas, and he greatly lamented its course and its outcome, which was the essential end of the Whig program for which he had labored most of his life. "At once triumphant and undone," Greeley sighed.[103]

And as far as Henry Clay knew, it was also the end of him as a public figure. During the summer, Governor William Owsley had offered to appoint him to fill Crittenden's vacated Senate post, but Clay declined.[104] He suspected it to be nothing more than an empty gesture, an attempt to soften the party's rebuke, only a little less meaningless than placing Fillmore on the ticket. And yet Owsley had said, "A patriot is never discharged but by death," words that gained a bit more resonance as the weeks wore on: the Free-Soilers met in Buffalo, the major parties put their heads in the sand, and the sections snarled and snapped at each other over the prize of the western territories. Clay gradually became aware of the changing mood of the country, a mood he found increasingly disturbing, even alarming. By the fall, he was restless and worried. The collapse of the Whigs as a coherent engine of change and improvement was disappointing, but the possibility that the Union could shatter was terrifying. A visitor to Lexington that October noted that a great many people expected Clay to be elected to the Senate over the winter. "It is confidently believed he will accept."[105]

CHAPTER FIFTEEN

"What Prodigies Arise"

A VISITOR TO Ashland in the fall of 1845 went out of his way to describe the plantation's slave quarters and their inhabitants in bright terms. The "negro cottages are exceedingly comfortable," he said, "all white-washed, clean and well furnished, and plenty of flowers in the windows and about the dwellings." Ashland's slaves, he observed, "possess more comforts of life, have better dwellings, are better clothed, and work less than a large majority of the day laborers of the North."[1]

Yet contradicting this glowing picture were other descriptions depicting Ashland as a place of brutal punishments where the purportedly compassionate master winked at a cruel overseer. Just months after newspaper accounts of Henry Clay's farm as a slave's Eden, the abolitionist press carried lurid stories about an escaped slave from Ashland named Lewis Richardson who claimed he had been viciously whipped at Clay's direction for a minor offense. According to Richardson, who told his story after reaching Canada, a total of 150 lashes had laid his back open after he had been suspended from a beam in one of Ashland's barns for almost an hour on a frigid December day. Richardson had run away after the whipping to tell this tale, one that was eagerly taken up by abolitionists to highlight not only Clay's depravity but to strip away the mask of benevolence he had affected with high talk of hating slavery while owning slaves.[2]

Yet the tale of Louis Richardson was not true, at least to the extent of Clay's involvement. In fact, Clay, who was on his way to New Orleans, did not know that a whipping had occurred. Richardson had received sixteen lashes, not 150, and according to Andrew Barnett, Clay's overseer, it was because of his frequent drunkenness, a circumstance attested to by reputable witnesses when Barnett defended himself against the charge of cruelty and vindicated his employer's reputation for kindness. Certainly it would have been out of character for Henry Clay to behave so cruelly, and under the weight of proof, even abolitionists let the matter fade away, especially when it was revealed that Clay made no effort to pursue or reclaim Richardson when he fled.[3]

As a young man just starting out in Kentucky, Henry Clay had urged the state constitutional convention of 1799 to adopt gradual emancipation, but in the years that followed he became a Kentucky planter who purchased slaves to work a growing farm. In doing this he essentially surrendered to circumstance and ambition. The circumstance was the world as he found it, first in Virginia and then in Kentucky. Slavery had always been part of that world, and though men he admired, such as George Wythe, had shown that it did not have to be that way, the life Clay chose pointed him in different, less admirable directions. After 1799, he gradually succumbed to the vice of slavery, a conclusion wrought by his ambition for status and local political prominence. Clay's behavior in all this was hypocritical, to be sure, and for that alone he merited at least a measure of the denunciation heaped on him by abolitionists.

He was in many ways a typical planter, and the claims of some friendly writers that Clay never sold a slave are false.[4] And yet in many ways he was not typical at all. While he did occasionally sell slaves, he also freed them, as in the case of Lottie Dupuy as well as her daughter Mary Ann and son Charles. Sometimes his purchases were made to unite families, and he was willing to help speed slaves to freedom when requested to by others. He was remarkably indifferent about recovering runaways. When a young slave named Levi disappeared while accompanying him during his travels in 1849, Clay casually remarked "that in a reversal of our conditions I would have done the same thing" and simply provided money to help Levi return to Ashland should he wish to, which he did. After Kentucky authorities arrested Vermont abolitionist Delia Webster in 1844 for inciting slaves to run away, Clay offered to defend her. Responding to defenders of slavery who hinted at reviving the African slave trade, he was unequivocal in condemning it as deserving the "detestation of mankind." He remained active in the American Colonization Society and served as its president from 1836 until his death.[5]

Clay believed that emancipated slaves could only prosper someplace other than America. In part that belief was born of the prejudices of his time, which he repeated in public and private statements: blacks were inferior, he felt, because of their race. But Clay also qualified the observation with caveats that slavery itself and the unrelenting prejudice of whites most thoroughly contributed to the degradation of blacks, a belief shared by Abraham Lincoln.[6] Clay insisted that whites would fare no better if made into slaves, and he rejected the argument that black inferiority justified black enslavement. That attitude, he said, was a spurious rationalization that could be insidiously used to justify the subjugation of anyone, given the right circumstances.[7]

Clay consistently denounced slavery as wrong, lamented its existence, and wished that it had never been established.[8] He would not consent to its extension, and where it did exist, he was eager to see it extinguished if that could be accomplished without undue injury to owners and excessive burdens placed on freed slaves. His embrace of gradual emancipation remained a constant throughout his life, despite his vagueness about methods and timetables. Gradualism would allow owners to absorb the economic shock of losing so great a capital investment. It would benefit slaves slated for freedom by giving them time to learn trades and gather the money necessary to go home, a place defined for Clay as that whence they had originated as a race, namely, Africa. The American Colonization Society for decades had been the vehicle to accomplish that objective, and Clay was among many important men who belonged to it, held high offices in it, contributed money to it, and lobbied for state and federal subsidization. By the 1840s, the idea had grown rather threadbare, although the organization still attracted new members. Nobody thought, however, that it would ever possess the financial means or political reach necessary for significant success, and in many respects it was always meant to be an example as well as an experiment.

Abolitionists grew to despise it. They castigated it for disguising overt racism behind a veil of humanitarianism. As slaveholders adopted a positive defense of slavery, they too attacked colonization and prevailed on state legislatures to outlaw practices friendly to it, such as bequests of slaves to the society with instructions for their transport to Africa. The American Colonization Society could have better countered these charges and stopped these attacks with evidence that its example was persuasive and the experiment was working, but proof on both counts was quite thin. Instances of emancipation remained rare, and many freed slaves showed no desire to go to Africa.[9]

In any case, Clay insisted that only slave owners could deal with the problem as it currently existed. He continued to oppose abolitionists because he thought that their radicalism damaged the cause of emancipation. Abolitionists not only hardened slaveholders' resolve to resist all solutions, even reasonable ones, they also goaded slaveholders into insisting that slavery was not a predicament at all and that it actually benefited slaves. Clay always branded this proslavery defense as odious and corrosive. People who defended slavery as a positive good undermined the very idea of freedom and endangered everyone's liberty, regardless of caste or color.[10] As the years went by and attitudes on both sides became more inflexible, Clay grew increasingly exasperated. Abolitionists moved in ways that entrenched slavery. Proslavery activists inched toward destroying the Union.

Meanwhile, he cried out that time was reason's greatest ally. Given enough time, a growing population would supply enough labor to make slavery obsolete, and it would then disappear.[11] He often made this prediction to abolitionists, but they did not believe him. Moreover, they opposed uncertain remedies and elastic schedules.

Abolitionists who genuinely admired him, believing that they could appeal to the better man in Henry Clay, urged him to free his slaves and set an example for his neighbors.[12] But slavery continued at Ashland. He was a benevolent master—too kind and lax, according to slave-owning neighbors—who by all objective accounts fed and clothed and lodged his slaves well. His slaves were allowed remarkable levels of liberty, allowed to come and go from Ashland as they wished to visit family on other plantations or in Lexington, often to stay overnight. Yet the fact remained that no matter how healthy and autonomous they were, they were still slaves, the property of Henry Clay. They had to eat and wear what was given to them, had to live where they were told to, always had to return to Ashland sooner rather than later from visits elsewhere.

At Ashland, Clay told his critics, one would find slaves in comfort from cradle to grave, which was as physically true as he could manage, and the paternalism soothed a kindhearted man who could boast that his elderly and infirm slaves were cosseted in their last years, not cast off to fend for themselves as were the "wage slaves" of the North. Yet such paternalism was part of the problem of slavery. The underlying consequences of paternalism were not as appalling or as emotionally evocative as the stories of brutal beatings and fractured families and violated women clutching mulatto children. Rather, the consequences of benevolent paternalism were insidious precisely because of their banality.

What happened at Ashland that December day in 1845 exposed the limits of benevolent paternalism. Clay was away, but the whipping happened. It mattered little that the punishment was "only" sixteen blows rather than 150. It had happened. The system allowed it to happen no matter what Henry Clay said or did, and that reality emphasized the immorality of slavery more than scandalous fabrications that played upon melodrama for sensational effect. That Henry Clay continued to own slaves while condemning slavery was nothing short of tragic, a fundamental flaw in an otherwise good and decent man.

THERE WERE FEW heroes in this predicament. As it did on the national scale, slavery jumbled Bluegrass political affiliations and tested class loyalties. Standing to the left of Henry Clay but to the right of radical abolitionists was Clay's second cousin, Cassius Marcellus Clay ("Cash" to those who knew him), son of the wealthy planter and slaveholder Green Clay. Cash was reckless with often toxic prose. A venomous pen was his first weapon of choice, a bowie knife his second, and because he was so effective with the one, he found it wise to have the other handy.

During his initial sojourn in the North while attending Yale and in his later travels in the North, Cash was impressed by the relative scarcity of poverty in the free states. Returning to Kentucky, he was ashamed to look on the lower-class southern whites who lived in filthy shacks and took pride in refusing to do work they perceived as suited only for slaves. Cash began emancipating those slaves he could, his authority over some being restricted by the laws of inheritance, and exhorted his fellow Kentuckians to follow his example. Such pronouncements made him many enemies, most notably the powerful Wickliffes, the state's wealthiest slaveholders. The feud with the Wickliffes produced at least one duel as well as a brawl during which Cash gouged out a man's eye and used his knife to slice off an ear. His famous cousin defended Cash in the ensuing trial.[13]

Cash's increasing activism with regard to slavery in Kentucky gradually estranged the two cousins, Henry Clay clinging to the idea that gradual emancipation presented the most realistic solution while Cash urged a firm date for Kentucky emancipation that would coerce slaveholders into cutting their eventual losses by selling their slaves to out-of-state buyers. Cash did not much worry about the fate of the slaves themselves, in whom he had little interest. Rather, he viewed emancipation as the best way to promote economic progress and white advancement. When a mob (James Clay included) disassembled the printing press of Cash's abolitionist newspaper, he blamed his older cousin, completing their estrangement.[14]

The Wickliffes and many other slave owners had long been obsessed with repealing the state's 1833 law banning the importation of slaves, a statute that had been widely violated but did have the salutary effect of keeping Kentucky's slave population relatively low. Intense lobbying and threats of political reprisals finally convinced the legislature to repeal the law in 1849. It was a major setback for antislavery advocates, one matched by their failure to control the constitutional convention of that same year. The central issue of the convention clearly would be the future of slavery in Kentucky.

In February, Henry Clay wrote a letter to provide a definitive statement of his views on this issue. Although addressed to his brother-in-law Richard Pindell, the letter was meant for publication and caused a stir.[15] In addition to repeating the claim that colonization was the most sensible way to effect emancipation, Clay lamented the failure of the state to address the problem fifty years earlier in its 1799 constitutional convention. Now a new opportunity was at hand, and he urged his fellow Kentuckians to adopt gradual emancipation as well as to fund colonization. Failing to act decisively this time could have terrible consequences, he said, for both Kentucky and the Union.[16]

"At no moment of Henry Clay's long and glorious career," proclaimed the Louisville *Courier,* "have we ever felt prouder of him."[17] Yet Clay correctly predicted that the Pindell letter would "bring on me some odium" in the South. Proslavery southerners saw Kentucky's convention as a bellwether for the fate of slavery in the Upper South, and Clay's statement confirmed their worst suspicions about his reliability on the subject. "Mr. Clay's name is no longer all powerful even in Kentucky," was a typical observation. "This letter completes his prostration with the masses."[18] Abolitionists were no happier. William Lloyd Garrison berated Clay's Pindell letter as "remorseless in purpose, cruel in spirit, delusive in expectation, sophistical in reasoning, tyrannous in principle." Yet Clay did not regret his statements. "I could not, towards the close of my life," he explained, "relinquish the inestimable privilege of freely expressing my sentiments on a great public matter, however they might be received by the public."[19]

In such an atmosphere, the campaign for the constitutional convention started in simmering rage and became ugly early. In one of its calmer and more decorous moments, Henry Clay presided over a meeting in Frankfort to promote emancipationist candidates, but other settings were freighted with the potential for violence as men went to meetings armed and angry.[20] Judge James Campbell shot Benedict Austin dead after a debate in Paducah. In June, tensions mounted in Madison County as Cash Clay aggressively spoke at public meetings for the emancipationist candidate and squared off against Squire Turner's family, who supported their patriarch's proslavery candidacy with snarls and threats. "It was now evident," said a newspaper account, "that there was some unpleasant feeling between them."[21] That observation was an incredible understatement. At a public meeting in Foxtown, the Turners set upon Cassius Clay with cudgels and knives. He was stabbed from behind. Thomas Turner pressed a revolver to Cash's head and pulled the trigger. The cap fired but not the chamber. Turner frantically pulled the trigger three more times without discharging a single shot. Cash ended the fracas by gutting Cyrus Turner with a bowie knife, a mortal wound. Everyone thought Cash Clay would die as well, but he again proved too stubborn to kill. As long as there was slavery, Cash's guardian angel would have his hands full.[22]

Kentucky showed the rest of the country that there would be slavery in the

Bluegrass State, presumably forever. Although emancipationists ran in twenty-nine counties, not a single one was elected, an ominous portent for the course of the constitutional convention. Proslavery Kentuckians marshaled forces to control every aspect of the meeting, adopting a constitution that not only endorsed slavery but bolstered it with protections that surpassed those of every other slave state's constitution.[23] The emancipationist cause in Kentucky was dead, and Clay was disheartened. In a few months, he was able to consider the matter philosophically. He was sure that slavery was destined for extinction, despite Kentucky's rejection of gradual emancipation. It would happen either "legally or naturally," he predicted with extraordinary foresight. "The chief difference in the two modes is that, according to the first, we should take hold of the Institution intelligently and dispose of it cautiously and safely." The alternative was to have slavery "some day or other take hold of us, and constrain us, in some manner or other, to get rid of it."[24] In his Pindell letter, Clay had voiced a grim warning: "in the event of a civil war breaking out . . . Kentucky would become the theater and bear the brunt" of it.[25] The question raised by those realities was how to gauge the number of years the country had left to control its own destiny, how long before the blight of slavery exerted its own dismal control.

As for himself, he made arrangements in his will to emancipate Ashland's slaves. All males born after January 1, 1850, were to be freed at age twenty-eight; all females born after that date, freed at twenty-five. Taking into account the possibility that financial necessity would require the sale of some slaves before their emancipation, he legally bound new owners to honor the schedule stipulated in his will. In any case, families subject to any sale were to be kept together. Only by their own consent could they be separated.[26]

As he laid these plans in 1851, he forlornly weighed the deteriorating status of free blacks. In that same year, Indiana adopted a constitution that prohibited free blacks from entering the state and contemplated the eviction of those in residence. Certain that other "free" states would eventually do the same, Henry Clay was heartsick. He therefore directed that his slaves be prepared for their freedom by receiving wages for their labor during the final three years of servitude. The money was to help them learn a trade and defray the cost of their transit to Africa. Furthermore, any children born to female slaves slated for freedom were to be free at birth, apprenticed to learn a trade, and taught reading, writing, and arithmetic.

In the end, he thought it was both the least and the best he could do. He had always hated slavery, had always lived with it as with a slumbering monster, vile in his eyes and disgraced by the considered judgment of enlightened men, but he had never hated the people who happened to be slaves, had never said of

them, as had Cassius Clay, that "God has made them for the sun and the ba-
nana."[27] Now, in places like Indiana, men and women who had so long been victims of slavery were to be made casualties of freedom. "What is to become of
these poor creatures?" he cried. "In the name of humanity, I ask what is to become of them—where are they to go?"[28]

IN LATE OCTOBER, just before the election of 1848, Clay invited Zachary
Taylor to Ashland. Taylor declined but said he wanted to meet during Clay's
visit to New Orleans that winter. Moreover, the president-elect claimed to lament
some people's efforts to generate bad feelings between them—the tireless Burnley, sworn enemy of Clay, was still much in Taylor's confidence—and rejoiced
that the attempts to poison their friendship had failed. That remained to be seen.
Clay had hopes for better times ahead with a Whig in the White House, and he
wanted to meet Taylor "to form an opinion whether that hope will be realized or
not." He left Ashland on December 20 for New Orleans and briefly ran into Taylor on the last leg of the journey, an accidental encounter too brief for anything
but idle pleasantries. The planned lengthier meeting in New Orleans never took
place. A cholera outbreak in the city was blamed, but other reasons kept them
apart. Clay claimed to bear Taylor no ill will over the events of 1848, but Taylor's
victory convinced Clay that he would have won had he been nominated. That
made his rejection by the Whigs even more disillusioning. Yet any lingering disappointment, said Clay, "should not affect our desire that the new administration
may honorably aquit [sic] itself, and for the advantage of our Country."[29]

On January 20, Clay had a bad fall in New Orleans "while carelessly descending a flight of stairs" and had to cancel a side trip to Mobile as a result. The
accident left him lame and his hands badly bruised. Such mishaps marked a
growing clumsiness as his gait grew uncertain and his balance shaky, a normal
consequence of age, but his halting step and chronic cough were worrisome.
"The fall was a service to me," Clay joked to his old friend Kit Hughes, claiming that it had awakened "some of my sleeping interior organs . . . to the performance of their duties." But he also wryly observed, "In youth our topics of
correspondence are our pleasures, in age our pains."[30] The whimsy disguised
gloomier reflections that clouded his days. He and Lucretia had started alone, he
recalled, and now, after eleven children, seven of them in their graves, only the
youngest, John, lived with them. Clay became increasingly pensive, and every
new loss pushed him in the conflicting directions of calm acceptance and mild
alarm. In one moment he was resigned to his own death, but in the next he worried that he might not live to see distant loved ones again. He worried when

friends fell silent, thinking the worst. Clay suspected something was amiss when Kit Hughes stopped answering letters in the summer of 1849. Hughes had stayed forever young to Clay, after all these years still the punster who had traveled mountainous seas on the *John Adams* thirty-five years earlier with him and Jonathan Russell, now dead for seventeen years. "If it be so ordered that we shall never see each other here below," Clay told Hughes, "I hope that we shall meet in the realms of bliss above."[31] Hughes died on September 18, 1849, making Henry Clay the sole survivor of the Ghent delegation. It was "a solemn warning that I too must soon follow them."[32]

Clay had always dreaded receiving bad news about those he loved, but in these final years the blows were more telling and his spirits less resilient. An amplified religiosity colored much of his temperament. When he learned of his brother Porter's death in early 1850, Clay's "greatest consolation" was that Porter "had long been a sincere, pious, and zealous Christian."[33] But sometimes even deep faith could not blunt his grief. In the summer of 1850, he heard that Anna Mercer, his dear friend William Mercer's daughter, was ill. He immediately wrote Mercer asking for a report, avowing trust in "an Allwise and Merciful God." He recalled how much Anna had suffered once when she wore tight shoes to a ball, and he mildly admonished her to "dance less, go to fewer parties, and avoid all excesses in your amusements." But Anna's health was delicate, for she too had tuberculosis. As the Mercers traveled abroad in 1851, she became ill again. That fall a letter told him that Anna had died three weeks earlier in Liverpool. He was as devastated as Mercer. It was as though his own girls were instantly gone all over again, a flood of grief over each one made newly raw by the thought of poor little Anna gone as well, never again to dance laughing and tender-footed at a Newport fancy ball.[34]

GOVERNOR OWSLEY HAD wanted to send Clay to the Senate when Crittenden resigned in the summer of 1848, but Clay had declined. Clay's friends soon revived the idea, but for a lengthy period at the end of the year he resisted. He had been quite ill that fall, and he was not convinced that his service would be of any use in the country's current situation. Friends holding up the example of John Quincy Adams left Clay unimpressed. Old Man Eloquent's stint in Congress, Clay thought, "had the tendency to diminish instead of augmenting his reputation."[35] Besides, he heard from Greeley, who was filling an unexpired congressional term at the end of the Thirtieth Congress, that the problems with the Mexican Cession would be settled soon by admitting the entire region as one or two states. There wouldn't be much point in Clay's going to Washington if

that were the case. Late in the year, he thought it unlikely the Kentucky legislature would consider him, and he did not want his friends to press his candidacy.
As usual, he feared it would be unseemly to appear to seek the office.[36]

Clay changed his mind, though. By January he no longer felt he could decline, because Greeley's cheerful forecast about the territorial question now appeared doubtful. Bills to admit California and New Mexico as one state never
even came to a vote. Some, however, suspected Clay was acting from the worst
motives. Did he harbor resentments that would prompt him to sabotage the administration? Bailie Peyton thought so and said Clay would "play hell." He recommended that Clay be frozen out, but Peyton was hardly an objective observer.
Not only was he a staunch Taylor Whig, he had once been embarrassed by
owing Clay money he could not repay.[37] People other than resentful debtors,
however, perceived in Clay a man bitter over his treatment in 1848 and inclined
to do something about it. James Buchanan predicted Clay "will raise the d[evi]l
there" as a "dying gladiator."[38]

Such expectations prompted Taylor's supporters to oppose Clay's return to
Washington, but through Bob Letcher, Clay let it be known that he bore no ill
will to anyone, and the pledge of benevolence persuaded Governor Crittenden
to support him. On February 1, Whig majorities in both houses of the Kentucky
legislature gave him an easy victory over Democrat Richard M. Johnson.[39]
Combs chuckled that Clay's return to the Senate would resemble "the sudden
entrance of an old tom cat into a room of cheese-stealing mice & rats."[40] Democrats even happily anticipated the prospect of Clay's making trouble, though a
clash with Taylor was less likely, friends said, because Clay's ambition was
"now rounded and smoothed by the corrections of time and religion." Buchanan
was counting on age to restrain the formerly impulsive Harry of the West. "Clay
may regain his influence," he mused, "but a man of seventy-three probably cannot do much."[41]

Clay jokingly admitted as much himself. He felt like "the day laborer . . .
who having worked all day by sun shine, is sent again at night into the fields to
work by moon light." He noted that he did "not apprehend any danger from lunacy," however.[42] Just how much work he intended to do, mischievous or otherwise, remained uncertain in any case. He did not attend the brief Senate session
in March that confirmed Taylor's appointments. When he went to the capital at
the end 1849, he said he would "take no leading part, either in support of, or in
opposition to the Administration." Instead, he merely wanted "to be a calm and
quiet looker on, occasionally offering a word of advice or pouring a little oil on
the tempestuous billows."[43]

Neither foe nor friend thought that likely. Buchanan gazed on with grudging admiration tinged with cynicism: "In life's last stage," he misquoted Samuel Johnson, "what prodigies arise."[44]

WARM WEATHER BROUGHT cholera to Lexington that summer, and Clay was reported to have died from it, a rumor that persisted until July 10.[45] He chose not to press his luck. The extended illness the previous fall, the accident in New Orleans early in the year, and the chronic cough that was now his constant companion persuaded him to head north. On July 24, he left Ashland with James and his family for a month-and-a-half journey through Ohio to Upstate New York and Newport, Rhode Island. James, Susan, and the children enjoyed this brief holiday before leaving for Europe, James having received an appointment as chargé d'affaires to Portugal. Clay was gratified by the exuberant, occasionally adulatory treatment he received along the way. Crowds flocked to train platforms to catch a glimpse of him through the window of his car as locomotives took on water and wood. Sometimes he spoke, but he was more often so weak that he remained seated and merely waved.[46]

In New York, he visited Martin Van Buren at his home, "Lindenwald." The two had a grand time, sitting down one afternoon to feast on "cruellers, ole-cocks, suckettush, owgreet cheese," and a large tureen of sauerkraut. Clay did not much care for the sauerkraut. With his handkerchief to his nose, he said, "Van, I've lived long, and encountered *as strong opposition* as any other man, but, to be frank with you, I have never encountered anything *quite so strong as this.*" At least, that was what the newspapers reported.[47]

Only a few weeks later, he was back at Ashland. The trip had started precariously and was mottled by ill health, but the crowds had been heartening, and Clay felt better. His cough would not go away, though. He began to suspect that it never would.[48]

WHILE CLAY TRAVELED, Taylor was bungling his first job as president, which was dispensing the patronage to solidify support for his administration and its programs. Immediately after the election, Whigs had clung to the hope that Taylor would sweep away the corruptions of "loco-foco misrule" to place "Departments . . . into new hands, and good, and things will go on more smoothly." Whigs could hardly wait for March and inauguration day. "Hurra for the Old Hero!" they cheered.[49]

But Taylor's decisions, beginning with his cabinet, were disappointing. Nine months passed between his inauguration in March and the opening of the Thirty-first Congress in December, and during that time Taylor went on something of a rampage, making appointments that made little sense. Gradually deemed incompetent, he was compared to a "half cooked mutton chop" that had been hurried too quickly to the table. Even before he left for Washington, Clay was convinced that Taylor would be a one-term president.[50]

Taylor's clumsy use of the patronage squandered the momentum of 1848, depriving the administration of the necessary clout to push through its program. Some appointments clearly should have been made. Crittenden was the logical choice for attorney general, and many expected it to be offered to him, but he was not asked and remained offstage in the governor's chair at Frankfort rather than in Washington, where he could have helped Taylor with the country's crises. Possibly Taylor was fearful that a Crittenden appointment would invite charges of a new "corrupt bargain," but that does not account for the trouble that Crittenden had in securing places for his friends. Such treatment by the Taylor administration verged on truculence.[51]

Another appointment that directly concerned Clay illustrated Taylor's public relations problem. Shortly after Taylor's inauguration, Clay asked him to appoint James to a diplomatic post, a request Clay felt was justified to balance John Tyler's spiteful refusal to honor William Henry Harrison's pledge to Henry Jr. eight years earlier. Taylor obliged by making James chargé d'affaires to Portugal. As the matter stood, it was so far so good, and had it been allowed to stand at that, it would have been the sort of gracious gesture that could heal breaches and salve wounds. Yet all the goodwill was lost when Taylor's supporters complained that the president was toadying to Clay, and Taylor defensively revealed that Clay had asked for the appointment. The administration thus countered the impression that Taylor had bargained for Clay's support by encouraging the perception that Clay's support could be purchased with a patronage appointment. John Clayton and Reverdy Johnson made gloating remarks that painted Henry Clay as just another office seeker grubbing for a place at the trough.[52]

Of all Taylor's mistakes with the patronage, this was among the most dreadful. The post itself—chargé to Portugal—was hardly a munificent boon, and Clay was mortified at being treated so gracelessly.[53] In Frankfort, John J. Crittenden was dismayed by the talk of Clay's supplication. Those who were saying this were "thoughtless or intemperate," he told John Clayton. Their remarks would "take off all the good & grace of the act, &, perhaps, make things worse." Crittenden said that Clay wanted to be Taylor's friend. "Little sparks," he warned, "are constantly falling around us that unless timely put out, might kindle a great fire."[54]

THE COUNTRY WAS in serious trouble when Zachary Taylor became president. Sectional harmony staggered under the weight of several controversies, some of long-standing and others of recent vintage. Northern agitation was on the rise to end slave trading in the District of Columbia, a national embarrassment for years. In earlier days, even southerners had found the trudging, forlorn coffles discomfiting. John Randolph one afternoon watched a lady making garments to send to Greek freedom fighters—a fashionable cause in the early 1820s—and motioned toward a group of young slaves in rags while acidly remarking: "Madam, the Greeks are at your door."[55] In 1849, Randolph's "Greeks" were still being bought and sold in the nation's capital, but southern uneasiness over it had all but vanished. Many southerners would not tolerate any position that challenged their insistence that all aspects of slavery were beneficial.

When the House of Representatives considered resolutions banning the D.C. slave trade, southerners came together as never before. In December 1848, a caucus of senators and representatives from the slave states watched John C. Calhoun's thundering rage over the growing assault on slavery. A committee drafted a Southern Address. Mostly Calhoun's creation, it was such a belligerent statement that southern Whigs and quite a few Democrats refused to sign it, but in the coming weeks, events eroded that restraint.[56]

Southern slaveholders brooded over the abolitionists' Underground Railroad, a supposedly vast network of safe houses that helped ferry fugitive slaves to freedom in Canada. The Underground Railroad was more menacing in the southern imagination than it was in fact, and even the incidence of runaway slaves was more exaggerated in lore than in reality. Southerners nevertheless demanded a more rigorous fugitive slave law, insisting that the federal government not only help reclaim fugitives but compel the northern states to do so as well. Virginia's James Mason was drafting a bill to accomplish this, and it was certain to unite the North in opposition.

Out west, Texas had a complaint of its own. As it had before the Mexican War, the Lone Star State still claimed that the enormous expanse east of the Rio Grande and north to the 42nd parallel was part of Texas. President Polk had supported the Texan position as one of the pretexts to provoke Mexico to war, but the federal government was determined to prevent Texas from expropriating half of provincial New Mexico. Quick-tempered Texans threatened to march on Santa Fe if necessary and take the disputed territory by force. The U.S. army was in Santa Fe. Texas did not care.

It was only one of the grave controversies involving the fate of the Mexican Cession. Early in 1848, even as Taylor's supporters were jockeying to secure his nomination, the discovery of gold in California and the rush of adventurers that followed created a completely unexpected state of affairs. The sudden influx of tens of thousands of people overwhelmed what passed for government in previously sleepy California. Little law and less order prevailed as prospectors came with shady pasts. Shady women quickly followed, and soon life in the goldfields was a dangerous mix of prostitution, thievery, claim jumping, murder, and vigilante justice. Upright and peaceable Californians, yearning for shelter from this human storm, tackled the task of erecting a government, a project surreptitiously supported by President Taylor. A convention drafted a constitution and audaciously proposed skipping the territorial stage by applying immediately to Congress for admission as a state. Clay wryly observed that northern Democrats like Senator Stephen A. Douglas should be pleased because Taylor had "produced a Democratic Child," but both Whigs and Democrats in the South were alarmed as they read California's proposed constitution. It excluded slavery.[57]

Under the weight of these controversies, the Union verged on disaster. Whig and Democrat differences crumbled in the South, and sectional unity to protect slavery at all costs took shape. As Clay prepared to head for Washington in October 1849, a bipartisan meeting in Mississippi called for a southern convention to assemble in Nashville the following June, its aim clearly to establish southern concord for action. The only question was how drastic that action would be.

WHEN CLAY ARRIVED in Washington, the news from home was troubling as winter raged in Kentucky. Eight inches of snow lay on the ground, and smallpox gripped Lexington. While the town set up hospitals and imposed quarantines, Clay tore into letters from Ashland, where a slave was ill and the family at risk. "John is lazy," Clay complained, "and his mother never writes." He felt guilty about leaving Lucretia, especially in the worst winter he could recall. He implored Thomas and Mary to look after her and hoped that duty and affection would make John attentive to her. "I do not think," he said, "I will leave her again another winter."[58]

He moved into Room 32, a bedchamber with an adjoining parlor at the National Hotel. Sir Henry L. Bulwer, British minister to the United States, and his wife, niece of the Duke of Wellington, were neighbors. Clay did not bring a slave to Washington but hired a free black named James Marshall. Clay grew fond of Marshall and was generous in large and little ways toward him, often giving him time off to visit his family in Virginia. Soon Clay had settled into a pleasant routine that included socializing with the Bulwers, though he usually stayed in at night and retired early.[59]

The mood in Washington disturbed him, and he feared that the anger of southern politicians would produce an "inflamed and perverted" response by the southern people. In mid-December, the House of Representatives struggled to elect a Speaker and fell into a round of coarse name-calling that degenerated into catcalls urging antagonists to "shoot" and jeering "Where is your bowie knife?" Clay watched from the gallery with Joshua Giddings. They were a study in contrasts. Several years of seeing such behavior had made Giddings numb to it, and he thought the scene in the House amusing. Clay looked "sober and grave." He soon urged his friends in Kentucky and New York to arrange public meetings supporting the Union and denouncing secession.[60]

He kept to his pledge to stay above the fray, requesting as the Senate organized committees that he not be appointed to any. The Senate chamber itself was comforting and familiar despite his long absence, still covered in the dark red carpet, its desks arranged in four tiers with galleries above. Before the renovation of 1835, only a bar behind the outermost desks separated the floor from the galleries, but now visitors were relegated to elevated seating that could accommodate about five hundred people and frequently did, many of them ladies eager to see political celebrities in action.[61] Senators prided themselves on keeping that action deliberative, dressing for the part with morning clothes their usual attire. Members had access to two large snuffboxes on Millard Fillmore's dais as well as wine and spirits, a custom retained from earlier days. That much was in Clay's recollection, but many of the people he was to serve with were new to him, known only by reputation if at all, and a casual survey of the semicircled desks revealed another sobering change that was startling: over half the Democrats were under fifty; all but five Whigs were older than that.[62]

Clay's reputation preceded him, and his return aroused curiosity among members and guests alike, eager to hear him speak but uneasy over the possibility that his mental as well as physical powers were fading. He looked old and feeble, and he paused often to bend under the rattling cough, but his wit was still sharp and spontaneous, his timing impeccable, and his audience responsive. When the Senate discussed an appropriation to repair a dam on the Ohio River, Clay related how he had once been near it while traveling on *Old Hickory*, "a steamboat bearing a name rather ominous, I confess." And in early December, one James Robertson appeared in the Senate gallery to announce that he intended to kill Henry Clay. The sergeant-at-arms took the man seriously and told Vice President Fillmore, who had Robertson arrested. Held for two weeks, he was clearly insane, and Clay judged him harmless as well. Upon his release, Robertson petitioned Congress for compensation, and Clay supported it in such a lighthearted way as to draw laughter and persuade Congress to give the man $100.[63]

He was soon as popular as ever, and even political opponents on Capitol Hill were deferential, which was fortunate because he would need every shred of goodwill he could muster for the work ahead. But his popularity was also a problem on the other end of Pennsylvania Avenue, where Zachary Taylor suspiciously watched the man his advisers were accusing of trying to reclaim the Whig Party. The relations between Clay and the administration were amiable in Clay's view, despite Taylor's never consulting him about anything. But the amiability was brittle. Clay declined to have dinner with Clayton and Reverdy Johnson, blaming his "cold." But he was still angry over Johnson's churlish remarks about James's appointment, and a visit to Clayton's office turned interminable when Clayton would not let him go, telling him about his official chores and many troubles. Not even brittle amiability described Clay's relationship with Taylor, and there were warning signs early. Clay was irked that Taylor had now invented another story about the contents of the November 1847 letter in which Taylor had promised to step aside for Clay. In a political sense, this was ancient history, but Clay bristled. He knew exactly where that letter was—tucked among a bundle of papers tied up in a pasteboard container in his upstairs office at Ashland—and he had Thomas send it to him.[64]

Letting the matter go would have been wise, but getting along with the president became increasingly difficult as Taylor nursed an exaggerated sensitivity. Clay took halting walks on the streets around the National Hotel, but he early discovered that if he made eye contact with anyone, he invited extended idle chatter. He was weary enough without the distractions. Taylor passed Clay one morning on Pennsylvania Avenue, concluded he had been snubbed, and was chilly when Clay called at the White House to assure him that nothing of the sort had been intended. Personalities and egos can pose petty obstacles to meaningful action, and the president was increasingly difficult to get along with.[65]

THE CALIFORNIA QUESTION rapidly became a crisis of the first order. Despite the South's dominance of national councils that included a slave-owning Louisiana planter in the White House, a preponderance in the cabinet, and a majority on the Supreme Court, the South was outnumbered in the House of Representatives, a result of the North's faster-growing population.[66] Only by sustaining equality in the Senate could it continue to block injurious schemes such as the Wilmot Proviso and protect its "peculiar institution." Southerners were deeply worried that California's admission would destroy the fragile balance of fifteen slave states and fifteen free states in the Senate. Likely avenues of slavery expansion were vanishing as well, making improbable the reestablishment of senatorial sectional balance. Campaigns were already under way in the rest of the Mexican Cession to sustain the Mexican law abolishing slavery, and southerners were angry that California's destiny, if unchecked, would go far to establish the pattern of free soil in a region obtained largely with the blood of southern soldiers.

The political problem within this otherwise complicated issue was itself simple. Northern Whigs wanted slavery barred from the western territories. Applying the Wilmot Proviso was an unlikely solution because southerners, whether Whig or Democrat, would not consent to it. The government could claim that because Mexico had abolished slavery in the region, it should not be reintroduced, hence doing nothing. Or the government could take California as the model to admit the entire Mexican Cession to the Union as a single state or multiple ones, bypassing territorial organization in order to absolve Congress of any responsibility for the region's slave or free status. Southern Whigs, if not southern Democrats, seemed willing to tolerate the prohibition of slavery as a function of extant Mexican law rather than as a new policy from Washington. The Taylor administration consequently pursued a policy of "non-action" to avoid riling southerners. It embraced immediate admission to preempt congressional debates sure to destroy the little sectional accord remaining.

Like the patronage plan, however, Taylor's approach to the western territories was better in theory than in practice. The political complexion of the Thirty-first Congress was a significant obstacle to the twin policies of non-action and admission. For one thing, Democrats were the majority in both houses and had to placate their powerful southern wing. Conversely, Whigs had to fashion a policy acceptable to their northern wing. Taylor did not help matters when special messages to both houses of Congress in late January revealed that he believed Congress possessed the authority to exclude slavery from the Mexican Cession. That admission gave northerners an opening, which frightened and angered southerners. Southern Whigs were especially troubled by indications that the president would not veto the Wilmot Proviso.[67]

After these revelations, Taylor's non-action plan was essentially dead on arrival. Southern Whigs began thinking about how they could use California's admission to bargain for concessions in the rest of the Mexican Cession. Ideally they could kill the Wilmot Proviso and give Texas its extension to the Rio Grande. In January 1850, Clay was rumored to have contrived a remedy that sought to accomplish these very goals. His enemies reacted by presuming that anything from his pen had the primary purpose of showing up Taylor in order to supplant him as the head of the party.[68] In short, it was to be the Old Chieftain versus Captain Tyler all over again, only this time with Old Zach—the same old story, just a different antagonist. Clay's motives for returning to Washington, however, were grounded more in patriotism than pride, for the vehemence of this new sectional dispute truly alarmed him. Possibly he was eager to rescue the Whig Party from Zachary Taylor, but the Union was foremost in his mind and saving the country was his primary goal. He started by going to the home of an old rival on a frigid, rainy January night.

It was January 21, the day the House received Taylor's troubling special message. That evening at seven o'clock, Clay's tall, gaunt form came haltingly to Daniel Webster's door on Louisiana Avenue, just blocks from Clay's rooms at the National Hotel. Clay did not have an appointment, but Webster instantly agreed to see him. They spent an hour together, Webster listening intently as Clay described his plan to resolve the crisis over the territories. Webster nodded and observed that Clay's ideas might well satisfy the North and reasonable southerners. Clay rose to leave, content at least that Webster would likely help him and certainly at this point not oppose him. Webster, in fact, was not so sure, but the visit touched and saddened him. His visitor had not been able to stop coughing, and only an hour's conversation had exhausted him. As he watched the faltering, sunken figure leave, Webster was certain of one thing if nothing else: Henry Clay was dying.[69]

Eight days later, on January 29, Clay stood on the Senate floor amid high expectations. "I hold in my hand," he said, "a series of resolutions I desire to submit to the consideration of this body." And thus it began. The relatively brief speech that followed outlined eight proposals that Clay hoped would be "an amicable arrangement of all questions in controversy between the free and slave states." He resorted to the most dramatic devices he could summon, even brandishing a fragment of Washington's coffin to goad those forgetful of the Union's glory.[70]

With this appearance Clay began his last grand legislative endeavor. From January 29 through August 1, he would be on his feet in debate no fewer than seventy times. Not every instance marked a major speech, but many of his remarks were extensive arguments and defenses of his proposals.[71] It was a killing pace for a man in his condition. Yet if sheer will could accomplish anything, he was determined to save his country. Webster knew that too—that at least Henry Clay would die trying.

CLAY'S JANUARY 29 speech was a brief preliminary to the major address concerning his proposal that he delivered a week later. People came from as far away as Boston to hear him. By midmorning on February 5, the Capitol was brimming with spectators so numerous they were blocking access to the Senate chamber. Galleries, cloakrooms, and corridors were jammed with people. The Rotunda overflowed, as did the library, and even the galleries of the House of Representatives sagged under the weight of a crowd that began emptying out toward the Senate as the time for Clay's speech neared.

Clay was sick, but he came up Pennsylvania Avenue from the National Hotel with a purpose. His cough forced him to stop more than once as he hung on the arms of companions. He steeled himself as the crowd parted to let him enter the Senate. Spectators broke into applause. For the rest of the morning, the Senate's routine business merely heightened anticipation. Finally, at one o'clock, Clay stopped writing and carefully put away his papers. As always, he spoke without notes. He stood slowly, partly from frailty, partly from habit. Ohio representative Salmon Chase's daughter, Kate, would later remark that Clay was so tall "he had to unwind himself to get up."[72] The galleries again broke into spontaneous applause. The throng outside realized he was about to begin and raised a prolonged cheer. Clay had to wait for the sergeant-at-arms to restore order. For the rest of the afternoon, his performance was so focused that he did not even go to his snuffbox. After more than two hours, he was spent but not done, and he concluded his address with another two-hour performance the next day.[73]

Clay tilted toward the North with his first four resolutions, which dealt with the Mexican Cession. Instead of making unpopulated expanses into states, as Taylor wanted, Clay relied on the fact that Mexican law had already excluded slavery in the region. He sought to satisfy southern demands that Texas have the Rio Grande boundary, but he wanted to lop off a considerable portion of northern Texas by running a new boundary from El Paso to the Sabine River. Everything north of that line would become part of the Mexican Cession. By virtue of Mexican law, Clay's new northern boundary for Texas would abolish slavery in a considerable portion of the state as it currently existed. Slave owners in Dallas and the surrounding regions would be forced to move south or lose their property. Moreover, the number of slaves that this plan would free was staggering— about twenty thousand—making Clay's initial proposal the most sweeping bid for mass emancipation until President Abraham Lincoln issued his proclamation twelve years later. Lincoln's Emancipation Proclamation occurred during the Civil War and had the force of arms behind it. Clay's proposal was a desperate attempt to prevent a civil war and had nothing other than the prescience of his contemporaries to recommend it. The idea did not stand a chance.

Clay tried to make the proffer more palatable to Texas with the federal treasury. From the start of the controversy, Clay had always believed that Texas would prove the most difficult problem to solve.[74] Too much pride was in play, and too much territory was at stake. Yet he thought he had hit on a workable solution. Texas was financially strapped and deeply in debt. Investors across the country who had purchased Texas bonds had a stake in preserving peace in the Southwest. Clay's friend Leslie Combs was a Texas bondholder, as was journalist Francis Grund. Clay hoped the bondholders would exert pressure for his boundary settlement in order to protect their interests. Grund, for one, had ties to William W. Corcoran, of the powerful bank Corcoran & Riggs, which would be brought into play in significant ways, such as canceling a large note it held from Daniel Webster. Clay reported that his neighbor Grund had taken "a wonderful liking" to him.[75]

Clay knew that wide support for this crucial part of the compromise was most likely to be garnered with a pledge to pay Texas bondholders with federal dollars. Southerners opposed to the compromise sourly agreed.[76] Clay's final resolutions, however, attempted to conciliate the South. He softened his call to abolish the slave trade in the District of Columbia by declaring that slavery itself should not be abolished in the District without Maryland and Virginia's consent. He recommended the adoption of a new fugitive slave law and stated that Congress had no authority to obstruct the slave trade between slave states.[77]

When he was done, he had spoken for almost five hours over the span of two days to deliver one of the finest, most masterful orations of his career. Despite its flawed endorsement of maintaining slavery—an obvious pander to the implacable South—there was much good in the speech. There was also a prophetic warning in its stirring conclusion. He described the horrors of the war that was certain to follow secession. Eleven years later, Abraham Lincoln would consult Clay's speech when framing his first inaugural address.[78]

The immediate response was mixed at best. Northerners had suspected that Clay's return to Washington was a plan to hoodwink them with a "second edition of the Missouri Compromise, and thus cheat the North again" by saving Taylor the trouble of vetoing the Wilmot Proviso.[79] "We think it would have been better for himself and his country, if he had remained at Ashland," complained one Ohio editorial.[80] Many southerners were no happier, and some were livid. Clay had firmly rejected the proposal of southern moderates to extend the Missouri Compromise line to the Pacific. "No earthly power," he said, "could induce me to vote for a specific measure for the introduction of slavery where it had not before existed, either south or north of that line."[81] The sentiment, along with his reliance on Mexican law, was simply a way to implement the Wilmot Proviso without invoking its name. Virginia radical Beverley Tucker was blunt: Clay was a "humbug" and "charlatan." Southern Democrats resolved to pick apart Clay's proposals even before formal debate on them began on February 11.[82]

The attacks by northern and southern extremists were to be expected. Clay was hoping to mobilize the center of both sections among the general population and in Congress by rousing what Lincoln would later call "the mystic chords of memory," the ardent attachment to the idea of the Union. Again, he foreshadowed Lincoln when he extemporaneously commented to the Senate: "I consider us all as one family, all as friends, all as brethren. I consider us all as united in one common destiny, and those efforts which I shall continue to employ will be to keep us together as one family, in concord and harmony; and above all, to avoid that direful day when one part of the Union can speak of the other as an enemy."[83]

In 1850, Clay prayed that the center was still large and strong enough to hold firm the bonds of Union, to embrace his words as worth living by. Lincoln too would speak eloquently of the sections being not "enemies, but friends," but by his time—just ten short years later—the center had crumbled away, and the words, while similar, had assumed an entirely different meaning. They had become worth dying for.

THE TAYLOR ADMINISTRATION rejected Clay's plan, but even with northern Whigs joining forces with Free-Soilers, the president did not have the votes to pass his own. Nevertheless, Taylor was confident, as he told Massachusetts congressman Horace Mann, that he could "save the Union without shedding a drop of blood." Mann also opposed Clay's proposals but thought overt northern resistance would only unite the South behind them. "If we from the North are still," predicted Mann, "it will be defeated by Southern votes and declamation."[84]

The crisis stalled into a tense stalemate. Southern Whigs like Alexander Stephens and Robert Toombs became adamant about the right to expand slavery into the Mexican Cession in exchange for California's admission as a free state. As far as Zachary Taylor was concerned, that was out of the question. Clay, as it turned out, was more flexible precisely because he had to secure the center. In the days after his speech of February 5 and 6, he realized his stand on sustaining Mexican law in New Mexico and Utah was alienating southern Unionists, a crucial part of that center. Thomas Ritchie exemplified that opposition. Friends during their youth in Richmond, the two had shared a few moments of pleasant conversation before Van Buren's inauguration in 1837, but mostly they had been estranged since Ritchie's condemnation of the "Corrupt Bargain" in 1825. Now, with the Union in jeopardy, they concluded it was time to put the past behind them.

Their reconciliation was a delicate matter that had to be accomplished quietly to avoid irritating their respective supporters, so long at odds. A mutual friend named James Simonton arranged a meeting, and late on the Sunday afternoon of February 10, while Washington drowsed, Ritchie and Virginia congressman Thomas Bayly came to Clay's rooms at the National Hotel. For the first time in years, the two old men sat across from each other and talked, at first reminiscing agreeably about their youthful days in Richmond. Clay said he always read the *Enquirer* and had followed Ritchie's career with friendly interest. They then moved to the reason for their meeting, a frank discussion of Clay's proposal. Ritchie had already suggested through Mississippi senator Henry S. Foote that Clay's plan should be referred to a select committee for formal presentation to the Senate as a package, and he repeated that suggestion with the stipulation that Clay drop his insistence on preserving the Mexican law that abolished slavery. That way, the South could be assured that the North would not admit a free California and then renege on opening the rest of the cession to slavery.

Clay pondered his options. He decided to give way on Mexican law. He agreed to push for territorial organization on the basis of popular sovereignty as a way to avoid making what was likely an unnecessary decision. Clay believed the region was unsuited to slavery in any case, and embracing popular sovereignty had the salutary effect of removing Ritchie's opposition to his plan. Clay remained firm, however, in resisting the formation of a committee to bundle his proposals. As he told the Senate four days later, he believed Foote's plan was "utterly impossible" as a way to settle the difficulties. In this regard, he was correct, for making one proposal reliant on all the others was bound to create more opposition in sum than the separate resolutions would provoke individually.

The old Whig and the aging Democrat parted amicably that Sunday evening, and Ritchie became a staunch ally in rallying moderate southern Democrats to the cause. Their rekindled friendship was soon common knowledge in Washington as Clay and Ritchie bantered at social events. Then one evening as he was seated across from Clay at a dinner, Ritchie jokingly referred to the Corrupt Bargain, and the table went as silent as it would have had Ritchie mentioned rope to a man on the eve of his hanging. "Shut your mouth, Tom Ritchie," Clay chuckled. "You know perfectly well that there never was a word of truth in that charge." Everyone laughed in relief. If Clay could save the Union, said Tom Ritchie, he would plant laurels on his grave. The old Whig and the aging Democrat understood each other at last.[85]

Northern Whigs and President Taylor were quite another matter, however, as were the angry Democrats of the South led by John C. Calhoun. Indeed, Calhoun, Webster, and Clay—the three leading lights of the Senate, dubbed the Great Triumvirate by contemporaries—could all have assumed sectional identities as the crises of 1850 evolved. Yet Clay, the slave-owning westerner, insisted on a national solution to the sectional problems menacing the Union.

Thus the formal debate on Clay's resolutions that commenced on February 11 became a prelude to what the other two members of the Great Triumvirate would have to say, and they did not weigh in until the first week of March. Calhoun on the fourth delivered—or rather, had delivered for him, because he was now so feeble that he could barely stand, let alone speak at length—a speech condemning northern political aggression and vowing resistance to requests for additional southern concessions on slavery. Few doubted that this definitive statement of the inflexible southern position was Calhoun's swan song, but they were less certain of its effectiveness. Had it preceded Clay's February address, it might have been more disruptive, but coming a month afterward it seemed oddly out of place and vaguely irrelevant.

That became more apparent three days later. Daniel Webster countered the blatant sectionalism of Calhoun's speech. In an address spanning three hours, Webster lauded the idea of the Union, denounced fire-eating secessionists, condemned rabble-rousing abolitionists, and made a shocking bid to appease southerners by promising to support a fugitive slave bill.[86] While some northern moderates, including many Boston merchants, appreciated Webster's attempt to restore sectional harmony, his pledge was unforgivable for most in the North and was especially appalling to New Englanders. Abolitionists denounced him outright. Zachary Taylor, for his own reasons, railed about Webster's rank disloyalty to the administration. Generally, though, Webster's tribute to the Union awakened the same sort of patriotic impulses stirred by Clay's brandishing of the splinter from Washington's coffin. Even better, Webster's demonstration of flexibility on a thoroughly southern issue halted secessionist momentum as it headed toward the Nashville convention.[87]

But what Webster did not do was also significant. He did not explicitly endorse Clay's compromise, and consequently did not rally northern Whigs behind it. From that perspective, the speech calmed passions without clarifying problems, and, upon reflection, disappointed those it did not offend. Taylor was not given much to reflection in the best of times, but he could take some comfort in the fact that Webster had not embraced Clay. The president now expected his advocate in the Senate, William Seward, to unite Whigs behind the administration's plan.

In the course of the year since Taylor's inauguration, Seward had emerged as the president's most influential adviser, which some Whigs found unfortunate. Webster thought Seward both "subtle and unscrupulous," and many suspected that the New Yorker was committed only to his own advancement. He was no friend of Clay's, and the administration expected him to demolish the Great Compromiser's scheme with a major address, Seward's first formal speech to the Senate. Seward had an arresting look about him—his gray-streaked red hair and aquiline nose made him look like an aging rooster—and though his voice tended to be droning rather than dramatic, he could say the most provocative things with an easy self-confidence that made men listen.[88]

On March 11, Seward spoke to rows of empty Senate desks, although the few men present were important. Webster was there, as were Thomas Hart Benton and Tom Corwin. Clay sat in a remote section of the empty chamber, but he soon rose to come nearer, troubled by Seward's words. As the New Yorker criticized compromises in general and Clay's in particular, it became clear that his speech would be the inflexible northern response to Calhoun's southern position. Any concessions to the South, Seward said, would endorse the idea that southerners had as much constitutional claim on the western territories as did northerners. Seward disagreed by citing what he called "a higher law than the Constitution," a phrase so provocative that it became emblematic of the speech and its most memorable (and, in the view of many, regrettable) contribution to the debate.[89] Aside from trying to spike sectional reconciliation, Seward's speech did nothing to advance any solution, including Taylor's. Seward's failure to promote the president's plan dismayed even the New Yorker's friends. After March 11, Taylor was angrier with Seward than with Webster or, if possible, even Clay, because Seward had grievously wounded the administration by alienating southern Whigs. Clay noted how Seward's "late Abolition Speech" had estranged him not just from the White House but everyone else as well. As for Taylor's presidency, Clay marveled that he had "never before seen such an Administration" that never consulted with Congress nor took a single prominent Whig into its confidence.[90]

As the end of March drew near, Clay judged events as cumulatively disastrous. John Bell introduced yet another compromise plan, and Stephen Douglas's Committee on Territories reported bills admitting California to the Union and organizing New Mexico and Utah as territories. Congressmen on opposing sides of these issues fell to fighting like common brawlers when they encountered one another on the streets and in taverns.

JOHN C. CALHOUN was dying. He had appeared only twice in the Senate since his March 4 address, once to hear Webster and finally to repeat briefly his opposition to any compromise that required the slightest southern concession. He was then confined to his rooms, weak but still alert. Clay wanted to see him. Hardly any but harsh words had passed between them for a quarter century, but Calhoun said to come ahead. Clay appeared for the appointment smiling and solicitous, but Calhoun's nature would not allow him to shed his animosity, not even for an hour. Calhoun's fellow South Carolinian Andrew Pickens Butler stood at the edge of the room and watched the two men, Clay with a kind smile murmuring idle pleasantries and Calhoun with a distant stare, giants in the twi-light.[91]

Calhoun died on March 31, a Sunday. The Great Triumvirate was no more. "From the old heroic race to which Webster and Clay and Calhoun belonged," New Yorker George Templeton Strong would lament, "down to the rising race of Sewards and Douglases and [Hamilton] Fishes is a dismal descent."[92] Both North and South saw giants in the twilight, passing.

Calhoun's death had the immediate effect of bringing the Senate to a stand-still on the sectional controversy while it eulogized him on April 2 and then on April 22 sent the customary delegation of six senators to Charleston to attend his funeral. During those three weeks, Clay reassessed the fate of his proposals. Whigs in both sections were not likely to support either his or Taylor's plan, and Clay had already abandoned sustaining Mexican law to support popular sover-eignty, a shift that essentially placed him in the moderate Democrat camp, or at least part of it. As the stalemate lengthened, it became difficult to trace tradi-tional alignments. Party labels blurred. Democrat Thomas Hart Benton sup-ported Taylor and opposed fellow Democrat Henry Foote, who continued to urge the creation of a committee to consider all proposals as one. Clay had long rejected what he derided as the Omnibus Plan, but he gradually realized that a broad range of political opinion wanted a comprehensive settlement. Moderate southerners had always been the key to a successful compromise, and they would not agree to a piecemeal arrangement that potentially had them giving up California without receiving any concessions.[93]

For these reasons, Clay finally consented to Foote's proposal to form a select committee. Almost everyone has judged Clay's decision to support the Om-nibus as a mistake, but he could see no other way to attract moderate southern-ers. Tempers were frayed by mid-April as the capital mourned Calhoun and suffered through "cold, damp, and rainy" weather.[94] The House was often in tu-mult, and finally the Senate too witnessed a shocking confrontation in which Henry Foote pulled a pistol on Thomas Hart Benton. After the pandemonium subsided, Clay wanted the two men to swear before a D.C. magistrate that they would not continue the quarrel, but Benton refused, insisting that he had done nothing wrong. Clay believed the country was running out of time.[95]

On April 18, the day after the Foote-Benton fracas, the Senate approved the creation of a Committee of Thirteen to consist of six free state and six slave state senators with Clay as the chairman. The committee was moderate and generally procompromise with members such as Cass, Jesse Bright, Webster, and John Bell. The only radicals were abolitionist Samuel Phelps of Vermont and James Mason of Virginia, the author of the Fugitive Slave Bill. Yet none of that mattered, for the committee never met as a group. Clay in fact was the committee, and Washington emptied out as he worked to draft a report, only occasionally consulting with the others about its particulars. At the end of April, he completed his labors at "Riverdale," Charles Calvert's home near Bladensburg.[96]

On May 8, Clay presented the report to the Senate. It revealed a remarkable change in his position. He detailed three bills with a lengthy justification. The first was Mason's Fugitive Slave Bill with a couple of amendments added, and the second was the elimination of the D.C. slave market. But it was the third bill, an enormous contrivance that would be called Clay's Compromise as well as the Omnibus Bill, that bundled together all the bills from the Committee on Territories organizing the Mexican Cession. Those proposals admitted a free California, established New Mexico and Utah territories on the basis of popular sovereignty, and adjusted the Texas boundary by having the state relinquish the Rio Grande for a payment of ten million dollars. He implored the Senate to enact these three bills, a plea he repeated on May 13.[97]

Clay's work was masterful in a way, a tribute to the classic political technique of reconciling diverse political interests without favoring any one of them to the extent of alienating the others. Southern Whigs found much to like in the plan, and Clay's proposal to deprive Texas of New Mexican land was meant to placate northern Whigs. In both of his speeches advocating acceptance of his report, he held out an olive branch to the Taylor administration by praising it for patriotically forming its own plan, one that had made sense in January, he said, but had now become outmoded by the welter of events.

The Taylor presidency was actually in no position to cavil over anything in Congress at just that moment. A scandal involving influence peddling within Taylor's cabinet led to a congressional investigation that tarnished the administration. "It is said that the President told the Cabinet that he liked them very much," Clay noted, "and they told him that they liked him very much, and so they agreed that they would not dissolve that union."[98] Even though the cabinet was exonerated of intentional wrongdoing, Taylor nevertheless lost the initiative in the compromise debates, leaving control of events to Henry Clay.

Taylor's intention to veto anything that included concessions for California's admission seemingly doomed Clay's efforts, though, and the Great Compromiser decided enough was enough. He appeared before the Senate on May 21 to deliver a response to the administration's obstruction and Zachary Taylor's obtuseness. Most accounts of Clay's May 21 speech describe it as a blistering denunciation of Taylor that surprised Whigs at first and then left them mildly angry because it seemed as though Clay did not care if he destroyed the party.[99] Yet the transcript of Clay's remarks does not warrant the venom that would be directed at him in the columns of the administration press. Clay was forceful but not vicious, and he was well into his remarks by the time he began parsing Taylor's plan, a task he described as a "painful duty." Clay said, "Let us here, and not in the columns of newspapers, have a fair, full, and manly interchange of argument and opinion."[100] More memorable than anything Clay said about Taylor, though, was his characterization of the stalled crisis over California, Texas, territorial organization, D.C. slave markets, and fugitive slaves as "five bleeding wounds" that would cause the death of the country if left untended. Taylor's shortsighted plan only partially treated one of these hemorrhaging problems, leaving the others to do their harm.[101]

Clay knew at last that trying to woo northern Whigs away from the president was a futile task, and he moved closer to a greater reliance on northern Democrats along with a smattering of procompromise Whigs to push through the Omnibus, if it were possible to enact it at all. Success appeared unlikely. Nothing had advanced a particle from the situation as it had existed in December, and the stalemate continued into June with Clay exhibiting diminishing patience and increasing anxiety. Friends and foes of his plan meanwhile quarreled day in and day out, tweaking his proposals with amendments, amending those amendments, adjusting changes with provisos, scrambling with stipulations to seize slight advantages. Meanwhile, Rome burned.[102]

Most depressing for Clay was a determined southern effort to extend slavery into the New Mexico and Utah territories. Southerners also adjusted his recommended Texas borders to give the Lone Star State more land, and lobbyists for Texas bondholders plied Congress to enhance the payout. These actions hurt the proposal by eroding its already reluctant northern support. The only cheerful news in an otherwise dreary June was that the radical plan to mount a secession movement had suffered a setback when the menacing Nashville convention sputtered to a tame conclusion. Yet any relief that that development afforded was soon dimmed by alarming news from Texas and New Mexico, where mounting Texas anger over the border and the presence of federal troops in Santa Fe moved the region closer to armed conflict. Indeed, as Congress drowned in words and floundered in parliamentary maneuver, the country confronted the sobering potential for civil war to break out in the arid Southwest. If many southerners were to be believed, it would spread eastward as Dixie drew daggers to defend the section's property and honor.

As alarming as the prospect was, it left Taylor unmoved and unfazed. Southern Whigs trooped into the White House to warn him of dire consequences, but such visits just left him more irritated and inflexible. When the Georgian George W. Crawford refused as secretary of war to sign orders sending additional troops to New Mexico, fearing it was striking a flint at a powder keg, Taylor reportedly said he would sign the orders himself. If Taylor sent additional soldiers to Santa Fe, Alexander Stephens declared after a stormy final interview, he would personally begin impeachment proceedings in the House.

Clay's count of votes for the compromise left him discouraged. The plan would fail unless he could muster more votes, especially with defections on the rise, the most disappointing one being that of Georgian John Berrien. Clay anxiously urged Willie Mangum to rush from North Carolina for the final contest at the end of the July.[103] Meanwhile, he kept up a façade of calm confidence. On the day before the Fourth of July recess, John Bell said Clay's refusal to meet Taylor halfway was "an exercise of his moral despotism" and cried out in exasperation to ask if "Mahomet will go to the mountain, or the mountain shall come to Mahomet." Clay spoke up: "I only wanted the mountain to let me alone." The Senate and galleries laughed.[104]

And there matters teetered as Washington sweltered. Zachary Taylor performed ceremonial duties of his office on an exceedingly hot and muggy Fourth. The event at the partially finished obelisk that would become the Washington Monument dragged on for hours under a blazing sun, and Taylor was parched and light-headed when he returned to the White House. He downed several glasses of iced milk and devoured bowls of fruits and vegetables. By that evening he was feeling poorly, his stomach cramping, and though he was intermittently at his desk during the next two days, the cramps and diarrhea drove him to his sickbed for good on July 7. The doctors then were able to work with a will at the business of killing him with cures. They dosed him with quinine and calomel, the latter a medicine laced with mercury, which might have been marginally effective for "cholera morbus," which the doctors had diagnosed. But it was lethal in treating gastroenteritis, which Taylor likely had. On June 9, he died. Just like the first Whig president nine years earlier, the second one died in office.[105]

Millard Fillmore became president amid a grave crisis. The new president could match anyone as to humble origins, for his youth was framed in want, hard men, and harder circumstances, exploited by an apprenticeship that worked him like a dog at the hands of masters intent upon keeping him ignorant and dependent. He rose above it with almost superhuman resolve to acquire an education in the law and to establish himself in politics, first in New York and then in Washington, gaining a reputation as a reliable worker and an unquestionably honest man. Along the way he acquired habits and manners that would have made him celebrated for sophistication had he not been so resolutely self-effacing. His manner in fact convinced many that he was a plodding, timid intellect, but not everyone fell into the trap of thinking simplicity equated with simpleness. Clay did not.[106]

Although retrospective accounts would claim that Fillmore's clear support for compromise immediately calmed the tense situation, actually nobody at the time was certain where the new president stood on the compromise. Fillmore knew that the country was in trouble and that the government stood amid a dozen deadly snares, each easily triggered by the slightest misstep. Clay at least thought the compromise had a much better chance of passage without the threat of a presidential veto hobbling it.[107] Fillmore moved deliberately, beginning with the formation of a new cabinet, correcting Taylor's bungling by making selections in consultation with Webster and Clay, with whom he established "intimate and confidential" relations.[108] Webster replaced John Clayton at the State Department with Clay's blessing. Fillmore very much wanted Crittenden for attorney general, but tapping him was a touchy business lest his estrangement from Clay spill over to the new administration. Clay, however, assured Fillmore that he would not mind seeing Crittenden go into the cabinet. Taking Clay's gracious gesture as an opening, mutual friends tried to reconcile him and Crittenden and restore "the pleasant days of old," but the effort failed.[109]

Fillmore reckoned the rising tensions in Texas and New Mexico as the most urgent crisis. A deadline of sorts prodded the administration to immediate action because a special session of the Texas legislature was scheduled for August 12 and everyone expected it to be belligerent, possibly even to act impulsively. In the latter part of July, Webster came out strongly in support of the Omnibus Bill with the clear intimation that Fillmore would sign it into law, and the Senate went into frenzied contortions to end its extended stalemate. On July 22, Clay delivered to the Senate what turned out to be his last major address in the national legislature. He was exhausted but spoke at considerable length, and fatigue with spontaneity resulted in a wandering speech that nevertheless flashed with passionate eloquence. When James Mason tried to interrupt him, Clay hurled back a thunderous verbal assault that brought the galleries to their feet. He scoffed at the prospect of a Southern Confederacy: "I say in my place never! Never! NEVER will we who occupy the broad waters of the Mississippi and its tributaries consent that any foreign flag shall float . . . upon the turrets of the Crescent City—never—never!" And he minced no words in condemning disunionists as traitors who deserved the fate of traitors. The galleries again exploded into such whistling, stamping, raucous cheers, and applause that David Rice Atchison nearly snapped his gavel and went hoarse repeatedly shouting *"Order!"* at the wall of noise.[110]

In the wake of Clay's speech, a baffling maze of attempts to tack on amendments and counteramendments to the Texas boundary adjustment consumed day after day. Clay's report had established that boundary on May 8, and it had gradually emerged as the principal stumbling block. All efforts to adjust it had failed, and it had remained unchanged for almost three months, until July 30.

On that day, Maine's James Bradbury, a Democrat, came up with the idea of postponing the decision about the border by authorizing a commission of Texans and federal officials to hammer out a resolution. Putting off the thorny problem would allow the rest of the compromise to become law. Bradbury's modification set off another dispiriting flood of amendments seeking to adjust it, but it was Georgia's William Dawson, a Whig, who successfully proposed that the New Mexico Territory not include the region east of the Rio Grande claimed by Texas until the commission fixed a boundary. Dawson's narrowly approved proviso was immediately and correctly perceived as a way to give Texas de facto authority over the disputed area, a backdoor way of making it more difficult to establish a border favorable to New Mexico. The fact that only one northern Whig supported Dawson's amendment revealed a surprising level of discontent and united sectional opposition.[111]

For weeks, Omnibus opponents from both North and South had been buoyant, confident that the bill would never be steered safely through the rocky shoals of Taylor's threatened veto and the clashing sectional currents of proslavery and antislavery.[112] Yet by the last day of July, these same men had become quite gloomy. Clay's adroit parliamentary skills, his tireless labors, his cajoling and coaxing, all seemed likely to accomplish the impossible: almost everyone suspected that he finally had the votes for Senate approval of the Omnibus. Clay himself was not absolutely certain of success, but he had reason to be more positive than at any time in the previous two months. As the Senate took up the legislation on July 31, though, Maryland Whig James A. Pearce gained the floor and objected to Dawson's proviso. Leaving Texas in control of the disputed region, he said, was clearly prejudicial to any claim New Mexico could subsequently lodge, and he moved to strike the portions that established the New Mexico Territory from the bill.[113]

Clay was stunned. Pearce had been on board for this compromise solution ever since Clay had reported it on May 8, and it was unthinkable that he could not have understood how fragile and precarious a structure it was. As with a house of cards, removing any one of them would collapse the whole. Some have suggested that Pearce was doing Fillmore's bidding, that the president and the Marylander had concocted this strategy with the aim of mollifying northern Whigs.[114] Pearce intended to remove New Mexico, thinking that he could quickly cleanse it of Dawson's distasteful amendment and then just as quickly reinsert New Mexico with no harm done and in fact everything much improved.

He was, of course, dead wrong, as Clay knew all too well. Opponents were all too willing—eager, in fact—to remove New Mexico from the bill, a move that put settling the Texas boundary in jeopardy. Now Clay's foes from both North and South saw their opening and lunged at it. Florida Democrat David Yulee led the successful effort to remove all provisions relating to Texas as well, an excision that knocked out every brace of support shoring up grudging southern acceptance of California's admission. Consequently, provisions relating to California were removed too, the final nudge to the rapidly collapsing house of cards that represented six months of grueling labor. All of Clay's bargaining, negotiating, conceding, maneuvering—all was shattered in the space of minutes. Clay and his supporters sat as if poleaxed while the Omnibus collapsed. As the roll calls progressed, Clay finally could stand it no longer. He slowly rose and pulled his withered frame down the aisle and out of the chamber. He looked a hundred years old. When it was over, his followers sat staring into the distance as their triumphant foes broke into strident celebrations, dancing in the Senate's aisles, slapping backs, and laughing wildly as if they were as smashed as Clay's work. Seward, more roosterlike than ever, almost crowed. They had beaten the man Benton acknowledged was one of the "best skilled parliamentarians . . . in America or Europe."[115]

All that remained of the Omnibus was the Utah Territorial Bill, which easily passed 31 to 18 on the following day. When the news was reported to the House of Representatives, it was greeted with loud, derisory laughter.[116]

Clay was mentally and physically exhausted. With Washington bathed in steaming temperatures, he came back into the Senate on August 1, primarily to vent his rage at a defensive James Pearce for ruining his work.[117] The discharge left Clay spent, and his heart and soul were drained, useless for any more toil on this thankless, futile task. He left the capital for the cooler ocean breezes of Newport. The Union remained in peril, but for the first time in his life, Henry Clay was too tired to care.

CHAPTER SIXTEEN

"The Best & Almost Only True Friend"

CLAY LEFT WASHINGTON on August 5 and that evening arrived in Philadelphia, where citizens "shouted him, hurrahed him, and made him address the multitude, sorely against his inclination."[1] Two days later he was on his way to Newport via steamboat. A large, cheering crowd greeted his arrival in New York City, and as he tried to board the *Empire State* at Pier 3, authorities had to control the surging multitude before he could reach his stateroom. Late that night, he arrived in Newport, and the next day he was honored at a reception in Bellevue House. The journey had the look of a triumphal tour. Clearly nobody blamed Clay for the failure of the Omnibus. "Clay has come out more nobly than ever," Robert C. Winthrop, who had filled Webster's Senate seat, observed, "and has evidently proved that his courage is of the sort that mounts with the occasion."[2]

Because Clay remained in Newport for most of August, it was easy to conclude that he had nothing to do with the ultimate success of the Compromise of 1850.[3] True enough, during Clay's absence from Washington, Democrats led by Stephen A. Douglas broke the Omnibus into its separate parts and relied on shifting majorities to pass the individual bills.[4] And it was also true that the bills Clay cobbled together during the spring and early summer had already been formulated by Douglas's Committee on Territories. In addition, by making the passage of one dependent on the passage of all, Clay had simply adopted Foote's plan. He abandoned his earlier insistence on Mexican law and agreed to popular sovereignty, a Democrat prescription for nonintervention. Taken in sum, such an evaluation reduces Clay's role to a secondary one at best; and considering the apparent mistake of pushing the Omnibus, which failed, rather than pursuing Douglas's successful strategy of securing its components' individual passage, Clay actually posed an obstacle to resolving the crisis. From that perspective, Clay failed to grasp the situation because he was too old or too ambitious or too egotistical or too out of touch. Worse, he was too stubborn to admit it.[5]

But all such criticisms stem from hindsight and treat the tactics that were ultimately successful as part of an obvious strategy. Those criticisms ignore the paralysis that greeted Douglas's initial attempts to bring his bills to a vote in the previous Congress. They ignore the passions that turned debates into shouting matches, impeded the election of a Speaker, and increasingly isolated the president from his own party. When Clay visited Webster and then introduced his resolutions at the start of 1850, Congress was adrift. Clay gave it direction. For the next six months, his speeches on the floor and his careful maneuvers between hostile camps and seemingly irreconcilable factions kept the idea of compromise alive during dark days that saw an elder statesman's death, a pistol drawn in the Senate chamber, and a dagger pointed at the heart of the Union. Clay's Omnibus failed, but Clay's idea of compromise did not. He was persuasive in ways that others could never match.

An incident in New York illustrated the unique power of his personality. The celebrated Mathew Brady asked him to sit for a photograph. Clay found this new, fascinating method of portraiture so much more convenient than tediously posing for a painter that he readily agreed. But he was in a hurry, and special arrangements had to be made to accommodate his schedule. The sitting was to take place during a break at a public reception in City Hall. The chief of police gained permission to tack up curtains in the Governor's Room, and the photographer set up his bulky camera. Because he was about to receive a delegation of ladies, Clay was well dressed in a satin stock and standing collar, and he was pleased that the room was quiet, for the corridors were packed with noisy crowds. Just as he prepared to pose, however, a throng of officials bustled into the room for their lunch break. The hubbub that arose when they spotted the famous visitor created a distraction sure to ruin the photograph. Suddenly, Clay raised his hand. The room immediately fell silent. He then rested his clasped hands in his lap and stared into the camera's uncovered lens. The seconds ticked by as the crowd remained perfectly still. As soon as the lens was covered and Clay stood, everyone broke into prolonged applause, a tribute to the man who could command instant silence with a wave of his hand.[6]

The people of Clay's time knew the truth of it back then. When news of the breakthrough on the compromise reached Newport, it only increased his celebrity. He attracted crowds on the beach when he ventured into the surf, and his walks on the resort's streets were met with spontaneous applause peppered with shouted hurrahs. He came back to Washington on August 27 to an enthusiastic greeting from fellow senators.[7] Stephen Douglas perceived what had happened through a partisan lens. "I must say," he noted, "that if Mr Clays name had not been associated with the Bills they would have passed long ago." He thought that Taylor had been jealous of Clay and that some Democrats did not want Clay to receive credit for the compromise. A contrasting figure in every way physically, Douglas stood almost a foot shorter than the old man; he was swarthy to Clay's gray pallor, and stout to Clay's slimness. Douglas was already "the Little Giant" to supporters, and his ego could match any man's, including Henry Clay's. But he gave the Whig devil his due: "let it always be said of old Hal that he fought a glorious and patriotic battle. No man was ever governed by higher & purer motives."[8]

Everyone's vision was limited in the gathering night of America's struggle over slavery. The compromise that passed in 1850 was deeply flawed in many ways. It did not accomplish a single one of its objectives except for admitting a free California. Slaves continued to be bought and sold in the capital because of loopholes. The complicated $10 million payoff to Texas to adjust the New Mexican border was never delivered to the state in a meaningful way. New Mexico and Utah's organization under popular sovereignty did not benefit the South. And the Fugitive Slave Law proved impossible to enforce as northern states thwarted it with personal liberty laws.

Just how blind the politicians of 1850 were to the real mood of the North was made most apparent by the Fugitive Slave Law. They had never thought it was anything more than a sop to southern extremists. The law, however, became the compromise's linchpin as southerners insisted that its enforcement was crucial to their continuance in the Union. Northern objections to it consequently raised anew the specter of southern secession, and Clay joined others in signing a congressional petition calling for its enforcement, in itself a gesture that highlighted the law's futility.[9] Any sense of political finality for this overarching moral controversy was illusory. Stephen Douglas informed the Senate just before Christmas that he had "determined never to make another speech on the slavery question," as though ignoring it would quiet the clamor. Such an attitude raised the question of just who was really blind to reality as the American dream gradually edged toward nightmare.[10]

By the time the Little Giant uttered his absurd statement, Clay had gone home. He had been heartened during the summer to hear that Lucretia was healthy and "enjoying more of society than she had been accustomed to."[11] He was eager to see her. When he arrived in Lexington on October 22, a large crowd escorted him to the Phoenix Hotel. What had once been Postlethwaite's Tavern was the site of many triumphant returns to Kentucky for Clay over the years, and the assembled citizens intended to make it yet another in gratitude for Clay's saving the country. His speech was brief, though, and after he assured the gathering that the Union was safe, he cut short his remarks. He stretched his hand toward Ashland. "But there lives an old lady about a mile and a half from here," he said, "whom I would rather see than any of you."[12]

Everyone laughed. Henry Clay was not joking.

CLAY WAS VERY proud of James, although his son's diplomatic mission to Portugal had ended in failure. Taylor's secretary of state, John Clayton, had sent the young man on the impossible errand of resolving a quarrel with the Portuguese that had been in dispute since the War of 1812. The disagreement had perplexed more experienced men than James, and Clay fretted, when he was not popping vest buttons with pride, hopeful that James had at last found his way. He hovered too, admonishing James to master French and scrutinizing his dispatches, which Clayton obligingly made available. Clay corrected their grammar and recommended that James soften their tone. Susan was receptive to the advice, even enrolling herself and the children in the French lessons along with James and dutifully reporting on everyone's progress. But James soon bristled. He was trying very hard to follow Clayton's instructions and live up to his father's expectations, but he found the Portuguese rude and dismissive. He thought that Clayton was behaving "as though cracked or drunk" and that his father was meddling—which he was, even covertly negotiating with the Portuguese consul general in Washington and asking British minister Henry Bulwer to lend assistance as well.[13]

Clayton had told James to take a threatening tone in order to break the deadlock with the Portuguese, and by the spring of 1850 a naval vessel was on the way to Lisbon to collect him. His instructions were to demand a final answer and if disappointed to ask for his passport.[14] All of this was unfolding as Clay labored to maintain good relations with the Taylor administration while preparing his committee's compromise report, and some have suggested that only after it was apparent that James's mission had failed did Clay break with the administration. There is, however, no evidence for this conclusion, and the concurrence of the two events was apparently coincidental.[15]

James was defensive about how things had played out in Lisbon. By the time Taylor died and Webster replaced Clayton at State, James and his family were heading home by way of London. Fillmore and Webster had nothing but praise for him, and Clay tried to help bring about a successful close of the Portuguese claims that could include James, even considering the possibility of his son's negotiating an agreement upon his return to Washington. Despite the peculiarity of someone other than the secretary of state concluding a diplomatic convention on American soil, Webster was not opposed to the idea, though Clay insisted that both his and James's wishes should be "entirely subordinate to convenience, and the public interest."[16] Time and distance thwarted Clay's plan and Webster's gesture, however, and James was not back in time to participate in the resolution of the dispute.

Clay meant well, but his constant suggestions, guidance, and tendency to hover irritated James in Lisbon just as they had in Lexington. As his son returned to America, Clay tried to help yet again, this time by selling James's house and finding him a better place to live. He conducted the transaction with James's consent, but the sale of the house was bungled to James's financial disadvantage, and Clay could not find a suitable replacement. He considered selling Ashland to James, but timing and finances quashed those plans. James moved his family to Missouri in 1851, settling near St. Louis, where he reported to his father that Thomas Hart Benton was befriending him. The information mildly wounded Clay, the implication being that Benton was a more competent mentor, and he warned that unless James became a Benton supporter, the young man and Old Bullion would not long be friends.[17]

Possibly James wanted to wound his father, but in only months, the young man's real sentiments were revealed when it became apparent that Clay was dying. James wrote to his mother a heartfelt admission: "He has been to me the best of fathers, and in losing him, I shall also lose the best & almost only true friend I have ever had."[18]

AFTER HIS STRENUOUS labors of the previous month, Clay was so persistently ill in the fall of 1850 that he feared death was near.[19] The weeks at Newport had not restored him as before, and he returned to Ashland exhausted and worried. Little rest awaited him in the days that followed, for Kentucky intended to celebrate his role in the compromise. Even before he left Washington, Lexington was planning a barbecue, and Clay supplied a list of dignitaries as well as all the state's representatives and senators to invite.[20] On the appointed day, an enormous crowd gathered at the fairgrounds to listen to speeches and feast on succulent meats that had turned for hours over glowing pits.

When Clay arrived, a great cheer erupted, and everyone flocked to the stand to hear him, but it appeared that the weather was going to disappoint everyone as inky clouds darkened the scene. Lightning flashed and thunder rumbled louder as the storm let loose a downpour. Not a soul moved. They all stood in the drenching rain, staring at the speaker's stand, and when Clay finally mounted it, their cheers mingled with the booming thunder. Holding an umbrella over Clay, Governor Thomas Metcalfe stood uncovered, his long white hair tousled by wind and matted by rain. Clay tried to stop after fifteen minutes but gave in to cries of "Go on! Go on!" When he shouted, "If you can stand it, God knows that I can," the cheer that rose in response was so deafening it bested the thunder. And by the time Clay finished forty-five minutes later, the sun was out. As the crowd headed to the pulled pork, everyone realized that they had seen something remarkable and heard in that voice itself something memorable, regardless of its message or meaning. The message now was always the same: Union forever, the country saved by reason and conciliation, and both abolitionism and secession condemned.[21]

Great anticipation surrounded Clay's appearance before the Kentucky legislature on November 15. Almost a half century had passed since he first entered that body as a freshman legislator to begin his public career, and its invitation touched him as much as any tribute ever had. He spoke at length about the state of the country and expressed optimism that the cooperation between Democrats and Whigs in the recent crisis marked a trend rather than a temporary circumstance. The speech revealed profound changes in Clay's political sentiments about the place of party in the country's increasingly fragile scheme of things. He evinced little affection for the Whigs, and praised the Democrats for behaving with high patriotism in the recent crisis. He plainly announced that the moment the Whig Party took up abolitionism, he would cease to be affiliated with it. Alarmed by agitation over the Fugitive Slave Law, he believed that it could lead only to the creation of two parties, one for the Union and one against it. He would cast his lot with the Union Party.[22]

For his entire career, Clay had worked to earn the respect of his colleagues, but at the end of it, he was more interested in their affection. All ambition, he declared, all aspiration was in his past. "I want no place whatever," he said, and then paused. "I beg pardon, sir, there is one place only which I desire, and that is a warm place in your hearts."[23]

He finally had that wish granted, even among long-standing foes, at least for that afternoon. The members on the floor and the spectators in the galleries were on their feet applauding. Women wept. Men did too.

CLAY RETURNED TO Washington at the end of 1850 in time to attend Jenny Lind's capital concert on December 16. The renowned "Swedish Nightingale" had charmed audiences in the Northeast. Her tour was sponsored by the tireless promoter and occasional humbug artist Phineas T. Barnum, but everything about Miss Lind was genuine, especially her talent. Clay sat with Webster at the performance, and though Webster afterward met the singer with an elaborate show of gallantry, it was Clay she wanted to see. She arranged to hear him argue a case before the Supreme Court and found his voice in speech as captivating as the world found hers in song. Clay called on her to pay his respects, and the newspapers delighted in the fact that the celebrities had been in the same room, a mutual admiration society of two.[24]

Within weeks of his return, though, these happy scenes gave way to increasing concerns about his declining health. The "perpetual cold" had become more than an irritation. It was alarming. He coughed all the time, suffering especially violent fits at night. "Expectoration is tough and difficult," he complained, "and what distresses me is that Nature seems less & less competent to carry them off, or to resist them."[25] Then an incident in the Senate suggested that impaired respiratory function was beginning to affect his mind. On February 11, a bill to help states care for the indigent insane was under discussion. The proposal was to grant a portion of the public lands to fund asylums. Clay praised the benevolent purpose but was concerned, he said, about placing so much of the public domain in the hands of one person. The remark caused everyone to pause, first in bewilderment and then in uncomfortable embarrassment. Either Clay had not read the bill or he had misunderstood its details. James Pearce patiently explained that the states, not a cabinet secretary, would be responsible for the grants, and Clay fumbled over a confession that he had not studied the matter carefully and would like to do so. It was more than awkward. For one thing, everyone knew about Theodore. And for another, it was obvious that Clay had slipped a mental cog over the simplest of proposals.[26]

Clay was also more impatient with adversaries about petty as well as significant matters. Regarding the latter, it became increasingly apparent to him that sustaining the Fugitive Slave Law was crucial to harmony in the Union, and he was irritated by those who treated southern anger about the issue casually. When New England caviled over the law, and it was suggested in the Senate that its modification or even its repeal should be debated, he exploded. Congress had debated and deliberated and decided this question just months before, he cried, and it was absurd to reopen it now under the threat of violent resistance to the law's enforcement.[27] He was just as vehement in his denunciation of southern hotheads. "Secession is treason," he said plainly. It should not, could not, be tolerated. He was adamant that if South Carolina seceded for any reason, the state should be quickly brought to heel. Only through such decisive action could the country survive.[28]

Colleagues who had noticed Clay's worsening health finally approached him. George W. Jones of Iowa later claimed to have suggested a trip to Cuba to relieve Clay's respiratory symptoms, but Clay had tried to go to Cuba five years earlier, possibly when he detected the first signs of tuberculosis, to follow close upon the example of his consumptive grandson Martin Duralde. That trip had not worked out, and it is evidence of Clay's growing alarm over his condition that he resolved to visit Cuba now, if for no other reason than to go home by way of the Caribbean and avoid mountains and rivers in a raw March. It would delay his return to Lucretia at Ashland, but that could not be helped.[29]

As February gave way to March, though, Fillmore called an extra session of the Senate to confirm his appointments and attend to other executive matters. Clay expected that the boat bound for Cuba would leave New York before adjournment. "It is perhaps of not much importance," he concluded, "as in any event, I cannot live a great deal longer."[30] He and his servant, James Marshall, took the trouble to acquire a passport, though, in those days simply a letter describing its bearer and including an official signature. Clay was thus marked as seventy-three years old, six feet tall, with a "high" forehead, blue eyes, a large nose, a wide mouth, his hair "grey," his complexion "fair." Secretary of State Daniel Webster signed the document.[31]

Clay hurried to New York and was happy to discover that the Cuba packet had not yet steamed after all. Following a farewell dinner and a ball at the recently rebuilt Niblo's Garden near Prince Street on Broadway, he left on the *Georgia* to arrive in Havana on March 17. The next day he wrote to Lucretia, "I have not yet seen much of this island, but enough to see that it is different from any thing I had ever before seen," and for the next three weeks, he enjoyed himself as much as his health would allow and saw as much as his waning stamina permitted.[32]

But the Cuban sojourn did him little physical good and, if anything, made him the worse for wear. When he arrived in New Orleans from Havana on April 5, he went into virtual seclusion at William Mercer's house on Canal Street. He declined to attend a public meeting in his honor, and friends had to disperse a crowd that gathered outside Mercer's expecting Clay to speak. On April 11, he left for Louisville, "very anxious once more to be at home," and arrived at Ashland on April 20, exhausted. "I think I shall not be tempted to leave it again," he said. At least the journey had been inexpensive. Clay had reached such a level of fame that people no longer let him pay for things.[33] In fact, when he looked into purchasing a cemetery plot that spring, John Lutz, the mathematics professor at Transylvania University who laid out Lexington Cemetery, arranged to assign him lots 37, 38, 54, and 55 in Section I. Lutz would take no money. They were a gift.[34]

In the weeks that followed, the simplest exertions, even writing letters, fatigued him.[35] On May 9, he began a letter to James but could manage only a few lines before putting down his pen and resorting to dictation. He always complained now about the debilitating cough. His physician, Benjamin W. Dudley, was either incompetent or an artful liar, for he told Clay that the cough was the result of a digestive disorder and that his lungs were not affected. "Be that as it may," Clay said, "I must get rid of the cough or it will dispose of me."[36]

Lucretia and John encouraged him to go on little outings, thinking that the time on horseback would be good exercise, and though the trips tired him, he did as they wished. Old memories beckoned, and he fought back weariness to visit nearby places he held in fond recollection. In May he returned to Peyton Short's old home, "Greenfield," where years earlier he and Short had regularly talked into the wee hours over libations after spending the day in the Versailles court. Short had been dead for a quarter century, and Clay found nothing of Greenfield remaining from the old days. He was unsentimental about such things and rejected the idea of properties becoming shrines to dead former owners.[37]

In the second week of July, Clay made arrangements to dispose of his property as he drafted his last will and testament. In addition to arranging for the gradual emancipation of his slaves, he provided for the distribution of his possessions and the care of his family. He left almost everything to Lucretia and instructed that her wants as well as needs were to be fulfilled, either at Ashland or elsewhere, at her wish. He was generous with his sons as well as the grandchildren. He gave to his son "the Mansfield house" that he had built for Thomas and Mary and forgave his considerable debts while leaving him $5,000. He gave John two hundred prime acres of Ashland, an interest in the horses, and several slaves. He provided for Theodore's maintenance with $600 per year, and stipulated that if Theodore ever recovered his senses, he was to receive $10,000 from the sale of Ashland after Lucretia's death. He set up a trust for Thomas and James, and bequeathed $7,500 to the Erwin children and an equal amount to Henry Jr.'s children. He distributed small but important mementoes: a pin containing a lock of Henry Jr.'s hair went to Henry III, William Mercer was to receive a snuffbox that had belonged to Peter the Great, a ring containing the famous splinter from George Washington's coffin went to a friend, and Lucy would be given a gold and diamond ring.[38]

Accomplishing the task marked an important admission, but he had always been careful to keep his affairs tidy. With the will drafted and his burial place settled, everything at last seemed in order. Yet that fall, Clay thought of something else. He had his mother's body moved from Woodford County, where she had been buried since her death in 1829. Her new grave was one of the gift lots, 38 in Section I, in Lexington Cemetery, and Clay had a marker erected that paid "tribute to her many domestic virtues," a gesture "prompted by the filial affection and veneration of one of her grateful sons—H. Clay."[39]

Friends surveyed the political landscape of the upcoming presidential election and talked of another Clay candidacy, but he was frank and resolute. He was old, he said, and he now freely admitted that his health was quite bad. Not only was the matter simply out of the question, the prospect held no appeal for him. He was certain it would be the Democrats' year, and he preferred Lewis Cass over Buchanan, who was neither honest nor sincere, in Clay's opinion. Webster was in the running for the Whigs, of course, but Winfield Scott seemed the favorite, another military man, and Clay preferred Cass over Scott as well.[40] He would never run again, Clay said, making clear at last that he really meant it. "I have not time, nor is it of any consequence," he wearily told one unflagging supporter, "to enter into a consideration of what has brought me to this conclusion."[41]

Clay informed his old friend William Mercer that he was trying "all the old womens [*sic*] remedies," but he was realistic. "My feelings indicate that the machine is nearly worn out," he said, "and that not one screw but several are out of place." Consumption still carried a stigma, and Clay was careful to say that his lungs were sound, but anyone who heard his cough and breathless wheezing had to doubt that. His enjoyments had fallen away one by one, his appetites were mainly memories, and his ties to life were all but broken. Neither he nor his friends could doubt that he had only a few more months. They indulged his little fictions.[42]

The horseback rides came to a stop, another of his pleasures passing away. James was sorry "to hear that Pa has got no better," for he had hoped that riding would improve things.[43] As fall came and October passed, the routines of the farm and household continued apace. The weather stayed warm enough to delay hog killing and required Ashland to buy extra bacon. Mary Watkins, Clay's niece by his half brother John, arrived for an extended visit, but despite the bustle of the impending harvest and the cheerful company in the house, he grew restless. He had forced himself to be sensible, but something in the air, something in the smell of autumn compelled him to defy the dwindling days and lengthening shadows. "My political life is ended," he conceded, "but I wish once more, and for the last time, to visit Washington." He weighed his time in that warm autumn and wondered, *How long?* "I hesitate," he said, "for I do not like to go there to be *brought* back!"[44]

Finally he decided to risk it, a decision that prompted criticism then and since for the seeming desertion of his aged wife during what he must have known were his final days. Soon after Clay's departure, Susan worried about her mother-in-law and wistfully contemplated her as lonely and neglected by her children. "They will never fully appreciate her goodness," she confided to her sister-in-law Mary. At least, not until her kind heart stopped and finally revealed, in absence, the great void it had filled for all of them. Susan paused over the possibility of vexing Thomas, but she spoke her mind anyway: all of the boys had always been *"spoiled children."*[45]

Although later observers would attribute his return to Washington to unstinting egotism, unabated ambition, and a desire to die on the national stage in order to become the center of the spectacle sure to ensue, nobody in the family seems to have objected to Clay's decision to leave Ashland that last November of his life. "We all ought to try and make him as happy as we can" was James's sentiment, one shared by everyone close to Henry Clay.[46] In addition, he was still a member of the Senate and wished "to exert any possible usefulness left to him."[47] He also had a commission to argue cases before the Supreme Court in the January 1852 session, a task that could fatten the estate's coffers with handsome fees.

Clay left Ashland on November 15 accompanied by a slave (possibly a servant) named Thornton, whom Clay sent home after boarding the *Allegheny Belle* at Maysville. As the sternwheeler churned toward Pittsburgh, Clay met a young New Yorker named Edwin Bryant who cheerfully took upon himself the task of looking after his famous but feeble traveling companion. Clay welcomed the help. Nothing ever dimmed his persistent faith in the goodness of people. He never ceased to believe that given the chance, people were inclined to behave decently.[48] Bryant was genuinely friendly, and a good thing that he was too, for Clay began coughing up a good deal of blood while vainly dosing himself with alum water. Clay reported his progress to Lucretia and aimed to put her at ease with the description of young Bryant as "very kind and attentive."[49] It was snowing on them as they rattled toward Maryland through the mountains, and a hard chill had settled in on the capital when they arrived there on November 23. Clay croaked his farewells to Bryant, who left for New York on his way to California, and settled into his old rooms at the National Hotel.[50]

On December 1, Clay limped into the Senate chamber, a shocking, frail ghost, and tried to participate in a dispute between Stephen Mallory and David Yulee about whose credentials were legitimate for Florida's Senate seat. Clay took Mallory's part in a short speech often interrupted by his racking cough, and he was near collapse when he finished. He made his way back to his rooms and wrote to Lucretia that he had attended the Senate, the beginning of his valiant but transparent effort to portray his circumstances in the best light possible.[51] It had not gone well at all, though. Clay fully intended to return to the Senate, but he never did. He blamed the blustery weather for keeping him in his rooms, and then he simply ceased mentioning the Senate altogether.[52]

Webster came to see him and was solicitous, taking special pains to praise James for his work in Portugal. President Fillmore sent an invitation for a private dinner at the White House, but Clay apologized that he was too weak to make the short trip up Pennsylvania Avenue. Fillmore refused to stand on ceremony. He came to see Clay right away and made a point of visiting him when he could, obviously a gesture of veneration but also because quiet, unassuming Millard Fillmore knew what it was like to be alone and cheerless.[53]

Clay's weight loss was now rapid and alarming. He had no appetite, and he confided that he very much regretted leaving Ashland. "My utmost wish," he said, "is to live to return."[54] To that end, he called in the best medical talent available. Dr. William W. Hall, a young specialist in throat and lung diseases, was soon joined by Dr. Samuel Jackson of Philadelphia, who observed Clay for two days. After poking, prodding, and consulting, they made their diagnosis, which Clay reported to Lucretia as acute bronchitis. Yet such a conclusion was highly unlikely, and Clay was evidently telling a soothing lie to his wife while keeping the grave confirmation of his actual illness to himself. Even years later, the Clay family would embrace this false information as fact, which attests to the continuing shame of tuberculosis as a presumed consequence of dissolute living. On the letter to Lucretia, someone (possibly Susan) later wrote, "it was bronchitis, not consumption."[55]

Clay knew much more than what he revealed to family at Ashland. On December 17, 1851, he resigned from the Senate effective the first Monday of September 1852.[56] Also, he told the artist John Neagle that his unsuccessful efforts to sell his full-length portrait of Clay to the Kentucky legislature would likely have a better prospect "when an event shall occur in regard to myself which cannot be very distant."[57]

Family in Kentucky knew he was gravely ill and were understandably worried. Thomas and Mary said they would come to Washington to look after him, but Clay continued to insist that it was unnecessary. He gave the same response to nearby friends, as when the novelist and Whig politician John P. Kennedy offered him a room in his home in Baltimore.[58]

CHRISTMAS AND NEW Year's came, and Clay planned to venture from his rooms for the first time in weeks. If he could argue at least two cases before the Supreme Court, he would receive his fees, but in the first week of January he was too ill to appear and had to secure the services of other lawyers, splitting the fees with them.[59]

Despite his fatigue, he agreed to meet the Hungarian separatist Louis Kossuth, who had come to the United States in an American frigate as an exile and commenced a tour to plead his country's case for independence from Austria. Regular Americans and government officials showered him with acclaim, treating him to banquets and turning out in droves to hear him speak. Kossuth was impressed by Clay's reputation as a champion of Latin American and Greek independence so many years before, and he seems to have been under the impression that Clay's influence could further his country's cause with Americans. He had been angling for an interview for weeks. The meeting finally took place in the early afternoon of January 9 in Clay's rooms. Clay was quite feeble, but he had dressed for the occasion and rose haltingly to greet his visitor, who arrived with an escort that included Lewis Cass and Thomas Ewing. Clay spoke admiringly of Kossuth and expressed sympathy with the troubles of his country, especially its victimization by Austrian oppression and Russian intervention, but he also insisted that neutrality was and always should be the bulwark of U.S. foreign policy.[60]

Clay was distressed by press accounts that described his health as rapidly failing and asserted "that one lung is almost entirely destroyed by rapidly progressing abscesses, and the other already gives indication of the incipient states of the disease."[61] He had explicitly stated to Lucretia and Mary that the family was not to believe newspaper reports about his condition, and in the wake of these latest stories, he took the time to write a fairly lengthy description of his circumstances with the best gloss he could manage. "If there be any change," he lied, "perhaps it is for the better."[62]

Meanwhile, a special tribute arranged by Whigs in New York helped alleviate winter's gloom. They were having a large gold medal cast in Clay's honor. Made from the purest California ore and mounted in a silver case, the medal featured his profile on its face and a list of his major accomplishments on its obverse. He was deeply touched and had provided the milestones: his first Speakership, the War of 1812, the Ghent peace, Missouri, the distribution of the public domain, preserving peace with France in 1835, and the Compromise of 1850.[63]

Clay wryly noted that he had nearly "emptied an apothecary's shop," but even a nightly opiate did not bring sleep. He spent his days in his rooms reading and occasionally answering letters, almost always now through dictation. When the cold abated a bit in February, he ventured out, but only a couple of times. Climbing the stairs to his upper-floor suite after a ride in a closed carriage so wore him out that he abandoned that pastime as well and thereafter never again left his rooms. In bed by eight, he did not rise until ten. His doctor came every day and streams of visitors appeared, but most were turned away. He could sit up only about seven hours a day.[64]

Clay hoped to gain enough strength to return to Ashland in late May or early June. When the time came, he planned to send for Thomas to accompany him. In late April, he told his son it would be best for him to leave for Washington in a few weeks.[65] In the days that followed, however, Clay's strength swiftly ebbed, and he became alarmed enough to amend his instructions to Thomas by telegram, a sure sign of urgency, calling for him to come as soon as he could.[66]

"I write to nobody in my hand writing, but to you," he told Lucretia. It must have taken him a long time to write this letter, for it was a laborious effort that produced his characteristically firm penmanship. The letter in its physical appearance gave no evidence that anything was wrong, but it was the last one he wrote to his wife of fifty-three years, a whispered promise that she alone at the end merited the immense effort of his pen touching paper, and in that respect it was a love letter.[67] At Ashland, as Thomas left for the capital, Lucretia retreated more into herself. She had to dismiss her gardener for drunkenness and did not replace him, as an economy, and Clay worried that she was overworking herself and scrimping on her needs.[68] James and Susan worried about her as well. "We wish you would make some one write to us occasionally about yourself," James entreated her from Missouri. "Months pass without our hearing of you & we think of you very often."[69]

When Thomas arrived in Washington on May 5, his father's appearance shocked him. The day before, Clay had experienced a crisis so serious that Senate chaplain Charles M. Butler had administered the sacrament of the Lord's Supper. Clay was extremely weak but alert enough to press his hands together in prayer and spread them in supplication. James Marshall was convinced that his employer was dying, but Butler's service seemed to revive him. Nonetheless, Thomas noted that his father was no longer merely gaunt but had become a wraith. He could speak for only a few minutes before the effort left him spent. The cough that had interrupted his sentences now disrupted words by the syllable. He no longer had the strength to walk and had to be carried from his bed to the couch in the parlor. Yet Thomas's arrival was a tonic, and for a few days Clay rallied. The opiates began to work, giving him a few comfortable nights, and Thomas even became cautiously optimistic. His father was "very feeble," he admitted, "but is not so much reduced in flesh as I had supposed before I came on here." Thomas added hopefully, "His lungs are not at all affected."[70]

Visitors continued to come to the National Hotel, but only a select few friends entered Room 32 in those dwindling days. There had been a few touching reconciliations. Francis Preston Blair had made his peace with Clay, and

along with Martin Van Buren he helped to smooth the progress of an understanding between Thomas Hart Benton and Clay. Van Buren sent Blair a portion
of Benton's memoir, *Thirty Years' View,* which discounted entirely the idea of
the Corrupt Bargain ever having occurred. The admission, coming after all these
years, was significant, and Blair told Clay about it "with the warm feelings of
earlier days." The long shadow finally lifted. "Mr. Clay was deeply moved," Van
Buren recalled.[71]

He was similarly touched by a gesture from Blair's wife, who had been
slower to forgive Clay for breaking with her husband so many years before,
even snubbing him on the floor of the Senate just months earlier. As the seriousness of his illness became apparent, Eliza Blair organized and led a circle of
ladies to keep him company and attend to his wants during the final days. The
soft voices and attentive care meant a lot to him, and Mrs. Blair's offer of a room
at her house on Pennsylvania Avenue where she could administer nonstop
"Kentucky nursing" made him cry.[72]

And then there was John J. Crittenden. For several years, friends had tried to
restore the good feelings of old, but the bitterness persisted. Clay suspected that
Crittenden had continued to block his patronage recommendations, and Kentucky factions attached to the two remained wary of each other. The previous
year, Washington hostess Julia Tayloe had invited Crittenden to dine with Clay
at her house by playfully quoting Shakespeare's *Two Gentlemen of Verona:* "Oh
Heaven! were man but constant, he were perfect; that one error Fills him with
faults." But the invitation came when Clay was already on his way to New York
to catch the packet to Cuba. Crittenden also might have noted what was surely
unintended irony in Mrs. Tayloe's dispatching her message on March 15, the
Ides.[73]

Thomas said that in the first week of that last June, his father asked to see
Crittenden. Their subsequent visit on June 6 presumably allowed them to settle
their differences, as just days later, Clay referred to Crittenden and himself as
"cordial friends." Thomas, however, noticed that Clay was "much depressed."
Yet his father also told him that everyone had been mistaken, that Crittenden
had not behaved dishonorably in 1848. Thomas said Clay implored him not to
hold anything against his old, newfound friend. There was certainly a visit—
Thomas was there to witness it—and evidence surfaced years later that suggested Clay had heard defenses of Crittenden and had mellowed about their
differences as early as 1850.[74] Yet James always doubted that his father ever forgave John J. Crittenden. After Clay's death, James arrived at Ashland to await
the arrival of the funeral party and found on Clay's desk a copy of the angry letter he had persuaded his father not to publish in 1848. Clay had apparently been

reviewing it just before leaving for Washington in November, suggesting to James that the wounds from Crittenden's betrayal had not healed and were in fact still fresh. Possibly both James and Thomas were correct: Clay might have been assessing this enormously important event of his life as he prepared for his journey. Yet once in Washington and aware of his rapidly approaching end, perhaps he decided it was pointless to leave the breach unmended. The former feeling would have been perfectly natural for any deeply wronged man, and the latter action would have been perfectly in character for Henry Clay.

When he found the letter at Ashland, James saw little point in its message. He burned it.[75]

BY THE TIME of Crittenden's visit, Thomas's optimism was ebbing. In only a few days, it vanished. Those allowed into the rooms found Henry Clay to be slowly disappearing, his deep voice reduced to a raspy whisper, the volume and violence of the cough terrifying. The entire city of Washington listened for news, expecting at any time to hear the worst. One of his congressional colleagues wrote to a friend that they all knew that Clay would die soon and lamented, "oh what a man will fall, when he falls," and observed that now that he was almost dead, "all men of all parties speak of him as 'the noblest Roman of them all.'"[76] Strangers continued to send him gifts or to bring them in person to leave at the hotel desk. These were often luscious treats for which he had no appetite. Yet it was truly the thought behind these presents that counted for Clay. He always said to Thomas when a new package arrived, "Was there ever a man who had such friends?" And he made certain that Thomas sent thank-you notes to everyone for even the slightest remembrance. "In the letter be kind," he instructed, "be very kind."[77]

The thermometer rose into the nineties, and the humidity rising from Washington's surrounding swamps made it seem even hotter. By mid-June, Clay was in a very bad way, profusely perspiring from the heat as well as his fever. His doctor rubbed him down from head to toe with brandy and alum. He pulled Thomas aside and told him that his father could not last much longer. "He now never gets out of bed," Thomas recorded in his diary.[78]

One of his last acts, and evidently the last document signed by Henry Clay, was to tie up a final loose end. James Marshall had given him a deed for a lot in Detroit as security for endorsing a note. Clay now noted that Marshall had paid everything he owed. He had overpaid, in fact, by two dollars. Clay wanted to make sure that the deed, which he had placed in a little trunk in Lucretia's room at Ashland, would be handed over to his servant, who as his companion had become his friend.[79]

The doctor tried to alleviate his patient's growing distress with larger doses of the opiate, and in late June, Clay began to hallucinate. He saw his mother. He saw Lucretia. "My dear wife," he murmured.[80] Finally he stopped eating altogether, and Thomas sadly noted that "taking even a single swallow of water is painful to him."[81]

On the morning of June 29, Clay asked James Marshall to shave him, but it was not long before something had clearly changed. James summoned Thomas. Clay looked up through watery eyes. "Sit near me, my dear son," he said. Thomas placed a chair next to the bed. "I do not wish you to leave me for any time today," his father whispered.

At ten o'clock, he asked Thomas for some cool water, but as he drank, his mind wandered. The silver tube he used for a straw remained dangling in his lips when the cup was taken away, and he had trouble swallowing. "I believe, my son, I am going," he mumbled. Thomas watched his father labor for breath. Clay whispered a request for Thomas to "button his shirt collar." He always liked things neat.

Thomas buttoned the collar, but as he withdrew his hand, Clay shakily grasped it and silently held it. Thomas sent for Senator James C. Jones, who had a room just above, and he soon joined Thomas and James at the bedside. Clay's eyes were closed, and his grip on Thomas's hand gradually relaxed. It was seventeen minutes past eleven.[82]

Before the clocks struck noon, Washington's church bells began to toll, a signal to the capital that it was over. The telegraph sent the news across the country, and soon the bells began to ring in cities and towns from the Atlantic coast to the deep interior. Thomas sent one of those first telegrams to Lexington: "My father is no more. He has passed without pain into eternity."[83] At Ashland, Lucretia received the hard news she had been expecting for months.

The bells in Lexington were already ringing.

Acknowledgments

WE ARE INDEBTED to countless people who helped us in our research to realize Henry Clay. The staffs of repositories across the country were often as enthusiastic as we were about our work and were unfailingly cheerful in assisting us to complete it, pointing us to undiscovered treasures and facilitating our investigation of them. We shrink from saying that Sarah Hartwell at Dartmouth's Rauner Special Collections Library or Christine M. Beauregard at the New York State Library or Eira Tansey at Tulane's Howard-Tilton Library is "typical" in any way, but they do exemplify the best of those who maintain the annals of the past and make them readily available to the people who try to understand that past. Eleanor Mills and Elizabeth Dunn at Duke University's Rare Book, Manuscript, and Special Collections Library, and Nelson Griffin and Matthew Turi at the Southern Historical Collection were more than accommodating during our visits. In fact, the kind people at all the archives we list in our bibliography have earned our respect and admiration, and on more than a few occasions have acted in a manner that could only be described as that of friends.

This was never more evident than at the Filson Historical Society in Louisville, Kentucky, where the Curator of Special Collections, James Holmberg, made sure that we had everything we needed, and an extraordinary group of people retrieved collections with such speed that during several days of labor we were never idle at our desks. Mike Veach not only found obscure items in a flash, he made flawless restaurant recommendations for both cuisine and soothing drink (what else but bourbon, naturally, of which Mike is a peerless connoisseur) that made our evenings restorative. Suzanne Maggard, Robin Wallace, and Sarah-Jane Poindexter were swift, thorough, and pleasant; and Jacob Lee took time from his chores calendaring important collections to advise us months after our departure about new and pertinent material he was running across. "Research" is not the term to describe working at the Filson: something more like "adventure framed in conviviality" comes closer to the mark.

Simply matchless as well are the extraordinary people at Ashland, the Henry Clay Estate, in Lexington. From our visit at the start of our labors through the conclusion of them, they have stood at our shoulders with encouraging words, indispensable advice, and a wealth of information, gently correcting our errors and making it possible for us to know Henry Clay as a husband, father, and friend in ways that would have certainly eluded us otherwise. While doing their outstanding and taxing work of presenting the home of the Clays to a grateful public, Anne Hagan-Michel, Eric Brooks, Sue Andrew, and Wendy Bright read our manuscript, in parts or in its entirety, sometimes repeatedly, and have been so generous with their time that our statement of thanks can be only a poor measure of our gratitude and an insufficient acknowledgment of our indebtedness. Wendy Bright allowed us to see her excellent master's thesis on Ashland just as it was being completed, and Sue Andrew provided a priceless trove of insights about Lucretia and the housekeeper Sarah Hall that would otherwise have remained tucked from our sight. Eric Brooks, the head curator at Ashland, served as liaison in correspondence that provided us with his and his colleagues' many suggestions and helpful queries, and he labored to make available for publication graphic materials ranging from portraits to photographs of artifacts. Some of the images that appear between these covers become accessible to a wide audience for the first time thanks to Eric Brooks. Though they are hardly special pleaders for their famous host, and indeed do not shrink from criticizing him when merited, we think that neither Henry Clay nor we ever had better friends. We also think that he would doubtless agree.

Many other friends have read the manuscript and have invariably found ways to improve it. We especially thank David Sckolnik, for our work on this biography likely would not have happened in his absence. Our agent, Geri Thoma, not only introduced us to the good people at Random House but also reviewed the work in progress, sometimes to give a gentle tug at the reins but mostly to hearten when we flagged and cheer when we could report progress. Jeanne's mother, Sarah, proved particularly strong-hearted in this regard, reading the manuscript and listening without complaint as we droned on about the minutiae of the early nineteenth century. At Random House, our editor, Jonathan Jao, first suggested we undertake this biography and upon its delivery applied a deft editorial hand with such surgical precision that virtually all of his recommendations have made it better. Emily DeHuff copyedited the manuscript with just the right mixture of insistence on proper forms and tolerance of our stylistic idiosyncrasies. We need not say, of course, that all slips of tongue and any errors of fact are our own, either because of our obstinacy about style or because it is inevitable that mistakes will mar any human endeavor.

Finally, our hats are off to the little lion who now forever sleeps, our constant companion through so much scribbling, so many books.

Notes

ABBREVIATIONS

AC	Annals of Congress
ADAH	Alabama Department of Archives and History
ASPFR	American State Papers, Foreign Relations
ASPMA	American State Papers, Military Affairs
Cong. Globe	Congressional Globe
Duke	Special Collections, Perkins Library, Duke University
Filson	Filson Historical Society
HCP	Papers of Henry Clay
LOC	Library of Congress
LOV	Library of Virginia
MHS	Maryland Historical Society
NYPL	New York Public Library
Reg. of Deb.	Register of Debates
SCHS	South Carolina Historical Society
UKY	Special Collections, University of Kentucky
UNC	Southern Historical Collection, University of North Carolina, Chapel Hill
UVA	Albert and Shirley Small Special Collections Library, University of Virginia, Charlottesville, Virginia
VHS	Virginia Historical Society
W&M	Swem Library, College of William and Mary

Prologue

1. Calvin Colton, editor, *The Private Correspondence of Henry Clay* (New York: A. S. Barnes, 1856), 636.

2. Executive Order, June 29, 1852, Henry Clay, *The Papers of Henry Clay,* 11 volumes, edited by James F. Hopkins, Mary W. M. Hargreaves, et al. (Lexington: University of Kentucky, 1959–1992), 10:968, hereafter cited as *HCP; Congressional Globe,* 46 volumes (Washington, DC: Blair & Rives, 1834–1873), 32 Cong., 1 sess., 1631; George Washington Ranck, *History of Lexington, Kentucky* (Cincinnati: Robert Clarke, 1872), 141; John Melish, *Travels Through the United States of America in the Years 1806 & 1807* (New York: Johnson Reprint, 1970), 213, 367; Marshall to Marshall, June 29, 1852, Bullitt Family Papers, Filson.

3. *Obituary Addresses on the Occasion of the Death of the Hon. Henry Clay, a Senator of the United States from the State of Kentucky, Delivered in the Senate and in the House of Representatives of the United States, June 30, 1852, and the Funeral Sermon of the Rev. C. M. Butler, Chaplain of the Senate, Preached in the Senate, July 1, 1852. Printed by Order of the Senate and House of Representatives* (Washington, DC: Robert Armstrong, 1852), 104. Hereafter cited as *Obituaries.*

4. Ibid., 9.

5. Ibid., 41, 48, 74, 76, 92. Seward had to swallow hard to say these words, because his attitude about emancipation clashed violently with Clay's insistence on gradualism. When abolitionists, Seward's wife included, objected to his kind words for Clay, Seward reminded her "how much of the misery of human life is derived from the indulgence of wrath!" Quoted in Doris Kearns Goodwin, *Team of Rivals: The Political Genius of Abraham Lincoln* (New York: Simon & Schuster, 2005), 153.

6. *Obituaries,* 107–8.

7. Ibid., 91, 101.

8. Ibid., 56.

9. Ibid., 23–28; see Allan Nevins, *Ordeal of the Union: Volume 1, Fruits of Manifest Destiny, 1847–1852* (New York: Charles Scribner's Sons, 1947), 279, for Hunter's devotion to Calhoun.

10. Blair to Martin Van Buren, July 4, 1852, Martin Van Buren Papers, LOC, microfilm edition.

11. *Obituaries,* 54, 115, 34.

12. *Cong. Globe,* 32 Cong., 1 sess., 1644.

13. Ibid., 1649.
14. *Obituaries,* 127.
15. Blair to Van Buren, July 4, 1852, Van Buren Papers.
16. Robert V. Remini, *Henry Clay: Statesman for the Union* (New York: W. W. Norton, 1991), 784. Embalming did not become customary until the 1860s.
17. Clay to Clay, June 29, 1852, Colton, *Private Correspondence,* 636. The quotation also appears with different punctuation in Thomas Hart Clay and Ellis Paxson Oberholtzer, *Henry Clay* (Philadelphia: George W. Jacobs, 1910), 379.
18. J. Thomas Scharf, *The Chronicle of Baltimore: Being a Complete History of "Baltimore Town" and Baltimore City from the Earliest Period to the Present Time* (Baltimore: Turnbull Brothers, 1874), 40.
19. *New York Times,* July 3, 1852. Some writers have confused the grand July 20 funeral in New York City with this more modest event. See, for example, Merrill D. Peterson, *The Great Triumvirate: Webster, Clay, and Calhoun* (New York: Oxford University Press, 1987), 488.
20. "Proclamation of the Special Committee of the Common Council," *New York Times,* July 3, 1852.
21. *New York Times,* July 7, 1852.
22. William H. Townshend, *Lincoln and the Bluegrass: Slavery and Civil War Kentucky* (Lexington: University Press of Kentucky, 1955), 202–3. For an example of the plans laid by other committees, see Committee of Citizens of Mercer County to Breckinridge, July 12, 1852, Robert J. Breckinridge Correspondence, Grigsby Collection, Filson.
23. Quoted from George M. Frederickson, "A Man but Not a Brother: Abraham Lincoln and Racial Equality," *Journal of Southern History* 41 (February 1975): 40. Carl Sandburg said Lincoln was disillusioned by what Sandburg described as Clay's selfish behavior that had helped injure the Whig Party and by his role in crafting the Compromise of 1850 and thus found it difficult to say laudatory things about Clay in a eulogy. See Sandburg, *Abraham Lincoln: The Prairie Years,* 2 volumes (New York: Harcourt, Brace & World, 1926), 420–22. Yet there is no evidence, other than Lincoln's support for Taylor in 1848—and that was for practical rather than principled reasons—to suggest that Lincoln was disenchanted with the man he had always tried and would continue to try to emulate. Sandburg probably relied on the diary of Gideon Welles for his conclusion, but Welles had acid views of his contemporaries, views secretly recorded in his diary while he himself seemed placid and benevolent.
24. Townshend, *Lincoln and the Bluegrass,*

132–35; Goodwin, *Team of Rivals,* 95. Townshend says that Mary had arranged a visit to Ashland for her husband in 1846, but other sources flatly deny Lincoln ever met Henry Clay, and Lincoln himself most tellingly never mentioned any such meeting, something he certainly would have done at some point in his life.
25. Roy P. Basler, *Abraham Lincoln: His Speeches and Writings* (Cleveland: World Publishing Company, 1946), 269.
26. Ibid., 269.
27. Elbridge Gerry, Jr., *The Diary of Elbridge Gerry, Jr.,* Preface and Footnotes by Claude G. Bowers (New York: Brentano's, 1927), 110–17.
28. *New York Times,* July 17, 1852.
29. Clay to Clay, July 11, 1852, Thomas J. Clay Collection, Henry Clay Papers, LOC.
30. *New York Times,* June 30, 1852; London *Times,* July 12, 1852.
31. Josiah Stoddard Johnston, Josiah Stoddard Johnston Diary, June 30, 1852, Filson.

CHAPTER ONE

The Slashes

1. *Register of Debates in Congress,* 14 volumes (Washington, DC: Gales and Seaton, 1824–1837), 23 Cong., 1 sess., 1481.
2. Bernard Mayo, *Henry Clay: Spokesman of the New West* (Boston: Houghton Mifflin, 1937), 6; Glyndon G. Van Deusen, *The Life of Henry Clay* (Boston: Little, Brown, 1937), 5; Clay and Oberholtzer, *Clay,* 16; "Genealogical Notes and Queries," *William and Mary College Quarterly Historical Magazine* 21 (January 1941): 61–62; Zachary F. Smith and Mary Rogers Clay, *The Clay Family* (Louisville, KY: J. P. Morton, 1983), 48.
3. Noah Webster is quoted in Stephanie Grauman Wolf, *As Various as Their Land: The Everyday Lives of Eighteenth-Century Americans* (New York: Harper Perennial, 1994), 257.
4. Smith and Clay, *Clay Family,* 6; Wesley M. Gewehr, *The Great Awakening in Virginia, 1740–1790* (Gloucester, MA: Peter Smith, 1965), 106; Clay and Oberholtzer, *Henry Clay,* 15. Specifically, John Clay founded the Chickahominy congregation over which he presided until his death in 1781 and the Black Creek congregation on the border between Hanover and Henrico counties. See Robert Baylor Semple, *A History of the Rise and Progress of the Baptists in Virginia* (Philadelphia: American Baptist Publication Society, 1894), 141, 145.
5. Rhys Isaac, *The Transformation of Virginia, 1740–1790* (Chapel Hill: University of North Carolina Press, 1982), 153–34, 162–65, 171, 174–75; Gewehr, *Great Awakening in Virginia,* 106, 108.

6. Mayo, *Clay*, 3–4; Isaac, *Transformation of Virginia*, 280; William Taylor Thom, *Struggle for Religious Freedom in Virginia: The Baptists* (Baltimore: Johns Hopkins University Press, 1900), 26.

7. Mayo, *Clay*, 4; Woody Holton, *Forced Founders: Indians, Debtors, Slaves, and the Making of the American Revolution in Virginia* (Chapel Hill: University of North Carolina Press, 1999), 147–48; Gewehr, *Great Awakening in Virginia*, 136; Thomas E. Buckley, *Church and State in Revolutionary Virginia, 1776–1787* (Charlottesville: University Press of Virginia, 1977), 38.

8. "Will of John Clay" in "Biographical and Genealogical Notes and Queries," *William and Mary College Quarterly Historical Magazine* 14 (April 1934): 174–75. The slave "Little Sam" appears to have been taken to Kentucky by Henry's mother and stepfather when they left Virginia in 1791. See Settlement of Accounts of Henry Watkins, October 27, 1797, *HCP* 1:1–2. Records do not indicate what happened to James. Perhaps he was one of the slaves taken by the British.

9. "Will of John Clay," 174.

10. Banastre Tarleton, *A History of the Campaigns of 1780 and 1781 in the Southern Provinces of North America* (New York: Arno Press, 1968), 294–95.

11. Smith and Clay, *Clay Family*, 15–19; Mayo, *Clay*, 5–6.

12. "Will of George Hudson, November 30, 1770," Smith and Clay, *Clay Family*, 8, 40, 54.

13. Wolf, *As Various as Their Land*, 162–66.

14. Mayo, *Clay*, 12–13; Calvin Colton, *The Life and Times of Henry Clay*, 2 volumes (New York: A. S. Barnes, 1846), 1:19.

15. Mayo, *Clay*, 14–16; Wolf, *As Various as Their Land*, 220–21.

16. Oscar Handlin and Mary Flug Handlin, *Facing Life: Youth and the Family in American History* (Boston: Little, Brown, 1971), 101.

17. *Reg. of Deb.*, 23 Cong., 1 sess., 1484; Van Deusen, *Clay*, 7; Mayo, *Clay*, 13–14; Colton, *Life and Times*, 1:19.

18. Wolf, *As Various as Their Land*, 132–36.

19. See "John Clay's Will"; Clay and Oberholtzer, *Clay*, 17; Epes Sargent, *The Life and Services of Henry Clay Brought Down to the Year 1844* (New York: Greeley & McElrath, 1844), 3; Smith and Clay, *Clay Family*, 43; Van Deusen, *Clay*, 9.

20. Horace Greeley and Robert Dale Owen, *The Autobiography of Horace Greeley, or Recollections of a Busy Life* (New York: E. B. Treat, 1872), 62.

21. Van Deusen, *Clay*, 423.

22. Mayo, *Clay*, 20; Albert J. Beveridge, *The Life of John Marshall*, 4 volumes (Boston: Houghton Mifflin, 1916), 1:190; François-Alexandre-Frédéric La Rochefoucauld–Liancourt, *Travels Through the United States of North America: The Country of the Iroquois, and Upper Canada, in the Years 1795, 1796, and 1797*, 4 volumes (London: R. Phillips, 1800), 3:60, 63–64.

23. Mayo, *Clay*, 20; Dumas Malone, *Jefferson and His Time*, 6 volumes (Boston: Little, Brown, 1948–1981), 3:89–91.

24. Colton, *Life and Times*, 1:20; Van Deusen, *Clay*, 10; Remini, *Clay*, 9.

25. Van Deusen, *Clay*, 10; Mayo, *Clay*, 22–23; Colton, *Life and Times*, 1:20–21.

26. Malone, *Jefferson*, 1:77–78.

27. Isaac Weld, Jr., *Travels Through the States of North America, and the Provinces of Upper and Lower Canada, During the Years 1795, 1796, and 1797*, 4th edition, 2 volumes (London: John Stockdale, 1807), 1:191.

28. Mayo, *Clay*, 22–23; La Rochefoucauld–Liancourt, *Travels* 3:76–79.

29. Colton, *Life and Times*, 1:25; Mayo, *Clay*, 32–39; Clay to Wickham, January 17, 1838, *HCP* 9:131.

30. Clay to Tinsley, January 9, 1793, Clay Letter, Special Collections, Transylvania University; Watkins to Clay, September 13, 1827, Henry Clay Family Papers, LOC.

31. Jefferson to Wythe, August 13, 1786, quoted in Malone, *Jefferson*, 1:281.

32. Ibid., 1:69.

33. Joyce Blackburn, *George Wythe of Williamsburg* (New York: Harper & Row, 1975), 108; Julian P. Boyd, "The Murder of George Wythe," *William and Mary Quarterly* 12 (October 1955): 516; La Rochefoucauld–Liancourt, *Travels*, 3:76; Mayo, *Clay*, 28–29; J. Drew Harrington, "Henry Clay and the Classics," *Filson Club Historical Quarterly* 61 (April 1987): 236–37.

34. Clay to Minor, May 3, 1851, *HCP* 10:886–89; Maurice G. Baxter, *Henry Clay the Lawyer* (Lexington: University Press of Kentucky, 2000), 17–18; Colton, *Life and Times*, 1:21–22; Mayo, *Clay*, 24–26; Blackburn, *George Wythe*, 125.

35. W. Edwin Hemphill, "George Wythe Courts the Muses: In Which, to the Astonishment of Everyone, That Silent, Selfless Pedant Is Found to Have Had a Sense of Humor," *William and Mary Quarterly* 9 (July 1952): 338.

36. Mayo, *Clay*, 29–30.

37. Ibid., 8, 29.

38. Ibid., 30–31; Malone, *Jefferson*, 1:119.

39. Malone, *Jefferson*, 1:67.

40. E. Lee Shepard, "Breaking In the Profession: Establishing a Law Practice in Antebellum Virginia," *Journal of Southern History* 48 (August 1982): 394–97, 402.

41. Colton, *Life and Times*, 1:24; Baxter, *Clay the Lawyer*, 18; Van Deusen, *Clay*, 12; Mayo, *Clay*, 41.

42. Mayo, *Clay*, 42–43; Van Deusen, *Clay*, 12; Baxter, *Clay the Lawyer*, 17; Francis Taliaferro Brooke, *A Family Narrative* (New York: New York Times, 1971), 38; License to Practice Law, *HCP* 1:2–3.

43. Mayo, *Clay*, 44; La Rochefoucauld–Liancourt, *Travels*, 76; Van Deusen, *Clay*, 15; Baxter, *Clay the Lawyer*, 18–19.

CHAPTER TWO

"My Hopes Were More than Realized"

1. Peterson, *Great Triumvirate*, 10; Mayo, *Clay*, 60; Neal O. Hammon, "Pioneer Routes in Central Kentucky," *Filson Club History Quarterly* 74 (2000): 143; Theodore G. Gronert, "Trade in the Blue-Grass Region, 1810–1820," *Mississippi Valley Historical Review* 5 (December 1981): 314a; Spratt to Bullitt, n.d., Bullitt Family Papers.

2. Moses Austin, "A Memorandum of M. Austin's Journey from the Lead Mines in the County of Wythe in the State of Virginia to the Lead Mines in the Province of Louisiana West of the Mississippi, 1796–1797," edited by George P. Garrison, *American Historical Review* 5 (April 1900): 524–25.

3. Stephen Aron, *How the West Was Lost: The Transformation of Kentucky from Daniel Boone to Henry Clay* (Baltimore: Johns Hopkins University Press, 1996), 6, 61–64; Steven A. Channing, *Kentucky: A Bicentennial History* (New York: W. W. Norton, 1977), 20, 27.

4. Mayo, *Clay*, 49.

5. Thomas Perkins Abernethy, *Three Virginia Frontiers* (Baton Rouge: Louisiana State University Press, 1940; reprint edition, Gloucester, MA: Peter Smith, 1962), 64–65; Channing, *Kentucky*, 44–47; Robert D. Mitchell, editor, *Appalachian Frontiers: Settlement, Society, and Development in the Pre-Industrial Era* (Lexington: University Press of Kentucky, 1991), 241–42; Craig Thompson Friend, "Merchants and Markethouses: Reflections on Moral Economy in Early Kentucky," *Journal of the Early Republic* 17 (Winter 1997): 556.

6. John W. Watkins was the son of Henry Clay's cousin John Watkins (his stepfather Henry's brother) and his aunt Mary Hudson Watkins. Watkins was among several family members who moved to New Orleans in the early nineteenth century and became one of that city's first American mayors. Mayo, *Clay*, 186.

7. Smith and Clay, *Clay Family*, 26.

8. Mayo, *Clay*, 60; Ranck, *Lexington*, 141; Melish, *Travels*, 400; Smith and Clay, *Clay Family*, 23; William Edward Railey, *History of Woodford County* (Versailles, KY: Woodford Improvement League, 1968), 54, 184; Clay to Robert Wickliffe, May 24, 1828, *HCP* 7:298.

9. Craig Thompson Friend, *Along the Maysville Road: The Early American Republic in the Trans-Appalachian West* (Knoxville: University of Tennessee Press, 2005), 55; Ranck, *Lexington*, 219; François Michaux, *Travels to the West of the Allegheny Mountains in the States of Ohio, Kentucky, and Tennessee, in the Year 1802* (London: R. Phillips, 1805), 56–57; Melish, *Travels*, 400.

10. Ranck, *Lexington*, 188, 194–95, 202; Mayo, *Clay*, 59; Richard C. Wade, *The Urban Frontier: The Rise of Western Cities, 1790–1830* (Cambridge, MA: Harvard University Press, 1959), 143; Humphrey Marshall, *History of Kentucky, Exhibiting an Account of the Modern Discovery, Settlement; Progressive Improvement; Civil and Military Transactions; and the Present State of the Country*, 2 volumes (Frankfort, KY: G. S. Robinson, 1824), 1:356; Clay and Oberholtzer, *Clay*, 22–23.

11. F. Garvin Davenport, *Ante-Bellum Kentucky: A Social History, 1800–1860* (Oxford, OH: Mississippi Valley Press, 1943), 195; William Henry Perrin, *The Pioneer Press of Kentucky, from the Printing of the First Paper West of the Alleghenies* (Louisville, KY: J. P. Morton, 1892), 9–14; Richard Miller Hadsell, "John Bradford and His Contributions to the Culture and the Life of Early Lexington," *Register of the Kentucky Historical Society* 62 (October 1964): 268; Mayo, *Clay*, 59.

12. Mayo, *Clay*, 61; Remini, *Clay*, 19; Ranck, *Lexington*, 206.

13. Colton, *Clay*, 1:78; Remini, *Clay*, 19; Mayo, *Clay*, 61.

14. E. L. Hawes, "Nicholas Family," *William and Mary Quarterly Historical Magazine* 16 (January 1936): 103; Mayo, *Clay*, 61, 63, 92–93; Ranck, *Lexington*, 151; William Henry Perrin, *History of Fayette County, Kentucky, with an Outline Sketch of the Blue Grass Region by Robert Peter, M.D.* (Chicago: O. L. Baskin, 1882), 339; Remini, *Clay*, 18; Baxter, *Clay the Lawyer*, 2.

15. Colton, *Clay*, 1:30.

16. Mayo, *Clay*, 88, 109–10; Aron, *Daniel Boone to Henry Clay*, 82; Baxter, *Clay the Lawyer*, 21, 32–33, 35; Legal Document, Papers of Thomas P. Hughes, UVA; Lowell H. Harrison, *John Breckinridge: Jeffersonian Republican* (Louisville, KY: Filson Club, 1969), 67.

17. Harrison, *Breckinridge*, 67.

18. Mayo, *Clay*, 61.

19. Retainer, July 3, 1799, Henry Clay Legal Documents, Filson; Mayo, *Clay*, 88; Clay to Taylor, November 1, 1799, Clay to Taylor, September 28, 1801, *HCP* 11:1, 4; Baxter, *Clay the Lawyer*, 21.

20. Sargent, *Clay*, 4.

21. Mayo, *Clay*, 98–99; Baxter, *Clay the Lawyer*, 24; Sargent, *Clay*, 4–5.

22. Mayo, *Clay*, 103.

23. Peterson, *Great Triumvirate*, 11; Mayo, *Clay*, 102.

24. Mayo, *Clay,* 108.
25. Abernethy, *Three Virginia Frontiers,* 86; *HCP* 1:8n.
26. Abernethy, *Three Virginia Frontiers,* 71, 83, 85; Peterson, *Great Triumvirate,* 12; Hadsell, "John Bradford," 268.
27. Lowell H. Harrison, *The Antislavery Movement in Kentucky* (Lexington: University Press of Kentucky, 1978), 1; Mayo, *Clay,* 78.
28. "Scaevola" letter, April 16, 1798, *HCP* 1:5; Harrington, "Clay and the Classics," 239.
29. Jeffrey Brooke Allen, "Were Southern White Critics of Slavery Racists? Kentucky and the Upper South, 1791–1824," *Journal of Southern History* 44 (May 1978): 187–88; Abernethy, *Three Virginia Frontiers,* 71, 83; Peterson, *Great Triumvirate,* 12; Harrison, *Breckinridge,* 99; Thomas D. Clark, *A History of Kentucky* (Lexington, KY: John Bradford Press, 1950), 202.
30. Aron, *Daniel Boone to Henry Clay,* 93; "Scaevola" letter, February 1799, *HCP,* 1:12; Mann Butler, *History of the Commonwealth of Kentucky* (Louisville, KY: Wilcox, Dickerman, 1834), 281; Mayo, *Clay,* 76–78.
31. Aron, *Daniel Boone to Henry Clay,* 93.
32. Mayo, *Clay,* 78; Ranck, *Lexington,* 219; Abernethy, *Three Virginia Frontiers,* 87; Peterson, *Great Triumvirate,* 13. Clay's progeny mirrored the fratricidal tragedy that the Civil War became in Kentucky, a state where divided loyalties were especially evident in its most prominent families. Thomas Hart Clay, the second oldest of Henry and Lucretia's sons, never joined the army but was a staunch Union man and supporter of Abraham Lincoln, who appointed him minister to Nicaragua in 1862. Yet Thomas's oldest and youngest sons, Harry and Thomas Jr., became officers in the Confederate army. James Brown Clay, the tenth of Henry and Lucretia's eleven children, also supported the Confederacy and was briefly imprisoned for treason. After James's release, Braxton Bragg appointed him a colonel, but following the Confederate defeat at Perryville, James fled to Cuba and then to Montreal, where he died in January 1864 of tuberculosis. James's oldest son, James Jr., fought for the Confederacy at Chickamauga but was with his father in Canada when he died. Returning to active duty, James Jr. earned the distinction of figuring in the final hours of the Confederate War Department, which accepted his resignation as its last official act in 1865.

    Henry Clay III, the eldest son of Henry Clay, Jr., joined the Union army at the start of the war, fought at Shiloh, and shortly after died of typhoid fever on June 5, 1862. The youngest of Henry Jr.'s children, Tommy, became a Confederate officer and was captured at Fort Donelson. Exchanged in August 1862, he returned to active service but died, ironically of typhoid fever just as his brother had, in October 1863. Tommy was twenty-three.

    Andrew Eugene Erwin (Eugene to the family), the fifth child of James and Anne Clay Erwin, became a lieutenant colonel in the Confederate army and was killed during the siege of Vicksburg in June 1863. Finally, Henry Jr.'s daughter, Anne (Nannie), married Henry Clay McDowell in 1857. McDowell joined the Union army, survived the war, and with Nannie restored Ashland to its prewar stateliness.

    We are grateful to Eric Brooks, curator of Ashland, the Henry Clay Estate, for this information about Henry Clay's descendants.
33. Harrison, *Breckinridge,* 74; Mayo, *Clay,* 73; Clark, *Kentucky,* 107; Ethelbert Dudley Warfield, *The Kentucky Resolutions* (New York: Putnam's, 1887), 42–43.
34. George T. Blakey, "Rendezvous with Republicanism: John Pope vs. Henry Clay in 1816," *Indiana Magazine of History* 62 (1966): 248; Warfield, *Kentucky Resolutions,* 43; Clark, *Kentucky,* 107; Mayo, *Clay,* 74.
35. Mayo, *Clay,* 75–76; Ranck, *Lexington,* 216.
36. Mayo, *Clay,* 89–91; Archibald Henderson, "The Creative Forces in Westward Expansion: Henderson and Boone," *American Historical Review* 20 (October 1914): 99, 106–7; Aron, *Daniel Boone to Henry Clay,* 61; Robert S. Cotterill, *History of Pioneer Kentucky* (Cincinnati: Johnson & Hardin, 1917), 74–75; *HCP* 1:15–16; Genealogical Records, Todd Family Papers, Filson.
37. Mayo, *Clay,* 90.
38. Wade, *Urban Frontier,* 51; Smith and Clay, *Clay Family,* 127; Peterson, *Great Triumvirate,* 10; Edna Talbott Whitley, "George Beck, An Eighteenth Century Painter," *Register of the Kentucky Historical Society,* 67 (January 1969): 20; Archibald Henderson, "The Transylvania Company, A Study in Personnel," *Filson Club History Quarterly* 21 (July 1947): 234–36; Mayo, *Clay,* 92; Hart Genealogy, Susanna Hart Price Papers, Filson.
39. Anya Jabour, *Marriage in the Early Republic: Elizabeth and William Wirt and the Companionate Ideal* (Baltimore: Johns Hopkins University Press, 1998), 13–14; Mayo, *Clay,* 91.
40. Memoir, Clay-Russell Papers, Filson.
41. Clay to Mercer, April 5, 1848, *HCP* 10:425.
42. Ranck, *Lexington,* 152; Memoir, Clay-Russell Papers; Mayo, *Clay,* 91.
43. Stephen Mintz and Susan Kellogg, *Domestic Revolutions: A Social History of American Family Life* (New York: Free Press, 1988), 43–45; David S. Heidler and Jeanne T. Heidler, *Daily Life in the Early American Republic: Creating a New Nation* (Westport, CT: Greenwood Press, 2004), 36–37; Jabour, *Marriage in the Early Republic,* 5.

44. Harrison, *Breckinridge,* 67; Land Sale Indenture, December 1799, Thomas Hart, Jr., to Thomas Hart, Sr., April 8, 1804, Agreement Between Jones and Hart, March 13, 1806, Thomas Hart Papers, UKY; Mayo, *Clay,* 113–14.

45. Peterson, *Great Triumvirate,* 12; Van Deusen, *Clay,* 30; Mayo, *Clay,* 115–16, 194–95.

46. Clay to Clay, July 6, 1804, Clay to Breckinridge, January 5, 1806, *HCP* 1:145, 215; Smith and Clay, *Clay Family,* 123; Harrison, *Breckinridge,* 181. During his Lexington years, Porter Clay worked as a furniture maker. Charles G. Talbert, "William Whitley, 1749–1813," *Filson Club History Quarterly* 25 (July 1951): 300; Brown to Price, Price Papers.

47. *HCP* 1:15–16; Gray to Hart, Hart Papers.

48. Mayo, *Clay,* 59, 209–15; Conditional Pledge to Transylvania University, April 1802, Agreement with Fisher, August 18, 1803, *HCP* 1:77–78, 114; Baxter, *Clay the Lawyer,* 33; Representation Agreement, September 7, 1804, Henry Clay Legal Documents.

49. Robert Charles Winthrop, *Memoir of Henry Clay* (Cambridge, MA: John Wilson, 1880), 39; Smith and Clay, *Clay Family,* 127; Jabour, *Marriage in the Early Republic,* 36.

50. Baxter, *Clay the Lawyer,* 22–25; Mayo, *Clay,* 105.

51. Van Deusen, *Clay,* 24; Mayo, *Clay,* 204–6.

52. Peterson, *Great Triumvirate,* 11.

53. Benjamin Perley Poore, *Perley's Reminiscences of Sixty Years,* 2 volumes (New York: W. A. Houghton, 1886), 1:62.

54. Mayo, *Clay,* 120–21; Tavern Bill, May 1803–March 1804, *HCP* 1:133–34.

55. Mayo, *Clay,* 208.

56. The area had been called Mud Licks when Hart acquired it. He, for obvious reasons, changed the name to Olympian Springs, after a nearby mountain. Hart financed the construction of a hotel and cabins that attracted Kentucky's upper class throughout the summer months. There, they "took the waters" for their health, socialized, played games (the men played a lot of cards, thus attracting to the resort an unsavory element of professional gamblers posing as tourists), and gossiped about their friends and enemies. Clay later acquired the resort from the estate of his father-in-law. The popularity of the Springs increased in 1803 when a weekly stage line was established from Lexington. J. Winston Coleman, Jr., "Old Kentucky Watering Places," *Filson Club History Quarterly* 16 (January 1942): 2.

57. Mayo, *Clay,* 148–49; Clay and Oberholtzer, *Clay,* 37; Butler, *History of Kentucky,* 308.

58. Timothy Flint, *Recollections of the Last Ten Years, Passed in Occasional Residences and Journeyings in the Valley of the Mississippi,*

introduction by George F. Berkhofer, Jr. (New York: Johnson Reprint, 1968), 77.

59. Mayo, *Clay,* 149–50.

60. Mayo, *Clay,* 150–52; Ranck, *Lexington,* 178.

61. Clay to Breckinridge, November 21, 1803, *HCP* 1:122; Mayo, *Clay,* 142–43, 151–52.

62. It was this very provision, originally enacted by Virginia and in force in the part of Virginia that became Kentucky, that confused the circumstances of Andrew and Rachel Jackson's marriage. Rachel only obtained permission from the Virginia legislature to pursue divorce from her husband in the courts. She did not do that, however, before she married Jackson. Because of this, political enemies would later charge that she was a bigamist and he an adulterer.

63. Act for Choosing Presidential Electors, December 24, 1803, Clay to Breckinridge, December 30, 1803, *HCP* 1:123–25; Mayo, *Clay,* 152–53.

64. Clay (Scaevola) to Daveiss, January 1803, *HCP* 1:93–95; Mayo, *Clay,* 153–54.

65. Mayo, *Clay,* 96–97.

66. Friend, "Merchants and Markethouses," 570; Ranck, *Lexington,* 222; Mayo, *Clay,* 158–60.

67. Joseph Howard Parks, *Felix Grundy, Champion of Democracy* (Baton Rouge: Louisiana State University Press, 1940), 24–27; Mayo, *Clay,* 160.

68. John Marshall's 1819 decision in the Dartmouth College case affirmed the Constitution's protection of contracts.

69. Brown to Clay, March 12, 1805, *HCP* 1:180.

70. Mayo, *Clay,* 164–66.

71. Parks, *Grundy,* 20–21.

72. Mayo, *Clay,* 167–68, 170–72; Parks, *Grundy,* 26.

73. Aron, *From Daniel Boone to Henry Clay,* 158–63; Mayo, *Clay,* 174–75.

74. Mayo, *Clay,* 175. The biblical imagery was drawn in part from Deuteronomy and Revelation.

75. Brown to Clay, February 27, 1806, *HCP* 1:221.

76. Alfred Leland Crabb, "Some Early Connections Between Kentucky and Tennessee," *Filson Club History Quarterly* 13 (July 1939): 148.

77. Randall Strahan et al., "The Clay Speakership Revisited," *Polity* 32 (2000): 567; Baxter, *Clay the Lawyer,* 33; Mayo, *Clay,* 180–81.

78. Amendments to Bill Providing Tax on Billiard Tables, November 27, 1804, *HCP* 1:158–59. The state senate raised the tax to $100.

79. Fortescue Cuming, *Sketches of a Tour to the Western Country Through the States of Ohio and Kentucky,* edited by Reuben Gold Thwaites (Cleveland: Arthur H. Clark, 1904), 184–85, 188–89.

80. Josiah Espy, *Memorandums of a Tour Made by Josiah Espy in the States of Ohio and Ken-*

tucky and Indian Territory in 1805 (Cincinnati: Robert Clarke, 1870), 8.

81. Melish, *Travels*, 400–401.

82. Mayo, *Clay*, 186–88, 218; Agreement with Banks, September 13, 1804, Transylvania University, Special Collections; Clay to Walter Beall, August 16, 1806, Beall-Booth Family Papers, Filson; Brown to Clay, December 18, 1804, Clay to Ballinger, September 6, 1806, *HCP* 1:65, 11:8.

83. Mayo, *Clay*, 125, 194.

84. Clay and Oberholtzer, *Clay*, 28.

CHAPTER THREE
"Puppyism"

1. For full discussions regarding the controversial election of 1800, see John E. Ferling, *Adams vs. Jefferson: The Tumultuous Election of 1800* (New York: Oxford University Press, 2004); Edward J. Larson, *A Magnificent Catastrophe: The Tumultuous Election of 1800, America's First Presidential Campaign* (New York: Free Press, 2007); and Bernard A. Weisberger, *America Afire: Jefferson, Adams, and the Revolutionary Election of 1800* (New York: William A. Morrow, 2000).

2. Nancy Isenberg, *Fallen Founder: The Life of Aaron Burr* (New York: Viking, 2007), 293; Mayo, *Clay*, 193; Blennerhassett to James Brown, December 9, 1805, William Harrison Safford, editor, *The Blennerhassett Papers: Embodying the Private Journal of Harman Blennerhassett and the Hitherto Unpublished Correspondence* (Cincinnati: Moore, Wilstach & Baldwin, 1864), 110–11.

3. Isenberg, *Burr*, 294.

4. Henry C. Castellanos, *New Orleans As It Was: Episodes of Louisiana Life* (Baton Rouge: Louisiana State University Press, 2006), 244–47; Isenberg, *Burr*, 296–97; Willard Rouse Jillson, "Aaron Burr's 'Trial' for Treason at Frankfort, Kentucky, 1806," *Filson Club History Quarterly* 17 (October 1943): 209; Mayo, *Clay*, 225. Territorial Governor William C. C. Claiborne later removed John Watkins as New Orleans mayor because of his complicity in Burr's schemes. See Thomas Perkins Abernethy, *The Burr Conspiracy* (New York: Oxford University Press, 1954), 277.

5. It was a common eighteenth- and nineteenth-century practice to give the mother's maiden name to at least one child as a middle name. Henry and Lucretia Clay did this with two of their children, Thomas Hart Clay and Susan Hart Clay. Lee Shai Weissbach, "The Peopling of Lexington, Kentucky: Growth and Mobility in a Frontier Town," *Register of the Kentucky Historical Society* 81 (1983): 119.

6. Milton Lomask, *Aaron Burr: The Conspiracy and Years of Exile, 1805–1836* (New York:

Farrar, Straus and Giroux, 1982), 126; Abernethy, *Burr Conspiracy*, 84, 90; Mayo, *Clay*, 239; Mary K. Bonsteel Tachau, *Federal Courts in the Early Republic: Kentucky, 1789–1816* (Princeton, NJ: Princeton University Press, 1978), 139; John Breckinridge died at home at the end of 1806 after a long illness, probably tuberculosis. James C. Klotter, *The Breckinridges of Kentucky, 1760–1981* (Lexington: University Press of Kentucky, 1986), 34.

7. Abernethy, *Burr Conspiracy*, 92; Mayo, *Clay*, 236; Remini, *Clay*, 42.

8. Ranck, *Lexington*, 266; Mayo, *Clay*, 227–29.

9. Aaron Burr, *Political Correspondence and Public Papers of Aaron Burr*, edited by Mary-Jo Kine, 2 volumes (Princeton, NJ: Princeton University Press, 1983), 2:999–1000; Mayo, *Clay*, 240.

10. Leland R. Johnson, "Aaron Burr: Treason in Kentucky?" *Filson Club History Quarterly* 75 (2001): 1–32; Burr to Clay, November 7, 1806, *HCP* 1:253; Burr, *Political Correspondence*, 2:1000; Mayo, *Clay*, 240; Lomask, *Aaron Burr*, 143; Innes to Daveiss, November 5, 1806, Daveiss to Innes, November 6, 1806, Papers of Harry Innes, LOC.

11. *Scioto* (Chillicothe, Ohio) *Gazette*, November 27, 1806; Robert McNutt McElroy, *Kentucky in the Nation's History* (New York: Moffat, Yard, 1909), 300–301; Mayo, *Clay*, 241.

12. Mayo, *Clay*, 244; Van Deusen, *Clay*, 40.

13. Mayo, *Clay*, 244–45; Remini, *Clay*, 43; Burr to Clay, November 27, 1806, *HCP* 1:256.

14. Van Deusen, *Clay*, 41; Burr to Clay, December 1, 1806, *HCP* 1:256; Abernethy, *Burr Conspiracy*, 97.

15. Mayo, *Clay*, 246–48; Lomask, *Aaron Burr*, 146–47; Abernethy, *Burr Conspiracy*, 97.

16. Mayo, *Clay*, 246–50; Lomask, *Aaron Burr*, 144; *National Intelligencer*, January 5, 1807; Marshall, *History of Kentucky*, 2:404–6.

17. *National Intelligencer*, January 5, 1807; Abernethy, *Burr Conspiracy*, 98; Lomask, *Aaron Burr*, 147.

18. Mayo, *Clay*, 252–53.

19. Everett Somerville Brown, editor, *William Plumer's Memorandum of Proceedings in the United States Senate, 1803–1807* (New York: Macmillan, 1923), 566; Lomask, *Aaron Burr*, 147–48; Abernethy, *Burr Conspiracy*, 98.

20. Mayo, *Clay*, 237, 256–57; Lomask, *Aaron Burr*, 149.

21. Marshall, *History of Kentucky*, 2:410–11.

22. Advertisement, December 8, 1806, Clay to Pindell, October 15, 1828, *HCP* 1:261, 7:501–2; Van Deusen, *Clay*, 43.

23. Mayo, *Clay*, 244; Remini, *Clay*, 43.

24. Clay to Street, December 17, 1806, *HCP* 11:9.

25. Mayo, *Clay*, 261–62.

26. Clay to Street, *HCP* 11:9; Melish, *Travels*, 144; Mayo, *Clay*, 262.

27. Brown, ed., *Plumer's Memorandum,* 570; Van Deusen, *Clay,* 44. Matthew Clay was Henry Clay's father John Clay's first cousin. Matthew was the brother of Green Clay, who had emigrated to Kentucky and formed another branch of the Clay family there. Henry Clay handled much of the legal work for his older cousin Green. Brief for Green Clay, 1801, Brief for Green Clay, 1805, Henry Clay Legal Documents.

28. *Annals of Congress,* 42 volumes (Washington, DC: Gales and Seaton, 1834–1856), 9 Cong., 2 sess., 24 (hereafter cited as *AC*); Brown, ed., *Plumer's Memorandum,* 547, 614; Senate Credentials, *HCP* 1:254–55.

29. Melish, *Travels,* 145.

30. Mayo, *Clay,* 270–71.

31. Brown, ed., *Plumer's Memorandum,* 547–48.

32. Clay to Innes, January 16, 1807, Clay to Todd, January 24, 1807, Clay to Hart, February 1, 1807, *HCP* 1:270, 272, 273; Mayo, *Clay,* 266.

33. Clay and Oberholtzer, *Clay,* 41, 44–45; Mayo, *Clay,* 266; Sargent, *Clay,* 7; Colton, *Clay,* 89.

34. Brown, ed., *Plumer's Memorandum,* 554; *AC,* 9 Cong., 2 sess., 27, 28, 32; Baxter, *Clay the Lawyer,* 33; Mayo, *Clay,* 272–73.

35. *AC,* 9 Cong., 2 sess., 40–43.

36. Brown, ed., *Plumer's Memorandum,* 565, 589. The House refused to suspend the writ. Mayo, *Clay,* 266.

37. Mayo, *Clay,* 273–74, 276–79; *National Intelligencer,* January 16, 1807; Strahan et al., "Clay Speakership," 567–68; Brown, ed., *Plumer's Memorandum,* 595, 628.

38. *National Intelligencer,* April 3, 1807; Brown, ed., *Plumer's Memorandum,* 634; Baxter, *Clay the Lawyer,* 34; Van Deusen, *Clay,* 46–48.

39. Charles Francis Adams, editor, *Memoirs of John Quincy Adams Comprising Portions of His Diary from 1785 to 1848,* 12 volumes (Philadelphia: J. B. Lippincott, 1874–1877), 1:444. Clay later expressed pride regarding his stand on this issue. Matthew Mason, "Slavery Overshadowed: Congress Debates Prohibiting the Atlantic Slave Trade to the United States, 1806–1807," *Journal of the Early Republic* 20 (Spring 2000): 74.

40. Brown, ed., *Plumer's Memorandum,* 595.

41. Hoadley to Evarts, February 5, 1807, George Hoadley Letter, VHS.

42. Clay to Hart, February 1, 1807, *HCP* 1:274.

43. Hoadley to Evarts, February 5, 1807, Hoadley Letter.

44. Brown, ed., *Plumer's Memorandum,* 628; Mayo, *Clay,* 274–75.

45. George Bancroft, "A Few Words About Henry Clay," *The Century Magazine* 30 (July 1885), 479.

46. Brown, ed., *Plumer's Memorandum,* 565, 608.

47. Ibid., 634; Mayo, *Clay,* 298.

48. Mayo, *Clay,* 300–301.

49. Ibid., 269, 303–5; Comegys to Clay, March 24, 1807, Brown to Clay, April 10, 1807, Clay to Jacoby, May 18, 1807, *HCP* 1:288, 289, 294; Blennerhassett to Blennerhassett, July 14, 1807, Safford, ed., *Blennerhassett Papers,* 259.

50. Mayo, *Clay,* 306; Lomask, *Aaron Burr,* 260; Blennerhassett to Blennerhassett, July 14, 1807, Extract from the *New World,* July 21, 1807, Safford, ed., *Blennerhassett Papers,* 259, 268–70; "Argument Relative to Harman Blennerhassett, July 15, 1807, Clay to Blennerhassett, July 22, 1807, Clay to Blennerhassett, March 14, 1842, *HCP* 1:298–99, 300–301, 9:678–80; *Pittsburgh Gazette,* August 11, 1807; Baxter, *Clay the Lawyer,* 32.

51. Deposition of Harry Innes, 1807, Harry Innes Papers, Filson; Mayo, *Clay,* 306–8.

52. Clay to Rodney, December 5, 1807, *HCP* 1:311; Bibb to Rodney, December 11, 1807, George Mortimer Bibb Papers, Filson.

53. Mayo, *Clay,* 309; Marshall, *History of Kentucky,* 2:447; Fowler to Innes, March 4, 1807, Innes Papers, LOC.

54. Resolution of Kentucky House and Senate, February 17, 1808, Innes Papers, LOC.

55. Mayo, *Clay,* 309–10; Clay acted as one of Innes's attorneys. Street eventually had to leave the state to avoid paying the court costs incurred in the libel suit. Trial Transcript, Innes Papers, Filson; Anderson C. Quisenberry, *The Life and Times of Hon. Humphrey Marshall* (Winchester, KY: Sun Publishing, 1892), 79.

56. "Regulus" to the People, ca. July 9, 1808, *HCP* 1:361–67.

57. *National Intelligencer,* March 9, 1808, March 18, 1808.

58. Quisenberry, *Marshall,* 100; George D. Prentice, *Biography of Henry Clay* (New York: John Jay Phelps, 1831), 42; Mayo, *Clay,* 336.

59. Amendment on Resolution on Foreign Relations, December 15, 1808, Debate on Foreign Relations, December 16, 1808, Further Amendment of Resolutions on Foreign Relations, December 16, 1808, *HCP* 1:388–90; Van Deusen, *Clay,* 53; Marshall, *History of Kentucky,* 2:459, 462; Mayo, *Clay,* 337.

60. Quisenberry, *Marshall,* 100; Van Deusen, *Clay,* 53–54; Mayo, *Clay,* 337–38.

61. Mayo, *Clay,* 338.

62. Clay to Marshall, January 4, 1809, *HCP* 1:397.

63. For discussions of duels or affairs of honor during the antebellum period, see Joanne B. Freeman, *Affairs of Honor: National Politics in the New Republic* (New Haven, CT: Yale University Press, 2001); Bertram Wyatt-Brown, *The Shaping of Southern Culture: Honor, Grace, and War, 1760s–1890s* (Chapel Hill: University of North Carolina Press,

2001); and Kenneth S. Greenberg, *Honor & Slavery: Lies, Duels, Noses, Masks, Dressing as a Woman, Gifts, Strangers, Humanitarianism, Death, Slave Rebellions, the Proslavery Argument, Baseball, Hunting, and Gambling in the Old South* (Princeton, NJ: Princeton University Press, 1996).

64. Marshall to Clay, January 4, 1809, *HCP* 1:398–99; Quisenberry, *Marshall,* 102; Clay and Oberholtzer, *Clay,* 50.

65. Clay to Hart, January 4, 1809, *HCP* 1:398; Charles Anderson Memoir, Filson.

66. Montpelier *Vermont Patriot,* November 2, 1844.

67. Payne to Payne, January 18, January 21, 1809, Letters from DeVall Payne to Hannah Payne, Miscellaneous Manuscripts Collection, University of Chicago Library; Mayo, *Clay,* 340; Clark, *Kentucky,* 287; Remini, *Clay,* 55.

68. Clay and Oberholtzer, *Clay,* 50.

69. Clay to Clark, January 19, 1809, Johnson to Clay, January 28, 1809, Barry to Clay, January 29, 1809, Resolution of Censure, January 24, 1809, *HCP* 1:400–402; Mayo, *Clay,* 341.

70. Van Deusen, *Clay,* 71; Remini, *Clay,* 74; Mayo, *Clay,* 194–95; for more on Ashland as a symbol, see Wendy S. Bright-Levy, "Ashland, the Henry Clay Estate, as House Museum: Private Home and Public Destination," M.A. thesis, University of Kentucky, 2008, and Eric Brooks, *Ashland, the Henry Clay Estate* (Charleston, SC: Arcadia Publishing, 2007).

71. Smith and Clay, *Clay Family,* 127.

72. Brown to Clay, September 16, 1804; Clay to Clay, March 10, 1814, *HCP* 1:149, 870–71; Lucretia Clay to Marshall and Harrison, September 18, 1856, Louisville *Journal,* reprinted in *New York Times,* September 26, 1856. The two surviving examples of Lucretia Clay's correspondence exist only as copies. The 1814 letter was loaned to Clay biographer Calvin Colton and never returned. Colton's careless disregard for returning loaned documents, in fact, strained his relationship with the family. Nor does Lucretia's 1856 letter to the *Journal* exist in the original. We are grateful to Eric Brooks, head curator at Ashland, the Henry Clay Estate, for this information.

73. Brown to Clay, September 16, 1804, Assignment by Henry Watkins, December 5, 1808, Clay to Mercer, April 5, 1848, *HCP* 1:149, 385, 10:424. Railey, *Woodford County,* 176; Brown to Price, May 1, 1806, Price Papers.

74. Last Will and Testament of Thomas Hart, August 31, 1807, Thomas J. Clay Collection, Henry Clay Papers.

75. Henderson, "Transylvania Company," 241; Mayo, *Clay,* 218; Memorandum, July 26, 1810, Hart Papers; Benton to Clay, September 18, 1810, Clay to Shelby, December 2, 1809, *HCP* 1:427, 490.

76. Wade, *Urban Frontier,* 109; Friend, *Maysville Road,* 221; Van Deusen, *Clay,* 30; Mayo, *Clay,* 197, 206.

77. Mayo, *Clay,* 343; Remini, *Clay,* 58; Resignation from Kentucky House of Representatives, January 4, 1810, *HCP* 1:33–34.

78. *National Intelligencer,* February 7, 1810; Clay to Thompson, March 14, 1810, *HCP* 1:458.

79. Garnett to Randolph, January 9, 1810, Randolph to Garnett, March 20, 1810, Papers of John Randolph of Roanoke, UVA.

80. Reginald Horsman, *The Causes of the War of 1812* (Philadelphia: University of Pennsylvania Press, 1962), 181.

81. *Maryland Gazette,* February 28, 1810.

82. *AC,* 11 Cong., 2 sess., 579–82.

83. Clay to Beatty, April 23, 1810, Clay to Unknown Recipient, March 21, 1810, Clay to Daveiss, April 19, 1810, *HCP* 1:470, 11:13–14; Gronert, "Blue-Grass Region," 316–18.

84. *AC,* 11 Cong., 2 sess., 623, 626–30; *National Intelligencer,* April 6, 1810.

85. *Raleigh Register and North Carolina Weekly Advertiser,* April 19, 1810; Van Deusen, *Clay,* 59–60.

86. Clay to the Electors of the Fifth Congressional District, May 14, 1810, Clay to Beatty, May 31, 1810, *HCP* 1:471, 473; *National Intelligencer,* August 24, 1810; Mayo, *Clay,* 360; Remini, *Clay,* 64.

87. Clay to Rodney, August 6, 1810, ibid., 1:481.

88. Margaret Bayard Smith, *The First Forty Years of Washington Society,* edited by Gaillard Hunt (Washington, DC: Government Printing Office, 1906), 85–86.

89. Clay to Ridgely, January 17, 1811, *HCP* 11:16; Smith, *Forty Years,* 86.

90. *AC,* 11 Cong., 3 sess., 44–62; *National Intelligencer,* December 29, 1810.

91. *AC,* 11 Cong., 3 sess., 63–64.

92. Ibid., 66; Mayo, *Clay,* 370.

93. *AC,* 11 Cong., 3 sess., 67–80; *National Intelligencer,* January 12, 1811; Octavius Pickering and Charles W. Upham, *The Life of Timothy Pickering,* 4 volumes (Boston: Little, Brown, 1867–1873), 4:175–82.

94. Mayo, *Clay,* 371; Remini, *Clay,* 67; Clay to Rodney, January 11, 1811, *HCP* 1:522.

95. Clay to Ridgely, January 17, 1811, *HCP* 11:16.

96. Richard Sylla et al., "Banks and State Public Finance in the New Republic: The United States, 1790–1860," *Journal of Economic History* 47 (June 1987): 392–93; Mayo, *Clay,* 375; Henry Adams, *The Life of Albert Gallatin* (Philadelphia: J. B. Lippincott, 1879), 428; Lucius P. Little, *Ben Hardin: His Times and Contemporaries, with Selections from His Speeches* (Louisville, KY: Courier-Journal, 1887), 62.

97. Mayo, *Clay,* 375; Philip Jackson Green, *The*

Life of William Harris Crawford (Charlotte: University of North Carolina, 1965), 17; Adams, *Gallatin,* 428; Norman K. Risjord, *The Old Republicans: Southern Conservatism in the Age of Jefferson* (New York: Columbia University Press, 1965), 113.

98. Speech on the Bill to Recharter the Bank of the United States, February 15, 1811, *HCP* 1:528.

99. Ibid., 1:529–39; Irving to Irving, February 16, 1811, Pierre M. Irving, *The Life and Letters of Washington Irving,* 3 volumes (New York: G. P. Putnam's Sons, 1883), 1:131.

100. Mayo, *Clay,* 377; Remini, *Clay,* 71; Evan Cornog, *The Birth of Empire: DeWitt Clinton and the American Experience, 1769–1828* (New York: Oxford University Press, 1998), 94.

101. Clay to Rodney, April 29, 1811, *HCP* 1:557.

CHAPTER FOUR

The Hawk and the Gambler

1. Mayo, *Clay,* 385, 391–95; Rental Agreement, April 5, 1811, Agreement with George Slaughter, Jr., April 6, 1811, Property Deed to William M. Nash, April 27, 1811, Graham to Clay, July 31, 1811, Clay to Rodney, August 17, 1811, *HCP* 1:553, 554, 556, 570–71, 574.

2. Clay to Rodney, August 17, 1811, Clay to Nicholson, October 8, 1811, Clay to Madison, ca. November 1811, *HCP* 1:574, 594, 11:18; Smith, *Forty Years,* 86; Van Deusen, *Clay,* 69.

3. Samuel Eliot Morison, *The Life and Letters of Harrison Gray Otis, Federalist, 1765–1848,* 2 volumes (Boston: Houghton Mifflin, 1913), 2:32.

4. Clay and Oberholtzer, *Clay,* 59; Irving H. Bartlett, *John C. Calhoun: A Biography* (New York: W. W. Norton, 1993), 70; Mark Zuehlke, *For Honour's Sake: The War of 1812 and the Brokering of an Uneasy Peace* (Toronto: Alfred A. Knopf Canada, 2006), 11; Remini, *Clay,* 78–79; Charles M. Wiltse, *John C. Calhoun, Nationalist, 1782–1828* (Indianapolis: Bobbs-Merrill, 1944), 53.

5. Speech, November 4, 1811, *HCP* 1:594; Lowndes to Lowndes, November 2, 1811, Harriott Horry Ravenel, *The Life and Times of William Lowndes, 1782–1822* (Boston: Houghton, Mifflin, 1901), 84; *Niles' Weekly Register,* November 9, 1811; Mayo, *Clay,* 404, 408–10.

6. For discussions of Clay and House committees, see James Sterling Young, *The Washington Community, 1800–1828* (New York: Harcourt, Brace, 1966); Gerald Gamm and Kenneth Shepsle, "Emergence of Legislative Institutions: Standing Committees in the House and Senate, 1810–1825," *Legislative Studies Quarterly* 14 (February 1989): 39–66; Jeffrey A. Jenkins, "Property Rights and the

Emergence of Standing Committee Dominance in the Nineteenth-Century House," *Legislative Studies Quarterly* 23 (November 1998): 493–519; Strahan et al., "Clay Speakership."

7. Edmund Quincy, *Life of Josiah Quincy of Massachusetts* (Boston: Fields, Osgood, 1869), 255.

8. Randolph Papers, University of Virginia; Robert J. Brugger, *Beverley Tucker: Heart Over Head in the Old South* (Baltimore: Johns Hopkins University Press, 1978), 90. Klinefelter's syndrome was first described by Dr. Harry Klinefelter in 1942 as caused by a chromosome abnormality.

9. Mayo, *Clay,* 408–10; Irving Brant, *James Madison,* 6 volumes (Indianapolis, IN: Bobbs-Merrill, 1941–1961), 5:381.

10. For different perspectives on the evolving role of the speakership, see Young, *Washington Community;* Randall Strahan, *Leading Representatives: The Agency of Leaders in the Politics of the U.S. House* (Baltimore: Johns Hopkins University Press, 2007); Randall Strahan, Matthew Gunning, and Richard L. Vining, Jr., "From Moderator to Leader: Floor Participation by U.S. House Speakers 1789–1841," *Social Science History* 30 (Spring 2006): 51–74; Ralph Volney Harlow, *The History of Legislative Methods in the Period before 1825* (New Haven, CT: Yale University Press, 1917); and Ronald M. Peters, Jr., *The American Speakership* (Baltimore: Johns Hopkins University Press, 1990).

11. Plumer to Clay, November 20, 1811, *HCP* 1:598; Plumer to Harper, November 22, 1811, William Plumer Papers, LOC.

12. Strahan et al., "Moderator to Leader," 51–54.

13. Ibid., 56; Robert Allen Rutland, *The Presidency of James Madison* (Lawrence: University Press of Kansas, 1990), 85–86.

14. Peters, *American Speakership,* 12, 33–37; Elaine K. Swift, "The Start of Something New: Clay, Stevenson, Polk, and the Development of the Speakership, 1789–1869," in Roger H. Davidson et al., *Masters of the House: Congressional Leadership over Two Centuries* (Boulder, CO: Westview Press, 1998), 13–14, 16, 21.

15. Clay to Daveiss, April 19, 1810, Clay to Parker, December 7, 1811, *HCP* 11:14–15, 1:599; *AC,* 12 Cong., 1 sess., 602; Mayo, *Clay,* 395–96; Van Deusen, *Clay,* 70; Ranck, *Lexington,* 143; Alfred Pirtle, *The Battle of Tippecanoe* (Louisville, KY: J. P. Morton, 1900), 57; Dorothy Goebel, *William Henry Harrison: A Political Biography* (Philadelphia: Porcupine Press, 1974), 122.

16. *AC,* 12 Cong., 1 sess., 588; Clay to Randall, December 28, 1811, *HCP* 1:602; *Niles' Weekly Register,* January 4, 1812.

17. *AC,* 12 Cong., 1 sess., 447–55; Larry James

Winn, "The War Hawks' Call to Arms; Appeals for a Second War with Great Britain," *Southern Speech Communication Journal* 37 (1972): 402–3; Van Deusen, *Clay,* 79; Donald R. Hickey, *The War of 1812: A Forgotten Conflict* (Urbana: University of Illinois Press, 1990), 72; William C. Bruce, *John Randolph of Roanoke, 1773–1833,* 2 volumes (New York: G. P. Putnam's Sons, 1922), 1:370.

18. *AC,* 12 Cong., 1 sess., 595–601.

19. Bradford Perkins, *Prologue to War: England and the United States, 1805–1812* (Berkeley: University of California Press, 1961), 5.

20. *AC,* 12 Cong., 1 sess., 601–2.

21. Ibid., 743; J.C.A. Stagg, *Mr. Madison's War: Politics, Diplomacy, and Warfare in the Early Republic, 1783–1830* (Princeton, NJ: Princeton University Press, 1983), 87; Randolph to Garnett, January 12, 1812, Randolph Papers, UVA.

22. *AC,* 12 Cong., 1 sess., 910–16; Van Deusen, *Clay,* 81–82; Rutland, *Presidency of Madison,* 89; L. W. Meyer, *Life and Times of Colonel Richard M. Johnson of Kentucky* (New York: Columbia University Press, 1932), 82.

23. Mayo, *Clay,* 447, 450–54; Randolph to Garnett, February 1, 1812, Randolph Papers, UVA.

24. For those who view Clay as the primary instigator of the war, see Zuehlke, *For Honour's Sake,* and Walter R. Borneman, *1812: The War That Forged the Nation* (New York: HarperCollins, 2004). For historians who present a more balanced picture of Clay's role, see Rutland, *Presidency of Madison;* Brant, *Madison,* volume 5; Harry Ammon, *James Monroe: The Quest for National Identity* (New York: McGraw-Hill, 1971; reprint edition, Charlottesville: University Press of Virginia, 1990); Ronald L. Hatzenbuehler, "The War Hawks and the Question of Congressional Leadership in 1812," *Pacific Historical Review* 45 (February 1976): 1–22; Norman K. Risjord, "1812: Conservatives, War Hawks and the Nation's Honor," *William and Mary Quarterly* 18 (April 1961): 196–210.

25. *Raleigh Register and North Carolina Gazette,* February 7, 1812; Mayo, *Clay,* 485.

26. Stagg, *Mr. Madison's War,* 93; Mayo, *Clay,* 490–91; Rutland, *Presidency of Madison,* 90.

27. Clay to Monroe, March 15, 1812, *HCP* 1:637; Stagg, *Mr. Madison's War,* 96.

28. *AC,* 12 Cong., 1 sess., 1588–92; Hickey, *War of 1812,* 39; Remini, *Clay,* 91.

29. Augustus John Foster, *Jeffersonian America: Notes on the United States of America Collected in the Years 1805–6–7 and 11–12 by Sir Augustus John Foster, Bart.,* edited by Richard Beale Davis (San Marino, CA: Huntington Library, 1954), 4, 90, 96, 183.

30. Brant, *Madison,* 5:435–36; Ammon, *Monroe,* 306; *National Intelligencer,* May 12, 1812.

31. Stagg, *Mr. Madison's War,* 107; James Madison, *The Papers of James Madison: Presidential Series,* edited by Robert Allen Rutland et al., 6 volumes (Charlottesville: University of Virginia Press, 1984–2008), 4:110; Clay to Worsley, May 24, 1812, Clay to unknown recipient, May 27, 1812, *HCP* 1:657, 659–60.

32. James Madison, *The Writings of James Madison,* edited by Gaillard Hunt, 9 volumes (New York: G. P. Putnam's Sons, 1900–1910), 8:192; Stagg, *Mr. Madison's War,* 109; Risjord, *Old Republicans,* 142.

33. *AC,* 12 Cong., 1 sess., 1451–78.

34. Remini, *Clay,* 92; Van Deusen, *Clay,* 87; Mayo, *Clay,* 521–25; Parks, *Grundy,* 59.

35. Mayo, *Clay,* 524–25; Wiltse, *Calhoun, Nationalist,* 65–66; Clay to Bledsoe, June 18, 1812, Clay to Worsley, June 20, 1812, *HCP* 1:674, 676.

36. Randolph to Garnett, April 14, 1812, Randolph Papers, UVA; Clay to *National Intelligencer,* June 17, 1812, Randolph to *National Intelligencer,* July 2, 1812, *HCP* 1:668–73, 686–91.

37. *AC,* 12 Cong., 1 sess., 1544–46; Hickey, *War of 1812,* 49.

38. Clay to Adams, June 18, 1812, *HCP* 11:23; Smith, *Forty Years,* 86–88.

39. Latrobe to Clay, June 20 and 24, 1812, *HCP* 1:676, 679; Gerry, *Diary,* 168–69; Bartlett, *Calhoun,* 75.

40. Charles Oscar Paullin and Frederic Logan Paxson, *Guide to Materials in the London Archives for the History of the United States Since 1783* (Washington, DC: Carnegie Institution of Washington, 1914), 39.

41. Clay to Worsley, July 21, 1812, Remarks, July 27, 1812, *HCP* 1:696–97; *National Intelligencer,* August 13, 1812.

42. Clay to Monroe, July 29, 1812, Clay to Eustis, July 31, 1812, Clay to Monroe, August 12, 1812, Speeches to Troops, August 14 and 16, 1812, *HCP* 1:697–99, 702–3, 712, 715.

43. Clay to Monroe, August 12, 1812, Clay to Eustis, August 22, 1812, ibid., 1:713–14, 717–18.

44. Clay to Eustis, August 22, 1812, ibid., 1:717–18.

45. Scott to Madison, August 25, 1812, Madison, *Papers, Presidential Series,* 5:202–3; Clay to Monroe, August 25, 1812, *HCP* 1:719–21; Stagg, *Mr. Madison's War,* 216; Goebel, *Harrison,* 136–37.

46. Harrison to Clay, August 29, August 30, 1812, *HCP* 1:723–25; Stagg, *Mr. Madison's War,* 218.

47. Clay to Monroe, September 21, 1812, *HCP* 1:728–29; Remini, *Clay,* 97.

48. Rutland, *Presidency of Madison,* 119; Remini, *Clay,* 96.

49. Clay to Harrison, November 7, 1812, Clay to Monroe, December 23, 1812, Clay to Rodney,

December 29, 1812, *HCP* 11:23–24,
1:748–49, 750.

50. *AC*, 12 Cong., 2 sess., 298–304.

51. *HCP* 1:747; Randolph to Garnett, December
7, 1812, Randolph Papers, UVA.

52. *AC*, 12 Cong., 2 sess., 540–70; Richard Buel,
Jr., *America on the Brink: How the Political
Struggle over the War of 1812 Almost Destroyed the Young Republic* (New York: Palgrave Macmillan, 2005), 171–72.

53. Van Deusen, *Clay,* 93; Speech, January 8–10,
1813, *HCP* 1:754–59; for Lincoln's Lyceum
speech, see Basler, *Lincoln Speeches,* 76–85.

54. Speech, *HCP* 1:759–62.

55. Remini, *Clay,* 99; Speech, *HCP* 1:762–73.

56. *Raleigh Register and North Carolina Gazette,*
February 19, 1813.

57. Quincy, *Life of Quincy,* 298–99; *AC,* 12
Cong., 2 sess., 677.

58. Washington, Kentucky, *Dove,* March 13,
1813; *Raleigh Register and North Carolina
Gazette,* March 19, 1813.

59. Brant, *Madison,* 6:147.

60. Clay to Taylor, April 10, 1813, Clay to
Hardin, May 26, 1813, *HCP* 1:782, 799.

61. Randolph to Quincy, June 20, 1813, Quincy,
Life of Quincy, 332.

62. Hickey, *War of 1812,* 119, 125; Remini, *Clay,*
102; *AC,* 13 Cong., 1 sess., 106.

63. Calhoun Remarks, May 31, 1813, John C.
Calhoun, *The Papers of John C. Calhoun,*
edited by Robert L. Meriwether et al., 28 volumes (Columbia: University of South Carolina Press, 1959–2003), 1:168–69; *Maryland
Gazette,* June 10, 1813.

64. Remarks, May 26, 1813, *HCP* 1:800; Webster
to Webster, May 26, 1813, Daniel Webster,
The Papers of Daniel Webster, edited by
Charles M. Wiltse et al., series 1, 7 volumes
(Hanover, NH: Dartmouth College by the University of New England Press, 1974–1988),
1:140.

65. Brant, *Madison,* 6:196–97; Hickey, *War of
1812,* 122.

66. Gerry, *Diary,* 149–50, 154, 202, 210.

67. Ibid., 154, 178, 188; Smith, *Forty Years,* 91;
Rutland, *Presidency of Madison,* 130.

68. Henry Barrett Learned, "Gerry and the Presidential Succession in 1813," *American Historical Review* 22 (October 1916): 94–97; Brant,
Madison, 6:187.

69. Stagg, *Mr. Madison's War,* 374; Brant, *Madi-
son,* 6:240; Remini, *Clay,* 103–4; Robert
Ernst, *Rufus King: American Federalist*
(Chapel Hill: University of North Carolina
Press, 1968), 331; *Maryland Gazette,* January
19, 1814, February 17, 1814; Plumer to
Adams, January 24, 1814, Plumer Papers.

70. *National Intelligencer,* January 20, 1814.

71. Monroe to American Commissioners, January
28 and 30, 1814, *American State Papers, Foreign Relations,* 6 volumes (Washington, DC:

Gales & Seaton, 1833–1858), 3:701–2;
Yancey to Ruffin, February 4, 1814, J. G. deR.
Hamilton, editor, *The Papers of Thomas Ruf-
fin,* 4 volumes (Raleigh: Edwards &
Broughton, 1918–1920), 1:143.

72. Clay to Brown, February 20, 1814, *HCP*
11:33; *National Intelligencer,* March 2, 1814;
Remini, *Clay,* 105.

73. Adams, *Memoirs,* 2:584; Bayard to Clay and
Russell, April 22, 1814, Gallatin to Clay,
April 22, 1814, *HCP* 1:881–85; George Milligan to Bayard, May 10, 1814, James A. Bayard, *Papers of James A. Bayard, 1796–1815,*
edited by Elizabeth Donnan (Washington, DC:
Annual Report of the American Historical Association of 1913, 1915), 293.

74. Clay to Russell, May 1, 1814, same to same,
May 4, 1814, Clay to Bayard and Gallatin,
May 2, 1814, Clay to Gallatin, May 2, 1814,
HCP 1:888–94; Milligan to Bayard, May 10,
1814, Bayard, *Papers,* 294; James Gallatin,
*The Diary of James Gallatin, Secretary to Al-
bert Gallatin: A Great Peace Maker,
1813–1827,* edited by Count Gallatin (New
York: Charles Scribner's Sons, 1916), 21;
Remini, *Clay,* 106.

75. Clay to Russell and Adams, May 31, 1814,
Clay to Crawford, July 2, 1814, *HCP*
1:928–29, 937; Remini, *Clay,* 108; Bayard
Journal, in Maris Stella Connelly, "The Let-
ters and European Travel Journal of James A.
Bayard, 1812–1815," Ph.D. dissertation,
Boston University, 2007, p. 447.

76. Hughes to Clay, May 15, 1814, *HCP* 1:914;
Gallatin to Castlereagh, June 9, 1814, Connelly, "Bayard," 436; Van Deusen, *Clay,* 97,
100; Remini, *Clay,* 108.

77. Bayard to Clay and Russell, April 22, 1814,
Gallatin to Clay, April 22, 1814, Clay to
Crawford, May 14, 1814, *HCP* 1:881–84,
909; Gallatin to Crawford, April 21, 1814,
Connelly, "Bayard," 406.

78. Adams, *Memoirs,* 2:656–57; Gallatin, *Diary,*
27; Adams to Adams, July 22, December 16,
1814, John Quincy Adams, *Writings of John
Quincy Adams,* edited by Worthington
Chauncey Ford, 7 volumes (New York:
Macmillan, 1913–1917), 5:66, 237–38.

79. Adams, *Memoirs,* 3:32, 39; Marie B. Hecht,
*John Quincy Adams: A Personal History of an
Independent Man* (New York: Macmillan,
1972), 230; Adams to Adams, August 23,
1814, Adams, *Writings,* 5:91.

80. Adams, *Memoirs,* 2:656; Crawford to Clay,
June 10, July 4, July 9, July 19, August 4, August 22, August 28, September 10, September
14, September 19, September 26, October 24,
November 11, December 12, 1814, Clay to
Crawford, July 2, July 25, August 8, August
11, August 18, August 22, September 20, October 17, 1814, *HCP* 1:932–36, 937–39,
941–49, 950, 960–61, 971–72, 974–75,

978–81, 988–90, 992–94, 11:34–36, 37–39, 40, 42–43.

81. Connelly, "Bayard," 17–22, 459; Castlereagh to His Majesty's Commissioners, July 23, 1814, *Correspondence, Despatches and Other Papers of Viscount Castlereagh, Second Marquess of Londonderry,* edited by Charles Vane, 12 volumes (London: Henry Colburn, 1848–1853), 10:67–72.

82. Bayard to Bayard, August 9, 1814, James A. Bayard and Richard H. Bayard Papers, LOC; Journal of Ghent Negotiations, August 7–10, 1814, Clay to Monroe, August 18, 1814, *HCP* 1:952–54, 962–67; British Memorandum of Substance, August 9, 1814, Arthur Wellesley, *Supplementary Despatches, Correspondence and Memoranda of Field Marshal Arthur, Duke of Wellington, K.G.,* 15 volumes (London: John Murray, 1858–1872), 9:179.

83. Journal of Ghent Negotiations, August 7–10, 1814, Journal of Ghent Negotiations, August 19, 1814, *HCP* 1:955–59, 968–70; Castlereagh to Commissioners, August 14, 1814, *Correspondence of Castlereagh,* 10:90.

84. Gallatin, *Diary,* 28; Hecht, *Adams,* 227.

85. Monroe to American Ministers, June 25, 1814, ASPFR, 3:703–4; Gallatin, *Diary,* 30; Goulburn to Earl Bathurst, August 23 and August 24, 1814, *Despatches of Wellington,* 9:189–90; Clay to Crawford, August 22, 1814, American Commissioners to British Commissioners, August 24, 1814, *HCP* 1:972–73.

86. Castlereagh to Lord Liverpool, August 28, 1814, *Correspondence of Castlereagh,* 10:102; Hecht, *Adams,* 229; Clay to Goulburn, September 5, 1814, *HCP* 1:973–74; Goulburn to Earl Bathurst, September 5, 1814, *Despatches of Wellington,* 9:222; Samuel Flagg Bemis, *John Quincy Adams and the Foundations of American Foreign Policy* (New York: Alfred A. Knopf, 1949), 207.

87. American to British Commissioners, September 30, 1814, *HCP* 1:981–82; Hickey, *War of 1812,* 291.

88. Goulburn to Clay, October 3, 1814, Clay to Crawford, October 17, 1814, *HCP* 1:982, 989; Gallatin, *Diary,* 32; Hecht, *Adams,* 231; Remini, *Clay,* 115; Wilbur Devereux Jones, "A British View of the War of 1812 and the Peace Negotiations," *Mississippi Valley Historical Review* 45 (December 1958): 481.

89. British to American commissioners, October 8, 1814, American to British commissioners, October 13, 1814, British to American commissioners, October 21, 1814, *ASPFR,* 3:721–25; Frank A. Updyke, *The Diplomacy of the War of 1812* (Gloucester, MA: Peter Smith, 1965), 276; Gallatin, *Diary,* 32.

90. American to British commissioners, October 24, 1814, British to American commissioners, October 31, 1814, *ASPFR,* 3:725–26.

91. Adams, *Memoirs,* 3:48–50.

92. Updyke, *Diplomacy,* 300–301; Gallatin, *Diary,* 32–33; Adams, *Gallatin,* 541.

93. Fred L. Engelman, *The Peace of Christmas Eve* (New York: Harcourt, Brace, 1960), 250–53; Wellington to Lord Liverpool, November 9, 1814, *Despatches of Wellington,* 9:424–26; Jones, "British View," 487.

94. British to American Commissioners, November 26, 1814, *ASPFR,* 3:735–41; Gallatin, *Diary,* 34; Adams, *Memoirs,* 3:71–78.

95. Hecht, *Adams,* 236; Adams, *Memoirs,* 3:101–3; British to American Commissioners, December 22, 1814, *HCP* 1:1005; Treaty of Ghent, December 24, 1814, *ASPFR,* 3:745–48; Engelman, *Peace of Christmas Eve,* 286.

96. Clay to Monroe, December 25, 1814, *HCP* 1:1007–8; Adams, *Memoirs,* 3:104.

97. Adams to Adams, December 16, 1814, Adams, *Writings,* 5:237, 239.

98. Adams, *Memoirs,* 3:133–34, 139, 143–44; Adams to Bayard, Clay, and Russell, January 2, 1815, Bayard Papers.

99. Adams, *Memoirs,* 3:155, 158; Van Deusen, *Clay,* 106–7.

100. Van Deusen, *Clay,* 107; Adams to Adams, April 24, 1815, Adams, *Writings,* 5:305; Clay to Crawford, March 23, 1815, *HCP* 2:11.

101. Clay to Monroe, March 25, 1815, Clay to Bayard, April 3, 1815, Minutes of Meeting, April 16, 1815, American Proposal, June 21, 1815, British to American commissioners, June 29, 1815, American commissioners to Monroe, July 3, 1815, *HCP* 2:12, 17, 19, 48–52, 54–57; Adams, *Gallatin,* 548–49; Adams, *Memoirs,* 3:190; Bayard, *Papers,* 384.

102. *National Intelligencer,* August 31, 1815, September 11, 1815; *Providence Patriot, Columbian Phenix,* September 9, 1815.

CHAPTER FIVE

Uncompromising Compromiser

1. Clay to Clay, March 10, 1814, *HCP* 1:870–71; Smith, *Forty Years,* 93.

2. Clay to Clay, April 15, 1835, Thomas J. Clay Collection, Henry Clay Papers.

3. Kendall to Flugel, May 14, 1814, Amos Kendall Papers, Filson; Amos Kendall, *Autobiography of Amos Kendall,* edited by William Stickney (reprint edition, New York: Peter Smith, 1949), 113–15; James D. Daniels, "Amos Kendall: Kentucky Journalist, 1815–1829," *Filson Club History Quarterly* 52 (January 1978): 47.

4. Kendall, *Autobiography,* 115, 131.

5. Ibid., 116–18, 123–24.

6. Ibid., 148–49, 172; Kendall to Flugel, August 16, 1815, October 11, 1815, Kendall Papers, Filson.

7. *National Intelligencer,* September 19, 1815;

Wade, *Urban Frontier,* 50; Gronert, "Blue-Grass Region," 321; Kirkpatrick to Este, July 4, no year, Marie Este Fisher Bruce Papers, VHS.

8. Kendall, *Autobiography,* 115, 141; Clay to Kendall, December 30, 1815, *HCP* 2:116.

9. Clay to Irving, August 13, 1817, *HCP* 11:62.

10. *National Intelligencer,* October 24, 1815; Trustees to Clay, October 5, 1815, Toasts, October 7, 1815, Clay to Hardin, October 13, 1815, *HCP* 2:65, 68–72, 99; Morrison to Innes, October 6, 1815, Innes Papers, LOC.

11. Agreement with Watkins, October 27, 1815, Acceptance of Speakership, December 4, 1815, *HCP* 2:86–88, 105.

12. Monroe to Clay, October 30, 1815, ibid., 2:88–89.

13. Annual Message, December 5, 1815, James D. Richardson, editor, *Compilation of the Messages and Papers of the Presidents,* 10 volumes (Washington, DC: Government Printing Office, 1896–1899), 1:562–69.

14. Quoted in Charles S. Sydnor, "One-Party Period of American History," *American Historical Review* 51 (April 1946): 450.

15. Hubbard to Hubbard, December 4, 1817, Papers of Thomas H. Hubbard, LOC.

16. Clay to Gallatin, December 21, 1815, *HCP* 2:109.

17. Carl J. Vipperman, *William Lowndes and the Transition of Southern Politics, 1782–1822* (Chapel Hill: University of North Carolina Press, 1989), 123.

18. For discussions of the expansion of the national government's role in economic development, see Harry L. Watson, "The Market and Its Discontents," *Journal of the Early Republic* 12 (Winter 1992): 464–70; Stephen Minicucci, "The 'Cement of Interest': Interest-Based Models of Nation-Building in the Early Republic," *Social Science History* 25 (Summer 2001): 247–74; John R. Van Atta, "Western Lands and the Political Economy of Henry Clay's American System, 1819–1832," *Journal of the Early Republic* 21 (Winter 2001): 633–65; Maurice G. Baxter, *Henry Clay and the American System* (Lexington: University Press of Kentucky, 1995); Harry L. Watson, *Liberty and Power: The Politics of Jacksonian America* (New York: Hill and Wang, 1990); and Charles Sellers, *The Market Revolution: Jacksonian America, 1815–1846* (New York: Oxford University Press, 1991).

19. Randolph to Garnett, February 2, 1816, Randolph Papers, UVA; Buchanan to Franklin, December 21, 1821, James Buchanan, *The Works of James Buchanan,* edited by John Bassett Moore, 12 volumes (Philadelphia: J. B. Lippincott, 1908–1911), 1:10; McLean to Este, February 15, 1816, Bruce Papers; Jewett to Dearborn, February 5, 1817, James C. Jewett, "The United States Congress of

1817 and Some of Its Celebrities," *William and Mary College Historical Quarterly* 17 (October 1908): 140.

20. John Lauritz Larson, " 'Bind the Republic Together': The National Union and the Struggle for a System of Internal Improvements," *Journal of American History* 74 (September 1987): 376.

21. *AC,* 14 Cong., 1 sess., 1249–52, 1834, 1877, 1878–79; Speech, January 29, 1816, *HCP* 2:140–58.

22. Charles E. McFarland and Nevin E. Neal, "The Nascence of Protectionism: American Tariff Policies, 1816–1824," *Land Economics* 45 (February 1969): 22–24; Remarks, March 22, 23, 1816, *HCP* 2:180.

23. For a history of the BUS, see Ralph C. H. Catterall, *The Second Bank of the United States* (reprint edition, Chicago: University of Chicago Press, 1968).

24. *AC,* 14 Cong., 1 sess., 1189; Speech, June 3, 1816, *HCP* 2:199–205.

25. McLean to Este, February 15, 1816, Bruce Papers.

26. Ammon, *Monroe,* 356.

27. Young, *Washington Community,* 116; Bailey to Payne, January 29, 1816, Papers of John Payne, LOC; William G. Morgan, "The Origin and Development of the Congressional Nominating Caucus," *Proceedings of the American Philosophical Society* 113 (April 1969): 193–94; Resolutions, March 16, 1816, Clay to Hardin, March 18, 1816, *HCP* 2:176–77.

28. C. Edward Skeen sees this event as a transformational moment, showing the move from deferential politics to popular politics. See Skeen, "*Vox Populi, Vox Dei:* The Compensation Act of 1816 and the Rise of Popular Politics," *Journal of the Early Republic* 6 (Autumn 1986): 253–74.

29. Remarks, March 7, 1816, *HCP* 2:171; *AC,* 14 Cong., 1 sess., 1174; Daniel Walker Howe, *What Hath God Wrought: The Transformation of America, 1815–1848* (New York: Oxford University Press, 2007), 86.

30. Blakey, "Pope vs. Clay," 233; Clay to Willis Field, March 25, 1816, *HCP* 2:181–82.

31. Blakey, "Pope vs. Clay," 241–45, 249; Perrin, *Fayette County,* 339.

32. Speech, June 3, 1816, July 25, 1816, "Pitt" to Clay, June 21, 1816, *HCP* 2:199–205; 208–9, 216–20.

33. Blakey, "Pope vs. Clay," 237.

34. Ibid., 239, 240–41, 250; Clay to Rodney, December 6, 1816, *HCP* 2:257.

35. Clay to Morris, February 5, 1817, Walsh to Clay, March 11, 1817, *HCP* 2:323, 11:58.

36. Clay to Morris, June 16, 1816, Clay to Irving, August 30, 1816, Agreement with Atkinson, October 7, 1816, Agreement with Long, October 24, 1816, Clay to McMahon, March 30,

1817, ibid., 2:236, 241, 333, 11:53, 55.

37. Clay to Madison, September 14, 1816, ibid., 2:233.

38. Madison to Clay, August 30, 1816, ibid., 2:226; Crawford to Gallatin, October 9, 1816, Albert Gallatin, *The Writings of Albert Gallatin*, edited by Henry Adams, 3 volumes (Philadelphia: J. B. Lippincott, 1879), 2:14; Noble E. Cunningham, Jr., *The Presidency of James Monroe* (Lawrence: University Press of Kansas, 1996), 22.

39. Clay to Hughes, December 8, 1816, Clay to Morris, December 14, 1816, *HCP* 2:260, 261–62; Smith, *Forty Years,* 130.

40. *AC,* 14 Cong., 2 sess., 495.

41. Henry Noble Sherwood, "The Formation of the American Colonization Society," *Journal of Negro History* 2 (July 1917): 211–22.

42. Eric Burin, *Slavery and the Peculiar Solution: A History of the American Colonization Society* (Gainesville: University Press of Florida, 2005), 14; Sherwood, "American Colonization Society," 222–27; Frankie Hutton, "Economic Considerations in the American Colonization Society's Early Effort to Emigrate Free Blacks to Liberia, 1816–36," *Journal of Negro History* 68 (Autumn 1983): 379; Charles I. Foster, "The Colonization of Free Negroes, in Liberia, 1816–1835," *Journal of Negro History* 38 (January 1953): 44–47; Speech, December 21, 1816, *HCP* 2:263–64.

43. Johnson to Clay, February 5, 1807, Bill of Sale, September 26, 1807, Deed of Emancipation, July 11, 1808, Bradford to Clay, October 3, 1816, Clay to Gales, October 14, 1817, Clay to Hart, November 15, 1817, Bill of Sale, April 7, 1821, Bill of Sale, December 19, 1817, Clay to Gurley, June 21, 1824, Speech, December 17, 1829, *HCP* 1:276–77, 303–4, 370, 2:391, 398, 417, 3:73, 7:147; 11:56, 178.

44. Ella Forbes, "African-American Resistance to Colonization," *Journal of Black Studies* 21 (December 1990): 211, 214; Rayford W. Logan, "Some New Interpretations of the Colonization Movement," *Phylon* 4 (1943): 329; Foster, "Colonization," 49–50.

45. *AC,* 14 Cong., 2 sess., 851–68; Jewett to Dearborn, February 5, 1817, Jewett, "Congress of 1817," 144.

46. Pamela L. Baker, "The Washington National Road Bill and the Struggle to Adopt a Federal System of Internal Improvement," *Journal of the Early Republic* 22 (Autumn 2002): 439–40, 442; Larson, "Internal Improvements," 377, 381.

47. Drew R. McCoy, *The Last of the Fathers: James Madison and the Republican Legacy* (Cambridge: Cambridge University Press, 1989), 92; Larson, "Internal Improvements," 381; Wiltse, *Calhoun, Nationalist,* 137.

48. Clay to Madison, March 3, 1817, *HCP* 2:322; Larson, "Internal Improvements," 382; Rutland, *Madison,* 206; Calhoun, *Papers,* 1:408.

49. Crawford to Gallatin, March 12, 1817, Gallatin, *Writings,* 2:25.

50. King to Gore, February 16, 1817, Charles R. King, editor, *Life and Correspondence of Rufus King,* 6 volumes (New York: G. P. Putnam's Sons, 1894–1900), 6:56; Crawford to Yancey, May 27, 1817, Bartlett Yancey Papers, UNC; Monroe to Jackson, March 1, 1817, John Spencer Bassett, editor, *The Correspondence of Andrew Jackson,* 7 volumes (Washington, DC: Carnegie Institution, 1927–1928), 2:276; Ammon, *Monroe,* 358–59; Roger J. Spiller, "John C. Calhoun as Secretary of War, 1817–1825," Ph.D. dissertation, Louisiana State University, 1977, 40–44.

51. Clay to Barbour, March 3, 1817, *HCP* 2:320; Van Deusen, *Clay,* 116; Brant, *Madison,* 6:418.

52. Clay to Monroe, May 21, 1817, Clay to Thompson, February 22, 1817, *HCP* 2:351, 11:58.

53. Clay to Hughes, October 9, 1817, *HCP* 2:390.

54. Clay to Russell, January 8, 1817, Clay to Tinsley, June 26, 1817, Toast, Reply, June 4, 1817, Clay to Hart, August 19, 1817, October 28, 1817, November 18, 1817, January 4, 1818, ibid., 2:353, 356, 374, 393, 394, 399, 423, 11:57; Crawford to Gallatin, October 27, 1817, Gallatin, *Writings,* 2:55.

55. Macon to Yancey, February 8, 1818, Yancey Papers; Cunningham, *Presidency of Monroe,* 134–35; Smith, *Forty Years,* 141; Clay to Adams, February 4, 1818, Clay to Hardin, February 22, 1818, *HCP* 2:433, 439; Crawford to Bibb, April 25, 1818, Governor William W. Bibb Papers, ADAH.

56. Cunningham, *Presidency of Monroe,* 50–52; Clay to Bodley, December 3, 1817, Speeches, March 7, 1818, March 13, 1818, *HCP* 2:406, 448–56, 467–89; McLane to McLane, February 11, 1818, Papers of Louis McLane, LOC; Richard C. Anderson Diary, May 1817, LOC.

57. Adams, *Memoirs,* 4:29.

58. Halford L. Hoskins, "The Hispanic American Policy of Henry Clay, 1816–1828," *Hispanic American Historical Review* 7 (November 1927): 462–66; Van Deusen, *Clay,* 117–23; Adams to Rodney, November 21, 1817, Caesar A. Rodney Papers, NYPL; Remarks, March 17, 1818, March 24, 1818, Speech, March 24–25, 1818, March 28, 1818, *HCP* 2:492, 509–10, 512–30, 553–59.

59. Adams to Rodney, November 11, 1817, Rodney Papers; Bemis, *Adams, Foreign Policy,* 308; Calhoun to Jackson, December 26, 1817, Andrew Jackson, *Papers of Andrew Jackson,* edited by Harold D. Moser et al., 7 volumes (Knoxville: University of Tennessee Press, 1980–2007), 4:163.

60. Fowler to Clay, May 23, 1818, Clay to Fowler, May 23, 1818, Speech, May 28, 1818, Clay to Tait, June 25, 1818, *HCP* 2:571–73, 580; *National Advocate*, August 27, 1818.

61. Clay to Tait, June 25, 1818, *HCP* 2:580.

62. For a full account of the First Seminole War, see David S. Heidler and Jeanne T. Heidler, *Old Hickory's War: Andrew Jackson and the Quest for Empire* (Baton Rouge: Louisiana State University Press, 2003).

63. Adams to Monroe, July 8, July 20, 1818, Adams, *Writings,* 6:383, 385; Calhoun to Monroe, September 1, 1818, Calhoun, *Papers,* 3:87; Ammon, *Monroe,* 421; William P. Cresson, *James Monroe* (Chapel Hill: University of North Carolina Press, 1946), 311.

64. John Niven, *John C. Calhoun and the Price of Union: A Biography* (Baton Rouge: Louisiana State University Press, 1988), 68–69.

65. Castlereagh to Bagot, August 18, 1818, same to same, September 2, 1818, Public Record Office Reference Foreign Office 115, volume 32, LOC; Bradford Perkins, *Castlereagh and Adams: England and the United States, 1812–1823* (Berkeley: University of California Press, 1964), 293; Adams to Erving, November 28, 1818, Adams, *Writings,* 6:474–75.

66. Adams, *Memoirs,* 4:119.

67. Anderson Diary, December 25, 1818.

68. Monroe's Second Annual Message, Richardson, *Messages and Papers,* 2:608–16; Heidler and Heidler, *Old Hickory's War,* 185.

69. Bibb to Tait, September 19, 1818, Tait Family Papers, ADAH.

70. *AC,* 15 Cong., 2 sess., 367–76.

71. Wirt to unknown recipient, January 2, 1819, William and Elizabeth Washington Gamble Wirt Papers, Duke.

72. Clay to Hardin, January 4, 1819, *HCP* 2:624; Majority Report and Minority Report, January 12, 1819, *American State Papers, Military Affairs,* 7 volumes (Washington, DC: Gales and Seaton, 1832–1861), 1:735–39; Anderson Diary, February 14, 1819.

73. *AC,* 15 Cong., 2 sess., 615–30; Risjord, *Old Republicans,* 189–90.

74. Jackson to Clay, October 25, 1806, *HCP* 1:250.

75. Nelson to Everette, December 1, 1818, Hugh Nelson Papers, LOC; Hubbard to Hubbard, January 20, 1819, Hubbard Papers.

76. Clay to Tait, June 25, 1818, *HCP* 2:580.

77. Smith, *Forty Years,* 145–47.

78. McLane to McLane, January 20, 1819, McLane Papers, LOC.

79. Speech, January 20, 1819, *HCP* 2:636–60.

80. Smith, *Forty Years,* 146.

81. Johnson to Desha, October 29, 1818, Joseph Desha Papers, LOC.

82. Peterson, *Great Triumvirate,* 55–56; Jackson to Lewis, January 25, 1819, January 30, Andrew Jackson Papers, LOC; Jackson to Donelson, January 31, 1819, Bassett, *Correspondence,* 2:408; *AC,* 15 Cong., 2 sess., 912–21; Adams, *Memoirs,* 4:239–40; Herbert Bruce Fuller, *The Purchase of Florida, Its History and Diplomacy* (Cleveland: Burrows Brothers, 1906), 264–65.

83. *AC,* 15 Cong., 2 sess., 256–66, 655–62, 674–721, 1132–33; Morrison to Clay, February 17, 1819, *HCP* 2:671–72.

84. *AC,* 15 Cong., 2 sess., 418, 1166.

85. Ibid., 1166.

86. Clay to Coburn, February 20, 1819, *HCP* 11:72–73.

87. *AC,* 15 Cong., 2 sess., 1170–1214, 1222–35; Robert Pierce Forbes, *The Missouri Compromise and Its Aftermath: Slavery and the Meaning of America* (Chapel Hill: University of North Carolina Press, 2007), 36–37; Alfred Lightfoot, "Henry Clay and the Missouri Question, 1819–1921: American Lobbyist for Unity," *Missouri Historical Review* 61 (1967): 149–50.

88. *AC,* 15 Cong., 2 sess., 1204, 1214, 1433–34.

89. For full discussions of the Missouri issue, see Glover Moore, *The Missouri Controversy, 1819–1821* (Lexington: University of Kentucky Press, 1953) and Forbes, *Missouri Compromise.*

90. Clay to Hardin, February 21, 1819, *HCP* 2:673–74; for *McCulloch v. Maryland,* see Richard E. Ellis, *Aggressive Nationalism: McCulloch v. Maryland and the Foundation of Federal Authority in the Young Republic* (New York: Oxford University Press, 2007).

91. Clay to Cheves, April 19, 1819, Clay to Holley, May 6, 1819, Lewis et al. to Clay, May 18, 1819, Clay to Lewis, May 18, 1819, Bill of Lading, May 26, 1819, Clay to Butler, July 19, 1819, Clay to Gales, July 19, 1819, *HCP* 2:687, 690–92, 693–94, 698, 700; *Orleans Gazette and Commercial Advertiser,* May 18, 1819; Randolph to Cunningham, July 20, 1819, Randolph Papers, VHS.

92. Van Atta, "Western Lands," 635; Clay to Cheves, July 19, 1819, November 14, 1819, Clay to Gales, July 19, 1819, *HCP* 2:699, 700–701, 720–22.

93. Adams, *Memoirs,* 4:471; Speech, December 6, 1819, *HCP* 2:726.

94. Van Deusen, *Clay,* 127–28; Adams, *Memoirs,* 4:276; Bemis, *Adams, Foreign Policy,* 336–37.

95. Watkins to Clay, October 5, 1820, Thomas J. Clay Collection, Henry Clay Papers.

96. Speech, December 30, 1819, *HCP* 2:740–48; *AC,* 16 Cong., 1 sess., 849.

97. Clay to Kendall, January 8, 1820, Clay to Beatty, January 22, 1820, Clay to Hardin, February 5, 1820, *HCP* 2:752, 766, 775; Adams, *Memoirs,* 4:525–26.

98. Clay to Hardin, February 5, 1820, Clay to Combs, February 5, 1820, *HCP* 2:774–75; Cunningham, *Presidency of Monroe,* 98.

99. Clay to Holley, February 17, 1820, *HCP* 2:781; Yancey to Austin, February 10, 1820, Austin-Twyman Papers, W&M.

100. *AC*, 16 Cong., 1 sess., 1586–87; Pleasants to Cabell, March 28, 1820, Joseph C. Cabell Papers, UVA; Taylor to Austin, March 28, 1820, Austin-Twyman Papers; Calhoun to DeSaussure, April 28, 1820, Henry William DeSaussure Papers, SCHS.

101. *AC*, 16 Cong., 1 sess., 1588–90.

102. Clay to Hunt, January 22, 1819, Clay to Beatty, March 4, 1820, *HCP* 2:662, 788; *Louisville Public Advertiser*, January 12, 1820; Adams, *Memoirs*, 5:110.

103. *AC*, 16 Cong., 1 sess., 1719–31; 2228–30; Van Deusen, *Clay*, 129–30; Bemis, *Adams, Foreign Policy*, 351–52; Alvin Laroy Duckett, *John Forsyth: Political Tactician* (Athens: University of Georgia Press, 1962), 56–62; Cresson, *Monroe*, 322–25; Clay to Crittenden, January 29, 1820, Clay to Kendall, April 16, 1820, *HCP* 2:769, 823; Randolph B. Campbell, "The Spanish American Aspect of Henry Clay's American System," *Americas* 24 (July 1967): 4–7.

104. Gronert, "Blue-Grass Region," 321–22; Wade, *Urban Frontier*, 169, 177; Clay to Harrison, September 11, 1831, Papers of George P. Fisher, LOC.

105. *National Intelligencer*, June 28, 1820; Advertisement, June 5, 1820, Clay to Cheves, March 15, 1820, November 5, 1820, June 23, 1822, Cheves to Clay, February 23, 1821, *HCP* 2:794, 869, 870–75, 900–901, 3:47–48, 238.

106. Clay to Leigh, December 7, 1819, December 18, 1819, December 26, 1819, May 1, 1820, receipt, January 14, 1820, *HCP* 2:726–27, 733, 735–36, 754, 849; Leigh to Clay, December 11, 1819, Benjamin Watkins Leigh Papers, VHS.

107. Clay to Dougherty, October 28, 1820, *HCP* 2:895.

108. Advertisement, October 2, 1820, Morrison to Clay, February 12, 1821, *HCP* 2:891, 3:33–34; Account Settlement, June 29, 1821, Hart Papers.

109. Clay to Ridgely, January 23, 1821, *HCP* 3:14–15.

110. Clay's old friend William Plumer cast the only vote against Monroe. He voted for John Quincy Adams because he did not like Monroe and believed Adams more qualified for the position.

111. Crawford to Gallatin, April 23, 1817, Gallatin, *Writings*, 2:35.

112. Floyd to McDowell, January 4, 1821, Papers of James McDowell, UVA; Remarks, January 23, 1821, *HCP* 3:15; C. Edward Skeen, "Calhoun, Crawford, and the Politics of Retrenchment," *South Carolina Historical Magazine* 73 (July 1972): 142, 147; Heidler and Heidler, *Old Hickory's War*, 230.

113. Van Deusen, *Clay*, 141–42; Moore, *Missouri Controversy*, 146; William N. Chambers, *Old Bullion Benton, Senator from the New West: Thomas Hart Benton, 1782–1858* (Boston: Little, Brown, 1956), 101–2.

114. Cabell to Cocke, December 2, 1820, Pleasants to Cabell, February 4, 1821, Cabell Papers.

115. Van Deusen, *Clay*, 142–43; George Dangerfield, *The Era of Good Feelings* (New York: Harcourt, Brace, 1952), 238; *AC*, 16 Cong., 2 sess., 1078–80, 1093–1146.

116. *AC*, 16 Cong., 2 sess., 1147–54.

117. Ibid., 1147–63; Adams, *Memoirs*, 5:276–77.

118. *AC*, 16 Cong., 2 sess., 1219, 1228, 1236–38; Van Deusen, *Clay*, 146–48; Clay to Cheves, March 5, 1821, *HCP* 3:58–59.

119. Clay to Monroe, March 1, 1821, Anderson to Clay, July 12, 1822, Clay to Adams, March 18, 1821, *HCP* 3:54, 70, 258; Adams, *Memoirs*, 5:311, 329.

120. Adams, *Memoirs*, 5:323–26, 330.

CHAPTER SIX

"I Injured Both Him and Myself"

1. Adams, *Memoirs*, 5:30; *St. Louis Enquirer*, May 19, 1821.

2. Van Deusen, *Clay*, 130; Hoskins, "Hispanic American Policy," 468–70; Ernest R. May, *The Making of the Monroe Doctrine* (Cambridge, MA: Belknap Press of Harvard University Press, 1975), 180.

3. Clay to Morris, February 25, 1822, March 8, 1822, March 21, 1822, *HCP* 11:100, 102–3.

4. Calhoun to Clay, May 19, 1821, Marriage Bond, April 22, 1822, Clay to Clay, December 13, 1822, ibid., 3:83, 198, 338.

5. Clay to Rodes, October 21, 1823, ibid., 3:502.

6. *National Intelligencer*, July 4, 1823; Clay to Graham, May 20, 1823, Graham Family Papers, VHS.

7. Baxter, *Clay and the American System*, 44–45; Credentials, December 22, 1821, Clay and Bibb to Randolph, January 31, 1822, *HCP* 3:151, 158.

8. Paul W. Gates, "Tenants of the Log Cabin," *Mississippi Valley Historical Review* 49 (June 1962): 20–21; Baxter, *Clay and the American System*, 45–46; Cary to Cary, February 11, 1822, Carr-Cary Family Papers, UVA; Speech, February 7, 1822, Clay to Brooke, March 9, 1823, *HCP* 3:161–70, 392–93; Clay to Grundy, July 7, 1822, Felix Grundy Papers, LOC; Clay to Burnet, August 27, 1822, Letters of Jacob Burnet, UVA; Clay to Leigh, February 15, 1823, Letters to Benjamin Watkins Leigh, UVA; Hernando de Soto, *The Mystery of Capital: Why Capitalism Triumphs in the West and Fails Everywhere Else* (New York: Basic Books, 2000), 151–52.

9. *Osborn v. United States*, 34 U.S. 573 (1824).

10. Paul E. Doutrich III, "A Pivotal Decision: The

1824 Gubernatorial Election in Kentucky," *Filson Club History Quarterly* 65 (January 1982): 16–18, 22; Mary W. M. Hargreaves, *The Presidency of John Quincy Adams* (Lawrence: University Press of Kansas, 1985), 15; Thomas William Howard, "Indiana Newspapers and the Presidential Election of 1824," *Indiana Magazine of History* 63 (September 1967): 188–89.

11. Warfield to Clay, December 18, 1821, Overton to Clay, January 16, 1822, Beatty to Clay, April 17, 1822, *HCP* 3:148–49, 156, 193.

12. Clay to Porter, April 14, 1822, Clay to Beatty, April 16, 1822, April 30, 1822, Hynes to Clay, June 30, 1822, Hammond to Clay, July 1, 1822, Benton to Clay, July 12, 1822, Leigh to Clay, November 9, 1822, ibid., 3:190–92, 243, 245, 318, 11:107, 109–10, 115; Clay to Burnet, October 5, 1822, Burnet Letters; *Augusta Chronicle,* October 31, 1822.

13. *AC,* 17 Cong., 1 sess., 733; Hecht, *Adams,* 337–38; Benton to Clay, April 9, 1822, *HCP* 11:103–4.

14. Benton to Clay, May 2, 1822, Kendall to Clay, June 20, 1822, Clay to Kendall, June 23, 1822, Clay to Hardin, June 23, 1822, Clay to Russell, July 9, 1822, September 4, 1822, *HCP* 3:204, 237, 238–39, 253–56, 283; Hecht, *Adams,* 342.

15. Clay to Gales and Seaton, November 15, 1822, Clay to Porter, February 4, 1823, *HCP* 3:322, 367; James Henry Rigali, "Restoring the Republic of Virtue: The Presidential Election of 1824," Ph.D. dissertation, University of Washington, 2004, 189–91; Adams, *Memoirs,* 6:49; Van Deusen, *Clay,* 171.

16. For a thorough examination of Jackson as a national symbol, see John William Ward, *Andrew Jackson: Symbol for an Age* (New York: Oxford University Press, 1955).

17. Hynes to Clay, July 31, 1822, Clay to Porter, August 10, 1822, Clay to Meigs, August 21, 1822, Meigs to Clay, September 3, 1822, *HCP* 3:265, 274, 282, 11:117.

18. Clay to Meigs, September 11, 1822, Clay to Sloane, October 22, 1822, Clay to Anderson, January 5, 1823, ibid., 3:285, 11:120–21, 129; John Lauritz Larson, *Internal Improvement: National Public Works and the Promise of Popular Government in the Early United States* (Chapel Hill: University of North Carolina Press, 2001), 153; Everett S. Brown, "The Presidential Election of 1824–1825," *Political Science Quarterly* 40 (September 1925): 389; Richard P. McCormick, *The Second American Party System: Party Formation in the Jacksonian Era* (Chapel Hill: University of North Carolina Press, 1966), 262.

19. Clay to Porter, October 22, 1822, Porter to Clay, January 29, 1823, Clay to Kendall, February 16, 1823, *HCP* 3:300–301, 356, 382–83; Richard P. McCormick, *The Presidential*

Game: The Origins of American Presidential Politics (New York: Oxford University Press, 1984), 116–18; Lillian B. Miller, *"If Elected—": Unsuccessful Candidates for the Presidency, 1796–1968* (Washington, DC: Smithsonian Institution Press, 1972), 87.

20. Clay to Porter, February 2, 1823, February 3, 1823, March 18, 1823, June 15, 1823, Porter to Clay, February 3, 1823, February 8, 1823, Astor to Clay, March 26, 1823, Tracy to Clay, April 27, 1823, *HCP* 3:362–66, 371–72, 401–3, 412, 432–34; Maxcy to Gaston, July 2, 1823, William Gaston Papers, UNC.

21. Clay to Brooke, January 8, 1823, February 26, 1823, August 28, 1823, Brooke to Clay, February 19, 1823, *HCP* 3:350–51, 384, 387–88, 477.

22. Carroll to Clay, February 19, 1823, Woods to Clay, May 22, 1823, Clay to Trimble, May 28, 1823, Benton to Clay, July 23, 1823, Clay to Godman, August 9, 1823, Wharton to Clay, August 13, 1823, Clay to Hammond, August 21, 1823, Clay to Jones, August 23, 1823, ibid., 3:385, 419, 460, 465, 466–67, 471, 11:141, 151; Jackson to Coffee, March 10, 1823, Jackson, *Papers,* 5:258; Calhoun to Jackson, March 30, 1823, Jackson to Calhoun, August 20, 1823, Calhoun, *Papers,* 7:550, 8:236; Jackson to Coffee, April 28, 1823, John Coffee Family Papers, LOC; *Providence Gazette,* December 2, 1823.

23. Albert Ray Newsome, *The Presidential Election of 1824 in North Carolina* (Chapel Hill: University of North Carolina Press, 1939), 104; Risjord, *Old Republicans,* 176; Plumer to Hale, April 5, 1820, Everett S. Brown, editor, *The Missouri Compromises and Presidential Politics, 1820–1825: From the Letters of William Plumer, Jr.* (St. Louis: Missouri Historical Society, 1926), 47.

24. Chase C. Mooney, *William H. Crawford, 1772–1834* (Lexington: University Press of Kentucky, 1974), 241.

25. Ibid.; Clay to Creighton, January 1, 1824, *HCP* 11:166; Saunders to Yancey, December 20, 1823, Yancey Papers; *Washington Republican and Congressional Examiner,* December 23, 1823; Beecher to Ewing, January 2, 1824, Papers of Thomas Ewing Family, LOC.

26. Clay to Epes Sargent, August 20, 1842, *HCP* 9:758.

27. *Niles' Weekly Register,* November 8, 1823, November 29, 1823; Carroll to Clay, October 1, 1823, Clay to Leigh, October 20, 1823, Clay to Porter, December 11, 1823, *HCP* 3:492, 501, 535; Saunders to Yancey, December 20, 1823, Yancey Papers; Van Deusen, *Clay,* 182.

28. Clay to Erwin, December 29, 1823, *HCP* 11:164–65; Saunders to Ruffin, February 5, 1824, Seawell to Ruffin, March 1, 1824, Thomas Ruffin Papers, UNC; Johnson to Wal-

worth, February 22, 1824, John Telemachus Johnson Papers, Filson; *Niles' Weekly Register,* November 15, 1823; McCormick, *Second American Party System,* 139–40; Kim T. Phillips, "The Pennsylvania Origins of the Jackson Movement," *Political Science Quarterly* 91 (Autumn 1976): 495–96.

29. *Argus of Western America,* December 31, 1823; Calhoun to Fisher, December 2, 1823, "Correspondence of John C. Calhoun, George McDuffie, and Charles Fisher Relating to the Presidential Campaign of 1824," edited by Albert Ray Newsome, *North Carolina Historical Review* 7 (October 1930): 484; Williams to Yancey, November 30, 1823, Yancey Papers; Brown, "Election of 1824," 391; Saunders to Yancey, December 4, 1823, "Letters of Romulus M. Saunders to Bartlett Yancey, 1821–1828," edited by Albert Ray Newsome, *North Carolina Historical Review* (1931): 435; Mangum to Cameron, December 10, 1823, *Papers of Willie Person Mangum,* edited by Thomas Henry Shanks, 5 volumes (Raleigh: North Carolina State Department of Archives and History, 1950), 1:82–83; Rochester to Clay, December 20, 1823, *HCP* 3:546–47.

30. Buchanan to Ewing, February 25, 1824, Ewing Family Papers; Robert V. Remini, *Martin Van Buren and the Making of the Democratic Party* (New York: Columbia University Press, 1959), 43–44.

31. Clay to Kendall, April 16, 1820, *HCP* 2:823; McCormick, *Presidential Game,* 108; Sydnor, "One-Party Period," 440; William G. Morgan, "The Decline of the Congressional Nominating Caucus," *Tennessee Historical Quarterly* 24 (1965): 246–47.

32. Saunders to Yancey, December 4, 1823, "Letters of Saunders," 435; Webster to Mason, November 30, 1823, Webster, *Papers,* 1:337; Clay to Erwin, December 29, 1823, Clay to Brooke, January 22, 1824, *HCP* 3:602–3, 11:164; Clay to Stuart, December 19, 1823, Henry Clay Papers, Duke; Campbell to Campbell, January 27, 1824, Campbell Family Papers, Duke.

33. McDuffie to unknown recipient, December 26, 1823, "Correspondence of Calhoun, McDuffie, and Fisher," 493–94; Brown, "Election of 1824," 392–93; Johnson to Walworth, February 22, 1824, John Telemachus Johnson Papers; *Mississippi State Gazette,* March 13, 1824.

34. Barbour to Clay, December 4, 1823, Clay to Brooke, December 20, 1823, *HCP* 3:530–31, 546; Sean Wilentz, *The Rise of American Democracy: Jefferson to Lincoln* (New York: W. W. Norton, 2005), 243; Campbell, "Spanish American Aspect," 9–10; Hoskins, "Hispanic American Policy," 470–71; Randolph B. Campbell, "Henry Clay and the Poinsett

Pledge Controversy of 1826," *Americas* 28 (April 1972): 429–30.

35. Webster to Everett, December 5, 1823, Webster, *Papers,* 1:338–39; Sylvia Neely, "The Politics of Liberty in the Old World and the New: Lafayette's Return to America in 1824," *Journal of the Early Republic* 6 (Summer 1986): 167; Remarks, January 20, 1824, Speech, January 23, 1824, *HCP* 3:597–99, 603–11; May, *Monroe Doctrine,* 236.

36. Clay to Harrison, March 10, 1824, Henry Clay Family Papers, LOC.

37. Wirt to Cabell, December 6, 1823, Cabell Papers; Brown to Price, December 23, 1823, February 4, 1824, May 23, 1824, Price Papers.

38. Johnson to Walworth, February 22, 1824, John Telemachus Johnson Papers.

39. Baker, "Washington National Road," 443; Larson, *Internal Improvement,* 149.

40. *AC,* 18 Cong., 1 sess., 1022–30.

41. Ibid., 1296–1311; Randolph to Garnett, January 16, 1824, Randolph Papers, UVA; Russell Kirk, *John Randolph of Roanoke: A Study in American Politics, with Selected Speeches and Letters* (Indianapolis: Liberty Press, 1978), 172.

42. *AC,* 18 Cong., 1 sess., 1312–13.

43. McFarland and Neal, "Tariff Policies," 25–28; Risjord, *Old Republicans,* 244; Howe, *What Hath God Wrought,* 271.

44. Van Atta, "Western Lands," 645, 649; Clay to Carey, January 2, 1824, *HCP* 11:166; Strahan et al., "Clay Speakership," 576–78.

45. Speech, March 30–31, 1824, *HCP* 3:683–727.

46. Adams, *Memoirs,* 6:258.

47. *Niles' Weekly Register,* April 24, 1824.

48. Charles M. Wiltse, "John C. Calhoun and the 'A.B. Plot,'" *Journal of Southern History* 13 (February 1947): 46–61; Cobb to Jackson, February 23, 1824, Jackson and Prince Family Papers, UNC; R. Carlyle Buley, *The Old Northwest: Pioneer Period, 1815–1840,* 2 volumes (Indianapolis: Indiana Historical Society, 1950), 2:16–17; William B. Hatcher, *Edward Livingston: Jeffersonian Republican and Jacksonian Democrat* (Baton Rouge: Louisiana State University Press, 1940), 307–8; Adams, *Memoirs,* 6:356–57; Clay to Brooke, May 28, 1824, *HCP* 3:767; Calhoun to Garnett, June 6, 1824, Calhoun, *Papers,* 9:139; Troup to Macon, June 15, 1824, Nathaniel Macon Papers, Duke.

49. Mangum to Polk, February 8, 1824, Brown-Ewell Family Papers, Filson; Haywood to Mangum, February 23, 1824, Mangum, *Papers,* 1:120; Mangum to Ruffin, January 20, 1824, Hamilton, *Papers of Ruffin,* 1:287; Clay to Bache, February 17, 1824, Clay to Blair, February 29, 1824, Clay to Erwin, June 19, 1824, *HCP* 3:645, 11:171.

50. McCormick, *Presidential Game,* 109–10; Robert P. Hay, "The Presidential Question:

Letters to Southern Editors, 1823–24," *Tennessee Historical Quarterly* 31 (1972): 171.

51. Adams, *Memoirs,* 6:372; McCormick, *Presidential Game,* 121–22; Duckett, *Forsyth,* 32.

52. Ingham to Gaston, April 24, 1824, Gaston Papers; Robert P. Hay, "The Case for Andrew Jackson in 1824: Eaton's *Wyoming Letters,*" *Tennessee Historical Quarterly* 29 (1970): 146–51; Philo-Jackson (pseudonym), *The Presidential Election, Written for the Benefit of the People of the United States but Particularly for Those of the State of Kentucky; Relating, Also, to the Constitution of the United States, and to Internal Improvements,* sixth series (Frankfort, KY: unknown publisher, 1824), 18–19.

53. *Cahawba Press and Alabama State Intelligencer,* June 7, 1823.

54. Mangum to Cameron, December 10, 1823, Mangum, *Papers,* 1:83.

55. Saunders to Yancey, February 1, 1823, Yancey Papers.

56. Lenoir to Lenoir, February 16, 1824, Lenoir Family Papers, UNC.

57. Seawell to Ruffin, Thomas Ruffin Papers; Haywood to Mangum, February 23, 1824, Mangum, *Papers,* 1:120.

58. Johnston to Clay, August 30, 1824, *HCP* 3:820.

59. Clay to Johnston, June 15, 1824, ibid., 3:777.

60. Clay to Johnston, August 31, 1824, Clay to Porter, September 2, 1824, *HCP* 3:821–23, 825; Peter L. Bernstein, *Wedding of the Waters: The Erie Canal and the Making of a Great Nation* (New York: W. W. Norton, 2005), 296–97; Robin Kolodny, "The Several Elections of 1824," *Congress and the Presidency* 23 (Fall 1996): 153.

61. Clay to Porter, September 2, 1824, Clay to Johnston, September 3, 1824, September 10, 1824, Johnston to Clay, September 4, 1824, September 11, 1824, Clay to Henry, September 14, 1824, *HCP* 3:825, 826, 829, 833, 836, 838; Remini, *Van Buren and Democratic Party,* 65.

62. Ruffin to Yancey, September 21, 1824, Dickins to Yancey, November 21, 1824, Yancey Papers; Lowrie to Gallatin, September 25, 1824, Adams, *Gallatin,* 602–3; Gallatin to Lowrie, October 2, 1824, *Writings of Gallatin,* 2:294; *Providence Gazette,* October 16, 1824; Charles Henry Ambler, *Thomas Ritchie: A Study in Virginia Politics* (Richmond: Bell Books & Stationery Company, 1913), 94–95; Clay to Hammond, October 25, 1824, *HCP* 3:870–72.

63. Clay to Crittenden, September 17, 1824, Clay to Johnston, September 19, 1824, October 2, 1824, Clay to Featherstonhaugh, October 10, 1824, *HCP* 3:842, 854, 11:180–82.

64. *Argus of Western America,* December 8, 1824; Donald J. Ratcliffe, *The Politics of Long Division: The Birth of the Second Party System in Ohio, 1818–1828* (Columbus: Ohio State University Press, 2000), 80, 105; Howard, "Indiana Newspapers," 195, 206.

65. Ruffin to Yancey, December 3, 1824, Thomas Ruffin Papers.

66. Jefferson to Holmes, April 22, 1820, Merrill D. Peterson, editor, *Jefferson: Writings* (New York: Viking, 1984), 1434.

67. Madison shared Jefferson's opinions about the current state of politics. Madison to Todd, December 2, 1824, Lucia Beverly Cutts, editor, *Memoirs and Letters of Dolly Madison, Wife of James Madison, President of the United States* (Boston: Houghton Mifflin, 1886), 167.

68. Memorandum, December 1824, Daniel Webster, *The Private Correspondence of Daniel Webster,* edited by Fletcher Webster, 2 volumes (Boston: Little, Brown, 1857), 1:371.

69. Clay to Brooke, November 26, 1824, *HCP* 3:888.

70. McCormick, *Second American Party System,* 116; "Correspondence of Calhoun, McDuffie, and Fisher," 481; Thurlow Weed, *Life of Thurlow Weed Including His Autobiography and a Memoir,* 2 volumes (Boston: Houghton Mifflin, 1883–1884), 1:126–27; Remini, *Van Buren and Democratic Party,* 74–79; Glyndon G. Van Deusen, *Thurlow Weed: Wizard of the Lobby* (Boston: Little, Brown, 1947), 30.

71. "Correspondence of Calhoun, McDuffie, and Fisher," 481; Remini, *Van Buren and Democratic Party,* 82; Wilentz, *American Democracy,* 250.

72. William to Yancey, December 6, 1824, Yancey Papers; Clay to Stuart, December 6, 1824, *HCP* 3:891.

73. Joseph G. Tregle, Jr., "Andrew Jackson and the Continuing Battle of New Orleans," *Journal of the Early Republic* 1 (Winter 1981): 381; Clay to Ford, December 13, 1824, Clay to Brooke, December 22, 1824, *HCP* 3:896, 900; Saunders to Yancey, December 10, 1824, "Letters of Saunders," 445.

74. McCormick, *Second American Party System,* 314; Clay to Brooke, December 22, 1824, *HCP* 3:900.

75. Martin Van Buren, *The Autobiography of Martin Van Buren,* edited by John C. Fitzpatrick (Washington, DC: Government Printing Office, 1920), 145; Weed, *Autobiography,* 1:128.

76. Clay to Erwin, December 13, 1824, Clay to Leigh, December 22, 1824, *HCP* 3:895, 901.

77. Edgar Ewing Brandon, *Lafayette, Guest of the Nation: A Contemporary Account of the Triumphal Tour of General Lafayette Through the United States in 1824–1825 as Reported by Local Newspapers,* 3 volumes (Oxford, OH: Oxford Historical Press, 1950–1957), 1:34; Stanley J. Idzerda, Anne C. Loveland, and Marc H. Miller, *Lafayette, Hero of Two*

Worlds: The Art and Pageantry of His Farewell Tour of America, 1824–1825 (Hanover, NH: University Press of New England, 1989), 52, 54, 63.

78. Idzerda et al., *Lafayette,* 55; Lafayette to Clay, December 26, 1815, Address, December 10, 1824, Clay to *National Intelligencer,* February 23, 1852, *HCP* 2:112–15, 3:893, 10:954–55.

79. Mangum to Ruffin, December 15, 1824, Thomas Ruffin Papers.

80. Clay to McClure, December 28, 1824, *HCP* 3:906; McCormick, *Presidential Game,* 127; Adams, *Memoirs,* 6:446–47, 452–53, 455–57; Albert D. Kirwan, *John J. Crittenden: The Struggle for the Union* (Lexington: University Press of Kentucky, 1962), 68–69; Paul C. Nagel, *John Quincy Adams: A Public Life, a Private Life* (New York: Alfred A. Knopf, 1997), 292.

81. *Southern Patriot and Commercial Advertiser,* January 11, 1825; Paul F. Boller, Jr., *Presidential Campaigns, from George Washington to George W. Bush* (New York: Oxford University Press, 2004), 38; McLane to McLane, January 13, 1825, McLane Papers, LOC.

82. Clay to Adams, January 9, 1825, Adams to Clay, January 9, 1825, *HCP* 4:11.

83. The most complete explanation of Clay's motives appears in a letter to fellow Kentuckian and future Jacksonian, Francis Preston Blair. Even though Clay obviously did not intend the letter for publication, he offered arguments to placate Kentucky over his decision to oppose Jackson in the House. See Clay to Blair, January 8, 1825, *HCP* 4:9–10.

84. McKee to Brown, January 26, 1825, Samuel Brown Papers, Filson; Green to Polk, January 29, 1825, Brown-Ewell Family Papers. For Jackson's behavior in New Orleans, see Matthew Warshauer, *Andrew Jackson and the Politics of Martial Law: Nationalism, Civil Liberties, and Partisanship* (Knoxville: University of Tennessee Press, 2006).

85. Clay to Featherstonhaugh, January 21, 1825, Clay to Brooke, January 28, 1825, Clay to Blair, January 29, 1825, *HCP* 4:34, 45, 47.

86. William G. Morgan, "John Quincy Adams v. Andrew Jackson: Their Biographers and the 'Corrupt Bargain' Charge," *Tennessee Historical Quarterly* 26 (1967): 43–44.

87. Adams, *Memoirs,* 6:464–65; Brown, "Election of 1824," 400.

88. McLane to McLane, January 2, 1825, McLane Papers, LOC.

89. Buchanan to Elder, January 2, 1825, Buchanan, *Works,* 1:120; Jackson to Coffee, January 6, 1825, Jackson, *Papers,* 6:7–8; Macon to Tait, January 9, 1825, Macon Papers; Mangum to Cameron, January 10, 1825, Cameron Family Papers, UNC.

90. Saunders to Yancey, January 11, 1825, January 18, 1825, "Letters of Saunders," 449–50;

Barry to Clay, January 10, 1825, Clay to Stuart, January 15, 1825, *HCP* 4:11–12, 19; Adams, *Memoirs,* 6:467–69, 473–78; McLane to McLane, January 13, 1825, McLane Papers, LOC; Taylor to Austin, January 23, 1825, Austin-Twyman Papers; *Niles' Weekly Register,* January 25, 1825; Ware to Brown, January 29, 1825, Samuel Brown Papers.

91. Adams, *Memoirs,* 6:483; Philadelphia *Columbian Observer,* January 25, 1825; Logan to Tazewell, January 31, 1825, Tazewell Family Papers, LOV; *Winyaw Intelligencer,* February 5, 1825; Cobb to Jackson, February 6, 1825, Jackson and Prince Family Papers.

92. Clay to Gales and Seaton, January 30, 1825, Kremer's Card, February 3, 1825, Clay to Erwin, February 25, 1825, *HCP* 4:48, 52, 82.

93. *Massachusetts Spy and Worcester Advertiser,* February 16, 1825; Adams, *Memoirs,* 6:494.

94. Appeal to the House, February 3, 1825, *HCP* 4:53–54.

95. McLane to McLane, February 5, 1825, McLane Papers, LOC; *Providence Gazette,* February 5, 1825; Clay to unknown recipient, February 4, 1825, Clay to Brooke, December 5, 1824, February 4, 1825, *HCP* 3:891, 4:55–6; Leigh to Lee, November 29, 1824, Benjamin Watkins Leigh Papers, VHS.

96. Adams, *Memoirs,* 6:495; William E. Foley, "The Political Philosophy of David Barton," *Missouri Historical Review* 58 (1964): 287; Alan S. Weiner, "John Scott, Thomas Hart Benton, David Barton and the Presidential Election of 1824: A Case Study in Pressure Politics," *Missouri Historical Review* 60 (July 1966): 481–83.

97. Weiner, "Election of 1824," 486–87; *Southern Patriot and Commercial Advertiser,* February 16, 1825.

98. Van Buren, *Autobiography,* 151; McLane to McLane, February 9, 1825, McLane Papers, LOC.

99. Van Buren, *Autobiography,* 151–52; Boller, *Presidential Campaigns,* 38–39; McLane to McLane, February 11, February 12, 1825, McLane Papers, LOC; Forsyth to O'Connor, February 25, 1825, John Forsyth Letters, UGA.

100. Adams, *Memoirs,* 6:501.

101. *National Intelligencer,* February 11, 1825; Smith, *Forty Years,* 183.

102. Gibbs to Ball, February 16, 1825, John Ball Papers, SCHS.

103. Jackson to Lewis, February 14, 1825, Jackson, *Papers,* 6:29–30.

104. Clay to Brown, January 23, 1825, Clay to Brooke, February 14, 1825, February 18, 1825, Crittenden to Clay, February 15, 1825, Kendall to Clay, February 19, 1825, Creighton to Clay, February 19, 1825, Clay to Hubbard, February 25, 1825, *HCP* 4:39, 67–69, 73–74,

76–77, 82; *New York Daily Advertiser,* March 5, 1825; Adams, *Memoirs,* 6:505, 508–9; Webster to Mason, February 14, 1825, Mason to Webster, February 20, 1825, Webster, *Papers,* 2:23, 28; Brockenbrough to Ruffin, February 19, 1825, Francis G. Ruffin Papers, UNC.

105. Jackson to Lewis, February 14, 1825, Jackson, *Papers,* 6:29–30.

106. *Louisiana Gazette,* February 28, 1825, March 1, 1825.

107. Henry Stuart Foote, *Casket of Reminiscences,* (Washington, DC: Chronicle Publishing Company, 1874), 27–28.

108. McLane to McLane, February 12, 1825, McLane Papers, LOC.

CHAPTER SEVEN

A Thousand Cuts

1. Clay to Whittlesey, March 26, 1825, *HCP* 4:178–79; Saunders to Yancey, February 22, 1825, Yancey Papers; *Daily National Journal,* March 9, 1825; Calhoun to Sterling, February 4, 1826, Calhoun, *Papers,* 10:72; Cocke to Gilmer, November 19, 1827, Tyler Family Scrapbook, W&M.

2. Kremer to Jackson, March 8, 1825, Bassett, *Correspondence,* 3:281–82; Atmore to Bryan, January 14, 1826, John Heritage Bryan Papers, Duke.

3. Address to the People, March 26, 1825, *HCP* 4:143–65.

4. Clay to Todd, March 27, 1825, Eaton to Clay, March 28, 1825, March 31, 1825, Clay to Eaton, March 30, 1825, April 1, 1825, Clay to Brooke, April 6, 1825, *HCP* 4:189, 191–92, 196–202, 221.

5. *The Microscope,* March 19, 1825; *Louisville Public Advertiser,* March 16, 1825; Brooke to Forsyth, March 13, 1825, Brooke Family Papers, VHS; Blair to Clay, March 7, 1825, Armstrong and Potts to Clay, March 9, 1825, Scott to Clay, March 9, 1825, Marshall to Clay, April 4, 1825, Mercer to Clay, April 7, 1825, Clay to Gaines, April 29, 1825, *HCP* 4:91, 97–98, 212, 228, 309–10; Harrison to Este, March 3, 1825, Bruce Papers.

6. Clay to Brooke, April 6, 1825, Clay to Vance, April 19, 1825, Kendall to Clay, April 28, 1825, Clay to Brown, May 9, 1825, *HCP* 4:221, 269, 305–6, 335–36; Van Deusen, *Clay,* 196–97.

7. Clay to Brown, May 9, 1825, *HCP* 4:335–36; Erwin to Mentelle, July 23, [1823?], Henry Clay Family Papers, UKY.

8. Clay to Hammond, May 23, 1825, Clay to Southard, June 17, 1825, *HCP* 4:388, 408–9, 447; *Augusta Chronicle,* June 29, 1825; Davenport, *Ante-Bellum Kentucky,* 26; Friend, *Maysville Road,* 157; Railey, *Woodford*

County, 184; Clay to Barbour, May 22, 1825, Papers of Henry Clay, UVA.

9. Dickson D. Bruce, Jr., *The Kentucky Tragedy: A Story of Conflict and Change in Antebellum America* (Baton Rouge: Louisiana State University Press, 2006), 128–30; *Niles' Weekly Register,* July 28, 1825, November 18, 1826; Kendall to Clay, February 19, 1825, *HCP* 4:66, 77; *Argus of Western America,* January 19, 1825; Andrew Forest Muir, "Isaac B. Desha, Fact and Fancy," *Filson Club Quarterly* 30 (October 1956): 319–21.

10. Frank F. Mathias, "Clay and His Kentucky Power Base," *Register of the Kentucky Historical Society* 78 (Spring 1980): 126; Kendall to Clay, October 4, 1825, *HCP* 4:718–20; Doutrich, "1824 Gubernatorial Election," 20–28; Buckner to Buckner, June 4, 1826, Buckner Family Papers, Filson.

11. Duralde to Clays, August 8, 1825, *HCP* 4:570–71.

12. Clay to Adams, June 28, 1825, July 21, 1825, Clay to Clay, August 24, 1825, Clay to Erwin, August 28, 1825, ibid., 4:489–90, 546, 589, 598; Adams, *Memoirs,* 7:46.

13. Adams, *Memoirs,* 7:46–48; Duralde to Clays, August 8, 1825, Clay to Clay, August 24, 1825, Clay to Erwin, August 28, 1825, *HCP* 4:571–71, 589–90, 598.

14. Clay to Bascom, August 30, 1825, Clay to Erwin, August 30, 1825, Clay to Parker, September 3, 1825, Webster to Clay, September 28, 1825, Clay to Brown, November 14, 1825, *HCP* 4:600, 601, 616, 698–99, 823.

15. Maureau to Clay, September 19, 1825, Eustis to Clay, September 20, 1825, ibid., 4:659, 665; *Philadelphia Aurora and Franklin Gazette,* October 20, 1825.

16. Clay to Mentelle, October 24, 1825, Clay to Brown, November 14, 1825, *HCP* 4:756, 822; Adams, *Memoirs,* 7:51–52; Brown to Price, December 12, 1825, November 23, 1826, Price Papers; Story to Denison, March 15, 1826, William N. Story, *Life and Letters of Joseph Story,* 2 volumes (Boston: Little, Brown, 1851), 1:495.

17. Paul C. Nagel, "The Election of 1824: A Reconsideration Based on Newspaper Opinion," *Journal of Southern History* 26 (August 1960): 328; Benton, *Thirty Years' View; or, A History of the Working of the American Government for Thirty Years, from 1820 to 1850,* 2 volumes (New York: D. Appleton, 1854–1856), 1:47; Larson, *Internal Improvements,* 149.

18. Peterson, *Great Triumvirate,* 146–47; Hammond to Clay, November 1, 1825, Creighton to Clay, November 14, 1825, *HCP* 4:780–83, 825; James E. Lewis, Jr., *The American Union and the Problem of Neighborhood: The United States and the Collapse of the Spanish Empire, 1783–1829* (Chapel

Hill: University of North Carolina Press, 1998), 199.

19. Adams, *Memoirs,* 7:61; Clay to Brown, December 12, 1825, Clay to Lafayette, December 13, 1825, *HCP* 4:895, 905–6; Kevin R. Gutzman, "Preserving the Patrimony: William Branch Giles and Virginia Versus the Federal Tariff," *Virginia Magazine of History and Biography* 104 (Summer 1996): 352–53.

20. Clay to Hammond, December 10, 1825, *HCP* 4:891.

21. Samuel Flagg Bemis, *The American Secretaries of State and Their Diplomacy,* 10 volumes (New York: Pageant Book Company, 1958), 4:124–28; Paul A. Varg, *United States Foreign Relations, 1820–1860* (East Lansing: Michigan State University Press, 1979), 64; Smith to Clay, June 25, 1825, Clay to Gallatin, February 24, 1827, *HCP* 4:468–75, 6:237; Gallatin, *Diary,* 267; Raymond Walters, Jr., *Albert Gallatin: Jeffersonian Financier and Diplomat* (New York: Macmillan, 1957), 330–31.

22. Adams, *Memoirs,* 7:59–60; Brown to Clay, September 13, 1827, *HCP* 6:1028.

23. Clay to Robertson, December 7, 1825, *HCP* 4:882–83; Lewis, *Problem of Neighborhood,* 193; John J. Johnson, *A Hemisphere Apart: The Foundations of United States Policy Toward Latin America* (Baltimore: Johns Hopkins University Press, 1990), 126–27; Van Deusen, *Clay,* 202.

24. Bemis, *Secretaries of State,* 4:131–32, 137; Adams, *Memoirs,* 7:71.

25. Campbell, "Spanish American Aspect," 10; Bemis, *Secretaries of State,* 4:137, 139.

26. Adams, *Memoirs,* 7:53; Campbell, "Spanish American Aspect," 10; Lester D. Langley, *Struggle for the American Mediterranean: United States–European Rivalry in the Gulf–Caribbean, 1776–1904* (Athens: University of Georgia Press, 1976), 47.

27. Campbell, "Spanish American Aspect," 12; Jackson to Branch, Branch Family Papers, UNC; Clay to Webster, ca. January 31, 1826, Webster, *Papers,* 2:82–83; McCormick, *Presidential Game,* 120; Henry Adams, *John Randolph* (Boston: Houghton Mifflin, 1882), 285.

28. Hoskins, "Hispanic American Policy," 475–76; Van Deusen, *Clay,* 208–9; Bemis, *Secretaries of State,* 4:149–53; Campbell, "Clay and Poinsett Pledge," 438–39; Langley, *American Mediterranean,* 47.

29. Johnson, *Hemisphere Apart,* 39; Bemis, *Secretaries of State,* 4:133–34, 154; Clay to Adams, July 2, 1827, Clay to Brown, August 10, 1827, Clay to Adams, August 23, 1827, *HCP* 6:738, 871, 950–51; Adams, *Memoirs,* 7:277; J. Fred Rippy, *Joel R. Poinsett, Versatile American* (Durham: Duke University Press, 1935; reprint edition, New York: Greenwood Press, 1968), 105–7, 121–25.

30. Eaton to Grundy, April 2, 1826, Felix Grundy Papers, UNC.

31. *Reg. of Deb.,* 19 Cong., 1 sess., 2:401.

32. Clay to Brooke, March 10, 1826, *HCP* 7:154; Clay to Randolph, March 31, 1826, Jesup to Underwood, March 4, 1853, Clay Family Papers, LOC.

33. Adams, *Randolph,* 259; Randolph to Clay, April 1, 1826, Clay Family Papers, LOC; Benton, *Thirty Years' View,* 1:70; Bruce, *Randolph,* 1:515.

34. Jesup to Tattnall, April 3, 1826, April 4, 1826, Tattnall to Jesup, April 3, 1826, Duel Terms, Clay Family Papers, LOC; Benton, *Thirty Years' View,* 1:71–74.

35. Benton, *Thirty Years' View,* 1:74.

36. Benton to Tucker, July 16, 1826, Clay Family Papers, LOC.

37. Van Buren, *Autobiography,* 204; Van Deusen, *Clay,* 221; Benton, *Thirty Years' View,* 1:75.

38. Jesup to Underwood, March 4, 1853, Clay Family Papers, LOC.

39. Account by Seconds, April 10, 1826, Benton to Tucker, July 16, 1826, Jesup to Underwood, March 4, 1853, Clay Family Papers, LOC; Van Deusen, *Clay,* 222; Benton, *Thirty Years' View,* 1:75–76.

40. Montpelier *Vermont Watchman and State Gazette,* May 2, 1826; Louisville *Public Advertiser,* April 26, 1826.

41. McLeod to McLeod, September 1826, McLeod Family Papers, VHS.

42. Jackson to Buchanan, April 6, 1826, Jackson to Houston, December 15, 1826, Jackson, *Papers,* 6:163, 243.

43. Edward Pessen, *Jacksonian America: Society, Personality, and Politics* (Homewood, IL: Dorsey Press, 1979), 179; John M. Belohlavek, *George Mifflin Dallas: Jacksonian Patrician* (University Park: Pennsylvania State University Press, 1977), 26.

44. Buchanan to Jackson, May 29, 1825, Jackson to Buchanan, June 25, 1825, Green to Buchanan, October 12, 1826, Buchanan, *Works,* 1:138–40, 217; Buchanan to Jackson, September 21, 1826, Jackson, *Papers,* 6:212–13; Memorandum, May 20, 1826, Bassett, *Correspondence,* 3:301. Duff Green had family ties in Kentucky and in fact was related to Humphrey Marshall, a connection that might at least partially explain his strong animosity to Clay. See W. Stephen Belko, *The Invincible Duff Green: Whig of the West* (Columbia: University of Missouri Press, 2006), 14–15.

45. Buchanan to Green, October 16, 1826, Buchanan, *Works,* 1:218–19.

46. Jackson to Beverley, June 5, 1827, Jackson, *Papers,* 6:330–31; Report of interview, ca. April 15, 1827, Clay, *Papers,* 6:448–49; Watkins to Gurley, May 1, 1827, Gurley Family Papers, Tulane.

47. Clay to Hammond, June 25, 1827, Clay to "the Public," July 4, 1827, Clay to Bealle, July 9, 1827, *HCP* 6:718–19, 728–30, 11:206.

48. Jackson to Buchanan, July 15, 1827, Jackson, *Papers,* 6:359–60; Buchanan to *Lancaster Journal,* August 8, 1827, Buchanan to Jackson, August 10, 1827, Buchanan, *Works,* 1:263–67, 269.

49. Estill to Barbour, August 26, 1827, Tyler Family Scrapbook; Clay to Southard, August 12, 1827, Maury to Clay, August 14, 1827, Webster to Clay, August 22, 1827, Clay to Blackford, August 24, 1827, Clay to Dallam, September 1, 1827, Ingersoll to Clay, October 6, 1827, *HCP* 6:891, 902, 949, 957–58, 985, 1118; McLaughlin to Ruffin, August 20, 1827, Hamilton, editor, *Papers of Ruffin,* 1:402; Leonard D. White, *The Jeffersonians: A Study in Administrative History, 1801–1829* (New York: Macmillan, 1959), 42.

50. Kendall to Clay, January 21, 1825, March 23, 1825, October 4, 1825, Clay to Kendall, October 18, 1825, Blair to Clay, January 24, 1825, Clay to Blair, December 16, 1825, *HCP* 4:35, 41, 136, 719, 747, 11:193; Donald B. Cole, *A Jackson Man: Amos Kendall and the Rise of American Democracy* (Baton Rouge: Louisiana State University Press, 2004), 97; Kendall to Flugel, April 4, 1839, Kendall Papers.

51. Kendall to Clay, March 23, 1825, October 4, 1825, December 25, 1825, Clay to Kendall, October 18, 1825, excerpt from *Argus of Western America, HCP* 4:136, 718–20, 746–48, 943, 6:1131–32; Elbert B. Smith, *Francis Preston Blair* (New York: Free Press, 1980), 30; Kirwan, *Crittenden,* 76; Daniels, "Kendall," 55; Donald B. Cole, *Martin Van Buren and the American Political System* (Princeton, NJ: Princeton University Press, 1984), 156.

52. Clay to Clay, February 22, 1827, Crittenden to Clay, November 15, 1827, *HCP* 6:222, 1264–65. A story, perhaps apocryphal, made the rounds of Washington that after Blair had gone public with his support for Jackson in 1828, he and Clay ran into each other outside a Frankfort, Kentucky, tavern. Clay immediately extended his hand and said, " 'How do you do, Mr. Blair?'" Blair stammered a bit and then extended his own hand, replying, "'Pretty well, I thank you sir. How did you find the roads from Lexington here?'" Clay answered, " 'The roads are very bad, Mr. Blair, very bad, and I wish, sir, that you would mend your ways.'" Story from *Perley's Reminiscences,* 1:104.

53. Clay to Blair, January 8, 1825, *HCP* 4:9.

54. Blair to Clay, October 3, 1827, November 14, 1827, Clay to Blair, October 11, 1827, October 19, 1827, ibid., 6:1106–7; Webster to Mason, January 9, 1828, Webster, *Papers,*

2:275; *Niles' Weekly Register,* January 5, 12, 1828.

55. Marshall to Clay, January 5, 1828, Madison to Clay, January 6, 1828, Ogden to Clay, January 8, 1828, Clay to Crittenden, February 14, 1828, Clay to Brooke, February 22, 1828, *HCP* 7:12, 14, 18, 94–95, 113; Cole, *Kendall,* 106; Clark, *Kentucky,* 150; Mathias, "Kentucky Power Base," 130–31; Webster to Mason, January 9, 1828, Webster, *Papers,* 2:275.

56. Kendall to Clay, February 6, 1828, May 28, 1828, October 1, 1828, Todd to Clay, February 18, 1828, Blair to Clay, March 4, 1828, Marshall to Clay, May 1, 1828, Clay to Harvie, June 5, 1828, *HCP* 7:81, 104, 139–40, 254–55, 306–7, 327–31, 480; Adams, *Memoirs,* 8:28.

57. Clay to Erwin, June 19, 1824, April 21, 1827, August 4, 1827, Erwin to Clay, May 21, 1827, Clay to Everett, May 2, 1827, Receipt from Decatur, June 5, 1827, Decatur to Clay, September 15, 1827, Clay to Adams, July 7, 1828, *HCP* 3:781, 6:471, 507, 576, 649, 849, 1038–39, 7:375.

58. Barraud to Baker, 1828, Barraud Family Papers, W&M; Clay to Crowninshield, March 18, 1827, Speech, June 20, 1827, Porter to Clay, November 22, 1827, *HCP* 6:320, 700–703, 1303–4.

59. Glyndon G. Van Deusen, *The Jacksonian Era, 1828–1848* (New York: Harper & Row, 1959), 33; William Seale, *The President's House: A History,* 2 volumes (Washington, DC: White House Historical Association, 1986), 1:172–73.

60. Michael F. Holt, *The Rise and Fall of the American Whig Party: Jacksonian Politics and the Onset of the Civil War* (New York: Oxford University Press, 1999), 10; Clay to Everett, May 22, 1827, Clay to Connant, October 29, 1827, Clay to Brooke, November 24, 1827, *HCP* 6:580, 1197, 1312; Barbour to Stuart, December 16, 1827, Papers of Alexander H. H. Stuart, UVA; Polk to Jackson, April 13, 1828, Jackson, *Papers,* 6:444–46; Harry L. Watson, *Jacksonian Politics and Community Conflict: The Emergence of the Second Party System in Cumberland County North Carolina* (Baton Rouge: Louisiana State University Press, 1981), 152; Warshauer, *Jackson and the Politics of Martial Law,* 58–59.

61. Van Deusen, *Clay,* 227–28; Norma Basch, "Marriage, Morals, and Politics in the Election of 1828," *The Journal of American History* 80 (December 1993), 891, 896; Clay to Hammond, December 23, 1826, Hammond to Clay, January 3, 1827, *HCP* 5:1023–24, 6:5; Jackson to Call, May 3, 1827, Jackson, *Papers,* 6:315–16; *United States Telegraph,* July 7, 1827.

62. Houston to Jackson, January 5, 1827, Hayne

to Jackson, June 5, 1827, Jackson, *Papers,* 6:256–57, 332–33; Eaton to Jackson, January 21, 1828, Bassett, *Correspondence,* 3:389–90; Clay to Erwin, August 4, 1827, Johnston to Clay, September 13, 1827, *HCP* 6:850, 1030.

63. Whittlesey to Clay, March 13, 1827, Sergeant to Clay, August 23, 1827, Johnston to Clay, September 13, 1827, Rochester to Clay, October 9, 1827, Clay to Webster, October 25, 1827, *HCP* 6:300, 1030, 1130, 1187; Major Wilson, "Republicanism and the Idea of Party in the Jacksonian Period," *Journal of the Early Republic* 8 (Winter 1988), 439; Van Deusen, *Jacksonian Era,* 29; Holt, *American Whig Party,* 8–9.

64. Porter to Clay, February 27, 1827, Brown to Clay, May 12, 1827, *HCP* 6:245–46, 544–47.

65. Lynn Hudson Parsons, *The Birth of Modern Politics: Andrew Jackson, John Quincy Adams, and the Election of 1828* (New York: Oxford University Press, 2009), 138; Clay to Brooke, January 18, 1828, February 2, 1828, March 1, 1828, Brooke to Clay, February 28, 1828, *HCP* 7:45, 73, 124, 135; Clay to Marshall, April 28, 1828, John Marshall Papers, W&M; Sweeny to Hooe, October 29, 1828, Papers of John Hooe, UVA.

66. Hammond to Clay, August 29, 1827, Fendall to Clay, September 1, 1827, Crittenden to Clay, September 6, 1827, Randolph to Clay, September 12, 1827, Clay to Randolph, September 15, 1827, *HCP* 6:974, 987, 1010, 1025, 1033; Cabell to Mercer, September 27, 1827, Cabell Papers.

67. Dangerfield, *Era of Good Feelings,* 405–6; Van Deusen, *Clay,* 215; Pickering to Randolph, April 12, 1828, Randolph Papers, UVA; Baxter, *American System,* 63–64; Daniel Feller, *The Jacksonian Promise: America, 1815–1840* (Baltimore: Johns Hopkins University Press, 1995), 72.

68. Dangerfield, *Era of Good Feelings,* 405–9; Branch to Jackson, May 23, 1828, Jackson, *Papers,* 6:459–60; Hayne to Jackson, September 3, 1828, Bassett, *Correspondence,* 3:432–35.

69. Hammond to Clay, August 10, 1827, Clay to Trumbull, December 27, 1827, Clay to Featherstonhaugh, February 18, 1828, *HCP* 6:877, 1384–85, 7:102; Van Deusen, *Clay,* 216.

70. *New York Times,* July 9, 1911; Clay to Erwin, February 1, 1827, Clay to Sloane, May 20, 1827, Clay to Southard, July 9, 1827, Clay to Dallam, September 1, 1827, Brown to Clay, September 6, 1827, Clay to Adams, September 24, 1827, Clay to Henry, September 27, 1827, Clay to Brown, October 28, 1827, Speech in Baltimore, May 13, 1828, Clay to Hammond, May 31, 1828, Speech in Virginia, summer 1828, Clay to Southard, July 2, 1828, Speech at Cincinnati, August 30, 1828, *HCP* 6:155, 572–73, 754, 985, 1007, 1063,

1073–76, 1194, 7:272–73, 314, 348–49, 373–74, 448–51; Adams, *Memoirs,* 7:113, 115, 291, 358.

71. George Ticknor, *Life, Letters, and Journals of George Ticknor,* 2 volumes (Boston: Houghton Mifflin, 1909), 1:381.

72. Adams, *Memoirs,* 7:439, 517.

73. Adams, *Memoirs,* 7:517; Clay to Adams, May 8, 1828, Physick and Chapman to Clay, May 11, 1828, *HCP* 7:262, 270.

74. Johnston to Clay, May 9, 1828, *HCP* 7:263.

75. Clay to Crittenden, January 25, 1827, Van Rensselaer to Clay, March 17, 1827, Hammond to Clay, March 28, 1827, Clay to Hammond, April 21, 1827, Learned to Clay, September 27, 1827, Street to Clay, October 8, 1827, Clay to Adams, May 8, 1828, Clay to Southard, July 2, 1828, ibid., 6:118, 315, 372, 473, 1077–81, 1125–26, 7:262–63, 374; Adams, *Memoirs,* 6:547.

76. Clay to Webster, June 13, 1828, Erwin to Clay, July 9, 1828, *HCP* 7:350, 377–78.

77. Erwin to Mentelle, October 27, 1827, Clay Family Papers, UKY; Erwin to Clay, July 17, 1827, Clay to Erwin, September 4, 1828, Clay to Breckinridge, October 1, 1828, *HCP* 6:799, 7:456, 478.

78. Rochester to Clay, October 12, 1827, Clay to Brooke, November 24, 1827, *HCP* 6:1141, 1311–12; Wilson, "Idea of Party," 439–41; David S. Heidler and Jeanne T. Heidler, " 'Not a Ragged Mob': The Inauguration of 1829," *White House History* 15 (Fall 2004): 17.

79. Whittlesey to Clay, August 15, 1828, Clay to Wattles, November 10, 1828, Clay to Beatty, November 13, 1828, *HCP* 7:429, 534, 536.

80. Clay to Beatty, November 13, 1828, ibid., 7:536.

81. Clay to Sloane, November 12, 1828, ibid.; Heidler and Heidler, "Inauguration of 1829," 18.

82. Clay to Brooke, November 18, 1828, *HCP* 7:541.

83. Niles to Clay, November 22, 1828, Clay to Niles, November 25, 1828, ibid., 7:544–45, 548.

84. Clay to Beall, November 18, 1828, Clay to Beatty, November 22, 1828, ibid., 7:544, 11:214; Smith, *Forty Years,* 246, 249.

85. Clay to Barbour, December 29, 1828, Clay Papers, UVA; Adams, *Memoirs,* 8:78, 82.

86. Clay to Webster, November 30, 1828, Crittenden to Clay, December 3, 1828, Clay to Brooke, December 29, 1828, January 10, 1829, *HCP* 7:552–53, 554, 575, 595; Bates to Bates, January 4, 1829, Edward Bates Papers, VHS.

87. Robert V. Remini, *Andrew Jackson and the Course of American Freedom, 1822–1832* (New York: Harper & Row, 1981), 150–51, 154; Robertson to Cabell, February 26, 1829, Cabell Papers.

88. Smith, *Forty Years,* 256, 259; Adams, *Memoirs,* 8:95.
89. Clay to Plumer, February 23, 1829, *HCP* 7:626; Memoir of Great-granddaughter, Clay-Russell Papers.
90. Davis to Bancroft, January 29, 1826, Webster, *Papers,* 2:81.
91. Smith, *Forty Years,* 277.
92. Ibid., 211, 246; Brown to Clay, May 12, 1827, *HCP* 6:545.
93. Smith, *Forty Years,* 277–78.
94. Donald B. Cole, *The Presidency of Andrew Jackson* (Lawrence: University Press of Kansas, 1993), 28–31; Clay to Brooke, February 21, 1829, Brooke to Clay, February 23, 1829, Clay to Caldwell, February 24, 1829, *HCP* 7:624–25, 626, 627; *Niles' Weekly Register,* March 21, 1829; William T. Barry, "Letters of William T. Barry, 1806–1810, 1829–1831," *American Historical Review* 16 (January 1911): 327.
95. Jackson to Coffee, March 19, 1829, Bassett, *Correspondence,* 4:13; Cambreleng to Van Buren, March 1, 1829, Van Buren Papers; Van Deusen, *Jacksonian Era,* 37–38; Cole, *Van Buren,* 204; Richard B. Latner, *The Presidency of Andrew Jackson* (Athens: University of Georgia Press, 1979), 61; Catherine Allgor, *Parlor Politics: In Which the Ladies of Washington Help Build a City and a Government* (Charlottesville: University Press of Virginia, 2000), 206.
96. Boyle to Clay, October 1, 1825, Overton to Clay, January 30, 1827, Wharton to Clay, March 6, 1829, Clay to Wharton, March 24, 1829, *HCP* 4:704–6, 6:139, 8:2–3, 11:222; Smith, *Forty Years,* 303.
97. Adams, *Memoirs,* 8:103.
98. Heidler and Heidler, "Inauguration of 1829," 15, 20–22.
99. Clay to U.S. Circuit Court, February 18, 1829, Condon to Clay, March 1, 1829, *HCP* 7:623, 632.
100. Jill LePore, *A Is for America: Letters and Other Characters in the Newly United States* (New York: Alfred A. Knopf, 2002), 128–30; Terry Alford, *Prince Among Slaves: The True Story of an African Prince Sold into Slavery in the American South* (New York: Oxford University Press, 1986); Speech, January 20, 1827, Rahahman to Clay, April 6, 1829, Mechlin to Clay, April 22, 1829, *HCP* 6:92–94, 8:28, 34.
101. Clay to U.S. Circuit Court, February 18, 1829, Condon to Clay, March 1, 1829, Clay to Davis, July 8, 1829, Clay to Fendall, August 7, 1830, September 10, 1830, December 5, 1830, *HCP* 7:623, 631–33, 8:72, 253, 261–62, 309; Richard L. Troutman, "The Emancipation of Slaves by Henry Clay," *Journal of Negro History* 40 (April 1955), 180–81. The 1869 census had Aaron and Lottie Dupuy living in Lexington.
102. Speech, March 7, 1829, *HCP* 8:4–5.

CHAPTER EIGHT

Losing the Bank, Saving the Union

1. Prentiss to Prentiss, September 3, 1836, George Lewis Prentiss, *Memoir of S. S. Prentice,* 2 volumes (New York: Scribner's Sons, 1855), 1:173.
2. Livestock Agreement, November 20, 1827, Stud Fees, October 12, 1832, Clay-Russell Papers; Clay to Thorton, November 2, 1828, Clay to Ewing, May 4, 1829, Clay to Brown, April 17, 1830, Clay to Treadwell, April 23, 1831, Clay to Jones, July 5, 1831, Berryman to Clay, October 5, 1831, Payne to Clay, October 12, 1832, *HCP* 7:525, 8:37–38, 192, 336, 371, 415, 582. During Clay's later years and in the years after his death, his son John Morrison Clay made Ashland Farms one of the most famous thoroughbred racehorse farms in the country.
3. Clay to Clay, February 6, 1828, October 21, 1828, ibid., 7:80
4. Clay to Clay, April 2, 1827, December 2, 1829, March 29, 1830, ibid., 6:385, 8:131–32, 185.
5. Clay to Clay, October 21, 1828, November 14, 1828, December 16, 1828, December 20, 1828, January 26, 1829, February 9, 1829, Clay to Clay, May 24, 1830 ibid., 7:511, 536, 569, 571, 606, 616, 8:213.
6. Adams, *Memoirs,* 7:297; Clay to Clay, March 27, 1827, *HCP* 6:365–66.
7. Erwin to Clay, July 9, 1829, Johnston to Clay, July 14, 1828, *HCP* 7:377, 385.
8. Clay to Clay, September 18, 1829, ibid., 8:103.
9. Clay to Clay, October 31, 1830, ibid., 8:284.
10. Erwin to Clay, May 15, 1830: ibid., 8:208.
11. Anne had four living children by 1830: Henry Clay Erwin, born in 1827, James Erwin, Jr., born in 1828, Lucretia Hart Erwin, born in 1829, and Andrew Eugene Erwin, born in 1830.
12. Claiborne to Clay, June 20, 1827, Clay to Erwin, September 3, 1827, Clay to Southard, December 2, 1830, *HCP* 6:703, 991, 8:308; Duralde to Clay, August 25, 1827, March 18, 1830, Clay Family Papers, LOC.
13. Watkins to Clay, September 13, 1827, Clay Family Papers, LOC; Clay to Clay, August 10, 1827, Clay to Clay, October 15, 1827, Clay to Clay, October 24, 1829, Clay to Hammond, August 27, 1832, Clay to Clay, August 28, 1832, *HCP* 6:876, 1149, 8:563, 566–67.
14. Claiborne to Clay, Clay to Clay, November 28, 1829, Clay to Clay, December 2, 1829, December 23, 1829, *HCP* 8:117, 130, 131, 161; Smith and Clay, *Clay Family,* 31.

15. Brown to Clay, August 13, 1827, Thomas J. Clay Collection of the Henry Clay Papers; Brown to Clay, August 30, 1827, October 13, 1827, October 28, 1830, Johnston to Clay, October 13, 1830, *HCP* 6:981, 1144; Brown to Price, December 29, 1828, February 10, 1829, November 3, 1830, Price Papers; Brown to Clay, February 9, 1830, Clay Family Papers, UKY; Baxter, *Clay the Lawyer,* 85; *Raleigh Register and North Carolina Gazette,* May 12, 1831.

16. Meyer, *Johnson,* 248; Clay to Adams, April 16, 1829, Clay to Hammond, September 9, 1829, *HCP* 8:27, 97; Webster to Agg, August 10, 1829, Webster, *Papers,* 2:422.

17. Clay to Sloane, May 30, 1829, Clay to Harrison, June 2, 1829, *HCP* 8:61–62, 64.

18. McLean to Graham, April 30, 1829, Graham Family Papers; Barry to Taylor, May 16, 1829, "Letters of Barry," 332; Harry L. Watson, "Old Hickory's Democracy," *Wilson Quarterly* 9 (1985): 122; Clay to Clay, April 19, 1829, Clay to Wharton, April 19, 1829, *HCP* 8:29, 31.

19. Clay to Brooke, March 12, 1829, *HCP* 8:8; Kendall to Kendall, February 14, 1829, March 22, 1829, Kendall, *Autobiography,* 283, 287, 303.

20. *National Intelligencer,* June 19, 1829.

21. Baxter, *Clay the Lawyer,* 89; Wickliffe to Clay, March 15, 1829, *HCP* 8:9; Colton, *Clay,* 1:90–91, Lexington *Gazette,* March 20, 1829.

22. *National Intelligencer,* July 21, 1829; Colton, *Clay,* 1:92–93.

23. Brooke to Clay, October 19, 1829, Brent to Clay, December 5, 1829, *HCP* 8:115, 133; Slidell to Cambreleng, October 11, 1829, John Slidell Letter, Historic New Orleans Collection.

24. Clay to Johnston, December 25, 1829, March 11, 1830, Speech, March 13, 1830, *HCP* 8:162, 179; Joseph G. Tregle, Jr., *Louisiana in the Age of Jackson: A Clash of Cultures and Personalities* (Baton Rouge: Louisiana State University Press, 1999), 240–44; *New-Hampshire Statesman and Concord Register,* February 20, 1830.

25. Norvell to Harrison, January 12, 1830, Jesse Burton Harrison Papers, VHS; Williams to Crawford, January 29, 1830, Crawford to unknown recipient, February 4, 1830, William Harris Crawford Papers, Duke; Calhoun to Monroe, February 21, 1830, James Monroe Papers, W&M; Letcher to Washington, April 26, 1830, Robert P. Letcher Miscellaneous Papers, Filson; Calhoun to Hamilton, March 28, 1830, Calhoun, *Papers,* 11:142; Clay to Letcher, April 1, 1830, *HCP* 11:229.

26. Ervin to Crawford, April 30, 1830, Crawford Papers, Duke; Crawford to Leigh, December 24, 1829, Leigh Papers, VHS; Crawford to Clay, March 31, 1830, Clay to Brooke, May 23, 1830, Clay to Brooke, April 24, 1831, *HCP* 8:185–86, 210, 338.

27. Peterson, *Great Triumvirate,* 186; Norma Lois Peterson, *Littleton Waller Tazewell* (Charlottesville: University of Virginia Press, 1983), 188; Jackson Memorandum, February 1831, Bassett, *Correspondence,* 4:231–36; Cole, *Presidency of Jackson,* 81–82.

28. Brown to Macon, April 29, 1830, Macon Papers.

29. For Calhoun's early role in the tariff and nullification crisis, see William W. Freehling, *Prelude to Civil War: The Nullification Controversy in South Carolina, 1816–1836* (New York: Harper & Row, 1965).

30. Herman Belz, editor, *The Webster-Hayne Debate on the Nature of the Union: Selected Documents* (Indianapolis, IN: Liberty Fund, 2000).

31. Maxcy to Calhoun, April 6, 1829, Calhoun, *Papers,* 11:15; Southard to Clay, July 23, 1829, Clay to Johnston, November 14, 1830, *HCP* 8:80, 297.

32. Clay to Thomas, October 5, 1829, *HCP* 11:228.

33. Clay to Webster, April 29, 1830, Clay to Washington, May 17, 1830, ibid., 8:196, 208.

34. Clay to Speed, May 1, 1831, ibid., 8:344.

35. Marshall to Hillhouse, May 26, 1830, Marshall Papers; Clay to Johnston, October 8, 1829, Clay to Porter, June 13, 1830, Clay to Everett, August 14, 1830, Clay to Greene, November 11, 1830, Clay to Citizens of Vincennes, October 18, 1831, *HCP* 8:113, 222, 249, 295–96, 420; Peter B. Knupfer, *The Union as It Is: Constitutional Unionism and Sectional Compromise* (Chapel Hill: University of North Carolina Press, 1991), 144.

36. Knupfer, *Union as It Is,* 22; Richard E. Ellis, *The Union at Risk: Jacksonian Democracy, States' Rights, and the Nullification Crisis* (New York: Oxford University Press, 1987), 166; Daniel Walker Howe provides invaluable insights into Clay's political philosophy in *What Hath God Wrought,* where he coins the felicitous term we quote. See page 124.

37. James C. Curtis, "In the Shadow of Old Hickory: The Political Travail of Martin Van Buren," *Journal of the Early Republic* 1 (Autumn 1982): 252; Van Deusen, *Clay,* 237.

38. Peterson, *Great Triumvirate,* 195; Clay to Webster, June 7, 1830, Clay to Beatty, June 8, 1830, Sergeant to Clay, July 7, 1830, *HCP* 8:220–21, 233; Norvell to Harrison, July 24, 1830, Harrison Papers; Combs to January, February 16, 1831, Leslie Combs Letters, Filson.

39. Clay to Conover, June 13, 1830, Clay to Everett, June 16, 1830, Clay to Evarts, August 23, 1830, Clay to Gunter, June 6, 1831, *HCP* 8:222, 226, 255, 358; Reginald Horsman, "The Indian Policy of an 'Empire of Liberty,'"

in Frederick E. Hoxie, Ronald Hoffman, and Peter J. Albert, editors, *Native Americans and the Early Republic* (Charlottesville: University Press of Virginia, 1999), 59; Ronald N. Satz, *American Indian Policy in the Jacksonian Era* (Lincoln: University of Nebraska Press, 1974), 39–40; Martin and Ridge to Ross, December 28, 1831, John Ross, *The Papers of Chief John Ross,* 2 volumes (Norman: University of Oklahoma Press, 1985), 1:234; Adams, *Memoirs,* 7:90, 219.

40. Patterson to Clay, June 13, 1831, *HCP* 8:362.
41. Clay to Williams, May 31, 1831, ibid., 8:352–53; Jackson to Van Buren, July 23, 1831, Bassett, *Correspondence,* 4:316; Story to Marshall, May 29, 1831, Marshall Papers; Thomas P. Govan, "John M. Berrien and the Administration of Andrew Jackson," *Journal of Southern History* 5 (November 1939): 452. For a full discussion of the Eaton affair, see John F. Marszalek, *The Petticoat Affair: Manners, Mutiny, and Sex in Andrew Jackson's White House* (New York: Free Press, 1997).
42. Quoted in Howe, *What Hath God Wrought,* 339; the actual quote from Shakespeare's *Antony and Cleopatra,* Act II, Scene 2, is "Age cannot wither nor custom stale her infinite variety."
43. Van Deusen, *Jackson Era,* 55–56; Louis P. Masur, *1831, Year of Eclipse* (New York: Hill and Wang, 2001), 89; Howe, *What Hath God Wrought,* 266–67; Holt, *American Whig Party,* 13.
44. Speech, April 16, 1821, Resolutions, March 9, 1822, *HCP* 3:74, 177–78; Ranck, *Lexington,* 143.
45. Southwick to Clay, December 3, 1827, Clay to Porter, March 24, 1828, Clay to Lawrence, November 21, 1830, Clay to Bailhache, November 24, 1830, Clay to Everett, June 12, 1831, August 20, 1831, *HCP* 6:1339, 7:186, 8:300, 303, 360, 388.
46. Sergeant to Clay, October 3, 1831, Johnston to Clay, October 8, 1831, ibid., 8:411, 417; Wirt to Chase, November 11, 1831, Wirt to Carr, January 5, 1832, John P. Kennedy, *Memoir of the Life of William Wirt,* 2 volumes (Philadelphia: Lee and Blanchard, 1850), 2:330, 333, 349, 358–59, 366; Wirt to Carr, September 30, 1831, October 5, 1831, Wirt Letterbook, MHS; Wirt to Carr, March 24, November 27, 1831, William Wirt Letters, LOV.
47. Kennedy, *Wirt,* 2:365; Van Deusen, *Clay,* 244; Clay to Johnston, August 20, 1831, Clay to Conover, August 26, 1831, Clay to Metcalfe, September 9, 1831, Clay to Southard, September 30, 1831, Clay to Greene, November 14, 1831, *HCP* 8:389, 391–92, 398, 409–10, 424.
48. Clay to Jamison, April 8, 1828, *HCP* 7:217.
49. Clay to Clay, November 11, 1825, Clay Family Papers, LOC.
50. Clay to Clay, March 15, 1827, January 16, 1828, February 25, 1828, February 10, 1829,

December 13, 1829, Statement of Assets, July 10, 1851, *HCP* 6:307, 7:38, 118, 616.
51. Theodore to Lucretia, September 1, 1830, Clay Family Papers, LOC.
52. Petition of William M. Brand, Fayette County Circuit Court Records, Kentucky Department of Libraries and Archives, Frankfort, Kentucky; Bodley to Sheriff, Fayette County, October 1831, Witness Subpoenas, October 1831, Finding of Jury, October 3, 1831, Fayette County Circuit Court Records; Davenport, *Ante-Bellum Kentucky,* 147; Clay to Clay, October 31, 1830, Clay to Clay, December 13, 1832, *HCP* 8:284, 603.
53. Clay to Clay, September 1, 1830, Clay Family Papers, LOC.
54. Clay to Williams, May 31, 1831, Lawrence to Clay, July 13, 1831, Clay to Brooke, August 15, 1831, Dearborn to Clay, September 3, 1831, Binns to Clay, September 10, 1831, Randall to Clay, September 13, 1831, Southard to Clay, September 18, 1831, McNairy to Clay, September 28, 1831, Worsley to Clay, October 22, 1831, *HCP* 8:353, 372, 385, 396, 399, 401, 404, 407, 421; Van Deusen, *Clay,* 244–45; Williams to Payne, July 21, 1831, Payne Papers; *United States Telegraph,* November 19, 1831; Clay to Clay, November 30, 1831, Clay Family Papers, LOC; Kirwan, *Crittenden,* 89–91.
55. Tazewell to Tazewell, January 29, 1832, Tazewell Family Papers; Smith, *Forty Years,* 324, 332; Clay to Erwin, December 25, 1831, Clay to Clay, December 7, 1831, January 8, 1832, May 20, 1832, Clay to Clay, January 17, 1832, March 26, 1832, April 9, 1832, June 7, 1832, Clay to Hunt, February 13, 1832, Clay to Clay, February 21, 1832, April 7, 1832, Erwin to Clay, April 1, 1832, Clay to Brown, October 23, 1832, *HCP* 8:427, 437–38, 442, 446, 462, 465, 480–81, 486, 488, 489, 520, 529, 587; Clay to Clay, February 28, 1832, Clay Family Papers, LOC.
56. Smith, *Forty Years,* 325.
57. Johnston to Clay, December 12, 1831, Clay to Livingston, December 13, 1831, Brown to Clay, December 16, 1831, *HCP* 8:431, 432, 433; Masur, *1831,* 95–96; Tregle, *Louisiana in Age of Jackson,* 254; Sergeant to Webster, April 9, 1831, Miner to Webster, September 8, 1831, Spencer to Webster, October 24, 1831, Webster, *Papers,* 3:109, 122, 130–32; McCormick, *Presidential Game,* 137; *Daily National Journal,* December 16, 1831.
58. Knupfer, *Union as It Is,* 145.
59. Prentiss, *Memoir,* 1:125.
60. *Perley's Reminiscences,* 1:143–44.
61. Moore to Edwards, December 31, 1831, Ninian Wirt Edwards, *History of Illinois, from 1778 to 1833: and Life and Times of Ninian Edwards* (Springfield: Illinois State Journal, 1870), 509.

62. Theodore D. Jervey, *Robert Y. Hayne and His Times* (New York: Macmillan, 1909), 300.

63. Bates to Bates, February 28, 1828, Bates Papers.

64. Johnston to Floyd, December 16, 1831, John B. Floyd Papers, W&M; Booker to Austin, August 20, 1831, Austin-Twyman Papers; Parker to Tazewell, February 6, 1832, Tazewell Family Papers; Clay to Snowden, September 25, 1831, *HCP* 8:405.

65. Samuel Flagg Bemis, *John Quincy Adams and the Union* (New York: Alfred A. Knopf, 1956), 282–86.

66. Clay to Adams, July 26, 1831, *HCP* 8:379.

67. Adams, *Memoirs*, 8:443.

68. Ibid., 8:444–47; Bemis, *Adams and the Union*, 244.

69. Van Deusen, *Jacksonian Era*, 58; Felix A. Nigro, "The Van Buren Confirmation Before the Senate," *Western Political Quarterly* 14 (March 1961): 151; Merrill D. Peterson, *Olive Branch and Sword: The Compromise of 1833* (Baton Rouge: Louisiana State University Press, 1982), 27; Floyd to Calhoun, January 2, 1832, Calhoun, *Papers,* 11:537.

70. Edwin A. Miles, "Andrew Jackson and Senator George Poindexter," *Journal of Southern History* 24 (February 1958): 54; Nigro, "Van Buren Confirmation," 152–55; Van Deusen, *Jacksonian Era,* 58; Clay to Porter, January 14, 1832, Speech, January 25, 1832, *HCP* 8:445, 450.

71. Nigro, "Van Buren Confirmation," 152, 157.

72. Tazewell to Tazewell, January 29, 1832, Parker to Tazewell, February 6, 1832, Tazewell Family Papers; Howe, *What Hath God Wrought,* 378; Jackson to Coffee, January 27, 1832, Bassett, *Correspondence,* 4:402; Van Deusen, *Jacksonian Era,* 58.

73. Comment in Senate, December 20, 1831, Niles to Clay, January 17, 1832, *HCP* 8:435, 446; Van Deusen, *Clay,* 250; Parks, *Grundy,* 187; Saunders to Mangum, January 23, 1832, Mangum, *Papers,* 1:463.

74. John A. Munroe, *Louis McLane: Federalist and Jacksonian* (New Brunswick, NJ: Rutgers University Press, 1973), 313; *Reg. of Deb.,* 22 Cong., 1 sess., 256.

75. *Reg. of Deb.,* 22 Cong., 1 sess., 257–64, 273–77.

76. Ibid., 266.

77. Ibid., 296–97.

78. Munroe, *Louis McLane,* 332.

79. O'Brien to Mangum, Mangum, *Papers,* 1:495.

80. Daniel Feller, *The Public Lands in Jacksonian Politics* (Madison: University of Wisconsin Press, 1984), 107, 147, 149; Van Atta, "Western Lands," 656; Van Deusen, *Clay,* 253; Peterson, *Compromise of 1833,* 31–32.

81. Clay to Brooke, March 28, 1832, *HCP* 8:481–82; Chambers, *Bullion Benton,* 190–91; Feller, *Public Lands,* 150–51; Van

Deusen, *Clay,* 253–54; Richard G. Miller, "The Tariff of 1832: The Issue That Failed," *Filson Club History Quarterly* 49 (July 1979): 223; Clay to Wolcott, April 18, 1832, Henry Clay Papers, Duke.

82. Peterson, *Compromise of 1833,* 33–38; Niven, *Calhoun,* 185; Bemis, *Adams and the Union,* 246; Wickham to Tazewell, June 18, 1832, Tazewell Family Papers; Clay to Brooke, June 29, 1832, Clay Papers, Duke.

83. Van Deusen, *Jacksonian Era,* 47; Latner, *Presidency of Jackson,* 108; Feller, *Jacksonian Promise,* 43; Lawrence Frederick Kohl, *The Politics of Individualism: Parties and the American Character in the Jacksonian Era* (New York: Oxford University Press, 1989), 191–92; Grundy to Jackson, October 22, 1829, Ingham to Jackson, November 26, 1829, November 27, 1829, Berrien to Jackson, November 27, 1829, Bassett, *Correspondence,* 4:83, 92–95. Ironically, one of the leaders of the pro-bank faction in Tennessee was Andrew Erwin, father of Clay's son-in-law James Erwin. See Charles G. Sellers, Jr., "Banking and Politics in Jackson's Tennessee, 1817–1827," *Mississippi Valley Historical Review* 41 (June 1954): 82.

84. Van Deusen, *Jacksonian Era,* 62; Clay to Biddle, September 11, 1830, *HCP* 8:263–64.

85. Jackson to Van Buren, December 6, 1831, Jackson to Randolph, December 22, 1831, Bassett, *Correspondence,* 4:379, 387; Smith, *Blair,* 67; Belohlavek, *Dallas,* 39; William O. Lynch, *Fifty Years of Party Warfare* (Indianapolis, IN: Bobbs-Merrill, 1931), 407; Howe, *What Hath God Wrought,* 377–78; Edwin J. Perkins, "Lost Opportunities for Compromise in the Bank War: A Reassessment of Jackson's Veto Message," *Business History Review* 61 (1987): 533–35; Clay to Biddle, December 15, 1831, Clay to Brooke, December 25, 1831, *HCP* 8:432–33, 437; Catterall, *Second Bank of the United States,* 215–17; Holt, *American Whig Party,* 16.

86. Howe, *What Hath God Wrought,* 378; Walter Buckingham Smith, *Economic Aspects of the Second Bank of the United States* (Cambridge, MA: Harvard University Press, 1953), 154; Perkins, "Lost Opportunities," 537; Clay to Brooke, June 29, 1832, Clay Papers, Duke; Clay to Conover, June 30, 1832, *HCP* 8:547; Jean Wilburn, *Biddle's Bank: The Crucial Years* (New York: Columbia University Press, 1967), 6.

87. Van Buren, *Autobiography,* 625; Watson, *Liberty and Power,* 143.

88. Richard P. Longaker, "Andrew Jackson and the Judiciary," *Political Science Quarterly* 71 (September 1956): 350–51; Amy Bridges, *A City in the Republic: Antebellum New York and the Origin of Machine Politics* (New York: Cambridge University Press, 1984), 26;

Feller, *Jacksonian Promise,* 170; Lynn L. Marshall, "The Authorship of Jackson's Bank Veto Message," *Mississippi Valley Historical Review* 50 (December 1963): 466–77.

89. *Reg. of Deb.,* 22 Cong., 1 sess., 1221–40, 1256–67, 1272.

90. Ibid., 1293.

91. Ibid., 1294.

92. Ibid., 1294–96.

93. McCaulley to Clay, July 15, 1832, Clay to Brooke, July 20, 1832, *HCP* 8:551, 554.

94. Robert S. Conte, "The Celebrated White Sulphur Springs of Greenbrier: Nineteenth Century Travel Accounts," *West Virginia History* 42 (Spring–Summer 1981): 191–201.

95. Biddle to Clay, August 1, 1832, *HCP* 8:556; Washington *Globe,* July 23, 1832.

96. Clay to Brooke, April 9, 1832, April 13, 1832, *HCP* 8:489, 491; Green to Calhoun, September 7, 1829, Calhoun, *Papers,* 11:74; Robert Seager, "Henry Clay and the Politics of Compromise and Non-Compromise," *Register of the Kentucky Historical Society* 85 (Winter 1987): 12; Clement Eaton, *Henry Clay and the Art of American Politics* (Boston: Little, Brown, 1957), 101–2.

97. Wirt to Carr, October 25, 1832, Kennedy, *Wirt,* 2:379–80; Ronald P. Formisano, *The Transition of Political Culture: Massachusetts Parties, 1790s–1840s* (New York: Oxford University Press, 1983), 205; Van Deusen, *Clay,* 261; Clay to Sloane, October 4, 1831, Clay to Watson et al., October 8, 1831, *HCP* 8:396, 415; Lee Benson, *The Concept of Jacksonian Democracy: New York as a Test Case* (Princeton, NJ: Princeton University Press, 1961), 60–61.

98. Latner, *Presidency of Jackson,* 138; Perry M. Goldman, "Political Virtue in the Age of Jackson," *Political Science Quarterly* 87 (March 1972): 47.

99. Clay to *National Intelligencer,* January 24, 1832, *HCP* 8:448–49.

100. Clay to Hammond, August 27, 1832, Clay to Thompson, August 27, 1832, Clay to Webster, August 27, 1832, Clay to Dearborn, September 6, 1832, Clay to Lawrence, September 6, 1832, Clay to Conover, September 8, 1832, ibid., 8:563, 565–66, 569–72, 11:240; McCalla to Blair, August 29, 1832, Francis Preston Blair Papers, LOC.

101. Webster to Clay, October 22, 1832, Papers of Daniel Webster, UVA; Clay to unknown recipient, October 27, 1832, Dearborn to Clay, October 29, 1832, October 30, 1832, Everett and Everett to Clay, October 29, 1832, *HCP* 8:590–91, 592, 593; Sprague to Dearborn, October 23, 1832, Joseph E. Sprague Letter, LOC.

102. Howe, *What Hath God Wrought,* 385; Van Deusen, *Clay,* 262.

103. Crittenden to Clay, November 17, 1832, *HCP* 8:599.

104. Clay to Mayer, January 21, 1832, ibid., 8:447.

105. Clay to Spencer, May 12, 1832, ibid., 8:511.

106. Clay to Hammond, November 17, 1832, ibid., 8:599.

107. Knupfer, *Union as It Is,* 121–22, 129; Williams to Floyd, April 16, 1832, George Frederick Holmes Papers, W&M; Clay to Greene, May 15, 1832, *HCP* 8:513.

108. Clay to Brown, December 9, 1832, *HCP* 8:602.

109. Clay to Caldwell, December 9, 1832, ibid.

110. Freehling, *Prelude to Civil War,* 262–64; Ellis, *Union at Risk,* 46; Jackson to Coffee, July 17, 1832, Bassett, *Correspondence,* 4:462; Clay to Brooke, March 28, 1832, *HCP* 8:482.

111. Stoddart to Clay, November 12, 1832, Clay to Brooke, December 12, 1832, *HCP* 8:597–98, 603; Smith, *Blair,* 265.

112. Peterson, *Compromise of 1833,* 52; Knupfer, *Union as It Is,* 111; Clay to Barbour, March 10, 1832, Clay to Davis, March 10, 1832, Draft Proposal, December 1832, *HCP* 8:472, 473, 604; Paul C. Nagel, *One Nation Indivisible: The Union in American Thought, 1776–1861* (New York: Oxford University Press, 1971), 29–30.

113. Clay to Clay, January 3, 1833, Clay to Helm, January 5, 1833, Clay to Brooke, January 17, 1833, January 24, 1833, *HCP* 8:608, 609, 613–14, 615; Knupfer, *Union as It Is,* 120; Charles Henry Ambler, *The Life and Diary of John Floyd, Governor of Virginia, an Apostle of Secession, and the Father of the Oregon Country* (Richmond, VA: Richmond Press, 1918), 210.

114. Peterson, *Compromise of 1833,* 65–66; Smith, *Blair,* 267; Cole, *Presidency of Jackson,* 171.

115. Clay to Webster, February 5, 1833, *HCP* 8:618; Webster to Hopkinson, February 9, 1833, Webster, *Papers,* 3:213; Peterson, *Compromise of 1833,* 54–55, 68; Adams, *Memoirs,* 8:524; Niven, *Calhoun,* 193; Howe, *What Hath God Wrought,* 407.

116. *Reg. of Deb.,* 22 Cong., 2 sess., 432, 462–73.

117. Ibid., 473–74, 478; Draft Proposal, December 1832, *HCP* 8:604; David E. Ericson, "The Nullification Crisis, American Republicanism, and the Force Bill Debate," *Journal of Southern History* 61 (May 1995): 253; Hammett to White, February 12, 1833, William Hammett Letters, VHS.

118. Peterson, *Compromise of 1833,* 72–76; Van Deusen, *Clay,* 268; Niven, *Calhoun,* 194; Clay to Brooke, February 14, 1833, *HCP* 8:623; Cole, *Presidency of Jackson,* 169; Ellis, *Union at Risk,* 174.

119. Latner, *Presidency of Jackson,* 159; Richard B. Latner, "The Nullification Crisis and Republican Subversion," *Journal of Southern History* 43 (February 1977): 24–25, 33; Speech, February 25, 1833, *HCP* 8:626–27; Ellis, *Union at Risk,* 173.

120. Comment, February 21, 1833, *HCP* 8:625; Cole, *Presidency of Jackson,* 173; Major L. Wilson, *The Presidency of Martin Van Buren* (Lawrence: University Press of Kansas, 1984), 11; Peterson, *Compromise of 1833,* 78. South Carolina repealed its ordinance of nullification for the tariff and, in a symbolic gesture, nullified the Force Act. See Ellis, *Union at Risk,* 177.

121. Peterson, *Compromise of 1833,* 83; Feller, *Public Lands,* 164; Major L. Wilson, " 'Liberty and Union': An Analysis of Three Concepts Involved in the Nullification Controversy," *Journal of Southern History* 33 (August 1967): 353–54; Howe, *What Hath God Wrought,* 409.

122. Knupfer, *Union as It Is,* 145; Ellis, *Union at Risk,* 94–95; Paul Murray, *The Whig Party in Georgia, 1825–1853* (Chapel Hill: University of North Carolina Press, 1948), 34; Hammett to White, February 11, 1833, Hammett Letters; Ambler, *Diary of John Floyd,* 212; Thomas B. Jones, "Henry Clay and Continental Expansion, 1820–1844," *Register of the Kentucky Historical Society* 73 (1975): 258–59; *United States Telegraph,* February 28, 1833; Clay to Johnston, March 15, 1833, *HCP* 8:633; Patton to Tazewell, April 1833, Tazewell Family Papers; Hall to Macon, February 22, 1833, Macon Papers; Emanuel to Carter, March 28, 1834, Carter Family Papers, W&M.

123. Comment, January 14, 1833, *HCP* 8:613.

124. Van Buren, *Autobiography,* 426; Van Deusen, *Clay,* 270; Peterson, *Compromise of 1833,* 51; Bruce, *Randolph of Roanoke,* 2:36; Knupfer, *Union as It Is,* 119; Clay to Brooke, March 11, 1833, *HCP* 8:631. A story, perhaps apocryphal, made the rounds that Randolph had asked that when he was buried he be positioned facing west so that he could always keep an eye on Henry Clay.

125. Robert Douthat Meade, "John Randolph of Roanoke: Some New Information," *William and Mary Quarterly* 13 (October 1933): 256; Lorenzo Sabine, *Notes on Duels and Dueling* (Boston: Crosby, Nichols, 1955), 110–11.

CHAPTER NINE
Whig

1. Clay to Williams, April 9, 1833, Clay to Biddle, April 10, 1833, Clay to Clay, April 14, 1833, Clay to Helm, April 20, 1833, Clay to Brooke, May 30, 1833, *HCP* 8:636, 637, 638, 644.

2. *National Intelligencer,* January 2, 1832; Washington *Globe,* November 20, 1833.

3. Kohn to Kohn, November 14, 1832, Carl Kohn Letterbook, Historic New Orleans Collection; Remark in Senate, June 27, 1832, Clay to Porter, July 2, 1833, *HCP* 8:545, 654;

Howe, *What Hath God Wrought,* 470; Nancy D. Baird, "Asiatic Cholera's First Visit to Kentucky: A Study in Panic and Fear," *Filson Club History Quarterly* 48 (July 1974): 228.

4. Clay to Clay, June 7, 1833, *HCP* 8:648; Baird, "Asiatic Cholera's First Visit to Kentucky," 230–31.

5. Natchez *Daily Courier,* May 24, 31, 1833; *United States Telegraph,* June 8, 1833; William Henry Sparks, *The Memories of Fifty Years: Containing Brief Biographical Notices of Distinguished Americans, and Anecdotes of Remarkable Men,* 3rd edition (Philadelphia: Claxton, Remsen & Haffelfinger, 1872), 460; Clay to Porter, June 16, 1833, *HCP* 8:651.

6. Letcher to Clay, December 26, 1829, Sibley to Clay, May 22, 1833, Clay to Everett, July 23, 1833, *HCP* 8:163, 642, 651, 660.

7. Howe, *What Hath God Wrought,* 23; *Niles' Weekly Register,* June 22, 1833, July 13, 1833.

8. Clay to Clay, July 23, 1833, Clay to Brown, October 8, 1833, Clay to Erwin, October 13, 1833, *HCP* 8:659, 664, 665.

9. Adams, *Memoirs,* 9:25; *National Intelligencer,* October 16, 1833.

10. Clay to Webster, June 17, 1833, Webster to Clay, June 22, 1833, Speech, October 21, 1833, Clay to Clay, December 1, 1833, *HCP* 8: 651, 653, 669, 11:252–54; Quincy, *Life of Quincy,* 301; Brooks, *Ashland,* 15.

11. Clay to Patrick, July 5, 1833, Clay to Clay, December 5, 1833, December 14, 1833, February 17, 1834, March 19, 1834, Clay to Erwin, October 13, 1833, December 21, 1833, Physick to Clay, April 19, 1834, *HCP* 8:655, 665, 671, 675–76, 681, 698, 706, 715; Van Deusen, *Clay,* 273.

12. Curtis, "Political Travail of Martin Van Buren," 253–54.

13. Jackson to Polk, December 16, 1832, Hamilton to Jackson, February 28, 1833, Taney to Jackson, March 1833, Jackson to Cabinet, March 19, 1833, Jackson to White, March 24, 1833, McLane to Jackson, May 20, 1833, Kendall to Van Buren, June 9, 1833, Bassett, *Correspondence,* 4:501, 5:22, 32–41, 46–47, 77–101, 106–8; Holt, *American Whig Party,* 24; McLane to Biddle, February 1, 1833, Louis McLane Papers, Duke; Kendall to Blair, May 12, 1829, Blair Papers, LOC.

14. Latner, *Presidency of Jackson,* 170; McLane to Jackson, May 20, 1833, Jackson to Duane, June 26, 1833, July 12, 1833, July 17, 1833, July 22, 1833, July 23, 1833, September 21, 1833, September 23, 1833, Duane to Jackson, July 22, 1833, Jackson to Van Buren, August 16, 1833, September 8, 1833, September 15, 1833, September 22, 1833, Jackson to Taney, September 15, 1833, September 23, 1833, Bassett, *Correspondence,* 5:77–101, 111–22, 128–29, 131–42, 159, 182, 187–88, 204–6; Jackson to Taney, March 12, 1833, August 11,

1833, Roger B. Taney Papers, MHS; Kearny to Smith, January 19, 1834, Philip Kearny Letter, Filson; Peter Temin, "The Economic Consequences of Bank War," *The Journal of Political Economy* 76 (March–April 1968): 258.

15. Remark, December 9, 1833, Clay to Brown, December 10, 1833, *HCP* 8:672, 673.

16. Jackson draft, September 1833, Bassett, *Correspondence,* 5:192–201; Parks, *Grundy,* 222; Cole, *Presidency of Jackson,* 205; Adams, *Memoirs,* 9:51; Clay to Clayton, December 12, 1833, Clay to Erwin, December 21, 1833, *HCP* 674, 681, 698; Mangum to Montgomery, December 18, 1833, Mangum, *Papers,* 2:55.

17. Clay to Tazewell, February 1, 1834, *HCP* 8: 693; Holt, *American Whig Party,* 24.

18. Clay to Brooke, December 16, 1833, *HCP* 8: 679.

19. *Reg. of Deb.,* 23 Cong., 1 sess., 74, 94; Harrington, "Clay and the Classics," 244; Catterall, *Second Bank of the United States,* 335, Clay to Porter, December 26, 1833, *HCP* 8:683.

20. Van Deusen, *Clay,* 281; Smith, *Blair,* 86; Cole, *Presidency of Jackson,* 205; Clay to Brooke, February 10, 1834, *HCP* 8:696.

21. Niven, *Calhoun,* 209; Bartlett, *Calhoun,* 205; Moore to McDowell, February 7, 1834, McDowell Papers.

22. *Reg. of Deb.,* 23 Cong., 1 sess., 826–30, 834; Benton, *Thirty Years,* 1:420; Wilson, *Presidency of Van Buren,* 35.

23. Clay to Brooke, March 23, 1834, *HCP* 8:706.

24. Comment, March 25, 1834, *HCP* 8:707; *Reg. of Deb.,* 23 Cong., 1 sess., 1187.

25. Speech, April 14, 1834, *HCP* 8:714.

26. Holt, *American Whig Party,* 27–29; Van Deusen, *Clay,* 277; Clay to Brooke, June 27, 1835, *HCP* 8:775; Clay to Caldwell, June 25, 1835, Clay Papers, Duke.

27. Clay to Sargent, September 23, 1843, *HCP* 9:861–62.

28. Speech, April 30, 1834, Clay to Caldwell, May 7, 1834, Remark, June 30, 1834, *HCP* 8:722, 724, 735, 775–76; Thomas Brown, "Southern Whigs and the Politics of Statesmanship, 1833–1841," *Journal of Southern History* 46 (August 1980): 364.

29. Speech, June 27, 1834, *HCP* 8:734; Parks, *Grundy,* 256; Richard Arden Wire, "John M. Clayton and Whig Politics During the Second Jackson Administration," *Delaware History* 18 (1978): 7.

30. Clay to Clay, March 10, 1834, Clay to Caldwell, May 7, 1834, Clay to Brown, August 2, 1834, *HCP* 8:704, 724, 738.

31. Clay to Caldwell, August 8, 1834, Clay to Chauncey, October 18, 1834, Clay to Lieber, December 3, 1834, Wines to Clay, April 30, 1836, ibid., 8:740, 749, 752, 847.

32. Jackson to Van Buren, August 8, 1834, Bassett, *Correspondence,* 5:281–82; Clay to

Gales, August 8, 1834, Clay to Speed, November 1, 1834, *HCP* 8:740, 750; Van Buren to Brown, September 7, 1834, Bedford Brown Papers, Duke; Clay to Leigh, October 22, 1834, Leigh Letters, UVA; Tucker to Cabell, September 5, 1834, Cabell Papers.

33. Wire, "John M. Clayton," 7; Clay to Clay, December 1834, Clay to Brooke, January 16, 1835, *HCP* 8:751, 756.

34. Remarks, January 6, 1835, *HCP* 8:754.

35. Jackson Annual Message, December 1, 1834, Richardson, editor, *Messages and Papers,* 3:104–7; Clay to Clay, December 1834, Remark, March 3, 1835, *HCP* 8:751–52, 766.

36. John M. Belohlavek, *"Let the Eagle Soar!": The Foreign Policy of Andrew Jackson* (Lincoln: University of Nebraska Press, 1983), 116.

37. Speech, January 14, 1835, Remark, March 3, 1835, *HCP* 8:755–56, 766; Francis D. Wormuth and Edwin B. Firmage, *To Chain the Dog of War: The War Power of Congress in History and Law* (Dallas, TX: Southern Methodist University Press, 1986), 37; *Niles' Weekly Register,* March 14, 1835; Belohlavek, *Foreign Policy of Jackson,* 118–19.

38. Clay to Biddle, March 4, 1835, *HCP* 8:767.

39. Clay to Brooke, June 27, 1835, ibid., 8:776.

40. Clay to Clay, November 19, 1835, ibid., 8:803.

41. Clay to Clay, December 3, 1835, December 9, 1835, Clay to Erwin, December 10, 1835, Smith to Clay, December 10, 1835, ibid., 8:804, 805, 806; Lexington *Intelligencer,* quoted in New York *Spectator,* December 28, 1835.

42. Smith, *Forty Years,* 375; Colton, *Clay,* 1:32; Clay to Clay, December 19, 1835, *HCP* 8:808.

43. Clay to Clay, December 19, 1835, *HCP* 8:808–9.

44. Erwin to Clay, December 15, 1835, Clay to Brooke, January 1, 1836, ibid., 8:807–8, 814; Clay to Clay, n.d., Clay to Clay, January 30, 1836, Clay-Russell Papers; Clay to Clay, April 15, 1835, Clay to Russell, January 1, 1836, Thomas J. Clay Collection, Henry Clay Papers.

45. Speech, December 29, 1835, Clay to Clay, January 23, 1836, Clay to Clay, January 25, 1836, *HCP* 8:812, 820, 821, 822.

46. Comment, March 28, 1832, Clay to Berry, June 15, 1833, Comment, March 9, 1836, ibid., 8:482–83, 650, 833; Betty L. Fladeland, "Compensated Emancipation: A Rejected Alternative," *Journal of Southern History* 42 (May 1976): 180–82.

47. Clay to Speed, August 23, 1831, Speech, June 18, 1836, Clay to Gurley, December 22, 1836, Clay to Huey, May 30, 1837, *HCP* 8:390, 853, 874, 9:47; Knupfer, *Union as It Is,* 150; Lonnie Edward Maness, "Henry Clay and the Problem of Slavery," Ph.D. dissertation, Mem-

phis State University, 1980, 103, 111, 121–22, 126–27; Seager, "Politics of Compromise," 17; Howe, *What Hath God Wrought,* 429, 513; William L. Van Deburg, "Henry Clay, the Right of Petition, and Slavery in the Nation's Capital," *Register of the Kentucky Historical Society* 68 (1970): 133–34; Remarks, January 27, 1837, Calhoun, *Papers,* 13:370–71.

48. Wilson, *Presidency of Van Buren,* 148.
49. Speech, June 18, 1836, *HCP* 8:855.
50. Clay to Whittier, July 22, 1837, ibid., 9:64; Belohlavek, *Foreign Policy of Jackson,* 237.
51. Howe, *What Hath God Wrought,* 545–46; Wilson, *Presidency of Van Buren,* 16.
52. Clay to Mangum, August 26, 1834, Willie P. Mangum Papers, Duke.
53. Holt, *American Whig Party,* 38; Clay to Brooke, July 20, 1835, *HCP* 8:791–92; Brown to Ewing, December 15, 1835, Ewing Family Papers; Powell Moore, "The Revolt Against Jackson in Tennessee, 1835–1836," *Journal of Southern History* 2 (August 1936): 345, 347–48, 355; Jonathan M. Atkins, "The Presidential Candidacy of Hugh Lawson White in Tennessee, 1832–1836," *Journal of Southern History* 58 (February 1992): 34–40.
54. Clay to Brooke, June 27, 1835, Clay to Bailhache, July 14, 1835, Clay to Southard, July 31, 1835, *HCP* 8:775–76, 782–84, 795; Clay to Barbour, July 18, 1835, Barbour Family Papers, VHS; Vance to Este, February 14, 1835, Bruce Papers.
55. Clay to Southard, July 31, 1835, Clay to Hughes, August 25, 1835, Brooke to Clay, August 31, 1835, *HCP* 8:795, 797–98.
56. Clay to Wines, April 30, 1836, Clay to Smith, May 14, 1836, Clay to Clay, May 12, 1836, May 19, 1836, Clay to Southard, September 27, 1836, ibid., 8:847, 850, 866.
57. Clay to Gilmer, January 1836, Remark, January 18, 1836, Speech, February 22, 1836, Clay to Patton et al., April 7, 1836, ibid., 8:819, 820, 829, 840; Clay to Brooke, January 25, 1836, Clay Papers, Duke; Peterson, *Compromise of 1833,* 103; Howe, *What Hath God Wrought,* 363.
58. Remark, March 31, 1836, *HCP* 8:839.
59. Peterson, *Compromise of 1833,* 103; Howe, *What Hath God Wrought,* 499.
60. Howe, *What Hath God Wrought,* 500; Peter L. Rousseau, "Jacksonian Monetary Policy, Specie Flows, and the Panic of 1837," *Journal of Economic History* 62 (June 2002): 457–58, 461; Richard H. Timberlake, Jr., "The Specie Circular and Distribution of the Surplus," *Journal of Political Economy* 68 (April 1960): 110–11, 117. Economic historian Richard Timberlake tried to demonstrate that the Specie Circular had little to do with the drain of specie from major banks, but Peter Rousseau, cited above, clearly demonstrated that it was a significant contributing factor.

61. Speech, July 26, 1836, Speech, January 11, 1837, *HCP* 8:860–61, 9:3–6; Howe, *What Hath God Wrought,* 500.
62. Clay to Fendall, November 5, 1836, Clay to Clay, December 16, 1836, *HCP* 8:868, 872; Jackson to Polk, September 15, 1835, Jackson to Armstrong, September 15, 1835, Bassett, *Correspondence,* 5:365, 366; Brown, "Southern Whigs," 364.
63. Clay to Brooke, February 26, 1836, *HCP* 8:831; Clement Eaton, "Southern Senators and the Right of Instruction, 1789–1860," *Journal of Southern History* 18 (August 1952): 312–15.
64. *Reg. of Deb.,* 24 Cong., 2 sess., 429.
65. Speech, January 16, 1837, *HCP* 9:12–14.
66. *Reg. of Deb.,* 24 Cong., 2 sess., 505; Jackson to Benton, January 17, 1837, Bassett, *Correspondence,* 5:450–51; Jon Meacham, *American Lion: Andrew Jackson in the White House* (New York: Random House, 2008), 337.
67. Clay to Clay, January 28, 1837, February 22, 1837, *HCP* 9:20, 31.
68. Clay to Brooke, February 10, 1837, Clay to Hughes, June 18, 1837, ibid., 9:27, 50.
69. Thomas Ritchie, *Thomas Ritchie's Letter, Containing Reminiscences of Henry Clay and the Compromise* (Richmond: n.p., 1952), 2–9.
70. Clay to Brooke, March 7, 1837, *HCP* 9:39.
71. Richardson, *Messages and Papers,* 3:313–20.
72. Howe, *What Hath God Wrought,* 502–3; Temin, "Economic Consequences of Bank War," 270; Rousseau, "Jacksonian Monetary Policy," 457–58.
73. Jackson to Van Buren, May 12, 1837, Bassett, *Correspondence,* 5:482; Wilson, *Presidency of Van Buren,* 67, 75; Howe, *What Hath God Wrought,* 506–7; David J. Russo, "The Major Political Issues of the Jacksonian Period and the Development of Party Loyalty in Congress, 1830–1840," *Transactions of the American Philosophical Society* 62 (1972): 37.
74. Clay to Stow, April 26, 1837, Clay to Clay, May 26, 1837, Clay to Hamilton, May 26, 1837, Clay to Hughes, June 18, 1837, Clay to Noble, June 20, 1837, Clay to Davis, July 3, 1837, Clay to Thompson, July 8, 1837, Clay to Wheatley, August 18, 1837, *HCP* 9:43, 45, 46, 49, 50–51, 55, 58.
75. Brown, "Southern Whigs," 370–72.
76. Speech, September 25, 1837, Remark, October 10, 1837, *HCP* 9:76, 85; Wilson, *Presidency of Van Buren,* 61, 76–77.
77. Clay to Hughes, June 18, 1837, Clay to Clay, August 27, 1837, September 8, 1837, Clay to Clay, October 8, 1837, *HCP* 9:50, 72, 73, 84.
78. Duralde to Clay, December 24, 1837, Clay to Clay, January 6, 1838, Thomas J. Clay Collection, Henry Clay Papers.
79. Duralde to Clay, December 24, 1837, ibid.
80. Clay to Clay, November 19, 1837, *HCP* 8:803.

81. Clay to Mangum, November 17, 1837, ibid., 9:92.

CHAPTER TEN
"I Had Rather Be Right than Be President"

1. Clay to Swartwout, August 10, 1838, *HCP* 9:216.
2. Clay to Sargent, August 11, 1838, Clay Papers, UVA; Clay to Wilde, June 24, 1839, *HCP* 9:329.
3. Clay to Prentice, August 14, 1837, *HCP* 9:69–70.
4. See, for example, Biddle to Webster, June 1, 1838, Webster, *Papers,* 4:303; Robert Gray Gunderson, *The Log-Cabin Campaign* (Lexington: University of Kentucky Press, 1957), 23–24.
5. Bryan to Clay, July 14, 1837, *HCP* 9:61–62; Sydney Nathans, *Daniel Webster and Jacksonian Democracy* (Baltimore: Johns Hopkins University Press, 1973), 108.
6. Clay to Hamilton, May 26, 1837, Clay to Letcher, May 30, 1837, Clay to Davis, July 3, 1837, Clay to Thompson, Jr., July 8, 1837, *HCP* 9:46, 48, 54–55, 58. Some of her contemporaries and Webster's recent biographer describe Caroline LeRoy Webster as unattractive, but the portrait by John Wesley Jarvis shows her to have had regular features pleasantly arranged. Possibly that likeness resulted from benevolent artistic license, but it seems unfair to find fault with her looks based on a few critical descriptions from people like Edward Everett. See Robert V. Remini, *Daniel Webster: The Man and His Time* (New York: W. W. Norton, 1997), 310.
7. Clay to Porter, June 3, 1838, *HCP* 9:198; Webster to Biddle, May 31, 1838, Webster, *Papers,* 4:302; Cole, *Van Buren,* 334–35.
8. Gunderson, *Log-Cabin Campaign,* 42; Holt, *American Whig Party,* 92.
9. Clay to the Committee of New York Whigs, August 8, 1837, *HCP* 9:67.
10. Clay to Swartwout, April 2, 1838, ibid., 9:167–68.
11. Henry A. Wise, *Seven Decades of the Union* (Philadelphia: J. B. Lippincott, 1872), 162–69; Clay to Porter, January 5, 1838. *HCP* 9:120; McCormick, *Presidential Game,* 120.
12. Holt, *American Whig Party,* 92–93; McCormick, *Presidential Game,* 175.
13. Clay to Clayton, June 14, 1838, Clay to Mangum, May 31, 1838, *HCP* 9:204, 194.
14. Clay to Porter, February 5, 1839, ibid., 9:276.
15. Webster to Curtis, June 12, 1839, Webster to Healy, June 12, 1838, "To the People of Massachusetts," Webster, *Papers,* 4:368–70.
16. Clay to Prentice, August 14, 1837, *HCP* 9:69.
17. Webb to Clay, December 15, 1837, ibid., 9:106.
18. Preston to Mangum, October 4, 1838, Mangum, *Papers,* 2:510.

19. Bell to Clay, May 21, 1839, *HCP* 9:317; Jones to Mangum, December 22, 1837, Mangum, *Papers,* 2:513.
20. Clay to Curtis, October 25, 1837, Clay to Lyman, November 22, 1837, Clay to Tallmadge, January 1838, Clay to Brooke, January 13, 1838, *HCP* 9:88, 93, 117, 130; Crittenden to Beatty, January 20, 1838, John Jordan Crittenden Papers, Filson.
21. Calhoun to Burt, December 24, 1838, Calhoun, *Papers,* 9:498.
22. Clay to Brooke, October 9, 1838, Clay to Rayner, June 2, 1839, *HCP* 9:239, 323; Clay to Tucker, October 10, 1839, Lyon Tyler, *The Letters and Times of the Tylers,* 3 volumes (Richmond, VA: Whittet & Shepperson, 1884), 1:601–2; Everett to Webster, July 26, 1839, Webster, *Papers,* 4:382.
23. Edgefield *Advertiser,* November 16, 1837; Holt, *American Whig Party,* 93.
24. *Cong. Globe,* 25 Cong., 2 sess., 55; Charles M. Wiltse, *John C. Calhoun: Nullifier, 1829–1839* (Indianapolis, IN: Bobbs-Merrill, 1949), 372–73.
25. Clay to Brooke, January 13, 1838, *HCP* 9:129; Preston to Tyler, December 30, 1837, Tyler, *Letters and Times of the Tylers,* 1:586.
26. Henry B. Stanton, *Random Recollections* (New York: Harper & Brothers, 1887), 152.
27. *Cong. Globe,* 25 Cong., 2 sess., Appendix, 60.
28. *Cong. Globe,* 25 Cong., 2 sess., 34; see also Van Deburg, "Henry Clay, the Right of Petition," 139–41; see Calhoun's remarks on May 6, 1812, regarding the right to petition, *AC,* 12 Cong., 1 sess., 1395.
29. *Cong. Globe,* 25 Cong., 2 sess., Appendix, 614–19; Clay to Clay, February 23, 1838, *HCP* 9:150; Preston to Mangum, March 28, 1838, Mangum, *Papers,* 2:517.
30. Nathan Sargent, *Public Men and Events from the Commencement of Mr. Monroe's Administration, in 1817, to the Close of Mr. Fillmore's Administration, in 1833,* 2 volumes (Philadelphia: J. B. Lippincott, 1875), 2:39; see *Cong. Globe,* 25 Cong., 2 sess., 176–81, for all of Calhoun's remarks.
31. *Cong. Globe,* 25 Cong., 2 sess., Appendix, 243–60; Preston to Mangum, March 28, 1838, Mangum, *Papers,* 2:517; see also Benton, *Thirty Years' View,* 2:98.
32. Clay to Biddle, February 20, 1838, *HCP* 9:149; Cole, *Van Buren,* 333; Remini, *Clay,* 517; Bartlett, *Calhoun,* 248.
33. Clay to Otis, June 26, 1838, *HCP* 9:208.
34. Seager, "Politics of Compromise," 2.
35. Clay to Erwin, April 26, 1837, Account and Receipts, Clay to Clay, May 21, 1838, *HCP,* 9:42, 52, 187.
36. Clay to Hughes, June 18, 1837, ibid., 9:50.
37. Clay to Clay, February 23, 1838, Clay to Clay, May 21, 1838, Clay to Erwin, April 10, 1839,

Clay to Brooke, May 24, 1839, ibid., 9:150, 187, 302, 314.

38. To Children of Unidentified Friend, February 18, 1838, ibid., 9:144–45.
39. Clay to Clay, May 22, 1839, ibid., 9:318.
40. Clay to Delavan, August 20, 1838, ibid., 9:218.
41. Clay to Otis, January 24, 1839, ibid., 9:275; Greene to Greene, January 19, 1840, Green Family Papers, Filson.
42. Clay to Lieber, February 2, 1838, *HCP* 9:142–43; Francis Lieber, *Political Hermeneutics, or On Political Interpretation and Construction; and Also on Precedents* (Boston: Little, Brown, 1837).
43. Clay to Clay, December 18, 1837, *HCP* 9:108.
44. Clay to Dod, June 1, 1838, ibid., 9:196.
45. Clay to Clay, January 7, 22, 23, March 23, 1838, ibid., 9:121, 133, 132–33, 165, 318.
46. Clay to Brooke, August 28, 1838, ibid., 9:224.
47. Samuel to Clay, April 12, 1837; see also Clay to January, October 6, 1838; *Fayette County Tax Assessor's Books,* 1841, ibid., 9:172, 238.
48. *Cong. Globe,* 25 Cong., 2 sess., 142–43; Appendix, 134.
49. Morehead to Crittenden, May 19, 1832, Charles Slaughter Morehead Papers, UKY.
50. Clay to Clay, May 11, 18, 1838, Duncan to Clay, July 16, 1838, *HCP* 9:184, 186, 213. Hart had done the work before his death. Clay paid his widow that September. See ibid., 185n1.
51. Clay to Hughes, January 1, 1838, Blackburn to Clay, September 17, 1838, March and Benson to Clay, September 18, 1838, Boulanger to Clay, May 1, 1838, Bayard to Clay, May 17, 1839, *HCP* 9:117, 181, 231, 311; Michael Birkner, *Samuel Southard: Jeffersonian Whig* (Rutherford, NJ: Fairleigh Dickinson University Press, 1984), 179–81; for an example of Corwin's cleverness, see *Cong. Globe,* 26 Cong., 1 sess., Appendix, 784–88.
52. Clay to Speed, March 2, 1838, Wood to Clay, March 8, 1838, Clay to Wood, March 22, 1838, *HCP* 9:153, 157, 164–65; Jeffrey L. Pasley, "Minnows, Spies, and Aristocrats: The Social Crisis of Congress in the Age of Martin Van Buren," *Journal of the Early Republic* 27 (Winter 2007): 649.
53. Clay to Biddle, September 12, 1838; Biddle to Clay, September 20, 1838, *HCP* 9:227, 231.
54. Clay to Joseph R. Ingersoll, June 24, 1839, ibid., 9:327.
55. George Templeton Strong, *Diary,* 4 volumes (New York: Macmillan, 1952), 1:81.
56. Cole, *Van Buren,* 323.
57. Clay to Porter, December 24, 1837, *HCP* 9:113–14.
58. *Cong. Globe,* 25 Cong., 2 sess., 80, 87.
59. Clay to Tallmadge, October 31, 1838, *HCP* 9:243.
60. Henry R. Mueller, *The Whig Party in Pennsyl-*

vania (New York: Columbia University Press, 1922), 57–58; McCormick, *Presidential Game,* 176.
61. Clay to Wyckoff, November 18, 1838, *HCP* 9:250; Payne to Payne, December 12, 1838, John Payne Papers.
62. Clay to Brooke, December 20, 26, 1838, *HCP* 9:258, 261–62; Pasley, "Social Crisis of Congress," 639.
63. Gunderson, *Log-Cabin Campaign,* 45–47.
64. Ibid., 43–45; Wise, *Seven Decades,* 165–66; Leigh to Barbour, October 27, 1839, Barbour Family Papers.
65. Clay to Brooke, January 18, 1839, *HCP* 9:273; Tyler, *Letters and Times of the Tylers,* 1:590–93.
66. Calhoun to Burt, December 24, 1838, Calhoun, *Papers,* 9:499.
67. Clay to Mangum, May 31, 1838, *HCP* 9:194; Jonathan H. Earle, *Jacksonian Antislavery and the Politics of Free Soil, 1824–1854* (Chapel Hill: University of North Carolina Press, 2004), 46.
68. Clay to Whittier, July 22, 1837, *HCP* 9:64.
69. Fladeland, "Compensated Emancipation," 183.
70. *Cong. Globe,* 25 Cong., 3 sess., 176, 177; New York *Spectator,* March 11, 1839; see also Clay to Birney, November 3, 1838, *HCP* 9:244.
71. Clay to Kennedy, May 16, 1839, *HCP* 9:314–15.
72. Clay to Crump et al., May 25, 1839, ibid., 9:319.
73. Clay to Rayner, June 2, 1839, ibid., 9:323.
74. Calhoun to Burt, February 17, 1839, Calhoun, *Papers,* 9:555.
75. *National Intelligencer,* March 30, 1839; Howe, *What Hath God Wrought,* 586–87.
76. Remini, *Clay,* 527; Van Deusen, *Clay,* 318n26; Holt, *American Whig Party,* 89.
77. Lathrop to Johnson, April 29, 1839, Charles C. Lathrop Letter, Filson.
78. Tappan to Clay, May 1, 1838, *HCP* 9:181–82.
79. Smith to Clay, March 21, 1839, Clay to Hammond, April 2, 1839, ibid., 9:298, 300.
80. Clay to Kennedy, May 16, 1839, ibid., 9:314–15.
81. Clay to Hamilton, February 24, 1839, ibid., 9:291.
82. Clay to Harriman, February 27, 1837, ibid., 9:33.
83. Clay to Kennedy, April 17, 1839, ibid., 9:306.
84. Washington *Globe,* January 29, 31, 1838; *Cong. Globe,* 25 Cong., 2 sess., Appendix, 134; 25 Cong., 3 sess., 55, 225–26; Clay to Estes, June 1, 1839, *HCP* 9:322.
85. Clay to Porter, May 14, 1839; Clay to Beverley Tucker, June 18, 1839, *HCP* 9:325–26, 312–13. For Clay's injury, see Clay to Bayard, May 3, 1839, *HCP* 11:274; Knupfer, *Union as It Is,* 151.

86. *National Intelligencer,* July 26, 1839; Everett to Webster, July 26, 1839, Webster, *Papers,* 4:382.

87. Glyndon G. Van Deusen, *William Henry Seward* (New York: Oxford University Press, 1967), 61.

88. Philip Hone, *The Diary of Philip Hone, 1828–1851,* edited by Bayard Tuckerman, 2 volumes (New York: Dodd, Mead, 1889), 1:374–75.

89. Ibid., 376.

90. Gunderson, *Log-Cabin Campaign,* 47.

91. Hone, *Diary,* 1:376; Clay to Clay, August 12, 1839, *HCP* 9:334–35.

92. Clay to Clay, August 12, 1839, *HCP* 9:334.

93. Glyndon G. Van Deusen, *Horace Greeley, Nineteenth-Century Crusader* (Philadelphia: University of Pennsylvania Press, 1953), 41; Thurlow Weed Barnes, *Memoirs of Thurlow Weed* (Boston: Houghton, Mifflin, 1884), 76.

94. John M. Taylor, *William Henry Seward: Lincoln's Right Hand* (Washington, DC: Brassey's, 1996), 49; *Niles' Weekly Register,* August 31, 1839.

95. Hone, *Diary,* 1:377; also see New York *Morning Herald,* August 22, 1839.

96. New York *Morning Herald,* August 26, 1839.

97. Charles D. Lowery, *James Barbour, a Jeffersonian Republican* (University: University of Alabama Press, 1984), 234; Norvell to Harrison, March 20, 1838, Harrison Papers; Henry H. Simms, *The Rise of the Whigs in Virginia, 1824–1840* (Richmond, VA: William Byrd Press, 1929), 140–41.

98. Graham to Mangum, October 11, 1839, Mangum, *Papers,* 3:19; Clay to Seward, September 26, 1839, Clay to Sargent, October 25, 1839, *HCP* 9:347, 352.

99. Norma Lois Peterson, *The Presidencies of William Henry Harrison and John Tyler* (Lawrence: University Press of Kansas, 1989), 23; Howe, *What Hath God Wrought,* 575.

100. Harrison to Clay, September 20, 1839, Clay to Leigh, September 25, 1839, Clay to Tompkins, October 12, 1839, *HCP* 9:342–43, 346, 11:277; Harrison to Crittenden, November 7, 1839, Anne Mary Butler Crittenden Coleman, *The Life of John J. Crittenden with Selections from His Correspondence and Speeches,* 2 volumes (Philadelphia: J. B. Lippincott, 1871), 1:112.

101. John J. Reed, "Battleground: Pennsylvania Antimasons and the Emergence of the National Nominating Convention, 1835–1839," *Pennsylvania Magazine of History and Biography* 122 (January–April 1998): 95–96; Mueller, *Whig Party in Pennsylvania,* 59; McCormick, *Presidential Game,* 176; Hans L. Trefousse, *Thaddeus Stevens: Nineteenth-Century Egalitarian* (Chapel Hill: University of North Carolina Press, 1997), 55, 64; Gunderson, *Log-Cabin Campaign,* 33.

102. Clay to Combs, December 3, 1838, *HCP* 9:359.

103. Minicucci, "Nation-building in the Early Republic," 262–63; David A. Crockett, "In the Shadow of Henry Clay: How to Choose a Successful Opposition Presidential Candidate," *Congress and the Presidency* 33 (Spring 2006): 51.

104. Arkansas had three votes in the convention, but only one delegate, B. H. Martin, chose to attend. If he had arrived in time, he would have cast the state votes for Clay. He was late, however, and found the convention had already chosen Harrison and Tyler. He endorsed the decision. See Martin to Penrose, December 10, 1839, in *Proceedings of the Democratic Whig National Convention: Which Assembled at Harrisburg, Pennsylvania, on the Fourth of December, 1839, for the Purpose of Nominating Candidates for President and Vice President of the United States* (Harrisburg, PA: R. S. Elliott, 1839), 26–27; Holt, *American Whig Party,* 103.

105. *Proceedings of the Democratic Whig National Convention,* 15–17, 18, 19; Combs to Clay, December 16, 1839, *HCP* 9:362; Gunderson, *Log-Cabin Campaign,* 57–59, 62; Benton, *Thirty Years' View,* 2:204; Howe, *What Hath God Wrought,* 571.

106. Gunderson, *Log-Cabin Campaign,* 61–62; Reed, "Emergence of National Nominating Convention," 112–13.

107. *Proceedings of the Democratic Whig National Convention,* 20; Holt, *American Whig Party,* 104.

108. Weed, *Autobiography,* 1:482.

109. Ibid., 1:482; Oliver Perry Chitwood, *John Tyler: Champion of the Old South* (New York: Russell & Russell, 1934), 167, 167n24; *Proceedings of the Democratic Whig National Convention,* 21.

110. Chitwood, *Tyler,* 171–72.

111. Wise, *Seven Decades,* 171–72.

112. Little, *Ben Hardin,* 354, 342.

113. Chitwood, *Tyler,* 162n12; *HCP* 9:364n2.

114. New York *Evening Post* quoted in the Montpelier *Vermont Patriot,* December 23, 1839; New York *Morning Herald,* December 16, 1839.

115. Clay to Metcalf, Combs, et al., November 20, 1839, *Proceedings of the Democratic Whig National Convention,* 23.

116. Clay to Clay, December 12, 1839; see also Clay to Clay, December 14, 1839, *HCP* 9:364, 365.

117. Speech in Washington, DC, December 11, 1839, ibid., 9:363; Gunderson, *Log-Cabin Campaign,* 69.

118. Harrison to Clay, January 15, 1840, *HCP* 9:374.

119. Clay to Browne, July 31, 1840, Clay to Smith, October 5, 1839, ibid., 9:438, 350; see also

Clay to Hamilton, June 20, 1840, ibid., 11:281.

120. Clay to Otis, December 19, 1840, Hammond to Clay, January 21, 1840, ibid., 9:368, 382.

121. Cole, *Van Buren,* 348–49, 357–58.

122. Harrison to Clay, August 6, 1840, *HCP* 9:438.

123. Baltimore *Republican,* December 11, 1839.

124. Gunderson, *Log-Cabin Campaign,* 75–76.

125. Turner to Mangum, November 22, 1840, Mangum Papers, Duke; Gunderson, *Log-Cabin Campaign,* 114; Cole, *Van Buren,* 377–78.

126. Hone, *Diary,* 2:85.

127. Clay to Gholson et al., July 21, 1840, *HCP* 9:433; Larry Schweikart, "Banking in the American South, 1836–1865," *Journal of Economic History* 45 (June 1985): 467.

128. Howe, *What Hath God Wrought,* 582–85.

129. Jackson to Van Buren, May 12, June 6, 1837, Bassett, *Correspondence,* 5:483, 487–88; Clay to Crittenden, December 5, 1843, *HCP* 9:898–99; Howe, *What Hath God Wrought,* 574; Peterson, *Harrison and Tyler,* 138.

130. Clay to Channing, December 13, 1837, Clay to Brooke, April 2, 1839, *HCP* 9:104, 298–99; Morehead to Crittenden, May 19, 1838, Morehead Papers; Howe, *What Hath God Wrought,* 584–85; Robert J. Morgan, *A Whig Embattled: The Presidency Under John Tyler* (Lincoln: University of Nebraska Press, 1954), 177.

131. Clay to Allen, June 22, 1840, *HCP* 9:425; see also Clay to Tucker, October 10, 1839, ibid., 11:279; White to unknown recipient, November 9, 1839, Hugh Lawson White Papers, Duke; Holt, *American Whig Party,* 90, 108–12; Howe, *What Hath God Wrought,* 574–75, 576.

132. Corwin to Crittenden, November 12, 1840, Coleman, *Crittenden,* 1:131.

133. Brown, "Southern Whigs," 375.

CHAPTER ELEVEN
Three Campaigns

1. Harrison's promise to serve a single term was applauded by Whig papers. See *Staunton Spectator* reprinted in the Natchez *Daily Courier,* June 8, 1840.

2. Clay to Clay, February 12, 1840, *HCP* 9:386.

3. Clay to Clay, January 24, February 12, 1840, ibid., 9:383, 386.

4. Tomlin to Barnes, November 21, 1840, Barnes Family Papers, W&M; Duralde to Clay, June 2, 1841, Clay Family Papers, UKY; Comment in Senate, June 30, 1838, Comment in Senate, July 10, 1840, Remark in Senate, July 11, 1840, *HCP* 9:210, 432.

5. Philadelphia *North American and Daily Advertiser,* January 17, 1840; James K. McGuire, editor, *The Democratic Party of the State of New York,* 2 volumes (New York: United States History Co., 1905), 1:239; the quotation is in "Political Portraits, No. XII, Silas Wright, Jr.," *United States Magazine and Democratic Review* 5 (1839), 417; *Cong. Globe,* 26 Cong., 1 sess., 138; Clay to Clay, January 24, 1840, *HCP* 9:383.

6. Niven, *Calhoun,* 236; *Ohio Statesman,* February 28, 1840.

7. Clay's speech on January 20, 1840, was widely reported. It appeared in the *Virginia Free Press,* March 12, 1840.

8. *Raleigh Register and North Carolina Gazette,* February 4, 1840.

9. Clay to Clay, ca. February 1840, February 18, 1840, *HCP* 9:388–90.

10. Clay to Clay, February 20, 1840, *HCP* 9:391.

11. New York *Morning Herald,* February 24, 1840; Clay to Clay, February 20, 1840, *HCP* 9:392.

12. New York *Morning Herald,* February 24, 1840; *National Intelligencer,* February 25, 1840; February 23, 1840, William Bolling Diary, VHS.

13. February 25, 1840, Bolling Diary.

14. Philadelphia *North American and Daily Advertiser,* March 2, 1840.

15. Boston *Courier,* March 5, 1840.

16. Ibid.

17. Clay to Clay, March 6, 1840, *HCP* 9:395.

18. Clay to Clay, April 2, 1840, ibid., 9:401.

19. Barbour to Taliaferro, April 10, 1840, Barbour Family Papers; Porter to Clay, December 16, 1839, *HCP* 9:367.

20. Clay to Clay, April 25, 1840, *HCP* 9:409.

21. Cincinnati *News* reprinted in the Natchez *Daily Courier,* June 5, 1840; Fayetteville *Observer,* January 6, 1841; Boston *Daily Atlas,* March 20, 1841.

22. Clay to Clay, February 20, 1840, *HCP* 9:392.

23. Gunderson, *Log-Cabin Campaign,* 5.

24. Sargent to Wise, June 23, 1840, Letter of Nathan Sargent, LOC; Clay to Green, May 12, 1840, *HCP* 9:411; Knupfer, *Union as It Is,* 152.

25. Cole, *Van Buren,* 377–78; Smith, *Blair,* 139; Jackson to Blair, July 28, 1840, Andrew Jackson Letters, Duke.

26. Clay to Clay, July 7, 1840, Clay to Gholson, July 21, 1840, *HCP* 9:430, 433; see also page 431n4; *New England Weekly Review,* July 25, 1840.

27. Clay to Sloane, July 27, 1840, Clay to Gholson, July 21, 1840, Clay to Committee of Gentlemen, July 23, 1840, Clay to Worthington, July 25, 1840, *HCP* 9:433, 454, 435.

28. Kirwan, *Crittenden,* 135.

29. Colton, *Life and Times,* 1:113; Parks, *Grundy,* 339; Little, *Ben Hardin,* 176.

30. Jonesborough *Whig,* August 26, 1840.

31. Speech in Nashville, August 17, 1840, *HCP* 9:440. By "Cuba allies," Clay was referring to the army's controversial use of Cuban blood-

hounds to track down Seminole Indians in Florida.

32. Jackson's letter was reprinted in the Nashville *Whig,* August 21, 1840.

33. To the Public, August 20, 1840, *HCP* 9:441–42.

34. For Jackson's continuing and absolute disdain for Clay and the Whigs, see Jackson to Blair, ca. 1841, Jackson Letters, McClung Collection, East Tennessee Historical Society.

35. Chitwood, *Tyler,* 194

36. Goebel, *Harrison,* 378–80.

37. Ashley to Green, November 29, 1840, Green Family Papers.

38. Jackson to Blair, February 19, 1841, Jackson Letters, McClung Collection; Tucker to Clay, December 16, 1839, *HCP* 9:367.

39. Clay to Otis, December 28, 1840, *HCP* 9:468.

40. Harrison to Clay, June 21, 1840, ibid., 9:424.

41. Harrison to Clay, November 2, 1840, Clay to Letcher, November 4, 1840, Harrison to Clay, November 15, 1840, ibid., 9:450–51, 452; Van Deusen, *Clay,* 337.

42. Goodwin, *Team of Rivals,* 283.

43. Kirwan, *Crittenden,* 142; New York *Morning Herald,* December 15, 1840; Mangum to Green, April 20, 1841, Mangum, *Papers,* 3:145.

44. Little, *Ben Hardin,* 211.

45. Ibid., 567; Wickliffe to Preston, January 20, 1841, Wickliffe-Preston Family Papers, UKY; Peter J. Sehlinger, *Kentucky's Last Cavalier: General William Preston, 1816–1887* (Lexington: University Press of Kentucky, 2004), 33.

46. Porter to Clay, November 29, 1840, *HCP* 9:455.

47. Clay to Porter, December 8, 1840, Clay to Brooke, December 8, 1840, ibid., 9:458–59; Kirwan, *Crittenden,* 138; George R. Poage, *Henry Clay and the Whig Party* (Chapel Hill: University of North Carolina Press, 1936), 16–17.

48. Philadelphia *North American and Daily Advertiser,* August 9, 1841.

49. Clay to Clayton, December 17, 1840, *HCP* 9:466.

50. Buckner to Buckner, December 14, 1840, Buckner Family Papers.

51. Clay to Saltonstall, November 22, 1840, *HCP* 9:454; Adams, *Memoirs,* 10:372.

52. Clay to Clay, January 19, 1841, Clay Family Papers, LOC; Clay to Clay, January 18, 1841, *HCP* 9:478–79.

53. Adams, *Memoirs,* 10:372, Clay to Letcher, December 13, 1840, *HCP* 9:462.

54. Calhoun to Colhoun, December 26, 1840, Calhoun, *Papers,* 15:402; Niven, *Calhoun,* 239.

55. New York *Herald,* December 21, 23, 1840.

56. Porter to Clay, January 4, 1841, *HCP* 9:471.

57. New York *Herald,* December 23, 1840.

58. Clay to Clayton, December 29, 1840, *HCP* 9:468.

59. Adams, *Memoirs,* 10:387.

60. *The South-Western Sentinel,* quoted in the Montpelier *Vermont Patriot,* May 25, 1840.

61. Boston *Daily Atlas,* March 13, 1841.

62. New York *Express* reprinted in the Cleveland *Daily Herald,* January 12, 1841; Calhoun to Clemson, January 3, 1841, Calhoun, *Papers,* 15:409–10.

63. *Groves v. Slaughter,* 40 U.S. 449 (1841).

64. John Quincy Adams Diary, 41, entry of February 19, 1841, 254, Adams Family Papers, Massachusetts Historical Society, online edition.

65. John Edward Semmes, *John H. B. Latrobe and His Times, 1803–1891* (Baltimore: Norman, Remington, 1917), 369–70.

66. New York *Express,* February 19, 1841. For Clay's appeal to ladies who flocked to hear him argue cases in any court throughout his career, see Greene to Greene, October 16, 1840, Green Family Papers.

67. Editors' note, *HCP* 9:476; Adams Diary, 41, entry of February 19, 1841, 254.

68. *Groves v. Slaughter,* 40 U.S. 503 (1941).

69. Ibid.

70. Tyler, *Letters and Times of the Tylers,* 2:10n4.

71. Richmond *Whig,* March 6, 9, 1840; *National Intelligencer,* May 27, 1840; Lyon Gardiner Tyler, editor, *Encyclopedia of Virginia Biography,* 5 volumes (New York: Lewis Historical Publishing, 1915), 3:41–42.

72. Clay to John M. Clayton, February 12, 23, 1841, *HCP* 9:499, 505.

73. Porter to Clay, January 4, 28, 1841, Clay to Porter, January 8, 1841, ibid., 9:471, 474, 485–86; Clark to Clay, August 28, 1841, Mangum, *Papers,* 3:224.

74. Porter to Clay, February 7, 20, 1841, *HCP* 9:497, 502–3; Hone, *Diary,* 1:319; Fitzwilliam Byrdsall, *The History of the Loco-foco, or Equal Rights Party: Its Movements, Conventions and Proceedings* (New York: Clement & Packard, 1842), 81.

75. Clay to Porter, February 7, 1841, *HCP* 9:497. Clay had made his remark about duplicitous Whigs during his visit to New York in December. See New York *Herald,* December 23, 1840.

76. Clay to Clayton, February 12, 1841, ibid., 9:499.

77. Goebel, *Harrison,* 370; Philadelphia *North American and Daily Advertiser,* March 6, 1841. The *Cong. Globe,* 26 Cong., 2 sess., 231, says that the Senate convened at 11:00, but it is likely that that is in error because of the several procedural matters that occupied it before commencing the inaugural ceremonies.

78. Philadelphia *North American and Daily Advertiser,* March 6, 1841. The proceedings of the special session of the Twenty-seventh

Congress that sat March 4–March 15 appear as a continuation of the *Congressional Globe* covering the Twenty-sixth Congress, second session. Therefore see *Cong. Globe,* 26 Cong., 2 sess., 232–36 here and afterward for this special session; Philadelphia *North American and Daily Advertiser,* March 6, 1841; Brown, "Southern Whigs," 377.

79. *Cong. Globe,* 26 Cong., 2 sess., 192, 236.

80. Ibid., 248.

81. Philadelphia *North American and Daily Advertiser,* March 13, 1841.

82. Ibid., March 12, 1841. Calhoun had changed his opinion by 1841. See Bartlett, *Calhoun,* 287.

83. Jean H. Baker, *James Buchanan* (New York: Macmillan, 2004), 25–26.

84. *Cong. Globe,* 26 Cong., 2 sess., 248–49; Boston *Daily Atlas,* March 13, 1841; Clay's pledge and bond is printed in the *Vermont Patriot,* November 2, 1844.

85. Adams, *Memoirs,* 10:442; Smith, *Blair,* 145.

86. New York *Herald,* March 13, 1841; *New England Weekly Review,* March 13, 1841; *Ohio Statesman,* March 16, 1841.

87. *Cong. Globe,* 26 Cong., 2 sess., 256–57; Elizabeth A. Linn and Nathan Sargent, *The Life and Public Services of Dr. Lewis F. Linn, for Ten Years a Senator of the United States from the State of Missouri* (New York: D. Appleton, 1857), 244–45; Poage, *Clay and the Whig Party,* 26.

88. "Notes for a Newspaper Editorial," February 4, 1841, Porter to Clay, February 20, 1841; *HCP* 9:495, 503; Weed to Granger, February 8, 1841, Barnes, *Memoirs of Thurlow Weed,* 89; Graves to Preston, February 7, 1841, Wickliffe-Preston Family Papers.

89. Harrison explained that the unsettled nature of the Tennessee delegation in Congress was a reason to delay an extra session. New representatives to be chosen in August would likely be Whigs, bolstering the party's majority in the House, and that alone was a reason to wait. The affiliation of Tennessee's two senators was also tied to the timing of an extra session; an early one was likely to yield Democrats.

90. Chitwood, *Tyler,* 188–89; Morgan, *Whig Embattled,* 28.

91. Clay to Harrison, March 13, 1841, Harrison to Clay, March 13, 1841, *HCP* 9:514, 515–16.

92. Sargent, *Public Men and Events,* 2:115–16; Adams Diary, 41, entry of March 13, 1841, 276.

93. Clay to Harrison, March 15, 1841, *HCP* 9:516–17.

94. Clay to Brooke, July 4, 1841, ibid., 9:557.

95. *National Intelligencer,* March 20, 1841; New York *Herald,* March 25, 1841.

96. Peterson, *Great Triumvirate,* 301; Holt, *American Whig Party,* 127.

97. Jackson to Blair, April 19, 1841, Jackson Letters, McClung Collection.

98. Clay to Conover, April 8, 1841, Clay to Lawrence, April 13, 1841, Clay to Starkweather, April 15, 1841, Clay to Berrien, April 20, 1841, Clay to Tayloe, April 21, 1841, *HCP* 9:518–19, 521.

99. Clay to Tucker, April 15, 1841, ibid., 9:520.

100. Kendall to Jackson, ca. 1841, Kendall Papers, Filson; Clay to Lawrence, April 13, 1841, *HCP* 9:519; Edward P. Crapol, *John Tyler: The Accidental President* (Chapel Hill: University of North Carolina Press, 2006), 3–4; Blair is quoted in Peterson, *Presidencies of Harrison and Tyler,* 45; Lambert to Mangum, May 7, 1841, Mangum, *Papers,* 3:154.

101. Morgan, *A Whig Embattled,* 18–21; Peterson, *Presidencies of Harrison and Tyler,* 52; Crapol, *Tyler,* 11.

102. Clay to Conover, April 9, 1841, *HCP* 9:518.

103. Clay to Lawrence, April 13, 1841, ibid., 9:519.

104. Clay to Porter, April 24, 1841, Clay to Ewing, April 30, 1841, ibid., 9:523, 524.

105. Peterson, *Presidencies of Harrison and Tyler,* 262–63.

106. Tyler to Clay, April 30, 1841, *HCP* 9:572–29.

107. Ewing to Clay, May 8, 1841, ibid., 9:530.

108. Simms, *Whigs in Virginia,* 154.

109. Morgan, *A Whig Embattled,* 31.

110. *Cong. Globe,* 27 Cong., 1 sess., 8, 12; Clay to Ewing, June 2, 1841, *HCP* 9:535.

111. David A. Martin, "The Changing Role of Foreign Money in the United Sates, 1782–1857," *Journal of Economic History* 37 (December 1977): 1009, 1018; *Cong. Globe,* 27 Cong., 1 sess., 129; Clay to Carey, June 11, 1841, *HCP* 9:543.

112. *Cong. Globe,* 27 Cong., 1 sess., 22.

113. Ibid., 48–49.

114. Clay to Letcher, June 11, 1841, *HCP* 9:543.

115. Wright to Van Buren, June 21, 1841, quoted in Chitwood, *Tyler,* 217.

116. Mangum to Cameron, June 26, 1841, Mangum, *Papers,* 3:184; *Cong. Globe,* 27 Cong., 1 sess., 97; Clay to Ewing, June 14, 1841, Ewing Family Papers.

117. Mangum to Cameron, June 26, 1841, Mangum, *Papers,* 3:182; Holt, *American Whig Party,* 132–33.

118. Chitwood, *Tyler,* 215. Chitwood calls this "a very probable tradition" because he regarded Lyon G. Tyler's biography of his father as "a very careful and reliable work" and presumed that Tyler's son must have "had some basis" for the account, concluding that "he may have had access to a paper that I have been unable to examine." See 215n39.

119. *Cong. Globe,* 27 Cong., 1 sess., 151–52; Clay to Clay, July 30, 1841, Clay Family Papers, UKY.

120. *Cong. Globe,* 27 Cong., 1 sess., 222–23, 328–29.

121. Poage, *Clay and the Whig Party,* 70; Thomas Ewing, "Diary of Thomas Ewing," *American Historical Review* 18 (October 1912): 99. Oliver Chitwood claimed Tyler was not deliberating, that he knew he would veto the bill before it passed. Chitwood speculated that Tyler wanted a bankruptcy bill to pass before he sent the veto message. See Chitwood, *Tyler,* 225–26. Crittenden to Clay, August 16, 1841, *HCP* 9:585–86.

122. *National Intelligencer,* August 17, 1841; *Cong. Globe,* 27 Cong., 1 sess., 337–38.

123. Howe, *What Hath God Wrought,* 591–92.

124. Peterson, *Presidencies of Harrison and Tyler,* 71–72.

125. Hampton to Clay, August 20, 1841, *HCP* 9:592.

126. Benton, *Thirty Years' View,* 2:344.

127. "Ewing Diary," 97–112.

128. *Cong. Globe,* 27 Cong., 1 sess., Appendix, 222–24, 364–66, 368–70; Chitwood, *Tyler,* 266n30; Webster to Ketchum, August 22, 1841, Webster, *Papers,* 5:146.

129. Clay to Spencer, August 27, 1841, *HCP* 9:594.

130. Adams, *Memoirs,* 10:545; Simmons to Simmons, August 29, 1841, James Fowler Simmons Papers, Filson.

131. New York *Herald,* August 31, 1841.

132. Clay to Clay, August 31, 1841, *HCP* 9:599; Letcher to Crittenden, September 3, 1841, Coleman, *Crittenden,* 161.

133. *Cong. Globe,* 27 Cong., 1 sess., Appendix, 344–45.

134. *Cong. Globe,* 27 Cong., 1 sess., 451.

135. Crittenden to Thompson, September 11, 1841, Crittenden Papers, Filson; Chitwood, *Tyler,* 273.

136. Chitwood, *Tyler,* 210n31.

137. See Chitwood, *Tyler,* 47; Poage, *Clay and the Whig Party,* 50–54; Van Deusen, *Clay,* 343–54; Remini, *Clay,* 584, for examples.

138. Crapol, *Tyler,* 16; *Cong. Globe,* 27 Cong., 1 sess., 42.

139. Lynchburg *Virginian* quoted in *Virginia Free Press,* September 2, 1841.

140. Neagle to Sartain, November 15, 1842, John Neagle Letter, Filson.

141. Mangum to Clay, July 4, 1842, *HCP* 9:728.

142. *National Intelligencer,* September 13, 1841; Ewing to Clay, November 1, 1843; see also Clay to Berrien, October 7, 1841, *HCP* 9:878, 612.

143. See the Jonesborough *Whig* for sample excerpts from papers.

144. Chitwood, *Tyler,* 273; Crapol, *Tyler,* 20.

CHAPTER TWELVE

Four Letters

1. Tallahassee *Floridian,* September 18, 1841.

2. *Ohio Statesman,* November 10, 1841.

3. Long to Mangum, July 7, 1842, Mangum, *Papers,* 3:366; Holt, *American Whig Party,* 135.

4. Clay to Spencer, August 27, 1841, *HCP* 9:594.

5. To the Whig caucus, September 13, 1841, ibid., 9:608.

6. *Cong. Globe,* 27 Cong., 1 sess., 344; Clay to Porter, October 24, 1841, *HCP* 9:616.

7. Clay to Tallmadge, October 30, 1841, Clay to Sargent, July 29, 1843, *HCP* 9:619, 841. Alexander McLeod was acquitted in October 1841. Tensions eased, and the following year, Webster concluded the Webster-Ashburton Treaty that settled the Maine border dispute.

8. Clay to Clayton, November 1, 1841, *HCP* 9:619–20.

9. Oliver Hampton Smith, *Early Indiana Trials: And Sketches* (Cincinnati: Moore, Wilstach, Keys, 1858), 593–94.

10. Ibid., 595–96. Dixon became seriously ill during the regular session of Congress and died on January 29, 1842.

11. Clay to Nye, October 29, 1841, *HCP* 9:618.

12. *The Southern Planter* (December 1841), 2:249, quoted in *HCP* 9:623.

13. Clay to Clay, March 7, 1842, ibid., 9:672.

14. Clay to Clay, June 6, 1841, Clay to Clay, December 24, 1841, ibid., 9:539, 624.

15. Van Deusen, *Clay,* 359; Poage, *Clay and the Whig Party,* 120; Clay to Editor, Philadelphia *North American and Daily Advertiser,* Clay to Clay, December 24, 1841, Deed of Trust for Ashland, November 15, 1842, Clay to Clay, March 13, 1842, Clay to Rogers, June 27, 1842, *HCP* 9:623, 624–25, 678, 720, 789–90.

16. Clay to Brooke, October 28, 1841, *HCP* 9:617.

17. Brown, "Southern Whigs," 377; Green to Mangum, November 17, 1841, Mangum to Green, March 2, 1842, Mangum, *Papers,* 3:252, 292; William J. Cooper, Jr., *The South and the Politics of Slavery, 1828–1856* (Baton Rouge: Louisiana State University Press, 1978), 153, 163.

18. Clay to Clay, December 10, 24, 1841, *HCP* 9:623, 624; Madison to Taylor, December 27, 1841, Allen C. Clark, *Life and Letters of Dolly Madison* (Washington, DC: W. F. Roberts, 1914), 306; *Pennsylvania Inquirer and Daily Courier,* November 16, 1841; *Milwaukee Journal,* January 19, 1842.

19. Clay to Clay, December 26, 1841, *HCP* 9:625.

20. *Cong. Globe,* 27 Cong., 2 sess., 164–66; Peterson, *Presidencies of Harrison and Tyler,* 97; Speech in Frankfort, October 26, 1842, *HCP* 11:288.

21. *Cong. Globe,* 27 Cong., 2 sess., 62, 69.

22. *Cong. Globe,* 27 Cong., 2 sess., 216.

23. Clay to Clay, February 13, 1842, *HCP* 9:652.

24. Davis to Payne, February 2, 1842, Payne Papers; Clay to Swartwout, January 14, 1842, *HCP* 9:631.

25. Beverley to Clay, February 8, 1842, *HCP* 9:648–49.

26. Clay to Beverley, February 17, 1842, Beverley to Clay, April 2, 1842, ibid., 9:659, 696–97; Concord *New-Hampshire Statesman and State Journal,* March 4, 1842.

27. Clay to Polk, May 20, 1843, *HCP* 9:818–19. The editors of the Clay Papers are not certain Clay sent this letter. It expressed his outrage over Polk's accusations and proposed that they debate the matter before a bipartisan panel, an event that never happened. See also *Raleigh Register and North Carolina Gazette,* April 26, 1844.

28. *Virginia Free Press,* September 9, 1841; Clay to Leigh, April 6, 1843, June 20, 1843, *HCP* 11:289, 9:826. *National Intelligencer,* February 25, 1842; Graves to Clay, February 26, 1842, Wise to Crittenden, February 26, 1842, Crittenden to Wise, February 27, 1842, Clay to Wise, February 28, 1842, Wise Family Papers, VHS; Wise to Clay, February 25, 1842, Clay to Plumer et al., August 1, 1844, *HCP* 9:661, 10:92; *Ohio Statesman,* March 16, 1842; "Mr. Wise's Speech," *William and Mary Quarterly* 18 (April 1919): 222–30.

29. *Cong. Globe,* 27 Cong., 2 sess., 235–36, Appendix, 145.

30. Clay to Hughes, November 15, 1841, *HCP* 9:622.

31. Clay to Tallmadge, October 30, 1841, Clay to Kentucky General Assembly, February 16, 1842, *HCP* 9:618–19, 626; Buckner to Buckner, March 2, 1842, Buckner Family Papers; Rives to Rives, March 8, 1842, Letters of William Cabell Rives, UVA.

32. *Raleigh Register and North Carolina Gazette,* April 8, 1842. Clay to Porter, February 7, 1842, Clay to Webb, February 12, 1842, *HCP* 9:647, 651; Kirwan, *Crittenden,* 160–61.

33. Clay to Porter, October 24, 1841, Clay to Allen, October 29, 1841, Clay to Clay, March 27, 1842, *HCP* 9:616, 617, 688.

34. *Cong. Globe,* 27 Cong., 2 sess., 376–77.

35. Kirwan, *Crittenden,* 161; Bartlett, *Calhoun,* 296.

36. *Ohio Statesman,* April 20, 1842; Hinton to Mangum, April 5, 1842, Mangum, *Papers,* 3:314.

37. Clay to Clay, March 13, 1842, *HCP* 9:677; New York *Weekly Herald,* May 21, 1842; Concord *New-Hampshire Statesman and State Journal,* May 27, 1842.

38. Clay to Van Buren, March 17, 1842, May 12, 1842, Clay to Sargent, May 31, 1842, Clay to Crittenden, June 3, 1842, *HCP* 9:680, 702, 704, 706.

39. Van Buren, *Autobiography,* 534; New York *Weekly Herald,* May 21, 1842.

40. Clay to Mangum, June 7, 1842, *HCP* 9:708; Philadelphia *North American and Daily Advertiser,* June 17, 1842; Lexington *Intelligencer,* June 10, 1842.

41. "Speech in Lexington," June 9, 1842, *HCP* 9:708–16.

42. Clay to Butler, August 8, 1842, ibid., 9:752.

43. Crittenden to Clay, July 2, 1842, ibid., 9:722; Letcher to Crittenden, June 21, 1842, Coleman, *Life of Crittenden,* 1:182–83.

44. Clay to McLeod, November 19, 1843, McLeod Family Papers; Johnston to Mangum, September 14, 1843, Mangum, *Papers,* 3:468.

45. Crittenden to Clay, July 2, 1842, Mangum to Clay, June 15, July 4, 1842, Clay to Sargent, July 31, 1842, *HCP* 9:717–18, 722, 724–28, 749.

46. United States Congress, House, *The Journal of the House of Representatives of the United States, 1841* (Washington, DC: Government Printing Office, 1789–), 1032–36.

47. Morgan, *A Whig Embattled,* 47; Crittenden to Clay, July 2, 1842, Clay to Berrien, July 21, 1842, *HCP* 9:722, 739.

48. Crittenden to Clay, August 3, 1842, Clay to Mangum, July 11, 1842, *HCP* 9:731, 749.

49. Walker to Clay, April 13, 1842, Crittenden to Clay, July 2, 1842, ibid., 9:698, 721; Crittenden to Letcher, June 23, 1842, Coleman, *Crittenden,* 1:184.

50. Pensacola *Gazette,* May 15, 1841.

51. Quoted in *Raleigh Register and North Carolina Gazette,* September 30, 1842.

52. *Cong. Globe,* 27 Cong., 1 sess., 430, 433.

53. Philadelphia *Whig Banner Melodist,* September 1844, vol. 1, no. 1.

54. Quoted in the Boston *Daily Atlas,* July 14, 1842.

55. Clay to Crook, July 25, 1842, *HCP* 9:744.

56. Sargent to Clay, August 6, 1842, *HCP* 9:752; Cleveland *Daily Herald,* October 7, 1842.

57. Clay to Sargent, July 16, 1842, *HCP* 9:736.

58. Clay to Littell, August 17, 1842, Clay to Colton, November 9, 1843, ibid., 9:757, 886.

59. New York *Herald,* September 30, 1842; Clay to Stratton, September 13, 1842, Speeches at Dayton, September 29, 1842, at Indianapolis, October 5, 1842, *HCP* 9:767, 773–77, 782–84; *Pennsylvania Inquirer and National Gazette,* October 5, 1842, Cleveland *Daily Herald,* October 7, 1842.

60. Mendenhall et al. to Clay, October 1, 1842, Speech in Richmond, Indiana, October 1, 1842, *HCP* 9:777–81; Thomas D. Hamm, *God's Government Begun: The Society for Universal Inquiry and Reform, 1842–1846* (Bloomington: Indiana University Press, 1995), 54–56.

61. Neagle to Sartain, November 15, 1842, Neagle Letter.

62. Speech in Columbus, Indiana, ca. October 6–9, 1842, *HCP* 9:785.

63. Clay to Branham and Bledsoe, July 23, 1843, Clay to Reigart, November 25, 1843, ibid., 9:838, 892–93.

64. Clay to Webb, March 15, 1842, November 8,

1843, Clay to Leigh, June 20, 1843, Clay to Clayton, June 21, 1843, ibid., 9:680, 827, 885; Mangum to Cameron, June 26, 1841, Mangum, *Papers,* 3:185.

65. Clay to Berrien, April 23, 1843, *HCP* 9:812; see also Clay to Clayton, August 8, 1842, June 28, 1843, ibid., 753, 831; Smith to Mangum, August 22, 1842, Leigh to Mangum, March 28, 1844, Atwell to Mangum, April 27, 1844, Mangum, *Papers,* 3:382, 4:79, 105.

66. Philadelphia *North American and Daily Advertiser,* October 4, 1842; *Pennsylvania Inquirer and National Gazette,* October 4, 1842; see also *National Intelligencer,* October 4, 1842; Boston *Daily Atlas,* October 1, 1842; New York *Herald,* October 2, 1842; Boston *Courier,* October 6, 1842.

67. Clay to Clayton, November 2, 1842, Clay to Sargent, July 29, 1843, Clay to Webb, October 27, 1843, *HCP* 9:787, 841, 876.

68. Clay to Porter, October 3, 1843, Porter to Clay, October 13, 1843, Clay to Lawrence, October 5, 1843, Clay to Clayton, October 10, 1843, Clay to Berrien, October 27, 1843, Clay to Webb, October 27, 1843, ibid., 9:864–66, 868–69, 870, 873, 874–76; Clay to Ewing, October 29, 1843, Ewing Family Papers.

69. Robert Tallant, *Romantic New Orleans* (New York: E. P. Dutton, 1950), 97–98; Deed of Trust for Ashland, November 15, 1842, Clay to Clay, December 9, 1842, January 3, 1843, Clay to Clay, December 12, 1842, Remittances from New Orleans, 1842–43, *HCP* 9:789–90, 792–93, 796, 815–16.

70. *Raleigh Register and North Carolina Gazette,* February 21, 1843; Jonesborough *Whig,* February 22, 1842; Milwaukee *Sentinel,* March 1, 1843; Clay to Clay, February 10, 1843, Speech in Lexington, April 10, 1843, Clay to Clayton, May 27, 1843, *HCP* 9:800, 810, 821.

71. Clay to Clay, March 7, 1842, Clay to Clayton, April 14, 1843, *HCP* 9:673, 812.

72. John E. Kleber, *The Encyclopedia of Louisville* (Lexington: University Press of Kentucky, 2001), 429–30; Clay to Clay, March 7, 1842, Clay to Clayton, April 14, 1843, *HCP* 9:673, 812; Jacob to James B. Clay, August 24, 1843, Jacob to Clay, March 22, 1844, Thomas J. Clay Collection, Henry Clay Papers; Clay to Clay, November 27, 1841, Clay Family Papers, LOC.

73. Clay to Letcher, August 15, 1843, *HCP* 9:844–45.

74. Clay to Moore et al., July 10, 1843, Clay to Pitts et al., December 12, 1843, Clay to Bayard, November 10, 1843, Clay to Porter, November 8, 1843, ibid., 9:833, 901, 834, 885; Knupfer, *Union as It Is,* 153.

75. Clay to Mangum, July 11, 1842, Clay to Leigh, April 6, 1843, *HCP* 9:732, 11:288.

76. Chitwood, *Tyler,* 284; Crapol, *Tyler,* 183–85; Corbin to Beverley, March 5, 1843, Beverley Family Papers, VHS.

77. Clay to Berrien, March 23, 1844, Clay to Miller et al., September 9, 1844, Clay to Clayton, August 29, 1844, Clay to Crittenden, March 24, 1844, Clay to Ray, September 26, 1844, *HCP* 10:13, 14, 105, 110, 127.

78. Mitchell to Preston, November 7, 1844, Wickliffe-Preston Family Papers; Swift to Pegram, September 24, 1844, Pegram-Johnson-Macintosh Family Papers, VHS; Clay to Simpson, August 15, 1843, Milwaukee *Sentinel,* December 2, 1843; Clay to Webb, October 25, 1844, *HCP* 9:845–46, 10:136.

79. Michael A. Morrison, *Slavery and the American West: The Eclipse of Manifest Destiny and the Coming of the Civil War* (Chapel Hill: University of North Carolina Press, 1997), 21–22, argues that Whig opposition to expansion had little to do with slavery but rather reflected a predisposition to resist anything that distracted the country from consolidating and developing its extant territory. Yet Republicans who inherited the Whig tradition (often the same people) did not oppose expansion after slavery ceased to be an issue, as William Seward's acquisitive foreign policy proves.

80. Clay to Oakley, May 30, 1843, Clay to Worthington, June 24, 1843, *HCP* 9:823, 828–29.

81. Clay to Saltonstall, December 4, 1843, ibid., 9:896.

82. Ibid.

83. Clay to Crittenden, December 5, 1843, Clay to Berrien, December 9, 1843, ibid., 9:898–99, 900.

84. Kendall to Clay, August 14, 1844, *HCP* 10:94, was published in *Kendall's Expositor,* August 27, 1844; see also Kendall to Green, June 7, 1844, Thomas J. Clay Collection, Henry Clay Papers; Clay to Sloane, June 14, 1844, Clay to Gales and Seaton, June 15, 1844, *HCP* 10:68–69; Cole, *Kendall,* 243; Peterson, *Presidencies of Harrison and Tyler,* 173.

85. New Orleans *Courier,* January 9, 1844; Trowbridge to Smith, January 14, 1844, Trowbridge Family Correspondence, Tulane; Frederick Pollock, editor, *Macready's Reminiscences and Selections from His Diaries and Letters,* 2 volumes (London: Macmillan, 1875), 2:239; Clay to James Brown Clay, January 22, 1844, *HCP* 10:3.

86. Murray, *Whig Party in Georgia,* 106; Clay to Crittenden, March 24, 1844, *HCP* 10:14.

87. Philadelphia *Whig Banner Melodist,* September 1844, vol. 1, no. 1.

88. Ibid.

89. Leigh to Mangum, April 22, 1844, Mangum, *Papers,* 4:114; Speech in Raleigh, April 13, 1844, *HCP* 10:18.

90. Clay to Crittenden, April 17, 1844, ibid., 10:40.

91. Clay to Crittenden, April 21, 1844, ibid.,

10:48; Howe, *What Hath God Wrought,* 680; Knupfer, *Union as It Is,* 154.

92. Jones, "Clay and Continental Expansion," 259–60; Cole, *Van Buren,* 393–94.

93. Stephens to Thomas, May 17, 1842, quoted in Holt, *American Whig Party,* 172.

94. Morrison, *Slavery and the American West,* 30–31.

95. Miller to Lee, May 16, 1844, Barnabas Lee Papers, Filson; Maness, "Clay and Slavery," 185–86; Reyburn et al. to Clay, September 11, 1844, Clay to Kennedy, September 16, 1844, *HCP* 10:116–17.

96. Clay to Weed, May 6, 1844, Clay Papers, Duke.

97. Yerby to Mangum, June 29, 1844, Mangum, *Papers,* 4:142; Clay to Green, August 24, 1844, *HCP* 10:103; Adams, *Memoirs,* 12:26.

98. Philadelphia *North American and Daily Advertiser,* May 7, 1848; *Emancipator and Weekly Chronicle,* June 26, 1844; Boston *Daily Atlas,* July 16, 1844; *Weekly Ohio Statesman,* August 7, 1844; Holt, *American Whig Party,* 192.

99. Combs to Clayton, November 20, 1844, John M. Clayton Papers, LOC; Wendell to Clay, March 11, 1848, *HCP* 10:414; Wales to Mangum, June 29, 1844, Mangum, *Papers,* 4:140; Galewood to Tazewell, June 15, 1844, Tazewell Family Papers; Peterson, *Presidencies of Harrison and Tyler,* 234–35.

100. Clay to Miller, July 1, 1844, *HCP* 10:78–79; Maness, "Clay and Slavery," 189–90.

101. Clay to Peters and Jackson, July 2, 1844, *HCP* 10:89–91; Jones, "Clay and Continental Expansion," 261–62.

102. Seward to Clay, September 10, 1844, Clay to Giddings, September 11, 1844, Clay to Green and Davis, September 23, 1844, Clay to Gales and Seaton, September 23, 1844, *HCP* 10:112, 114–15, 122–24.

103. Weaver to Crittenden, February 20, 1844, Drake to McDuffie, March 28, 1844, John J. Crittenden Papers, LOC; Clay to Wickliffe, September 2, 1844, Clay to Bond, September 10, 1844, Clay to Clay, September 11, 1844, Clay to Giddings, September 11, 1844, *HCP* 10:108–9, 111, 112, 114–15; Starkweather to Mangum, September 30, 1844, Mangum, *Papers,* 4:201.

104. Boston *Daily Atlas,* November 11, 1844; Mitchell to Preston, November 7, 1844, Wickliffe-Preston Family Papers; Allison to Bullitt, September 3, October 1844, Bullitt to Robertson, October 29, 1844, Bullitt Family Papers.

105. Crittenden to Clay, November 13, 1844, *HCP* 10:146; Beatty to Stevenson, December 28, 1844, Beatty-Quisenberry Family Papers, Filson.

106. Frelinghuysen to Clay, November 9, 1844; Clay to LeVert, November 21, 1844, *HCP* 10:143, 154.

107. Clay to Leakin et al., December 9, 1844, *HCP* 10:277.

108. Ibid., 10:176–77.

CHAPTER THIRTEEN
"Death, Ruthless Death"

1. Roman to Clay, December 2, 1844, *HCP* 10:169–70.

2. Beatty to Stevenson, December 28, 1844, Beatty-Quisenberry Family Papers; Central Clay Committee to Clay, March 4, 1845, Henry Clay Papers, LOV.

3. Combs to Boardman, November 2, 1844, Combs Letters, Filson.

4. Underwood's remarks and Clay's response are in *HCP* 10:170–72.

5. Crittenden to Combs, December 16, 1844, John Jordan Crittenden Letters, UKY.

6. Clay to Crittenden, November 28, 1844, *HCP* 10:161.

7. See, for example, Clay to Schenck, April 8, 1847, Hampton to Clay, June 3, 1845, Clay to Grinnell and Nye, September 27, 1845, Clay to White et al., December 16, 1845, Speech to McNairy, November 12, 1846, Clay to Washington, November 13, 1846, *HCP* 10:318, 228, 243, 253, 286, 288; see also the Philadelphia *North American and Daily Advertiser,* January 4, 1845.

8. Tilford to Clay, February 17, 1845, *HCP* 10:200.

9. See, for example, Clay to Lawrence, March 20, 1845, ibid., 10:209.

10. Clay to Tilford, February 22, 1845, ibid., 10:201. See also Clay to LeVert, May 20, 1845, ibid., 10:226.

11. Mercer to Clay, April 22, 1845, ibid., 10:217.

12. Clay to Tilford, August 4, 1845, ibid., 10:233.

13. Clay to Wedgewood, July 30, 1845, ibid., 10:275; Lexington *Gazette,* April 15, 1893.

14. These accounts also named Tilford as "Littford," another discrepancy that casts doubt on the story as a whole. See the *Scioto* (Chillicothe, Ohio) *Gazette,* March 17, 1847. Clay's friends protested the publicity from the start. See the Boston *Daily Atlas,* May 8, 1845.

15. *Milwaukee Daily Sentinel,* October 12, 1845; Madeleine McDowell, "Recollections of Henry Clay," *Century Magazine* 50 (September 1895): 766.

16. Neagle to Sartain, November 15, 1842, Neagle Letter; Simmons to Simmons, June 6, 1841, Simmons Papers.

17. Clay to Clay, May 6, 1845, *HCP* 10:224; Clay Lancaster, "Major Thomas Lewinski: Émigré Architect in Kentucky, *Journal of the Society of Architectural Historians* 11 (December 1952): 14, 18.

18. Clay to Clayton, April 14, 1843, ibid., 9:812.

19. Philadelphia *North American and Daily Advertiser,* October 14, 1845.

20. Ibid.; McDowell, "Recollections," 765–66.
21. Clay to Burnham, 1851, *HCP* 10:838.
22. One such article was derived from an October 1830 speech to the Hamilton County, Ohio, Agricultural Society and appeared in that year's *The Western Agriculturist and Practical Farmer's Guide.* See *HCP* 8:272–78, Clay to Colman, March 4, 1842, ibid., 9:671–72.
23. Clay to Garrett & Sons, July 31, 1843, Clay to Sargent, July 31, 1842, Clay to Clayton, August 8, 1842, *HCP* 9:749, 754, 841–42. "Why can't we furnish our navy and merchant vessels [with native hemp]?" asked a concerned patriot. "We shall never be independent till we do. And in case of war with England, we would be in a pretty box if that nation blockaded the Baltic." See Stevenson to Beatty, March 12, 1841, Beatty-Quisenberry Family Papers.
24. James F. Hopkins, "Henry Clay, Farmer and Stockman," *Journal of Southern History* 15 (February 1949): 89–90; Jeff Meyer, "Henry Clay's Legacy to Horse Breeding and Racing," *Register of the Kentucky Historical Society* 99 (Autumn 2002): 473–96.
25. Cleveland *Daily Herald,* January 28, 1846.
26. Clay to LeVert, June 25, 1846, *HCP* 10:247.
27. Preston to Preston, July 1, 1846, Wickliffe–Preston Family Papers.
28. *New York Times,* January 2, 1883.
29. Frankfort *Commonwealth,* July 7; Boston *Daily Atlas,* July 24, 1846; Duralde to Duralde, July 29, 1846, Martin Duralde III Letterbook, Library of Virginia.
30. The article entitled "Armistead Churchill," *William and Mary Quarterly,* volume 9 (April 1901), 249, states that Alexander and Mary Bullitt had only two children, Polly and a son, Thomas. Yet the biographical article on Alexander Scott Bullitt in John E. Kleber, *The Kentucky Encyclopedia* (Lexington: University Press of Kentucky, 1992), 139, lists three children: Polly, Thomas, and James.
31. Bullitt to Bullitt, December 12, 1845, Bullitt Family Papers.
32. Mary Ellen Doyle, *Pioneer Spirit: Catherine Spalding, Sister of Charity of Nazareth* (Lexington: University Press of Kentucky, 2006), 166.
33. Samuel D. Gross, *Autobiography of Samuel D. Gross, M.D.,* 2 volumes (Philadelphia: G. Barrie, 1887), 1:122.
34. Ibid.; Bullitt to Bullitt, May 1849, Bullitt Family Papers; McDowell, "Recollections," 765.
35. Bullitt to Bullitt, May 8, 1849, Bullitt Family Papers. See also the Louisville *Daily Journal,* April 30, May 7, 8, 9, 1849.
36. Clay to Sargent, January 11, 1845, *HCP* 10:189.
37. Clay to Bayard, May 7, 1846, ibid., 10:267.
38. Clay to Clay, June 21, 1845, ibid., 10:229;

Oliver Frazer said that Clay was "the worst sitter in the world." See McDowell, "Recollections," 767. See also *National Intelligencer,* May 10, 1845; Philadelphia *North American and Daily Advertiser,* July 3, 1845. Jackson's death was not unexpected, but his cult of personality was enduring. Rumors had circulated up until he breathed his last that he might run for a third term. *Niles' Weekly Register,* November 8, 1845, 47:145.
39. Johnston to Mangum, May 20, 1854, Mangum, *Papers,* 5:292.
40. McDowell, "Recollections," 767.
41. Clay to Stevenson, April 27, 1846, *HCP* 10:265.
42. Clay to Clay, December 17, 1846, Clay to Clay, December 17, 1845, Clay Family Papers, UKY.
43. Clay to Clay, October 5, 1849, Clay to Clay, April 8, 1845, *HCP* 10:623, 215.
44. Clay to Clay, July 22, 1845, ibid., 10:233.
45. Neagle to Sartain, November 14, 1842, Neagle Letter.
46. McDowell, "Recollections," 767.
47. Clay to Clay, March 17, April 8, 1845, *HCP* 10:208, 215.
48. Clay to Clay, May 13, 1851, ibid., 10:891; Duralde to Duralde, August 8, 1846, Duralde to Clay, July 1, 1846, Duralde Letterbook.
49. Clay to Clay, February 18, 1851, *HCP* 10:862.
50. Duralde to Clay, July 1, 1846, Duralde Letterbook.
51. Duralde to Clay, July 1, 1846, ibid.; Clay to Clay, August 27, 1837, May 21, 1838, Clay to Clay, January 22, 1838, *HCP* 9:72, 187, 133.
52. Clay to Lee, April 20, 1839, *HCP* 9:308.
53. Clay to Clay, April 2, 1845, ibid., 10:212–13.
54. Clay to Clay, April 5, 1845, ibid., 10:213.
55. Such stories were given renewed currency when Theodore died in 1870. See *New York Times,* May 19, 1870.
56. Cleveland *Daily Herald,* July 29, 1845; Clay to Clay, April 8, 1845, April 27, 1845, May 6, 1845, Clay to Clay, July 1, September 6, 1850, Clay to Clay, July 18, 1850, Clay to Clay, July 18, 1850, January 4, February 11, 1851, Clay to Clay, January 13, 1851, *HCP* 10:215, 220–21, 224, 759, 763, 767, 806, 840, 854.
57. Clay to Clay, March 13, 1852, *HCP* 10:958.
58. McDowell, "Recollections," 766. Clay marveled at the little girl's courage when she fearlessly played in the surf at Newport as a five-year-old. He would leave her a gold and diamond ring in his will, one of the more valuable bequests he made to his grandchildren. Her life was troubled by chronic illness, and she died at eighteen from diphtheria. See Clay to Clay, August 13, 1849, *HCP* 10:611. Last Will and Testament, July 10, 1851, *HCP* 10:900–904.
59. Duralde to Clay, February 23, 1846, Clay

Family Papers, UKY; Clay to Clay, January 18, 1843, Clay to Clay, February 8, 1847, Clay to Erwin, July 19, 1851, Clay to Cowles, September 14, 1851, *HCP* 9:798, 10:304, 906, 911.

60. Clay to Cowles, October 24, 1851; Schmidt to Clay, December 13, 1851, *HCP* 10:926–27, 937. For a sympathetic treatment of Margaret Johnson Erwin, see John Seymour Erwin, *Like Some Green Laurel: Letters of Margaret Johnson Erwin* (Baton Rouge: Louisiana State University Press, 1981).

61. Newspapers consistently reported James Erwin, Jr.'s death as a suicide. See, for example, the Fayetteville *Observer,* April 18, 1848, and *The Liberator,* April 21, 1848; *Weekly Raleigh Register,* August 24, 1859; Clay to Erwin, September 14, 1851, Clay to Cowles, September 14, 1851, *HCP* 10:913, 911.

62. Such to Clay, March 11, 1841, Duralde to Clay, November 22, 1849, Owen to Clay, September 11, 1850, Clay to Turner, November 24, 1850, Clay to Clay, December 26, 1850, *HCP* 9:513, 10:626–57, 808–9, 833, 836–37.

63. Clay to Paulding, May 3, 1839, Clay to Warrington, May 3, 1839, Paulding to Clay, May 24, 1839, Clay to Paulding, June 8, 1839, ibid., 9:310–11.

64. Clay to Clay, March 17, 1845, Clay to McClellan, September 24, 1846, ibid., 10:203, 208; Duralde to Clay, July 1, 1846, Duralde to Clay, July 9, 1846, Duralde Letterbook.

65. Duralde to Clay, July 20, 1846, Duralde Letterbook.

66. Duralde to Clay, July 24, August 23, 1846, Duralde to Duralde, August 8, 1846, ibid.; McClellan to Clay, September 17, 1846, Clay to McClellan, September 24, 1846, *HCP* 10:279–80. Martin's physician in Philadelphia was originally Dr. Nathaniel Chapman, but he was called away to Baltimore and the final crisis came soon after. The matter fell to Dr. George McClellan, a celebrated ophthalmic surgeon, whose care of a respiratory patient would have seemed irregular except there was nothing a specialist could have done for Martin Duralde at that point. McClellan was the father of George B. McClellan, who would assume supreme command of the Union armies in 1861.

67. Clay to Bayard, February 4, 1845, *HCP* 10:197.

68. Clay to Kennedy, January 31, 1845, Clay to Tucker, January 11, 1845, Clay to Thompson, April 23, 1845, ibid., 10:194, 189, 219.

69. Abel Upshur, Tyler's secretary of state whose death in the *Princeton* accident led to his replacement by Calhoun, was so obsessed with annexing Texas that he described it as the most important deed of his life's work and pledged to retire from office after accomplishing it. See Edmund Berkeley to Lewis Berkeley, May 8, 1844, Berkeley Family Papers, UVA; Tyler was anxious about there being no diversity of accounts regarding his administration's drive for annexation, and he labored to have Calhoun and everybody else, including Polk, erase any variations of the narrative. He drafted and had Calhoun review a lengthy account of the cabinet consultations and communications with Polk in the four days over which the joint resolution was considered and the plan for it adopted. See Tyler to Mason, November 27, 1848, Letters from John Tyler, VHS.

70. Clay to Lord Ashburton, May 14, 1845, *HCP* 10:266.

71. Clay to Sargent, April 28, 1846, ibid., 10:265.

72. Coutee to Berkeley, January 19, 1846, Berkeley Family Papers.

73. May 16, 1846.

74. Smith and Clay, *Clay Family,* 179.

75. Clay to LeVert, June 25, 1846, *HCP* 10:274.

76. Quoted in *Weekly Raleigh Register,* May 16, 1846.

77. Clay to Clay, June 18, 1846, Clay Family Papers, UKY; Perrin, *History of Fayette County,* 439.

78. Clay to Clay, February 12, 1847, *HCP* 10:305.

79. Ibid.

80. *National Intelligencer,* January 9, 1847.

81. Clay to Clay, February 24, 1848, *HCP* 10:310.

82. Raymond, Mississippi, *Gazette,* January 22, 1847; Cleveland *Daily Herald,* April 15, 1847; Clay to Clay, February 12, 1847, *HCP* 10:307.

83. Toast at the New England Society of Louisiana Dinner, December 22, 1846, New Orleans *Daily Picayune,* December 23, 1846; Hughes to Clay, September 14, 1847, *HCP* 10:351.

84. See, for example, his admonitions about writing letters in his note to Henry III, March 9, 1846, Clay Family Papers, UKY.

85. Clay to Clay, February 8, 1847, ibid.

86. Clay to Clay, March 8, 1847, *HCP* 10:313.

87. Clay to Lawrence, February 23, 1847, ibid., 10:310.

88. Clay to Clay, March 13, 1847, ibid., 10:314.

89. Clay to Mercer, April 1, 1847, Clay to Bayard, April 16, 1847, ibid., 10:315, 321.

90. Polk judged the fight a useless encounter. See James K. Polk, *Polk: The Diary of a President, 1845–1849,* edited by Allan Nevins (New York: Longmans, Green, 1952), 208–9.

91. McMurtry to Stevenson, March 2, 1847, Walter J. McMurtry Miscellaneous Papers, Filson.

92. W.M.W. to L.R.W., May 28, 1848, W.M.W. Letter, Filson; Perrin, *History of Fayette County,* 440.

93. Perrin, *History of Fayette County,* 440; Cleveland *Herald,* April 7, 1847.

94. Fry to Clay, March 22, 1847, *HCP* 10:314.

95. Clay to Mercer, April 13, 1847, ibid., 10:320.

96. Taylor to Clay, March 1, 1847, *National Intelligencer,* April 14, 1847.
97. Clay to Mercer, April 13, 1847, *HCP* 10:320.
98. Ray Holder, "Parson Winans and Mr. Clay: The Whig Connection, 1843–1846," *Louisiana History* 25 (Winter 1984): 61; also see Clay to Bayard, February 4, 1845, *HCP* 10:197; Bullitt to Bullitt, April 17, 1847, Bullitt Family Papers.
99. Holt, *American Whig Party,* 276.
100. According to newspaper accounts, the reason Clay was baptized at Ashland was because Christ Church was undergoing extensive renovations and could not accommodate the ceremony. See the Cleveland *Daily Herald,* July 16, 1847.
101. Editorial note, *HCP* 10:338.
102. Perrin, *History of Fayette County,* 441; *Raleigh Register and North Carolina Gazette,* August 11, 1847; Clay to Bayard, August 7, 1847, *HCP* 10:344.
103. Clay to Randall, April 2, 1847, *HCP* 10:316.
104. Clay to Wilde, April 10, 1847, Clay to Delegation of Citizens from New York City, Trenton, New Haven, and Philadelphia, August 20, 1847, ibid., 10:319, 347.
105. Clay to Bayard, August 7, 1847, ibid., 10:344.
106. Converse and Company Legal Document, page 10, Filson. Henry Jr. drafted the will on June 29, 1846, at Camp Oakland, naming his father and father-in-law its executors. Ironically, it was probated on April 12, 1847, his father's birthday, but even more peculiar was the fact that six years later on the day his son had drafted the document, Henry Clay died.
107. Clay to Clay, April 4, 1847, Clay Family Papers, UKY.

CHAPTER FOURTEEN
The Last Gamble

1. LeVert to Clay, December 6, 1844, *HCP* 10:147, Crittenden to Combs, December 16, 1844, Crittenden Letters, UKY; Caperton to Caperton, December 4, 1847, John Caperton Letters, Filson; White to Crittenden, September 29, 1845, Crittenden Papers, LOC; Holt, *American Whig Party,* 207.
2. Sargent to Clay, February 27, 1847, Clay to Mercer, November 14, 1846, *HCP* 10:311, 289.
3. Philadelphia *North American and Daily Advertiser,* October 14, 1845.
4. Clay to Clayton, April 16, 1847, Clay to Daniel Ullmann, May 12, 1847, *HCP* 10:323, 328; Holt, *American Whig Party,* 264–65.
5. Gaither to Bullitt, May 28, 1847, Bullitt Family Papers. Taylor's lack of party identification had Democrats musing about his possible nomination as their candidate. See Ficklin to Richie, April 24, 1847, Richie-Harrison Papers, W&M.
6. Clay to Ullmann, May 12, 1847, *HCP* 10:329.
7. Summers to Blackburn, April 19, 1847, Blackburn Family Papers, Filson.
8. Stevenson to Letcher, April 23, 1847, Crittenden Papers, LOC.
9. "J. J. Crittenden did more to induce Genl Taylor to offer his name for nomination than any other man," states a bitter note in the Thomas J. Clay Collection, Henry Clay Papers. The remark appears on the obverse of a list of Kentucky delegates showing how they voted at the Philadelphia Convention in June 1848. Also see Kirwan, *Crittenden,* 211.
10. Burnley to Crittenden, April 4, 1848, Crittenden Papers, LOC.
11. Stevenson to Crittenden, May 1, 1847, ibid.; Todd to Todd, May 29, 1848, Charles Stewart Todd Papers, Filson.
12. White to Clay, September 4, 1847, *HCP* 10:349; for rumors about the activities of Clay's Kentucky friends, see Ullmann to Clay, July 12, 1847, *HCP* 10:339, and Harvey to Mangum, June 3, 1847, Mangum, *Papers,* 5:66; and for Clay's humiliation over the Taylor movement in Kentucky, see Clay to Crittenden, September 26, 1847, *HCP* 10:305.
13. Clay to White, September 20, 1847, *HCP* 10:353.
14. Clay to Crittenden, September 21, 1847, ibid., 10:350.
15. Clay to Crittenden, September 26, 1847, ibid., 10:355.
16. Burnley to Crittenden, April 4, 1848, Crittenden Papers, LOC.
17. Combs to Crittenden, February 27, 1848, ibid.
18. Tyler to Wickliffe, August 24, 1845, Tyler Letters, VHS.
19. Wickliffe to Preston, July 28, 1847, November 21, 1847, Wickliffe-Preston Family Papers; *Emancipator and Weekly Chronicle,* August 27, 1845.
20. Bullitt to Bullitt, November 16, 1844, Bullitt Family Papers.
21. Clay to Clay, February 6, 1846, Clay Family Papers, UKY; Bullitt to Bullitt, December 5, 1846, Bullitt Family Papers; Philadelphia *North American and Daily Advertiser,* September 11, 1846; Boston *Daily Atlas,* December 29, 1845, December 22, 1846.
22. Speech in Philadelphia, August 14, 1847, *HCP* 10:345; Clay to Carter et al., August 17, 1847, Clay Papers, UVA.
23. Clay to Clay, August 18, 1847, *HCP* 10:346.
24. Tyler to Wickliffe, August 24, 1845, Tyler Letters, VHS.
25. Clay to Clay, February 7, 1846, Clay Family Papers, UKY; Clay to Clay, January 12, 1846; Clay to Clay, January 24, February 2, 1846, *HCP* 10:256, 257, 259.
26. Clay to Greeley, November 21, 1846; Clay to LeVert, December 19, 1846, *HCP* 10:294, 298.

27. Clay to Sargent, November 18, 1846, ibid., 10:293.
28. Clay to Ullmann, August 4, 1847, ibid., 10:343.
29. Clay to Warrington, May 3, 1839, ibid., 9:310; also see *Reg. of Deb.*, 24 Cong., 2 sess., 947–55.
30. One of Clay's grandsons referred to his chances in the 1848 election in just this way. See Erwin to Clay, January 29, 1848, Thomas J. Clay Collection, Henry Clay Papers.
31. Clay to Clay, February 12, 1847, *HCP* 10:305.
32. Taylor to Wood, September 14, 1847, quoted in K. Jack Bauer, *Zachary Taylor: Soldier, Planter, Statesman of the Old Southwest* (Baton Rouge: Louisiana State University Press, 1985), 227.
33. Hawley to Weed, September 7, 1847, quoted in Bauer, *Taylor,* 227; see also Taylor to Crittenden, May 5, 1847, Crittenden Papers, LOC; Taylor to Wood, September 23, 1847, Thomas Bangs Thorpe, *The Taylor Anecdote Book: Anecdotes and Letters of Zachary Taylor* (New York: D. Appleton, 1848), 19–20.
34. Bullitt to Taylor, August 21, 1847, Bullitt Family Papers; Taylor to Wood, October 12, 1847, Zachary Taylor Letters, UKY.
35. Clay to Ullmann, August 4, 1847, *HCP* 10:342.
36. Clay to Crittenden, September 26, 1848, ibid., 10:355.
37. Poage, *Clay and the Whig Party,* 168. No evidence links Clay to the circular, but he certainly knew about it, and it is likely that he had a hand in the project. See also Holt, *American Whig Party,* 277.
38. Letcher to Crittenden, December 23, 1847, Crittenden Papers, LOC.
39. Speech in Lexington, November 13, 1847, *HCP* 10:361–73.
40. Gaither to Bullitt, May 28, 1847, Bullitt Family Papers.
41. Taylor to Wood, October 12, 1847, Taylor Letters, UKY.
42. Clay to Clayton, April 16, 1847, *HCP* 10:322.
43. Clay to Greeley, November 22, 1847, ibid., 10:378.
44. Greeley to Clay, November 30, 1847, ibid., 10:381.
45. Poage, *Clay and the Whig Party,* 161–63.
46. Taylor to Clay, November 4, 1847, *HCP* 359.
47. Taylor to Crittenden, November 1, 1847, Crittenden Papers, LOC.
48. Taylor to Clay, December 28, 1847, *HCP* 10:392–93.
49. Poage, *Clay and the Whig Party,* 175.
50. Taylor to Peyton, May 20, 1848, Bullitt Family Papers.
51. Crittenden to Burnley, January 8, 1848, Coleman, *Crittenden,* 1:290–92.
52. Bibb to Crittenden, December 25, 1847, Crittenden Papers, LOC.
53. McLean to Ewing, October 6, 1847, Ewing Family Papers; Holt, *American Whig Party,* 271.
54. Burnley to Crittenden, April 4, 1848, Crittenden Papers, LOC.
55. Tucker to Berkeley, September 26, 1845, Berkeley Family Papers.
56. Greeley to Clay, November 20, 1848, *HCP* 10:381; Crockett, "Shadow of Henry Clay," 65, Holt, *American Whig Party,* 288.
57. Letcher to Crittenden, December 23, 1847, Crittenden Papers, LOC.
58. Poage, *Clay and the Whig Party,* 168; Clay to Clay, February 4, February 18, 1848, Clay to Mercer, April 5, 1848, *HCP* 10:300, 403, 424; Mangum to Graham, January 23, 1848, February 15, 1848, Mangum, *Papers,* 5:90, 93, 98.
59. Lewis to Noland, January 26, 1848, Berkeley Family Papers.
60. Mangum to Swain, January 12, 1848, Mangum, *Papers,* 5:91.
61. Clay to Mercer, February 7, 1848; Clay to Clay, February 1, 1848, February 21, 1848, Clay to Clay, February 18, 1848, *HCP* 10:399, 400, 404, 408.
62. Stevenson to Clay, May 22, 1848, ibid., 10:470.
63. Hill to Kemper, February 8, 1848, James Lawson Kemper Papers, Library of Virginia; Erwin to Clay, January 29, 1848, Thomas J. Clay Collection, Henry Clay Papers.
64. Speech at Independence Hall, February 26, 1848, Clay to Hughes, February 22, 1848, *HCP* 10:409, 410; Kirwan, *Crittenden,* 214.
65. Philadelphia *Bulletin,* February 25, 1848.
66. Holt, *American Whig Party,* 301; Hill to Kemper, February 8, 1848, Kemper Papers.
67. Morehead to Combs, March 7, 1848, Morehead Papers; Holt, *American Whig Party,* 311–13.
68. Letcher to Crittenden, February 21, 1848, Crittenden Papers, LOC.
69. Clay to Combs, February 18, 1848, *HCP* 10:404; Taylor to Preston, March 28, 1848, Preston to Taylor, February 26, 1848, Taylor Letters, VHS.
70. Holt, *American Whig Party,* 308; Poage, *Clay and the Whig Party,* 175–76.
71. Stevenson to Duncan, April 12, 1848, Letter of Thomas B. Stevenson, LOC; Corwin to Clay, May 3, 1848, Forrer to Clay, April 7, 1848, Wendell to Clay, March 11, 1848, Bebb to Clay, April 4, 1848, *HCP* 10:414–15, 422–23, 426; Poage, *Clay and the Whig Party,* 173–74.
72. Pierce to Clay, March 24, 1848, Gartrell to Clay, April 15, 1848, *HCP* 10:419, 442.
73. Lexington *Observer & Kentucky Reporter,* April 12, 1848.
74. Hunt to Weed, April 1848, Barnes, *Weed,* 167.
75. Claiborne to Clay, April 26, 1848, *HCP* 10:446.

76. Toombs to Thomas, April 16, 1848, quoted in Poage, *Clay and the Whig Party,* 167n4.

77. Clay to Hughes, May 8, 1848, Clay to Stevenson, April 12, 1848, Stevenson to Clay, May 18, 1848, Clay to Stevenson, May 20, 1848, *HCP* 10:433–34, 459, 465–69.

78. Crittenden to Clay, May 4, 1848, *HCP* 10:458–59.

79. Kirwan, *Crittenden,* 227–28; Joseph G. Rayback, "Who Wrote the Allison Letters: A Study in Historical Detection," *Mississippi Valley Historical Review* 36 (June 1949): 57n17, 71.

80. Crockett, "Shadow of Henry Clay," 54.

81. Taylor to Crittenden, March 25, 1848, Crittenden Papers, LOC.

82. Taylor to Clay, April 30, 1848, *HCP* 10:451–52.

83. Clay to Harvey, April 18, 1848, Clay to Hughes, May 8, 1848, ibid., 10:440, 459.

84. Munford to Bullitt, May 8, 1848, Bullitt Family Papers.

85. Todd to Todd, May 29, 1848, Charles Stewart Todd Papers.

86. Holt, *American Whig Party,* 330.

87. Clay to Fendall, June 6, 1848, *HCP* 10:480.

88. Greeley to Clay, May 29, 1848, Harlan to Clay, June 2, 1848, ibid., 10:474–76, 478.

89. Wickliffe to Preston, September 18, 1847, Wickliffe-Preston Family Papers; Clay to Brooks, April 13, 1848, White to Clay, May 26, 1848, Scott to Clay, July 19, 1848, Clay to Stevenson, August 5, 1848, Stevenson to Clay, August 10, 1848, *HCP* 10:435, 471–72, 511, 518, 519.

90. Lawrence to Clay, June 9, 1848, ibid., 10:481.

91. Poage, *Clay and the Whig Party,* 181, 181n27.

92. Erwin to Burnley, July 18, 1848, Crittenden Papers, LOC.

93. Kirwan, *Crittenden,* 218; Underwood to Crittenden, June 19, 1852, Crittenden Papers, LOC.

94. Clay to Stevenson, June 14, 1848, *HCP* 10:488.

95. Clay to Beatty, April 28, 1851, ibid., 10:885.

96. Richmond *Enquirer,* July 4, 1848.

97. Ewing to Taylor, July 22, 1848, Ewing Family Papers, LOC.

98. Clay to Worsley et al., June 27, 1848, Clarke to Clay, August 22, 1848, Meade, King, et al. to Clay, August 31, 1848, Clay to Cincinnati Whigs, September 1, 1848, Clay to Clarke, September 12, 1848, Ullmann to Clay, September 9, 1848, Clay to Ullmann, September 16, 1848, Dean to Clay, October 5, 1848, *HCP* 10:504–5, 522, 529, 536, 537–38, 543, 550; Mower to Mangum, September 11, 1848, Mangum, *Papers,* 5:111; Clayton to Crittenden, August 11, 1848, Crittenden Papers, LOC.

99. Hoar to Webster, August 13, 1848, Webster Papers, Dartmouth.

100. *National Intelligencer,* August 14, 1848.

101. Clay to Greeley, June 15, 1848, Clay to Graham, June 16, 1848, Clay to Harlan, June 22, 1848, Morehead to Clay, June 22, 1848, Clay to McMichael, September 16, 1848, *HCP* 10:489, 492, 500, 541–42.

102. The Lexington *Observer & Kentucky Reporter* carried reports on his condition throughout the month, although the precise nature of his illness was never revealed.

103. Greeley, *Autobiography,* 214–15.

104. Owsley to Clay, June 20, 1848, Clay to Harlan, June 22, 1848, *HCP* 10:498, 500.

105. Blaine to Ewing, October 9, 1848, James Gillespie Blaine Papers, Filson.

CHAPTER FIFTEEN
"What Prodigies Arise"

1. Philadelphia *North American and Daily Advertiser,* October 14, 1845; *Milwaukee Daily Sentinel,* October 13, 1845.

2. *The Liberator,* April 10, 1846; *The Emancipator,* May 27, 1846.

3. *The Emancipator,* July 1, 1846.

4. Ivan E. McDougle, "Public Opinion Regarding Emancipation and Colonization," *Journal of Negro History* 3 (July 1918): 314; Clay to John M. Clay, April 20, 1852, Clay Papers, UVA.

5. Deed of Emancipation for Charles Dupuy, December 9, 1844, *HCP* 10:176–77; *Cong. Globe,* 31 Cong., 1 sess., Appendix, 1633. In December 1844, Delia Webster was convicted of abducting slaves bound for Ohio and sentenced to two years in the Kentucky state penitentiary. Governor Owsley pardoned her, and she returned to Vermont in February 1846. Eight years later, she again returned to Kentucky to rescue slaves, but the state banished her.

6. Goodwin, *Team of Rivals,* 206–8.

7. Speech to the American Colonization Society, January 21, 1851, Clay to Hunkey, May 10, 1851, *HCP* 10:845, 890; *National Intelligencer,* December 19, 1844. The saga of Levy is related in Clay to Clay, September 3, 1849, October 2, 1849; Clay to Clay, September 5, 1849, Clay to Hodges, September 15, 1849, *HCP* 10:614, 615, 616, 620.

8. Clay to Giddings, October 6, 1847, *HCP* 10:356.

9. Certificate of Membership in the American Colonization Society, March 16, 1846, for Mrs. Emmeline Rockwell, Clay Papers, UVA; Davis to Clay, February 20, 1847, Thornton to Clay, June 8, 1846, November 1, 1847, Clay to McClain, June 5, 1847, *HCP* 10:272–73, 308, 333, 359; Giles Badger Stebbins, *Facts and Opinions Touching the Real Origin, Character, and Influence of the American Colonization Society: Views of Wilberforce,*

Clarkson and Others, and Opinions of the Free People of Color of the United States (Boston: J. P. Jewett, 1853).

10. Clay to Baldwin, August 28, 1838, *HCP* 9:223.

11. Clay to Coates, October 18, 1851, ibid., 10:925.

12. Smith to Clay, March 21, 1839, ibid., 9:298.

13. David L. Smiley, *Lion of White Hall: The Life of Cassius M. Clay* (Madison: University of Wisconsin Press, 1962), 52, 61–62. Accounts vary as to the number of shots exchanged in Clay's duel with Robert Wickliffe. See Sehlinger, *Kentucky's Last Cavalier,* 40.

14. Cassius Marcellus Clay and Horace Greeley, *The Writings of Cassius Marcellus Clay: Including Speeches and Addresses* (New York: Harper, 1848), 301–7, 337–40; Harold D. Tallant, *Evil Necessity: Slavery and Political Culture in Antebellum Kentucky* (Lexington: University Press of Kentucky, 2003), 118–19; Smiley, *Lion of White Hall,* 56–57; Clay to Clay, September 25, 1845, *HCP* 10:241; Clement Eaton, "Mob Violence in the Old South," *Mississippi Valley Historical Review* 29 (December 1942): 361–62.

15. The Pindell letter was printed first in the Lexington *Observer & Kentucky Reporter* and then by newspapers across the nation. See *National Intelligencer,* June 26, 1849.

16. Clay to Pindell, February 17, 1849, *HCP* 10:574–79.

17. Quoted in Gettysburg *Star and Banner,* March 16, 1849.

18. Clay to Clay, March 3, 1849, *HCP* 10:582; Collins to Blackburn, March 5, 1849, Blackburn Family Papers.

19. Garrison to Clay, March 16, 1849, Clay to McMichael, April 7, 1849, *HCP* 10:585, 588.

20. Clement Eaton, editor, "Minutes and Resolutions of an Emancipation Meeting in Kentucky in 1849," *Journal of Southern History* 14 (November 1948): 541–43.

21. *Daily Sanduskian,* June 28, 1849.

22. Ibid.; H. Edward Richardson, *Cassius Marcellus Clay: Firebrand for Freedom* (Lexington: University Press of Kentucky, 1976), 69–70; Hambleton Tapp, "Robert J. Breckinridge and the Year 1849," *Filson Club History Quarterly* 12 (July 1938): 142–43.

23. Eaton, "Emancipation Meeting in Kentucky in 1849," 541.

24. Clay to Hamilton, October 2, 1849, *HCP* 10:621–22.

25. Clay to Pindell, February 17, 1849, ibid., 10:579.

26. Last Will and Testament, July 10, 1851, ibid., 10:902–3.

27. Smiley, *Lion of White Hall,* 56.

28. Clay to Morrison, September 30, 1851, *HCP* 10:915.

29. Taylor to Clay, November 17, 1848, Clay to Mercer, December 10, 1848, Clay to Hughes, December 16, 1848, Clay to Stephenson, January 31, 1849, ibid., 10:559, 561, 563, 568.

30. Clay to Hughes, January 26, 1849, ibid., 10:567.

31. Clay to Hughes, August 4, 1849, Clay to Dean, September 1849, ibid., 10:609, 619–20.

32. Clay to Hughes, September 29, 1849, ibid., 10:618–19. Albert Gallatin had died just a month earlier than Hughes.

33. W. E. Whitfield to Clay, February 17, 1850, Clay to Clay, March 7, 1850, Clay to Farris, March 11, 1850, ibid., 10:677, 684, 686. Porter Clay died on February 16, 1850, in Camden, Arkansas.

34. Clay to Mercer, July 21, 1850, Clay to Mercer, August 1, 1850, Clay to Mercer, August 1, 1851, Clay to Mercer, November 2, 1851, ibid., 10:771, 790, 908, 928.

35. Clay to Mercer, December 10, 1848, ibid., 10:561.

36. Clay to Stevenson, December 18, 1848, Clay to Harlan, January 26, 1849, ibid., 10:564, 567.

37. Nevins, *Ordeal of the Union,* 1:234; Clay to Clay, December 24, 1841, *HCP* 9:624–25.

38. Buchanan to Bancroft, January 8, 1849, Buchanan, *Works,* 11:483.

39. Stevenson to Clay, April 20, 1849, *HCP* 10:594–95.

40. Combs to Clayton, January 22, 1849, quoted in Holt, *American Whig Party,* 398.

41. *The Mississippian,* January 12, 1849; Cincinnati *Atlas,* quoted in Hamilton, Ohio, *Telegraph,* February 1, 1849; Buchanan to Bancroft, February 5, 1849, Buchanan, *Works,* 11:484.

42. Clay to Underwood, February 11, 1849, *HCP* 10:569–70.

43. Clay to Bayard, June 16, 1849, Clay to Stevenson, June 18, 1849, ibid., 10:602–4.

44. Buchanan to Bancroft, February 5, 1849, Buchanan, *Works,* 11:484. The quotation is from *The Vanity of Human Wishes* and correctly reads "In Life's last Scene what Prodigies surprise," followed by "Fears of the Brave, and Follies of the Wise?"

45. Philadelphia *North American and Daily Advertiser,* July 6, 1849; New York *Daily Herald,* July 7, 1849; *National Intelligencer,* July 10, 1849.

46. Clay to Bayard, June 16, 1849, *HCP* 10:602; New York *Daily Herald,* August 4, 8, 1849; Boston *Emancipator and Republican,* August 23, 1849.

47. Norwalk *Huron Reflector,* November 6, 1849.

48. Clay to Mr. and Mrs. Hollister, September 19, 1849, *HCP* 10:617.

49. Webb to Blackburn, November 13, 1848, Blackburn Family Papers.

50. Mayer to Todd, September 8, 1849, Charles Stewart Todd Papers; Combs to Fillmore, Au-

gust 20, 1849, Combs Letters, Filson; Clay to Stevenson, June 29, 1849, Clay to Clay, October 5, 1849, *HCP* 10:606, 623.

51. Crittenden to Mason, November 29, 1848, Crittenden to Clayton, May 26, 1849, Crittenden Papers, Filson.

52. Clay to Taylor, May 12, 1849, Taylor to Clay, May 28, 1849, *HCP* 10:595–96, 599–600; Kirwan, *Crittenden,* 250.

53. Clay to Stevenson, June 29, 1849, *HCP* 10:606.

54. Crittenden to Clayton, June 29, 1849, Crittenden Papers, LOC.

55. Bruce, *Randolph,* 2:203.

56. David S. Heidler, *Pulling the Temple Down: The Fire-Eaters and the Destruction of the Union* (Mechanicsburg, PA: Stackpole Books, 1994), 22.

57. *Cong. Globe,* 31 Cong., 1 sess., 178.

58. Clay to Combs, December 10, 1849, Clay to Clay, December 15, 1849, Clay to Brown, Clay, December 29, 1849, Clay to Clay, January 8, 1850, Clay to Clay, January 11, 1850, *HCP* 10:631, 346, 347, 350, 369, 634.

59. Clay to Bayard, December 15, 1849, Clay to Clay, December 28, 1849, January 2, 21, 1850, ibid., 10:632, 342, 350, 368.

60. Nevins, *Ordeal of the Union,* 1252n116; Clay to Combs, December 22, 1849, Clay to Ullmann, February 2, 1850, *HCP* 10:635–36, 660.

61. Benjamin Brown French, *Witness to the Young Republic: A Yankee's Journal, 1828–1870,* edited by Donald B. Cole and John J. McDonough (Hanover: University Press of New England, 1989), 61.

62. Nevins, *Ordeal of the Union,* 1:268–69; Holman Hamilton, *Prologue to Conflict: The Crisis and Compromise of 1850* (Lexington: University Press of Kentucky, 1964), 32.

63. *Cong. Globe,* 31 Cong., 1 sess., 197–98, 356, 644–46.

64. *Cong. Globe,* 31 Cong., 1 sess., 39–40; Clay to Bayard, December 14, 1849, Clay to Stevenson, December 31, 1849, Clay to Clay, December 28, 1850, Clay to Clay, January 12, 1850, *HCP* 10:633, 635, 638, 648.

65. Nevins, *Ordeal of the Union,* 1:274.

66. Clay to Harvie, August 18, 1848, *HCP* 10:522.

67. Richardson, *Messages and Papers,* 5:26–30. This is the message to the Senate that replicates the one sent to the House on January 21.

68. Clay's motives remained a target of suspicion throughout the compromise debate. See Hubard to Hubard, June 19, 1850, Correspondence of Robert Thruston Hubard, UVA.

69. George Ticknor Curtis, *Life of Daniel Webster,* 2 volumes (New York: D. Appleton, 1870), 2:397–98; see also Robert A. Brent, "Between Calhoun and Webster: Clay in 1850," *Southern Quarterly* 8 (1970): 296; Michael Birkner,

"Daniel Webster and the Crisis of Union," *Historical New Hampshire* 37 (1982): 151–52.

70. *Cong. Globe,* 31 Cong., 1 sess., 244, 246.

71. A. H. Carrier, *Monument of the Memory of Henry Clay* (Philadelphia: D. Rulison, 1859), 123–24.

72. Goodwin, *Team of Rivals,* 158.

73. *Cong. Globe,* 31 Cong., 1 sess., Appendix, 115–27; Hamilton, *Prologue to Conflict,* 55–56; Poage, *Clay and the Whig Party,* 201–2.

74. Clay to Stevenson, June 18, 1849, *HCP* 10:604.

75. Clay to Stevenson, April 25, 1850, ibid., 10:710; Hamilton, *Prologue to Conflict,* 131–32.

76. Barnwell to Hammond, August 14, 1850, quoted in Hamilton, *Prologue to Conflict,* 129.

77. *Cong. Globe,* 31 Cong., 1 sess., 246.

78. William H. Herndon and Jesse W. Weik, *Herndon's Lincoln: The True Story of a Great Life* (Springfield, IL: Herndon's Lincoln Publishing, 1888), 478.

79. Hamilton, Ohio, *Telegraph,* February 1, 1849.

80. Norwalk *Huron Reflector,* January 29, 1850.

81. Speech in Senate, January 29, February 6, 1850, *HCP* 10:658, 671.

82. Washington *Union,* February 2, 1850; Tucker to Hammond, February 2, 1850, quoted in Hamilton, *Prologue to Conflict,* 60.

83. *Cong. Globe,* 31 Cong., 1 sess., 405.

84. Hamilton, *Prologue to Conflict,* 70; David D. Van Tassel, "Gentlemen of Property and Standing: Compromise Sentiment in Boston in 1850," *New England Quarterly* 23 (September 1950): 309.

85. Clay to Simonton, February 8, 1850, *HCP* 10:673; Ambler, *Ritchie,* 279–82, 288; *Cong. Globe,* 31 Cong., 1 sess., 368; Henry S. Foote, *Casket of Reminiscences* (Washington, DC: Chronicle Publishing, 1874), 278. Some cynics believed Clay purchased Ritchie's support with the pledge of lucrative printing contracts, but no evidence supports the claim. See Hamilton, *Prologue to Conflict,* 122; see also William Kauffman Scarborough, editor, *The Diary of Edmund Ruffin: Toward Independence, October 1856–April 1861* (Baton Rouge: Louisiana State University Press, 1972), 267.

86. Hamilton, *Prologue to Conflict,* 80–81. Hamilton suggests that the speech Webster delivered on March 7 was considerably more inclined to the South than the one that was printed for distribution.

87. Dudley to Webster, May 4, 1850, Webster Papers, Dartmouth; Birkner, "Webster and the Crisis of Union," 169–73.

88. Nevins, *Ordeal of the Union,* 1:298–99. "He was a good deal given to facetiousness," Henry Foote would later recall, "but I never

heard him utter a decidedly brilliant witticism in my life." See Foote, *Casket of Reminiscences,* 124.

89. *Cong. Globe,* 31 Cong., 1 sess., Appendix, 265.

90. Clay to Harlan, March 16, 1850, *HCP* 10:689.

91. Bancroft, "A Few Words About Henry Clay," 481.

92. Strong, *Diary,* 2:107.

93. *Cong. Globe,* 31 Cong., 1 sess., 356, 365–69.

94. Clay to Clay, April 25, 1850, *HCP* 10:709.

95. *Cong. Globe,* 31 Cong., 1 sess., 747–64.

96. Clay to Clay, April 25, 1850, *HCP* 10:709; Hamilton, *Prologue to Conflict,* 94.

97. *Cong. Globe,* 31 Cong., 1 sess., 644–51; Senate Reports, 31 Cong., 1 sess., no. 123.

98. Clay to Stevenson, April 25, 1850, *HCP* 10:710.

99. See, for example, Nevins, *Ordeal of the Union,* 1:319, and Holt, *American Whig Party,* 502.

100. *Cong. Globe,* 31 Cong., 1 sess., Appendix, 614.

101. Ibid., 615.

102. Clay to Brooke, June 11, 1850; Speech at Ellicott's Mills, Maryland, June 23, 1850, *HCP* 10:745, 755–56; *Cong. Globe,* 31 Cong., 1 sess., Appendix, 861–62, 865–67.

103. Clay to Mangum, June 25, Mangum, *Papers,* 5:178.

104. *Cong. Globe,* 31 Cong., 1 sess., Appendix, 1092.

105. For descriptions of the unpleasant heat in Washington that summer, see Hubard to Hubard, June 19, 1850, Hubard Correspondence, and Clay to Clay, July 6, 1850, *HCP* 10:763. Proving that conspiracy theories are not merely modern phenomena, stories soon circulated that Taylor was poisoned because he opposed extending slavery into the western territories. The persistence of such tales led to Taylor's exhumation in June 1991. The examination ruled out poison as the cause of death. See *New York Times,* September 11, 1881, June 15, 1991; Pittsburgh *Post-Gazette,* June 26, 1991. See also http://www.ornl.gov/info/ornlreview/rev27-12/text/ansside6.html.

106. Robert J. Rayback, *Millard Fillmore: Biography of a President* (Buffalo, NY: H. Stewart, 1959), is the standard biography of this much underestimated man.

107. Clay to Clay, July 13, 1850, Clay to Mercer, July 21, 1850, *HCP* 10:764, 771.

108. Clay to Mercer, July 18, 21, 1850, Clay to Fillmore, August 10, 1850, ibid., 10:767, 771, 792.

109. Clay to Clay, August 6, 1850, ibid., 10:791; Pindell to Crittenden, August 12, 1850, Crittenden Papers, LOC; Kirwan, *Crittenden,* 275.

110. *Cong. Globe,* 31 Cong., 1 sess., Appendix, 1405–15.

111. *Cong. Globe,* 31 Cong., 1 sess., 1481–82.

112. Hubard to Hubard, June 25, July 2, 1850, Hubard Correspondence, UVA.

113. *Cong. Globe,* 31 Cong., 1 sess., Appendix, 1473–74.

114. Rayback, *Fillmore,* 247–52. Hamilton, *Prologue to Conflict,* 113, said there was no evidence to support this speculation.

115. *Cong. Globe,* 31 Cong., 1 sess., 751; Hamilton, *Prologue to Conflict,* 109–11; Poage, *Clay and the Whig Party,* 255–56.

116. New York *Express,* August 6, 1850.

117. *Cong. Globe,* 31 Cong., 1 sess., Appendix, 1487–88.

CHAPTER SIXTEEN
"The Best & Almost Only True Friend"

1. Hone, *Diary,* 387.

2. Winthrop to Everett, August 1, 1850, quoted in Nevins, *Ordeal of the Union,* 1:341.

3. Holman Hamilton subscribed to this view. See Hamilton, *Prologue to Conflict,* 148–49; see also Holt, *American Whig Party,* 486.

4. The House of Representatives passed the bills in somewhat different fashion during September.

5. Holman Hamilton, "Democratic Senate Leadership and the Compromise of 1850," *Mississippi Valley Historical Review* 41 (December 1954), 405.

6. "Webster, Clay, Calhoun, and Jackson: How They Sat for the Daguerreotypes," *Harper's New Monthly Magazine* 38 (May 1869):788.

7. Nevins, *Ordeal of the Union,* 1:344.

8. Douglas to Lanphier and Walker, August 3, 1850, Robert W. Johannsen, editor, *The Letters of Stephen A. Douglas* (Urbana: University of Illinois Press, 1961), 192–93.

9. Hamilton, *Prologue to Conflict,* 172.

10. Nevins, *Ordeal of the Union,* 1:349.

11. Clay to Clay, August 15, 1850, *HCP* 10:795.

12. McDowell, "Recollections," 766.

13. Clay to Clay, October 2, December 4, 29, 1849, January 2, 8, 1850; Clay to Clayton, December 6, 1849, Clay to Clay, December 15, 1849, Clay to Clay, February 2, 1850, Clay to Clay, February 18, November 15, 1850, *HCP* 10:620, 629–30, 639–40, 631, 633, 641–42, 645–46, 660, 678–79, 828; Bearss, "Claims Against Portugal," 173–74.

14. Bearss, "Claims Against Portugal," 177.

15. Bearss makes this claim. See ibid., 178.

16. Clay to Clay, August 22, 31, 1850, Clay to Webster, August 22, 1850, Clay to Fillmore, August 17, 20, 1850, *HCP* 10:779, 793, 798, 801.

17. Clay to Clay, October 26, 1851, Clay to Clay, January 3, 1852, *HCP* 10:927, 943.

18. Clay to Clay, June 1, 1852, Thomas J. Clay Collection, Henry Clay Papers.

19. Clay to Clay, October 16, 1850, *HCP* 10:822.

20. Clay to Harrison, [summer 1850], Papers of James O. Harrison, LOC.
21. McDowell, "Recollections," 766–67.
22. In these last years, Clay was as willing to recommend Democrats as Whigs for patronage posts. See George W. Jones to Clay, November 2, 1850, Clay to Stuart, November 7, 1850, Stuart Papers, UVA.
23. *National Intelligencer,* November 27, 1850.
24. Clay to Clay, December 23, 1850, *HCP* 10:835; *National Intelligencer,* December 18, 1850; New York *Herald,* December 19, 1850.
25. Clay to Clay, February 27, 1851, Clay to Clay, March 5, 1851, *HCP* 10:876, 880–81.
26. *Cong. Globe,* 31 Cong., 2 sess., 506.
27. Ibid., 597. See also Fish to Clay, February 18, 1851, Clay to Fish, February 23, 1851, *HCP* 10:864–65, 870–71.
28. Clay to Stevenson, May 17, 1851, ibid., 10:891.
29. *Obituaries,* 53; Clay to Clay, February 27, 1851, Clay to Clay, March 5, 1851, *HCP* 10:876, 880–81.
30. Clay to Clay, March 7, 1851, *HCP* 10:881.
31. Passport, March 8, 1851, Clay Legal Documents.
32. March 18, 1851, *HCP* 10:883.
33. Clay to Clay, March 18, April 7, 1851, Clay to Hunt, April 9, 1851, ibid., 10:881, 884.
34. Lutz to Clay, May 23, 1851, Clay to Lutz, May 26, 1851, ibid., 10:892, 893.
35. Clay to Hopkins, July 17, 1851, ibid., 10:905.
36. Clay to Clay, May 9, 1851, ibid., 10:889.
37. Clay to Short, June 16, 1851, ibid., 10:898; see also Thomas Speed, *The Political Club, Danville Kentucky, 1786–1790: Being an Account of Early Kentucky Society from the Original Papers Recently Found* (Louisville, KY: John P. Morton, 1894), 77–78; *Cong. Globe,* 31 Cong., 1 sess., 225.
38. Last Will and Testament, July 10, 1851, *HCP* 10:900–904.
39. J. Winston Coleman, *Last Days, Death and Funeral of Henry Clay* (Lexington: Winburn Press, 1951), 2.
40. Clay to Ullmann, June 14, September 26, 1851, *HCP* 10:896–97, 914.
41. Clay to McLeod, November 15, 1851, McLeod Family Papers.
42. Clay to Mercer, August 1, 1851, 1850, *HCP* 10:908.
43. Clay to Clay, July 22, 1851, Thomas J. Clay Collection, Henry Clay Papers; Clay to Clay, July 28, 1851, Clay-Russell Papers.
44. Clay to J.D.H., November 15, 1851; see also Clay to Clay, October 31, November 16, 1851, Clay to Clay, November 5, 1851, *HCP* 10:927, 928, 929, 931.
45. Clay to Clay, December 2, 1851, Thomas J. Clay Collection, Henry Clay Papers.
46. Gross, *Autobiography,* 1:122; Clay to Clay, July 28, 1851, Clay-Russell Papers.

47. Coleman, *Final Days,* 3.
48. Clay to Clay, November 16, 1851, Clay to Brooke, November 3, 1838, *HCP* 10:931–32, 9:245.
49. Clay to Clay, November 19, 1851, ibid., 10:933.
50. Clay to Clay, November 23, 1851, ibid.
51. *Cong. Globe,* 32 Cong., 1 sess., 2, 4; Clay to Clay, December 1, 1851, *HCP* 10:934.
52. Clay to Clay, December 3, 1851, *HCP* 10:935.
53. Clay to Clay, December 6, 1851, Clay to Clay, December 9, 1851, Fillmore to Clay, June 7, 1851, ibid., 10:936, 967; Rayback, *Fillmore,* 350.
54. Clay to Clay, December 6, 1851, *HCP* 10:936.
55. Clay to Clay, December 18, 1851, Thomas J. Clay Collection, Henry Clay Papers.
56. Clay to Kentucky General Assembly, December 17, 1851, *HCP* 10:938.
57. Clay to Neagle, December 21, 1851, ibid., 10:940.
58. Clay to Clay, December 25, 1851, Kennedy to Clay, December 25, 1851, Clay to Kennedy, December 31, 1851, Clay to Allibone, January 11, 1852, ibid., 10:940, 941, 946.
59. Clay to Clay, January 4, 1852, ibid., 10:943.
60. *National Intelligencer,* January 10, 1851.
61. *New York Times,* January 12, 1852.
62. Clay to Clay, December 9, 1851, Clay to Clay, December 25, 1851, Clay to Clay, January 20, 1842, *HCP* 10:396, 940, 949.
63. Clay to Ullmann, September 26, 1851, March 6, 18, 1852, Clay to Citizens of New York, February 9, 1852, Ullmann to Clay, February 9, 1851, ibid., 10:914, 951, 952–53, 960.
64. Clay to Clay, January 12, March 3, 1852, Clay to Clay, February 28, 1852, ibid., 10:947, 956, 957.
65. Clay to Clay, April 7, 1852; Clay to Clay, April 21, 1852, *HCP* 10:964, 965.
66. Clay to Harrison, April 28, 1852, ibid., 10:966.
67. Clay to Clay, April 25, 1852, Thomas J. Clay Collection, Henry Clay Papers.
68. Clay to Clay, December 1, 1851, March 3, 1852, *HCP* 10:934, 957.
69. Clay to Clay, June 1, 1852, Thomas J. Clay Collection, Henry Clay Papers.
70. *Obituaries,* 632–33; Clay to Clay, May 8, 1852, Colton, *Private Correspondence,* 631, 633.
71. Blair to Clay, January 22, 1852, *HCP* 10:949; Van Buren, *Autobiography,* 535.
72. Van Buren, *Autobiography,* 667.
73. Tayloe to Crittenden, March 15, 1851, Crittenden Papers, LOC. The letter is incorrectly dated in the Crittenden Papers as March 19, 1851, by a hand other than Julia Tayloe's. Yet it contains her notation "Saturday morning." Because March 19 was a Wednesday, we have concluded that the invitation was dispatched the previous Saturday, the fifteenth, and per-

tained to a dinner party on the following
Wednesday, the nineteenth.

74. Colton, *Private Correspondence,* 634; Simmons to Crittenden, November 30, 1859, Crittenden Papers, LOC; Underwood to Crittenden,
June 19, 1852, Coleman, *John J. Crittenden,*
2:37; see also Kirwan, *Crittenden,* 284.

75. James Brown Clay Diary, entry, Thomas J.
Clay Collection, Henry Clay Papers. We are
grateful to Eric Brooks, head curator at Ashland, the Henry Clay Estate, and to Dr. Lind-
sey Apple, the accomplished scholar of the
Clay family, for providing us with a photo-
copy of this document.

76. Morehead to Ruffin, June 24, 1852, Hamilton,
Papers of Ruffin, 2:327–28.

77. Coleman, *Final Days,* 5–6; Colton, *Private
Correspondence,* 635.

78. Colton, *Private Correspondence,* 635.

79. Memorandum of H. Clay, late June 1852,
HCP 10:968.

80. Coleman, *Final Days,* 6.

81. Colton, *Private Correspondence,* 635.

82. Coleman, *Final Days,* 6–7; Clay to Clay, June
29, 1852, Colton, *Private Correspondence,*
636.

83. Colton, *Private Correspondence,* 636.

Bibliography

PRIMARY SOURCES

Manuscript Collections

Alabama Department of Archives and History, Montgomery, Alabama
Governor William W. Bibb Papers
Tait Family Papers

Special Collections Research Center, University of Chicago Library
Letters of DeVall Payne to Hannah Payne, Miscellaneous Manuscripts Collection

Rauner Special Collections Library, Dartmouth College, Hanover, New Hampshire
Daniel Webster Papers

Duke University Rare Book, Manuscript, and Special Collections Library, Durham, North Carolina
Bedford Brown Papers
John Heritage Bryan Papers
Campbell Family Papers
Henry Clay Papers
William Crawford Papers
Andrew Jackson Letters, 1796–1843
Nathaniel Macon Papers
Willie Person Mangum Papers
Louis McLane Papers
Hugh Lawson White Papers
William and Elizabeth Washington Gamble Wirt
     Papers

East Tennessee Historical Society
Jackson Letters, McClung Collection

Filson Historical Society, Louisville, Kentucky
Charles Anderson Memoir
Beall-Booth Family Papers
Beatty-Quisenberry Family Papers
George Mortimer Bibb Papers
Blackburn Family Papers
James Gillespie Blaine Papers

M. W. Boyd Letter
Samuel Brown Papers
Brown-Ewell Family Papers
Buckner Family Papers
Bullitt Family Papers
John Caperton Letters
John Chambers Letters
Henry Clay Legal Documents
Clay-Russell Papers
Leslie Combs Letters
Converse & Co. Legal Document
John Jordan Crittenden Papers
Joseph Ficklin Papers
Green Family Papers
Grigsby Collection, Robert J. Breckinridge Corre-
     spondence
Harry Innes Papers
John Telemachus Johnson Papers
Josiah Stoddart Johnston Diary
Philip Kearny Letter
Amos Kendall Papers
Charles C. Lathrop Letter
Barnabas Lee Papers
Robert P. Letcher Miscellaneous Papers
Walter J. McMurtry Miscellaneous Papers
John Neagle Letter
Susannah Hart Price Papers
James Fowler Simmons Papers
Charles Stewart Todd Papers
Todd Family Papers
W.M.W. Letter

Hargrett Rare Book and Manuscript Library, University of Georgia, Athens, Georgia
John Forsyth Letters

Kentucky Department of Libraries and Archives
Fayette County Circuit Court Records

University of Kentucky Special Collections, Lexington, Kentucky
Henry Clay Family Papers
Leslie Combs Letters

John Jordan Crittenden Letters
Thomas Hart Papers
Robert P. Letcher Letters
Charles Slaughter Morehead Papers
Zachary Taylor Letters
Wickliffe-Preston Family Papers

Library of Congress, Manuscript Division, Washington, D.C.
Richard C. Anderson Diary
James A. Bayard and Richard H. Bayard Papers
Francis Preston Blair Papers
Henry Clay Family Papers
Thomas J. Clay Collection, Henry Clay Papers
John M. Clayton Papers
John Coffee Family Papers
John J. Crittenden Papers
Joseph Desha Papers
Papers of Thomas Ewing Family
Papers of George P. Fisher
Felix Grundy Papers
James O. Harrison Papers
Papers of Thomas H. Hubbard
Papers of Harry Innes
Andrew Jackson Papers
Thomas Sidney Jesup Papers
Louis McLane Papers
Hugh Nelson Papers
Papers of John Payne
William Plumer Papers
Public Record Office, Reference Foreign Office
 115, volume 32
Letter of Nathan Sargent
Letter of Joseph E. Sprague
Letter of Thomas B. Stevenson
Martin Van Buren Papers

Manuscripts Department, Maryland Historical Society Library, Baltimore, Maryland
Roger B. Taney Papers
William Wirt Letterbook

Massachusetts Historical Society, Boston, Massachusetts
Adams Family Papers

Historic New Orleans Collection, New Orleans, Louisiana
Carl Kohn Letterbook
John Slidell Letter

New York Public Library, New York, New York
Caesar Rodney and Caesar A. Rodney Papers

South Carolina Historical Society, Charleston, South Carolina
John Ball Papers
Henry William DeSaussure Papers

Southern Historical Collection, University of North Carolina, Chapel Hill, North Carolina
Branch Family Papers

Cameron Family Papers
William Gaston Papers
Felix Grundy Papers
Jackson and Prince Family Papers
Lenoir Family Papers
Francis G. Ruffin Papers
Thomas Ruffin Papers
Bartlett Yancey Papers

Transylvania University, Lexington, Kentucky
Cuthbert Banks Agreement
Henry Clay Letter, 1793

Tulane University, New Orleans, Louisiana
Gurley Family Papers
Trowbridge Family Correspondence

Albert and Shirley Small Special Collections Library, University of Virginia, Charlottesville, Virginia
Berkeley Family Papers
Letters of Jacob Burnet
Joseph C. Cabell Papers
Carr-Cary Family Papers
Papers of Henry Clay
Papers of John Hooe
Correspondence of Robert Thruston Hubard
Papers of Thomas P. Hughes
Letters to Benjamin Watkins Leigh
Papers of James McDowell
Papers of John Randolph of Roanoke
Letters of William Cabell Rives
Papers of Alexander H. H. Stuart and Related Stuart and Baldwin Families
Papers of Daniel Webster

Virginia Historical Society, Richmond, Virginia
Barbour Family Papers
Edward Bates Papers
Beverley Family Papers
William Bolling Diary
Brooke Family Papers
Marie Este Fisher Bruce Papers
Graham Family Papers
William Hammett Letters
Jesse Burton Harrison Papers
George Hoadley Letter
Benjamin Watkins Leigh Papers
McLeod Family Papers
Pegram-Johnson-McIntosh Family Papers
William C. Preston Papers
William Selden Papers
Zachary Taylor Letters
Letters from John Tyler
Wise Family Papers

Library of Virginia, Richmond, Virginia
Henry Clay Papers
Martin Duralde III Letterbook
James Lawson Kemper Papers

Tazewell Family Letters

William Wirt Letters

Manuscript Department, Swem Library, College of William and Mary, Williamsburg, Virginia

Austin-Twyman Papers

Barnes Family Papers

Barraud Family Papers

Brown, Coulter, Tucker Papers

Carter Family Papers

John B. Floyd Papers

George Frederick Holmes Papers

John Marshall Papers

James Monroe Papers

Richie-Harrison Papers

Tyler Family Scrapbook

Published Primary Sources

Adams, Charles Francis, editor. *Memoirs of John Quincy Adams, Comprising Portions of His Diary from 1785 to 1848.* 12 volumes. Philadelphia: J. B. Lippincott, 1874–1877.

Adams, John Quincy. *Writings of John Quincy Adams.* 7 volumes. Edited by Worthington Chauncey Ford. New York: Macmillan, 1913–1917.

Ambler, Charles Henry. *The Life and Diary of John Floyd, Governor of Virginia, an Apostle of Secession, and the Father of the Oregon Country.* Richmond, VA: Richmond Press, 1918.

American State Papers, Foreign Relations. 6 volumes. Washington, DC: Gales & Seaton, 1833–1858.

American State Papers, Military Affairs. 7 volumes. Washington, DC: Gales & Seaton, 1832–1861.

Annals of Congress. 42 volumes. Washington, DC: Gales & Seaton, 1834–1856.

Austin, Moses. "A Memorandum of M. Austin's Journey from the Lead Mines in the County of Wythe in the State of Virginia to the Lead Mines in the Province of Louisiana West of the Mississippi, 1796–1797." Edited by George P. Garrison. *American Historical Review* 5 (April 1900): 518–42.

Bancroft, George. "A Few Words About Henry Clay." *The Century Magazine* 30 (July 1885): 479–81.

Barnes, Thurlow Weed. *Memoirs of Thurlow Weed.* Boston: Houghton, Mifflin, 1884.

Barry, William T. "Letters of William T. Barry, 1806–1810, 1829–1831." *American Historical Review* 16 (January 1911): 327–36.

Basler, Roy P., editor. *Abraham Lincoln: His Speeches and Writings.* Cleveland: World Publishing Company, 1946.

Bassett, John Spencer, editor. *The Correspondence of Andrew Jackson.* 7 volumes. Washington, DC: Carnegie Institution of Washington, 1927–1928.

Bayard, James A. *Papers of James A. Bayard, 1796–1815.* Edited by Elizabeth Donnan. *Annual Report of the American Historical Association.* Washington, DC: Government Printing Office, 1915.

Belz, Herman, editor. *The Webster-Hayne Debate on the Nature of the Union: Selected Documents.* Indianapolis, IN: Liberty Fund, 2000.

Benton, Thomas Hart. *Thirty Years' View; or, A History of the Working of the American Government for Thirty Years, from 1820 to 1850.* 2 volumes. New York: D. Appleton, 1854–1856.

Brandon, Edgar Ewing, editor. *Lafayette, Guest of the Nation: A Contemporary Account of the Triumphal Tour of General Lafayette Through the United Sates in 1824 and 1825 as Reported by Local Newspapers.* 3 volumes. Oxford, OH: Oxford Historical Press, 1950–1957.

Brooke, Francis Taliaferro. *A Narrative of My Life; for My Family.* New York: New York Times, 1971.

Brown, Everett S., editor. *The Missouri Compromises and Presidential Politics, 1820–1825: From the Letters of William Plumer, Jr.* St. Louis: Missouri Historical Society, 1926.

———, editor. *William Plumer's Memorandum of Proceedings in the United States Senate, 1803–1807.* New York: Macmillan, 1923.

Buchanan, James. *The Works of James Buchanan.* Edited by John Bassett Moore. 12 volumes. Philadelphia: J. B. Lippincott, 1908–1911.

Burr, Aaron. *Political Correspondence and Public Papers of Aaron Burr.* Edited by Mary-Jo Kine. 2 volumes. Princeton, NJ: Princeton University Press, 1983.

Byrdsall, Fitzwilliam. *The History of the Locofoco, or Equal Rights Party: Its Movements, Conventions and Proceedings.* New York: Clement & Packard, 1842.

Calhoun, John C. "Correspondence of John C. Calhoun, George McDuffie, and Charles Fisher, Relating to the Presidential Campaign of 1824." Edited by Albert Ray Newsome. *North Carolina Historical Review* 7 (October 1930): 477–504.

———. *The Papers of John C. Calhoun.* Edited by Robert L. Meriwether, W. Edwin Hemphill, Clyde N. Wilson, et al. 28 volumes. Columbia: University of South Carolina, 1959–2003.

Clark, Allen C. *Life and Letters of Dolly Madison.* Washington, DC: W. F. Roberts, 1914.

Clay, Cassius Marcellus, and Horace Greeley. *The Writings of Cassius Marcellus Clay: Including Speeches and Addresses.* New York: Harper, 1848.

Clay, Henry. *The Papers of Henry Clay.* Edited by James F. Hopkins, Mary W. M. Hargreaves, et al. 11 volumes. Lexington: University Press of Kentucky, 1959–1992.

Coleman, Anne Mary Butler Crittenden, editor. *The Life of John J. Crittenden with Selections from His Correspondence and Speeches.* 2 volumes. Philadelphia: J. B. Lippincott, 1871.

Colton, Calvin. *The Life and Times of Henry Clay.* 2 volumes. New York: A. S. Barnes, 1846.

————, editor. *The Private Correspondence of Henry Clay.* New York: A. S. Barnes, 1956.

Congressional Globe. 46 volumes. Washington, DC: Blair & Rives, 1834–1873.

Cuming, Fortescue. *Sketches of a Tour to the Western Country Through the States of Ohio and Kentucky.* Edited by Reuben Gold Thwaites. Cleveland: Arthur H. Clark, 1904.

Cutts, Lucia Beverly, editor. *Memoirs and Letters of Dolly Madison, Wife of James Madison, President of the United States.* Boston: Houghton Mifflin, 1886.

Douglas, Stephen A. *The Letters of Stephen A. Douglas.* Edited by Robert W. Johannsen. Urbana: University of Illinois Press, 1961.

Eaton, Clement, editor. "Minutes and Resolutions of an Emancipation Meeting in Kentucky in 1849." *Journal of Southern History* 14 (November 1948): 541–43.

Edwards, Ninian Wirt. *History of Illinois, from 1778 to 1833: and Life and Times of Ninian Edwards.* Springfield: Illinois State Journal, 1870.

Erwin, John Seymour. *Like Some Green Laurel: Letters of Margaret Johnson Erwin, 1821–1863.* Baton Rouge: Louisiana State University Press, 1981.

Espy, Josiah. *Memorandums of a Tour Made by Josiah Espy in the States of Ohio and Kentucky and Indian Territory in 1805.* Cincinnati: Robert Clarke, 1870.

Ewing, Thomas. "Diary of Thomas Ewing." *American Historical Review* 18 (October 1912): 97–112.

Flint, Timothy. *Recollections of the Last Ten Years, Passed in Occasional Residences and Journeyings in the Valley of the Mississippi.* New York: Johnson Reprint, 1968.

Foote, Henry S. *Casket of Reminiscences.* Washington, DC: Chronicle Publishing, 1874.

Foster, Augustus John. *Jeffersonian America: Notes on the United States of America Collected in the Years 1805–6–7 and 11–12 by Sir Augustus John Foster, Bart.* Edited by Richard Beale Davis. San Marino, CA: Huntington Library, 1954.

French, Benjamin Brown. *Witness to the Young Republic: A Yankee's Journal, 1828–1870.* Edited by Donald B. Cole and John J. McDonough. Hanover, NH: University Press of New England, 1989.

Gallatin, Albert. *The Writings of Albert Gallatin.* Edited by Henry Adams. 3 volumes. Philadelphia: J. B. Lippincott, 1879.

Gallatin, James. *The Diary of James Gallatin, Secretary to Albert Gallatin, a Great Peace Maker, 1813–1827.* Edited by Count Gallatin. New York: Charles Scribner's Sons, 1916.

Gerry, Elbridge, Jr. *The Diary of Elbridge Gerry, Jr.* New York: Brentano's, 1927.

Gibbon, Edward. *Memoirs of the Life and Writings of Edward Gibbon.* Oliver Farrar Emerson, editor. Boston: Ginn & Company, 1898.

Greeley, Horace, and Robert Dale Owen. *The Auto-biography of Horace Greeley, or Recollections of a Busy Life.* New York: E. B. Treat, 1872.

Gross, Samuel D. *Autobiography of Samuel D. Gross, M.D.* 2 volumes. Philadelphia: G. Barrie, 1887.

Hamilton, J. G. deR., editor. *The Papers of Thomas Ruffin.* 4 volumes. Raleigh, NC: Edwards & Broughton, 1918–1920.

Hamilton, Stanislaus Murray, editor. *The Writings of James Monroe.* 7 volumes. New York: G. P. Putnam's Sons, 1898–1903.

Herndon, William H., and Jesse W. Weik. *Herndon's Lincoln: The True Story of a Great Life.* Springfield, IN: Herndon's Lincoln Publishing, 1888.

Hone, Philip. *The Diary of Philip Hone, 1828–1851.* Edited by Bayard Tuckerman. 2 volumes. New York: Dodd, Mead, 1889.

Irving, Pierre M. *The Life and Letters of Washington Irving.* 3 volumes. New York: G. P. Putnam's Sons, 1883.

Jackson, Andrew. *Papers of Andrew Jackson.* Edited by Harold D. Moser et al. 7 volumes. Knoxville: University of Tennessee Press, 1980–2007.

Jewett, James C. "The United States Congress of 1817 and Some of Its Celebrities." *William and Mary College Quarterly Historical Magazine* 17 (October 1908): 139–44.

Kendall, Amos. *Autobiography of Amos Kendall.* Edited by William Stickney. New York: Peter Smith, 1949.

Kennedy, John P. *Memoir of the Life of William Wirt.* 2 volumes. Philadelphia: Lee and Blanchard, 1850.

King, Charles R., editor. *Life and Correspondence of Rufus King.* 6 volumes. New York: G. P. Putnam's Sons, 1894–1900.

La Rochefoucauld–Liancourt, François-Alexandre-Frédéric. *Travels Through the United States of North America: The Country of the Iroquois, and Upper Canada, in the Years 1795, 1796, and 1797.* 4 volumes. London: R. Phillips, 1800.

Lieber, Francis. *Political Hermeneutics, or On Political Interpretation and Construction; and Also on Precedents.* Boston: Little, Brown, 1837.

Linn, Elizabeth A., and Nathan Sargent. *The Life and Public Services of Dr. Lewis F. Linn, for Ten Years a Senator of the United States from the State of Missouri.* New York: D. Appleton, 1857.

Madison, James. *The Papers of James Madison: Presidential Series.* Edited by Robert Allen Rutland et al. 6 volumes. Charlottesville: University of Virginia Press, 1984–2008.

————. *The Writings of James Madison.* Edited by Gaillard Hunt. 9 volumes. New York: G. P. Putnam's Sons, 1900–1910.

Mangum, Willie Person. *The Papers of Willie Person Mangum.* Edited by Thomas Henry Shanks. 5 volumes. Raleigh: North Carolina State Department of Archives and History, 1950.

Marshall, Humphrey. *History of Kentucky, Exhibiting an Account of the Modern Discovery; Settlement; Progressive Improvement; Civil and Military Transactions; and the Present State of the Country.* Frankfort, KY: G. S. Robinson, 1824.

McDowell, Madeline. "Recollections of Henry Clay." *Century Magazine* 50 (September 1895): 766–70.

Mearns, David C. *The Lincoln Papers: The Story of the Collection, with Selections to July 4, 1861.* 2 volumes. Garden City, NY: Doubleday, 1948.

Melish, John. *Travels Through the United States of America in the Years 1806 & 1807.* New York: Johnson Reprint, 1970.

Michaux, François. *Travels to the West of the Allegheny Mountains in the States of Ohio, Kentucky, and Tennessee, in the Year 1802.* London: R. Phillips, 1805.

"Mr. Wise's Speech in 1843." *William and Mary Quarterly* 18 (April 1919): 222–31.

Newsome, Albert Ray, editor. "Letters of Romulus M. Saunders to Bartlett Yancey; 1821–1828." *North Carolina Historical Review* 8 (1931): 427–62.

Obituary Addresses on the Occasion of the Death of the Hon. Henry Clay, a Senator of the United States from the State of Kentucky, Delivered in the Senate and in the House of Representatives of the United States, June 30, 1852, and the Funeral Sermon of the Rev. C. M. Butler, Chaplain of the Senate, Preached in the Senate, July 1, 1852. Printed by Order of the Senate and House of Representatives. Washington, DC: Robert Armstrong, 1852.

Paullin, Charles Oscar, and Frederic Logan Paxson. *Guide to Materials in the London Archives for the History of the United States Since 1783.* Washington, DC: Carnegie Institution, 1914.

Peterson, Merrill D., editor. *Jefferson: Writings.* New York: Viking, 1984.

Philo-Jackson (pseudonym). *The Presidential Election, Written for the Benefit of the People of the United States but Particularly for Those of the State of Kentucky; Relating, Also, to the Constitution of the United States, and to Internal Improvements.* Sixth series. Frankfort, KY: by author, 1824.

"Political Portraits, No. XII, Silas Wright, Jr." *United States Magazine and Democratic Review* 5 (1839): 409–18.

Polk, James K. *Polk: The Diary of a President, 1845–1849.* Edited by Allan Nevins. New York: Longmans, Green, 1952.

Pollock, Frederick, editor. *Macready's Reminiscences and Selections from His Diaries and Letters.* 2 volumes. London: Macmillan, 1875.

Poore, Benjamin Perley. *Perley's Reminiscences of Sixty Years.* 2 volumes. New York: W. A. Houghton, 1886.

Prentice, George D. *Biography of Henry Clay.* New York: John Jay Phelps, 1831.

Prentiss, George Lewis. *Memoir of S. S. Prentice.* 2 volumes. New York: Scribner's Sons, 1855.

Proceedings of the Democratic Whig National Convention: Which Assembled at Harrisburg, Pennsylvania, on the Fourth of December, 1839, for the Purpose of Nominating Candidates for President and Vice President of the United States. Harrisburg, PA: R. S. Elliott, 1839.

Quincy, Edmund. *Life of Josiah Quincy of Massachusetts.* Boston: Fields, Osgood, 1869.

Ravenel, Harriott Horry. *The Life and Times of William Lowndes, 1782–1822.* Boston: Houghton Mifflin, 1901.

Register of Debates in Congress. 14 volumes. Washington, DC: Gales & Seaton, 1825–1837.

Richardson, James D., editor. *Compilation of the Messages and Papers of the Presidents.* 10 volumes. Washington, DC: Government Printing Office, 1896–1899.

Ritchie, Thomas. *Thomas Ritchie's Letter, Containing Reminiscences of Henry Clay and the Compromise.* Richmond: n.p., 1852.

Ross, John. *The Papers of Chief John Ross.* Edited by Gary E. Moulton. 2 volumes. Norman: University of Oklahoma Press, 1985.

Safford, William Harrison, editor. *The Blennerhassett Papers: Embodying the Private Journal of Harman Blennerhassett and the Hitherto Unpublished Correspondence.* Cincinnati: Moore, Wilstach & Baldwin, 1864.

Sargent, Epes. *The Life and Services of Henry Clay Brought Down to the Year 1844.* New York: Greeley & McElrath, 1844.

Sargent, Nathan. *Public Men and Events from the Commencement of Mr. Monroe's Administration, in 1817, to the Close of Mr. Fillmore's Administration, in 1853.* 2 volumes. Philadelphia: J. B. Lippincott, 1875.

Scarborough, William Kauffman, editor. *The Diary of Edmund Ruffin: Toward Independence, October 1856–April 1861.* Baton Rouge: Louisiana State University Press, 1972.

Smith, Margaret Bayard. *The First Forty Years of Washington Society.* Edited by Gaillard Hunt. Washington, DC: Government Printing Office, 1906; reprint edition, New York: Frederick Ungar, 1965.

Smith, Oliver Hampton. *Early Indiana Trials: And Sketches.* Cincinnati: Moore, Wilstrach, Keys, 1858.

Sparks, William Henry. *The Memories of Fifty Years: Containing Brief Biographical Notices of Distinguished Americans, and Anecdotes of Remarkable Men.* 3rd edition. Philadelphia: Claxton, Remsen & Haffelfinger, 1872.

Stanton, Henry B. *Random Recollections.* New York: Harper & Brothers, 1887.

Stebbins, Giles Badger. *Facts and Opinions Touching the Real Origin, Character, and Influence of the American Colonization Society: Views of Wilberforce, Clarkson & Others, and Opinions of the Free People of Color of the United States.* Boston: J. P. Jewett, 1853.

Story, William W. *Life and Letters of Joseph Story.* 2 volumes. Boston: Little, Brown, 1851.

Strong, George Templeton. *Diary.* 4 volumes. New York: Macmillan, 1952.

Tarleton, Banastre. *A History of the Campaigns of 1780 and 1781 in the Southern Provinces of North America.* New York: Arno Press, 1968.

Thorpe, Thomas Bangs. *The Taylor Anecdote Book: Anecdotes and Letters of Zachary Taylor.* New York: D. Appleton, 1848.

Ticknor, George. *Life, Letters, and Journals of George Ticknor.* 2 volumes. Boston: Houghton Mifflin, 1909.

Tyler, Lyon G. *The Letters and the Times of the Tylers.* 3 volumes. Richmond, VA: Whittet & Shepperson, 1884.

United States Congress, House. *Journal of the House of Representatives of the United States.* Washington, DC: Government Printing Office, 1789–.

Van Buren, Martin. *The Autobiography of Martin Van Buren.* Edited by John C. Fitzpatrick. *Annual Report of the American Historical Association.* Washington, DC: Government Printing Office, 1920.

Vane, Charles W., editor. *Correspondence, Despatches and Other Papers of Viscount Castlereagh, Second Marquess of Londonderry.* 12 volumes. London: H. Colburn, 1848–1854.

"Webster, Clay, Calhoun, and Jackson: How They Sat for the Daguerreotypes." *Harper's New Monthly Magazine* 38 (May 1869): 788.

Webster, Daniel. *The Papers of Daniel Webster.* Edited by Charles M. Wiltse, Harold D. Moser, et al. Series 1, 7 volumes. Hanover, NH: University Press of New England, 1974–1988.

———. *The Private Correspondence of Daniel Webster.* Edited by Fletcher Webster. 2 volumes. Boston: Little, Brown, 1857.

Weed, Thurlow. *Life of Thurlow Weed Including His Autobiography and a Memoir.* 2 volumes. Boston: Houghton Mifflin, 1883–1884.

Weld, Isaac, Jr. *Travels Through the States of North America, and the Provinces of Upper and Lower Canada, During the Years 1795, 1796, and 1797.* 4th edition. 2 volumes. London: John Stockdale, 1807.

Wellesley, Arthur. *Supplementary Despatches, Correspondence and Memoranda of Field Marshal Arthur Duke of Wellington, K. G.* 15 volumes. London: John Murray, 1858–1872.

"Will of John Clay" in "Biographical and Genealogical Notes and Queries." *William and Mary College Quarterly Historical Magazine* 14 (April 1934): 174–79.

Winthrop, Robert Charles. *Memoir of Henry Clay.* Cambridge, MA: John Wilson, 1880.

Wise, Henry A. *Seven Decades of the Union: The Humanities and Materialism, Illustrated by a Memoir of John Tyler with Reminiscences of Some of His Great Contemporaries.* Philadelphia: J. B. Lippincott, 1872.

Newspapers and Periodicals

The American Whig Review
Argus of Western America
Augusta Chronicle
Baltimore *Republican*
Bangor *Daily Whig & Courier*
Boston *Courier*
Boston *Daily Atlas*
Boston *Emancipator and Republican*
Cahawba Press and Alabama State Intelligencer
Carolina Observer
Cleveland *Daily Herald*
Cleveland *Plain Dealer*
Columbian Star
Concord *New-Hampshire Statesman and State Journal*
Daily National Journal
Daily Sanduskian
Edgefield *Advertiser*
The Emancipator
Emancipator and Weekly Chronicle
Fayetteville *Observer*
Frankfort *Commonwealth*
Gettysburg *Star and Banner*
Hamilton, Ohio, *Telegraph*
Jonesborough *Whig*
Kendall's Expositor
Lexington *Gazette*
Lexington *Intelligencer*
Lexington *Kentucky Reporter*
Lexington *Observer & Kentucky Reporter*
The Liberator
London *Times*
Louisiana Gazette
Louisville *Daily Journal*
Louisville Public Advertiser
Maryland Gazette
Massachusetts Spy and Worcester Advertiser
The Microscope
Milwaukee Daily Sentinel
Milwaukee Journal
Milwaukee Sentinel
Mississippi State Gazette
The Mississippian
Montpelier *Vermont Patriot and State Gazette*
Nashville *Whig*
Natchez *Daily Courier*
National Advocate
National Intelligencer
New England Weekly Review
New-Hampshire Statesman and Concord Register
New Orleans *Daily Picayune*
New York Daily Advertiser
New York *Express*
New York *Herald*
New York *Morning Herald*
New York *Spectator*
New York Times
New York *Weekly Herald*
Niles' Weekly Register
Norwalk *Huron Reflector*

Ohio Statesman
Orleans Gazette and Commercial Advertiser
Pennsylvania Inquirer and National Gazette
Pensacola Gazette
Philadelphia Aurora and Franklin Gazette
Philadelphia Bulletin
Philadelphia Columbian Observer
Philadelphia North American and Daily Advertiser
Philadelphia Whig Banner Melodist
Pittsburgh Gazette
Pittsburgh Post-Gazette
Providence Gazette
Providence Patriot, Columbian Phenix
Raleigh Register and North Carolina Gazette
Raymond, Mississippi, Gazette
Richmond Enquirer
Richmond Whig
Scioto (Chillicothe, Ohio) Gazette
Southern Patriot and Commercial Advertiser
St. Louis Enquirer
Tallahassee Floridian
The True American
United States Telegraph
Virginia Free Press
Washington Globe
Washington, Kentucky, Dove
Washington Republican and Congressional Examiner
Washington Union
Weekly Ohio Statesman
Weekly Raleigh Register
Winyaw Intelligencer

SECONDARY SOURCES

Books

Abernethy, Thomas Perkins. *The Burr Conspiracy.* New York: Oxford University Press, 1954.
———. *Three Virginia Frontiers.* Baton Rouge: Louisiana State University Press, 1940; reprint edition, Gloucester, MA: Peter Smith, 1962.
Adams, Henry. *John Randolph.* Boston: Houghton Mifflin, 1882.
———. *The Life of Albert Gallatin.* Philadelphia: J. B. Lippincott, 1879; reprint edition, New York: Peter Smith, 1943.
Alford, Terry. *Prince Among Slaves: The True Story of an African Prince Sold into Slavery in the American South.* New York: Oxford University Press, 1986.
Allgor, Catherine. *Parlor Politics: In Which the Ladies of Washington Help Build a City and a Government.* Charlottesville: University Press of Virginia, 2000.
Ambler, Charles Henry. *Thomas Ritchie: A Study in Virginia Politics.* Richmond, VA: Bell Book & Stationery Company, 1913.
Ammon, Harry. *James Monroe: The Quest for National Identity.* New York: McGraw-Hill, 1971; reprint edition, Charlottesville: University Press of Virginia, 1990.

Aron, Stephen. *How the West Was Lost: The Transformation of Kentucky from Daniel Boone to Henry Clay.* Baltimore: Johns Hopkins University Press, 1996.
Baker, Jean H. *James Buchanan.* New York: Macmillan, 2004.
Barlett, Irving H. *John C. Calhoun: A Biography.* New York: W. W. Norton, 1993.
Bauer, K. Jack. *Zachary Taylor: Soldier, Planter, Statesman of the Old Southwest.* Baton Rouge: Louisiana State University Press, 1985.
Baxter, Maurice G. *Henry Clay and the American System.* Lexington: University Press of Kentucky, 1995.
———. *Henry Clay the Lawyer.* Lexington: University Press of Kentucky, 2000.
Beach, Moses Yale, editor. *The Wealth and Biography of the Wealthy Citizens of the City of New York.* New York: New York *Sun,* 1846.
Belko, W. Stephen. *The Invincible Duff Green: Whig of the West.* Columbia: University of Missouri Press, 2006.
Belohlavek, John M. *George Mifflin Dallas: Jacksonian Patrician.* University Park: Pennsylvania State University Press, 1977.
———. *"Let the Eagle Soar!": The Foreign Policy of Andrew Jackson.* Lincoln: University of Nebraska Press, 1983.
Bemis, Samuel Flagg. *The American Secretaries of State and Their Diplomacy.* 10 volumes. New York: Pageant Book Company, 1958.
———. *John Quincy Adams and the Foundations of American Foreign Policy.* New York: Alfred A. Knopf, 1949.
———. *John Quincy Adams and the Union.* New York: Alfred A. Knopf, 1956.
Benson, Lee. *The Concept of Jacksonian Democracy: New York as a Test Case.* Princeton, NJ: Princeton University Press, 1961.
Bernstein, Peter L. *Wedding of the Waters: The Erie Canal and the Making of a Great Nation.* New York: W. W. Norton, 2005.
Beveridge, Albert J. *The Life of John Marshall.* 4 volumes. Boston: Houghton Mifflin, 1916.
Birkner, Michael. *Samuel Southard: Jeffersonian Whig.* Rutherford, NJ: Fairleigh Dickinson University Press, 1984.
Blackburn, Joyce. *George Wythe of Williamsburg.* New York: Harper & Row, 1975.
Boller, Paul F., Jr. *Presidential Campaigns, from George Washington to George W. Bush.* New York: Oxford University Press, 2004.
Borneman, Walter R. *1812: The War That Forged a Nation.* New York: HarperCollins, 2004.
Brant, Irving. *James Madison.* 6 volumes. Indianapolis, IN: Bobbs-Merrill, 1941–1961.
Bridges, Amy. *A City in the Republic: Antebellum New York and the Origin of Machine Politics.* New York: Cambridge University Press, 1984.
Brooks, Eric. *Ashland, the Henry Clay Estate.* Charleston, SC: Arcadia Publishing, 2007.
Bruce, Dickson D., Jr. *The Kentucky Tragedy: A*

Story of Conflict and Change in Antebellum America. Baton Rouge: Louisiana State University Press, 2006.

Bruce, William C. John Randolph of Roanoke, 1773–1833. 2 volumes. New York: G. P. Putnam's Sons, 1922.

Brugger, Robert J. Beverley Tucker: Heart over Head in the Old South. Baltimore: Johns Hopkins University Press, 1978.

Buckley, Thomas E. Church and State in Revolutionary Virginia, 1776–1787. Charlottesville: University Press of Virginia, 1977.

Buel, Richard J. America on the Brink: How the Political Struggles over the War of 1812 Almost Destroyed the Young Republic. New York: Palgrave Macmillan, 2005.

Buley, R. Carlyle. The Old Northwest: Pioneer Period, 1815–1840. 2 volumes. Indianapolis: Indiana Historical Society, 1950.

Burin, Eric. Slavery and the Peculiar Solution: A History of the American Colonization Society. Gainesville: University Press of Florida, 2005.

Butler, Mann. History of the Commonwealth of Kentucky. Louisville, KY: Wilcox, Dickerman, 1834.

Carrier, A. H. Monument to the Memory of Henry Clay. Philadelphia: D. Rulison, 1859.

Castellanos, Henry C. New Orleans As It Was: Episodes of Louisiana Life. Baton Rouge: Louisiana State University Press, 2006.

Catterall, Ralph C. H. The Second Bank of the United States. Chicago: University of Chicago Press, 1902 (reprint edition).

Chambers, William N. Old Bullion Benton, Senator from the New West: Thomas Hart Benton, 1782–1858. Boston: Little, Brown, 1956.

Channing, Steven A. Kentucky: A Bicentennial History. New York: W. W. Norton, 1977.

Chitwood, Oliver Perry. John Tyler: Champion of the Old South. New York: Russell & Russell, 1934.

Clark, Thomas D. A History of Kentucky. Lexington, KY: John Bradford Press, 1950.

Clay, Thomas Hart, and Ellis Paxson Oberholtzer. Henry Clay. Philadelphia: George W. Jacobs, 1910.

Cole, Donald B. A Jackson Man: Amos Kendall and the Rise of American Democracy. Baton Rouge: Louisiana State University Press, 2004.

———. Martin Van Buren and the American Political System. Princeton, NJ: Princeton University Press, 1984.

———. The Presidency of Andrew Jackson. Lawrence: University Press of Kansas, 1993.

Coleman, J. Winston, Jr. Last Days, Death and Funeral of Henry Clay. Lexington, KY: Winburn Press, 1951.

Cooper, William J., Jr. The South and the Politics of Slavery, 1828–1856. Baton Rouge: Louisiana State University Press, 1978.

Cornog, Evan. The Birth of Empire: DeWitt Clinton and the American Experience, 1769–1828. New York: Oxford University Press, 1998.

Cotterill, Robert S. History of Pioneer Kentucky. Cincinnati: Johnson & Hardin, 1917.

Crapol, Edward P. John Tyler: The Accidental President. Chapel Hill: University of North Carolina Press, 2006.

Cresson, William P. James Monroe. Chapel Hill: University of North Carolina Press, 1946.

Cunningham, Noble E., Jr. The Presidency of James Monroe. Lawrence: University Press of Kansas, 1996.

Curtis, George Ticknor. Life of Daniel Webster. 2 volumes. New York: D. Appleton, 1870.

Dangerfield, George. The Era of Good Feelings. New York: Harcourt, Brace, 1952.

Davenport, F. Garvin. Ante-Bellum Kentucky: A Social History, 1800–1860. Oxford, OH: Mississippi Valley Press, 1943.

Doyle, Mary Ellen. Pioneer Spirit: Catherine Spalding, Sister of Charity of Nazareth. Lexington: University Press of Kentucky, 2006.

Duckett, Alvin Laroy. John Forsyth: Political Tactician. Athens: University of Georgia Press, 1962.

Earle, Jonathan H. Jacksonian Antislavery and the Politics of Free Soil, 1824–1854. Chapel Hill: University of North Carolina Press, 2004.

Eaton, Clement. Henry Clay and the Art of American Politics. Boston: Little, Brown, 1957.

Ellis, Richard E. Aggressive Nationalism: McCulloch v. Maryland and the Foundation of Federal Authority in the Young Republic. New York: Oxford University Press, 2007.

———. The Union at Risk: Jacksonian Democracy, States' Rights, and the Nullification Crisis. New York: Oxford University Press, 1987.

Engleman, Fred L. The Peace of Christmas Eve. New York: Harcourt, Brace, 1960.

Ernst, Robert. Rufus King: American Federalist. Chapel Hill: University of North Carolina Press, 1968.

Feller, Daniel. The Jacksonian Promise: America, 1815–1840. Baltimore: Johns Hopkins University Press, 1995.

———. The Public Lands in Jacksonian Politics. Madison: University of Wisconsin Press, 1984.

Ferling, John E. Adams vs. Jefferson: The Tumultuous Election of 1800. New York: Oxford University Press, 2004.

Forbes, Robert Pierce. The Missouri Compromise and Its Aftermath: Slavery and the Meaning of America. Chapel Hill: University of North Carolina Press, 2007.

Formisano, Ronald P. The Transformation of Political Culture: Massachusetts Parties, 1790s–1840s. New York: Oxford University Press, 1983.

Freehling, William W. Prelude to Civil War: The Nullification Controversy in South Carolina, 1816–1836. New York: Harper & Row, 1965.

Freeman, Joanne B. Affairs of Honor: National Pol-

itics in the New Republic. New Haven, CT: Yale University Press, 2001.

Friend, Craig Thompson. *Along the Maysville Road: The Early American Republic in the Trans-Appalachian West.* Knoxville: University of Tennessee Press, 2005.

Fuller, Hubert Bruce. *The Purchase of Florida, Its History and Diplomacy.* Cleveland: Burrows Brothers, 1906.

Gewehr, Wesley M. *The Great Awakening in Virginia, 1740–1790.* Gloucester, MA: Peter Smith, 1965.

Goebel, Dorothy. *William Henry Harrison: A Political Biography.* Philadelphia: Porcupine Press, 1974.

Goodwin, Doris Kearns. *Team of Rivals: The Political Genius of Abraham Lincoln.* New York: Simon & Schuster, 2005.

Green, Philip Jackson. *The Life of William Harris Crawford.* Charlotte: University of North Carolina at Charlotte, 1965.

Greenberg, Kenneth S. *Honor and Slavery: Lies, Duels, Noses, Masks, Dressing as a Woman, Gifts, Strangers, Humanitarianism, Death, Slave Rebellions, the Proslavery Argument, Baseball, Hunting, and Gambling in the Old South.* Princeton, NJ: Princeton University Press, 1996.

Grigsby, Hugh Blair. *Discourse on the Life and Character of the Hon. Littleton Waller Tazewell.* Norfolk, VA: J. D. Ghiselin, 1860.

Gunderson, Robert Gray. *The Log-Cabin Campaign.* Lexington: University of Kentucky Press, 1957.

Hamilton, Holman. *Prologue to Conflict: The Crisis and Compromise of 1850.* Lexington: University Press of Kentucky, 1964.

Hamm, Thomas D. *God's Government Begun: The Society for Universal Inquiry and Reform, 1842–1846.* Bloomington: Indiana University Press, 1995.

Handlin, Oscar, and Mary Flug Handlin. *Facing Life: Youth and the Family in American History.* Boston: Little, Brown, 1971.

Hargreaves, Mary W. M. *The Presidency of John Quincy Adams.* Lawrence: University Press of Kansas, 1985.

Harlow, Ralph Volney. *The History of Legislative Methods in the Period Before 1825.* New Haven, CT: Yale University Press, 1917.

Harrison, Lowell H. *The Antislavery Movement in Kentucky.* Lexington: University Press of Kentucky, 1978.

———. *John Breckinridge: Jeffersonian Republican.* Louisville, KY: Filson Club, 1969.

Hatcher, William B. *Edward Livingston: Jeffersonian Republican and Jacksonian Democrat.* Baton Rouge: Louisiana State University Press, 1940.

Hecht, Marie B. *John Quincy Adams: A Personal History of an Independent Man.* New York: Macmillan, 1972.

Heidler, David S. *Pulling the Temple Down: The Fire-Eaters and the Destruction of the Union.* Mechanicsburg, PA: Stackpole Books, 1994.

Heidler, David S., and Jeanne T. Heidler. *Daily Life in the Early American Republic: Creating a New Nation.* Westport, CT: Greenwood Press, 2004.

———. *Old Hickory's War: Andrew Jackson and the Quest for Empire.* Reprint edition, Baton Rouge: Louisiana State University Press, 2003.

Hickey, Donald R. *The War of 1812: A Forgotten Conflict.* Urbana: University of Illinois Press, 1990.

Holt, Michael F. *The Rise and Fall of the American Whig Party: Jacksonian Politics and the Onset of the Civil War.* New York: Oxford University Press, 1999.

Holton, Woody. *Forced Founders: Indians, Debtors, Slaves, and the Making of the American Revolution in Virginia.* Chapel Hill: University of North Carolina Press, 1999.

Horsman, Reginald. *The Causes of the War of 1812.* Philadelphia: University of Pennsylvania Press, 1962.

Howe, Daniel Walker. *The Political Culture of the American Whigs.* Chicago: University of Chicago Press, 1979.

———. *What Hath God Wrought: The Transformation of America, 1815–1848.* New York: Oxford University Press, 2007.

Idzerda, Stanley J., Anne C. Loveland, and Marc H. Miller. *Lafayette, Hero of Two Worlds: The Art and Pageantry of His Farewell Tour of America, 1824–1825.* Hanover, NH: University Press of New England, 1989.

Isaac, Rhys. *The Transformation of Virginia, 1740–1790.* Chapel Hill: University of North Carolina Press, 1982.

Isenberg, Nancy. *Fallen Founder: The Life of Aaron Burr.* New York: Viking, 2007.

Jabour, Anya. *Marriage in the Early Republic: Elizabeth and William Wirt and the Companionate Ideal.* Baltimore: Johns Hopkins University Press, 1998.

Jervey, Theodore D. *Robert Y. Hayne and His Times.* New York: Macmillan, 1909.

Johnson, John J. *A Hemisphere Apart: The Foundations of United States Policy Toward Latin America.* Baltimore: Johns Hopkins University Press, 1990.

Kehl, James A. *Ill Feeling in the Era of Good Feeling: Western Pennsylvania Political Battles, 1815–1825.* Pittsburgh: University of Pittsburgh Press, 1956.

Kirk, Russell. *John Randolph of Roanoke: A Study in American Politics, with Selected Speeches and Letters.* Indianapolis: Liberty Press, 1978.

Kirwan, Albert D. *John J. Crittenden: The Struggle for the Union.* Lexington: University Press of Kentucky, 1962.

Kleber, John E. *The Encyclopedia of Louisville.* Lexington: University Press of Kentucky, 2001.

———. *The Kentucky Encyclopedia.* Lexington: University Press of Kentucky, 1992.

Klotter, James C. *The Breckinridges of Kentucky, 1760–1981.* Lexington: University Press of Kentucky, 1986.

Knupfer, Peter B. *The Union as It Is: Constitutional Unionism and Sectional Compromise.* Chapel Hill: University of North Carolina Press, 1991.

Kohl, Lawrence Frederick. *The Politics of Individualism: Parties and the American Character in the Jacksonian Era.* New York: Oxford University Press, 1989.

Langley, Lester D. *Struggle for the American Mediterranean: United States–European Rivalry in the Gulf-Caribbean, 1776–1904.* Athens: University of Georgia Press, 1976.

Larson, Edward J. *A Magnificent Catastrophe: The Tumultuous Election of 1800, America's First Presidential Campaign.* New York: Free Press, 2007.

Larson, John Lauritz. *Internal Improvement: National Public Works and the Promise of Popular Government in the Early United States.* Chapel Hill: University of North Carolina Press, 2001.

Latner, Richard B. *The Presidency of Andrew Jackson.* Athens: University of Georgia Press, 1979.

LePore, Jill. *A is for American: Letters and Other Characters in the Newly United States.* New York: Alfred A. Knopf, 2002.

Lewis, James E., Jr. *The American Union and the Problem of Neighborhood: The United States and the Collapse of the Spanish Empire, 1783–1829.* Chapel Hill: University of North Carolina Press, 1993.

Little, Lucius P. *Ben Hardin: His Times and Contemporaries, with Selections from His Speeches.* Louisville: *Courier-Journal,* 1887.

Lomask, Milton. *Aaron Burr: The Conspiracy and Years of Exile, 1805–1836.* New York: Farrar, Straus and Giroux, 1982.

Lowery, Charles D. *James Barbour, A Jeffersonian Republican.* University: University of Alabama Press, 1984.

Lynch, William O. *Fifty Years of Party Warfare.* Indianapolis, IN: Bobbs-Merrill, 1931.

Malone, Dumas. *Jefferson and His Time.* 6 volumes. Boston: Little, Brown, 1948–1981.

Marcus, Jacob Rader. *United States Jewry, 1776–1985.* Detroit: Wayne State University Press, 1989.

Marszalek, John F. *The Petticoat Affair: Manners, Mutiny, and Sex in Andrew Jackson's White House.* New York: Free Press, 1997.

Mason, Matthew. *Slavery and Politics in the Early American Republic.* Chapel Hill: University of North Carolina Press, 2006.

Masur, Louis P. *1831, Year of Eclipse.* New York: Hill and Wang, 2001.

May, Ernest R. *The Making of the Monroe Doctrine.* Cambridge, MA: Belknap Press of Harvard University Press, 1975.

Mayo, Bernard. *Henry Clay: Spokesman of the New West.* Boston: Houghton Mifflin, 1937.

McCormick, Richard L. *The Party Period and Public Policy: American Politics from the Age of Jackson to the Progressive Era.* New York: Oxford University Press, 1986.

McCormick, Richard P. *The Presidential Game: The Origins of American Presidential Politics.* New York: Oxford University Press, 1982.

———. *The Second American Party System: Party Formation in the Jacksonian Era.* Chapel Hill: University of North Carolina Press, 1966.

McCoy, Drew R. *The Last of the Fathers: James Madison and the Republican Legacy.* Cambridge: Cambridge University Press, 1989.

McElroy, Robert McNutt. *Kentucky in the Nation's History.* New York: Moffat, Yard, 1909.

McGuire, James K., editor. *The Democratic Party of the State of New York.* 2 volumes. New York: United States History Company, 1905.

Meacham, Jon. *American Lion: Andrew Jackson in the White House.* New York: Random House, 2008.

Meyer, L. W. *Life and Times of Colonel Richard M. Johnson of Kentucky.* New York: Columbia University Press, 1932.

Miller, Lillian B. *"If Elected—": Unsuccessful Candidates for the Presidency, 1796–1968.* Washington, DC: Smithsonian Institution Press, 1972.

Mintz, Stephen, and Susan Kellogg. *Domestic Revolutions: A Social History of American Family Life.* New York: Free Press, 1988.

Mitchell, Robert D., editor. *Appalachian Frontiers: Settlement, Society, and Development in the Pre-Industrial Era.* Lexington: University Press of Kentucky, 1991.

Mooney, Chase C. *William H. Crawford, 1772–1834.* Lexington: University Press of Kentucky, 1974.

Moore, Glover. *The Missouri Controversy, 1819–1821.* Lexington: University Press of Kentucky, 1953.

Morgan, Robert J. *A Whig Embattled: The Presidency Under John Tyler.* Lincoln: University of Nebraska Press, 1954.

Morison, Samuel Eliot. *The Life and Letters of Harrison Gray Otis, Federalist, 1765–1848.* 2 volumes. Boston: Houghton Mifflin, 1913.

Morrison, Michael A. *Slavery and the American West: The Eclipse of Manifest Destiny and the Coming of the Civil War.* Chapel Hill: University of North Carolina Press, 1997.

Mueller, Henry R. *The Whig Party in Pennsylvania.* New York: Columbia University Press, 1922.

Munroe, John A. *Louis McLane: Federalist and Jacksonian.* New Brunswick, NJ: Rutgers University Press, 1973.

Murray, Paul. *The Whig Party in Georgia, 1825–1853.* Chapel Hill: University of North Carolina Press, 1948.

Nagel, Paul C. *John Quincy Adams: A Public Life, a Private Life.* New York: Alfred A. Knopf, 1997.

———. *One Nation Indivisible: The Union in*

American Thought, 1776–1861. New York: Oxford University Press, 1971.

Nathans, Sydney. *Daniel Webster and Jacksonian Democracy.* Baltimore: Johns Hopkins University Press, 1973.

Nevins, Allan. *Ordeal of the Union: Volume 1, Fruits of Manifest Destiny, 1847–1852.* New York: Charles Scribner's Sons, 1947.

Newsome, Albert Ray. *The Presidential Election of 1824 in North Carolina.* Chapel Hill: University of North Carolina Press, 1939.

Niven, John. *John C. Calhoun and the Price of Union: A Biography.* Baton Rouge: Louisiana State University Press, 1988.

Parks, Joseph Howard. *Felix Grundy, Champion of Democracy.* Baton Rouge: Louisiana State University Press, 1940.

Parson, Lynn Hudson. *The Birth of Modern Politics: Andrew Jackson, John Quincy Adams, and the Election of 1828.* New York: Oxford University Press, 2009.

Perkins, Bradford. *Castlereagh and Adams: England and the United States, 1812–1823.* Berkeley: University of California Press, 1964.

———. *Prologue to War: England and the United States, 1805–1812.* Berkeley: University of California Press, 1961.

Perrin, William Henry, editor. *History of Fayette County, Kentucky, with an Outline Sketch of the Blue Grass Region by Robert Peter, M.D.* Chicago: O. L. Baskin, 1882.

———. *The Pioneer Press of Kentucky, from the Printing of the First Paper West of the Alleghenies.* Louisville, KY: J. P. Morton, 1892.

Pessen, Edward. *Jacksonian America: Society, Personality, and Politics.* Homewood, IL: Dorsey Press, 1979.

Peters, Ronald M., Jr. *The American Speakership.* Baltimore: Johns Hopkins University Press, 1990.

Peterson, Merrill D. *The Great Triumvirate: Webster, Clay, and Calhoun.* New York: Oxford University Press, 1987.

———. *Olive Branch and Sword: The Compromise of 1833.* Baton Rouge: Louisiana State University Press, 1982.

Peterson, Norma Lois. *Littleton Waller Tazewell.* Charlottesville: University of Virginia Press, 1983.

———. *The Presidencies of William Henry Harrison and John Tyler.* Lawrence: University Press of Kansas, 1989.

Pickering, Octavius, and Charles W. Upham. *The Life of Timothy Pickering.* 4 volumes. Boston: Little, Brown, 1867–1873.

Pirtle, Alfred. *The Battle of Tippecanoe.* Louisville, KY: J. P. Morton, 1900.

Poage, George R. *Henry Clay and the Whig Party.* Chapel Hill: University of North Carolina Press, 1936.

Quisenberry, Anderson C. *The Life and Times of Hon. Humphrey Marshall.* Winchester, KY: Sun Publishing, 1892.

Railey, William Edward. *History of Woodford County.* Versailles, KY: Woodford Improvement League, 1968.

Ranck, George Washington. *History of Lexington, Kentucky.* Cincinnati: Robert Clarke, 1872.

Ratcliffe, Donald J. *The Politics of Long Division: The Birth of the Second Party System in Ohio, 1818–1828.* Columbus: Ohio State University Press, 2000.

Rayback, Robert J. *Millard Fillmore: Biography of a President.* Buffalo, NY: H. Stewart, 1959.

Remini, Robert V. *Andrew Jackson and the Course of American Freedom, 1822–1832.* New York: Harper & Row, 1981.

———. *Daniel Webster: The Man and His Time.* New York: W. W. Norton, 1997.

———. *Henry Clay: Statesman for the Union.* New York: W. W. Norton, 1991.

———. *Martin Van Buren and the Making of the Democratic Party.* New York: Columbia University Press, 1959.

Richardson, H. Edward. *Cassius Marcellus Clay: Firebrand for Freedom.* Lexington: University Press of Kentucky, 1976.

Rippy, J. Fred. *Joel R. Poinsett, Versatile American.* Durham, NC: Duke University Press, 1935.

Risjord, Norman K. *The Old Republicans: Southern Conservatism in the Age of Jefferson.* New York: Columbia University Press, 1965.

Rutland, Robert Allen. *The Presidency of James Madison.* Lawrence: University Press of Kansas, 1990.

Sabine, Lorenzo. *Notes on Duels and Dueling.* Boston: Crosby, Nichols, 1855.

Sandburg, Carl. *Abraham Lincoln: The Prairie Years.* 2 volumes. New York: Harcourt, Brace & World, 1926.

Satz, Ronald N. *American Indian Policy in the Jacksonian Era.* Lincoln: University of Nebraska Press, 1974.

Scharf, J. Thomas. *The Chronicle of Baltimore: Being a Complete History of "Baltimore Town" and Baltimore City from the Earliest Period to the Present Time.* Baltimore: Turnbull Brothers, 1874.

Seale, William. *The President's House: A History.* 2 volumes. Washington, DC: White House Historical Association with the cooperation of the National Geographic Society, 1986.

Sehlinger, Peter J. *Kentucky's Last Cavalier: General William Preston, 1816–1887.* Lexington: University Press of Kentucky, 2004.

Sellers, Charles. *The Market Revolution: Jacksonian America, 1815–1846.* New York: Oxford University Press, 1991.

Semmes, John Edward. *John H. B. Latrobe and His Times, 1803–1891.* Baltimore: Norman, Remington, 1917.

Semple, Robert Baylor. *A History of the Rise and Progress of the Baptists in Virginia.* Philadelphia: American Baptist Publication Society, 1894.

Simms, Henry H. *The Rise of the Whigs in Virginia, 1824–1840.* Richmond, VA: William Byrd Press, 1929.

Smiley, David L. *Lion of White Hall: The Life of Cassius M. Clay.* Madison: University of Wisconsin Press, 1962.

Smith, Elbert B. *Francis Preston Blair.* New York: Free Press, 1980.

Smith, Walter Buckingham. *Economic Aspects of the Second Bank of the United States.* Cambridge, MA: Harvard University Press, 1953.

Smith, Zachary F., and Mary Rogers Clay. *The Clay Family.* Louisville, KY: J. P. Morton, 1899.

Speed, Thomas. *The Political Club, Danville, Kentucky, 1786–1790: Being an Account of Early Kentucky Society from the Original Papers Recently Found.* Louisville, KY: John P. Morton, 1894.

Stagg, J.C.A. *Mr. Madison's War: Politics, Diplomacy, and Warfare in the Early Republic, 1783–1830.* Princeton, NJ: Princeton University Press, 1983.

Strahan, Randall. *Leading Representatives: The Agency of Leaders in the Politics of the U.S. House.* Baltimore: Johns Hopkins University Press, 2007.

Tachau, Mary K. Bonsteel. *Federal Courts in the Early Republic: Kentucky, 1789–1816.* Princeton, NJ: Princeton University Press, 1978.

Tallant, Harold D. *Evil Necessity: Slavery and Political Culture in Antebellum Kentucky.* Lexington, NJ: University Press of Kentucky, 2003.

Tallant, Robert. *Romantic New Orleans.* New York: E. P. Dutton, 1950.

Taylor, John M. *William Henry Seward: Lincoln's Right Hand.* Washington, DC: Brassey's, 1996.

Thom, William Taylor. *Struggle for Religious Freedom in Virginia: The Baptists.* Baltimore: Johns Hopkins University Press, 1900.

Townshend, William H. *Lincoln and the Bluegrass: Slavery and Civil War Kentucky.* Lexington: University Press of Kentucky, 1955.

Trefousse, Hans L. *Thaddeus Stevens: Nineteenth-Century Egalitarian.* Chapel Hill: University of North Carolina Press, 1997.

Tregle, Joseph G., Jr. *Louisiana in the Age of Jackson: A Clash of Cultures and Personalities.* Baton Rouge: Louisiana State University Press, 1999.

Tyler, Lyon Gardiner, editor. *Encyclopedia of Virginia Biography.* 5 volumes. New York: Lewis Historical Publishing, 1915.

Updyke, Frank A. *The Diplomacy of the War of 1812.* Gloucester, MA: Peter Smith, 1965.

Van Deusen, Glyndon G. *Horace Greeley, Nineteenth-Century Crusader.* Philadelphia: University of Pennsylvania Press, 1953.

———. *The Jacksonian Era, 1828–1848.* New York: Harper & Row, 1959.

———. *The Life of Henry Clay.* Boston: Little, Brown, 1937.

———. *Thurlow Weed, Wizard of the Lobby.* Boston: Little, Brown, 1947.

———. *William Henry Seward.* New York: Oxford University Press, 1967.

Varg, Paul A. *United States Foreign Relations, 1820–1860.* East Lansing: Michigan State University Press, 1979.

Vipperman, Carl J. *William Lowndes and the Transition of Southern Politics.* Chapel Hill: University of North Carolina Press, 1989.

Wade, Richard C. *The Urban Frontier: The Rise of Western Cities, 1790–1830.* Cambridge, MA: Harvard University Press, 1959.

Walters, Raymond, Jr. *Albert Gallatin: Jeffersonian Financier and Diplomat.* New York: Macmillan, 1957.

Ward, John William. *Andrew Jackson: Symbol for an Age.* New York: Oxford University Press, 1955.

Warfield, Ethelbert Dudley. *The Kentucky Resolutions.* New York: Putnam's, 1887.

Warshauer, Matthew. *Andrew Jackson and the Politics of Martial Law: Nationalism, Civil Liberties, and Partisanship.* Knoxville: University of Tennessee Press, 2006.

Watson, Harry L. *Jacksonian Politics and Community Conflict: The Emergence of the Second Party System in Cumberland County North Carolina.* Baton Rouge: Louisiana State University Press, 1981.

———. *Liberty and Power: The Politics of Jacksonian America.* New York: Hill and Wang, 1990.

Weisberger, Bernard A. *America Afire: Jefferson, Adams, and the Revolutionary Election of 1800.* New York: William A. Morrow, 2000.

White, Leonard D. *The Jeffersonians: A Study in Administrative History, 1801–1829.* New York: Macmillan, 1959.

Wilburn, Jean. *Biddle's Bank: The Crucial Years.* New York: Columbia University Press, 1967.

Wilentz, Sean. *The Rise of American Democracy: Jefferson to Lincoln.* New York: W. W. Norton, 2005.

Wilson, Major L. *The Presidency of Martin Van Buren.* Lawrence: University Press of Kansas, 1984.

Wiltse, Charles M. *John C. Calhoun, Nationalist, 1782–1828.* Indianapolis, IN: Bobbs-Merrill, 1944.

———. *John C. Calhoun, Nullifier, 1829–1839.* Indianapolis, IN: Bobbs-Merrill, 1949.

Wolf, Stephanie Grauman. *As Various as Their Land: The Everyday Lives of Eighteenth-Century Americans.* New York: Harper Perennial, 1994.

Wormuth, Francis D., and Edwin B. Firmage. *To Chain the Dog of War: The War Power of Congress in History and Law.* Dallas, TX: Southern Methodist University Press, 1986.

Wyatt-Brown, Bertram. *The Shaping of Southern Culture: Honor, Grace, and War, 1760s–1890s.* Chapel Hill: University of North Carolina Press, 2001.

Young, James Sterling. *The Washington Community, 1800–1828.* New York: Harcourt, Brace, 1966.

Zuehlke, Mark. *For Honour's Sake: The War of 1812 and the Brokering of an Uneasy Peace.* Toronto: Alfred A. Knopf Canada, 2006.

Articles

Allen, Jeffrey Brook. "Were Southern White Critics of Slavery Racists? Kentucky and the Upper South, 1791–1824." *Journal of Southern History* (May 1978): 169–90.

"Armistead Churchill." *William and Mary Quarterly* 9 (April 1901): 246–49.

Atkins, Jonathan M. "The Presidential Candidacy of Hugh Lawson White in Tennessee, 1832–1836." *Journal of Southern History* 58 (February 1992): 27–56.

Baird, Nancy D. "Asiatic Cholera's First Visit to Kentucky: A Study in Panic and Fear." *Filson Club History Quarterly* 48 (July 1974): 228–40.

Baker, Pamela L. "The Washington National Road Bill and the Struggle to Adopt a Federal System of Internal Improvement." *Journal of the Early Republic* 22 (Autumn 2002): 437–64.

Basch, Norma. "Marriage, Morals, and Politics in the Election of 1828." *Journal of American History* 80 (December 1993): 890–918.

Baylor, Orval W. "The Life and Times of John Pope, 1770–1845." *Filson Club History Quarterly* 15 (April 1941): 59–77.

Bearss, Sara B. "Henry Clay and the American Claims Against Portugal, 1850." *Journal of the Early Republic* 7 (Summer 1987): 167–80.

Birkner, Michael. "Daniel Webster and the Crisis of Union, 1850." *Historical New Hampshire* 37 (1982): 151–73.

Blakey, George T. "Rendezvous with Republicanism: John Pope vs. Henry Clay in 1816." *Indiana Magazine of History* 62 (1966): 233–50.

Boyd, Julian P. "The Murder of George Wythe." *William and Mary Quarterly* 12 (October 1955): 513–42.

Brent, Robert A. "Between Calhoun and Webster: Clay in 1850." *Southern Quarterly* 8 (1970): 293–308.

Brown, David. "Jeffersonian Ideology and the Second Party System." *The Historian* 62 (1999): 17–30.

Brown, Everett S. "The Presidential Election of 1824–1825." *Political Science Quarterly* 40 (September 1925): 384–403.

Brown, Thomas. "Southern Whigs and the Politics of Statesmanship, 1833–1841." *Journal of Southern History* 46 (August 1980): 361–80.

Campbell, Randolph B. "Henry Clay and the Poinsett Pledge Controversy of 1826." *Americas* 28 (April 1972): 429–40.

———. "The Spanish American Aspect of Henry Clay's American System." *Americas* 24 (July 1967): 3–17.

Coleman, J. Winston, Jr. "Old Kentucky Watering Places." *Filson Club History Quarterly* 16 (January 1942): 1–26.

Conte, Robert S. "The Celebrated White Sulphur Springs of Greenbrier: Nineteenth Century Travel Accounts." *West Virginia History* 42 (Spring-Summer 1981): 191–221.

Crabb, Alfred Leland. "Some Early Connections Between Kentucky and Tennessee." *Filson Club History Quarterly* 13 (July 1939): 147–56.

Crockett, David A. "In the Shadow of Henry Clay: How to Choose a Successful Opposition Presidential Candidate." *Congress & the Presidency* 33 (Spring 2006): 47–74.

Curtis, James C. "In the Shadow of Old Hickory: The Political Travail of Martin Van Buren." *Journal of the Early Republic* 1 (Autumn 1981): 249–67.

Daniels, James D. "Amos Kendall: Kentucky Journalist, 1815–1829." *Filson Club History Quarterly* 52 (January 1978): 46–65.

Doutrich, Paul E., III. "A Pivotal Decision: The 1824 Gubernatorial Election in Kentucky." *Filson Club History Quarterly* 56 (January 1982): 14–29.

Eaton, Clement. "Mob Violence in the Old South." *Mississippi Valley Historical Review* 29 (December 1942): 351–70.

———. "Southern Senators and the Right of Instruction, 1789–1860." *Journal of Southern History* 18 (August 1952): 303–19.

Ericson, David F. "The Nullification Crisis, American Republicanism, and the Force Bill Debate." *Journal of Southern History* 61 (May 1995): 249–70.

Fladeland, Betty L. "Compensated Emancipation: A Rejected Alternative." *Journal of Southern History* 42 (May 1976): 169–86.

Foley, William E. "The Political Philosophy of David Barton." *Missouri Historical Review* 58 (1964): 278–89.

Folsom, Burton W., II. "The Politics of Elites: Prominence and Party in Davidson County, Tennessee." *Journal of Southern History* 39 (August 1973): 359–78.

Forbes, Ella. "African-American Resistance to Colonization." *Journal of Black Studies* 21 (December 1990): 210–23.

Formisano, Ronald P. "Political Character, Antipartyism and the Second American Party System." *American Quarterly* 21 (1969): 683–709.

Foster, Charles I. "The Colonization of Free Negroes, in Liberia, 1816–1835." *Journal of Negro History* 38 (January 1953): 41–66.

Frederickson, George M. "A Man but Not a Brother: Abraham Lincoln and Racial Equality." *Journal of Southern History* 41 (February 1975): 39–58.

Friend, Craig Thompson. "Merchants and Markethouses: Reflections on Moral Economy in Early Kentucky." *Journal of the Early Republic* 17 (Winter 1997): 553–74.

Gamm, Gerald, and Kenneth Shepsle. "Emergence of Legislative Institutions: Standing Committees in the House and Senate, 1810–1825." *Legislative Studies Quarterly* 14 (February 1989): 39–66.

Gates, Paul W. "Tenants of the Log Cabin." *Mississippi Valley Historical Review* 49 (June 1962): 3–31.

"Genealogical Notes and Queries." *William and Mary College Quarterly Historical Magazine* 21 (January 1941): 61–68.

Goldman, Perry M. "Political Virtue in the Age of Jackson." *Political Science Quarterly* 87 (March 1972): 46–62.

Govan, Thomas P. "John M. Berrien and the Administration of Andrew Jackson." *Journal of Southern History* 5 (November 1939): 447–67.

Gronert, Theodore G. "Trade in the Blue-Grass Region, 1810–1820." *Mississippi Valley Historical Review* 5 (December 1918): 313–23.

Gutzman, Kevin R. "Preserving the Patrimony: William Branch Giles and Virginia Versus the Federal Tariff." *Virginia Magazine of History and Biography* 104 (Summer 1996): 341–72.

Hadsell, Richard Miller. "John Bradford and His Contributions to the Culture and the Life of Early Lexington." *Register of the Kentucky Historical Society* 62 (October 1964): 265–77.

Hamilton, Holman. "Democratic Senate Leadership and the Compromise of 1850." *Mississippi Valley Historical Review* 41 (December 1954): 403–18.

Hammon, Neal O. "Pioneer Routes in Central Kentucky." *Filson Club History Quarterly* 74 (2000): 125–43.

Harrington, J. Drew. "Henry Clay and the Classics." *Filson Club History Quarterly* 61 (April 1987): 234–46.

Hatzenbuehler, Ronald L. "The War Hawks and the Question of Congressional Leadership in 1812." *Pacific Historical Review* 45 (February 1975): 1–22.

Hawes, E. L. "Nicholas Family." *William and Mary Quarterly Historical Magazine* 16 (January 1936): 103–7.

Hay, Robert P. "The Case for Andrew Jackson in 1824: Eaton's *Wyoming Letters*." *Tennessee Historical Quarterly* 29 (1970): 139–51.

———. "The Presidential Question: Letters to Southern Editors, 1823–24." *Tennessee Historical Quarterly* 31 (1972): 170–86.

Heidler, David S., and Jeanne T. Heidler. " 'Not a Ragged Mob': The Inauguration of 1829." *White House History* 15 (Fall 2004): 14–23.

Hemphill, W. Edwin. "George Wythe Courts the Muses: In Which, to the Astonishment of Everyone, That Silent, Selfless Pedant Is Found to Have Had a Sense of Humor." *William and Mary Quarterly* 9 (July 1952): 338–45.

Henderson, Archibald. "The Creative Forces in Westward Expansion: Henderson and Boone."
American Historical Review 20 (October 1914): 86–107.

———. "The Transylvania Company, A Study in Personnel." *Filson Club History Quarterly* 21 (July 1947): 228–42.

Hockett, Homer C. "The Influence of the West on the Rise and Fall of Political Parties." *Mississippi Valley Historical Review* 4 (March 1918): 459–69.

Holder, Ray. "Parson Winans and Mr. Clay: The Whig Connection, 1843–1846." *Louisiana History* 25 (Winter 1984): 57–75.

Hopkins, James F. "Henry Clay, Farmer and Stockman." *Journal of Southern History* 15 (February 1949): 89–96.

Horsman, Reginald. "The Indian Policy of an 'Empire of Liberty.'" In Frederick E. Hoxie, Ronald Hoffman, and Peter J. Alberts, editors, *Native Americans and the Early Republic*. Charlottesville: University Press of Virginia, 1999.

Hoskins, Halford L. "The Hispanic American Policy of Henry Clay, 1816–1828." *Hispanic American Historical Review* 7 (November 1927): 460–78.

Howard, Thomas William. "Indiana Newspapers and the Presidential Election of 1824." *Indiana Magazine of History* 63 (September 1967): 177–206.

Hutton, Frankie. "Economic Considerations in the American Colonization Society's Early Effort to Emigrate Free Blacks to Liberia, 1816–36." *Journal of Negro History* 68 (Autumn 1983): 376–89.

Jenkins, Jeffery A. "Property Rights and the Emergence of Standing Committee Dominance in the Nineteenth-Century House." *Legislative Studies Quarterly* 23 (November 1998): 493–519.

Jillson, Willard Rouse. "Aaron Burr's 'Trial' for Treason, at Frankfort, Kentucky, 1806." *Filson Club History Quarterly* 17 (October 1943): 202–29.

Johnson, Leland R. "Aaron Burr: Treason in Kentucky?" *Filson Club History Quarterly* 75 (January 2001): 1–32.

Jones, Thomas B. "Henry Clay and Continental Expansion, 1820–1844." *Register of the Kentucky Historical Society* 73 (October 1975): 241–62.

Jones, Wilbur Devereux. "A British View of the War of 1812 and the Peace Negotiations." *Mississippi Valley Historical Review* 45 (December 1958): 481–87.

Kaplan, Lawrence S. "France and the War of 1812." *Journal of American History* 57 (June 1970): 36–47.

Kolodny, Robin. "The Several Elections of 1824." *Congress and the Presidency* 23 (Fall 1996): 139–64.

Lancaster, Clay. "Major Thomas Lewinski: Émigré Architect in Kentucky." *Journal of the Society of Architectural Historians* 11 (December 1952): 13–20.

Larson, John Lauritz. " 'Bind the Republic Together':

The National Union and the Struggle for a System of Internal Improvements." *Journal of American History* 74 (September 1987): 363–87.

Latner, Richard B. "The Nullification Crisis and Republican Subversion." *Journal of Southern History* 43 (February 1977): 19–38.

Learned, Henry Barrett. "Gerry and the Presidential Succession in 1813." *American Historical Review* 22 (October 1916): 94–97.

Lightfoot, Alfred. "Henry Clay and the Missouri Question, 1819–1821: American Lobbyist for Unity." *Missouri Historical Review* 61 (1967): 143–65.

Logan, Rayford W. "Some New Interpretations of the Colonization Movement." *Phylon* 4 (1943): 328–34.

Longaker, Richard P. "Andrew Jackson and the Judiciary." *Political Science Quarterly* 71 (September 1956): 341–64.

Marshall, Lynn L. "The Authorship of Jackson's Bank Veto Message." *Mississippi Valley Historical Review* 50 (December 1963): 466–77.

Martin, David A. "The Changing Role of Foreign Money in the United States, 1782–1857." *Journal of Economic History* 37 (December 1977): 1009–27.

Mason, Matthew. "Slavery Overshadowed: Congress Debates Prohibiting the Atlantic Slave Trade to the United States, 1806–1807." *Journal of the Early Republic* 20 (Spring 2000): 59–81.

Mathias, Frank F. "Henry Clay and His Kentucky Power Base." *Register of the Kentucky Historical Society* 78 (Spring 1980): 123–39.

Mayo, Edward L. "Republicanism, Antipartyism, and Jacksonian Politics: A View from the Nation's Capital." *American Quarterly* 31 (1979): 3–20.

McCormick, Richard P. "The Jacksonian Strategy." *Journal of the Early Republic* 10 (1990): 1–17.

McDougle, Evan E. "Public Opinion Regarding Emancipation and Colonization." *Journal of Negro History* 3 (July 1918): 303–28.

McFarland, Charles E., and Nevin E. Neal. "The Nascence of Protectionism: American Tariff Policies, 1816–1824." *Land Economics* 45 (February 1969): 22–30.

Meade, Robert Douthat. "John Randolph of Roanoke: Some New Information." *William and Mary Quarterly* 13 (October 1933): 256–64.

Meyer, Jeff. "Henry Clay's Legacy to Horse Breeding and Racing." *Register of the Kentucky Historical Society* 99 (Autumn 2002): 473–96.

Miles, Edwin A. "Andrew Jackson and Senator George Poindexter." *Journal of Southern History* 24 (February 1958): 51–66.

Miller, Ricard G. "The Tariff of 1832: The Issue That Failed." *Filson Club History Quarterly* 49 (July 1979): 221–30.

Minicucci, Stephen. "The 'Cement of Interest': Interest-Based Models of Nation-building in the Early Republic." *Social Science History* 25 (Summer 2001): 247–74.

Moore, Powell. "The Revolt Against Jackson in Tennessee, 1835–1836." *Journal of Southern History* 2 (August 1936): 335–59.

Morgan, William G. "The Decline of the Congressional Nominating Caucus." *Tennessee Historical Quarterly* 24 (1965): 245–55.

———. "John Quincy Adams v. Andrew Jackson: Their Biographers and the 'Corrupt Bargain' Charge." *Tennessee Historical Quarterly* 26 (1967): 43–58.

———. "The Origin and Development of the Congressional Nominating Caucus." *Proceedings of the American Philosophical Society* 113 (April 1969): 184–96.

Muir, Andrew Forest. "Isaac B. Desha, Fact and Fancy." *Filson Club History Quarterly* 30 (October 1956): 319–23.

Nagel, Paul C. "The Election of 1824: A Reconsideration Based on Newspaper Opinion." *Journal of Southern History* 26 (August 1960): 315–29.

Neely, Mark E., Jr. "American Nationalism in the Image of Henry Clay: Abraham Lincoln's Eulogy on Henry Clay in Context." *Register of the Kentucky Historical Society* 73 (1975): 31–60.

Neely, Sylvia. "The Politics of Liberty in the Old World and the New: Lafayette's Return to America in 1824." *Journal of the Early Republic* 6 (Summer 1986): 151–71.

Nigro, Felix A. "The Van Buren Confirmation Before the Senate." *Western Political Quarterly* 14 (March 1961): 148–59.

Pasley, Jeffrey L. "Minnows, Spies, and Aristocrats: The Social Crisis of Congress in the Age of Martin Van Buren." *Journal of the Early Republic* 27 (Winter 2007): 599–653.

Perkins, Edwin J. "Lost Opportunities for Compromise in the Bank War: A Reassessment of Jackson's Veto Message." *Business History Review* 61 (1987): 531–50.

Phillips, Kim T. "The Pennsylvania Origins of the Jackson Movement." *Political Science Quarterly* 91 (Autumn 1976): 489–508.

Rayback, Joseph G. "Who Wrote the Allison Letters: A Study in Historical Detection." *Mississippi Valley Historical Review* 36 (June 1949): 51–72.

Reed, John J. "Battleground: Pennsylvania Antimasons and the Emergence of the National Nominating Convention, 1835–1839." *Pennsylvania Magazine of History and Biography* 122 (January–April 1998): 77–115.

Risjord, Norman K. "1812: Conservatives, War Hawks and the Nation's Honor." *William and Mary Quarterly* 18 (April 1961): 196–210.

Rousseau, Peter L. "Jacksonian Monetary Policy, Specie Flows, and the Panic of 1837." *Journal of Economic History* 62 (June 2002): 457–88.

Russo, David J. "The Major Political Issues of the Jacksonian Period and the Development of Party Loyalty in Congress, 1830–1840." *Transactions of the American Philosophical Society* 62 (1972): 3–51.

Schweikart, Larry. "Banking in the American South, 1836–1865." *Journal of Economic History* 45 (June 1985): 465–67.

Seager, Robert II. "Henry Clay and the Politics of Compromise and Non-Compromise." *Register of the Kentucky Historical Society* 85 (Winter 1987): 1–28.

Sellers, Charles G., Jr. "Banking and Politics in Jackson's Tennessee, 1817–1827." *Mississippi Valley Historical Review* 41 (June 1954): 61–84.

Shepard, E. Lee. "Breaking In the Profession: Establishing a Law Practice in Antebellum Virginia." *Journal of Southern History* 48 (August 1982): 393–410.

Sherwood, Henry Noble. "The Formation of the American Colonization Society." *Journal of Negro History* 2 (July 1917): 209–28.

Shields, Johanna Nicol. "Whigs Reform the 'Bear Garden': Representation and the Apportionment Act of 1842." *Journal of the Early Republic* 5 (Autumn 1985): 355–82.

Skeen, C. Edward. "Calhoun, Crawford, and the Politics of Retrenchment." *South Carolina Historical Magazine* 73 (July 1972): 141–75.

———. "*Vox Populi, Vox Dei:* The Compensation Act of 1816." *Journal of the Early Republic* 6 (Fall 1986): 253–74.

Strahan, Randall, Matthew Gunning, and Richard L. Vining, Jr. "From Moderator to Leader: Floor Participation by U.S. House Speakers, 1789–1841." *Social Science History* 30 (Spring 2006): 51–74.

Strahan, Randall, Vincent G. Moscardelli, Moshe Haspel, and Richard S. Wike. "The Clay Speakership Revisited." *Polity* 32 (Summer 2000): 561–93.

Swift, Elaine K. "The Start of Something New: Clay, Stevenson, Polk, and the Development of the Speakership, 1789–1869." In Roger H. Davidson, Susan Webb Hammond, and Raymond W. Smock, editors, *Masters of the House: Congressional Leadership over Two Centuries.* Boulder, CO: Westview Press, 1998.

Sydnor, Charles S. "A Description of Sargent S. Prentiss." *Journal of Southern History* 10 (November 1944): 475–79.

———. "One-Party Period of American History." *American Historical Review* 51 (April 1946): 439–51.

Sylla, Richard, John B. Legler, and John J. Wallis. "Banks and State Public Finance in the New Republic: The United States, 1790–1860." *Journal of Economic History* 47 (June 1987): 391–403.

Talbert, Charles G. "William Whitley, 1749–1813." *Filson Club History Quarterly* 25 (July 1951): 300–316.

Tapp, Hambleton. "Robert J. Breckinridge and the Year 1849." *Filson Club History Quarterly* 12 (July 1938): 125–50.

Temin, Peter. "The Economic Consequences of the Bank War." *Journal of Political Economy* 76 (March–April 1968): 257–74.

Timberlake, Richard H., Jr. "The Specie Circular and Distribution of the Surplus." *Journal of Political Economy* 68 (April 1960): 109–17.

Torrence, William Clayton. "Henrico County, Virginia: Beginnings of Its Families: Part I." *William and Mary College Quarterly Historical Magazine* 24 (October 1915): 116–42.

———. "Henrico County, Virginia: Beginnings of Its Families: Part IV." *William and Mary College Quarterly Historical Magazine* 25 (July 1916): 52–58.

Tregle, Joseph G., Jr. "Andrew Jackson and the Continuing Battle of New Orleans." *Journal of the Early Republic* 1 (Winter 1981): 373–93.

Troutman, Richard L. "The Emancipation of Slaves by Henry Clay." *Journal of Negro History* 40 (April 1955): 179–81.

Van Atta, John R. "Western Lands and the Political Economy of Henry Clay's American System, 1819–1832." *Journal of the Early Republic* 21 (Winter 2001): 633–65.

Van Deburg, William L. "Henry Clay, the Right of Petition, and Slavery in the Nation's Capital." *Register of the Kentucky Historical Society* 60 (1970): 132–46.

Van Tassel, David D. "Gentlemen of Property and Standing: Compromise Sentiment in Boston in 1850." *New England Quarterly* 23 (September 1950): 307–19.

Watson, Harry L. "The Market and Its Discontents." *Journal of the Early Republic* 12 (Winter 1992): 464–70.

———. "Old Hickory's Democracy." *Wilson Quarterly* 9 (1985): 101–33.

Wehle, H. B. "A Portrait of Henry Clay Reattributed." *The Metropolitan Museum of Art Bulletin* 20 (September 1925): 209–16.

Weiner, Alan S. "John Scott, Thomas Hart Benton, David Barton and the Presidential Election of 1824: A Case Study in Pressure Politics." *Missouri Historical Review* 60 (July 1966): 460–94.

Weissbach, Lee Shai. "The Peopling of Lexington, Kentucky: Growth and Mobility in a Frontier Town." *Register of the Kentucky Historical Society* 81 (1983): 115–33.

Wells, Camille. "The Planter's Prospect: Houses, Outbuildings, and Rural Landscapes in Eighteenth-Century Virginia." *Winterthur Portfolio* 28 (Spring 1993): 1–31.

Whitley, Edna Talbott. "George Beck, An Eighteenth Century Painter." *Register of the Kentucky Historical Society* 67 (January 1969): 20–36.

Wilson, Major L. "'Liberty and Union': An Analysis of Three Concepts Involved in the Nullification Controversy." *Journal of Southern History* 33 (August 1967): 331–55.

———. "Republicanism and the Idea of Party in the Jacksonian Period." *Journal of the Early Republic* 8 (Winter 1988): 419–42.

Wiltse, Charles M. "John C. Calhoun and the 'A. B. Plot.'" *Journal of Southern History* 13 (February 1947): 46–61.

Winn, Larry James. "The War Hawks' Call to Arms: Appeals for a Second War with Great Britain." *Southern Speech Communication Journal* 37 (1972): 402–12.

Wire, Richard Arden. "John M. Clayton and Whig Politics During the Second Jackson Administration." *Delaware History* 18 (1978): 1–16.

Theses and Dissertations

Bright-Levy, Wendy S. "Ashland, the Henry Clay Estate, as House Museum: Private Home and Public Destination." M.A. thesis, University of Kentucky, 2008.

Connelly, Maris Stella. "The Letters and European Travel Journal of James A. Bayard, 1812–1815." Ph.D. dissertation, Boston University, 2007.

Maness, Lonnie Edward. "Henry Clay and the Problem of Slavery." Ph.D. dissertation, Memphis State University, 1980.

Rigali, James Henry. "Restoring the Republic of Virtue: The Presidential Election of 1824." Ph.D. dissertation, University of Washington, 2004.

Spiller, Roger J. "John C. Calhoun as Secretary of War, 1817–1825." Ph.D. dissertation, Louisiana State University Press, 1977.

Index

NOTE: HC refers to Henry Clay.

ABOUT THE AUTHORS

DAVID S. HEIDLER and JEANNE T. HEIDLER have written numerous scholarly books and articles dealing with the history of the early American republic, the antebellum period, and the Civil War. David is associated with the Department of History at Colorado State University–Pueblo, and Jeanne is professor of history at the United States Air Force Academy, where she is the senior civilian member of her department.